John Paul II's
Book of Saints

BUNSON
MATTHEW AND MARGARET

Our Sunday Visitor Publishing Division
Our Sunday Visitor, Inc.
Huntington, Indiana 46750

Pictures used in this book are from a variety of sources. Pictures from *Faces of Holiness*, © 1998 by Our Sunday Visitor Publishing, are used with permission of author Ann Ball. The picture of Blessed Marie Rivier was provided by the Sisters of the Presentation of Mary, Methuen Province, with permission by Sister Helen Bissionnette, P.M., Provincial Superior. Other pictures are from the Our Sunday Visitor files.

Text of Pope John Paul II's speeches © 2005 by Libreria Editrice Vaticana. Used with permission.

The authors and publisher are grateful to all copyright holders without whose material this book could not have been completed. Every reasonable effort has been made to determine copyright holders of excerpted materials and to secure permissions as needed. If any copyrighted materials have been inadvertently used in this work without proper credit being given in one form or another, please notify Our Sunday Visitor in writing so that future printings of this work may be corrected accordingly.

Our Sunday Visitor Publishing Division
Our Sunday Visitor, Inc.
200 Noll Plaza
Huntington, IN 46750

ISBN: 978-1-59276-244-6 (Inventory No. T295)
LCCN: 2006936404

Cover design by Monica Haneline
Cover photo: OSV file photo
Interior design by Sherri L. Hoffman
PRINTED IN THE UNITED STATES OF AMERICA

ACKNOWLEDGMENTS

There are many individuals to whom special gratitude is owed for their assistance and cooperation in the completion of this work. Without their charity and generosity this book would not have been possible. Particular gratitude must be given to the Congregation of the Causes of Saints and to the literally dozens of postulators of the saints and beati presented in this work; they are an inspiration to all for their faithful service to the Church and their patience and devotion in laboring on behalf of the truly remarkable men and women who have been raised to the altars by Pope John Paul II. We are indebted to His Eminence, Edouard Cardinal Gagnon, for his kindness and inestimable aid. We also thank Greg Erlandson, Publisher of Our Sunday Visitor, for his enthusiasm and confidence; and Jackie Lindsey, Acquisitions Editor. Additional thanks are owed to: Carrie Bannister; Ann Ball, for contributing pictures from her book *The Faces of Holiness;* the Orders, institutions, and individuals who contributed pictures; Mark Thiel; Edward Wells; Kim Clanton-Green; Marie Cuglietta; and the staffs of several libraries, including Marquette University and Sahara West Library.

The Church proposes the example of numerous saints who bore witness to and defended moral truth even to the point of enduring martyrdom, or who preferred death to a single mortal sin. In raising them to the honor of the altars, the Church has canonized their witness and declared the truth of their judgment, according to which the love of God entails the obligation to respect his commandments, even in the most dire of circumstances, and the refusal to betray those commandments, even for the sake of saving one's own life.

— *Veritatis Splendor* (91.3)

The martyrologium of the first centuries was the basis of the veneration of the saints. By proclaiming and venerating the holiness of her sons and daughters, the Church gave supreme honor to God himself; in the martyrs she venerated Christ, who was at the origin of their martyrdom and holiness. In later times there developed the practice of canonization, a practice which still continues in the Catholic Church and the Orthodox churches. In recent years the number of canonizations and beatifications has increased. These show the vitality of the local churches, which are much more numerous today than in the first centuries and in the first millennium. The greatest homage which all the churches can give to Christ on the threshold of the third millennium will be to manifest the redeemer's all-powerful presence through the fruits of faith, hope, and charity present in men and women of many different tongues and races who have followed Christ in the various forms of the Christian vocation.

— *Tertio Millennio Adveniente* (37)

FOREWORD

Beatifications and canonizations were an outstanding feature of Pope John Paul II's magisterium during the twenty-plus years of his pontificate. It is fitting that we be invited to get acquainted with the women and men the Holy Father proposed as models for us to imitate and as patrons on whom we can rely in forwarding our praises and requests to God and helping us in our necessities.

This is done here through a collection of well-researched and finely-drawn portraits of people who are close to God — and closer to us than we would expect.

Officially proclaiming Blesseds and Saints was not something marginal or occasional in the Pope's pastoral solicitude. In fact, he saw the centuries-old practice as a most effective means to carry out his mission as Vicar of Christ and head of the Church — a mission that entails the triple power and duty to govern, to teach, and to sanctify.

To govern the Church means to be responsible for its unity and dynamism. For canonizations and beatifications, the Holy Father invites faithful from all places to gather in unity and proclaim the same faith. Those present, and those who follow the event from afar, are led to understand that one does not become a saint in isolation but as an active member of the Body of Christ, in what the *Credo* calls the Communion of Saints.

Unity is possible only by the interaction of the diverse functions and charism of bishops, priests, and religious or lay men and women. All have a special role in giving the Church its vitality, making it present in all fields of human endeavor. The condition is that talents and creativity be at the service of charity and tend to one final purpose of glorifying the Lord. By raising to the glory of the altar some of her sons and daughters, the Church tells us that they have done precisely that.

As head of the Church, the Pope also revealed himself to be a great leader for humanity. He never missed an occasion to remind those responsible for the government of nations that there are God-given values to be protected.

He was listened to when he received them in audience or made it a duty to meet them in his journeys.

Official representatives of nations attend beatifications because the new saints are from their country and they cannot but realize the great part they have played for the common good of society by unselfish dedication to popular education, the care of the needy, social and rural development, and other similar causes. The Holy Father never missed telling them that it is the Holy Spirit who has sustained their generosity, their faith in the human person, their awareness of the needs of their brothers, their spirit of initiative, and most of all, the holiness of life which has brought success to their efforts.

Pope John Paul II was a great teacher, taking the Gospel to the limits of the earth, never caring about his health or security. *Gospel* means "Good News," and what better "News" can we receive than that of being shown that the Holy Spirit is ever active and powerful in bringing out the best in us and drawing us to perfection?

After he officially affirmed the holiness of a servant of God and granted the faculty to render him a public cult, the Holy Father always commented on the liturgical texts and explained how holiness is simply putting God's Word into practice. His homilies, showing how the saints have lived the Word of God in the variety of their personalities, their outstanding virtues and their accomplishments, became a unique commentary on the Scriptures.

In what is called the mission of sanctifying are included the mission of leading the Church in prayer and that of caring for the sanctity of the Church and its members. John Paul II was a man of prayer, which could be seen wherever he went, and preserving the beauty and purity of the Liturgy was always one of his concerns. Beatifications are an invitation to pray, following the example of the new saints, and add a dimension to divine cult by making us render homage to God for his saints and together with them.

Beatifications are also a reminder of our call to perfection. Vatican II has reaffirmed the actuality of the vocations of the people that the Pope proposed as models — people who are close to us and have been in duties and situations similar to ours.

I remember well twenty years ago, at the Committee for the Family, having had a long conversation with the Archbishop of Hanoi, at a time when the Church in Vietnam was already under a regime of persecution. He was almost miraculously allowed to attend a Synod of Bishops. Knowing the tremendous problems he had to face, we asked him what we could do for him. To our surprise he answered, "Send us lives of saints!" He explained that his people need more than anything else to see that it is possible to follow in Christ's footsteps and to remain faithful, even when that requires heroism.

The Pope, too, found that the usual pretext to resist Christ's call to obey his Father's commandment is to say that His Church's ideal of virtue, of moral behavior and self-renouncement, is out of reach for most of us. How often, in encounters with family groups, retreats for youth, or even for priests and religious, have I heard the response, "This is impossible, Christ cannot demand so much. This is not for people like me." Beatifications are the Pope's answer to our lack of confidence in God's overwhelming grace, in the power of the Holy Spirit who dwells in us and, to quote Pope Paul IV, "makes the impossible possible."

The great variety of gifts and personalities in the new saints and Blesseds shows that the Holy Spirit is never inactive. They come from the most diverse social and cultural backgrounds; they have had important functions or simple, ordinary lives; their pilgrimage on earth has been long or short; they have lived in poverty or in affluence. And they invite all of us to strive toward perfection.

They have certain common features. In the last ten years, I have been what is called the *cardinal ponens* — that is, the relator presenting to the College of Cardinals the conclusions of the long work involved in Causes of Saints before they make a final recommendation to the Holy Father on validity of the case. In all the Causes, a reality I have always encountered is that the saints have been accepted to bear the Cross of Christ. The cross of daily fidelity to the simple duties of one's state, the cross of physical pain supported with peace or even joy, the cross of spiritual suffering in periods of doubt or the conscience of our human frailty, the cross of sharing in and trying to alleviate the suffering of others, the cross of misunderstanding and even persecution.

Another common feature is the simplicity and humility with which they have accepted the common devotions to the Child Jesus, to the Eucharist, the Passion, the Sacred Heart, the Blessed Mother in her diverse mysteries, to St. Joseph, or some other favorite saint. There, they have found the strength to bear the Cross and the inspiration for the accomplishments in which they have become instruments of divine love.

The degree of intimacy with Christ they have attained can be traced back, for instance, to the first spiritual experience of their communion or to the long hours they have spent in adoration before the Tabernacle.

Pope John Paul II made us the gift of proposing to us models and intercessors for all occasions. Among the holy men and women introduced to us in this book, the Spirit might make some seem more akin to us, more relevant to our conditions and aspirations. The broad panorama offered by the authors should encourage us to study more in-depth the action of grace in one or the other. They have the merit of making us proud of our Church and more confident in our call to imitate our Savior a little more every day.

— EDOUARD CARDINAL GAGNON

INTRODUCTION

The saints and blesseds of the pontificate of Pope John Paul II have been our constant companions for these past many months. It has been an honor and a privilege to record their lives, their contributions to the world, and their spiritual splendors.

The Holy Father sought to remind the world that the glory of the Church is neither limited to one or two continents or countries nor to a specific age in human history. The faith is found throughout the whole of the world and has a relevance and meaning to all human beings, in every setting and era, and from every ethnic, cultural, and economic background. Many of the Saints and Blesseds walked upon the earth during our lifetime, assuring us that the age of miracles and holiness is not a thing of the past, but alive, vital, and relevant in our modern world. While they may be different in the details of their lives, each one of these remarkable human beings brought their individual talents to bear on the tasks at hand, responding to grace and the will of God with heroic generosity and fidelity. We pray that the spirit of these holy men and women will inspire the faithful throughout the Church in the days to come.

We have also experienced the kindness and generosity of postulators and the men and women who are carrying on the labors, spiritual visions, and heroism of these saints and blesseds in completing this work. Their kindness and encouragement reflect the ideals of their founders, and their participation in this work had added to our edification and growth in the Faith.

Editorial Note:

Owing to the considerable multiplicity of spellings of the names and places of origins among the saints and blesseds of Pope John Paul II, this work utilizes the English spelling and version of most place and personal names. Most of the names are well-known, but some are relatively obscure, necessitating spellings and presentations that are more accessible to all readers. Additionally, the excerpts used throughout the text are taken directly from the addresses, homilies, and writings of Pope John Paul II. As these are official texts, no attempt has been made to edit or revise the specific language used, as customarily found in papal documents such as those published by *L'Osservatore Romano*, though some stylistic changes have been made for consistency and for American-English spelling. Cross-references have been used throughout for greater ease in finding a specific saint or blessed under one of the many alternate names by which they are commonly known.

✜

The Saints of
Pope John Paul II

$\mathcal{A}$

✠

Agnes of Bohemia (c. 1205 – March 6, 1282)

Princess and Foundress

Agnes of Bohemia was the daughter of King Ottocar, the ruler of Bohemia — now a part of the modern Czech Republic — and Queen Constance, the daughter of the king of Hungary. Born in about 1205, in the city of Prague, she is often called Agnes of Prague by historians.

Her education — a requirement of Agnes's rank and future role in the society of the time — took place at Trebnitz, under the care of the Cistercian Nuns. In their convent, she received the grace of a religious vocation. The realities of royal life, however, intervened; at the age of three, following the customs of the period, Agnes had been betrothed to Prince Boleslaus. When Prince Boleslaus died very young, she was next betrothed to Prince Henry, the son of Emperor Frederick II of the Holy Roman Empire.

When Prince Henry married an Austrian duchess for political reasons, Emperor Frederick subsequently asked for Agnes' hand in marriage, having seen her and determined that she would make a worthy consort. She was thus betrothed for the third time.

But, despite her strict upbringing and her filial duties to her parents, Agnes refused to accept marriage to the emperor. Court officials, naturally, urged her to marry him, but she defied them and appealed to Pope Gregory IX, asking him to intercede and to permit an annulment of the betrothal. The Holy Father and all of Europe knew of Agnes' religious vocation — to the point that, upon hearing of her refusal, Emperor Frederick said, "If she had left me for a mortal man, I would have taken vengeance with the sword, but I cannot take offense, because in preference to me she has chosen the King of Heaven."

Related to St. Elizabeth of Hungary on her mother's side, Agnes knew that this former queen had become a tertiary, then a nun at Marburg. The courts of Europe at the time had been quite shocked by this royal dedication, wondering what could have prompted such a drastic retreat into the religious life. But Agnes understood: St. Elizabeth had responded to the grace of God, a response that she planned to imitate with the same enthusiasm.

In 1225, the Friars Minor had arrived in Prague, introducing the Franciscan spirit to the capital. Agnes was drawn to that spirit and allowed it to form her aspirations. She obtained a grant of land from her brother, King Wenceslaus I, and on that property erected a Franciscan hospital for the poor and needy. Agnes then established the Confraternity of the Crusaders of the Red Star to staff the hospital and the attached clinics. In 1234, she founded a Poor Clare Convent, St. Savior, in Prague. In order to make sure that the rule and spiritual ideals of the Poor Clares were firmly instilled in St. Savior, Agnes wrote to Clare of Assisi, asking her aid in this endeavor. Clare responded by sending five nuns from Assisi to establish the rule and the cloister routine successfully.

Agnes and Clare never met face to face, but they corresponded by letter for two decades, and the correspondence was preserved. Agnes entered St. Savior on Pentecost Sunday, 1234, and remained cloistered for almost half a century. In time, she became abbess of the convent and was revered as a model of the religious life. Given the gifts of healing and prophecy, Agnes predicted events happening in the world, including her brother Wenceslaus' victory over the Duke of Austria.

Agnes served as a Poor Clare for forty-six years, dying in St. Savior Convent in Prague. Pope John Paul II canonized her on November 12, 1989, in Rome, declaring:

> Agnes of Bohemia, although she lived in a period far removed from ours, still remains a shining example of the Christian faith and heroic charity, which invites us to reflection and imitation.

Feast day: March 6.

✢

Agostina Livia Pietrantoni
(March 27, 1864 – November 13, 1894)
Heroic Martyr of Charity

Livia Pietrantoni was born near Rieti, Italy, one of ten children in a devout peasant family. Her father suffered from severe arthritis, so she had to help her mother care for him and the other children. Livia tended cattle, made shoes, and took part in the annual olive harvests. Along with other young women, she worked on the roads as well.

She was popular and had many would-be suitors, but she had received the grace of a religious vocation, and despite the pleas of her family, Livia refused marriage proposals until she was twenty-one. On August 3, 1886, she joined the Sisters of Charity in Rome and was given the religious name of Agostina. She then worked for two years at the Santo Spirito Hospital in the Eternal City. In the summer of 1889, she began working with patients suffering from tuberculosis, then considered incurable.

Agostina contracted the disease around the time of her profession, in September 1893, and suffered severely over the next years; at one time she became so ill that she received the Last Rites.

Eventually recovering enough to perform her duties, Agostina continued to care for the tuberculosis patients despite her own infirmities, taking care to safeguard other patients from contracting the same disease. The patients in her care were all males, and their frustrations sometimes led them to violence, placing Agostina in constant danger. But despite the threats, she transformed her nursing care into an endless spiritual work of mercy.

One of the patients under her care, however, a man named Giuseppe Romanelli, became so angry and violent that he was expelled from the hospital. He became convinced that Agostina was responsible for his expulsion, and on the morning of November 13, 1894, he entered the unguarded main entrance and hid in a hallway, seeking revenge. When Agostina passed him, he lunged at her with a knife and stabbed her seven times. She cried out, but help did not arrive in time to save her life. Agostina died assuring her fellow sisters that she was content with God's will.

Her death was greeted with immense grief in Rome, and she was honored immediately as a heroine, a woman of deep prayer, and a "martyr of charity." She was buried originally in the Campo Verano, but her remains were transferred on March 15, 1941, to the motherhouse of the congregation. Pope Paul VI beatified Agostina on November 12, 1972. Pope John Paul II canonized her on April 18, 1999.

Feast day: November 13.

✠

Agostino Roscelli (July 27, 1818 – May 7, 1902)

Founder of the Institute of Sisters of the Immaculata

Agostino was born in Casarza Ligure, Italy, the son of a local farming family. Reserved as a child but bright and sensitive, he was entrusted with the care of the family's flock of sheep. He spent hours with the animals, learning to pray and to seek union with God while on lonely hillsides. This spiritual union led him to a parish mission in 1835, where he received the grace of a religious vocation.

Generous Catholic friends of the family sponsored Agostino's seminary training, and he was ordained to the priesthood in 1846. His first assignment was as an assistant of St. Martin d'Albaro Parish. Later, in 1854, he became pastor of the Church of Consolation. He devoted his life to aiding those forgotten or abused by society and was gifted with the grace of contemplation. Concerned about the young women of the area, Agostino founded a residential center for them in Genoa and provided educational and professional training programs.

In 1874, he became chaplain of a provincial orphanage and served as well as a prison chaplain. His congregation, the Institute of Sisters of the Immaculata, was founded in 1876 to serve in the residential women's centers.

After his death in Genoa, Agostino was deeply mourned by the faithful of the region. Pope John Paul II beatified him on May 7, 1995, and canonized him on June 10, 2001. The Holy Father declared:

> The love of God for men is revealed with special emphasis in the life of St. Agostino Roscelli, whom we contemplate today in the splendour of holiness. His existence, entirely permeated by deep faith, can be considered a gift offered for the glory of God and the good of souls.

Feast day: May 7.

✝

Albert (Adam) Chmielowski of Krakow
(August 20, 1845 – December 25, 1916)
Founder of the "Gray Brothers and Sisters"

Albert Chmielowski was born in Adamin Iglomia, Poland, near Krakow, during a turbulent period in Europe. He felt committed to the people and events of his own age from his earliest years; when he was only seventeen, he lost a leg while taking part in an insurrection for Poland's freedom.

Recovering, Albert turned to art as an expression of faith, gaining considerable popularity and fame for his works, but he was still concerned about the evils of the times. This concern led him to enter the Franciscans as a member of the Third Order, taking the name of Br. Albert. In 1887, Albert put on a coarse gray habit and founded a religious society that would become the Brothers of the Third Order of St. Francis, Servants of the Poor, also known as the Albertines; in 1891, he established a similar congregation for women. They organized shelters and soup kitchens and undertook other charitable enterprises for the poor and the abandoned. Albert died while performing his charitable labors in Krakow on Christmas Day.

Pope John Paul II beatified Albert on June 22, 1983, in Krakow, Poland, and canonized him on November 12, 1989. Declaring that this new saint understood the necessity of "giving one's soul," the Holy Father praised his "tireless, heroic service on behalf of the marginalized and the poor." Pope John Paul II also beatified a spiritual daughter of Albert's, Maria Bernardina Jablonska, on June 6, 1997.

Feast day: June 17.

✠

Alfonso Rodriquez — see Paraguay, Jesuit Martyrs of

✠

Alphonsus de Orozco, O.S.A.
(October 17, 1500 – September 19, 1591)
"Royal Preacher" of King Charles V of Spain

Alphonsus de Orozco was born in Oropesa, near Toledo, Spain, and was the son of the governor of the local castle. He began his studies in the nearby Talavera de la Reina, and for three years, was a choirboy in the Cathedral of Toledo, where he developed a fondness and talent for music.

At the age of fourteen, Alphonsus' parents took him to the University of Salamanca, where one of his elder brothers was already studying. During the Lenten sermons in 1520, Alphonsus was attracted by the prayerful atmosphere of the Friary of St. Augustine, and there, made his profession of vows at the hands of St. Thomas of Villanova.

Soon after his ordination to the priesthood in 1527, Alphonsus impressed his superiors with his profound spirituality and obvious abilities as a preacher. They consequently appointed him to the post of preaching, the first of many offices that he would hold over his lifetime. Alphonsus, however, was determined to devote his life to the missions and sailed for Mexico as a missionary in 1549. On his way to the New World, he suffered a severe bout of arthritis in the Canary Islands and received medical attention. His doctors, fearing for his life, refused him permission to continue his journey or his dream of missionary labors in the New World.

Back in Spain, Alphonsus was named "royal preacher" to the court of the emperor Charles V in 1554, and lived at Valladolid, a city that then served as the seat of the royal court. When the court was moved to Madrid in 1561, Alphonsus moved as well to the new capital. But even though he held an important post in the court, Alphonsus continued to live only as a humble friar, maintaining personal austerity and poverty. Customarily, he ate one meal, at midday, and slept no more than three hours, using a table as a bed and cut vines for his pillow. His room was decorated with one chair, a candle, a broom, and some books.

Alphonsus' room was also chosen specifically to be near the front door of the Augustinian friary of St. Philip so that he would always be available to the poor, who came in great numbers to ask his help. He was a beloved figure in the city, known as the "Saint of St. Philip's." He visited the sick in hospitals, prisoners in jail, and the poor in the streets and in their homes. When he was not ministering to the people, he was in prayer, writing books, or preparing sermons.

Alphonsus wrote many books, in both Latin and Spanish. These included *Rule for a Christian Life* (1542), *Garden of Prayer and the Mount of Contemplation* (1544), *Memorial of Holy Love* (1576), *Spiritual Treasury* (1551), *The Art of Loving God and Neighbor* (1567), *The Book of the Gentleness of God* (1576), and *Tract on the Crown of Our Lady* (1588).

At the same time, he had an abiding love of his own Augustinian order and wrote about its history and spirituality, both in the hope of attracting new vocations and inducing its members to imitate the true Augustinian way of life. To bring further reform, he helped establish the first foundations of the later movement of recollection in the Order. He founded Augustinian monasteries, friaries, and houses of contemplative nuns.

In August 1591, Alphonsus fell ill with a fever, but he managed to celebrate his daily Mass. He did not recover from the illness, however. But before his passing he was visited by the king, Philip II, Princess Isabel, and the Cardinal Archbishop of Toledo, Gaspar de Quiroga, who personally fed him, then asked for his blessing. Alphonsus died in the College of the Incarnation, which he had founded two years before. (Today, this building is the seat of the Spanish Senate.)

News of his death caused grief throughout Madrid, and a large crowd burst into the church of the college, seeking some relic: a splinter from the bed, a piece of Alphonsus' clothes, shoes, or hair shirt. The Cardinal Archbishop kept for himself the wooden cross Alphonsus had long carried with him.

Pope Leo XIII beatified Alphonsus de Orozco on January 15, 1882. Pope John Paul II canonized him on May 19, 2002, declaring:

> His pastoral dedication to serving the poorest in the hospitals and prisons makes him a model for all who, under the guidance of the Spirit, base their entire life on the love of God and of their neighbor, following the great commandment of Jesus.

Feast day: September 19.

✠

Andrew Dung Lac — see Martyrs of Vietnam

✠

Andrew Kim and Companions — see Martyrs of Korea

✠

Ángela de la Cruz (María de los Ángeles Guerrero González) (January 30, 1846 – March 2, 1932)
"Angel" to the Poor

Ángela de la Cruz González was born in Seville, Spain, and given the baptismal name of Maria of the Angels Guerrero Gonzalez.

Her father worked as a cook in the convent of the Trinitarian Fathers, where her mother also worked in the laundry. They had fourteen children, although only six reached adulthood.

Little Maria made her First Communion when she was eight and her Confirmation when she was nine. She had little formal education, beginning work as a young girl in a shoe shop. Her boss and teacher of shoe repair, Antonia Maldonado, was a holy woman, and Canon José Torres Padilla of Seville became Maria's spiritual director, having a considerable influence on her life.

When Maria was nineteen, she asked to enter the Discalced Carmelites in Santa Cruz but was refused admission because of her poor health. Instead, following the advice of Canon Torres, she began caring for destitute cholera patients, victims of an epidemic spreading rapidly among the poor.

In 1868, she tried once again to enter the convent, this time the Daughters of Charity of Seville. Although she was still frail, she was admitted. The sisters tried to improve her health, sending her to Cuenca and Valencia, but to no avail. She was forced to leave the Daughters of Charity during her novitiate and returned home to continue working in the shoe shop.

Under Canon Torres' direction, in November 1871 Maria made a private vow to live the evangelical counsels. In 1873, she understood her mission in the world was to be "poor with the poor in order to bring them to Christ."

So Maria continued to work in the shoe shop, until August 2, 1875. At that time, three other women joined her, in a rented room in Seville, and began community life as the Sisters of the Company of the Cross. She became Mother Angela of the Cross and directed her companions in their visits and their aid to the poor, day and night.

When not working among the poor, the Sisters lived as contemplatives, and soon more women wished to join them. In 1877, a second community was founded in Utrera, in the province of Seville; a year later, another followed in Ayamonte (the same year Canon Torres died). While Mother Angela was alive, another twenty-three convents were established, and she became known as "Mother of the Poor."

Mother Angela of the Cross died in Seville. Pope John Paul II beatified her on November 5, 1982, and canonized her in Spain on May 4, 2003.

Feast day: March 2.

✠

Arnold Janssen (November 5, 1837 – January 15, 1909)
Founder of the Divine Word Missionaries

Arnold Janssen was born in Goch, a small city in lower Rhineland, Germany, the second of ten children. His parents fostered his vocation to the priesthood, and he was ordained on August 15, 1861, for the diocese of Muenster. Arnold was then assigned to teach natural sciences and mathematics in a secondary school in Bocholt, and because of his profound devotion to the Sacred Heart of Jesus, he was named Diocesan Director for the Apostleship of Prayer. This apostolate encouraged Arnold to open himself to ecumenical activities with Christians of other denominations, and he decided to dedicate his life to awakening the German church to its missionary responsibility.

In 1873, he resigned from his teaching post and, soon after, founded *The Little Messenger of the Sacred Heart*. This popular monthly magazine presented news of missionary activities and encouraged German-speaking Catholics to do more to help the missions.

But soon, difficult times came for the Catholic Church in Germany. Bismarck unleashed the *Kulturkampf,* a systematic repression of the Church in the country, with a series of anti-Catholic laws. This led to the expulsion of priests and religious and to the imprisonment of many bishops. Arnold proposed that some of the expelled priests could go to the foreign missions or at least help in the preparation of missionaries. Slowly, but surely — and with a little prodding from the Apostolic Vicar of Hong Kong — Arnold discerned that God was calling him to undertake this difficult task personally. With the support of a number of bishops, he inaugurated the mission house on September 8, 1875, in Steyl, Holland; thus began the Divine Word Missionaries.

Aware of the importance of publications for attracting vocations and funding, Arnold started a printing press just four months after the inauguration of the house. Thousands of generous lay people contributed their time and effort to mission animation in German-speaking countries by helping to distribute the magazines from Steyl.

The new congregation developed as a community of both priests and Brothers, but volunteers at the mission house included women as well as men. Virtually from its very beginning, a group of women, including Blessed Maria Helena Stollenwerk, served the community. They wished to serve the mission as Religious Sisters, so Arnold was inspired to found the mission congregation of the Servants of the Holy Spirit (SSpS) on December 8, 1889, and the first Sisters left for Argentina in 1895. In 1896, Arnold selected some of the Sisters to form a cloistered branch, the Servants of the Holy Spirit of Perpetual Adoration (SSpSAP).

Arnold was beatified on October 19, 1975, by Pope Paul VI and was canonized by Pope John Paul II on October 5, 2003, in St. Peter's Square. He declared:

> "Nations shall come to your light" (Is 60: 3). The prophetic image of the New Jerusalem that spreads divine light on all the peoples clearly illustrates the life and tireless apostolate of St. Arnold Janssen. He zealously carried out his priestly work, spreading the Word of God by means of the new mass media, especially the press.
>
> Obstacles did not dismay him. He liked to repeat: "Proclamation of the Good News is the first and most significant expression of love for one's neighbour." He now helps his religious family from Heaven, to continue

faithfully along the tracks he marked out that witness to the permanent value of the Church's evangelizing mission.

Feast day: January 15.

☩

Augustine Chao and 119 Companions, Martyrs of China
Heroes in Persecution

The long list of the Martyrs of China extends over several centuries and is a litany of heroism and dedication to the faith, even unto death. On October 1, 2000, Pope John Paul II honored 120 of the martyrs of China. They are comprised of many missionaries from Europe, but they were also mostly Chinese Catholics. These men, women, and children embraced the Catholic faith with such fervor that they willingly died rather than abjure Christ, even in the face of arrest, imprisonment, severe torture, and death.

The first martyr of China was Francis Fernández de Capillas, a priest of the Order of Preachers (Dominicans). He was put to death on January 15, 1648, at the hands of the Manchus, after suffering severe torture. He was beheaded while, with others, he recited the Sorrowful Mysteries of the Rosary. Blessed Francis Fernández de Capillas has been proclaimed by the Holy See as the Protomartyr of China.

Five Spanish missionaries who had carried out their activity between 1715 and 1747 were put to death as a result of a new campaign of persecution that commenced in 1729, receded for a time, then erupted once more in 1746 at the command of the anti-Christian emperor Yung-Cheng and of his son, K'ien-Lung. Peter Sans i Yordà, O.P, Bishop, was martyred in 1747, at Fuzou. All four of the following were killed on October 28, 1748: Francis Serrano, O.P., Priest; Joachim Royo, O.P., Priest; John Alcober, O.P., Priest; Francis Diaz, O.P., Priest. Blessed Peter Sans i Yordà, O.P, Bishop, was martyred in 1747, at Fuzou.

New persecutions were launched throughout the nineteenth century. Emperor Kia-Kin (r. 1796-1821) issued new decrees against all members of the Christian faith: the first in 1805, against Christians; two more in 1811, against Chinese studying to receive sacred orders, and against priests who were propagating the Christian religion. Finally, a decree 1813 exonerated voluntary apostates from every punishment.

Even the thought of being exempted from punishment did not tempt the faithful, however. The chief Catholic martyrs in this period were: Peter Wu,

22

a Chinese lay catechist strangled on November 7, 1814; and Joseph Zhang Dapeng, a lay catechist and merchant strangled to death on March 12, 1815.

In 1815, two more decrees gave encouragement to the persecutions. The immediate result was the cruel beheading of Monsignor Dufresse, of the Paris Foreign Missions Society, and some Chinese Christians. More martyrs followed them: John Gabriel Taurin Dufresse, M.E.P., Bishop, arrested on May 18, 1815, taken to Chengdu, condemned and executed on September 14, 1815; Augustine Zhao Rong, a Chinese diocesan priest, arrested and subjected to such cruel tortures that he died, in 1815; John da Triora, O.F.M., priest, strangled on February 7, 1816; Joseph Yuan, a Chinese diocesan priest arrested in August 1816, condemned, and strangled on June 24, 1817; and Francis Regis Clet of the Congregation of the Mission (Vincentians), who labored for thirty years in the Chinese missions and was arrested after being betrayed by a Christian. He endured horrendous tortures and was killed by strangling on February 17, 1820.

Others who died: Thaddeus Liu, a Chinese diocesan priest, strangled on November 30, 1823; Peter Liu, a Chinese lay catechist, arrested in 1814 and condemned to exile in Tartary. He remained in exile for almost twenty years, but then returned home, was again arrested, and was strangled on May 17, 1834. Joachim Ho, a Chinese lay catechist, was strangled on July 9, 1839; Augustus Chapdelaine, M.E.P., a priest of the diocese of Coutances and member of the Paris Foreign Missions Society, was arrested in 1856, tortured, condemned to death in prison, and died in February 1856; Laurence Bai Xiaoman, a Chinese layman, beheaded on February 25, 1856; and Agnes Cao Guiying, a widow, arrested and condemned to death in prison. She was executed on March 1, 1856.

Three Chinese catechists — Jerome Lu Tingmei, Laurence Wang Bing, and Agatha Lin Zao (known as the Martyrs of MaoKou, in the province of Guizhou) — were killed on January 28, 1858.

Two seminarians and two lay people — one, a farmer, the other, a widow who worked as a cook in the seminary — suffered martyrdom together on July 29, 1861. They are known as the Martyrs of Qingyanzhen (Guizhou): Joseph Zhang Wenlan, seminarian; Paul Chen Changpin, seminarian; John Baptist Luo Tingying, layman; Martha Wang Luo Mande, laywoman.

On February 18 and 19, 1862, the Martyrs of Guizhou were put to death. They were John Peter Neel, a priest of the Paris Foreign Missions Society; Martin Wu Xuesheng, lay catechist; John Zhang Tianshen, lay catechist; John Chen Xianheng, lay catechist; Lucy Yi Zhenmei, lay catechist.

A change took place in 1840 in China with the start of the terrible Opium War. The conflict — in which China struggled unsuccessfully to rid itself of the opium trade and which it lost to Great Britain and its allies — ended in 1842, when China had to sign the first international treaty of modern times. This was followed by other treaties with America and France.

Taking advantage of this opportunity, France replaced Portugal as the European power protecting the missions and soon issued a decree in two parts. The first, in 1844, permitted the Chinese to follow the Catholic religion; the second, in 1846, abolished all penalties against Catholics. Henceforth, the Church was free to conduct its missionary activity. The result was the widespread success of the Church, except for the brief period of anti-Christian activity during the Boxer Rebellion (the uprising of the "Society for Justice and Harmony") early in the twentieth century.

This rebellion sprang from a deep resentment toward Christians, who were seen as foreign invaders forced upon China by the European powers. Hatred culminated with a new decree issued on July 1, 1900, that marked a new era of persecution and martyrdom. Several missionaries and many Chinese were put to death in the period immediately following the decree.

The Martyrs of Shanxi, killed on July 9, 1900, all were Franciscan Friars Minor: Gregory Grassi, Bishop; Francis Fogolla, Bishop; Elias Facchini, Priest; Theodoric Balat, Priest; Andrew Bauer, Religious Brother.

The Martyrs of Southern Hunan, also Franciscan Friars Minor, were Anthony Fantosati, Bishop (martyred on July 7, 1900); Joseph Mary Gambaro, Priest (martyred on July 7, 1900); and Cesidio Giacomantonio, Priest (martyred on July 4, 1900).

Also martyred were seven Franciscan Missionaries of Mary, of whom three were French, two Italian, one Belgian, and one Dutch. These were Mary Hermina of Jesus; Mary of Peace; Mary Clare; Mary of the Holy Birth; Mary of St. Justus; Mary Adolfine; and Mary Amandina. Eleven Secular Franciscans were martyred, all Chinese: John Zhang Huan, seminarian; Patrick Dong Bodi, seminarian; John Wang Rui, seminarian; Philip Zhang Zhihe, seminarian; John Zhang Jingguang, seminarian; Thomas Shen Jihe, layman and a manservant; Simon Qin Cunfu, lay catechist; Peter Wu Anbang, layman; Francis Zhang Rong, layman and a farmer; Matthew Feng De, layman and neophyte; Peter Zhang Banniu, layman and laborer. To these are joined a number of Chinese lay faithful: James Yan Guodong, farmer; James Zhao Quanxin, manservant; Peter Wang Erman, cook.

During the height of the Boxer Rebellion, Chinese Christians were hunted down and murdered in the thousands. Joining them in death for the

Faith were four French Jesuit missionaries. At least fifty-two Chinese lay Christians have been noted and remembered: men, women, and children — the oldest of them seventy-nine years old and the youngest aged only nine. All suffered martyrdom in July 1900: Leo Mangin, S.J., Priest; Paul Denn, S.J., Priest; Rémy Isoré, S.J., Priest; Modeste Andlauer, S.J., Priest. The names and ages of the Chinese lay Christians were as follows: Mary Zhu born Wu, aged about 50 years; Peter Zhu Rixin, aged 19; John Baptist Zhu Wurui, aged 17; Mary Fu Guilin, aged 37; Barbara Cui born Lian, aged 51; Joseph Ma Taishun, aged 60; Lucy Wang Cheng, aged 18; Mary Fan Kun, aged 16; Mary Chi Yu, aged 15; Mary Zheng Xu, aged 11 years; Mary Du born Zhao, aged 51; Magdalene Du Fengju, aged 19; Mary du born Tian, aged 42; Paul Wu Anjyu, aged 62; John Baptist Wu Mantang, aged 17; Paul Wu Wanshu, aged 16; Raymond Li Quanzhen, aged 59; Peter Li Quanhui, aged 63; Peter Zhao Mingzhen, aged 61; John Baptist Zhao Mingxi, aged 56; Teresa Chen Tinjieh, aged 25; Rose Chen Aijieh, aged 22; Peter Wang Zuolung, aged 58; Mary Guo born Li, aged 65; Joan Wu Wenyin, aged 50; Zhang Huailu, aged 57; Mark Ki-T'ien-Siang, aged 66; Ann An born Xin, aged 72; Mary An born Guo, aged 64; Ann An born Jiao, aged 26; Mary An Linghua, aged 29; Paul Liu Jinde, aged 79; Joseph Wang Kuiju, aged 37; John Wang Kuixin, aged 25; Teresa Zhang born He, aged 36; Lang born Yang, aged 29; Paul Lang Fu, aged 9; Elizabeth Qin born Bian, aged 54; Simon Qin Cunfu, aged 14; Peter Liu Zeyu, aged 57; Ann Wang, aged 14; Joseph Wang Yumei, aged 68; Lucy Wang born Wang, aged 31; Andrew Wang Tianqing, aged 9; Mary Wang born Li, aged 49; Chi Zhuze, aged 18; Mary Zhao born Guo, aged 60; Rose Zhao, aged 22; Mary Zhao, aged 17; Joseph Yuan Gengyin, aged 47; Paul Ge Tingzhu, aged 61; Rose Fan Hui, aged 45.

In addition to these martyrs was Alberic Crescitelli, a priest of the Pontifical Institute of Foreign Missions of Milan, who was martyred on July 21, 1900. Several years later, more martyrs came from the members of the Salesian Society of St John Bosco: Louis Versiglia, bishop, and Callistus Caravario, priest. They were killed together on February 25, 1930.

The first of the martyrs were beatified on May 27, 1900, under Pope Leo XIII. Pope John Paul II canonized all of the martyrs together on Oct. 1, 2000. On that day, the Holy Father proclaimed:

"The precepts of the Lord give joy to the heart" (Responsorial Psalm). These words of the Responsorial Psalm clearly reflect the experience of Augustine Zhao Rong and his 119 companions, martyrs in China. The testimonies which have come down to us allow us to glimpse in them a state of mind marked by deep serenity and joy.

Feast day for the Martyrs of China: September 28.

B

✠

Benedetta Cambiagio Frassinello
(October 2, 1791 – March 21, 1858)
Married and Religious

The founder of the Benedictine Sisters of Providence, Benedetta Cambiago Frassinello labored with her husband to promote education. She was born in Langasco, near Genoa, Italy, the daughter of Giuseppe and Francesca Cambiagio. The devout and faithful family moved to Pavia while Benedetta was still young. There, Benedetta, at the age of twenty, had a profound mystical experience and became devoted to prayer and penance.

She married Giovanni Battista Frassinella on February 7, 1816, in compliance with her family's wishes, and the couple lived a normal married life for two years. Then Giovanni, impressed by Benedetta's holiness, agreed to live with her as brother and sister. The couple was taking care of Benedetta's younger sister Maria at the time. When Maria died of intestinal cancer in 1825, Giovanni entered the Somaschan Fathers, and Benedicta became an Ursuline.

One year later, Benedetta became ill and left the convent to return to Pavia, where she began an apostolate among young women of the region. Giovanni was recalled from his monastery to aid in this work, and the couple took vows of perfect chastity. So successful were they in Pavia that Benedetta was appointed "Promoter of Public Instruction." Unfortunately, civil and Church authorities criticized Benedetta because of the unusual relationship she shared with her husband; so, in 1838, she turned her work over to the bishop of Pavia and withdrew to Ronco Scrivia. There, the couple and five companions founded the Congregation of the Benedictine Sisters of Providence and opened a school.

Benedetta died in Ronco Scrivia on 1858. Pope John Paul II beatified Benedetta on May 10, 1987, declaring that her remarkable piety inspired others to heroic sanctity and to unstinting service of those in need. The Holy Father canonized Benedetta on May 19, 2002, proclaiming:

> Guided by divine grace, the new saint was concerned to accomplish God's will with fidelity and coherence. With boundless confidence in the Lord's

goodness, she abandoned herself to his "loving Providence," deeply convinced, as she liked to repeat, that one must "do everything for love of God and to please him."

Feast day: March 21.

✠

Benedetto Menni, O.H. (March 11, 1841 – April 24, 1914)
Crusader for Reform

Benedetto Menni was born in Milan, Italy, and raised firmly in the Catholic Faith. When he had completed his education, Benedetto worked in a bank and became involved in the political upheavals of the time. He was drawn into military service, where he labored as a stretcher-bearer in the Battle of Magenta and witnessed the horrors of war on a close, personal basis. After his release from the military, he prayed to know the will of God for his life and visited a local hermit, who recognized unique spiritual abilities in Benedetto and advised him to become a religious.

Benedetto entered the Order of the Hospitallers of St. John of God, receiving his habit on May 13, 1860. In 1866, he was ordained a priest in Rome.

On January 14, 1867, Pope Blessed Pius IX (r. 1846-1878) received Benedetto in an audience. The Holy Father knew that the Fr. General of the Order had asked Benedetto to go to Spain to restore the Order there. Pope Blessed Pius IX encouraged Benedetto to accomplish this task.

Benedetto had many trials in Spain, including a threat to his life, and he was expelled once for his activities. However he continued his labors and restored the Order in Portugal, Mexico, and Spain. He also founded the Hospitaller Sisters of the Sacred Heart of Jesus with Maria Josefa Recio and Maria Augustias Jimenez. The congregation was founded in Ciempozuelos, Spain, in May 1881.

Finally, exhausted by his ministries, Benedetto died in Dinan, in northern France, in 1914.

Pope John Paul II beatified Benedetto on June 23, 1985, and canonized him on November 21, 1999, observing:

> His spirituality was born of his own experience of God's love for him. ...
> He carried out his service to the order and to society with a humility based
> on hospitality and blameless integrity, which made him a model for many.

Feast day: April 24.

✠

Bernardo of Corleone (February 6, 1605 – January 12, 1667)
"The Finest Blade in Sicily"

This future Franciscan Capuchin friar was born Filippo Latino in Corleone, Sicily. His home was popularly known as "the house of saints" — his father, Leonardo, a skilled cobbler and leather craftsman, brought home the poor and homeless and cared for them. Filippo and his brothers and sisters learned about the Faith watching their saintly parents.

Filippo, however, was a celebrated dueler who gained fame when he wounded the hand of one of his boasting challengers, causing the swordsman to lose his arm. The incident left Filippo severely shaken with guilt and shame, and he begged forgiveness from the wounded man, who later became his friend.

Receiving the grace of a religious vocation, Filippo took the habit of the Capuchin Franciscans on December 13, 1631, at the age of twenty-seven. He was given the religious name of Bernardo and spent the next years moving from one friary to another in the province, serving as a cook or assistant cook. He also took care of the sick and became well known as a launderer to the friars.

At the same time, however, he was revered for his spiritual insights, advice, and personal mortifications. Such was his level of contemplative prayer that he passed into ecstasies. He also remained in churches throughout the night because he did not wish to leave the Blessed Sacrament alone, and he received daily Communion, something that was highly unusual in that era.

Bernardo was beatified by Pope Clement XIII on May 15, 1768, and canonized by Pope John Paul II on June 10, 2001, who announced:

> The evangelical witness of St Bernardo of Corleone, elevated to the honour of the altars today, observed within the mystery of the Trinity gains a particular effectiveness. All wondered and asked how a simple lay brother could discourse so well about the mystery of the Trinity. In fact, his life was entirely directed toward God, by a constant ascetical exertion joined with prayer and penance. Those who knew him agreed in testifying that "he was always at prayer," "never ceased to pray," "prayed constantly" (*Summ.* 35).

Feast day: January 12.

C

✠

Cirilo Bertrán and 8 Companions and Inocencio de la Immaculada (The Martyrs of Asturias) (October 1934)

Christian Brothers and Martyrs of Spain

During the Spanish Civil War, Communist-led rebel forces were in control of Asturias, and on October 4, 1934, they used heavy military force to annihilate opponents of the Second Republic. In Turon, they put their anti-Catholic regime into action, destroying or profaning sacred structures and hunting down Catholics, both laypeople and clergy.

The Christian Brothers operated a school in Turon for the sons of local coal miners. Cirilo Bertrán Tejedor and his fellow teachers defied the rebels by continuing instruction in religion and by urging attendance at Mass. They were not intimidated by threats. On the First Friday of October 1934, the local Communist authorities entered the Christian Brothers' residence and discovered Passionist Fr. Manuel Arnau (Inocencio de la Immaculada) preparing to celebrate Mass. He and the Christian Brothers were arrested, marched to a local cemetery, and shot. The martyrs were:

Cirilo Bertrán Tejedor, born José Sanz Tejedor, in Lerma, Spain, on March 20, 1888, became a Christian Brother in 1907. Cirilo taught in many schools of the congregation and served as Superior in Santander in 1925. In 1933, he was sent to Turon, and he started this assignment by making a thirty-day retreat. An eyewitness to the execution of Cirilo Bertrán and his companions stated that the martyrs heard their sentence calmly and walked to their doom with dignity and soft prayers.

Marciano José (Filomeno) Lopez, born in 1900 in Spain, was assigned to Turon only six months before his martyrdom. He did not teach because he was deaf and had severe health problems.

Julian Alfredo (Vilfridio Fernández) Zapico, a Christian Brother born in 1903, was transferred to Turon only one month before his martyrdom. He was assigned to that troubled region because he was viewed as a religious with a firm resolve and character, one needed in such a crisis.

Victoriano Pio (Claudio Bernabé) Cano was a Christian Brother who arrived in Turon only twenty days before his martyrdom. Born in 1905, he was honored for his brilliant musical abilities.

Benjamin Julian (Vicente Alonso) Andres, born in 1908, had been sent to Turon because he had a sound sense of political matters. Benjamin was also beloved for his sense of joy and optimistic outlook on life.

Augusto Andres (Román Martin) Fernández (1910) was sent to Turon when his school was closed earlier by anti-religious rebels. Augustino taught in the town for about one year before being martyred.

Benito de Jesús (Hector Valdivieso) Sáez, born in Argentina in 1910, was involved in Spain's Eucharistic Crusade and was recognized as a talented writer.

Aniceto Adolfo (Manuel Seco) Gutierrez was a Christian Brother only twenty-two years old when he was martyred.

Innocencio Canoura Arnau, a Passionist priest born in 1887, taught literature, philosophy, and theology. He was at the Christian Brothers' residence to hear the confessions of students in preparation for First Friday liturgies on October 5 when he was marched out with the Christian Brothers to be shot.

Pope John Paul II beatified the Martyrs of Asturias on April 29, 1990, and canonized them on November 21, 1999, along with St. Jaime Hilario Barbal. The Holy Father declared:

> Not afraid to shed their blood for Christ, they conquered death and now share in the glory of God's kingdom. This is why I have the joy of enrolling them among the saints today, holding them up to the universal Church as models of Christian life and our intercessors with God . . . Joined with the group of martyrs of Turón is Bro. Jaime Hilario, of the same religious congregation, who was killed in Tarragona three years later. While forgiving his executioners, he said, "My friends, to die for Christ is to reign."

Feast day: October 9.

✠

Claude de la Colombière, S.J.
(February 2, 1641 – February 15, 1682)
Spiritual Director of Margaret Mary Alacoque

A Jesuit priest, Claude de la Colombiére was one of the leaders in the spread of the devotion to the Sacred Heart.

He was born at Saint-Symphorien d'Ozen, near Lyons, France, in 1641, and was formally educated at the Jesuit College in Lyons. Entering the Society of Jesus in 1659, he was sent to Avignon and Paris for advanced studies by the Jesuits and ordained to the priesthood in the society. Claude then served as tutor to the son of the powerful French minister Maurice Colbert, acquiring as well a reputation as a preacher.

In 1675, Claude became the Superior of Paray-le-Monial College, demonstrating academic brilliance and an intense loyalty to the precepts of the Faith. While serving at Paray-le-Monial, he met the future St. Margaret Mary Alacoque. He became her confessor and aided her in spreading devotion to the Sacred Heart of Jesus. In a vision, Margaret Mary was told that Claude was Christ's "perfect friend," and that Claude's gift was "to lead souls to God." He then was assigned by the order to England to serve as a chaplain to Mary Beatrice d'Este, the duchess of York.

At this point, however, the Titus Oates Plot was launched. This was a spurious claim purported by Titus Oates that a vast Jesuit conspiracy was at work to assassinate King Charles II, install his brother, the duke of York — the future King James II — on the throne, and bring England back to the Catholic Faith. During the hysteria that gripped the kingdom, Claude was falsely charged as a participant in this plot, charges made because of the resentment caused by Claude's loyal service to the duchess of York and his respected position in her court. He was imprisoned and was harshly treated (most especially because he was a Jesuit) before receiving banishment from England, but he never fully recovered from the torments visited on him by the British.

He was able to return to Paray-le-Monial in 1679, where he was welcomed as a "dry" martyr for the faith, meaning that he had suffered every indignity and cruelty but had not shed his blood, nor had he suffered execution. Claude remained in poor health, however, physically broken by his many ordeals. He died of hemoptysis (coughing up blood from the lungs), and his sufferings were widely known within the Church of his era.

Pope Pius XI beatified him on June 16, 1929, and Pope John Paul II canonized Claude in Rome on May 31, 1992, declaring:

The past three centuries allow us to evaluate the importance of the message which was entrusted to Claude. . . . In a period of contrasts between the fervor of some and the indifference or impiety of many, here is a devotion centered on the humanity of Christ, on his presence, on his love of mercy and on forgiveness . . . devotion to the Heart of Christ would be a source of balance and spiritual strengthening for Christian communities so often faced with increasing unbelief over the coming centuries.

Feast day: February 15.

✠

Claudine Thévenet (March 30, 1774 – February 3, 1837)
Aid and Protector of Young Women

The founder of the Congregation of the Sisters of Jesus and Mary, Claudine Thévenet (Marie de St. Ignatius) was born in Lyons, France, and raised in a devout family acutely attuned to the injustices of her era. Claudine saw her brothers, Louis and Francis, taken prisoner by the government authorities of the French Revolution for remaining true to the faith. In January 1794, she saw them paraded to their deaths in Lyons and followed so that she could witness their martyrdoms while comforting them with her loving presence.

Soon after, Claudine began to take an interest in the young women active in the workforce of Lyons. In 1816, after years of labors on her own, she established a pious union with the aid of Fr. André Coindre. This led to the founding of the Congregation of the Sisters of Jesus and Mary two years later. Taking the religious name of Mary of St. Ignatius, she gathered pious companions and formed a community designed to provide young women with a Christian education conformable to their positions in a changing society, while instructing these women in the Faith.

In this program, Claudine established boarding schools, academies, and residences for young women of the working classes who had few resources in the secular world. She was a true model of charity, demonstrating as well an understanding of the era in which she lived. Countless young women looked to Claudine for education, respect, and secure lodgings in a turbulent period. She even conducted residences for ladies involved in the literary profession, a pressing need at the time. The Congregation of the Sisters of Jesus and Mary established houses at Le Puy, Rodes, and Remíremont. The motherhouse had to be established in Rome when the persecutions started in France. The sisters also started a college in Rome, imbued with the foundress' spirit of adapting to new needs.

Claudine Thévenet died in Lyons. Ten years later, Pope Blessed Pius IX approved the constitution of her congregation, and in 1842, members of her religious congregation opened missions in India and Pakistan, including Bombay, Poonah, Lahore, Simla, and Agra. In 1850, the sisters established a house in Spain, and one was opened in Mexico in 1902. The congregation started serving in Canada in 1855 and in the United States in 1877.

Pope John Paul II beatified Marie on October 4, 1981, and canonized her on March 21, 1993, declaring:

> In the frailty of a child, Claudine Thévenet discerned the power of God the Creator, in the child's poverty the glory of the Almighty, who does not cease calling and who calls us to share the fullness of life which he possesses; in the child's abandonment, Christ crucified and risen, who is ever present in his brothers and sisters, the least of people. . . . Her concept of education combines a sense of human realities with a sense of the divine. Were not the homes which she founded for the poorest girls called "Providences?" Indeed, it was necessary to teach the young girls to manage a good household, doing the smallest chores with as much care and love as the greatest. A burning charity places her at the service of the young with respect and affection in order to permit each one to give the best of herself. . . . She ceaselessly invoked God's goodness.

Feast day: February 3.

✠

Clelia Barbieri (February 13, 1847– July 13, 1870)
Youngest Foundress of a Religious Congregation

The founder of The Little Sisters of Our Lady of Sorrows, Clelia Barbieri was born in Budrio, Emilia, Italy, the daughter of Joseph and Hyacintha Nanetti Barbieri. Her father died in 1855, leaving her family endangered financially, and Clelia had to assume many responsibilities at an early age. She became a catechist for the local parish, even though there was political unrest and an anti-religious feeling sweeping through the area.

The local pastor encouraged Clelia to start educating young women as well, and a friend, Teodora Baraldi, joined her in the task. The Little Sisters of Our Lady of Sorrows (also called the Minims of Our Lady of Sorrows) developed from Clelia's efforts, and another young woman, Orsola Donati, aided in the founding of the congregation on May 1, 1868. The archbishop of Bologna, Lucida Maria Cardinal Parocchi, blessed the Little Sisters and

their work. In 1949, the institute was given pontifical status and was attached to the Servite Order. The Minims work in Europe, Tanzania, and India.

Clelia understood the modern demands upon religious and, accordingly, she designed the congregation as both an active and a contemplative apostolate. Dedicated to Christ in the Holy Eucharist, Clelia demonstrated this love with unique fidelity to the everyday, parish-level activities that brought the Faith to her neighbors. She died very suddenly, at the age of twenty-three, at Budrio. Giorgio Cardinal Gusmini wrote her biography, and the faithful of the region honored her immediately, calling Clelia "the mother."

Clelia was beatified on October 2, 1968, by Pope Paul VI. Pope John Paul II canonized her on April 9, 1989, declaring:

> . . . Clelia Barbieri is not the fruit of a particular school of spirituality but the genuine product of that first and fundamental school of holiness which was the parish church of her village. The Eucharist is the theological location both of the mystical experiences of Clelia — from the first Communion to the termination of her life — and of that reality which she herself will name the glorious inspiration, the charism of foundation. From the devotion to the Eucharist springs forth her multiple charitable activities in the form of evangelization and education, assistance and immediate intervention on behalf of the poor, the sick, the marginalized, by means of a simple and ingenious creativity which makes her worthy of the title given to her by her people: "Mother, Mother Clelia."

Feast day: July 13.

✠

Crispin of Viterbo (November 13, 1668 – May 19, 1750)
The "Little Beast of Burden"

Crispin of Viterbo was born in Viterbo, Italy; when he was five, his mother consecrated him to the Blessed Virgin. Seeing a procession of Friars Minor

Capuchin, Crispin was inspired to embrace the religious life, and he was accepted into the Franciscans as a lay brother assigned to menial tasks.

He served as a cook in the Viterbo Capuchin monastery and was then assigned to other tasks in Tolfa, Rome, and Albano. Going about his chores without a hat, Crispin was asked by a passerby why he went on his rounds bareheaded. He had long been nicknamed the "Little Beast of Burden" — thus, he replied, "An ass does not need a hat."

Crispin, however, developed a profound holiness and soon attracted the notice of men and women outside of his community, who visited him for his counsel and guidance. He also began to receive visits almost every day from bishops, cardinals, and others of note, and was even consulted by the Holy Father. He did not take their ranks and titles too seriously, viewing them instead as children of God who needed reminders about the eternal aspects of salvation and the need for self-awareness and truth. Crispin brought a heavenly perspective on human affairs to people of all ranks.

When Crispin became infirm due to his age, austere penances, and labors, he was sent to Rome to rest. He died there, surrounded by his mourning Franciscan companions and leaders of the Church. This hidden, humble lay brother had touched the lives of hundreds and had communicated his wisdom, fervor, and devotion face to face with those who sought him out. He was a font of spiritual perfection, and his body, which was discovered still remarkably preserved, is enshrined under a side altar in the Capuchin church in Rome.

Crispin was beatified by Pope Pius VII in 1806 and canonized by Pope John Paul II on June 20, 1982, the first saint raised to the altars in his remarkable pontificate. During the ceremonies, the Holy Father praised this humble monk as a giant of the spiritual life, a gentle soul who perceived the secrets of the saints and perfection.

Feast day: May 19.

✠

Cristóbal Magallanes Jara and Companions (1915-28)
Martyrs of the Catholic Action Movement in Mexico

Early in the twentieth century, Mexican authorities tried to impose a "Mexican Church" on the nation, replacing Catholic bishops with schismatic prelates. Foreign missionaries were expelled, and schools and seminaries were closed by government order.

Pope Pius XI (r. 1922-1939) had worked with the Mexican bishops to find a way of preserving the faith; in retaliation, the government closed the churches. Priests were hunted down, and devout laypeople were warned to abjure the Church and Christian worship.

Catholic Action responded to the challenge, blunting the message of secular humanism and keeping the faithful inspired. Priests and laymen who belonged to Catholic Action were therefore singled out for persecution. Fifteen priests were martyred in Jalisco, four in Zacatecas, and one each in Chihuahua, Colima, Durango, Guanajuato, Guerrero, and Morelos. Most died at the hands of firing squads, and all were tortured hideously before their martyrdoms. The three laymen, David, Manuel, and Salvador, died with their parish priest, Luis Batis Sáinz. All of the martyrs symbolize the other Mexican men and women who made the ultimate sacrifice for the Faith during the same period of ordeal.

The Catholic Action Martyrs are:

Cristóbal Magallanes Jara (1869-1927); Román Adame Rosales; Rodrigo Aguilar Aleman; Julio Álvarez Mendoza; Luis Batis Sáinz; Agustín Caloca Cortés; Mateo Correa Megallanes; Atilano Cruz Alvarado; Miguel De La Mora; Pedro Esqueda Ramírez; Margarito Flores García; José Isabel Flores Varela; David Galván Bermudes; Salvador Lara Puente; Pedro de Jesús Maldonado Lucero; Jesús Méndez Montoya; Manuel Morales; Justino Orona Madrigal; Sabas Reyes Salazar; José María Robles Hurtado; David Roldán Lara; Toribio Romo González; Jenaro Sánchez Delgadillo; Tranquilino Ubiarco Robles; David Uribe Velasco.

Pope John Paul II beatified Cristóbal and his companions on November 22, 1992, and canonized them on May 21, 2000. In his homily, the Holy Father spoke of the martyrs, saying:

Most of them belonged to the secular clergy and three were laymen seriously committed to helping priests. They did not stop courageously exercising their ministry when religious persecution intensified in the beloved land of Mexico, unleashing hatred of the Catholic religion. They all freely and calmly accepted martyrdom as a witness to their faith, explicitly forgiving their persecutors. Faithful to God and to the Catholic faith so deeply rooted in the ecclesial communities which they served by also promoting their material well-being, today they are an example to the whole Church and to Mexican society in particular.

After the harsh trials that the Church endured in Mexico during those turbulent years, today Mexican Christians, encouraged by the witness of these witnesses to the faith, can live in peace and harmony, contributing the wealth of Gospel values to society. The Church grows and advances, since she is the crucible in which many priestly and religious vocations are born, where families are formed according to God's plan, and where young people, a substantial part of the Mexican population, can grow up with the hope of a better future.

May the shining example of Cristóbal Magallanes and his companion martyrs help you to make a renewed commitment of fidelity to God, which can continue to transform Mexican society so that justice, fraternity and harmony will prevail among all.

Feast day: May 25.

✠

Cunegunda (Kinga) (1224 – July 24, 1292)
Royal Saint

The Patroness of Poland and Lithuania, Cunegunda, also called Kinga, founded a Poor Clare convent. She was the daughter of King Bela IV of Hungary and the niece of St. Elizabeth of Hungary. At the age of sixteen, she married King Boleslaus V of Poland, but she asked her husband to allow her to remain celibate. He agreed to this for one year, but eventually he and Cunegunda took a vow of celibacy before the Bishop of Krakow, Prandota of Bialaczew. Henceforth, Boleslaus was called "the Chaste." Together, the two led an austere life at court, devoting both their time and royal resources to charity and the poor. Biographies from the period testify that Cunegunda was called by her people "comforter," "physician," "holy mother," and "nurse."

She also promoted the cultural development of Poland through literature, such as the first book written in the Polish language: *Zoltarz Dawidów*, the Psalter of David. With the Bishop of Kraków, Cunegunda worked tirelessly for the canonization of the martyr of Kraków, Bishop Stanislaus of Szczepanów. A great influence on her spirituality was also almost certainly exercised by St. Hyacinth, who lived during that time.

After Boleslaus' passing in 1279, Cunegunda became a Poor Clare at the Convent of Stary Sacz, a monastic retreat that she had founded. She also built churches and hospitals, ransomed Christians captured by the Turks, and served the poor and ill. In 1287, she led her nuns to refuge in a castle during an onslaught by the Tartar Mongols. The castle seemed doomed to destruction by the Tartars, who were leaving no fortress or village in their path untouched. Cunegunda, however, saved her nuns entirely by prayer. The Tartars departed the region, leaving the fortress unmolested.

Even before her death, Cunegunda was revered for her holiness and her miraculous abilities in prayer. Her cult was confirmed in 1690, and in 1715 she was declared the patroness of both Poland and Lithuania. On June 16, 1999, Pope John Paul II declared her a saint. The pontiff proclaimed:

> St. Kinga teaches us that both marriage and virginity lived in union with Christ can become a path to holiness. Today St. Kinga rises to safeguard these values. She reminds us that the value of marriage, this indissoluble union of love between two persons, cannot be brought into question under any circumstances. Whatever difficulties may arise, one may not abandon the defence of this primordial love which has united two persons and which is constantly blessed by God. Marriage is the way of holiness, even when it becomes the way of the Cross. The walls of the Convent of Stary Sacz, which St. Kinga founded and where she came to the end of her life, seem today a testimony of how much she esteemed chastity and virginity, rightly seeing in this state an extraordinary gift whereby man experiences in a special way his own freedom. He can make of this inner freedom a place of encounter with Christ and with others on the path of holiness.

Feast day July 24.

Ꝺ

✠

Daniel Comboni (March 15, 1831 – October 10, 1881)
Apostle to Africa

Daniel Comboni was born at Limone, Lake Gorda, in northern Italy. One of eight children, he was the only one to survive to maturity. While attending the school operated by Fr. Nicholas Mazza, who was training missionaries for Africa, Daniel was inspired by accounts of the martyrs of Japan. He studied for the priesthood and was ordained in December 1854. He also underwent medical training, and when a plague struck Verona, he aided countless victims.

In September 1857, Daniel and five companions were sent to Africa. They spent three months in Khartoum, then went to the Holy Cross Mission in southern Sudan. There, the group was overcome by malaria, and Daniel and the survivors had to leave the area in January 1859. He returned to Fr. Mazza's Institute to train more missionaries.

Daniel was one of the first Europeans interested in educating Africans and establishing a native clergy for the continent. He spoke six European languages, as well as Arabic and six dialects of Dinko, Bari, and Nuba. When he was given seven African slaves, rescued by the British, he restored several to their villages and educated the rest. With these slaves in mind, Daniel founded the Institute of the Good Shepherd for the Regeneration of Africa in 1867, a group called the Comboni Missionaries. Five years later, he founded the Verona Sisters to aid the priests in the mission apostolate. From 1867 until his death, Daniel made eight long and dangerous journeys to Africa, working successfully to stem the slave trade.

During the Sudan rebellion, the religious leader of the rebels, the Mahdi, captured some of Daniel's priests and nuns. Although Mahdi forces killed Lord Gordon at Khartoum, they showed respect for the Catholic religious; the modesty, charity, and humility displayed by the Comboni missionaries won them their freedom, and they were returned unharmed.

In 1872, Daniel was appointed pro-vicar apostolic of Central Africa, responsible for administering missions in Egypt, Sudan, and southward to the region of the Lakes. In 1877, he was named vicar apostolic and was consecrated a bishop, and one year later, was involved in relieving Khartoum in a dire famine.

He died in Khartoum of malaria, and Pope Leo XIII (r. 1878-1903) called his death "a great loss." Other Comboni missionary groups have since been established to carry on his visioned apostolate; they arrived in the U.S. by 1940.

Pope John Paul II beatified Daniel on March 17, 1996, declaring:

Leading humanity to the light of eternal life: Daniel Comboni's ideal continues today in the apostolate of his spiritual sons and daughters. They still maintain strong ties in Africa, particularly in Sudan, where their founder spent a great part of his energy as a tireless evangelizer and where he died at a young age, worn out by his labors and illness. The unconditional trust he had in the power of prayer (cf. Scritti, n. 2324) is effectively expressed in the "Cenacles of missionary prayer" which are being set up in many parishes and represent a significant way to promote and renew missionary spirituality.

The pope subsequently canonized him on October 5, 2003.

Feast day: October 10.

$\mathcal{E}$

✠

Edith Stein (Teresa Benedicta of the Cross)
(October 12, 1891 – August 9 or 10, 1942)
Philosopher, Convert, Martyr

Edith Stein (Teresa Benedict of the Cross), was born in Breslau, Germany, the youngest of seven children in a prominent Jewish family. She abandoned Judaism as early as 1904, becoming a self-proclaimed atheist. Her brilliant intellect was seeking truth, however, and she entered the University of Göttingen, where she became a protégé of the famed philosopher Edmund Husserl. She was also a proponent of the philosophical school of phenomenology, both at Göttingen and Freiburg in Breisgau. She earned a doctorate in 1916 and emerged as one of Europe's brightest philosophers.

One of her primary endeavors was to examine phenomenology from the perspective of Thomistic thought, and in that process, her interest in Catholic teaching began to grow. Propelled by her reading of the autobiography of St. Teresa of Ávila, she was baptized on January 1, 1922. Following her baptism, she gave up her university post and became a teacher in the Dominican school at Speyer. In 1932, she received the post of lecturer at the Educational Institute of Munich, but a year later, was forced to resign. Adolf Hitler had come to power in 1933, and the first anti-Jewish campaigns had begun. In 1934, Edith entered the Carmelite Order, receiving the name Teresa Benedicta of the Cross.

In the cloister, she was able to continue her philosophical research, but the Nazis did not recognize her conversion and intended to send her to a concentration camp. Edith was taken out of Germany and sent to a Carmelite cloister in the Netherlands in 1938. When the Nazis occupied that land, however, the Gestapo arrived at the cloister and arrested her in 1942. Her sister, Rosa, also a convert, was arrested at the same time as part of the order by Hitler to liquidate all non-Aryan Catholics. Edith Stein was taken to Auschwitz, the notorious death camp, and died there in one of the gas chambers.

Following her death and the end of the war, her extensive spiritual and philosophical writings were collected and published, receiving promotion by the Archivum Carmelatinum Edith Stein at Louvain, Belgium. Her Cause was formally opened in 1962.

Pope John Paul II beatified Edith on May 1, 1987, in the cathedral at Cologne, Germany, and canonized her on October 11, 1998. At her canonization, the pontiff praised the Carmelite martyr for her fidelity to the truth and to the love of Christ. The pontiff also named her a co-patroness of Europe, with St. Bridget of Sweden and St. Catherine of Siena, on October 1, 1999. At her canonization, Pope John Paul II declared:

> The spiritual experience of Edith Stein is an eloquent example of . . . extraordinary interior renewal. A young woman in search of the truth has become a saint and a martyr through the silent workings of divine grace: Teresa Benedicta of the Cross, who from heaven repeats to us today all the words that marked her life: "Far be it from me to glory except in the Cross of our Lord Jesus Christ."
>
> Dear brothers and sisters! Because she was Jewish, Edith Stein was taken with her sister Rosa and many other Catholic Jews from the Netherlands to the concentration camp in Auschwitz, where she died with them in the gas chambers. Today we remember them all with deep respect. A few days before her deportation, the woman religious had dismissed the question about a possible rescue: "Do not do it! Why should I be spared? Is it not right that I should gain no advantage from my Baptism? If I cannot share the lot of my brothers and sisters, my life, in a certain sense, is destroyed.". . .
>
> This woman had to face the challenges of such a radically changing century as our own. . . . The modern world boasts of the enticing door which says: everything is permitted. It ignores the narrow gate of discernment and renunciation. I am speaking especially to you, young Christians . . . . Your life is not an endless series of open doors! Listen to your heart! Do not stay on the surface, but go to the heart of things! And when the time is right, have the courage to decide! The Lord is waiting for you to put your freedom in his good hands.

Feast day: August 10.

✠

Egidio Maria of St. Joseph (Francis Anthony Postillo) (November 16, 1729 – February 7, 1812)

Aegidius and Giles Mary of St. Joseph

A future Franciscan lay brother, Egidio was born in Taranto, Apulia, Italy, and baptized Francesco. His family and neighbors were simple, devout Catholics, and Francesco matured in the Faith, becoming a rope maker in his hometown. In 1754, he made his application to the Discalced Friars Minor of St. Peter of Alcántara in Naples. Because he lacked the formal education necessary to train for the priesthood, he was received as a novice lay brother and took the name Egidio.

After making his vows as a Franciscan, he was assigned as a porter, or a gatekeeper, at the local Franciscan seminary. Porters normally served as intermediaries for religious houses, answering the bell at the gate and greeting the people who visited there. Egidio served faithfully in this post, but his overwhelming compassion and charity led him into far-flung sections of Naples and beyond. The Franciscans at the seminary recognized his piety and faithful service, but they did not know the scope of his activities or the day-to-day valor he displayed.

Skilled in caring for the sick, Egidio brought a tender concern to the men and women who sought him out at his post. He was busy every day with the wounded or diseased, and he walked outside the city limits offering aid and comfort to the most pitiful people in the region. In keeping with the spiritual legacy of St. Francis, Egidio made certain to wash and minister to all lepers who needed his aid. He refused no one in his solicitous ministry.

Egidio reached the age of eighty while performing this endless ministry of compassion and care. When he died at prayer in Naples on February 7, 1812, thousands mourned his passing. Vast crowds overwhelmed Egidio's funeral with their sorrow. His Cause was opened soon after his death, and Pope Leo XIII beatified him in 1888. Pope John Paul II canonized Egidio on June 2, 1996. At his canonization ceremony Pope John Paul II praised him as a glory of the Franciscan crown, a humble follower of Christ and *il Poverello* who left the indelible mark of his love and sanctity on the city of Naples and on the modern Church.

Feast day: February 7.

✠

Enrique de Ossó y Cercelló
(October 16, 1840 – January 27, 1896)

Pioneer of Evangelization through Modern Communications

Enrique de Ossó y Cercelló was born in Vinebre, a small town in Tarragona province, Spain, the son of Jaime and Micaela de Ossó y Cervelló. His mother fostered his priestly vocation, but his father was opposed the entire idea and sent Enrique to an uncle to study the textile business. Enrique was only twelve when he made this move to Quinto de Ebro, and within a few months became seriously ill. Enrique's father tried again to apprentice him elsewhere — this time in Reus — but once more, illness brought the boy home.

In September 1854, Enrique's mother died of cholera during a terrible epidemic, and his father sent him again to Reus. This time, he fled the textile training by going to Montserrat Monastery, where his brother, Jaime, found him and took him home. Finally, Enrique's father recognized the possibility of a priestly vocation for his son and agreed to allow the young man to pursue the matter.

Moved by a lecture on the life of St. Teresa of Ávila, Enrique took the decisive step of entering the priesthood. He studied at Barcelona and Tortosa and was ordained on September 21, 1867, celebrating his first Mass at Montserrat.

One of his classmates was Emmanuel Domingo y Sol, who declared that the life of St. Teresa of Ávila had spurred Enrique's priestly vocation, and that he had taken upon himself the arduous task of reforming and renewing the Faithin Spain.

Appointed a teacher of mathematics in the Tortosa seminary, Enrique continued his apostolate of preaching and missions until the local bishop removed him from his faculty obligations, which allowed him to dedicate himself full-time to education and catechetics. He was tireless in his efforts, using modern methods to appeal to young and old, and he established many programs, including the Institute of Josephine Brothers and the Teresian Missionaries. The Company, or Congregation of St. Teresa, was his crowning achievement. This congregation was dedicated to forming "Teresians" who would carry the Carmelite spirit into the world, and the congregation received papal approval in 1877, extending its mission to Algiers in 1885. Today, these sisters serve in Spain, Portugal, Africa, and Mexico.

Enrique also recognized the growing impact of the press on the society of his day and viewed the arena of communication as a distinct apostolate that had to be undertaken by the faithful. A prodigious writer, he started a weekly publication, *El Hombre* (*The Man*), and another called *El Amigo del Pueblo* (*The Friend of the People*). These books were followed by the publishing of the *Revista Teresiana* (*The Teresian Review*), a magazine of Carmelite tradition that became popular in Spain.

Enrique understood and praised the unique apostolate of women in the world, and he offered them specialized publications on prayer and the spiritual life. He hoped to establish a foundation for men, the Josephites, but he was not able to achieve this goal. He went to Valencia to see Emmanuel Domingo y Sol but, while there, suffered a stroke. He died soon after in Gilet and was buried there.

In July, 1908, his remains were transferred to the chapel of the Company of St. Teresa in Tortosa. Pope John Paul II beatified Enrique on October 14, 1979, and canonized him in Madrid on June 16, 1993, declaring that this new saint was faithful to God's call, understanding that his "first and fundamental contribution to the building of the Church itself" was his own holiness. The Holy Father said that the Catalan province of Spain could rejoice in a son who served as a symbol of the spiritual wealth of the Faith in the region.

Feast day: January 27.

✠

Eugene de Mazenod (August 1, 1782 – May 21, 1861)
Founder and Archbishop

Charles Joseph Eugene de Mazenod was born in Aix, Provence, France, the son of a devout noble family, and shared in their exile to Italy because of the terrors of the French Revolution. Although he was the last of his noble line, Eugene studied for the priesthood and was ordained at Amiens on December 21, 1811.

He served in parishes in Aix, where he was moved by the plight of the faithful as a result of the revolution. Gathering a small group of missionaries, Eugene sent them into the rural areas of Provence to instruct the local populace. The Missionary Oblates of Mary Immaculate, the outcome of this original group of home visitors, became a congregation on January 25, 1816. Pope Leo XII gave it his final approval as the Congregation of the Oblates of Mary Immaculate on February 17, 1826.

Eugene also aided his uncle, the aged archbishop of Marseilles, in administering that archdiocese and succeeded him in that see. He was initially consecrated a titular bishop in early 1837, succeeding his uncle in 1851. Pope (and future Blessed) Pius IX bestowed the pallium upon him.

As archbishop of Marseilles, Eugene displayed a brilliant grasp of political and religious affairs and an almost heroic fidelity to the faith. Focused on Church renewal and reform, he introduced the theological system of St. Francis de Sales into Marseilles. He also protected the young people of his region and declared apostolic freedom again and again in the face of adamant civil powers trying to repress the Church in France. He took an active part in defining the dogma of the Immaculate Conception in 1854 and supported papal infallibility with elegance and firmness.

As a result of his valiant service to his native land, he was created a Peer of France. He was given the rank of cardinal by the Holy See as well but died in Marseilles before he could be elevated to the Sacred College of Cardinals. His remains were enshrined in the cathedral of Marseilles, mourned by the thousands who attended his funeral.

Pope Paul VI beatified Eugene de Mazenod on October 19, 1975; Pope John Paul II canonized him on December 3, 1995. At the ceremony, Eugene was praised for his vision, tenacity, and exquisite conformity to the will of God. His nobility allowed him to transcend the social, political, and religious barriers of his turbulent era, and his fidelity to the Faith provided him with a charity that communicated Christ's love to one and all.

Feast day: May 21.

✠

Eustochia Smeraldo Calafato (1434 – c. January 20, 1491)
Patroness of Messina

A religious founder, Eustochia Smeraldo Calafato was born in Annunziata, Italy, the daughter of Bernardo and Macaldo Romano Colonna and was baptized Smeralda, Sicilian for Emerald. She was raised in the Faith by her fervent mother and received a vision of Christ Crucified.

When she attempted to enter the Poor Clare Convent of Santa Maria di Basicó, her brothers became enraged and threatened to burn down the convent, forcing Smeralda to placate them. In 1449, however, seeing her determination, her brothers finally relented. She took vows and received the name Eustochia in religion. Somewhat disappointed, however, with the Poor Clares of that convent — they did not practice an extreme penitential life within the cloister — Eustochia sought another convent in which to serve as a Poor Clare. She received permission from Pope Callistus III to join a community where reforms were being implemented, went into Santa Maria Acommodata Convent, and was soon joined by others who valued her vision. Her niece, Paula, and her own sister entered as well.

Eustochia had great devotion to the Passion of Christ and spent her nights in prayer before the Blessed Sacrament. The sick and needy of Messina benefited from her charity; in 1463, they flocked to Montevergine — also called Monte della Vergini, the "Maiden's Hill" — where she built a cloister large enough to accommodate her community. During her tenure as Superior, she faced such difficulties and obstacles that she appealed to the Holy See for redress; but the people of Messina considered Eustochia their patroness, especially in times of earthquake.

She reportedly died at Montevergine in 1491, but may have died earlier. Eustochia's body remains incorrupt.

In 1777, the senate of Messina voted to make two visits a year to her tomb, where her body is still exposed for veneration. She was beatified at Rome by Pope Pius VI in 1782.

Pope John Paul II canonized Eustochia at Messina on June 11, 1988. He declared:

> St. Eustochia is a splendid example . . . . Learning assiduously in the school of Christ Crucified, she grew in knowledge of him and, meditating on the splendid mysteries of grace, she conceived a faithful love for him. For our saint, the cloistered life was not a mere flight from the world in order to take refuge in God. Through the severe asceticism which she imposed upon herself, she certainly wanted to be united to Christ, gradually eliminating whatever in her, as in every human person, was fallen; at the same time, she felt united to all. From her cell in the monastery of Montevergine she extended her prayer and the value of her penances to the whole world. In such a way she wanted to be near to each brother and sister, alleviate every suffering, ask pardon for the sins of all.

Feast day: January 20.

✝

Ezequiel Moreno y Díaz (April 9, 1848 – August 19, 1906)
Colombian Bishop

Ezequiel Moreno y Diaz was born in Alfaro Tarazona, Colombia, where the Faith was a strong presence in the lives of the people. Drawn to the spiritual-

ity of the Augustinian Recollects he entered that ancient order. He was ordained and assigned to Augustinian ministries, displaying fervor and dedication in each undertaking.

Ezequiel was elevated to the episcopacy and was consecrated as the titular bishop of Pinara on October 23, 1893. On December 2 of that year, he was named the bishop of Pasto, a diocese erected by Pope Blessed Pius IX in Colombia in 1859 — a relatively new diocese located at the base of La Galera volcano. Here, Ezequiel distinguished himself through his care for the needs of his flock, his charity, and his generosity. He died in Montegudo and was mourned by the faithful in the entire region.

Pope Paul VI beatified Ezequiel on November 1, 1975, and Pope John Paul II canonized him in Santo Domingo during a visit to the Dominican Republic, on October 11, 1992. At the ceremony, Ezequiel was revered for his fidelity to Christ, his consummate episcopal charity, and his personal holiness.

Feast Day: August 19.

F

✠

Francesco Antonio Fasani
(August 6, 1681 – November 29, 1742)
Francis of Lucera

Francesco Antonio Fasani was born at Lucera, Italy; consequently, he is sometimes honored in devotions as Francis of Lucera.

The son of Joseph and Isabella Della Monaco Fasani, he was baptized Donato Antonio Giovanni, and was called Giovanniello. Giovanniello's father died when the child was only ten, and he was sent to study under the Franciscans (the Friars Minor Conventual) in Lucera after his mother remarried. There, his spirituality and maturity were recognized; there, he received the grace of a religious vocation. At the age of fifteen, he joined the Franciscans and went to Monte St. Angelo Gorgano for religious training and preparation for seminary.

After completing his seminary training as a Franciscan and his studies for the priesthood, he was ordained a priest at the tomb of St. Francis of Assisi on September 19, 1705. Taking the name Francesco Antonio, he then returned to the university to further his knowledge of the Faith, earning a doctorate in theology in Rome. His first assignment, in 1707, was to teach philosophy in the St. Francis Convent in Lucera. Within a short time, he had earned the title of "Padre Maestro," acknowledging his learning and erudition, but especially because of his perfect imitation of St. Francis of Assisi.

Through the years, he fulfilled many positions in the Order, including superior, then provincial. Francesco conducted charities, started a Christmas collection for the poor, and spent hours caring for local prisoners, who were treated badly by officials in the region. Devoted to Our Lady, he was one of the first in Italy to conduct novenas to the Blessed Virgin under the title of Immaculate Conception. He preached throughout Italy for thirty-five years, was gifted with many spiritual graces, and even predicted his own death at Lucera.

Pope Pius XII beatified Francesco Anthony in 1957. Pope John Paul II canonized him on April 13, 1986, honoring him as a glory of the Franciscans and as a promoter of the Immaculate Conception and Our Lady.

Feast day: November 27.

✠

Faustina Kowalska (August 25, 1905 – October 5, 1938)
Saint of Divine Mercy

The first saint of the new millennium, Faustina Kowalska was born in Glogowiec, Poland, the third child of a devout peasant family, and was baptized Helena in the parish church of Swinice, Warckie. María Faustina had only

three years of formal education before she went to live and work as a domestic in Aleksandrow, near Lodz, at age sixteen.

Even as a small child, Faustina had reported seeing bright lights during her prayers at night, and this continued in Aleksandrow. One afternoon, she stepped into the courtyard of her employers' home and saw it engulfed in flames. Her screams brought the mistress of the house, who didn't see flames, but did see Faustina faint. A doctor summoned by the family pronounced Faustina healthy, but she resigned her position and went home.

Upon her return, she announced to her parents that she desired a religious vocation. Her father refused to give his permission, even though he and Faustina's mother had long recognized an intense spirituality in their daughter. Disheartened, Faustina took a second job as a domestic and tried to live like other girls her age. While at a dance with one of her sisters, Faustina experienced a vision of Christ suffering. This was all the prompting she needed. The next day Faustina packed her belongings and went to Warsaw.

Within the year (1925), she was permitted to enter the Congregation of the Sisters of Our Lady of Mercy and served as a cook, gardener, and portess, or doorkeeper, in the congregation's convents in Krakow and Plock, Poland, and Vilnius, Lithuania. Maria Faustina was kind and charitable, but throughout her life, few understood her profound spiritual interior graces. She experienced visions, prophecies, and an internal stigmata.

On the evening of February 22, 1931, Sr. Faustina experienced a vision like none before. She saw Jesus, clothed in a white garment, with one hand raised in a blessing, the other touching his garment at his breast. From his breast emanated two rays. He told Faustina, "Paint an image according to the pattern you see, with the signature *Jesus, I trust in you.*"

But Faustina was not a painter or an artist; she had to struggle to have anyone believe her. Finally, her spiritual advisor, Rev. Michael Sopocko, helped locate an artist to do the painting, and the image of the Divine Mercy was displayed to the public for the first time on April 28, 1935.

Devotion to the Divine Mercy continued to grow just as Faustina continued to unite herself with Christ. Following the instructions of Fr. Sopocko, Faustina recorded her visions and prophecies in a diary, and these mystical writings have been translated into many languages. Faustina even predicted the date of her own death from tuberculosis at age thirty-three.

Pope John Paul II beatified Maria Faustina on April 18, 1993, and canonized her on April 30, 2000. He declared at the canonization:

Today my joy is truly great in presenting the life and witness of Sr. Faustina Kowalska to the whole Church as a gift of God for our time. By divine Providence, the life of this humble daughter of Poland was completely linked with the history of the twentieth century, the century we have just left behind. In fact, it was between the First and Second World Wars that Christ entrusted his message of mercy to her. Those who remember, who were witnesses and participants in the events of those years and the horrible sufferings they caused for millions of people, know well how necessary was the message of mercy. Jesus told Sr. Faustina, "Humanity will not find peace until it turns trustfully to divine mercy" (Diary, p. 132). Through the work of the Polish religious, this message has become linked for ever to the twentieth century, the last of the second millennium and the bridge to the third. It is not a new message but can be considered a gift of special enlightenment that helps us to relive the Gospel of Easter more intensely, to offer it as a ray of light to the men and women of our time.

In August 2002, the pontiff journeyed to Poland to dedicate the Shrine of Divine Mercy in Krakow. The pope declared that the theme of his visit was to emphasize the divine mercy of God and the practice of mercy in daily life. The Holy Father declared on August 17:

"O inconceivable and unfathomable Mercy of God, Who can worthily adore you and sing your praises? O greatest attribute of God Almighty, You are the sweet hope of sinners" (*Diary*, 951).

Dear Brothers and Sisters! Today I repeat these simple and straight-forward words of St. Faustina, in order to join her and all of you in adoring the inconceivable and unfathomable mystery of God's mercy. Like St. Faustina, we wish to proclaim that apart from the mercy of God there is no other source of hope for mankind. We desire to repeat with faith: Jesus, I trust in you! This proclamation, this confession of trust in the all-powerful love of God, is especially needed in our own time, when mankind is experiencing bewilderment in the face of many manifestations of evil.

Feast day: October 5.

G

✠

Gaspar Bertoni (October 9, 1777 – June 12, 1835)
Founder of the Stigmatine Congregation

An apostolic missionary and mystic, Gaspar Bertoni was born at Verona, Italy, the son of Francis (a prosperous lawyer and notary) and Brunora Ravelli Bertoni. Gaspar was educated first at home, then at St. Sebastian's School. There, Jesuits served on the faculty, as the order had been suppressed in 1774, and the Jesuits had to find employment in other institutions. The Marian Congregation was also involved in Gaspar's training.

On the day of his first Holy Communion, Gaspar received his first mystical experience and the grace of a priestly vocation. He was in his first year at seminary in 1796 when the revolutionary troops of France entered northern Italy. Beginning on June 1 of that year, these troops occupied Verona, where they would remain entrenched for two decades. Wanting to alleviate the sufferings caused by such an occupation, Gaspar joined the Gospel Fraternity for Hospitals, an association dedicated to the care of the sick and wounded, and cared for the victims of the war. He was ordained to the priesthood on September 20, 1800.

One of Gaspar's first priestly ministries was to serve as a chaplain to the sisters founded by St. Magdalen Canossa. He aided Leopoldine Naudet and Teodora Campestrini (whose Causes have been opened by the Church) in discerning the Will of God in their lives as well. Gaspar demonstrated unflinching loyalty to the pope during these difficult days, becoming famous as a spiritual director and preacher.

When Pope Pius VII was seized by the French and removed to a place of imprisonment at the command of the French emperor Napoleon Bonaparte, Gaspar was a conspicuous leader in the European-wide movement to offer prayers and support for the captive pontiff. He also established Marian Oratories, organized free schools for disadvantaged youngsters, and became the spiritual director for the diocesan seminary.

In 1816, just one year after the final defeat of Napoleon at the famed battle of Waterloo, Gaspar was at last able to found the Stigmatines, with the aim of having them serve as "apostolic missionaries for the assistance of the bishops." Sts. Mary and Joseph were designated as patrons of the congregation. The Stigmatines, the Congregation of the Sacred Stigmata of Our Lord Jesus Christ, was founded on November 4, 1816. One year later, Pope Pius VII conferred upon Gaspar the title of "Apostolic Missionary."

Gaspar also spread devotion of the Espousal of Mary and Joseph and of the Five Wounds of Christ. His physical sufferings began in 1812, when he suffered an attack of fever following an ecstasy. Toward the end of his life, these physical trials increased; he endured 300 operations on his infected right leg, calling his hospital bed "the School of God." He continued to inspire and guide others throughout his physical ordeals, offering his life as an oblation, even as he served as the "angel of counsel" for many.

Gaspar's death brought a great response from the faithful of Verona and Rome. His spiritual sons in the Stigmatine Congregation today labor in Italy, the United States, Brazil, Canada, Chile, the Ivory Coast, England, Tanzania, Thailand, and the Philippines.

Pope Paul VI beatified Gaspar Bertoni on November 11, 1975. Pope John Paul II canonized him on November 1, 1989, declaring:

> It is significant to note that St. Gaspar Bertoni drew up a project of Christian life which foresaw for all people, regardless of their state of life, the call to holiness; not only for priests, but also for husbands and wives, following the example of the Holy Couple of Nazareth. It was a call to youth, to workers, and to every other type of person.

Feast day: June 12.

✠

Genoveva Torres Morales
(January 3, 1870 – January 5, 1956)
Provider of Spiritual Havens for the Physically Impaired

Genoveva Torres Morales was born in Almenara, Castille, Spain, the youngest of six children. By the time she was eight years of age, both her parents and four of her siblings had died, leaving Genoveva to care for the home and her brother, José. Although he treated her with respect, José was very demanding and taciturn. Being deprived of affection and companionship from her early years, Genoveva became accustomed to solitude.

At the age of thirteen, Genoveva suffered an injury, and her left leg had to be amputated in order to stop the gangrene that developed from an infection. The amputation was done in her home; the anesthesia was not sufficient, and her pain was excruciating. Unfortunately, her leg continued to give her pain and difficulties throughout her life, to the point where she was forced to use crutches.

From 1885 to 1894, she lived at the Mercy Home operated by the Carmelites of Charity. Her routines with the sisters and the other children in the home allowed Genoveva to deepen her life of piety and perfect her sewing skills. It was also in these years that Fr. Carlos Ferrís, a diocesan priest and future Jesuit — who would eventually found a leprosarium in Fontilles — guided the beginnings of her spiritual and apostolic life. She received the gift of "spiritual liberty," something she would endeavor to practice throughout her life. Reflecting on this period at the Mercy Home, she later would write: "I loved freedom of heart very much, and worked and am working to achieve it fully. . . . It does the soul so much good that every effort is nothing compared with this free condition of the heart."

Genoveva intended to join the Carmelites of Charity, but she was not accepted because of her physical condition. So, in 1894, she left the Carmelites of Charity's home and went to live briefly with two women who supported themselves by their own work. Together they shared the solitude and poverty. In 1911, Canon Barbarrós, who had come to know her, suggested that she begin a new religious community to care for the many poor women who could not afford to live on their own and thus suffered much hardship. For years, Genoveva had thought of starting a religious congregation that would be solely concerned with meeting the needs of such women — and she knew of no one engaged in this work.

With the h ꞌarrós and Fr. Martín Sánchez, S.J., she established the first ꞇ ꞌncia. Soon after, other women arrived, and
other communit. ꞇd in other parts of Spain. In 1953, the
Congregation of t. ꞅf Jesus and the Holy Angels received
Pontifical approval.

Mother Genoveva ꞅ later, in 1956, and was beatified by
Pope John Paul II on Jaꞇ During her canonization on May 4,
2003, the Holy Father saiꞇ

St. Genoveva Torres was an ꞇ Ꞇrument of God's tender love for lonely
people in need of love, comfort and physical and spiritual care. The char-
acteristic note that fuelled her spirituality was adoration of the Eucharist
for the expiation of sins, which formed the basis of an apostolate full of
humility and simplicity, of self-denial, and charity.

Feast day: January 5.

┽

Gianna Beretta Molla (October 4, 1922 – April 28, 1962)
Martyr for Motherhood

A medical doctor and a mother, Gianna Beretta Molla sacrificed her own life
to insure the birth of her daughter.

Born in Magenta (Milan), Italy, Gianna was active in Catholic Action
and in the St. Vincent de Paul Society. After earning degrees in medicine and
surgery from the University of Pavia in 1949, she opened a medical clinic in

Mesero (near Magenta) in 1950. She specialized in pediatrics at the University of Milan
in 1952, and thereafter gave special attention
to mothers, babies, the elderly, and the poor.

While working in the field of medicine,
which she considered a "mission," she
increased her generous service to Catholic
Action, especially among the "very young."
She became engaged to Pietro Molla, and
they were married on September 24, 1955, in
the Basilica of St. Martin in Magenta.
Gianna gave birth to three children — Pier-
luigi, Mariolina, and Laura — and harmo-
nized the demands of being a mother, wife, and doctor with a passion for life.

57

In September 1961, toward the end of the second month of another pregnancy, she developed a fibroma in her uterus. Surgery would be required to treat this condition, but the risk to her unborn child was too great. Conscious of the risk that her continued pregnancy brought, she still pleaded with the surgeon to save the life of the child she was carrying, and entrusted herself to prayer and Providence. A few days before the child was due, Gianna told the doctors, "If you must decide between me and the child, do not hesitate; choose the child — I insist on it."

On the morning of April 21, 1962, Gianna Emanuela was born. Despite all efforts and treatments to save both of them, on the morning of April 28, in terrible pain and after repeated exclamations of "Jesus, I love you. Jesus, I love you," Gianna died.

Her funeral was an occasion of profound grief, faith, and prayer, and she was buried in the cemetery of Mesero (4 km from Magenta). Pope Paul VI remembered her at the Sunday Angelus of September 23, 1973, as "a young mother from the diocese of Milan who, to give life to her daughter, sacrificed her own, with conscious immolation." The Holy Father in these words clearly refers to Christ on Calvary and in the Eucharist.

Pope John Paul II beatified Gianna on April 24, 1994, during the International Year of the Family, and he canonized her on May 16, 2004. He declared:

> Gianna Beretta Molla was a simple, but more than ever, significant messenger of divine love. In a letter to her future husband a few days before their marriage, she wrote: "Love is the most beautiful sentiment the Lord has put into the soul of men and women."
>
> Following the example of Christ, who "having loved his own . . . loved them to the end" (Jn 13: 1), this holy mother of a family remained heroically faithful to the commitment she made on the day of her marriage. The extreme sacrifice she sealed with her life testifies that only those who have the courage to give of themselves totally to God and to others are able to fulfil themselves.
>
> Through the example of Gianna Beretta Molla, may our age rediscover the pure, chaste, and fruitful beauty of conjugal love, lived as a response to the divine call!

Feast day: April 28.

✠

Giovanni Calabria (October 8, 1873 – December 4, 1954)
Correspondent with C. S. Lewis

Giovanni Calabria was born in Verona, Italy, where his family was profoundly in need. Giovanni's father died when he was twelve, making it necessary for him to get employment as an errand boy. He received the grace of a religious vocation as he matured, and he entered the seminary, living on meager amounts of food to survive.

His seminary education was interrupted by a two-year military tour of duty that placed Giovanni in service at the military hospital of the city. During this period of mandatory service, Giovanni founded a charitable union for the assistance of the sick poor. He also volunteered to care for typhus victims, and he suffered an attack of the disease as a result.

When able to return to the seminary, Giovanni completed his studies and was ordained a priest by Cardinal Bacilieri of Verona on August 11, 1901. He was then assigned to parishes, where he began charitable programs for soldiers and chimney sweeps. On November 26, 1907, Giovanni founded the Casa Buoni Fanciulli, a home for orphaned or abandoned boys. He educated and trained the boys but also founded programs and facilities for the elderly and ill. As his coworkers and aides grew in number, Giovanni began a religious congregation, the Poor Servants of Divine Providence, dedicated to the care of the most desperate of God's beings. The congregation of the Poor Women Servants of the Divine Providence brought dedicated young women to the cause as well. He also founded a lay institute, the Family of External Brothers, hoping to have an impact upon the secular life of Verona.

Giovanni was a devout promoter of Christian unity and wrote to many people to advance this union. One of his faithful correspondents in this concern was the English writer C.S. Lewis. He also taught his coworkers and associates a simple but sure lesson, saying, "It is no longer the time for compromises! We Christians must be strictly dedicated to holiness."

Exhausted by his labors, Giovanni died, and his remains were placed in the congregation's motherhouse in Verona. He was declared Venerable in 1986; Pope John Paul II beatified Giovanni on April 17, 1988, in Verona, Italy, with Blessed Joseph Nascimeni. Pope John Paul II then canonized Giovanni Calabria on April 18, 1999, declaring that Giovanni was an example of "ardent faith, authentic charity, the spirit of sacrifice, the love of the poor, zeal of love, and fidelity to the Church."

Feast day: December 4.

✢

Giuseppe Marello (December 26, 1844 – May 30, 1895)
Founder of the Oblates of St. Joseph

Giuseppe Marello was born in Turin, Italy, the son of Vincenzo and Anna Maria Marello. Anna Maria died very young, and the family moved to Santi Martino Alfieri, where Giuseppe was raised. At age twelve he entered the seminary, desiring a priestly vocation and a life of true service. When he suffered a bout of typhus in 1863, he made a vow to complete his studies if he regained his health. He did recuperate, and he attributed this renewal of his physical well being to Our Lady of Consolation. Upon completion of his studies, he was ordained on September 19, 1868.

He was made a secretary to Bishop Carlo Savio of Asti and served in this capacity for thirteen years. Giuseppe accompanied his bishop to the First Vatican Council (1869-1870). During this part of his ministry, he also took over a retirement home to save it from financial ruin, served as a spiritual director, and taught catechism.

In 1878, Giuseppe founded the Oblates of St. Joseph, a religious community of priests and brothers, designed to assist bishops and clergy in evangelization. On February 17, 1889, Giuseppe was consecrated the bishop of Asti. He worked untiringly there for the young and the abandoned, visited visited every parish in his diocese, and wrote six pastoral letters for the faithful.

Even as he performed such charitable labors, he was not exempt from suffering. Another religious congregation spread slanderous lies about him, lies that were exposed in time but caused him much humiliation until eventually, he was cleared of all charges.

In May 1895 he went to Savona, to take part in the celebration of the third centennial of St. Philip Neri. There, he suffered a cerebral hemorrhage and died suddenly in the bishop's residence.

Pope John Paul II beatified Giuseppe on September 26, 1993, in the Campo del Palio of Asti, and described him as a model Pastor of the People of God. Pope John Paul II also canonized him on Nov. 21, 2001. The pontiff declared:

"It pleased God to make every fullness dwell in him Christ" (Col. 1:19). St Giuseppe Marello participated in that fullness, as priest of the clergy of Asti and as Bishop of the Diocese of Acqui. Fullness of grace, fostered in him by an intense devotion to the Blessed Virgin Mary; fullness of the priesthood, which God conferred on him as gift and mission; fullness of holiness which he achieved, by being conformed to Christ, the Good Shepherd. Bishop Marello was formed in the golden period of holiness in the Piedmont area, when, in the midst of numerous forms of hostility against the Church and the Catholic faith, the champions of the spirit and of charity flourished, Sts. Cottolengo, Cafasso, Don Bosco, Murialdo, and Allamano.

Joseph was a good and intelligent young man, enthusiastic about cultural and social movements, but our saint only found in Christ the synthesis of every ideal and was consecrated to him in the priesthood. "To take care of the interests of Jesus" was his motto in life, and for this reason he wanted to imitate St Joseph, the spouse of Mary, the custodian of the Redeemer. What strongly attracted him to St Joseph was the life of hidden service, joined with deep interior life. He knew how to transmit this style to the Oblates of St Joseph, the Congregation he founded. He liked to repeat to them, "Be extraordinary in ordinary things," and he added, "Be Carthusians inside your house and apostles outside." The Lord wanted to use his robust personality for his Church, calling him to govern the Diocese of Acqui, where, in the span of a few years, he spent himself for his flock, leaving a memory that has only grown with time.

Feast day: May 30.

✠

Giuseppe Moscati (July 25, 1880 – April 12, 1927)
Bringing Christ Into the Practice of Medicine

A physician of Naples, Giuseppe Moscati labored endlessly to better the lives of the poor in his city.

He was born in Benevento, Italy, where he was raised devoutly in a troubled political era that caused much suffering for the poor of the land. He had a keen interest in medical matters from an early age and began the formal study of medicine in Benevento, then in Naples. From Naples University, he received a medical degree with a specialty in research.

Giuseppe became famous for his medical skills and soon was appointed a professor at the university. An inspiration for young doctors, he sought always to bring Christ into the realm of medicine and conducted himself with amiable piety. He emulated Christ by using his skills and knowledge to benefit those who were most in need; for many hours each morning, he conducted clinics for the poor in the region, assisting them with programs to improve the living conditions and the health of their children. He had a special concern for the families condemned to live in the slums of the area around Naples. He exposed the squalor, filth, and despair of the Neapolitan slums and brought order, cleanliness, and, above all, Christian charity to the sick, abandoned, and destitute. His presence in these wretched communities prompted other leaders to take an interest, especially in the welfare of the very young children of the city. As for

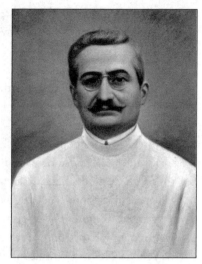

Giuseppe, he declined to use his position in society for his own benefit, instead laboring among the poor until his death.

Pope Paul VI beatified Giuseppe Moscati in 1975 as a model of medical charity. Pope John Paul II canonized him on October 25, 1987. At the ceremony, the Holy Father declared:

> In his constant rapport with God, Giuseppe Moscati found the light to better understand and diagnose illnesses and the warmth to be able to draw near to those who, in their suffering, looked for sincere participation on the part of the doctor assisting them. From this deep and constant reference to God he drew the strength that sustained him and that allowed him to live with the honesty and rectitude in his delicate and complex setting, without giving in to any form of compromise. He was a Head Physician in the hospital, but without ambition for positions: if he was appointed to them, it was because his merits could not be denied, and when he occupied them, it was with total integrity and for the good of others.

Feast day: April 12.

☦

Giuseppe Maria Cardinal Tomasi
(September 12, 1649 – January 1, 1713)
Confessor to Pope Clement XI

Giuseppe Maria Cardinal Tomasi was born in Alicata, Licata, Sicily. As the son of the Duke of Palermo, he was destined by his princely family for court service. But instead, he received the grace of a religious vocation and joined the Clerks Regular of the Theatine Order at Palermo on March 24, 1665. This was no small sacrifice — in order to become a Theatine, Giuseppe Maria had to renounce his princely titles and privileges in favor of his brother — but one he made willingly. He was professed on March 25, 1666.

Sent to Messina to continue his studies, Giuseppe Maria was delayed by a bout of poor health, but soon recovered and went on with his seminary training at Ferrara, Modena, Rome, and Palermo. He was ordained a priest on December 25, 1673. The years that Giuseppe Maria spent in seminary brought him considerable attention because of his intellectual prowess and his skills in language. He knew Greek, Ethiopian, Arabic, Syriac, Chaldaic, and Hebrew, converted one of his professors from Judaism through his intellectual sincerity and faith, and specialized in the study of Scripture, the Psalms, and Patristic writings.

He wrote many treatises and liturgical works, including an edition of Augustine's *Speculum, Antiphonarium,* the *Codices Sacramentorum,* and a *Psalterium.* Many of his works appeared under the pseudonym of J.M. Carus. He taught that true wisdom rests in the restoration and maintenance of past revelations and knowledge, not just in the embrace of new information alone.

Also revered for his holiness and spiritual graces, Giuseppe Maria was summoned to the Vatican by Pope Innocent XII (r. 1691-1700) in 1697, and appointed theologian to the Congregation of Discipline of Regulars in 1704. Giuseppe Maria became confessor to Cardinal Albani and ordered him, under pain of mortal sin, to accept the papacy as Pope Clement XI in 1700. He was, in turn, forced to accept the cardinalate in 1712 from Pope Clement XI on the same condition.

Giuseppe continued his labors for the Church, but he also experienced visions, cared for the poor, taught catechism to children, and was famed for the abiding pastoral concerns he took for his titular parish in Rome. As his mystical experiences increased, he was known to perform miracles of healing and was provided with many abilities of prayer and grace. Giuseppe Maria died in Rome and was mourned by all of Romans, from the pope and College of Cardinals to the humblest and poorest of the Eternal City.

Pope Pius VII beatified Giuseppe Maria in 1803. Pope John Paul II canonized him on October 12, 1986. During the ceremonies the holy prince of the Church was lauded as a true servant of Christ and the "prince of liturgists." His mystical graces and his total surrender to Christ mark him as one of the unique saints of his century.

Feast day: January 1.

H

✠

Hannibal Maria Di Francia (July 5, 1851 – June 1, 1927)
Apostle to the Poor

Hannibal Maria Di Francia was born in Messina, Italy, the son of a knight, the Marquises of St. Catherine of Jonio, Papal Vice-Consul and Honorary Captain of the Navy. His mother, Anna Toscano, also belonged to an aristocratic family. The third of four children, he lost his father when he was only fifteen months old.

Hannibal, especially devoted to the Eucharist, was seventeen and at prayer in front of the Blessed Sacrament when was given the "revelation of *Rogate*"; that is, he deeply felt that vocations in the Church come only through prayer. Subsequently, he found that such prayer is commanded by Jesus in the Gospel when He says: "Ask *[Rogate]* the Lord of the harvest to send out laborers to gather his harvest" (Mt. 9:38; Lk. 10:2). These words became the fundamental insight to which he dedicated his entire life.

Hannibal possessed a lively intelligence and remarkable literary abilities, which he dedicated to study for the priesthood, and he was ordained on March 16, 1878. A few months before his ordination, he met an almost blind beggar, Francesco Zancone, a providential encounter which led him to discover the sad social and moral reality of one of the poorest neighborhoods in the outskirts of Messina (Case Avignone). With the permission and the encouragement of his bishop, Msgr. Joseph Guarino, he made the Avignone ghetto his home and dedicated himself completely to the redemption of its inhabitants. In 1882 he started his orphanages, called "Anthonian Orphanages" because they were placed under the patronage of St. Anthony of Padua.

Hannibal also believed that the "*Rogate*" was the real answer. He wrote:

> What are these few orphans we attend to, these few people we bring the good news to, compared to the millions who are lost and abandoned as sheep without a shepherd? . . . I looked for an answer and I found a complete one in the words of Jesus: "Ask the Lord of the harvest to send out

laborers to gather his harvest." I concluded then that I had found the secret key to all good works and to the salvation of all souls.

He founded two religious Congregations: the Daughters of Divine Zeal, in 1887, and the Rogationists ten years later. Hannibal wanted both institutions to live the Rogate as a fourth vow. The institutions were canonically approved on August 6, 1926.

To spread the prayer for vocations Hannibal promoted several initiatives: he had personal epistolary contacts with the Popes of his time, and he instituted a "Holy Alliance," a movement of prayer for vocations intended for the clergy, and the "Pious Union of the Evangelical Rogation" for all the faithful. He published the periodical "God and Neighbor," to involve everyone in these ideals.

When Hannibal died in Messina, people began to say: "Let us go to see the sleeping saint." He died comforted by the vision of the Blessed Virgin Mary, whom he had loved so much during his life, and he was buried in the Shrine of the "Evangelical Rogation." Pope John Paul II beatified him on October 7, 1990 and defined him as the "authentic forerunner and zealous master of the modern pastoral care for vocations." He was canonized on May 16, 2004.

Feast day: June 1.

✠

Hedwig (1374 – July 17, 1399)
Saintly Queen of Poland

Hedwig was born in Buda, Hungary, in 1374, the daughter of King Louis of Poland. At the age of nine, she was betrothed to William, duke of Austria, and she came to love him. But the Diet, or parliament, of Poland did not have romantic ideals and did not consider Hedwig's personal needs as vital elements of the succession to the throne. The members of the Diet ruled against the marriage and the subsequent alliance with Austria and dissolved the betrothal without allowing Hedwig a personal opinion. William then tried to elope with her, hoping to force the Diet into accepting him, but he failed in his efforts.

In 1384, the ten-year-old Hedwig was crowned the queen of Poland. From the moment of her coronation, she understood the duties of the crown, surrendered any thought of marrying William, and accepted the will of God that she should serve her people. In 1386, she married Grand Duke Ladislas Jagiello of Lithuania, forming a political alliance that served both countries well. Before the wedding, tradition reports that Hedwig covered herself with a thick black veil and went to the cathedral of Krakow. There, she prayed for courage and resolve and to receive the grace to keep to the obligations of her station in life. Hedwig left the black veil draped over the crucifix in the cathedral to symbolize her acceptance of her own cross. She was still a child, but she knew enough about crowns and courts to recognize her own destiny. This act was a token of her surrender to God's will for her and for her people.

Hedwig was married to the Grand Duke in a wedding ceremony that was the social highlight of the era. For Hedwig, the wedding symbolized in a new and terribly personal way the sacrifices that she was being called to make for her country. Jagiello's father had died in 1377, and the new duke faced a rival for the throne of Lithuania, a cousin named Vytautas. By marrying Hedwig, he consolidated his political position and became the king of Poland. A pagan, Jagiello agreed to have himself and the entire population of Lithuania baptized if he married Hedwig. He also agreed to compensate William, duke of Austria, for losing his regal love.

Both Hedwig and Jagiello faced difficulties because of the political unrest in the region. Aided by Hedwig, Jagiello baptized the people of Lithuania; thus, the Teutonic Knights, who were attacking both countries, could not use the excuse that they were invading a pagan country or one with a pagan king. The kingdom soon became one of the truly devout Christian regions in Europe, remaining firm in the Faith into the modern age. Having offered her title, her talents, and her entire life to service of Christ, Hedwig obtained permission from Pope Boniface IX to establish a faculty of theology at Krakow University and instituted programs for the sick and poor of many nations, putting her devotion to Christ into charitable actions.

Hedwig and her firstborn child, a daughter, died in childbirth in Krakow on July 17, 1399. She was beatified in 1896 by Pope Leo XIII, honored for her commitment to the duties of her throne and the demands of her station as a royal. Pope John Paul II canonized Hedwig on June 8, 1997, on the Blonia Esplanade in Krakow, in the presence of more than one and a half million of her devout countrymen and women. There, the Holy Father declared:

> I thank Divine Providence that this privilege has been given to me, that I have been allowed to fix my gaze, together with you, on this figure who reflects the splendor of Christ, and to learn what it means to say "the greatest thing is love. . . ." She gave the whole nation the example of love of

Christ and of man, of man who is hungry for faith and knowledge, as he is also for daily bread and clothing. God grant that this example will also be drawn from today, so that the joy of the gift of freedom may be complete.

Feast day: February 28.

✠

Humilis de Bisignano (August 26, 1582 – November 26, 1637)
Counselor to Two Popes

Humilis de Bisignano was born in Bisignano (Cosenza), Italy, the son of Giovanni Pirozzo and Ginevra Giardino, and received the name of Luca Antonio at baptism. From childhood he demonstrated extraordinary piety and wanted to enter the religious life; however, he was twenty-seven years old when at last he entered the novitiate of the Friars Minor at Mesoraca (Crotone). He made his religious profession, receiving the name Humilis, on September 4, 1610.

As a lay brother of the Order, Humilis begged for alms, attended the community Mass, tended the garden, and performed other manual works. Even in the novitiate, he was distinguished for his spiritual maturity and fervor in the observance of the Rule, and his charity made him beloved by all. From his youth he had demonstrated the gift of continuous ecstasy, to such an extent that he was called "the ecstatic Friar." He was also blessed with extraordinary gifts of prophecy, miracles, and, especially, of infused knowledge. Although he was illiterate and without education, he responded to questions on Sacred Scripture and on any point whatsoever of Catholic doctrine with a precision that astounded theologians. On various occasions, he was examined by assemblies of secular and religious individuals, and he responded with such wisdom that he surprised his examiners.

Humilis also enjoyed the confidence of the Popes Gregory XV and Urban VIII, who called him to Rome and made use of his prayers and advice. He remained many years in Rome, residing most of the time in the Convent of St. Francis of Ripe, except for a few months spent in that of St. Isidore. He also lived for a time in the Convent of the Holy Cross in Naples, where he was tireless in spreading the cult of Blessed John Duns Scotus.

Humilis died in Bisignano. Pope Leo XII beatified him on January 29, 1992, and Pope John Paul II canonized him on May 19, 2002.

Feast day: November 27.

$\mathcal{J}$

✝

Ignazio da Santhía (June 5, 1686- September 21, 1770)
Father of Sinners and the Lost

Ignazio da Santhía was baptized Lorenzo Maurizio Belvisotti when he was born in Santhiá, in the Vercelli region of Northern Italy, the fourth of six children of the upper-class Belvisotti family. He received his early education from a priest, who helped him discern his vocation to the priesthood. Ordained initially a diocesan priest in 1710, he joined the Capuchin Friars six years later in order to pursue more fully the spiritual life to which he felt called and to embrace the simple life established by St. Francis of Assisi.

Ignazio made his religious profession on May 24, 1717, and then was sent over the next years to various Franciscan houses across Italy. He served variously as sacristan and novice master, earning a reputation for his gifts as a confessor and spiritual advisor. In 1731, he was sent to the monastery of Mondovì, where he was made master of novices and vicar of the monastery. He was in charge of the novitiate for fourteen years; there, his work as novice director earned him great fame among the Capuchins.

In 1744, he was afflicted with a mysterious eye ailment that led to near blindness, and he was forced to leave the novitiate and go to Turin. Upon his partial cure, he returned to ministry in time to perform charitable heroism. The war that broke out in Piedmont from 1743-1746 necessitated the labors of the Capuchins in caring for the wounded, sick, and refugees. Ignazio was made head chaplain in the hospitals of Asti, Vinovo, and Alessandria.

Following the war, he returned to the convent in Turin-Monte. There, he remained for twenty-four years as spiritual director and confessor. Among his labors were visits to the sick and begging for food and clothing for the poor. He died in the midst of these ministries at Turin-Monte, repeating, "Paradise is not made for slackers. Let's get to work!"

Pope Paul VI beatified Ignatius of Santhiá on April 17, 1966, and Pope John Paul II canonized him on May 19, 2002, declaring:

"Receive the Holy Spirit: whose sins you shall forgive, they are forgiven" (Jn. 20:22-23). With these words, the Risen One bestows on the Apostles the gift of the Spirit and with it the divine power to forgive sins. The Capuchin priest Ignatius of Santhiá lived uniquely the mission of forgiving sins and of guiding men and women on the paths of evangelical perfection. For the love of Christ and to advance more quickly in evangelical perfection he walked in the footsteps of the Poverello of Assisi. In the Piedmont of his time, Ignatius of Santhiá was father, confessor, counsellor, and teacher of many — priests, religious, and lay people — who sought his wise and enlightened guidance. Even today he continues to remind everyone of the values of poverty, simplicity, and authentic Christian life.

Feast day: September 22.

J

+

Jan Sarkander (December 20, 1576 – March 17, 1620)

Martyr of the Confessional

Jan Sarkander was a victim of the Protestant Reformation.

He was born at Skotschau, Silesia, in the modern Czech Republic, where he was raised devoutly. During those years, the region was deeply divided by the Protestant Reformation and the lingering hostility of the Hussites, zealous reformers who fought a long and bitter war with orthodox Catholics and plunged Bohemia and Moravia into chaos.

Jan was educated by the Jesuits at the Society's college in Prague and went to the seminary to complete his studies. In 1607, he was ordained a priest at Grozin, where he was already demonstrating holiness and a staunch loyalty to Catholic doctrines and ideals. His first assignment in 1613 was to Boskowitz, where he served as a curate. Jan was then transferred to the town of Holleschau, in the diocese of Olmütz, in modern Slovakia, in 1616. As he tried to serve the Catholic people of the region, he was continually harassed by a local landowner, Bitowsky von Bystritz, who intended harm to the Church. Jan was not intimated by the landowner, however, and his constancy and courage made Bitowsky a fervent and unforgiving enemy. Undaunted, Jan converted two hundred Hussites and Bohemian brethren with the assistance of Jesuit priests. His patron in this ministry was Baron von Labkowitz of Moravia.

The eruption of the Thirty Years' War in 1618 engulfed Hollenschau and the faithful. Protestants raised armies to put down Catholic authorities and occupied Hollenschau, prompting Jan to go to Krakow, Poland, for a time. He could not leave his parishioners defenseless, however, and resolved to stand with them no matter what perils came his way. Jan returned to Hollenschau and faced the Protestant insurgents.

In 1620, Polish troops moved into the region, and Jan, carrying the Blessed Sacrament, went to the military commanders to plead for the safety of Hollenschau. His courage saved the region from further bloodshed, and the people gave thanks to God for being spared the same ravages that were destroying so much of Europe. Bitowsky von Bystritz, however, realized that this act of bravery on Jan's part provided him with a ready excuse for revenge. The landowner denounced Jan as a Polish spy and traitor. Jan's protection of Hollenschau was used as evidence, and he was arrested and taken to Olmütz. There, a committee of Protestants employed terrible punishments in an attempt to make Jan break the confessional seal and condemn Baron von Labkowitz. The torture was attended by a Catholic judge, Johann Scintilla, who reported the grim proceedings to Franz Cardinal von Dietrichstein.

Jan was placed on the rack, and on three separate days he was racked for two or three hours at a time. When he remained true to his priestly vows and did not incriminate Baron von Labkowitz, the Protestants soaked Jan in sulfur and feathers and set him on fire. Pitch and oil were hurled at him to increase the burns. Even after such horrific tortures, Jan did not break his silence, and he was thrown into a cell by his frustrated captors. There, he lingered in agony for almost a month, receiving additional cruelties by the guards. Immediately upon his death, Jan was declared a martyr for the faith. His remains were placed in the cathedral of Olmütz.

Pope Blessed Pius IX beatified Jan Sarkander in 1859, and Pope John Paul II canonized him at Olomouc, in the Czech Republic, on May 21, 1995. During the ceremonies, Jan's fearless defense of the Faith and his overwhelming charity were honored. He was praised for his suffering in order to protect the confessional seal, and his courage and charitable ministry to his parish were declared hallmarks of his holy life.

Feast day: March 17.

✠

Japan, Martyrs of (1613), Lawrence Ruiz and Dominican Religious

Courageous Ministers to the Persecuted in Japan

Lawrence Ruiz and his companions are honored as martyrs in Japan. Members of this group were put to death during a five-year period, joining thousands who died rather than deny Christ and the faith. This was a time of severe persecution of the Church in Japan, and though the Church was faced with near-extinction under the weight of the oppression, it survived and flowered.

Lawrence Ruiz was a layman from Manila in the Philippines. Married and a devout Catholic, he devoted himself to assisting the Dominicans in their mission activities in the Philippines, demonstrating both selfless devotion and courage in often difficult and hostile situations.

As a skilled mariner, Lawrence was asked by the Dominicans to aid them in making a secret voyage to Japan, an island nation in the throes of a bitter persecution of the Church. The Dominicans — and Lawrence — were acutely aware that they risked torture and death in journeying to bring the sacraments to Catholics residing there. Lawrence discussed the voyage with the friars Dominic Ibañez de Erquicia, Jacob Kyshei Tomonaga, and thirteen other members of the Order (including Frs. Michael Anzaraza, Anthony Gonzales, William Cowtet, Vincent Shiwozuka, and Lazarus of Kyoto), then agreed without hesitation to assist the Dominicans.

The vessel was soon caught in a severe storm at sea and veered off course. After a long ordeal on the high seas, the ship crashed on the shore of Okinawa. Japanese authorities arrived on the scene quickly and arrested Lawrence and his Dominican passengers.

Every member of the party endured unspeakable torture at the hands of their captors, lingering for many days in abject agony. They were treated with special cruelty for being members of a religious Order. Gradually, one by one, they died from their injuries, but not one had abjured the faith, and each displayed astonishing courage, determination, and loyalty to Christ and his Church.

The Martyrs of Japan were canonized by Pope John Paul II on October 18, 1987. The pope had beatified Lawrence and the Dominicans in Manila, the Philippines, in 1981. At the canonization ceremony, the heroism and zeal of these missionaries and their lay companions were honored. These martyrs, and their thousands of Japanese comrades in death, remain symbols of one of the most remarkable compilations of sacrifice in the history of the Church.

Feast day: October 1.

(NOTE: These Martyrs of Japan canonized by Pope John Paul II should not be confused with the other Martyrs of Japan made famous by the example of St. Paul Miki and his companions. They were martyred in the late sixteenth century and were canonized in 1862 by Pope Pius IX.)

⊹

Jean-Gabriel Perboyre (January 6, 1802 – September 11, 1840)
Victim of Chinese Persecutions

Jean-Gabriel Perboyre was born in Le Puech, in the diocese of Cahors in southern France, the son of Pierre and Marie Rigal Perboyre. One of eight children in the family, he had great devotion to his brother, Louis, while serving as a model for their childhood companions.

Jean-Gabriel attended a preparatory school with Louis at Montauban, where he received the grace of a religious vocation. With his brother, he entered the Congregation of the Missions of St. Vincent de Paul in December 1818. Two years later, he made his vows as a Vincentian and studied for the priesthood. He was ordained in Paris, then assigned to the seminary at Saint-Fleur, where he taught dogmatic theology.

In 1832, he became assistant director of the Vincentian novitiate in Paris, but his heart was in the missions of China. Louis had sailed to these missions and had died there, prompting Jean-Gabriel to want to take his brother's place in the Far East. He received permission to go in 1835, left Europe on March 21 of that year, and arrived in Macao on August 29. There, he studied Chinese and adjusted to the new climate and the exotic culture.

He began his mission in June 1836, and two years later was assigned to Hebei (or Hou-Pé) in the area of the Yangtze Lakes, where he taught the Faith and watched with growing concern the mounting official attitude of hostility toward Europeans and the Christian religion — instigated by England's attacks on China in 1839, as part of the terrible First Opium War. Now, the Chinese were retaliating against missionaries throughout the land.

Jean-Gabriel tried to carry on his labors by avoiding the authorities, but a neophyte catechist betrayed him. He was arrested and brought to trial at Cha-Yuen-Keu on September 16, 1839. Stripped of his priestly garments, he was clothed in rags and dragged from village to village, tortured at each new hearing; he was regularly hanged by his thumbs and beaten with bamboo rods.

In the face of this inhuman cruelty, however, Jean-Gabriel did not swerve from his love of Christ or the Chinese faithful. He endured his torments with resignation to God's will, giving praise even as his life was drained in excruciating suffering. Upon reaching the town of Wuhang, after even more torture, he was condemned to death along with seven criminals. Jean-Gabriel was tied to a cross on the crest of a hill, called "the red mountain," and strangled with a rope.

He was declared venerable by Pope Gregory XVI in 1843, and was beatified by Pope Leo XIII on November 9, 1889. Pope John Paul II canonized Jean-Gabriel on June 2, 1996, declaring his heroism and generosity in service, even unto death.

Feast day: September 11.

☩

Jeanne Delanoue (June 18, 1666 – August 17, 1736)
Businesswoman Turned Benefactress

Born in Samur, Anjou, France, Jeanne Delanoue was the youngest of twelve children in the Delanoue family. Her father was a draper, and her mother operated a religious-goods business in Samur. Bright and ambitious, Jeanne took over the religious business when her mother died in 1691, and proved capable of assuming the rough-and-tumble competition in that era. Jeanne earned the respect of other tradespeople by being a wise, shrewd woman who understood the value of work and profits.

Her life took an abrupt turn, however, prompted by the Holy Spirit. During the season of Pentecost, in 1698, she experienced two separate revelations about the truth of human life and labors. She had a vision and heard the pious exhortation of a widowed pilgrim from Rennes, a woman named Frances Souchet. The two events entirely changed Jeanne's outlook; her concern about profits and success paled in the light of Christ's command of charity. Her tidy life seemed a sterile wasteland when she took a hard look at the suffering around her.

Jeanne closed her shop — much to the astonishment of her neighbors — and began to visit the poor, sick, and abandoned. The orphans of Samur became her special concern; for them, she furnished three houses donated by admiring benefactors, turning them into havens for all in need. More and more companions joined Jeanne in her apostolate, including her niece. In 1704, with her young relative and two trusted members of her group, Jeanne founded the Sisters of St. Anne of Providence of Samur. She herself then became Jeanne of the Cross.

Two years later, encouraged by St. Louis de Montfort, Jeanne leased a large house from the Oratorians. She began caring for children, poor women, and the sick of Samur and received canonical approval from the bishop of Angers. She also practiced penance and mortification and was revered for her miracles of healing. By 1721, her sisters were starting new foundations throughout France. Fifteen years later, she died in Fencet.

Pope Pius XII beatified Jeanne in 1947; Pope John Paul II canonized her on October 31, 1982. The Holy Father called Jeanne "a great prodigy of charity," declaring:

> . . . when we proclaim the holiness of Jeanne Delanoue, it is important to try to understand the spiritual secret of her peerless dedication. It does seem that her temperament led her to an interest in the poor through sentimentality or pity. But the Holy Spirit himself led her to see Christ in the poor, the Christ-Child in their children — she had a particular devotion to him — Christ the friend of the poor. Christ himself, humiliated and crucified. And with Christ she wished to show to the poor the tenderness of the Father. To this God she had recourse with the audacity of a child, expecting everything from him, from his Providence, the name with which she designated her homes and her foundation from their very origin, the Congregation of St. Anne of Providence. Her constant devotion to Mary was inseparable from that of the Blessed Trinity.

Feast day: August 17.

☩

John Dukla (c. 1414 – September 29, 1484)
Hermit and Missionary

John Dukla was born in Dukla, Galicia, Poland, in a vast farming area. An intensely prayerful man, he began his religious life as a hermit, living away from the world in silence. In time, however, he came to understand that he was to minister to the world and to souls seeking salvation.

Accordingly, John entered the Conventual Franciscans and was ordained to the priesthood. From 1440 to 1463 he labored as a preacher, and he was elected Superior of the monastery because of his holiness and sound judgment.

After serving his term in the monastery, John traveled as a missionary to the area of Lvov, in the Ukraine. There, a group of Observant Franciscans, called the Bernardines, were conducting their ministries. John was attracted by the Bernardine spirit and transferred to that branch of the Order.

Combining the contemplative and active life styles, John was able to continue his recollected prayer and yet serve the needs of the faithful of the area. He preached and heard confessions every day; people recognized his intense holiness and flocked to him.

Even when he was stricken with blindness in the last years of his life, he didn't retire from his pastoral duties. He would still preach — and find his way to the confessional by groping along the pews.

He died in Lvov, a beloved priest and a mourned counselor, and his remains were buried in the local cemetery. In 1945 his body was taken to Rzeszow, then to Dukla, where the Bernardine Fathers serve as custodians of his shrine.

Pope Clement XII beatified John in 1733. Pope John Paul II canonized John in Krosno, Poland, on June 10, 1997, during a visit to that country. The canonization ceremony was witnessed by half a million people, and the Holy Father prayed at John's tomb, pronouncing:

> Blessed John earned fame as a wise preacher and zealous confessor. Crowded around him were people hungry for sound doctrine of God, to hear his preaching or, at the confessional grille, to seek comfort and counsel. . . . The written accounts say that despite old age and his loss of sight, he continued to work, and asked to have his sermons read for him so as to be able to go on. He would grope his way to the confessional so as to be able to convert and lead them to God.

Feast day: October 3.

✠

José Maria de Yermo y Parres
(November 10, 1851 – September 20, 1904)
Patron of the Needy of Mexico

The founder of the Congregation of the Servants of the Sacred Heart of Jesus and the Poor, José Maria de Yermo y Parres was a member of an upper-class family, demonstrated an intellectual brilliance early in life, and was educated by tutors and in private schools.

In 1867, he became a member of the Congregation of the Missions and was sent to Paris to continue his theological education. Upon returning to Mexico, he left his religious community to prepare for the diocesan priesthood, and in 1879, was ordained for the Diocese of León. There, he aided the diocesan curia and was active in academic concerns. However, his health failed, and he was assigned as a chaplain for two missions just outside of León. When he discovered the state of poverty in the area, José's life was changed forever.

In December 1885, José opened the Sacred Heart Hospice and founded the Congregation of the Servants of the Sacred Heart of Jesus and the Poor. These missionary women served the destitute and aided him in his ministry. Four years later, he went to Puebla, where he started the apostolate of Christian Mercy, a program to free women from prostitution. The Christian Mercy program provided many such women with education and training until the Mexican government suppressed it in 1928, but José worked unceasingly in Puebla de los Angeles until his death.

Pope John Paul II beatified José Maria at the Basilica of Our Lady of Guadalupe in Mexico City on May 6, 1990, and canonized him on May 21, 2000. The Holy Father declared:

> "This is his commandment, that we should believe in the name of his Son Jesus Christ and love one another, just as he has commanded us" (1 Jn. 3:23). The command par excellence that Jesus gave to his disciples is to love one another fraternally as he has loved us (cf. Jn. 15:12). In the second reading we heard, the command has a twofold aspect: to believe in the person of Jesus Christ, the Son of God, confessing him at every moment, and to love one another because Christ himself has commanded us to do so. This command is so fundamental to the lives of believers that it becomes the prerequisite for the divine indwelling. Faith, hope and love lead to the existential acceptance of God as the sure path to holiness.
>
> It could be said that this was the path taken by José María de Yermo y Parres, who lived his priestly commitment to Christ by following him with all his might, distinguishing himself at the same time by an essentially prayerful and contemplative attitude. In the Heart of Christ he found guidance for his spirituality and, in reflecting on his infinite love for men, he desired to imitate him by making charity the rule of his life.

Feast day: September 20.

✠

José María Rubio y Peralta (July 22, 1864 – May 2, 1929)
Apostle of Madrid

José María Rubio y Peralta was born in Dalías, Spain, one of twelve children, six of whom died at a young age. He was given a Christian upbringing and, in 1875, began secondary school in Almería. As José María felt called to the priesthood, he transferred to the diocesan seminary in 1876 to continue his academic pursuits. In 1878, he moved to the major seminary of Granada, where over the years he completed studies in philosophy, theology, and canon law. On September 24, 1887, he was ordained a priest.

At this time, he also felt called to become a Jesuit, but since he was impeded by circumstances — he took care of an elderly priest who needed assistance — he could not fulfill this wish for nineteen years. In the years after his ordination, José María was also busy as an assistant parish priest in Chinchón, then as pastor in Estremera. In 1890, the Bishop called him to Madrid, where he was given the responsibility of synodal examiner. He also taught metaphysics, Latin, and pastoral theology at the seminary in Madrid and was chaplain to the nuns of St Bernard.

In 1906, after a pilgrimage to the Holy Land the previous year, he finally entered the Jesuit novitiate in Granada. On October 12, 1908, he made his religious profession.

José María was exemplary in his pastoral ministry, sustained and nurtured by his profound spiritual life. The Bishop of Madrid called him "The Apostle of Madrid," and the faithful sought him out from the early morning hours for confession and spiritual direction. He was known for his incisive, simple preaching that moved many to conversion. He also had particular devotion to the poor, always providing them with the material and spiritual assistance they needed.

Through his preaching and spiritual direction, José María was also able to attract and guide many laypeople who wanted to live their Christian faith authentically and assist him in the mission of helping the poor. Under his guidance, they opened tuition-free schools that offered academic formation as well as instruction in various trades. They also assisted the sick and disabled and tried to find work for the unemployed. José María was always the heart and soul of these charitable endeavors, but he remained in the background, preferring to let his lay assistants receive the credit for such programs.

Eucharistic adoration was a profound aspect of his priestly life, and he taught his followers to keep prayer their primary occupation so that they would receive the strength needed for their labors. He was a faithful laborer himself until his death in Aranjuez.

Pope John Paul II beatified him on October 6, 1985, and canonized him on May 4, 2003. The Holy Father declared at the ceremony:

> St. José María Rubio lived his priesthood first as a diocesan priest and then as a Jesuit, giving himself totally to the apostolate of the Word and

of the Sacraments, dedicating long hours to the confessional and directing numerous spiritual retreats in which he formed many Christians who would later die as martyrs in the religious persecution in Spain. 'Do what God wants and want what God does!' was his motto.

Feast day: May 2.

✠

Josemaría Escrivá de Balaguer
(January 9, 1902 – June 16, 1975)
Founder of Opus Dei

Josemaría Escrivá de Balaguer was the author of monumental spiritual guides.

He was born in Barbastro, Spain, the second of six children born to José Escrivá and María Dolores Albás. His parents were devout Catholics and provided a solid upbringing and a happy home. Starting in 1910, however, a series of tragic events befell the family. First, his three younger sisters died, and in 1914, his family suffered financial ruin. In 1915, the Escrivás moved to Logroño, a nearby town, where their father found a job.

Josemaría entered the Seminary of Saragossa in 1920. While preparing for ordination, he also studied law at the university. At the age of twenty-two, he was appointed an inspector, or prefect, in the Seminary by the Archbishop of Saragossa. On March 28, 1925, Josemaría was ordained a priest and was then sent to Perdiguera, a small country village, to serve as assistant pastor. In April 1927, with the consent of his Archbishop, he moved to Madrid to study for a doctorate in civil law, working as an instructor in law to support his family following the death of his father in 1924.

It was thus while in Madrid that Josemaría first recognized his calling to establish Opus Dei. On October 2, 1928, he received an understanding of the need for such an apostolate. Initially open only to men, Opus Dei membership was expanded on February 14, 1930, to women. The rest of his life was devoted to the promotion and development of Opus Dei.

In 1934, Josémaría published *Spiritual Considerations*, the first version of *The Way*, one of the most popular devotional works in modern history; *The Way* has been published in 372 printings in forty-four languages, with over four and a half million copies in print.

In 1943, he came to realize the need within Opus Dei for a way in which priests could be incardinated for service to the members of Opus Dei and the wider Church. On June 25, 1944, three engineers were ordained to the priesthood, the first of thousands of members of the Priestly Society of the Holy Cross.

In the period following the war, Josemaría embarked upon plans to expand Opus Dei beyond the confines of Spain. The first step in this was his journey to Rome in 1946 to obtain papal recognition for Opus Dei. On February 24, 1947, Pius XII granted Opus Dei the *decretum laudis*, or decree of praise. Three years later, on June 16, 1950, the pontiff gave Opus Dei definitive approval. The headquarters of Opus Dei were then established in Rome, rather than in Spain, in order to stress that Opus Dei seeks only to serve the Church. Opus Dei subsequently spread across Europe and Latin America.

Despite increasingly poor health, Josemaría was at the forefront of this growth and development. On March 28, 1975, he celebrated the Golden Jubilee of his ordination. Only a few months later, he died suddenly from a heart attack.

At the time of his passing, Opus Dei claimed over 60,000 members from 80 countries and all five continents. In 1982, Pope John Paul II gave to Opus Dei its definitive status in Church Law as a Personal Prelature.

On May 17, 1992, Pope John Paul II beatified Josemaría Escrivá, in a ceremony attended by hundreds of thousands of pilgrims. The pontiff canonized him October 6, 2002, declaring:

> St. Josemaría was a master in the practice of prayer, which he considered to be an extraordinary "weapon" to redeem the world. He always recommended: "in the first place prayer; then expiation; in the third place, but very much in third place, action" (*The Way*, n. 82). It is not a paradox but a perennial truth: the fruitfulness of the apostolate lies above all in prayer and in intense and constant sacramental life. This, in essence, is the secret of the holiness and the true success of the saints.

Feast day: May 17.

✠

José Manyanet y Vives (January 7, 1833 – December 17, 1901)
Devotee of the Holy Family

José Manyanet y Vives was born in Tremp, in the province of Lleida, Spain, and was baptized on the same day at his parish Church of our Lady of Valldeflors, patroness of the city. He had to work in order to complete studies with the Piarist Fathers in Barbastro and at the Seminaries of Lleida and Urgell, but he did complete them and was ordained a priest on April 9, 1859.

For the next twelve years, José served the Diocese of Urgell as private secretary of the bishop, librarian of the seminary, administrator of the chancery, and secretary for pastoral visitations. He then felt God's call to become a religious priest and to found two religious congregations. In 1864, with the approval of his bishop, he established the religious congregations of the Sons of the Holy Family Jesus, Mary, and Joseph and, in 1874, the Missionary Daughters of the Holy Family of Nazareth. These communities were designed to aid in spreading devotion to the Holy Family of Nazareth and in the Christian formation of families, especially through Catholic education.

José guided and encouraged the formation and expansion of his Institutes for almost four decades, opening schools and centers of ministry in several towns in Spain. He wrote several books and booklets to spread the devotion of the Holy Family and founded the magazine *La Sagrada Familia*.

José suffered poor health all of his life, and his labors exhausted him. He died in his school for children in Barcelona, praying: "Jesus, Mary, and Joseph, may I breathe forth my soul in peace with you."

Pope John Paul II beatified José Manyanet y Vives in 1984 and canonized him in Rome, on May 16, 2004. At his canonization, John Paul II declared:

> From the beginning, the Holy Spirit has brought forth men and women who have remembered and spread the truth revealed by Jesus. One of these was St. José Manyanet, a true apostle of the family. Inspired by the school of Nazareth, he carried out his plan of personal sanctity and heroically devoted himself to the mission that the Spirit entrusted to him. He founded two religious congregations. A visible symbol of his apostolic zeal is also the temple of the Holy Family of Barcelona.

Feast day: December 17.

⊹

Joseph Freinademetz (April 15, 1852 – January 28, 1908)
"A Chinese Among the Chinese"

A missionary of the Society of the Divine Word, Joseph was born in Oies, a small hamlet of five houses situated in the Dolomite Alps of northern Italy, in the region known as South Tyrol. Joseph was baptized on the day he was born.

Studying in the diocesan seminary at Bressanone (Brixen), he was ordained a priest on July 25, 1875, and assigned to the community of St. Martin. However, he deeply wanted to dedicate his life to the foreign missions and spoke to the future St. Arnold Janssen, the founder of a mission house that had quickly developed into the Society of the Divine Word. Joseph entered the mission house in Steyl, Netherlands, in August 1878. On March 2, 1879, he received his mission cross and departed for China with Fr. John Baptist Anzer, another Divine Word Missionary.

Five weeks later, they arrived in Hong Kong, where they remained for two years, preparing for actual mission work by learning the language, customs, and traditions of China. In 1881, the priests went to their new mission in South Shantung, a province with twelve million inhabitants and only 158 Christians.

The work was demanding, marked by long, arduous journeys, bandit attacks, and opposition from local authorities as they formed the first Christian communities. As soon as Fr. Joseph founded a community and stabilized it, the Bishop would send him to another region to begin the work over again.

Joseph trained the laity to assume responsibilities, especially as catechists. He dedicated much energy to their formation and prepared a catechetical manual in Chinese. At the same time, together with Anzer (who had become bishop) he put great effort into the preparation, spiritual formation, and ongoing education of Chinese priests and other missionaries. His whole life was marked by an effort to become a Chinese among the Chinese, so much so that he wrote to his family, "I love China and the Chinese. I want to die among them and be laid to rest among them."

In 1898, Joseph was quite ill with laryngitis and showed the first signs of tuberculosis as a result of his labors. He was sent to Japan for a rest, with the hope that he could regain his health; he returned to China somewhat recuperated, but not fully cured. When the bishop had to travel outside of China in 1907, Joseph took on the added burden of the administration of the diocese. During this time, there was a severe outbreak of typhus. He went throughout the region, offering aid and comfort, until he collapsed with the disease. He returned to Taikia, the seat of the diocese, where he died on January 28, 1908, and was buried at the twelfth station on the Way of the Cross. Joseph's grave soon became a pilgrimage site for Christians.

Beatified on October 19, 1975, by Pope Paul VI, he was canonized by Pope John Paul II on October 5, 2003. At the canonization, Pope John Paul declared:

With the tenacity typical of mountain people, this generous "witness of love" made a gift of himself to the Chinese peoples of southern Shandong. For love and with love he embraced their living conditions, in accordance with his own advice to his missionaries: "Missionary work is useless if one does not love and is not loved." An exemplary model of Gospel enculturation, this Saint imitated Jesus, who saved men and women by sharing their existence to the very end.

Feast day: January 28.

✛

Josephine Bakhita (c. 1869 – February 8, 1947)
The "Madre Moretta"

Future Canossian Sister Josephine Bakhita was born in the Sudan, in northeastern Africa and, at the age of nine, was stolen by slavers. The slave traders gave her the name *Bakhita,* meaning "the Lucky One." She escaped from these slavers only to be caught by another, who took her as a gift to his daughter in El Obeid.

There, she was treated well until she broke a vase. Then, she was sold to a Turkish officer, who sold her again in the market in Khartoum. The Italian vice-counsel bought Josephine and took her to Italy, where she was given to a Signora Michieli in Genoa. Signora Michieli sent Josephine to a convent to be educated by the Daughters of Charity of Canossa. Josephina became a Christian on January 9, 1890, and was baptized by the cardinal patriarch. Despite the demands of Signora Michieli, who claimed ownership, Josephina refused to leave the convent after discovering her religious vocation. The cardinal patriarch and the king's procurator were called upon to mediate the matter, and they decided in favor of Josephine's vocation.

Josephine was welcomed into the Canossian convent, made her novitiate, and took religious vows. Her holiness and devotion were demonstrated in her labors as a cook, gate keeper, and keeper of linens. In time, however, Josephine, called the *Madre Moretta* (Black Mother), traveled throughout Italy to raise funds for the missions, inspiring countless individuals who recognized that God had brought her out of slavery to honor him. She served as a Canossian for half a century, dying in Schio, Italy, revered by the people of her adopted land. The people of the Sudan have not forgotten her, either. Her portrait hangs in the cathedral at Khartoum.

Pope John Paul II beatified Josephine on May 17, 1992, in the presence of three hundred Canossian Sisters and pilgrims, many from the Sudan. On October 1, 2000, the Holy Father canonized Josephine, proclaiming:

> In today's world, countless women continue to be victimized, even in developed modern societies. In St. Josephine Bakhita we find a shining advocate of genuine emancipation. The history of her life inspires not passive acceptance but the firm resolve to work effectively to free girls and women from oppression and violence, and to return them to their dignity in the full exercise of their rights. My thoughts turn to the new saint's country, which has been torn by a cruel war for the past 17 years, with little sign of a solution in sight. In the name of suffering humanity I appeal once more to those with responsibility: open your hearts to the cries of millions of innocent victims and embrace the path of negotiation. I plead with the international community: do not continue to ignore this immense human tragedy. I invite the whole Church to invoke the intercession of St. Bakhita upon all our persecuted and enslaved brothers and sisters, especially in Africa and in her native Sudan, that they may know reconciliation and peace.

Feast day: February 8.

✠

Józef Sebastian Pelczar (January 17, 1842 – March 28, 1924)
Polish Bishop and Founder

Józef Sebastian Pelczar was born in the small town of Korczyna in southwestern Poland. There, he spent his childhood; after he had completed two years of elementary education at the local primary school, his parents sent him to the district town of Rzeszow to continue his education. Even at this tender age, Józef wanted to devote himself to the service of God. In his diary he wrote, "Earthly ideals are fading away. I see the ideal of life in sacrifice, and the ideal of sacrifice in priesthood."

He entered the Minor Seminary and, in 1860, began theological studies at the Major Seminary of Przemysl. Ordained to the priesthood on July 17, 1864, Józef was sent to Sambor, to a parish in the Diocese of Przemysl, where he worked for a year and a half as a curate. In 1866, he was sent to Rome and spent two years there, studying at Collegium Romanum (presently known as the Gregorian University) and the Institute of St. Apollinaris (now known as the Lateran University). He returned to Poland with doctorates in theology and canon law and became a professor of the Major Seminary of Przemysl (1869-1877). Later, he was appointed as professor and Dean of the Theological Department of the Jagiellonian University in Krakow (1877-99).

Józef quickly earned a reputation as a wise and scholarly man and a friend to young people. As a sign of their high esteem for him, the academic community entrusted him with the honorable responsibility of Rector of the University (1882-83), Krakow's Alma Mater.

Józef served in many capacities at this time besides academic work. He was involved in social and charitable activities, such as the St. Vincent de Paul Society and the Society for the Education of the People. In the latter, he served as President for sixteen years. During that time, he erected hundreds of libraries, delivered numerous free lectures, published and distributed more than a thousand books, and opened a school for servants.

In 1891, Fr. Pelczar established the Fraternity of Our Lady, Queen of the Polish Crown. Besides its religious commitment, the Fraternity was founded to care for the poor, orphans, apprentices, and servants, especially those who were sick and unemployed. In 1894, he founded the Congregation of the Sister Servants of the Most Sacred Heart of Jesus in Krakow, with the aim of spreading the Kingdom of the love of the Heart of Jesus. He wanted the Sisters to be signs and instruments of this love for girls, for the sick, and for all people in need.

Five years later, in 1899, he was named Auxiliary Bishop of the Diocese of Przemysl. Upon the death of Bishop L. Solecki in 1900, Józef succeeded to the see of Przemysl. He served a quarter of a century in the diocese with avid devotion to the people. He made regular pastoral visits to the parishes and devoted special attention to raising the moral and intellectual awareness of the clergy. Through his efforts, the number of churches and chapels increased, and many churches were restored. He sympathized with workers who were unjustly treated, and with those who were forced to emigrate because of the difficult economical situation. He emphasized the necessity of implementing the social doctrine of the Church as expressed in the social documents of Leo XIII. Józef authored numerous theological, historical, and canonical books, pastoral letters, sermons, addresses, as well as prayer books and textbooks, before he died. The relics of Józef Sebastian Pelczar rest in the Cathedral Church in Przemysl.

Pope John Paul II beatified Józef on June 2, 1991, in Rzeszow, Poland. The Holy Father canonized him on May 18, 2003. The pontiff proclaimed:

"Perfection is like that city in the Apocalypse (Rev. 21) with 12 gates that open toward every part of the world, as a sign that the men of every nation, every State and every age may pass through them . . . No condition, no age is an obstacle to a perfect life. Indeed, God is not concerned with external things . . . but the soul . . . and demands no more than what we are able to give."

With these words, our new Saint, Joseph Sebastian Pelczar, expressed his faith in the universal call to holiness. He lived out this conviction as priest, teacher, and Bishop. He himself strove for holiness and he led others towards it. He was zealous in all things, but in such a way that in his service Christ himself was the Master.

His motto in life was: "All for the Most Sacred Heart of Jesus through the immaculate hands of the Most Blessed Virgin Mary." This motto shaped his spiritual life, which consisted in the entrustment of himself, his life and his ministry to Christ through Mary.

His gift to Christ was intended above all as a response to His love, contained and revealed in the sacrament of the Eucharist. He would say: "Every person must be struck with amazement at the thought that the Lord Jesus, destined to go to the Father on a throne of glory, lived on earth with men. It was His love that invented this miracle of miracles, instituting the Most Holy Sacrament." He ceaselessly inspired in himself and in others this wonderment of faith. It was this that led him also to Mary. As an expert theologian, he could not but see in Mary the One who "in the mystery of the Incarnation also anticipated the Eucharistic faith of the Church"; the One who, bearing in her womb the Word who became flesh, was in a certain sense the "tabernacle" — the first "tabernacle" in history (cf. *Ecclesia de Eucharistia*, n. 55).

Therefore, he turned to her with filial devotion, the love he had learned in his family, and he encouraged this love in others. He wrote to the Congregation of the Sisters Servants of the Most Sacred Heart of Jesus, which he founded: "One of the most ardent desires of the Sacred Heart of Jesus is that his Most Holy Mother be venerated and loved by all: firstly, because the Lord himself has ineffable love for her, and then because he made her the mother of all men, so that with her sweetness she might attract to herself even those who flee the Holy Cross, and bring them to the Divine Heart."

Feast day: January 19.

☩

Juan Diego Cuauhtlatoatzin (c. 1474 – 1548)
Witness of Our Lady of Guadalupe

Juan Diego Cuauhtlatoatzin was a Native Mexican given the name "Cuauht-latoatzin" ("the talking eagle") at his birth in Cuautlitlán, today part of Mexico City, Mexico. He was a member of the Chichimeca people, one of the indigenous communities that resided in the Anáhuac Valley. Little is known about his life prior to conversion, but when he was fifty years old, he was baptized by a Franciscan priest, Fr. Peter da Gand, one of the first Franciscan missionaries in Mexico.

On December 9, 1531, Juan Diego was on his way to morning Mass when the Blessed Mother appeared to him on Tepeyac Hill. She asked him to go to the bishop and request in her name that a shrine be built at Tepeyac. There, she promised, she would pour out her grace upon those who invoked her. But Bishop Juan de Zumárraga, a Franciscan missionary prelate, did not believe Juan Diego and demanded some kind of proof that the apparition was true.

On December 12, Juan Diego returned to Tepeyac. The Blessed Mother appeared again and instructed him to climb the hill and to pick the flowers that he would find there. Juan Diego obeyed, and although it was winter, he found magnificent roses in bloom. He gathered up the flowers and carried them to Our Lady. She placed them in his *tilma* (the long cloak made of *maguey* and worn by high-ranking Aztecs in many eras) and told him to keep the roses hidden there until he could give them to Bishop Zumárraga, as the proof that had been demanded.

At the bishop's residence, where he was again received by the prelate, Juan opened his *tilma,* and the roses fell onto the floor. The bishop and his attendants knelt suddenly, an act that startled Juan until he looked down and saw the image of Our Lady of Guadalupe, exactly as she had appeared to him, imprinted on his *tilma.*

That image became a national treasure of Mexico instantly, then a holy object enshrined in Mexico City. The bishop finally accepted Juan Diego's claim and granted him permission to live the rest of his life as a hermit in a small hut near the chapel, where the bishop had commanded the miraculous image be preserved.

Juan Diego devoted his remaining life to the care of the church and the many pilgrims who came to visit and pray to Our Lady. He died in 1548 and was buried in the first chapel dedicated to the Virgin of Guadalupe.

Pope John Paul II beatified Juan Diego on May 6, 1990, in the Basilica of Our Lady of Guadalupe in Mexico City. On July 31, 2002, during his fifth pastoral visit to Mexico, Pope John Paul II canonized Juan as a saint (a canonization also celebrated in the Basilica of Our Lady of Guadalupe). At that time, the Holy Father declared:

> "The Guadalupe Event," as the Mexican Episcopate has pointed out, "meant the beginning of evangelization with a vitality that surpassed all expectations. Christ's message, through his Mother, took up the central elements of the indigenous culture, purified them and gave them the definitive sense of salvation" (May 14, 2002, No. 8). Consequently Guadalupe and Juan Diego have a deep ecclesial and missionary meaning and are a model of perfectly inculturated evangelization. [...] The noble task of building a better Mexico, with greater justice and solidarity, demands the cooperation of all. In particular, it is necessary today to support the indigenous peoples in their legitimate aspirations, respecting and defending the authentic values of each ethnic group. Mexico needs its indigenous peoples and these peoples need Mexico!
>
> Blessed Juan Diego, a good, Christian Indian, whom simple people have always considered a saint! We ask you to accompany the Church on her pilgrimage in Mexico, so that she may be more evangelizing and more missionary each day.

Feast day: December 9.

✠

Juan Grande Román, O.H. (1546 – June 3, 1600)
"The Great Sinner"

Juan Grande Román was born in Carmona, Andalusia, Spain, and went to Seville at the age of fifteen to apprentice in the linen business with a relative before returning home to start his own shop. At age twenty-two, however, he recognized that he had a religious vocation, and became a hermit near Marcena.

Discovering the daily sufferings of people around him, Juan abandoned his hermitage and went to Jerez de la Frontera, where he cared for prisoners for three years and called attention to the terrible conditions in a local hospital. With the patronage of a wealthy couple in the area, Juan established a new hospital that he affiliated with the Order of Hospitallers. He became a member of the Order, bringing his unique abilities and virtues to the Order's various ministries (blessed with mystical gifts, Juan even foretold the destruction of the Spanish Armada).

He continued to care for prisoners and orphans and established projects and institutions for their nurturing; he gave dowries to poor young women so they could find husbands; and he fed and clothed prisoners and fugitive Spaniards from Cadiz. At the same time, he demonstrated holiness and inspired all who came into contact with him. Juan did not expect gratitude from those he served. He also did not give in to the officials who resented the standards that he imposed upon them and their charitable institutions.

In 1600, a plague struck Jerez de la Frontera, killing 300 citizens in a day. Juan devoted his time and energies to caring for such victims, eventually falling ill himself. He died at Jerez de la Frontera, mourned by all who had long regarded him as the guardian of the region.

Pope Blessed Pius IX beatified Juan Grande Román in 1853. Pope John Paul II canonized him on June 2, 1996. At the ceremony, Juan was honored not only for his heroic service to others, but for his intense prayer life that served as a wellspring of grace, energies, and compassion. "Juan, the Great Sinner" is a favorite saint of Spain.

Feast day: June 3.

$$\mathcal{K}$$

✠

Katharine Marie Drexel (November 26, 1858 – March 3, 1955)
Heiress Missionary

A missionary and founder of Xavier University in New Orleans, Katharine Marie Drexel was a patroness of Native Americans and Afro-Americans.

She was born in Philadelphia, the second daughter of Francis A. Drexel and Hannah, who died one month later. Francis then married Emma M. Bouvier, a Catholic, who raised Katharine and her sister in the Faith.

Katharine made her debut in Philadel-phia society in 1879, but was beginning to feel inclined toward the religious life. Then her stepmother, Emma, died that same year, and Katharine's father died in 1901. As a result, Katharine and her sister each received an inheritance amounting to one thousand dollars a day.

In 1886, Katharine became ill and went to Germany to recover at a spa. After recommending the establish-ment of a Catholic bureau to handle the endeavor, she recruited European priests and nuns for the American Indian missions. The following year, she built schools in the Dakotas, Wyoming, Montana, California, Oregon, and New Mexico. When she had an audience with Pope Leo XIII (r. 1878-1903), however, Katharine was amazed when he advised her to become a missionary herself.

In 1889, acting on that advice, she entered the Sisters of Mercy novitiate, receiving her habit on November 7 from Archbishop Ryan of Philadelphia. In 1891, Katherine professed her vows as the first member of the Sisters of the Blessed Sacrament for Indians and Colored People. She opened a novitiate and, by the end of the year, at Cornwall Heights (near Philadelphia), there were twenty-one religious in the congregation. The first mission was St. Catherine's in Santa Fe, New Mexico. Other missions and schools followed, and Pope St. Pius X (r. 1903-1914) granted the preliminary approval of the congregation in 1907. She also received prudent counsel on religious affairs from a contemporary, Francis Cabrini.

Katharine instituted a fourth vow in the congregation, beside those of poverty, chastity, and obedience. She vowed "to be the mother and servant of the Indians and Negro races according to the rule of the Sisters of the Blessed Sacrament, and not to undertake any work which would lead to the neglect or abandonment of the Indian and Colored races."

Elected Superior General, Katharine continued to expand the scope of her congregation's labors. In 1912, while in New Mexico, she contracted typhoid fever and was forced to spend time recuperating. After her recovery she resumed her work; in 1915, she founded Xavier University in New Orleans, the first U.S. Catholic institution of higher education for Blacks.

Katharine did not stop her many projects or the dispensing of her millions of inherited dollars until 1935, when a heart attack forced her to retire as Superior. She went to the convent infirmary to pray and mature in the contemplative life. She died in Cornwell Heights.

Pope John Paul II beatified Katharine Marie Drexel on November 20, 1988, and canonized her on Oct. 1, 2000, announcing:

"See what you have stored up for yourselves against the last days!" (Jas. 5:3). In the second reading of today's liturgy, the Apostle James rebukes the rich who trust in their wealth and treat the poor unjustly. Mother Katharine Drexel was born into wealth in Philadelphia in the United States. But from her parents she learned that her family's possessions were not for them alone, but were meant to be shared with the less fortunate.

As a young woman, she was deeply distressed by the poverty and hopeless conditions endured by many Native Americans and Afro-Americans. She began to devote her fortune to missionary and educational work among the poorest members of society. Later, she understood that more was needed. With great courage and confidence in God's grace, she chose to give not just her fortune but her whole life totally to the Lord.

To her religious community, the Sisters of the Blessed Sacrament, she taught a spirituality based on prayerful union with the Eucharistic Lord and zealous service of the poor and the victims of racial discrimination. Her apostolate helped to bring about a growing awareness of the need to combat all forms of racism through education and social services. Katharine Drexel is an excellent example of that practical charity and generous solidarity with the less fortunate which has long been the distinguishing mark of American Catholics.

Feast day: March 3.

✠

Korea, Martyrs of (1864)
Andrew Kim and Companions

The title Martyrs of Korea has been bestowed upon Andrew Kim and 102 companions who died at the hands of brutal opponents of the Faith over a period of years. These martyrs represent the more than 8,000 Koreans who died in demonstration of the Faith in their native land, displaying calm bravery and heroic fidelity.

The Catholic Faith was brought to Korea in a unique fashion: the result of curiosity by the intellectuals of the land, who were anxious to learn as much about the outside world as possible. They discovered some Christian books produced through Korea's embassy to the Chinese capital, and one Korean, Yi Sung-hun, went to Beijing in 1784 to study Catholicism. There, he was baptized by Peter Ri. Returning to Korea, he took up residence in a simple house (now the site of Myongdong Cathedral) and began to convert many others.

In 1791, when these Christians were suddenly viewed as foreign traitors, two of Ri's own converts, Paul Youn and Jacques Kuen, were martyred. This is hardly surprising, even though it was tragic; Korea had long been the victim of foreign aggression, in particular by Japan. The Hermit Kingdom — as Korea has traditionally been termed — was always concerned about alien powers overcoming the nation once again. As the Empires of Europe were at that time extending their spheres of influence across Asia, the Koreans were doubly disturbed by the Christian faith, seeing it as a prelude to possible Western attack and as a threat to traditional Korean life.

Despite these obstacles, the Catholic Faith endured in Korea so strongly that three years after the martyrdoms of Youn and Kuen, Fr. James Tsiou, a Chinese, entered the kingdom and discovered more than 4,000 Catholics awaiting his arrival. He labored in the country until 1801, when Korean authorities martyred him.

Pope Leo XII (r. 1832-1829) established the Prefecture Apostolic of Korea in response to a plea from Korean Catholics, who needed a greater Church structure for the growing community. On September 9, 1831, the vicariate apostolic of Korea was established, and in 1837, Bishop Laurent Marie Joseph Imbert entered the country. Fr. Pierre Mauban and Fr. Jacques Honoré Chastan aided the bishop. Some 9,000 Koreans were Catholics at the time. These lay Catholics hid and supported the missionaries, under the risk of martyrdom. Nobles and simple farmers worked side by side to protect the priests and bishop. When the persecutions were intensified, the Catholics simply kept moving from one safe house to the next. Seoul was the center of Catholic activities, and people from other areas contributed to the support funds freely.

In 1839, the French missionaries were revealed to the Korean government. Bishop Imbert and the two priests surrendered in order to avoid investigations that would implicate the lay people. They were beheaded at Saenamt'o on September 21. Their remains were buried on Mount Samsongsam and transferred later to Myongdong Cathedral.

The laity was not spared, however. Between May 20, 1839, and April 29, 1844, sixty-seven Korean Catholics were martyred. Most were tortured, stripped, and beheaded. The Church was not demolished, however, despite the suffering. Three young Koreans had been sent to Macao in 1837 to complete seminary studies. Kim Tae-gon returned to Korea, then left to bring Bishop Joseph Ferréol and Fr. Antoine Daveluy into the country. Fr. Kim Tae-gon was ordained by Bishop Ferréol, becoming the first native-born Korean priest, on August 17, 1845. He was arrested in June 1846, imprisoned for three months, and then beheaded on September 16, 1846.

Severe persecutions continued, and Korean Catholics fled to the mountainous regions, where they established new parishes in exile. In 1864, the Korean government instituted a new persecution that claimed the lives of two bishops, six French missionaries, a Korean priest, and 8,000 Korean men, women, and children. Some of the better-known martyrs are:

Andrew Kim — the first priest to die for the Catholic Faith in that nation. He is sometimes called Andrew Kim Taegon. Andrew was a member of one of the highest-ranked noble families in Korea. He was educated in the Faith, and despite the threat of persecution, he maintained his devotion even when a government-sponsored program began in earnest in 1939 in all regions of the land. Andrew went to Macao, where he received seminary training and was ordained. He returned to Korea to labor in the missions but was arrested by the authorities almost immediately after reaching his homeland. Joining his countrymen and European missionaries in prison, Andrew was martyred by Korean officials.

Lawrence Imbert — born in Aix-en-Provence, France, Lawrence entered the Paris Foreign Missions Society and was ordained with the express hope of serving the Church in its distant missions. His aspirations were fulfilled in 1825 when his superiors decided he was ready for missionary work and sent him to China. There, he labored for over a decade and proved himself so capable and respected a missionary that he was named titular bishop of Capse. In 1837, he entered Korea in secret and devoted himself to the very difficult task of assisting the Faith in the kingdom. Known as *Bom* among the Koreans, he added his strength to the growing Catholic population, eventually surrendering to Korean authorities in 1839 when the persecutions worsened. Korean Catholics were being tortured to reveal the whereabouts of foreign missionaries, and, rather than have innocent men, women, and children die to shield him, Bishop Imbert gave himself up as did Fathers Philibert Maubant and James Honoré Chastan on August 11. After severe beatings, they were beheaded in Gae Nam Do, near Seoul, on September 21, 1839.

Columba Kim — a devout laywoman, Columba was martyred with her sister, Agnes, in 1839. She was twenty-six when arrested. Imprisoned, the women were pierced with red hot awls and scorched without mercy. Stripped of their clothes, they were placed in a cell with male criminals, but, to the surprise of their captors, the prisoners refused to harm them. Columba complained about such treatment for women, even Catholics — who were criminals in the eyes of the Korean government — and the authorities heeded her objection, ceasing the practice. Nevertheless, Columba and Agnes were sentenced to death and were beheaded at Seoul on September 26.

Peter Ryau — a Christian Korean, Peter was only thirteen when he presented himself to the authorities as was demanded by the law of the land. For what his captors considered obstinate devotion to an outlaw creed, Peter was tortured with such excessive cruelty that his arms and legs were shredded. To demonstrate to the judges the severity of his treatment, Peter pulled away some of his torn flesh and threw it at their feet. The horrified judges were joined by an equally stricken group of onlookers, and Peter was taken back to the prison and strangled on December 31, 1839.

Companions: Others are commemorated in this glorious gathering of the blessed, including: thirteen-year-old Peter Yu Tae-Chol, slain for confessing the Faith; Anna Pak A-gi, a simple woman who was not advanced in her doctrinal knowledge but went faithfully to death as a disciple of Christ and his Mother; John Nam Chong-sam, a high-ranked noble who served as a model of chastity, charity, and poverty until he was slain; Damien Nam

Myong-hyok and Mary Yi Yon-hui, both models of family life; and John Yi Kwong-hai, who dedicated himself to the service of the Church.

Pope John Paul II canonized the Martyrs of Korea on May 6, 1984, in Seoul, Korea. At the ceremony, the Holy Father declared that the Church in Korea was a community unique in the history of the Church. The Holy Father said, "The death of the martyrs is similar to the death of Christ on the Cross, because, like his, theirs has become the beginning of new life."

Feast day: September 20.

✟

Košice, Martyrs of (1619)
Victims of Calvinist Persecution

Marek Krizin (also known as Marek Korosy or Mark Krizevcanin) became a martyr for the Faith with two Jesuit companions, Stephen Pongracz and Melchior Grodecz. They were put to death at Košice, Slovakia, by Calvinist troops invading the region.

Marek was from a well-known Croat family. He studied at the Germanicum in Rome, then became a canon in Esztergom, Hungary. Concerned deeply about the loss of the Faith in the region around Košice, and inspired by the model of St. Peter Canisius, he accepted assignment to Košice with the express hope of regaining Catholic vigor among the inhabitants. His Jesuit companions came from different backgrounds. Stephen Pongracz was a Hungarian, and Melchior Grodecz, also called Melchior Grodziecky, was a Czech.

Taken prisoner by the Calvinist forces, the three priests suffered abuse and torments, but they did not deny the Faith. Their captors, enraged by their loyalty to the pope and the Church, killed them. All were honored as martyrs and were beatified in 1905 by Pope St. Pius X.

Pope John Paul II canonized the priests on July 2, 1995, as the Martyrs of Košice, declaring:

> The Apostles bore this witness to Jesus by their words, their example and their blood. After them countless others down the centuries have put these words of Christ into practice, even to the point of making the supreme sacrifice. The Holy Martyrs of Košice also belong to these noble ranks. By their example and their intercession, they also encourage believers of the present generation not to draw back when faced with the difficulties which faithful adherence to the demands of the Faith can occasion.

Feast day: September 5.

$\mathcal{L}$

✠

Léonie Françoise de Sales Aviat
(September 16, 1844 – January 10, 1914)

Patroness of French Working Girls

Léonie Françoise de Sales Aviat was born in Sezánne, France, in the region of Champagne. Léonie Françoise saw the problems of her own era and desired to promote the well-being of French working girls, who were exploited and endangered by many factions of society.

On October 30, 1868, the young founder was clothed with the religious habit and received the name of Sr. Françoise de Sales Aviat. Sr. Françoise worked among the girls, then founded the Sister Oblates of St. Francis de Sales in Troyes, taking vows in 1871. Fr. Louis Brisson, knowing the pressing need for such an apostolate, aided her in this work; Sr. Françoise, a spiritual daughter of St. Francis de Sales, adopted the Salesian rule for her congregation. She opened homes and schools in France and watched her Sister Oblates expand their missions to meet the needs of many areas. They also conducted retreats as part of their apostolate.

Mother Aviat had to leave France in 1903 because of anti-religious legislation. Undeterred, she started again in Perugia, Italy, and directed her sisters from there. She drafted the congregation's constitution and saw it approved by Pope St. Pius X (r. 1903-1914) in 1911, shortly before her death in Perugia.

The Sister Oblates of St. Francis de Sales arrived in the United States in 1952; some forty years later, Pope John Paul II beatified Mother Aviat, on September 27, 1992. He then canonized her on Nov. 25, 2001. The Holy Father declared:

> The loving plan of the Father "who has made us enter the kingdom of his beloved Son" found a splendid realization in St. Frances de Sales Aviat: who lived her self-offering to the end. At the heart of her dedication and of her apostolate, Sr. Frances de Sales put prayer and union with God, where she found the light and the energy to overcome trials and difficulties, and to persevere to the end of her life in the life of faith, desiring to

be led by the Lord: "O my God, let my happiness be found in sacrificing my will and my desires for you!" The resolution which distinguished Mother Aviat so well, "Forget oneself completely," is also for us an appeal to go against the current of egotism and easy pleasures, and open ourselves to the social and spiritual needs of our time.

Dear Oblate Sisters of St. Francis-de-Sales, at the school of your foundress, in profound communion with the Church and wherever God has placed you, be determined to receive the present graces and to benefit from them, for it is in God that we find the light and the help necessary in every circumstance! Trusting in the powerful intercession of the new saint, accept with joy the invitation to live, with renewed fidelity, the intuitions which she so perfectly lived.

Feast day: January 11.

✠

Leopold Mandic (Castronovo)
(May 12, 1866 – July 30, 1942)
"Missionary" at Home

Leopold Mandic (Castronovo) was born in Castelnuovo, on the southern tip of Dalmatia, Croatia, the son of a devout local Croat family. The twelfth child born to the Mandics, he was baptized Adeodatus. Though always small in stature (he stood only four feet, five inches tall as an adult), he wanted to be a foreign missionary, declaring that in his heart and mind he was always "beyond the seas."

In response to the grace of a priestly vocation, he entered the Capuchin Franciscans at Udine, Italy, and was professed in the Order in 1885. Leopold completed his studies in the Franciscan seminary and was ordained a priest in Venice in 1890. He was given various assignments in the Order's houses, among them Padua in 1906.

World War I shattered Italy and the rest of Europe in the following decade. Leopold was taken prisoner by Austrians and spent one year in a camp, where he ministered as a priest to his fellow inmates. When he was released, he asked to be sent to the foreign missions; but his holiness and unique insight into human souls led his superiors to assign him to various Capuchin monasteries instead, where he labored as a confessor and spiritual director. He possessed a remarkable ability to discern graces and was much needed in the ongoing care of the faithful. Despite his longing for mission duty, Leopold served as a spiritual director and confessor for the next four decades of his life.

Always frail, he suffered from severe stomach ailments and chronic arthritis. These conditions were aggravated by his unending labors in parish confessionals, though Leopold did not complain and did not seek rest. In time, he walked with a pronounced stoop, and arthritis crippled his hands severely. He maintained his grueling schedule and kept his devotion to Our Lady of Sorrows.; and, although he never gave up his desire for the foreign missions, he resolved to accept the will of God.

He died in Padua in the midst of the Second World War. His funeral was attended by the many souls who had been touched by his pastoral gifts.

Pope Paul VI beatified Leopold Mandic in 1976. Pope John Paul II canonized Leopold on October 16, 1983, declaring:

> His greatness lay ... in immolating himself, in giving himself, day after day, for the entire span of his priestly life, for fifty-two years ... [Leopold was] the confessor who was a "missionary" in another sense.

Feast day: July 30.

✠

Luigi Orione (June 23, 1872 – March 12, 1940)
Don Orione of a Turbulent Era

Luigi Orione was born in Pontecurone, diocese of Tortona, on June 23, 1872. At thirteen years of age, he entered the Franciscan Friary of Voghera (Pavia), but he left after one year because of poor health. From 1886 to 1889, he was a pupil of John Bosco at the Valdocco Oratory (Youth Centre) in Turin.

On October 16, 1889, he joined the diocesan seminary of Tortona. As a young seminarian, he devoted himself to the care of others by becoming a member of both the San Marziano Society for Mutual Help and the Society of St. Vincent de Paul. His first Oratory was opened in Tortona on July 3, 1892, to provide for the Christian training of boys. In the following year, Luigi, still a seminarian, started a boarding school for poor boys in the St. Bernardine estate.

He was ordained on April 13, 1895, and within a short time opened new houses at Mornico Losana (Pavia), Noto, as well as in Sicily, Sanremo, and Rome.

Seminarians and priests joined Luigi to form the first core group of the Little Work of Divine Providence. In 1899, he founded the branch of the

Hermits of Divine Providence. The Sons of Divine Providence — composed of priests, lay brothers and hermits — was approved in March 1903.

Luigi aided the victims of the earthquakes of Reggio and Messina (1908) and the Marsica region (1915), and by appointment of Pope St. Pius X, was made Vicar General of the diocese of Messina for three years. On June 29, 1915, he founded the Congregation of the Little Missionary Sisters of Charity, then the Blind Sisters, Adorers of the Blessed Sacrament, and the Contemplative Sisters of Jesus Crucified. For lay people, he set up the associations of the Ladies of Divine Providence, the Former Pupils, and the Friends. More recently, the Don Orione Secular Institute and the Don Orione Lay People's Movement have come into being.

Following World War I (1914-1918), the number of Don Luigi's schools, boarding houses, agricultural schools, and charitable and welfare works increased. Among his most enterprising and original works, he set up the "Little Cottolengos" for the care of the suffering and abandoned, which were usually built in the outskirts of large cities.

His religious congregations also served the missions. In 1913, he sent his first religious to Brazil, then to Argentina and Uruguay (1921), Palestine (1921), Poland (1923), Rhodes (1925), the USA (1934), England (1935), and Albania (1936). From 1921-1922 and from 1934-1937, he himself made two missionary journeys to Latin America — to Argentina, Brazil, and Uruguay, and going as far as Chile.

In the winter of 1940, he went to the Sanremo house to aid his health. There, he died, sighing, "Jesus, Jesus! I am going."

At its first exhumation in 1965, his body was found to be intact and has been exposed to the veneration of the faithful in the shrine of Our Lady of Safe Keeping in Tortona ever since Pope John Paul II beatified him on October 26, 1980. Pope John Paul II canonized Don Luigi Orione on May 16, 2004, declaring:

"Men who have risked their lives for the sake of Our Lord Jesus Christ" (Acts 15:26). These words taken from the Acts of the Apostles can be well-applied to St. Luigi Orione, a man who gave himself entirely for the cause of Christ and his Kingdom. Physical and moral sufferings, fatigue, difficulty, misunderstandings and all kinds of obstacles characterized his apostolic ministry. "Christ, the Church, souls," he would say, "are loved and served on the cross and through crucifixion or they are not loved and served at all" (*Writings*, 68, 81).

The heart of this strategy of charity was "without limits because it was opened wide by the charity of Christ" (ibid., 102, 32). Passion for Christ was the soul of his bold life, the interior thrust of an altruism without reservations, the always fresh source of an indestructible hope.

This humble son of a man who repaired roads proclaimed that "only charity will save the world" (ibid., 62, 13), and to everyone he would often say that "perfect joy can only be found in perfect dedication of oneself to God and man, and to all mankind" (ibid).

Feast day: March 12.

✠

Luigi Scrosoppi (August 4, 1804 – April 3, 1884)
Apostolate to the Poor and Abandoned

An Oratorian priest and founder born in Udine, Italy, Luigi Scrosoppi is revered as an Apostle of Charity.

He began preparing for the priesthood at the Udine diocesan seminary at the age of twelve, and was ordained in 1827, at age twenty-three. At his side were his two brothers, Carlos and Giovanni Baptist, both of whom were also priests.

Luigi began his apostolate immediately, dedicating his priestly life to the care of the poor and abandoned, using his family fortune for their welfare. After he founded an institute of Providence for the formation of young women and the Opere program for deaf-mute girls, young women came to aid him in his ministry. Out of this group, he founded the Sisters of Divine Providence and placed the congregation under the patronage of St. Cajetan. On February 1, 1837, nine women made their vows; others soon joined, from all walks of life.

Luigi entered the Congregation of the Oratory of St. Philip Neri, and the Oratory served as a center for his labors. He taught love of Christ, loyalty to the pope and the Church, and total dedication to "the little ones," the vulnerable of society.

At the close of 1883, increasingly poor health forced Luigi to give up all of his labors, and word spread that he was failing. Large crowds of the faithful from Udine and the surrounding countryside went to visit him and to pray for his recovery, then to mourn his passing.

Pope John Paul II beatified Luigi Scrosoppi on October 4, 1981, and canonized him on June 10, 2001. At that time, the Holy Father declared:

Charity was the secret of his long and untiring apostolate, nourished by a constant contact with Christ, contemplated and imitated in the humility and poverty of his birth at Bethlehem, in the simplicity of his life of hard work at Nazareth, in the complete immolation on Calvary, and in the astonishing silence of the Eucharist. Consequently, the Church holds him up to priests and to the faithful as a model of a deep and effective union of communion with God and the service of his neighbour. In other words, he is a model of a life lived in intense communion with the Holy Trinity.

Feast day: April 3.

$$\mathscr{M}$$

＋

Magdalen of Canossa (March 1, 1774 – April 10, 1835)
Founder of the Canossian Daughters of Charity

She was born Magdalen Gabrielle in Verona, Italy, the daughter of the Marquis Ottavio of Canossa and Marchioness Maria Teresa Szlugh. Her father was a naturalist and geologist, a descendant of an ancient aristocratic family. Her mother was a court attendant and lady-in-waiting to Empress Marie Therese's court in Vienna, Austria.

When Magdalen was only five, her father died suddenly. While her mother followed all the customary customs of mourning and maintained the family estate, when she remarried two years later, she left Magdalen and her four siblings in the care of their uncle Jerome and the estate servants. Magdalen suffered a number of major illnesses as a child, but her strength increased as she matured. Uncle Jerome and others discovered as well that she had dedicated herself to Christ and intended to embrace the religious life.

She made a prolonged retreat at a nearby Carmelite convent, and, for a time, she wanted to be a Carmelite. This proved impossible when she assumed the burdens of the family estate at age nineteen. Magdalen demonstrated herself to be a skilled administrator, even when Napoleon, some of his officers, and a troop of his cavalry arrived at her castle door seeking lodgings. The French leader called Magdalen "an angel" and treated her with much respect throughout his stay.

By 1803, Magdalen's family members had started assuming responsibilities for the affairs of the estate, freeing to start her own apostolate, which centered on needy children and on the dream of providing every young boy or girl an education.

She opened a school in 1805 in an abandoned Augustinian monastery reportedly ceded to her by Napoleon, who was now Emperor of France. The young women who joined her in the school became the first sisters of her congregation, the Canossian Daughters of Charity. Magdalen started the congregation in 1808 and saw her sisters laboring in Bergamo, Milan, Trent, and Venice. Today there are about 4,000 members of the congregation, with 395 houses in many countries.

She displayed great holiness in this work, using what she called "the fire" of charity to aid others. Spiritually, Magdalen was a gifted mystic, known to have received many graces. She experienced ecstasies and visions and was said to levitate during prayer. A model of charity, she also suffered severe physical problems in her later years, bearing them heroically.

Magdalen died in Verona, and her remains were enshrined in a marble sarcophagus. Pope Pius XII beatified her in 1941, and Pope John Paul II canonized her on October 2, 1988, declaring:

> When she realized the frightful sufferings which material and moral misery had spread among the population of her town, she saw that she could not love her neighbor "as a lady," that is by continuing to enjoy the privileges of her social class, and merely sharing her possessions without giving herself . . . charity consumed her like a fever, charity towards God, driven to the heights of mystical experience; charity toward her neighbor, carried to the furthest consequences of self-giving to others.

Feast day: April 10.

✠

Marcellin Joseph Benoît Champagnat
(May 20, 1789 – June 6, 1840)
"A Heart Without Borders"

Marcellin Joseph Benoît was born at Hameau du Rosey, Lyon, France, to a peasant family and dropped out of school at the age of eight. His formal education did not begin again until he was fifteen, and within a short time, he recognized a vocation to the priesthood. Marcellin entered the major seminary of Lyons, France, at the age of sixteen and was a fellow student with John Marie Vianney, the future Curé of Ars.

Ordained to the priesthood on July 22, 1816, Marcellin was sent to serve as an associate pastor in LaValla, a small village of the Massif Central in the heart of France. During one of his pastoral journeys through the parish, he encountered a dying young man completely ignorant of the most rudimentary elements of the Faith, and the memory subsequently haunted the young priest. That experience set the tone for Marcellin's apostolate, becoming the basis for his founding of the Society of Mary.

On January 2, 1817, he presided over two young men who took vows to become the first members of the Little Brothers of Mary, or Marist Brothers. A few weeks later, three other young men became part of the community. The congregation centered on poverty, humility, and total trust in God under Mary's protection. Its members would serve as teachers, catechists, and educators of young people.

After Marcellin instructed the first members, they were certified to teach catechism to the children and adults of the parish. In November 1819, he assigned his first Brothers to the schools of LaValla and Marlhes. Many more candidates arrived to join the congregation, inspiring him to embark upon an extensive building program and, in 1824, he asked permission to leave his parish work and devote full time to his apostolate. He spent the rest of his life working to expand the congregation and develop its resources.

In 1836, the Holy See gave official recognition to the Society of Mary and entrusted it with the missions of Oceania. Today, there are Marist Brothers in seventy-two countries, living proof of their founder's motto: "A heart without borders."

Marcellin died at the age of fifty-one. Pope Pius XII beatified him on May 25, 1955, and Pope John Paul II canonized him on April 18, 1999. The pope declared:

> St. Marcellin announced the Gospel with an ardent heart. He was sensitive to the spiritual and educational needs of his time, especially the prevailing religious ignorance, and the abandonment which youth were experiencing. . . . he was a model for all parents and educators to help them look upon youth with hope, to encourage them with total love, which will make a true human, moral, and spiritual formation possible.

Feast day: June 6.

✠

Marguerite Bourgeoys (April 17, 1620 – January 12, 1700)
Foundress of the Congregation of Notre Dame of Montréal

Marguerite Bourgeoys was a remarkable pioneer in education in Canada.

She was born in Troyes, France, the sixth child of twelve in the family of Abraham Bourgeoys and his wife, Guillemette Garnier. Raised devoutly and educated by her family, at age twenty, Marguerite received the grace of a vocation during her prayers on the Feast of Our Lady of the Rosary.

However, when she applied at the convents of the Carmelites and the Poor Clares, she was not accepted in either convent.

Marguerite was a Sodalist, however, attached to the convent of Augustinian Canonesses. A priest in whom she confided her disappointment, Abbé Gendret, advised her that God perhaps had chosen her for an active apostolate. Subsequent events soon bore out his prediction.

In 1653, Paul Chomody de Masonneuse, the governor of the French settlement in Canada, then a fort called Ville-Marie (now modern Montreal) arrived in Troyes to visit his sister, an Augustinian Canoness. He was introduced to Marguerite and decided that she was the woman destined to start educational programs in Ville-Marie. Marguerite accepted the governor's invitation and set sail in June 1653, landing in Québec in September and going overland to Ville-Marie to begin her labors.

Two hundred people lived there at the time, and the fort was equipped with a small hospital and a Jesuit mission chapel. Marguerite looked after the colony's children and helped in the school, located in a stone stable. Although she had an assistant, she quickly realized that more young women were needed for the apostolate. So Marguerite returned to Troyes to recruit other teachers, including her friend, Catherine Crolo. She returned with three young women and expanded the school to meet the needs of the growing colony.

When the Iroquois War ended in 1667, Marguerite, seeing the city of Montréal taking shape in the wilderness, added classes for Indian children and introduced a Marian Sodality. In 1670, she returned to France to recruit more teachers and to receive a letter of patent — an authorization from King Louis XIV — for her school. Marguerite brought six more young women with her; this last contingent made it possible for her to start the Congregation of Notre Dame, canonically erected by the Bishop of Québec, Blessed François Montmorency de Laval, in 1676.

Marguerite, having envisioned an active apostolate, had to stand firm over the years to keep her sisters from being enclosed or made part of the Ursulines. The sisters persevered without formal religious profession until June 24, 1698, when the rule and constitution were formally approved.

Her apostolate was far from easy. She endured fires, the deaths of two of her sisters — including her niece — and extreme poverty. Because she did not distinguish between the races in her apostolate, Marguerite set a precedent in the New World when she received two Iroquois young women dedicated to Notre Dame de Bon Secours. On Mount Royal in Montréal, she also opened a school for Indian girls. That school moved to Sault au Recollect in 1701 and to the Lake of the Two Mountains in 1720.

In 1689, she was invited by Bishop de Saint-Vallier to start a house of the congregation in Québec. Though advanced in age, she made the long journey there on foot. Four years later, at the age of seventy-three, Marguerite was finally allowed to resign as the Superior of the congregation; she had given her life to the people of Montréal, all the while demonstrating unfailing devotion to the Faith and to the apostolate of her congregation.

In 1699, as Marguerite's health declined, she prayed that she might die in the place of the young novice mistress of the congregation, who was seriously ill. The young novice mistress recovered, and three days later, Marguerite died serenely.

She was declared venerable in 1878 and beatified in 1950, by Pope Pius XII.

Pope John Paul II canonized Marguerite on October 31, 1982, declaring:

> ... in particular she contributed to building up that new country (Canada), realizing the determining role of women, and she diligently strove toward their formation in a deeply Christian spirit. . . . Marguerite Bourgeoys deemed it no less indispensable to do all in her power to lay the foundations for sound and healthy families. She had then to contribute to the solution of a problem very particular to that place and time. . . . Marguerite Bourgeoys went in search, with her great educative know-how, of robust French girls of real virtue. And she watched over them as a mother, with affection and confidence, she received them into her home in order to prepare them to become wives and worthy mothers, Christians, cultured, hard-working, radiant mothers.

Feast day: January 12.

✠

Marguerite d'Youville (October 15, 1701 – December 23, 1771)
Mother of Universal Charity

The founder of the Sisters of Charity, Marguerite d'Youville was the first Canadian proclaimed a saint.

She was born Mary Marguerite Dufrost de Lajemmerais in Varennes, Canada, to Christopher and Renée de Varennes Dufrost de Lajemmerais. Her brother was Lavérendrye, the famed explorer who discovered the Rocky Mountains.

Marguerite was educated by the Ursulines in Québec but, at age twelve, had to return home to aid her widowed mother. In 1722, she married

François d'Youville and bore him six children, four of whom died young. François was engaged in the illegal liquor trade and was a wastrel. He treated Marguerite rather indifferently, but when he fell ill, she cared for him for two years until he died in 1730.

Marguerite had to take up a trade in order to support her children and pay off her dead husband's debts. At the same time, she was caring for the poor.

While working and raising her remaining sons, who became priests, Marguerite still found time and energy to support the Confraternity of the Holy Family in Québec. She had particular devotion to the Eternal Father, trusting in his divine providence. During this period, Marguerite was

also able to save a local hospital, originally founded in 1694. She administered the hospital and gathered companions to form a new congregation designed to offer the people of Québec medical care imbued with Christian charity. The women lived in a small house, and in June 1753, received permission to incorporate their activities. On August 25, 1755, Marguerite and her companions received a gray habit. (The rule of the Sisters of Charity, called the Gray Nuns, had been approved years before.)

In 1747, Marguerite was given charge of General Hospital in Montréal. Under her leadership the hospital cared for disabled soldiers, epileptics, the aged, the insane, the incurables, and lepers, providing as well a haven for orphans and abandoned children. Hôtel Dieu, as it was called, rose as a medical testimony of Christian virtue. The sisters made clothing for military troops in order to maintain themselves and their patients. During the French and Indian War — as the Seven Years' War was called in North America — Marguerite cared for English prisoners captured by French forces. She also defended the institution against meddlesome government bureaucrats who would have limited her charity.

When the hospital was destroyed by fire in 1766, Marguerite knelt in the ashes to sing the *Te Deum*, accepting the terrible loss with religious calm. She died two days before Christmas 1771, in Montréal.

Declared venerable in 1890 by Pope Leo XIII, Marguerite d'Youville was beatified in 1959 by Pope John XXIII. Pope John Paul II canonized Marguerite on December 9, 1990, declaring, "More than once the work which Marguerite undertook was hindered by nature or people. In order to work to bring that new world of justice and love closer, she had to fight some hard and difficult battles." The Holy Father added that Marguerite's holiness "continues to bear fruit."

Feast day: April 11.

Maria Crescentia Höss
(October 20, 1682 - Easter Sunday 1744)

Franciscan Reformer

Maria Crescentia Höss was born in Kaufbeuren, Bavaria, in the Diocese of Augsburg, the seventh of the eight children of Matthias Höss and Lucia Hoermann. In 1703, despite family problems and the reluctance of the Superior of the community, she was granted admission to the Franciscan Tertiaries of Mayerhoff and was professed in 1704.

From 1709 to 1741, Maria Crescentia held a variety of offices in the convent — porter, novice mistress, and Superior — fulfilling each with talent and immense charity. Especially notable was her service as novice mistress from 1726 to 1741. In 1741, she was elected Superior of the community over her repeated objections, and she brought various reforms to the house, encouraging her sisters to observe silence and undertake constant spiritual reading, especially the Gospels.

In her three years as Superior of the community of Mayerhoff, she earned the title of second foundress of the community. Central to her reforms for the spiritual renewal of Mayerhoff included absolute trust in divine providence, devotion to Christ in daily life, a love of silence, and devotion to Jesus Crucified, the Eucharist, and the Blessed Mother. One of the other keys to her success was her extreme selectivity in accepting new vocations.

When Maria Crescentia died, her remains were interred in the chapel of her monastery. Long beloved in Bavaria, she was beatified by Pope Leo XIII in 1900. Pope John Paul II canonized her on November 25, 2001. At that time, the pontiff said:

> Give glory to Christ the King: this wish inspired St. Maria Crescenzia Höss from her childhood. It was for his service that she used her talents. God gave her a beautiful voice. Already as a young lady she could sing a solo part, not to display herself but to sing and to play for Christ the King.
>
> Her knowledge of her fellow men she placed at the service of the Lord. This Franciscan was an esteemed advisor. To her convent came many visitors: [both] simple men and women, princes and empresses, priests and religious, abbots and bishops. In a certain way she became a kind of "midwife" and helped those seeking counsel to bring forth the truth in their hearts. Sorrow did not spare the saint. "Mobbing" took place in her time. She endured the intrigues of her own community, without ever doubting her own vocation. The long period of suffering allowed her to grow in the virtue of patience. That was helpful for her when she became superior: for her to direct meant spiritually to serve. She was generous with the poor, motherly with her sisters, and kind to all who needed a kind word. St. Crescenzia lived what the Kingdom of Christ means: "Whatever you do to the least of your brothers, that you do to me" (Mt. 25:40).

Feast day: April 5.

✠

María de Jesus Sacramentado Venegas de la Torre
(September 8, 1868 – July 30, 1959)
First Mexican Woman Canonized

María de Jesus Sacramentado Venegas de la Torre was born in Jalisco, Mexico, and raised devoutly by her family. From an early time in her youth, she devoted herself to many hours of prayer in the local parish church. On December 8, 1898, she joined the Children of Mary and, later, received the grace of a religious vocation. Exactly seven years later — December 8, 1905 — she entered the community of the Daughters of the Sacred Heart of Jesus in Guadalajara.

The Daughters of the Sacred Heart of Jesus had been founded by Guadalupe Villaseñor de Perez Verdia, a noblewoman of Guadalajara, with the assistance of Canon Atenógenes Silva y Alvarez Tostado. María de Jesus subsequently proved an important figure in the congregation's receiving canonical recognition as a religious institute. For this reason, she is honored as a founder.

The main apostolate of the community was the Sacred Heart Hospital of Guadalajara. Throughout her life, María de Jesus was the crucial figure in the development of the congregation. When she died, the entire region went into mourning, and a vast crowd attended her funeral.

Pope John Paul II beatified María de Jesus on November 22, 1992, and canonized her on May 21, 2000, with other Mexican saints. The pope declared:

St. María de Jesús Sacramentado Venegas, the first Mexican woman to be canonized, knew how to remain united to Christ during her long earthly life and thus she bore abundant fruits of eternal life. Her spirituality was marked by an exceptional Eucharistic piety, since it is clear that an excellent way to union with the Lord is to seek him, to adore him, to love him in the most holy mystery of his real presence in the Sacrament of the Altar.

She wanted to continue his work by founding the Daughters of the Sacred Heart of Jesus, who today in the Church follow her charism of charity to the poor and the sick. Indeed, the love of God is universal; it is meant for all human beings and for this reason the new saint understood that it was her duty to spread it, generously caring for everyone until the end of her days, even when her physical energy was declining and the heavy trials that she had to endure throughout her life had sapped her strength.

Very faithful in her observance of the Constitutions, respectful to Bishops and priests, attentive to seminarians, St. María de Jesús Sacramentado is an eloquent example of total dedication to the service of God and to suffering humanity.

Feast day: July 30.

✠

Maria De Mattias (February 4, 1805 – August 20, 1866)
Coworker with Gaspar Del Bufalo

She was born at Vallecorsa, the southernmost town of the Papal States, in the geographical province of Frosinone. Her family was well-to-do and highly educated. Her father read the Scriptures to her when she was still very young, and she developed a great love for Christ.

Maria had begun a series of spiritual transformations while young and, in 1822, she met Gaspar Del Bufalo, who was preaching a mission at Vallecorsa. She witnessed the change in the local people as a result of the mission and offered herself for the same apostolate. Under the guidance of one of Gaspar's companions, Fr. Giovanni Merlini, she founded the Congregation of the Sisters Adorers of the Blood of Christ in Acuto (Frosinone) on March 4, 1834, at the age of twenty-nine.

Earlier, she had been called by the Administrator of Anagni, Bishop Giuseppe Lais, to teach the local young girls, and as a result Maria had learned to read and write on her own. She did not limit her activity to the school but also gathered mothers and young boys to catechize them as well. Customs of the time forbade her to speak to men, but they came spontaneously anyway to listen to her, even in hiding. The shepherds, abandoned to their own resources, asked to be instructed by her, even after sundown. People flocked to the religious functions to listen to the teacher.

Maria was able to open about seventy communities during her lifetime, three of which were in Germany and England. Almost all were in small isolated towns of Central Italy, except for Rome, to which she was called by Pope Blessed Pius IX for the San Luigi Hospice and for the school of Civitavecchia.

Maria De Mattias died at Rome and was buried in Rome's Verano Cemetery, according to the desire of Pope Pius IX, who chose a tomb for her and commissioned a bas-relief on it depicting the vision of Ezekiel: "Dry bones, hear the word of the Lord."

On October 1, 1950, Pope Pius XII beatified Maria. Pope John Paul II canonized her on May 18, 2003, declaring:

> Maria De Mattias was won over in the depths of her spirit by the mystery of the Cross and founded the Institute of the Sisters Adorers of the Blood of Christ "under the emblem of the Divine Blood." Love for Jesus crucified was expressed in her in passion for souls and in humble devotion to her brothers and sisters, her "beloved neighbour," as she liked to say. "Let us encourage one another," she urged, "to suffer willingly out of love of Jesus who with such great love shed his blood for us. Let us work hard to win souls for heaven." St. Maria De Mattias entrusts this message to her spiritual sons and daughters today, spurring all to follow the Lamb who gave himself in sacrifice for us, even to the point of giving up their life.

Feast day: February 4.

✠

María Josefa of the Heart of Jesus Sancho de Guerra
(September 7, 1842 – March 20, 1912)
The First Basque Canonized Saint

Co-founder of the Servants of Jesus of Charity, María Josefa of the Heart of Jesus Sancho de Guerra was born in Vitoria, Spain, to a poor family, the eldest daughter of Bernabe Sancho and Petra de Guerra. Her father died when she was seven years old, and her mother was forced to send her to Madrid when she was fifteen; there, her relatives could provide her with an education. Eventually, she returned to Vitoria and expressed a desire to enter the religious life. She was, in fact, preparing to enter the Conceptionist contemplative convent of Aranjuez in 1860, when she fell victim to typhus during an outbreak of the disease.

Upon her recovery, María Josefa was accepted into the Institute of the Servants of Mary, recently founded in Madrid by (St.) Soledad Torres Acosta. She was sent into the poorest districts of Madrid and distinguished herself during the plague of 1865, when she worked for many days without rest. However, over time she came to a difficult decision: she would leave the Institute of the Servants of Mary and devote herself to a new religious community focused exclusively upon assisting the sick in the hospitals and in their homes.

Three other Servants of Mary joined María Josefa, and they were granted permission by the Cardinal Archbishop of Toledo to establish a new foundation in Bilbao in the spring of 1871. At that time, Maria Josefa was twenty-nine years old; for the next forty-one years, she was Superior of the new Institute of the Servants of Jesus of Charity. Her final years were marked by long periods of illness that confined her in the house of Bilbao. By the time of her death, however, there were forty-three houses supported by over 1,000 sisters. In time, the Servants of Jesus of Charity spread to other European countries, Latin America, and Asia.

Pope John Paul II beatified María Josefa on September 27, 1992, and canonized her on October 1, 2000, proclaiming:

> In the life of the new saint, the first Basque to be canonized, the Spirit's action is remarkably visible. He led her to the service of the sick and prepared her to be the Mother of a new religious family. St. María Josefa lived her vocation as an authentic apostle in the field of health, since her style of care sought to combine motherly and spiritual attention, using every means to achieve the salvation of souls. Although she was ill for the last

twelve years of her life, she spared no effort or suffering and was unstinting in her charitable service to the sick in a contemplative atmosphere, recalling that "care does not only consist in giving the sick medicine and food; there is another kind of care . . . and it is that of the heart, which tries to adapt itself to the suffering person."

May María Josefa of the Heart of Jesus help the Basque people to banish violence forever, and may Euskadi be a blessed land and a place of peaceful and fraternal coexistence, where the rights of every person are respected and innocent blood is no longer shed.

Feast day: March 20.

⁜

María Maravillas de Jesús, Pidal y Chico de Guzmán
(November 4, 1891 – December 11, 1974)

Carmelite Monastery Foundress

María Maravillas de Jesús was born in Madrid, Spain, the daughter of Luis Pidal y Mon, the Marquis of Pidal, and Cristina Chico de Guzmán y Muñoz. At the time, her father was the Spanish Ambassador to the Holy See, and she grew up in a devout Catholic family.

María made a vow of chastity at the age of five and devoted herself to charitable work. After coming into contact with the writings of St. John of the Cross and St. Teresa of Jesus, she felt called to become a Discalced Carmelite. Her father, whom she had faithfully assisted when he became ill, died in 1913, and her mother was at first reluctant to accept her daughter's decision to enter the Carmelite monastery. On October 12, 1919, however, María finally did enter the Discalced Carmelites of El Escorial in Madrid, and made her simple vows on May 7, 1921.

Before her final profession on May 30, 1924, María had already received a special call from God to found the Carmel of Cerro de los Ángeles, and the foundation was inaugurated on October 31, 1926, with three other Carmelites. This was the first of the series of Teresian Carmelite Monasteries that she would establish, according to the Rule and Constitutions of the Discalced Carmelites.

On June 28, 1926, the Bishop of the Diocese of Madrid-Alcalá appointed her prioress of the new monastery. In 1933, she established another foundation in Kottayam, India; from this Carmel came other foundations in India.

Her role as prioress would be permanent in the various monasteries she founded throughout her life. During the Spanish Civil War, the nuns of Cerro de los Ángeles lived in an apartment in Madrid. In September 1937, another Carmel in the Batuecas, Salamanca, was founded. In 1939, the Carmel of Cerro de los Ángeles was restored. In the following years, foundations were established in other parts of Spain. Mother Maria Maravillas de Jesús also restored and sent nuns to her original Carmel of El Escorial and to the venerable Carmel of the Incarnation in Avila. In order to unite these monasteries, she founded the Association of St. Teresa, which received official approval from the Holy See in 1972.

On December 8, 1974, the Solemnity of the Immaculate Conception, Maria Maravillas de Jesús was anointed and received Holy Communion. Three days later, surrounded by her community in the Carmel of La Aldehuela, Madrid, she died. At the time of her death, her sisters report that she kept repeating the phrase, "What happiness to die a Carmelite!"

Pope John Paul II beatified Maria Maravillas de Jesús on May 10, 1998; he then canonized her on May 4, 2003, paying tribute to her with these words:

> St. Maravillas of Jesus was motivated by a heroic faith that shaped her response to an austere vocation, in which she made God the centre of her life. Having overcome the painful circumstances of the Spanish Civil War, she established new foundations for the Order of Carmel, imbued with the characteristic spirit of the Teresian reform. Her life of contemplation and monastic enclosure did not prevent her from responding to the needs of the persons she dealt with and promoting social and charitable works around her.

Feast day: December 11.

✠

Maria Rosa Doloribus Molas y Vallvé
(March 24, 1815 – June 11, 1876)
Pioneer in the Care of the Mentally Ill

Maria Rosa Doloribus Molas y Vallvé was born in Reus, Spain, near Tarragona. Her parents operated a small store in Reus, and Maria Rosa was raised in a very devout environment. Maria Rosa had long desired a religious vocation, but when she was seventeen, her mother fell victim to an outbreak of cholera and died, and after her mother's death, her father would not allow her to leave home for several years.

She remained with her father until she was twenty-six. Then, at last, she went to join a group of nuns operating a hospital and almshouse. Maria Rosa demonstrated not only religious virtues as a nun but a practical awareness of order, discipline, and the need for administrative skills in providing care to the sick and needy. Her greatest trial in this area came when she was made Superior of the House of Mercy in Tortona, Spain, a dumping ground for the mentally ill. Some three hundred inmates filled that institution, and the medical care being administered was inadequate and injurious to the patients. Maria Rosa established modern methods of hygiene, proper medical procedures, and common-sense order to the entire institution. She separated the vulnerable infants and established wards that employed medical standards and improved care.

For eight years, Maria Rosa maintained an institution that met the improved medical requirements of the time. She then discovered that the congregation in which she was professed was not constituted in a valid manner. Debating their next move, Maria Rosa and twelve companions placed themselves under the jurisdiction of the local bishop. He had witnessed Maria Rosa's dedication, administrative skills, and personal holiness and had no doubts about allowing her to found the Sisters of Our Lady of Consolation in 1857. These sisters were organized to care for people everywhere, and they have focused on the poorer regions of the world, carrying on Maria Rosa's apostolate of mercy.

Maria Rosa did not confine her work to the hospital — she also served as a mediator in disputes; in 1843, she crossed a military battle line in order to negotiate a ceasefire during an attack on the city of Reus.

Maria Rosa was beatified in 1977 by Pope Paul VI. Pope John Paul II canonized her on December 11, 1988, announcing:

> The existence of this woman, imbued with charity, totally committed to the neighbor, is a prophetic proclamation of the mercy and consolation of God. . . . The life of Maria Rosa, spent in doing good, translated for the people of her time and for those of today into a message of consolation and hope . . . . Mother Maria Rosa is one of those persons chosen by God to proclaim to the world the mercy of the Father. She had the charism to be an instrument of reconciliation and of spiritual and development.

Feast day: June 11.

✠

Maximilian Kolbe (January 7, 1894 – August 14, 1941)
Saint of Auschwitz

This modern saint was born in Zdunska-Wola, near Lodz, Poland, and baptized Raymond. The boy had a devotion to the Blessed Mother even as a child, but his life would change forever when had a vision in which the Blessed Mother offered him two crowns, one of purity and one of martyrdom. Fearlessly, he chose both.

On September 4, 1910, Raymond received the habit of the Conventual Franciscans and the name in religion — Maximilian — by which he is revered on earth. He was ordained a priest in Rome in 1918, having earned a doctorate in theology and having founded the Militia of Mary Immaculate to advance Marian devotion. (This group is also called the Knights of the Immaculata.)

In 1920, Maximilian suffered a bout of tuberculosis and was confined to a convalescent home for two years, after which he returned to Krakow, Poland, and continued his ministry in the Knights of the Immaculata. He then went to Japan and India, spreading the special devotion to those countries. Recalled to Poland in 1939, Maximilian faced the Nazi occupiers of his homeland and realized that his apostolate was being targeted. In that year, he was arrested by the Gestapo, but was fortunate enough to be released. In February 1941, he was arrested again and confined in Warsaw.

On May 28, 1941, with 250 other prisoners, Maximilian was sent to Auschwitz, the Nazi extermination camp. He and the other priest prisoners were singled out for special punishment details and beaten. Throughout, Maximilian assured his companions that the Nazis "will not kill our souls." He added, "And when we die, then we die pure and peaceful, resigned to God in our hearts."

In August 1941, Maximilian saw a Polish soldier, Francis Gajowniczek, chosen as a victim of retaliatory execution for the escape of a prisoner. He announced to the startled German commandant, "I am a Catholic priest from Poland. I would like to take his place, because he has a wife and children." Francis Gajowniczek was returned to the ranks, and Maximilian became a condemned victim.

With the nine other chosen prisoners, Maximilian was placed in a starvation unit, deprived of food and water. They did not cry or weep but recited the Rosary and sang Marian hymns. A Nazi officer was so impressed by the piety and the courage that he kept careful documentation of the days of suffering. At the end of two weeks, Maximilian and three other prisoners were still alive. They were given lethal injections by the camp executioner, and their remains were cremated the next day.

Pope Paul VI beatified Maximilian in 1971. Pope John Paul II canonized Maximilian Kolbe as a martyr on October 10, 1982, declaring him the "patron of our difficult century." In describing Maximilian's heroism and devotion, the Holy Father said:

> The reality of death through martyrdom is always a torment; but, the secret of that death is the fact that God is greater than the torment. So then, we have before us a martyr — Maximilian Kolbe — the minister of his own death — stronger still in his love, to which he was faithful, in which he grew throughout his life, in which he matured in the camp at Auschwitz. . . . That maturing of love which filled the whole life of Fr. Maximilian and reached its definitive fulfillment on Polish soil in the act at Auschwitz, that maturing was linked in a special way to the Immaculate Handmaid of the Lord. . . .
>
> Maximilian Kolbe, like few others, was filled with the mystery of the divine election of Mary. His heart and his thoughts were concentrated in a particular way upon that 'new beginning,' which — through the work of the Redeemer — was signified by the Immaculate Conception of the Mother of his earthly incarnation. . . . Maximilian Kolbe penetrated this mystery in a particularly profound way and complete way: not in the abstract, but in the life-filled context of the Triune God, Son and Holy Spirit, and in the life-filled context of the divine salvific plan for the world. . . . Once there arose, in the Middle Ages, the legend of St. Stanislaus. Our time, our age will not create a legend of St. Maximilian. The eloquence of the facts themselves, the testimony of his life and martyrdom, is strong enough.

Feast day: August 14.

+

Meinard (c. 1130 – August 14, 1196)

Augustinian Bishop Praised By Two Popes

Meinard was born in Germany and entered the monastery Segelberg, founded by St. Vicelino. While studying for the priesthood, Meinard was imbued with the missionary spirit of that saint and the dedication and valor of the Augustinian Canons Regular.

Ordained a priest, he went to Livonia (which was still a pagan region) and established himself at Ykescola, near Riga, Latvia. Consecrated a bishop in 1186, he was the first prelate of Livonia.

In the castle of Ykescola, Meinard formed a community of Canons Regular, and trained members of the community were brought from Segelberg for the new foundation. They aided Meinard in forming a regional clergy and in establishing seminary standards. He was tireless in his efforts to evangelize the region and carefully consolidated the diocesan gains among the local pagans. He forged a solid Christian base before he died, ensuring growth and stability, because he was prudent and alert to the customs and views of the local peoples.

Meinard's successes in evangelization and administration were results of his heroic virtue and spiritual maturity. Both Pope Clement III (r. 1189-1191) and Pope Celestine III (r. 1191-1198) attested to Meinard's labors in their letters.

Meinard died in his Livonian castle and was buried there, but his remains were translated from Ykescola to the cathedral of Riga in the thirteenth century. A monument and a sepulcher still honor his memory in the region.

During the Reformation of the sixteenth century, with its political and social impacts, Meinard was forgotten by the outside world. Pope John Paul II reintroduced this missionary giant to the faithful. He canonized Meinard in Riga on September 8, 1993, calling upon the Christians of this era to take up the Cross of Christ and the ministry of evangelization with renewed zeal.

Feast day: October 11.

✠

Miguel Febres Cordero
(November 7, 1854 – February 9, 1910)
Walking by the Grace of God

Miguel Febres Cordero was born in Cuenca, Ecuador, to a prominent family and suffered from malformed feet. At the age of five, the boy had a vision and started walking for the first time. His family understood this event as a sign of God's favor and raised him with care and fervor, calling him Pancho in the family.

In 1863, after being tutored at home, Miguel Febres entered the nearby de la Salle Christian Brothers' school, demonstrating his brilliance in the classrooms. He received the grace of a religious vocation while at the school, but his family wanted him to pursue a career in the world. In time they settled on a priestly vocation and sent Miguel Febres to the seminary at Cuenca. There, he became quite ill.

Miguel Febres returned to the Christian Brothers when he recovered and, in 1868, at the age of fourteen, received the habit. He was the first native Ecuadorian to become a Christian Brother. His novitiate was made in Cuenca because of his poor health, but he flourished and started writing books in his late teens. He published his first book at age twenty — a work dedicated to Spanish grammar — and was a gifted teacher revered for his sense of humor and common sense. His personal prayer life was also intense.

Miguel Febres' research earned him considerable fame, and he became a member of the Academies of France, Ecuador, and Spain. He had great devotion as well to the Sacred Heart and to the Blessed Virgin Mary. Men and women in the scientific and educational fields learned to respect him and appreciate the deep spiritual values that prompted all that he accomplished.

In 1907, Miguel Febres visited New York, en route to Belgium. There, he was asked to translate texts, and there his health deteriorated once more. He went to Premia del Mar, in Spain, to the junior novitiate of his congregation to recover, but the political unrest in that nation swept up both him and his students.

In July, 1909, when the Spanish nation was overwhelmed by a revolution, Premia del Mar was attacked. Miguel Febres took the Blessed Sacrament from the chapel and led his novices calmly to safety. But the stress of this exertion was too much for him; he contracted pneumonia and died. He was mourned by the faithful in many different countries around the world, who had given support to his many labors.

On July 21, 1936, Premia del Mar was attacked by Spanish Communists, who set fire to the chapel. During the assault, Miguel's coffin was opened, and his body was found to be intact. His remains were subsequently returned to Ecuador, where a young crippled boy was miraculously cured by touching the coffin in the procession through the streets of Quito.

Miguel Febres was beatified on October 30, 1977, by Pope Paul VI. Pope John Paul II canonized him on October 21, 1984. The Holy Father declared that the Church looked to St. Miguel Febres Cordero, the "apostle of the school, who was also an exemplary missionary, an evangelizer of Latin America..." The Holy Father concluded, "He never hesitated to present an exacting and demanding Christianity to the young men sent to him," and he "shared heroically in the sufferings of Christ."

Feast day: February 9.

✠

Mutien-Marie Wiaux (March 20, 1841 – January 30, 1917)
Evangelization Through Art and Music

Mutien-Marie Wiaux was born in Mellet, Belgium, in a village in the French-speaking region. His father was a prosperous blacksmith, and his mother operated a small café located in part of the family residence. The devout family ran a very proper café, and every night ended in the establishment with recitation of the Rosary.

A leader of the children of the area, Mutien-Marie was educated in the village, then went to work at his father's blacksmith forge; however, he was not physically equipped to follow his father's trade. Rather, he had an abiding interest in the Christian Brothers, who had arrived in the area in 1855. He entered the congregation that same year, recommended by his local pastor. Completing his novitiate at Namur, Mutien-Marie was assigned to St. Bertuin's, a school in Malonne, Belgium.

His first teaching experience ended in disaster, but a Br. Maixentis, who taught art and music, defended Mutien-Marie and had him appointed as his assistant. The young Mutien-Marie set about learning art and music, having no experience in those fields. In time, he played a variety of musical instruments. He also lived the rule of the congregation perfectly for fifty-eight years, serving all that time at St. Bertuin's. When not in the classroom, Mutien-Marie labored as a prefect and parish catechist.

The simple beauty of his life, as noted by Pope Paul VI in his beatification homily, rested in the day-to-day transformations of routine tasks into moments of devotion and true sanctity.

Noted for his dedication to the Blessed Sacrament and to the Blessed Virgin Mary, he did not treat art and music as mere adjustments of life, but incorporated them into the human quest for salvation. He accepted as well the physical infirmities that plagued him from 1875 until 1906. He spent all of his time praying the Rosary for the Christian Brothers and their charges.

In January 1917, Mutien-Marie collapsed from a final and severe bout of illness. He grew weaker steadily until finally, on January 29, he recited a litany and died the next morning. Miracles were quickly attributed to his intercession, and a shrine was erected in Malonne honoring this gentle, caring Christian Brother.

Pope Paul VI beatified him in 1977. Pope John Paul II canonized Mutien-Marie on December 10, 1989, declaring that Mutien-Marie "has all the greatness of the humble." The Holy Father added,

> His message is not expressed in terms of this world's. Rather, he shows his brothers, teachers, and students the true fruitfulness of a life that is humbly offered.

Feast day: January 30.

$\mathcal{N}$

✠

Nimatullah Youssef Kassab Al-Hardini
(1808 – December 14, 1858)

Saint of Kfifan

A Maronite priest, Nimatullah Youssef Kassab Al-Hardini was a model religious.

He was born in 1808 in Hardin, Lebanon. As a child, he was strongly influenced by the monastic tradition of the Maronite Church. Four of his brothers became priests or monks, and Youssef entered the Lebanese Maronite Order in 1828.

He began religious life at the monastery of St. Anthony in Qozhaya, near the Qadisha (Holy Valley), where he remained for two years until he started his novitiate and was given the name Nimatullah. During the novitiate, he deepened his life of personal and community prayer and dedicated time to the manual labor of learning to bind books. On November 14, 1830, he made his religious profession and was sent to the monastery of Sts. Cyprian and Justina in Kfifan to study philosophy and theology. On December 25, 1833, he was ordained a priest and became a professor and director of the Scholasticate.

During the two civil wars of 1840 and 1845, he suffered greatly with his people. In 1845, the Holy See appointed him Assistant General of the order. A man of culture, Fr. Nimatullah asked the Superior General to send monks to further their studies at the new college founded by the Jesuits in Ghazir. He served as Assistant General for two more terms but refused to be appointed Abbot General. "Better death than to be appointed Superior General," he is reported as saying.

In December 1858, while teaching at the monastery of Kfifan, he became gravely ill as a result of the bitter cold in that region. His condition worsened, leading to his death. He died holding an icon of the Blessed Virgin and saying, "O Mary, to you I entrust my soul." He was fifty years old.

While still alive, Fr. Nimatullah was known as the "Saint of Kfifan," a monk who gave himself completely to his brother monks and neighbors during a time of suffering in his Land and difficulty within his Order.

Pope John Paul II beatified Nimatullah on May 10, 1998, and canonized him on May 16, 2004, declaring:

A man of prayer, in love with the Eucharist which he adored for long periods, St. Nimatullah Kassab Al-Hardini is an example for the monks of the Order of Lebanese Maronites as he is for his Lebanese brothers and sisters and all Christians of the world. He gave himself completely to the Lord in a life full of great sacrifices, showing that God's love is the only true source of joy and happiness for man. He committed himself to searching for and following Christ, his Master and Lord.

Feast day: December 14.

$\mathcal{P}$

✠

Paola Elisabetta Cerioli
(January 28, 1816 – December 24, 1865)
"The Mother of Many Orphans"

Paola Elisabetta Cerioli was born Costanza in Soncino, Italy, the last of sixteen children born into the noble family of Francesco Cerioli and Francesca Corniani. She was a frail child plagued by a heart condition throughout her life and remained at home until she was eleven years old, when she was sent off to school in Bergamo.

At age nineteen, Paola Elisabetta returned to Soncino, where a planned marriage awaited her; fifty-nine-year-old Gaetano Busecchi, widow of a countess, was set to be her husband. Seeing it as God's will, she accepted this proposal and was married on April 30, 1835.

Her marriage lasted nineteen years and was marked by suffering on all sides: her husband's difficult character and poor health weighed on her, and three of the four children that she gave birth to died prematurely; Carlo, her greatest "consolation," died in January 1854, telling his mother just before he died, "Mama, do not cry . . . the Lord will give you other children." At the end of that same year, on December 25, Gaetano also died.

Paola Elisabetta began to visit and assist the sick and to share her belongings with the poor and orphans. She gave all her wealth to the poor and opened her home to welcome orphans. Even before giving away all her assets, she made a perpetual vow of chastity on December 25, 1856. And, with her confessor's approval, she made vows of poverty and obedience on February 8, 1857.

Other young women joined her, and Paola Elisabetta drew up a Rule for the community that would become the Sisters of the Holy Family, which was founded on December 8, 1857, in Comonte, Italy. From that day onward, Paola Elisabetta dedicated herself to the growth and development of the religious community, On November 4, 1863, in Villacampagna, she founded a male branch, the Religious of the Holy Family. Both congregations were dedicated to the special protection of St. Joseph; thus, the orphans under their care were known as the "sons and daughters of St. Joseph."

Mother Paola Elisabetta died unexpectedly in Comonte on December 24, 1865. She was forty-nine years old. Pope Pius XII beatified her on March 19, 1950, the Solemnity of St. Joseph. Pope John Paul II canonized her on May 16, 2004, declaring:

> Contemplating the Holy Family, Paola Elisabetta understood that families remain strong when the bonds among their members are sustained and kept together by sharing the values of faith and a Christian way of life. To spread these values, the new Saint founded the Institute of the Holy Family. She was convinced that in order for children to grow up sure of themselves and strong, they needed a family that was healthy and united, generous and stable. May God help Christian families to welcome and witness in every situation to the love of the merciful God.

Feast day: December 24.

✠

Paola Frassinetti (March 3, 1809 – June 11, 1882)
Friend of John Bosco

Paola Frassinetti was born in Genoa, Italy, the only daughter of John and Angela Frassinetti (her four brothers became priests). Raised in a devout and happy home, Paola suffered the tragedy of her mother's death when she was only nine. Seeking consolation, Paola turned to the Blessed Mother, dedicating herself to Mary.

An aunt came to raise the family but died within three years, leaving Paola to manage the household. She learned her lessons from her father and brothers, who educated her faithfully in home classes. At the age of twenty, she developed bronchial problems and went to live with her brother, a priest at Quinto, a village on the west coast near Genoa. There, she recovered her health and served as the parish housekeeper.

As his housekeeper, she demonstrated a prayerful spirit and a genuine concern for the poor of the parish, particularly the young children. She opened a school in Quinto for poor girls, a project in which her brother helped her, training them in the spiritual life as she educated them for life in the world.

In 1834, Paola founded the Sisters of St. Dorothy in Genoa, a congregation dedicated to the education of poor children. Her spirit brought about many vocations to her congregation and increased the benefits of the poor. Paola saw her sisters expand their labors in the world, going to Portugal, then to Brazil. In 1835, an epidemic of cholera ravaged northern Italy, and

Paola and her sisters served faithfully until all of the victims had received adequate care. She labored until 1876, when she suffered a paralyzing stroke. She endured two more such attacks in 1879 and 1882. During her last attack, the future St. John Bosco came to visit her, announcing her virtues and her coming death.

Paula contracted pneumonia and began a rapid decline. Upon her death in Rome, her remains were enshrined at St. Onofria, the Dorothean motherhouse in the Eternal City. In 1906, her body was found to be incorrupt, and it was placed in a silver and crystal casket, a gift from the faithful of Brazil.

Pope Pius XI beatified Paola Frassinetti Paula in 1930; Pope John Paul II canonized Paola on March 11, 1984, declaring:

> Paola Frassinetti is . . . a splendid fruit of the redemption always active within the Church. It has been said that in order to determine if a work is Christian, it is necessary to see if there is the seal of the redeeming Cross. . . . In fact, she was convinced that whoever wants to undertake a path to perfection cannot renounce the Cross, mortification, humiliation, and suffering, which assimilate the Christian to the divine model, who is Crucified. . . . Not only did the Cross not frighten her, but it was for her the powerful spring which moved her, the secret source from which sprang her tireless activity and her indomitable courage.

Feast day: June 11.

✠

Paraguay, Martyrs of (November 1628)

First South American Martyrs Raised to the Altars

The Martyrs of Paraguay, all Jesuits, were three native Paraguayans who traveled from the estuary of the La Plata River, beyond the Mbaracayu Mountains, to the areas now part of southern Brazil, in order to preach the Gospel. Entire villages and communities came into existence because of their efforts, and they brought a message of love and spiritual union to the native populations. These three Jesuit missionaries were led by Roch Gonzalez, accompanied by Alphonsus Rodriguez and John de Castillo.

Roch Gonzalez was born in Anuncíon, Paraguay, in 1576, to a noble Spanish family. Educated well, he studied for the priesthood and was ordained at age of twenty-three. He joined the Society of Jesus in 1609 and immediately became a forceful advocate of the so-called "reductions" (from the Spanish *reducciónes*, or settlements), the Jesuit missions where Native

Americans lived in self-sufficient communities free from the exploitation that was a sad aspect of Spanish colonial activities in South and Central America. He headed the first reduction in Paraguay and founded six others in the Paraná and Uruguay River areas. Dedicated to the care of all the Paraguayan tribes, Roch and his companions strongly opposed the colonial policies of Spain, the operations of the Inquisition, and the enslavement of native peoples.

In 1626, Roch joined his Jesuit companions, Alphonsus and John, in founding a new reduction called All Saints. Working together, the missionaries decided to expand their efforts and involve other, more distant tribes. Roch and Alphonsus went to Caaró, in what is now a region in the southern tip of the nation of Brazil. There, they opened All Saints chapel and began mission programs.

Roch found himself the target of a local medicine man's hatred. While they tried to make friends, the Jesuits were rebuffed and resented. On November 15, 1628, Roch was hanging a small bell at the Church of All Saints when one of the henchmen of the medicine man came up from behind and struck him with a hatchet. Alphonsus was attacked as well, his body placed in the chapel beside Roch. The henchmen then set fire to the chapel. John received word of the martyrdom two days later. He was himself attacked soon after — the native tribesmen bound him, then stoned and beat him to death.

Pope Pius XI beatified the three Jesuits in 1934 by Pope Pius XI as the Martyrs of Paraguay, the first South American martyrs to be so honored. Pope John Paul II canonized Roch and his companion martyrs in Asunciòn, Paraguay, on May 16, 1988, calling them models of holiness for all Christians. The Holy Father announced:

> Neither the obstacles of the wilderness, the misunderstanding of people, nor the attacks of those who saw their evangelizing activity as a threat to personal interests, could intimidate these champions of the Faith. Their unreserved self-offering led them to martyrdom. . . . The entire life of (Roch) Gonzalez de Santa Cruz and his companion martyrs was completely characterized by love: love for God and, in him, for all people, particularly the most needy, those who did not know of Christ's existence or had not yet been liberated by his redeeming grace . . . the fruits did not take long in coming. As a result of their missionary activity, many people abandoned pagan worship to open themselves up to the light of the true faith.

Feast day: November 17.

☩

Paula Montal Fornés de San José de Calasanz
(October 11, 1799 – February 26, 1889)
Foundress of the Daughters of Mary

Paula was born in Arenys de Mar, near Barcelona, Spain, the daughter of Ramon and Vicenta Fornes Montal. Paula's childhood in a seaside village appears to have been difficult, and she became prayerful and recollected, aware of the suffering of others.

At the age of thirty, still unmarried and devout, Paula realized the grace of a religious vocation and went with a friend, Inez Busquets, to Gerona, where they opened a school to provide the young with proper education and spiritual guidance. The school was a success, prompting Paula to establish a college in May, 1842, and a third educational institute in 1846.

On February 2, 1847, she founded the Daughters of Mary, taking the religious name of Paula of St. Joseph of Calasanz. Three companions joined her in this holy foundation, with Paula providing the vision and leadership for attracting other young women and for expanding the congregation's educational efforts.

The Daughters of Mary, "the Pious School Sisters," received papal approval from Pope Pius IX (r. 1846-1878) in May 1860. Five years later, Queen Isabel II (r. 1833-1868) of Spain recognized the Daughters of Mary as well. The Daughters arrived in the United States in 1954.

Paula, exhausted by her labors, died faithful to the Piarist rule at Olesa de Montserrat. She was declared venerable in 1988.

Pope John Paul II beatified Paula on April 18, 1993, praising her for following in the footsteps of St. Joseph Calasanz and for bringing a profound charism to the Piarist of Scalopian spirit. Her life of service and devotion was honored.

The pontiff canonized her on November 25, 2001, saying:

"I say to you: today you will be with me in Paradise" (Lk. 23:43). St. Paula Montal Fornés de San José de Calasanz, foundress of the Institute of the Daughters of Mary, Sisters of the Pious Schools, was received in paradise, into the fullness of the kingdom of God, after a life of holiness. First in her native city, Arenys del Mar, she was involved in many apostolic activities and in prayer and interior devotion she was led into the mystery of God; then as foundress of a religious family, inspired by the slogan of St. Joseph Calasanz, "Piety and Letters," she gave herself to advancing women and the family with her ideal: "Save the family, educating the young girls in a holy fear of God"; in the end, she was to give proof of the authenticity, the firmness and the beauty of her spirit, a spirit shaped by God during the thirty years of hidden life in Olesa de Montserrat.

The new saint belongs to the group of founders of religious orders who in the nineteenth century came forward to meet the many needs that were present and that the Church, inspired by the Gospel and by the Spirit, wanted to respond to for the good of society. The message of St. Paula is still valid today and her educational charism is a source of inspiration in the formation of the generations of the third Christian millennium.

Feast day: February 26.

✠

Pauline of the Agonizing Heart of Jesus (*Amabile Visintainer*) (December 16, 1865 – July 9, 1942)
First Saint Raised in Brazil

The founder of the Daughters of the Immaculate Conception, Pauline of the Agonizing Heart of Jesus was actually born in Vigola Vattaro (Trento), Italy — but in September 1875, her family, together with many other people from Trent, migrated to the area of St. Catherine in Brazil. They created by their very arrival the town of Vigolo, presently part of the community of Nova Trento.

At age fifteen, she and a companion, Virginia Rosa Nicolodi, moved into a shack to look after a woman dying of cancer. From this single act of charity was begun the Congregation of the Little Sisters of the Immaculate Conception, which obtained the approval of the congregation from Bishop José de Camargo Barros of Curitiba in 1885. In December of the same year, Pauline, together with her first two companions, Virginia and Teresa Anna Maule, professed her religious vows and took the name of Sr. Pauline of the Agonizing Heart of Jesus.

Pauline was elected for one term as Superior General but then returned to caring for the sick. In 1903, Mother Pauline left Nova Trento in order to take care of the orphans, the children of former slaves, and the old and abandoned slaves in the district of Ipiranga of São Paulo. In 1909, Bishop Duarte Leopoldo e Silva, Archbishop of São Paulo, sent her to work with the sick at "Santa Casa" and the elderly of the Hospice of St. Vincent de Paul at Bragança Paulista. He also forbade her from having an active role in her Congregation, but she accepted the decree by the bishop with patience, hoping only that the Congregation of the Little Sisters might continue to prosper.

She was at last acknowledged as the "Venerable Mother Foundress" on May 19, 1933. In her later years, Pauline lived in prayer in the motherhouse, suffering from diabetes. She eventually went blind and lost an arm because of the disease.

Pope John Paul II beatified Pauline in Florianopolis (São Paulo), Brazil, on October 18, 1991, and canonized her on May 19, 2002, declaring:

> The action of the Holy Spirit is revealed in a special way in the life and mission of Mother Pauline. He inspired her to build a home, with a group of young women friends that was later called by the people the "Little Hospital of St. Virgilius" and destined to provide material and spiritual assistance to the suffering and the marginalized. Thus in response to the plans of Providence, is born the first religious community in Southern Brazil: named the Congregation of the Little Sisters of the Immaculate Conception. It was in this hospital that "being-for-others" became the guiding motive for Mother Pauline. In service to the poor and the suffering, she became a manifestation of the Holy Spirit who is "the best comforter; the soul's most welcome guest, sweet refreshment here below."

Feast day: July 9.

☩

Pedro de San José de Betancurt
(May 16, 1619 – April 25, 1667)
The St. Francis of the Americas

A Franciscan Tertiary Missionary, Pedro de San José de Betancurt was born in Villaflores, on the island of Tenerife, on 1619. A descendant of the Canary Island conqueror, Juan de Betancur, Pedro was raised as a simple shepherd. He spent his youth in the field and pastures, where he developed an intense prayer life and union with Christ.

At the age of thirty-one, Pedro left Tenerife and his shepherd's life to go to Guatemala. After a long and arduous journey, he arrived in Guatemala City, where local Franciscans and Jesuits befriended him. There, he started studies for the priesthood at the Jesuit College in San Borgia, although he later withdrew. Still drawn to the religious life, Pedro took private vows and became a Third Order Franciscan, taking the name Pedro of St. Joseph.

In 1658, he moved to the vacant hut of the famous mystic, Maria de Esquivel. He also founded a hospital named for Our Lady of Bethlehem, a hostel, schools, and an oratory, all designed to aid the needy. Organizing the many generous young men who followed him, Pedro founded the Hospitaller Bethlehemites to provide adequate medical care and Christian charity. He rented a house in a part of Guatemala City called "Calvary" and established his hospital there, supporting the hospital and his other charitable institutions by begging on the streets. Pedro wore a Franciscan habit as he entered poor sections of the city to build chapels and shrines for the local families, and he promoted devotions and prayed for the souls in Purgatory.

Beloved and revered, Pedro started the custom of gathering children for the recitation of the Franciscan Rosary on each February 18. He also started the popular *Posada* celebrations that continue today throughout South America.

In 1667, Pedro, "the St. Francis of the Americas," died in Guatemala City. His Cause was opened in 1709, as the so-called minstrel of Christ who changed the lives of all who knew him and benefited from his generosity.

Pope John Paul II beatified Pedro de San José de Betancurt on June 22, 1980, honoring the humility, dedication, and service of the Blessed, all of which reflected Franciscan joy, trust, and delight in caring for God's own. The Holy Father canonized him on July 30, 2002, during a pastoral visit to Guatemala, declaring:

> Already in the land of his birth, as in every phase of his life, Br. Pedro was a deeply prayerful man, especially here where, at the hermitage of Calvary, he diligently sought God's will at every moment. Thus he is an outstanding example for Christians today, whom he reminds that training in holiness "calls for a Christian life distinguished above all in the art of prayer" (*Novo millennio ineunte*, 32). I therefore renew my exhortation to all the Christian communities of Guatemala and other countries to be authentic schools of prayer where all activity is centred on prayer. An intensely devout life always bears abundant fruit. Br. Pedro modeled his spirituality in this way, particularly in contemplation of the mysteries of Bethlehem and of the Cross. If, in the birth and childhood of Jesus, he immersed himself deeply in the fundamental event of the Incarnation of the Word — which led him to discover spontaneously, as it were, the face of God in man — then, in meditating on the Cross, he found the strength to practice mercy heroically with the lowliest and the most deprived.

Feast day: April 18.

✠

Pedro Poveda Castroverde (December 3, 1874 – July 28, 1936)
Founder of the Teresian Association

Born in Linares, Spain, to a solidly Christian family, Pedro Poveda Castro-verde felt called to become a priest from his early childhood. In 1889, he entered the diocesan seminary in Jaén. Because of financial difficulties, how-ever, he transferred to the Diocese of Guadix, Grenada, where the Bishop had offered him a scholarship. He was ordained a priest on April17, 1897.

After ordination, Pedro taught in the seminary and served the diocese in many other matters. In 1900, he completed a licentiate in theology at Seville and later began an apostolate among the "cave-dwellers" — those who lived in dugouts in the hills outside of Guadix. There, he built a school for children and workshops for adults, providing professional training and Christian for-mation. He was challenged by other locals, however; he had to leave this spe-cial ministry for the solitude of Covadonga, in the mountains of northern Spain. There, in 1906, he was appointed canon of the Basilica of Covadonga in Asturias, where the Blessed Virgin is venerated under this title.

In Covadonga, he devoted much time to prayer and reflected particularly on the problem of education in Spain. He came to understand that the Lord was inviting him to open new paths in the Church and in the society of his time. He began to publish articles and pamphlets on the question of the pro-fessional formation of teachers and was also in contact with other persons who felt the need for the presence and action of Christians in society.

In 1911, he opened the St. Teresa of Ávila Academy as a residence for stu-dents and the starting point of the Teresian Association, dedicated to the spiritual and pastoral formation of teachers. The following year he joined the Apostolic Union of Secular Priests and started new pedagogical centers and some periodicals. To further his work, Pedro moved to Jaén, where he taught in the seminary, served as spiritual director of *Los Operarios* Cate-chetical Centre, and worked at the Teacher Training College. In 1914, he opened Spain's first university residence for women in Madrid.

Meanwhile, the Teresian Association continued to develop, spreading to various groups and areas, and leading to its ecclesiastical and civil approval in Jaén. Pedro offered the Teresian Association as a new path of Christian life and evangelization created with and for laypersons, forming them to be wit-nesses of the Gospel. In 1921, he moved to Madrid and was appointed a chaplain of the Royal Palace; a year later, he was named a member of the Central Board against illiteracy. But most of his time was devoted to the

Teresian Association, which received papal approval in 1924. Although he did not direct the Association, as its founder, he worked to consolidate and promote the various dimensions of its mission as it spread to Chile and, later, to Italy (1934).

It was during the religious persecution in Spain that Pedro was given the opportunity to sacrifice his life for the Faith. He was taken prisoner by the Communist Spanish; at dawn on July 28, 1936, when told by his persecutors to identify himself, he said, "I am a priest of Christ." He died because of his allegiance to Christ.

Pope John Paul II beatified Pedro Poveda Castroverde on October 10, 1993.

The Holy Father canonized him on May 4, 2003, in Spain, declaring:

> St. Pedro Poveda, grasping the importance of the role of education in society, undertook an important humanitarian and educational task among the marginalized and the needy. He was a master of prayer, a teacher of the Christian life and of the relationship between faith and knowledge, convinced that Christians must bring essential values and commitment to building a world that is more just and mutually supportive. His life ended with the crown of martyrdom.

Feast day: July 28.

✠

Pio da Pietrelcina, O.F.M., Cap. (Padre Pio)
(May 25, 1887 – Sept. 23, 1968)
Stigmatic

A Franciscan friar, Pio da Pietrelcina was revered as a spiritual advisor and stigmatic and known the world over as Padre Pio.

He was born at Pietrelcina in the Archdiocese of Benevento, the son of Grazio Forgione and Maria Giuseppa De Nunzio. Baptized the next day, he was given the name Francesco. At the age of twelve, he received the Sacrament of Confirmation and made his First Holy Communion.

On January 6, 1903, at the age of sixteen, he entered the novitiate of the Capuchin Friars at Morcone. There, on January 22, he took the Franciscan habit and the name Brother Pio. At the end of his novitiate year, he took simple vows, and on January 27, 1907, made his solemn profession. After he was ordained a priest on August 10, 1910, at Benevento, he remained with his family until 1916 due to the debilitating effects of tuberculosis. In September of that year, he was sent to the friary of San Giovanni Rotondo and remained there until his death.

In 1911, he first began suffering the pains of the stigmata. The stigmata became more apparent by 1918, when he received visible wounds on his side and hands. The stigmata remained part of his life until the night before his death, when it disappeared.

Padre Pio committed himself for his entire ministry to relieving the pain and suffering of many families. In 1925, he opened a small hospital in the area, an institution that anticipated the much larger foundation of the Casa Sollievo della Sofferenza (House for the Relief of Suffering) that was established on May 5, 1956. He was especially devoted to prayer, declaring: "In books we seek God, in prayer we find him. Prayer is the key which opens God's heart." In assisting the thousands who came to him for counsel, he demonstrated to an exemplary degree the virtue of prudence, acting and counseling in the light of God.

Padre Pio was investigated and cleared during several Vatican inquiries into charges of sexual misconduct and fraud. His troubles included being suspended from all forms of ministry except for celebrating Mass from 1931-32. He accepted the investigations with humility and resignation.

He died on Sept. 23, 1968, at the age of eighty-one. Thousands attended his funeral, and eight million people visit his tomb annually. On May 2, 1999, Pope John Paul II beatified Padre Pio of Pietrelcina, naming September 23 as the date of his liturgical feast. A crowd of more than 200,000 people watched the beatification on television screens in St. Peter's Square.

Pope John Paul II canonized him on June 16, 2002, before the largest crowd ever gathered for a canonization. The Holy Father proclaimed:

"But may I never boast except in the cross of Our Lord Jesus Christ" (Gal. 6:14).

Is it not, precisely, the "glory of the Cross" that shines above all in Padre Pio? How timely is the spirituality of the Cross lived by the humble Capuchin of Pietrelcina. Our time needs to rediscover the value of the

Cross in order to open the heart to hope. Throughout his life, he always sought greater conformity with the Crucified, since he was very conscious of having been called to collaborate in a special way in the work of redemption. His holiness cannot be understood without this constant reference to the Cross . . . "I am the Lord who acts with mercy" (Jer. 9:23).

Padre Pio was a generous dispenser of divine mercy, making himself available to all by welcoming them, by spiritual direction and, especially, by the administration of the sacrament of Penance. I also had the privilege, during my young years, of benefiting from his availability for penitents. The ministry of the confessional, which is one of the distinctive traits of his apostolate, attracted great crowds of the faithful to the monastery of San Giovanni Rotondo. Even when that unusual confessor treated pilgrims with apparent severity, the latter, becoming conscious of the gravity of sins and sincerely repentant, almost always came back for the peaceful embrace of sacramental forgiveness.

Feast day: September 23.

R

✝

Rafqa Pietra Choboq Ar-Rayès (Rebecca de Himlaya) (1832 – March 23, 1914)

Victim Soul

Rafqa Pietra Choboq Ar-Rayès was born in the mountain village of Himlaya, Lebanon, sometime in 1832. Called Petra Ar-Rayes at her Maronite baptism, she grew up blessed with devout Maronite relatives — she was raised by a stepmother after her own mother's death when she was only seven — and received the grace of a religious vocation.

In 1853, Rafqa entered the Marianist Sisters and was given the name Anissa in religion. She taught young girls in the congregation's schools from 1856-1871, but was drawn more and more to the contemplative life. In that year, the Marianist Congregation was dissolved, an event that allowed Rafqa to enter the Maronite Order of St. Anthony, and she became a member of the community of St. Simeon. She was given the name Rafqa in her new community.

On Rosary Sunday, 1885, Rafqa prayed to become a victim of divine love. She was struck blind that night and endured terrible pain in her right eye. That eye was eventually removed in an operation without an anesthetic. Rafqa had hemorrhages from her eye two or three times a week ever after as a result, yet this suffering did not stop her from performing all of her normal convent duties. She did the washing, baking, and weaving, and even memorized the Divine Office so that she could join her sister religious in choir services.

In 1897, Rafqa was assigned to the monastery of St. Joseph of Gerabta. There, she suffered paralysis from disarticulation of her bones. Rafqa faced death with a calm spirit of joyful surrender, saying, "I am not afraid. I have been waiting for my Lord for a long time." After her death at As-Sahr, more than 2,600 miracles were reported at her tomb.

Pope John Paul II beatified Rafqa on November 17, 1985, and canonized her on June 10, 2001, declaring:

> By canonizing Blessed Rafqa Choboq Ar-Rayès, the Church sheds a very particular light on the mystery of love given and received for the glory of God and the salvation of the world. This nun of the Lebanese Maronite Order desired to love and to give her life for her people. In the sufferings which never left her for twenty-nine years of her life, St. Rafqa always showed a passionate and generous love for the salvation of her brothers, drawing from her union with Christ, who died on the cross, the force to accept voluntarily and to love suffering, the authentic way of holiness. May St. Rafqa watch over those who know suffering, particularly over the peoples of the Middle East who must face a destructive and sterile spiral of violence. Through her intercession, let us ask the Lord to open hearts to the patient quest for new ways to peace and so hasten the advent of reconciliation and harmony.

Feast day: March 23.

☩

Raphael Kalinowski, O.C.D.
(September 1, 1835 – November 15, 1907)
Martyr of the Confessional

Raphael Kalinowski was born Josef Kalinowski in Vilna, Lithuania, of Polish descent and was raised in an era of military expansion and unrest. He attended the military academy at Pietroburgo; upon graduation, he was assigned to Brest, Litowski, in Belarus, where he worked as an engineer and attained the rank of captain. Witnessing the Czar's occupation of Poland in 1863, he joined the insurrection and was arrested. In 1864, he was sentenced to ten years in the hard-labor camps of Siberia for his part in the uprising.

Josef returned to Poland at the end of his imprisonment, in 1874, with a deeply profound spiritual vocation. He taught for a time; one of his students was August Czartoryski, one of the first Salesians, whose Cause is also open. Drawn to the contemplative life, he entered the Discalced Carmelites in Austria, took the religious name Raphael, completed his novitiate and seminary studies, and, on January 15, 1882, was ordained a priest.

He was a superb confessor and spiritual director who fought valiantly for Church unity in a troubled era. He also fostered intense devotion to the Blessed Virgin Mary; the future St. Albert Chmielowski, the founder of the Albertines, met Raphael and was guided by his wisdom.

Raphael died in the Carmelite monastery at Wadowice after decades of faithful service in the confessional and in the direction of souls. He was a spiritual giant of Poland, mourned by the people of that land.

Pope John Paul II beatified Raphael on June 23, 1983, at Krakow, Poland. The pope canonized him on November 17, 1991, naming him a "Martyr of the Confessional." The Holy Father declared as well:

> Ordained a priest, Raphael . . . set to work in Christ's vineyard. He was as esteemed confessor and spiritual director. He guided souls in the sublime knowledge of the love of God, Christ and Our Lady, the Church and neighbor. He dedicated many hours to this humble apostolate. He was always recollected, always ready to make a sacrifice, to fast, to practice mortification. The man "conquered by Christ." The man whose spirit, after all the difficult experiences of his former life — and even through the experiences which caused him much suffering — discovers the full meaning of the words which Christ spoke in the Upper Room: "As the father loves me, so also I love you . . ." (Jn. 15:9,13).

The pope added that with St. Albert Chmielowski, Raphael provided Poland with new horizons of faith, saying:

> These two great sons of the Polish land, who showed the paths to holiness to their contemporaries and to the succeeding generations, ended their lives at the dawn of this century, on the eve of the regained independence of Poland.

Feast Day: November 19.

✠

Richard Pampuri, O.H. (August 2, 1897- May 1, 1930)
Physician and Founder

He was born Erminio Filippo Pampuri in Trivolizi, Italy, the tenth child of a prosperous, pious family. His mother died when he was three, and the child was sent to Torino to live with his grandfather and an aunt. An uncle, Carlo, trained Erminio in medical practices, instilling in him a deep love of serving the sick. In 1907, his father was killed in an accident, but he survived the tragedy with calm.

Putting aside his original desire to become a foreign missionary, Erminio entered medical school. His sister entered the convent, and he became a Franciscan tertiary, saluting her for her full commitment to the religious life. He also took part in Catholic associations at a time when anticlericalism was rampant in Italy. Conscripted into the army, Erminio served in the medical corps in World War I, receiving a decoration for conspicuous bravery. In 1918, he continued his studies, graduating in medicine and surgery on July 6, 1921. The following year he completed his internship and, in 1923, was registered at Pavia University as a general practitioner and surgeon.

As a student, he had been active in the Conference of St. Vincent de Paul and other service organizations. So, when he went to Milan, he founded the Band of Pius X, a group dedicated to medical care for the poor. While working to raise funds to provide food and clothing for the needy, he was realizing his own religious vocation as well.

On June 22, 1927, Erminio became Richard, a Hospitaller of St. John of God, dedicating his medical skills entirely to the service of Christ and his poor. He took his vows on October 28, 1928, and was assigned to a clinic in Brescia. There, he continued his apostolate to the poor, earning fame for healing the sick. Ironically enough, however, his own health was not very good: after he was assigned to Milan, he suffered a severe lung affliction which soon became pneumonia. Richard then prophesied when he would die — and true to his prediction, he expired at the age of thirty-three.

Pope John Paul II beatified Richard in 1981 and canonized him on November 1, 1989, declaring that the saint was "close to our times, but even closer to our problems and our sensibilities." The Holy Father also said that Richard's life shines with "the mystery of eternal holiness of the Triune God." With St. Gaspar Bertoni, canonized on the same day, Richard displayed the content of the evangelical Beatitudes. The pope concluded, "They are two witnesses to Christ's love, in different times and different kinds of life."

Feast day: May 1.

✠

Roque (Roch) González de Santa Cruz (1576 – 1628) (+1628) and two Spanish Companions, Alonso Rodríguez and Juan de Castillo, S.J. — see Paraguay, Martyrs of

✠

Rose-Philippine Duchesne
(August 29, 1769 – November 18, 1852)
"The Woman Who Prays Always"

A religious pioneer in America, Rose-Philippine Duchesne was born in Grenoble, France, the daughter of Pierre François Duchesne, a prominent lawyer. Her mother belonged to the distinguished Periér family, ancestors of Casimir Periér, the president of France in 1894.

Desiring a religious vocation, Rose Philippine joined the Visitation Sisters at age seventeen but saw her convent caught up in the tragic persecutions of the French Revolution. The convent was closed, and Rose Philippine was sent home in order to save her life. When the Revolution ended, she returned to the convent, hoping to revive the branch of the Visitation Congregation. Unable to achieve this, she invited Madeleine Sophie Barat to assume control of the convent for her own ministry. Madeleine could not expand her congregation's work in that fashion , howver, and had to decline the offer.

Rose Philippine had already demonstrated her courage and constancy during a period of intense trial and danger. After being sent home from the convent, she had provided havens for the clergy being hunted by anti-religious forces and had cared for political prisoners. Recognizing the fortitude and spiritual maturity on the part of Rose Philippine, the future St. Madeleine invited her to become a member of the Society of the Sacred

Heart. On December 31, 1804, Rose Philippine took vows in that congregation and immediately demonstrated qualities of leadership and generosity.

In 1818, when Rose Philippine was forty-nine, she was chosen to lead four companions to the United States, and Bishop Louis Dubourg of New Orleans welcomed her to the city. She did not speak English, but she opened a school in St. Charles, Missouri, and pioneered Indian schools, orphanages, and a Sacred Heart novitiate. She recognized the sacrifices demanded of the Church and missionaries in the New World, saying, "Poverty and Christian heroism are here, and trials are the riches of priests in this land."

When Rose Philippine was on the Potowátomi reservation, although unable to learn the tribal language, she earned the admiration of the Indians through her holiness and recollections. The Potowátomi called her "the Woman Who Prays Always." She suffered keen disappointments in her labors of more than three decades, but she continued to lead the way in establishing educational and charitable institutions.

Rose Philippine died in St. Charles, Missouri, at the age of eighty-three, and a shrine was erected there in her memory. In the process of her beatification, Rose Philippine's remains were exhumed in 1940 and found to be incorrupt. The only true photograph of her was taken on that occasion.

Rose Philippine Duchesne was beatified on May 12, 1940, by Pope Pius XII. Pope John Paul II canonized her on July 3, 1988, declaring:

> . . . her whole life was transformed and enlightened by her love for Christ in the Eucharist. During the long hours she spent before the Blessed Sacrament she learned to live continually in the presence of God. . . . The radical commitment of Mother Duchesne to the poor and the outcast of society, remains a very dynamic source of inspiration for her own Congregation, and for all religious today. . . . Her absolutely unique example is valid for all Christ's disciples, especially for those who live in the underprivileged parts of the world . . . With missionary courage, this great pioneer looked to the future with the eyes of the heart — a heart that was on fire with God's love.

Feast day: November 18.

S

✠

Simón de Rojas, O.S.S.
(October 28, 1552 – September 28, 1624)
Royal Confessor

A Trinitarian tutor, Simon de Rojas founded a secular pious association.

He was born in Valladolid, Spain, the third of four children of noble parents, Gregorio Ruiz de Navamanuel and his wife, Costanza de Rojas. Educated, and displaying a keen mind as he grew older, Simon also maintained a profound spirit of recollection. He entered the Trinitarians at the age of twelve and was professed eight years later, in the Valladolid Trinitarian monastery. Simon was sent to Salamanca for philosophy and theology training and was ordained a priest in 1577. During this period, he dedicated his life to the Blessed Mother.

His academic brilliance and administrative abilities led to his appointment to religious offices in the Trinitarians, and he served as a Superior as well. Simon's sermons and obvious piety brought him to the attention of the Spanish court of King Philip III, a deeply religious ruler. Philip was not particularly active as a monarch — leaving the task of government to the Duke de Uceda — but recognized Simon's holiness and ordered him to serve as confessor to the court. In time, Simon was appointed tutor to the heir, Prince Philip, who inherited the throne as Philip IV in 1621 and ruled until 1665. He was also confessor to Queen Isabella of Bourbon.

Even with his royal duties, however, Simon did not forsake his Trinitarian ministry. He refused two appointments as bishop and gave his personal funds to aid the poor. He was particularly devoted to the Holy Eucharist. He also spread devotion of total consecration to Mary throughout Spain and Germany, founding the Congregation of the Servants of the Most Sweet Name of Mary, a secular organization promoting this cause. Pope Gregory XV (r. 1621-1623) joined in this total consecration.

Toward the end of Simon's life, he was able to spend more time in prayer and private penance. After his death in Madrid, he was given royal honors and mourned by the people of Spain.

Simon was beatified in 1766 and canonized by Pope John Paul II on July 3, 1988. At that time, the pontiff declared that the new saint:

> . . . gave full meaning to his life as a Christian, as a priest, in his contemplation of the mystery of the God of Love. Faithful to the redeeming and merciful charism of his Order, "Fr. Rojas" — as he was familiarly called by his people — was very aware of all kinds of needs in his neighbor, especially of the poor and the outcast, as he was aware of the needs of Christians imprisoned for their faith. On their part, the poor saw in him their guardian champion and father.

The Holy Father also stated that Simon's active apostolate was "not an obstacle to his contemplative prayer, nor to his dedication of long periods of time for prayer during the day, and still more during the night after the sung office at midnight."

Feast day: September 28.

$\mathcal{T}$

⊹

Teresa Benedicta of the Cross — see Edith Stein

⊹

Teresa de Jesús "de los Andes" Solar
(July 13, 1900 – April 2, 1920)
Chilean Contemplative

Teresa de Jesús "de los Andes" was born Juana Enriquita Josephine of the Sacred Hearts Soler in Santiago, Chile, the daughter of Michael Fernandez Jaraquemada and Lucia Solar Armstrong of that city. Teresa was well educated by her parents and displayed a unique religious fervor even as a small child.

She recognized the grace for a Carmelite vocation and entered the Carmelite Convent of the Andes on May 7, 1919, receiving the habit of Carmel and the religious name Teresa of Jesus on October 14, 1919. As a Carmelite, she received many mystical graces and displayed rare contemplative gifts. Teresa became united in her prayers to Christ, the Divine Victim, and experienced many spiritual encounters, even as her health began to fail and she was diagnosed with typho correpta, a severe form of typhus. After receiving the Last Sacrament, she made her profession as a cloistered nun on April 6. Six days later, she died.

Pope John Paul II beatified Teresa of Jesus on April 3, 1987. On March 21, 1993, the pontiff canonized her before a crowd of one million of her countrymen in Santiago, Chile. At the ceremony, the Holy Father declared:

Sr. Teresa "de los Andes," Teresa of Jesus, is the light of Christ for the whole Chilean Church; the Discalced Carmelite, the first fruit of holiness of the Teresian Carmel of Latin America, today is enrolled among the saints of the Universal Church . . . God made shine forth in her in an admirable way the light of his Son, Jesus Christ, so that she could be a beacon and guide to a world which seems to be blind to the splendour of the divine. In a secularized society which turns its back on God, this Chilean

Carmelite, whom to my great joy I present as a model of the perennial youth of the Gospel, gives the shining witness of a life which proclaims to the men and women of our day that it is in the loving, adoring, and serving God that the human creature finds greatness and joy, freedom, and fulfillment. The life of Blessed Teresa cries out continually from within her cloister: "God alone suffices!" She shouts it out particularly to the young people who hunger for the truth and seek a light which will give direction to their lives. To young people who are being allured by the continuous messages and stimuli of an erotic culture, a society which mistakes the hedonistic exploitation of another for genuine love which is self-giving, this young virgin of the Andes today proclaims the beauty and happiness that come from a pure heart.

Feast day: July 13.

✠

Teresa Eustochio Verzeri (July 31, 1801- March 3, 1852)
Pioneer in Catholic Education

The founder of the Congregation of the Daughters of the Sacred Heart of Jesus, Teresa Eustochio Verzeri was a pioneer in Catholic education. She was born in Bergamo, Italy, the first of the seven children of Antonio Verzeri and the countess Elena Pedrocca-Grumelli. Her brother, Girolamo, became Bishop of Brescia.

Her mother was an important figure in developing her spiritual and intellectual development, as was Canon Giuseppe Benaglio, a local cleric who took over as advisor after the death of her father. It was in this environment that Teresa developed her vocation. She entered the Benedictine Monastery of St. Grata, but she could not be given the habit because she was only sixteen. Returning home, Teresa again entered the monastery in August 1821. Once more she departed, and once more she returned. Finally, she left the monastery for good in order to establish the Congregation of the Daughters of the Sacred Heart of Jesus on February 8, 1831, in Bergamo. More women came to be part of the community, including her sisters and her mother. They concentrated on educating middle-class girls, finding homes for abandoned orphans, and promoting Christian doctrine among the sick and the poor.

After opening two schools in Bergamo, the new community expanded over 1831-32 to other cities in Lombardy, Parma, Piacenza, the Papal States, the Tyrol, and Venice. In 1836 Canon Benaglio died, and Teresa dedicated herself totally to the continued growth and development of her sisters. The bishop of Bergamo approved the formal rules for the congregation in 1842, and Pope Blessed Pius IX granted the formal approval of the Holy See in 1847. Today, the Daughters of the Sacred Heart of Jesus continue to serve in Italy, Brazil, Argentina, Bolivia, the Central African Republic, Cameroon, India, and Albania.

Teresa Verzeri died in Brescia after caring for countless sick during a cholera outbreak. Pope Pius XII beatified her in 1946, and Pope John Paul II canonized her on June 10, 2001, declaring:

Teresa Eustochio Verzeri, whom today we contemplate in the glory of God, in her brief but intense life knew how to be led with docility by the Holy Spirit. God revealed himself to her as a mysterious presence before whom we must bow with profound humility. Her joy was to be considered under constant divine protection, feeling herself in the hands of the heavenly Father, whom she learned to trust in forever.

Feast day: March 3.

⊹

Thomas of Cori (June 4, 1655 – January 11, 1729)
Noted Confessor

Thomas of Cori (Tommasso da Cori) was born Francesco Antonio Placidi in Cori, Layina, Italy; he was orphaned at the age of fourteen and left to care for his younger sister. After developing his foundations for a prayer life, Francesco discerned a vocation and entered the Franciscan novitiate at Orvieto, taking the name Thomas in religion.

Ordained a priest in 1683, he was soon appointed novice master at Holy Trinity Friary in Orvieto. After several years, however, he was transferred to Civitella (Bellegra). This transfer permitted him to fulfill his hope of becoming a hermit in order to devote himself entirely to prayer.

As a hermit, Thomas wrote a rule and was fond of declaring that we must "become a prayer." Although Thomas' own spiritual life was marked by long periods of aridity, in subsequent travels in the region around Civitella, he became renowned for his abilities and gifts as a confessor, preacher, and retreat master. He also was reputed to be a miracle worker, and died in the midst of his labors.

Pope John Paul II beatified Thomas of Cori on April 29, 1990, and canonized him on November 21, 1999, announcing:

"I myself will search for my sheep, and will seek them out" (Ez. 34:11). Tommasso of Cori, a priest of the Order of Friars Minor, was the living image of the Good Shepherd. As a loving guide, he knew how to lead the brothers entrusted to his care towards the pastures of faith, ever inspired by the Franciscan ideal. In the friary he showed his spirit of charity, making himself available for any need, even the humblest. He lived the kingship of love and service, according to the mind of Christ who, as today's liturgy sings, "offered his life on the altar of the Cross and redeemed the human race by this one perfect sacrifice of peace" (Preface of Christ the King). As a genuine disciple of the "Poverello" of Assisi, St. Thomas of Cori was obedient to Christ, the King of the universe. He meditated upon and incarnated in his life the Gospel requirement of poverty and of self-giving to God and neighbour. Thus his whole life appears as a sign of the Gospel, a witness to the heavenly Father's love revealed in Christ and active in the Holy Spirit for human salvation.

Feast day: January 11.

$\mathcal{U}$

✠

Urszula Ledóchowska (1865 – May 29, 1939)
Instrumental in the History of Europe and the Church

She was born Giulia Ledóchowska, but on the day of her religious profession in the Ursuline convent of Krakow, she took the name Maria Urszula of Jesus. Hers was a unique family, boasting many politicians, military men, ecclesiastics, and consecrated people involved in the history of Europe and of the Church. The first three children in her family, including M. Urszula, chose the consecrated life: Maria Teresa (beatified in 1975) founded the future Society of St. Peter Claver, and the younger brother, Vladimiro, became the general Preposito of the Jesuits.

Urszula lived in the convent at Krakow for twenty-one years. Her love for the Lord, her educational talent, and her sensibility toward the needs of youngsters in the changing social, political, and moral conditions of those times, put her at the center of attention. When women earned the right to study in universities, she succeeded in organizing the first boardinghouse in Poland for female students — not only a safe place to live and study, but a place that afforded them a solid religious preparation.

This passion, together with the blessing of Pope St. Pius X, gave her the strength to move into the heart of Russia, which was hostile towards the Church. She and another Sister left for Petersburg in civilian clothes; religious habits were prohibited in that city. In Petersburg, Urszula had a growing community of nuns and established an autonomous structure of the Ursulines, even though she and her community were under constant surveillance by the secret police.

When war started in 1914, Urszula had to leave Russia. She headed for Stockholm and, during her Scandinavian travels through Sweden, Denmark, and Norway, concentrated her activities on education and on the life of the local Church, aiding war victims and ecumenical programs. The house where she lived with her nuns became a point of reference for people of different political and religious orientations.

In 1920 Urszula, her sisters, and a vast number of orphan children of immigrants returned to Poland. Her congregation became officially the Ursulines of the Sacred Agonizing Heart of Jesus. The community developed quickly, and in 1928, the Generalate, or Motherhouse, was established in Rome. The Sisters began to work in the poor suburbs of Rome and, in 1930, were established in France.

Wherever possible, Urszula founded educational and instructional work centers. She sent the nuns to catechize and to work in the poor parts of town. When Urszula died in Rome, people said of her, "She died a saint."

Pope John Paul II beatified Urszula Ledóchowska on June 20, 1983, in Poznan. On May 18, 2003, Pope John Paul II canonized her, declaring:

> She knew that for believers, every event, even the least important, becomes an opportunity to carry out God's plans. What was ordinary, she made extraordinary; what was part of daily life, she transformed so that it became eternal; what was banal, she made holy. If today St. Ursula has become an example of holiness for all believers, it is because her charism can be grasped by those who, in the name of the love of Christ and of the Church, want to witness effectively to the Gospel in today's world. We can all learn from her how to build with Christ an ever more human world — a world in which values such as justice, freedom, solidarity, and peace will be more and more fully achieved. From her we can learn how to put into practice every day the "new" commandment of love.

Feast day: May 26.

$\mathcal{V}$

✠

Virginia Centurione Bracelli
(April 2, 1587 – December 15, 1651)

Patroness of Young People

The founder of a religious congregation, Virginia Centurione Bracelli was born in Genoa, the daughter of Giorgio Centurione, duke of the Republic in the year 1621-1622, and Lelia Spinola. Both of them were of ancient noble origin. Virginia was baptized two days after her birth and received her first religious and literary formation from her mother and private tutor. She soon desired a cloistered life but had to agree to her father's command that she marry Gaspare Grimaldi Bracelli on December 10, 1602.

Gaspare's family was both illustrious and wealthy, but he was wholly taken up with gambling and had a dissolute life. Virginia gave birth to two daughters, Lelia and Isabella; Gaspare, meanwhile, did not abandon his lifestyle, which led to his death on June 13, 1607, in Alessandria. Widowed at the age of twenty, Virginia pronounced a private perpetual vow of chastity, refusing the occasion of a second marriage proposed by her father. She lived in her mother-in-law's house, believing strongly that God was asking her to serve him through the poor.

In the autumn of 1624-1625, the war between the Ligurian Republic and the Duke of Savoy, supported by France, increased the unemployment in the region and brought starvation to some. Virginia took in fifteen abandoned young people. In August 1625, the death of her mother-in-law allowed her to expand her care. She started an organization to offer aid, and during the plague and famine of 1629-1630, she rented the empty convent of Monte Calvario. Three years later, Virginia was caring for 300 patients in three houses.

Giving up Monte Calvario because it was too expensive, Virginia bought two villas next to Carignano's Hill that, with the construction of the new annex of the Church, were dedicated to Our Lady of Refuge. She founded two religious congregations: the Sisters of Our Lady of Refuge on Mount Calvary and the Daughters of Our Lady on Mount Calvary. Virginia continued aiding the poor and intervened in political rivalries in order to bring peace. She died at the age of sixty-four, having attained union with God in mystical experiences.

Pope John Paul II beatified Virginia Centurione Bracelli on the occasion of his Apostolic Visit in Genoa on September 22, 1985. He canonized her on May 18, 2003, in St. Peter's Square, announcing:

> In response to the exhortation of the Apostle John, she wanted to love not only "with words," "or with her lips," but "with deeds and in truth" (cf. I Jn 3: 18). Disregarding her noble origins, she devoted herself to assisting the lowliest with extraordinary apostolic zeal. The effectiveness of her apostolate stemmed from her unconditional adherence to God's will, which was nourished by ceaseless contemplation of, and obedient listening to, the word of the Lord.
>
> In love with Christ and for his sake ready to give herself for her brothers and sisters, St. Virginia Centurione Bracelli leaves the Church the witness of a simple and active saint. Her example of courageous fidelity to the Gospel also continues to exert a powerful influence on people in our time. She used to say: when God is one's only goal, "all disagreements are smoothed out, all difficulties overcome" (*Positio*, n. 86).

Feast day: December 15.

✠

Vietnam, Martyrs of (1745 – 1862)
Victims of Ferocious Persecution

The story of the Catholic Church in Vietnam opens in 1533, when a Portuguese missionary arrived in the kingdom. An imperial edict against Christianity soon made it impossible for the Faith to take root until 1615, when the Jesuits established a permanent mission in the central region of the kingdom.

In 1627, Jesuit Fr. Alexander de Rhodes established a northern mission. He was expelled in 1630, after baptizing 6,700 Vietnamese. Fr. de Rhodes reportedly returned to Vietnam, but was banished once more in 1645. He then went to France, where the Paris Seminary for Foreign Missions was founded — the Society for Foreign Missions. Priests trained in the Society soon arrived in Vietnam, and the Faith underwent a period of swift growth.

Between 1798 and 1853 — a period of intense political rivalry and civil wars in Vietnam — sixty-four known Christians were executed. Pope Leo XIII beatified them in 1900.

In 1833, all Christians were ordered to renounce the Faith and to trample crucifixes underfoot. Up to 300,000 people suffered in some way from persecution during the next fifty years. In 1847, French warships arrived to "protect" the missionaries and Catholics; this motive, however, proved to be a mere pretext for France's long-term colonial ambitions in Vietnam. Gradually, French authorities seized control of the kingdom through treaties in 1862, 1874, and 1884. Persecutions nevertheless continued in parts of the country until 1883.

The bishops and priests, all Europeans, were slain in unbelievably inhuman fashion. In 1841 the persecutions abated, as France threatened to intervene with warships, but in 1848, bounties were placed on the heads of the missionaries by a new emperor. Two priests, Frs. Augustin Schöffler and John Louis Bonnard, were beheaded as a result. In 1855, the persecution took on a new ferocity, and in the following year wholesale massacres began. Thousands of Vietnamese Christians were slain, including four bishops and twenty-eight Dominicans. Reportedly, between 1857 and 1862, 115 native priests, 100 Vietnamese nuns, and more than 5,000 of the faithful were martyred. Convents, churches and schools were destroyed, and as many as 40,000 Catholics were dispossessed of their lands and exiled from their own regions. Twenty-eight martyrs from this era were beatified in 1909.

At long last, the Peace of 1862 — brought about by the surrender of Saigon and other regions to French colonial forces — and the payment of indemnities to France and Spain put an end to the persecutions.

Also called the Martyrs of Tonkin or Annam, the Martyrs of Vietnam include ninety-six Vietnamese, eleven Spaniards, and ten French missionaries. Among the better-known martyrs of this group are the following:

Andrew Dung Lac An Tran, a native of Vietnam, was educated in the Faith and ordained a priest. He served in the Catholic missions in Vietnam until the persecutions brought about untold sufferings among the Vietnamese Christians. The priests associated with the Foreign Mission Society of Paris were particularly singled out for harsh treatment, and Andrew was arrested with St. Peter Thi and joined his fellow martyrs in prison, where they were tortured and abused. Andrew shared his sufferings with St. Théophane Venard, St. Thomas Thien Tran, St. Emmanuel Phung Van Le, St. Hieronymous Hermosila, St. Bishop Valentine Berriochoa, and more than one hundred others. He was beheaded on December 21, 1839.

Andrew Thong Kim Nguyen was born in 1790 in Vietnam and grew up a respected member of his village, even serving as mayor. When persecution began, Andrew was exiled from his village because of his devotion to the Catholic Faith. He died from exhaustion and dehydration during the forced march of all Christian prisoners to Mi-Tho in 1855.

Andrew Trong Van Tram, a native of Vietnam, was born in 1817 and, while raised a Catholic, decided to follow a military career in his native land. He also aided the Paris Foreign Mission Society, which was then conducting missionary and parochial operations in Vietnam. Discovered by Vietnamese authorities in 1834, Andrew was stripped of his military rank and put into prison in Hué. The following year Andrew joined his companions in martyrdom after refusing to abjure the Faith. His mother was present at her son's death in Hué; when Andrew was beheaded, she knelt beside the executioner's block to catch his severed head in her lap.

Anthony Quynh (Nam) was born in 1768 and studied medicine, becoming a physician. A Catholic, he aided the Paris Foreign Mission Society in Vietnam and was arrested for his association with the European missionaries in 1838. He was kept in prison for two terrible years. During his imprisonment, Anthony cared for his fellow martyrs and endured many tortures and abuses. He was strangled in prison in 1840.

Anthony Dich Nguyen was a wealthy farmer, much esteemed. He supported the Paris Foreign Mission Society in Vietnam and was a generous patron of the Church. He also sheltered priests fleeing government authorities (among them James Nam) during the persecutions in that land. The authorities discovered Anthony's activities and arrested him. After torture and abuse, he was beheaded in 1838.

Augustine Huy Viet Phan was born in Vietnam and served for a time as a soldier. A Catholic, he joined fellow soldier Nicholas Thé in aiding the missionary labors of the Church. Both were arrested and condemned to death in 1839. They were stretched on a rack and sawed in half.

Augustine Moi Van Nguyen was a native Vietnamese who worked as a day laborer. He studied the Faith and became a Dominican tertiary known for his piety and charity. When the persecution of the Church raged in Vietnam, he was ordered by authorities to step on a crucifix as a visible sign of his abjuring the Faith. He refused and was strangled.

Augustine Schöffler was born in Mittelbronn, Lorraine, France, in 1822, and studied for the priesthood. After receiving training as a member of the Paris Foreign Mission Society, Augustine was sent to Vietnam in 1848. He was soon caught up in the persecution of that era and was arrested by the authorities. He was martyred by beheading in 1851.

Bernard Due Van Vo was born in Vietnam in 1755 and converted to the faith. After becoming a Catholic, Bernard studied for the priesthood. He was ordained and subsequently served for decades in various missionary labors on behalf of the Faith in the country. Bernard was eighty-three when he was arrested and beheaded by government authorities in 1838.

Dominic (Nicholas) Dat Dinh embraced the Faith and served in the army. (He may also have been a Dominican tertiary.) Refusing to deny the Faith, Dominic was stripped of his military position and strangled in 1839.

Dominic Henares, a Spaniard by birth, became bishop-coadjutor to Ignatius Delgado in Vietnam, serving as vicar apostolic of the region. When persecution of the Church started, Dominic was arrested with his catechist, Francis Chieu. They were imprisoned and beheaded. Dominic died praising God and proclaiming his faith.

Dominic Trach (Doai) was a native of Vietnam, born in 1792. A devout Catholic, he became a Dominican tertiary, then a priest. He was ordained for the mission in his native land and labored in his own country until his arrest in 1842. He was beheaded by the Vietnamese.

Dominic Uy Van Bui, born in Vietnam in 1813, lived as a devout Catholic for many years, performing duties as a catechist for the local community. When the persecution erupted in Vietnam, he was seized and ordered to abjure the Faith. He refused and was strangled at age twenty-six in 1839.

Dominic Hanh Van Nguyen, a native of Vietnam, was a devout Catholic and studied for the priesthood. After ordination, he labored in his country for decades. At the time of the severe persecution of the Church in Vietnam, Dominic was arrested and martyred at age sixty-seven.

Dominic Xuyen Van Nguyen, a native of Vietnam, was ordained for the Dominican missions and gave his life to the cause of advancing the Faith among his people. When the persecutions started, he was arrested with Thomas Du. They were beheaded.

Emmanuel Trieu Van Nguyen, born in Vietnam in 1756, was raised a Christian. After serving in the army, Emmanuel entered the seminary to become a priest of the Paris Foreign Mission Society. He returned to Vietnam after ordination and was arrested while visiting his mother. Taken to a prison, he was beheaded by government officials.

Francis Xavier Can Nguyen was a native of Vietnam, born in 1803 in Sou Mieng, and a catechist. Francis aided the efforts of the Paris Foreign

Mission Society and was arrested by government authorities. He was strangled in prison when he refused to abjure the Faith.

Francis Chieu Van Do, a native of China, was born in 1796, embraced the Faith, then devoted himself to aiding the priests in their Vietnamese mission. He was arrested by government authorities with Dominic Henares, a bishop, whom he was serving. They were beheaded together in 1838.

Francis Gil de Frederich was born in Tortosa, Spain, in 1702, and was educated at Barcelona, He entered the Dominicans and, after his studies, was sent to the as a missionary to the Philippines. In 1732, he was assigned to Vietnam, where he performed his missionary duties until his arrest in 1742 (or 1743) and his martyrdom by beheading.

Francis Isidore Gagelin was born in Montperreaux, France, in 1799 and entered the Paris Foreign Mission Society. He was sent to Vietnam in 1822 and was ordained to the priesthood there. When the government instituted a renewed persecution of the Church, Francis surrendered to authorities at Bong-son. He was placed in a prison, where he was martyred by strangulation in 1833.

Francis Jaccard was born in 1799 at Onnion, in Savoy, France. Entering the Paris Foreign Mission Society, he was ordained a priest and was sent to Vietnam in 1826. He labored there until his arrest. He was martyred for the Faith by strangulation in 1838.

Francis Trung Von Tran, a native of Vietnam, was born in Phan-xa in 1825 and embraced the Catholic Faith. A corporal in the Vietnamese army, he was arrested and commanded to abjure Christ. When he refused, he was beheaded at An-hoa in 1858.

Hyacinth Casteñeda was born in Sétavo, Spain. After entering the Dominicans, he was ordained and sent to the mission in China, then to Vietnam. There, he was arrested by government authorities and beheaded with Vincent Liem in 1773.

Ignatius Delgado y Cebrián was born in Spain in 1761. Raised in a prayerful family, he became a professed Dominican and worked for half a century in the missions in Vietnam on behalf of the Faith. A skilled preacher and administrator, he was named vicar apostolic for the eastern region of that land and consecrated a bishop. Thus, when the persecutions of the Faith were launched, Ignatius was arrested by government authorities and placed in a cage for public ridicule. He died in his cage from hunger and exposure. Pope Leo XIII beatified him in 1900.

James Nam, a native Vietnamese priest, was associated with the Paris Foreign Mission Society. Arrested in the great persecutions by government authorities, he was imprisoned and beheaded in 1838 with Anthony Dich and Michael My.

Jerome Hermosilla was an important leader of the Church in Vietnam during one of its darkest eras. Born in La Calfada, Spain, he was professed as a Dominican and was assigned to the mission of the order in Manila, in the Philippines. There, he was ordained and, in 1828, was sent to Vietnam to serve in the Dominican missions in the eastern region. Jerome succeeded Ignatius Delgado as vicar apostolic. Consecrated a bishop, he was soon singled out for arrest by government authorities because of his prominent position. Jerome was tortured cruelly in prison, and then beheaded in 1861 with Bishop Valentine Berriochoa.

John Dat, a native of Vietnam, was born in 1764 and ordained a priest in 1798. Arrested by authorities for preaching the Gospel, he was kept imprisoned for three months before being beheaded in 1798.

John Louis Bonnard was a member of the Paris Foreign Mission Society, and thus dedicated to the apostolate in Vietnam. He was arrested by government authorities and beheaded in 1852, at the age of twenty-eight.

John Baptist Con was a native of Vietnam, born in 1805. A true adherent of the Faith, he married and served the Church in his area as a lay catechist. In the midst of the severe persecution of the Church in the country, John was arrested and imprisoned. He was martyred by beheading in 1840.

John Charles Cornay was born in Loudon, France, in 1809. Ordained a priest of the Paris Foreign Mission Society, he was sent to Vietnam to work for the faith. He was arrested and kept as a chained prisoner in a cage for three months, and was then beaten and beheaded on September 20, 1837.

John Hoan Trinh Doan was born about 1789 at Kim-long, Vietnam, and was educated by the missionaries of the Church in that country. Such was his faith that he entered the seminary and was ordained a priest. In 1861, John was arrested by the troops of King Tu-Duc and executed for the Faith. Pope St. Pius X beatified him in 1909.

John Thanh Van Dinh, a native Vietnamese, served as a catechist with the Paris Foreign Mission Society, bringing the Faith to his people. Arrested and tortured, he was martyred for the Faith.

Joseph Canh Luang Hoang, born in 1765, was a native of Vietnam. He studied medicine and became a Dominican tertiary. As a prominent Catholic, he was arrested by government authorities and beheaded in 1838.

Joseph Fernandez was born in Spain in 1775 and entered the Dominicans as a young man. Sent to Vietnam in 1805, he completed his studies and was ordained a priest with the express purpose of serving in that mission.

Unfortunately, soon after being named provincial vicar, he was arrested by authorities and martyred by beheading. He was beatified in 1900 by Pope Leo XIII.

Joseph Hien Quang Do, a native Dominican of Vietnam, served as a priest in his own land, laboring in the Dominican missions until his arrest by government authorities in 1840. He was beheaded for the Faith at Nam-Dinh that same year.

Joseph Khang Duy Nguyen is remembered as the servant of Jerome Hermosilla, the Dominican bishop in Vietnam. When the bishop was imprisoned in 1861, Joseph tried to help him escape from his captivity but was caught by the authorities, beaten, tortured, then beheaded.

Joseph Luu Van Nguyen, a native Vietnamese, was born in 1790 and became a devout supporter of the Church and the Vietnamese missions. Arrested by government authorities, he died of tortures and abuse in a prison in Vinh-long in 1854.

Joseph Marchand was another member of the Paris Foreign Mission Society. A native of Passavant, France, he entered the Society and was assigned to the missions in Vietnam. He labored there until his arrest in 1835, and was martyred by having his flesh torn apart by tongs.

Joseph Vien Dinh Dang, a native of Vietnam, was born in 1786 and raised a Catholic. Ordained a priest, he worked in the missions until his arrest. Joseph was beheaded.

Joseph Nghi (Kim), a native priest, was associated with the Paris Foreign Mission Society. He was arrested by government authorities during the persecution and beheaded for the Faith in 1840.

Joseph Thi Dang Le was a Vietnamese soldier in the service of King Tu-Duc until his faith was discovered. Arrested, Joseph refused to deny Christ and was garroted in 1860.

Joseph Uyen Dinh Nguyen, a Dominican tertiary, was a native of Vietnam, born in 1778. Aiding the missions of the Church, Joseph was arrested by government authorities. He died of torture and abuse in prison in 1838.

Lawrence Huong Van Nguyen was a native of Vietnam, born about 1802. Ordained as a priest and committed to the cause of the Church in his native land, he worked for a number of years until caught up in the persecutions, arrested and imprisoned. He suffered martyrdom by beheading in 1856.

Luke Loan Ba Vu, a revered elderly priest, was born in Vietnam in 1756 and educated in the Faith. Called to a vocation, he studied for the priesthood and was ordained. He served many long decades of service to the Church and his own people before was arrested by government authorities and beheaded in 1840.

Martin Tho, a native of Vietnam, suffered martyrdom with aged Martin Tinh. Tho was a tax collector and a devout Catholic. During the time of the persecutions, he refused to abjure the Faith and was martyred in 1840.

Martin Tinh Duc Ta, a native Vietnamese priest, was executed at the age of eighty after laboring for decades before falling victim to the persecution. He died with Martin Tho.

Matthew Gam Van Le was a native of Vietnam, born in 1812. Joining the Paris Foreign Mission Society, he dedicated himself to promoting the faith. One of his achievements was to bring Christian missionaries from Singapore to Vietnam on his fishing boat. Arrested for such service in 1846, Matthew was tortured and beheaded the next year.

Matthew Alonzo Leziniana was born in Navas del Rey, Spain. Entering the Dominicans, Matthew was ordained and assigned to the Order's missions in the Philippines. He was then sent to Vietnam. After a period of service, he was arrested and beheaded in a persecution in 1745.

Matthew Dac (Phuong) Nguyen was a native Vietnamese. Born in 1801, he served as a catechist for the Faith for some years until his arrest by authorities. He was beheaded near Dong-hai in 1861.

Michael Hy Dinh-Ho was born about 1808 and was a Vietnamese nobleman in a Christian family. Rising in the royal administration, he became powerful as the superintendent of Vietnam's silk mills. Michael was not involved in the persecutions at first. He became more and more concerned, however, and began to take a role in protecting the faithful. For this, Michael was arrested and beheaded near Hué.

Michael My Huy Nguyen, a native Vietnamese, was the father-in-law of Anthony Dich. Married with a family and a farmer by profession, he served the Church with great fidelity. Michael gave special assistance to Anthony in his efforts to protect the missionaries during the persecution. When Anthony tried to hide James Nam in 1838, he and James were arrested with Michael. All three were martyred.

Nicholas Thé (Duc Bui), a soldier of Vietnam, served the rulers of the country with loyalty until a persecution was launched against the faith. Nicholas refused to deny Christ when arrested and was racked and sawed in half for proclaiming the Catholic faith.

Paul Tong Buong, a captain of the royal bodyguard of Vietnam, served King Minh-Menh. Because he was a Catholic who supported the programs of the Paris Foreign Mission Society in Vietnam, he was arrested in 1832, stripped of his military rank, and imprisoned. Paul suffered for months before being beheaded in 1833.

Paul Hanh was one of the most unique of the Vietnamese martyrs; he was an outlaw who secretly supported the Christian community. When he was arrested, he openly professed his belief in Christ. For this, he endured terrible tortures before his beheading, near modern Saigon (Ho Chi Minh City) in 1859.

Paul Khoan Khan Pham was born in Vietnam and studied with the Paris Foreign Mission Society. Ordained, he labored for four decades before his arrest. He was beheaded for the Faith in 1840, after enduring two years of extreme abuse in a prison.

Paul Loc Van Le was a native Vietnamese, born in 1831, and was a veteran of Vietnam's army before studying for the priesthood. Paul was arrested soon after his ordination and beheaded in 1859.

Paul Tinh Bao Le was a priest of the missions of Vietnam who studied for ordination in order to aid the evangelization of his land. When the persecution caught him, he was imprisoned, then beheaded at Sontay in 1857.

Peter Duong Van Troung, a native Vietnamese, served with Peter Truat as a catechist, aiding the European and Vietnamese missionaries in their evangelizing programs. For these acts of loyalty, the two were taken in the persecution of the Church and martyred in 1838.

Peter Hieu Van Nguyen, a member of the Paris Foreign Mission Society, was a native catechist who aided the missions. He was arrested and refused to deny Christ. Peter and two companions were beheaded in 1840.

Peter Francis Néron was born in Jura, France, in 1818. He studied with the Paris Foreign Mission Society, was ordained in 1948, and was assigned to the missions in Hong Kong before being sent to Vietnam. There, he headed the Society's central seminary. When the persecution was launched once more by the Vietnamese government, Peter was arrested. He endured harsh treatment and suffered martyrdom by beheading in 1861.

Peter Quy Cong Doan was born at Bung, Vietnam, and was a devout Christian. Ordained as a priest, he worked to evangelize his native land until his arrest. He was tortured and beheaded at Chaudoc in 1859.

Peter Thi Van Truong (Pham) was born in Vietnam in 1763. He became a devout priest who labored in the Catholic missions. Elderly at the time of his arrest in 1839, he was beheaded for the Faith.

Peter Tuan Ba Nguyen was born in 1766. A faithful missionary priest, he would not abjure the Faith and was condemned to death. He died in prison in 1838 from wounds received from his captors.

Peter Tuy Le, a native Vietnamese priest, had been raised devoutly and studied enthusiastically for ordination. Many years later (1833), at the age of seventy, he was arrested and beheaded.

Peter Van Van Doan, born about 1780, was dedicated to the evangelization of his native land. To make his contribution, Peter served as a catechist. He was arrested, refused to deny Christ, and was beheaded for his heroic loyalty in 1857.

Philip Minh Van Phan was born in 1815 and entered the Paris Foreign Mission Society. After studies and ordination, he returned to Vietnam and labored there until his arrest. Philip was beheaded at Vinh-hong in 1853.

Simon Hoa Dac Phan was a Catholic physician and mayor of his native village in Vietnam. Arrested in 1840, he was cruelly tortured and beheaded. Simon was beatified in 1909.

Stephen (Etienne-Theodore) Cuenot was a French missionary bishop who gave his life for Christ. Born in Beaulieu, France, in 1802, Stephen was ordained and made a member of the Paris Foreign Mission Society. In 1833, he was made vicar apostolic of Vietnam and was consecrated in Singapore as a bishop. He labored in the missions, expanding the faith, until his arrest in 1861. Stephen died in prison on November 14, possibly by poisoning, just before his slated execution.

Stephen Vinh, a devout peasant, was a Dominican tertiary. When he refused to abjure the Faith, Stephen was strangled at Ninh-Tai with four companions.

Théophane Venard, a French priest and martyr of Vietnam, is remembered for his service to the Faith and for chanting hymns on the way to his execution. He was born in Pic-St. Loup, France and was raised devoutly in the Faith. Aspiring to the missions, he entered the Paris Foreign Missions Society, received seminary training, and was ordained on June 5, 1852, for the Society's missions. On September 19 of that year, he sailed to Hong Kong, where he worked for the next fifteen months. He was then assigned to Vietnam, to an area called Tonkin at the time.

A Vietnamese royal edict condemning Christianity began Théophane's heroic ordeals on the mission. He was forced to hide in Christian villages and to conduct his ministries at night. He was also plagued by serious physical problems, to the point where his courage was tried severely in serving his Vietnamese faithful.

Théophane maintained this grueling labor for almost four years before his capture on November 30, 1860. He was tried and condemned to death by authorities, but was not given the grace of a sudden martyrdom. Instead, he was put into a cage, abused, and tortured. He did not complain. Indeed, in a letter to his father, he described his coming martyrdom by likening himself to "the spring flower which the Master of the garden gathers for his pleasure."

On February 2, 1861, Théophane was carried to the site of his execution, where, as he described the act in a letter, "a slight saber-cut will separate my head from my body." Ill and wounded by his tormentors, Théophane sang hymns on his way to death. When he was slain, his head was placed on a pole and exhibited as a victory for the Vietnamese authorities. His remains were saved and eventually transferred to a shrine in Paris. He was beatified on May 2, 1909.

Thomas De Van Nguyen, a layman of Vietnam, was a tailor by profession and a Dominican tertiary who sheltered missionaries. He was arrested in 1839 for his activities and subsequently strangled with four companions for refusing to deny the Faith.

Thomas Thien Tran (also listed as Thomas Dien) was a seminarian of Vietnam and preparing to be ordained when he was arrested in 1838. He was only eighteen when Vietnamese authorities scourged and strangled him.

Thomas Du Viet Dinh, a Dominican tertiary and ordained priest of Vietnam, Thomas worked in the missions in Nam-Dingh. He was arrested in 1839, at the age of sixty-five and, after hideous tortures, was beheaded.

Thomas Toan was a catechist when arrested in 1840, at the age of seventy-three. He showed signs of apostatizing at first, but then repented this weakness and stayed firm in the Faith, despite being scourged and exposed to the sun and natural elements for twelve days. He died of his torments, still faithful to Christ.

Valentine Berriochoa served as a bishop of Vietnam and was a companion of Jerome Hermosilla. Valentine was born in Elloria, Spain, later entered the Dominicans, and became known as an especially devout member of his Order. Professed and ordained, he was sent originally to the Dominican missions in the Philippines, where he distinguished himself by faithful service. In 1858, Valentine was consecrated a bishop and appointed vicar apostolic of the Dominican mission territories of Vietnam.

Upon his arrival, he faced the ordeals of the Vietnamese persecutions and worked under extreme difficulties. He was arrested in 1861, imprisoned, and tortured with another Dominican bishop, Jerome Hermosilla; the two were beheaded at the same time. He was beatified in 1909 by Pope St. Pius X.

Vincent Diem The Nguyen was the first Dominican martyr of Vietnam and a noble by birth in his native land. Raised as a Catholic, Vincent became a Dominican and was ordained for the priesthood. He was soon assigned to assist Hyacinth Castañeda in his endeavors. Arrested in 1773, he was beheaded with Hyacinth.

Vincent Yen Do was ordained in 1808. When the persecutions began in 1832, he went into hiding and managed to conduct his priestly ministry in secret. He was betrayed to authorities, however, and in 1838 was arrested and beheaded.

Pope John Paul II canonized all of the Martyrs of Vietnam on June 19, 1988, praising the courage and loyalty of these stalwart martyrs who aided the faithful of that land during the terrible years of persecution. The Holy Father canonized ninety-six Vietnamese, eleven Spaniards, and ten French martyrs. During the ceremony in St. Peter's Square, he stated:

> The Vietnamese martyrs "sowing in tears," in reality initiated a profound and liberating dialogue with the people and culture of their nation, proclaiming above all the truth and universality of faith in God and proposing, moreover, a hierarchy of values and duties particularly suited to the religious culture of the entire Oriental world.
>
> Under the guidance of the first Vietnamese catechism, they gave testimony that it is necessary to adore the one Lord as the one personal God who made heaven and earth. Faced with the coercive impositions of the authorities with regard to the practice of the Faith, they affirmed their freedom to believe, holding with humble courage that the Christian religion was the only thing that they could not abandon, that they could not disobey the supreme Sovereign: the Lord. Moreover, they vigorously affirmed their desire to remain loyal to the authorities of the country, observing all that is just and right: they also taught that one should respect and venerate one's ancestors, according to the customs of their land, in the light of the mystery of the resurrection.
>
> The Vietnamese Church, with its martyrs and its witness, has been able to proclaim its desire and resolve not to reject the cultural traditions and the legal institutions of the country; rather, it has declared and demonstrated that it wants to incarnate them in itself, in order to contribute faithfully to the true building up of the country.... Once again, we can say that the blood of the martyrs is for you, Christians of Vietnam, a well-spring of grace to make progress in the faith. In you, the Faith of our fathers continues and is carried on to new generations. This faith remains the foundation of the perseverance of all those who, considering themselves authentically Vietnamese, faithful to their land, also want to continue to be true disciples of Christ.

Feast day: November 24.

✠

Vietnam, Dominican Martyrs of (1856 – 1862)
Members of the Order of Preachers (the Dominicans) and Martyrs

King Tu-Duc, ruler of the central region of Vietnam — known also as Tonkin, Indo-China, and Assam — ascended to the throne in 1848. He followed the pattern of religious persecution set by his anti-Christian predecessors, then increased the scope and fury of the oppression. His persecutions continued until 1862, when he was compelled to sign a peace treaty with France and Spain that ended his repression and demanded the protection of European missionaries and their converts.

The persecution of the European missionaries had been both merciless and efficient. In 1848, a price was set on the heads of foreign missionaries, and in 1851, it was decreed that all European and native priests were to be slain. By 1855, Christians were commanded to abjure the Faith, and rewards for European missionaries were offered everywhere. In July 1856, wholesale massacres of Christians began, resulting in such atrocities as the burning of entire Christian villages and their inhabitants.

Although Dominicans faced torture, imprisonment, and martyrdom in Vietnam before 1856, the Dominican Martyrs of this era are especially honored. Bishops Joseph Diaz Sanjuro, Jerome Hermosillo, and their fellow Dominicans were slain during the reign of Tu-Duc. Some were tortured to death, strangled, or abused until they died. Included in this list are: Dominic Kham Viet Pham, Joseph Khang, Melchior Garcia Sampedro, Dominic Ninh, Lawrence Ngon, Luke Thin Viet Pham, Joseph Tuc, Paul Duong, Thomas Khuong, Dominic Cam, Joseph Tuan Van Tran, Dominic Huyen, Dominic Toai, Dominic Mau, Vincent Duong, Peter Tuan, Peter Dung Van Dinh, Peter Da, Dominic Nhi, Andrew Tuong, Dominic Nguyen, Vincent Tuong, Dominic Mao. The fervor and fidelity of these martyrs has long brought fame and honor upon the Dominicans. They were canonized by Pope John Paul II on June 19, 1988, among one hundred seventeen Martyrs of Vietnam. As members of the Order of Preachers, however, they deserve special recognition.

(See Martyrs of Vietnam for additional details.)

Feast day: November 24.

(W-X-Z)

Z

☩

Zdislava de Lemberk (c. 1220 – c. January 1, 1252)

Model Lay Religious

A Bohemian Dominican Tertiary, Zdislava de Lemberk (also called Zdislava Berka) was born in Krizanov, Moravia, now Letomerice, Bohemia (in the modern Czech Republic). Of an aristocratic family, Zdislava was forced to marry a nobleman allied to her clan, and she and her husband resided in a castle at Gabel that became a haven for the people of the surrounding region. Hundreds of local men and women journeyed there in times of trial, assured that Zdislava would find a way to ease their sufferings.

When the Mongol invasions of the area brought about upheavals and disaster, refugees swarmed about Gabel. Zdislava cared for them all.

Her husband was so impressed with Zdislava's goodness and compassion that he allowed her to become a member of the Dominican Third Order, a rare privilege in that era. Embracing the tertiary rule and lifestyle, she grew in prayer and received many singular mystical graces and experiences. Zdislava founded St. Lawrence Priory, establishing this religious house as a source of faith in her area.

Zdislava died at Jablone, Bohemia. She was beatified in 1907 by Pope St. Pius X. and canonized by Pope John Paul II at Olomanc, in the Czech Republic, on May 21, 1995. At that time, the pontiff said:

> St. Zdislava of Lemberk, heroine of charity and the family, is as it were a reflection of Mary. During her life she imitated Mary's tenderness and concern for neighbor, especially the poor and the sick.

Feast day: January 1.

The Blesseds of Pope John Paul II

"'Jesus Christ: though he was rich, he became poor for your sake, to make you rich out of his poverty" (2 Cor. 8:9). . . . This phrase, taken from the Letter of St. Paul to the Corinthians, is a sort of introduction to the Gospel and the parable of the rich man and Lazarus. At the same time the Church, assembled near the tomb of St. Peter, pronounces this phrase while looking to all the Servants of God who are proclaimed blessed. . . . To each of them Jesus showed the way to holiness, first becoming poor and making himself a model for all, he who was the Son of God, of one being with the Father. He revealed the mystery of this poverty which makes one rich to each of the new Blessed. In this way he showed each of them the way to holiness. Today, the Church rejoices for these sons and daughters who have traveled the way indicated by the Divine Master.

— Pope John Paul II, Beatification Mass, October 1, 1983

A

✠

Adeodata Pisani (December 28, 1806 – February 25, 1853)
Embracing the "Hidden Life"

An aristocrat of Malta, Maria Adeodata Pisani astounded the people of her social class by renouncing wealth, titles, and privileges in order to embrace the hidden life of a dedicated religious. She was born in Naples, the daughter of the Maltese Baron of Frigenuini, who was experiencing problems because of the changing Italian political scene at that time. In 1820, the Baron was arrested in Italy and exiled to Malta, and Adeodata and her mother followed him into exile. In time, her parents separated, and the young girl experienced the trauma of such a domestic tragedy.

Prayerful and trusting in the mercy of God, she received the grace of a religious vocation and, on July 16, 1828, entered the Benedictine Monastery of St. Peter in Medina. Her entrance into the convent disturbed many nobles on Malta, as it was unheard of in that era. No aristocratic woman of that historical period willingly surrendered titles, social standing, and the prospect of a wealthy marriage. Adeodata's entrance into the religious life consternated her friends and relatives, and many attended her ceremony of vows on March 8, 1830.

Contrary to the predictions of her peers that she would leave the convent, Adeodata remained a Benedictine nun, and in 1847 became the Mistress of Novices of the Benedictines. She was elected Abbess in 1851.

Adeodata suffered from poor health — a heart disease that sapped her strength — but remained dedicated and a model religious until her death. Many of the faithful, of all walks of life, were inspired by her commitment to Christ and by her fidelity to her vows.

Pope John Paul II beatified Maria Adeodata Pisani in Malta on May 9, 2001. During the ceremony, the Pope declared:

> Prayer, obedience, service of her sisters, and maturity in performing her assigned tasks: these were the elements of Maria Adeodata's silent holy life. Through her prayer, work and love, she became a well-spring of that

spiritual and missionary fruitfulness without which the Church cannot preach the Gospel as Christ commands.

✠

Adolph Kolping (December 8, 1813 – December 4, 1865)
Patron of the Victims of Industrialization

Adolph Kolping was born in Kerpen, a village near Cologne in Germany, and entered the local work force at an early age. Thus, he experienced the cruel realities of working in the plants and factories of Germany at the time.

Always faced with delicate health and physical sufferings, Adolph worked as much as twelve hours a day and studied at night in order to respond to a call to the priesthood. He conducted his seminary studies while earning his own living until his ordination in 1845, using that experience to guide his apostolate. As a priest, he was assigned to the cathedral of Cologne, where he began a series of projects to aid the young workingmen of his area. A choir that he founded developed into the Young Workmen's Society, designed to uplift the moral life of the working classes. The "Kolping Societies" — or, as they were called, the *Gesellenvereine* — spread quickly throughout Europe and were popular in America. Adolph formed one in Cologne in 1849 and another in St. Louis, Missouri, in 1856. At the time of his death, there were more than four hundred *Gesellenvereine* in the world.

He was also a strong defender of the family and always available to the poor and the downtrodden. Adolph spent his life defending their rights and trying to better their working conditions. He was a pioneer in this cause, bringing his own experiences and faith to the work and recognizing the harsh demands of an industrialized people. Adolph died in Cologne, and the news of his passing brought thousands of mourners to the large funeral. The working people came to lay him to rest with reverence and genuine grief.

Pope John Paul II beatified Adolph Kolping on October 27, 1991, and met with pilgrims who had come to Rome for the ceremony. The Holy Father described Blessed Adolph as a man who "stood with both feet planted firmly on the earth, and was oriented toward heaven . . . in the world, but not of the world."

✠

Agnes Phila — see Thailand Martyrs

✠

Agnes Phuta — see Thailand Martyrs

✠

Agnes of Jesus Galand de Langeac
(November 17, 1602 – October 19, 1634)
"Pray to My Son for the Abbot of Prébrac"

A Dominican religious, Agnes of Jesus Galand de Langeac was a remarkable mystic chosen by God to perform a particular task that would benefit the Church in France.

She was born in Puy-en-Velay, France and, at the age of five, was entrusted to the Congregation of the Holy Virgin for her education. At the convent, she demonstrated great piety; when she was seven, she volunteered to become "a slave of the Holy Virgin," making this private vow freely. In 1623, Agnes of Jesus responded to divine grace and entered the Dominican Convent at Langeac. There, she matured spiritually and was elected prioress four years later. She was later deposed from this office, but she accepted that event with calm and grace.

Her devotion to the Blessed Virgin continued, and in 1631, the Blessed Mother of God appeared to her, saying, "Pray to my Son for the Abbot of Prébrac." Agnes of Jesus knew nothing about this abbot, never having met him, but she spent the next three years praying and making sacrifices for the man. She then appeared in a vision to the famous abbot and preacher, Jean-Jacques Olier, abbot of Prébac, during his retreat under the direction of Vincent de Paul. As a result of her supernatural appearance before him, the abbot began a search for her. When they were face to face, she told him, "I have received orders from the Holy Virgin to pray for you. God has destined you to open the first seminaries in France."

The abbot was called to Paris in 1634, to begin the labors that would lead to the opening of those seminaries, and Agnes of Jesus, knowing that her mission was completed, died in peace in her monastery.

Pope John Paul II beatified Agnes of Jesus on November 20, 1994, declaring:

> Truly blessed, Agnes de Langeac was able, without the slightest reservation, to enter into God's plan for her, offering her intellect, will, and freedom to the Son of Man that he might transform them and harmonize them totally with his own!

╬

Alanus de Solminihac
(November 25, 1593 – December 31, 1659)
"Faith and Valor"

An aristocrat and bishop of France, Alanus de Solminihac was born in the family's castle in Belet, and considered by many to be a remarkable gift from God. Raised devoutly and well educated, Alanus longed even as a young child to serve the Faith as a Knight of Malta, as he was attracted to the military discipline and the courageous commitment of that Order. In 1613, however, at the age of twenty, he entered the Canons Regular of St. Augustine at Chancelade Abbey, near Périqueux. There, he started an intense spiritual life that aided him when he was sent to Paris to continue his theological and spiritual studies and to complete his ordination programs.

In 1623, Alanus returned to Chancelade Abbey, where he was installed as Superior and entrusted with the enormous task of restoring the Augustinian rules and ideals. His fervor and holiness inspired the members of his abbey to undertake the reformation with zeal. Other religious communities in the region responded with the same ardor.

In 1636, Pope Urban VIII (r. 1623-1644) consecrated Alanus as the bishop of Cahors, France. He brought a spirit of reform to that city, but he also demonstrated a genuine pastoral concern that took him on many visits to the parishes, where he was able to be among the people. He attended the council of Trent and followed the lead of Charles Borromeo in enforcing the council's decrees.

Alanus convened a diocesan synod, held an episcopal council, and restored traditions and religious customs. He actually visited each one of his parishes nine times — no mean feat, considering that there were 800 parishes under his jurisdiction! He also started a priestly seminary, sponsored regular parish missions and charitable organizations, and promoted Eucharistic adoration. Three years before his death, Alanus preached at the diocesan jubilee. He died, revered by his contemporaries for his holiness and asceticism, in Mercues.

Pope John Paul II beatified Alanus de Solminihac on October 4, 1981. The Holy Father praised the new Blessed as a singular bishop who had "the courage to evangelize the modern world fearlessly."

✠

Alberto Hurtado Cruchaga
(January 22, 1901 – August 18, 1952)
"The Friend of God and Man"

Alberto Hurtado Cruchaga was born in Vina del Mar, Chile, and was raised with both an awareness of local injustices and of new technological approaches to spreading the doctrines of the Church. Alberto's father died when he was young, and his family was poor, yet he was well educated; he earned an academic scholarship and learned about modern communication methods prior to entering the Society of Jesus.

Ordained to the priesthood in 1933, Alberto made his final vows and began his ministry as a teacher and retreat master. In time, he would spearhead the Church's efforts for the poor and support innovative and effective social programs in Chile, starting with his best-selling book *Is Chile a Catholic Country?*

Vivacious, enthusiastic, and open to all, he was a true "Father of Chile." He had a devotion to the poor, especially those who were helpless victims, and he ministered to their needs through charitable projects with a personal commitment based on the faith. He wrote and lectured throughout Chile to awaken the Christian conscience, using his first-hand knowledge and his personal experiences as a missionary to arouse his fellow countrymen.

Because of his preaching and ceaseless efforts, Alberto inspired the Christian Democratic Movement in Chile and aided the organization of Christian labor unions that were designed to protect workers from abuse. Many social action groups in Chile, such as *Centro Bellarmino*, *El Hugar de Cristo*, and the Rural Institute for Education, trace their origins to Albert's preaching and concern for social justice in the region. He also founded the Chilean Trade Union Association and the journal, *Mensaje*. When he died of pancreatic cancer in Santiago, Chile, at a comparatively young age, thousands came to mourn him and to demonstrate grief for Chile's loss. On his deathbed, he said: "I am happy, Lord."

Pope John Paul II beatified Alberto Hurtado Cruchaga on October 16, 1994. During the ceremony, he declared:

> "The friend of God and man" was praised for daring to use modern methods to spread the Gospel of Christ. Blessed Alberto was revered for serving as a true pastor of the abandoned and betrayed.

✠

Alberto Marvelli (March 21, 1918 – October 5, 1946)
President of Catholic Action

Born in Ferrara, Italy, the second of six children to Luigi Marvelli and Maria Mayr, Alberto demonstrated from an early age a zeal for charity that found expression in his labors for Catholic Action. Under his mother's influence, he devoted himself to the care of the poor and the sick; even as a child, he regularly gave away food to the hungry.

In June 1930, he and his family moved to Rimini, where Alberto attended the Salesian Oratory and Catholic Action group in the parish. There, his determination to be holy found rapid development. In March 1933, however, his father died unexpectedly and, later that year, Alberto began to keep a spiritual diary. This proved to be an eloquent record of his spiritual life, including Mass every day and recitation of the rosary. In 1936, he was elected president of Catholic Action, a position that permitted him to direct the organization's concern for the poor.

During the Second World War, he and his family moved to Vergiano, near Rimini, to avoid the air raids, but he went back repeatedly to help the wounded and homeless. He was especially noted for his effort to save as many people as possible from deportation to the concentration camps. The German occupiers of Italy after the fall of the regime of Mussolini sent thousands to their deaths in the camps, and Alberto heroically rescued as many as he could from the sealed carriages of the trains just before they would leave the station of Santarcangelo.

After the liberation of Rimini in September 1945, he moved his family back to the city — but they found only ruins from the terrible fighting, and Alberto was soon appointed an administrator for housing. He was quickly named a town councilor and a member of the Italian Society of Civil Engineers. To assist the needy, he opened soup kitchens and distributed food to the places where it might be needed most. Beloved by the average people, he was encouraged to run for office with the Christian Democrats and was an immensely popular candidate in local elections. But, while on his way to a meeting, he was hit by an army truck and died a few hours later. His mother was soon elected in his place.

He was beatified by Pope John Paul II on September 5, 2004.

✛

Alexandrina Maria da Costa
(March 30, 1904 – October 13, 1955)
Member of the Union of Salesian Cooperators

Alexandrina Maria was a profound model for those determined to offer up their sufferings to be conformed with Christ.

She was born in Balasar, Portugal, to a devoted family that provided for her a solid Christian education. Even as a child, she was able to perform long feats of labor and so assisted her family with badly needed income. She fell ill, however, when she was twelve and nearly died from an infection. This proved only the first event in what became her life as a victim soul.

Two years later, on Holy Saturday in 1918, Alexandrina and two other young women were assaulted by three men. To save her purity, Alexandrina jumped from a window. She suffered severe injuries from the leap, including permanent and growing paralysis. Despite the terrible suffering, she literally dragged herself to Mass until the paralysis left her completely immobilized from April 1925 until her death. She spent those years bedridden.

Throughout her ordeal, Alexandrina prayed ceaselessly to the Blessed Mother for strength and to ask to be healed in the hope of becoming a missionary. She understood, though, that her true vocation was to be a victim soul, and she embraced the Cross with all of her heart. As she said, "Our Lady has given me an even greater grace: first, abandonment; then, complete conformity to God's will; finally, the thirst for suffering." To express her conformity with Christ's Passion, Alexandrina celebrated the Stations of the Cross every Friday from 1938 to 1942.

Especially remarkable was that, from March 1942 until her death, Alexandrina received no nourishment of any kind, save for the Holy Eucharist. How this was possible remained an absolute mystery to her doctors, and even more perplexing to them was the joy that characterized Alexandrina's demeanor even to the very end. The Salesian priest, Fr. Umberto Pasquale, proved a valuable friend and spiritual director; in 1944, he assisted Alexandrina in entering the Union of Salesian Cooperators. Alexandrina's last words were "I am happy, because I am going to Heaven." She was beatified by Pope John Paul II on April 25, 2004.

✛

Alfonso Maria Fusco
(March 23, 1839 – February 8, 1910)
Education for the Poor

The founder of a congregation of religious, Alfonso Maria Fusco was born in Angri Salerno, Italy. His birth was actually the result of fervent prayers on the part of his parents — and a Redemptorist priest, Fr. Francesco Saverio Pecorelli, who predicted his birth.

Alfonso was a pious child, receiving the grace of a priestly vocation at a very young age, declaring at the age of eleven that he wanted to enter the seminary. He enrolled in the Seminary of Nocera dei Pagani and was ordained on May 29, 1863. He was then assigned to the College of St. John the Baptist, and there he met Maddalena Caputo, a holy woman who desired the religious life. Alfonso joined with her and co-founded the congregation called the Baptistine Sisters of the Nazarene.

The congregation flourished, but Alfonso was slandered and harassed by many in the area and suffered insults from officials and even the members of the congregation that he had helped to found. He endured with a steadfast heart throughout the terrible ordeals and finally was recognized for his patience, honor, and holiness. Cleared of all slanderous charges, he was able to found houses of the congregation without opposition before he died in Angri.

Pope John Paul II beatified Alfonso on October 7, 2001, in Rome. During the ceremonies, the Holy Father declared:

> With the characteristic inner calm of saints that stems from absolute faith in God and his Providence, he managed to make the 'dream' of his life come true: to found a women's congregation which would assist poor young people and provide them with an education. Today, the Sisters of St. John the Baptist carry his message to many parts of the world.

✛

Alfredo Ildephonse Schuster —
see Ildephonse (Alfredo) Schuster

╬

Aloysius (Alojzije) Stepinac (May 8, 1898 – February 10, 1960)
"Without Hatred Towards Anyone, and Without Fear from Anyone"

Called Alojzije in his native Croatia, Aloysius Stepinac was born in Krasíc (Brezaric, Croatia), Yugoslavia. He was educated locally and completed military service in World War I, during which he was an Italian prisoner for a time. He returned to civilian life in 1919, then began his ministerial studies. In Rome, Aloysius attended the Pontifical Germanicum-Hungaricum College and earned doctorates at the Pontifical Gregorian University. He was ordained a priest on October 26, 1930.

His first assignment was in the Archdiocese of Zagreb as a parish priest, but he distinguished himself by founding the archdiocesan Caritas programs in 1931. Three years later, at the age of thirty-six, he was appointed coadjutor archbishop of Zagre. He created twelve new parishes and promoted the Catholic press, defending the rights of the Church during the Concordat between Yugoslavia and the Holy See. Aloysius was installed as archbishop of Zagreb when his predecessor died on December 7, 1937.

The advance of the Nazis alerted him to the sufferings of refugees, and he founded charitable organizations, including the Action for Assistance for Jewish Refugees, in 1938. His writings clearly demonstrate his concerns: "The Catholic Church does not recognize races that rule and races that are enslaved."

Initially optimistic about the Church's position in Croatia when Ante Pavelic and the Ustasha regime came to power, he was soon appalled at the fascist policies of the government and protested the treatment of the Church, Jews, Serbs, and Gypsies, writing on May 23, 1941: "Every day we witness measures that are ever more severe against people who, often, are totally innocent."

World War II brought about terrible ordeals, and Aloysius was most concerned about the plight of Jews and Orthodox Christians. To save as many as possible, he permitted all priests to accept as a convert any Jew or Orthodox Christian without the requirement of special catechetical knowledge and with the understanding that they would return to their original faiths "when these times of madness and savageness are over."

At the end of the fighting, however, Aloysius and his Catholic people found themselves under the control of the Communists. He was arrested in 1945 for speaking out against the murders of priests by Communist militants and for refusing to accept anything less than full freedom for the Church and a continuation of the unity of the Church in Croatia with the Holy See. Josip Broz, Tito, the new Communist leader of Yugoslavia, tried to pressure Aloysius into creating a nationalized Croatian Catholic Church without allegiance to Rome. This he and the other bishops of Yugoslavia refused to do, and so the full fury of the Communists was leveled at him.

He was vilified in the press, ridiculed by Communist spokesmen, and made the target of hate campaigns. Arrested on the spurious charges of war crimes, he was put on trial in September 1946, and sentenced on October 11, 1946, to sixteen years of hard labor for defending the Holy See and Church unity.

The Jews of Yugoslavia openly protested this sentence, declaring that Aloysius was one of the few men in Europe who risked all by defending their rights. He was imprisoned until 1951, when his health deteriorated. Put under house arrest in Krasíc, he still managed to write more than five thousand letters and to serve as a priest.

On June 23, 1953, Pope Pius XII elevated Aloysius to the rank of cardinal, citing him as "an example of apostolic zeal and Christian strength." Yugoslavia retaliated against the pope's action by breaking diplomatic ties with the Vatican. The new Cardinal remained under house arrest until 1959, when he was ordered to testify at the trial of the spiritual director of the seminary. He refused, citing the abuses he had endured and the need for the freedom of the Church in Croatia. He died soon after, almost certainly as the result of poisoning by his Communist captors, as an examination of his bones in 1996 indicated.

Pope John Paul II beatified Aloysius Cardinal Stepinac on October 3, 1998, at Marija Bistrica, the Marian shrine near Zagreb, before 500,000 Croatians and other faithful. The Holy Father declared at this ceremony:

Blessed Alojzije Stepinac did not spill his blood in the strict sense of the word. His death was caused by the long suffering he endured; the last fifteen years of his life were a continual succession of trials, amid which he courageously endangered his own life in order to bear witness to the Gospel and the unity of the Church. In the words of the psalmist, he put his very life in God's hands (cf. Ps 16 [15]: 5).

Very little time separates us from the life and death of Cardinal Stepinac: barely thirty-eight years. We all know the context of his death. Many present here today can testify from direct experience how much the sufferings of Christ abounded in those years among the people of Croatia and those of so many nations on the continent. Today, reflecting on the words of the Apostle, we wish to express the heartfelt hope that after the time of trial, the comfort of the crucified and risen Christ may abound in all who live in this land.

For all of us, a particular cause for comfort is today's beatification. This solemnity takes place in the Croatian national shrine of Marija Bistrica on the first Saturday of the month of October. Beneath the gaze of the Most Blessed Virgin, an illustrious son of this blessed land is raised to the glory of the altars, on the 100th anniversary of his birth. It is an historic moment in the life of the Church and of your nation. The Cardinal Archbishop of Zagreb, one of the outstanding figures of the Catholic Church, having endured in his own body and his own spirit the atrocities of the communist system is now entrusted to the memory of his fellow countrymen with the radiant badge of martyrdom.

✠

Aloysius Versiglia — see Luigi Versiglia

✠

Alphonsa Muttathupandatu (August 19, 1910 – July 28, 1946)
Victim of Love

A Clarist mystic, Alphonsa Muttathupandatu took drastic measures to dedicate her life to Christ. She was born into the Syro-Malabar rite of the Church in Arpukara (Kudamaloor, Kerala), India, and was called Annakutti, or Anna, by her loving family. The child's life changed when her mother died and she was raised by her aunt, Annamma, who was devout and set in the old customs of the region.

Anna received a good education and was expected to marry a young man chosen by her family. But she refused all offers of marriage, expressing her belief that Christ had called her to the religious life. When pressed by family members to wed, she went to the local fire pit, where she intended to burn and disfigure her feet to discourage suitors. She fell into the pit accidentally, however, and suffered severe burns over her entire body.

This act of self-immolation and the resulting weeks of pain while she was recuperating convinced the family that she was adamant in her desire for the convent. She was allowed to recover in peace and was then given reluctant permission to enter the Clarist Sisters, a Franciscan tertiary congregation in the Syro-Malabar rite, in 1927. She received the name Alphonsa of the Immaculate Conception and displayed spiritual maturity and spiritual gifts, including prophecy. She also experienced a vision of St. Thérèse, the Little Flower, and entered into a mystical union in prayer. Alphonsa offered herself as a victim for others until she died at the Clarist convent in Bharananganam. Just before her last breath, she announced that she was at peace.

The funeral held for her astounded the Clarist Sisters, as people of all faiths came to honor the memory of Alphonsa. Her grave became an instant ecumenical pilgrimage destination, and men and women wept over her life and death. They called her "Sister Alphonsa of India." Hindus, Muslims, and Christians alike visited her tomb and asked for her intercessions.

Pope John Paul II beatified Alphonsa Muttathupandatu on February 8, 1986, in Changanachery (Kottayam), India, praising her as a victim of love who embraced Christ Crucified. Blessed Alphonsa was honored as a pure soul of India who achieved greatness through humility.

♱

Ambrosio Francisco Ferro and 28 Companions
(unknown — October 3, 1645)
The Protomartyrs of Brazil

The Spanish originally discovered the land known today as Brazil, but the Portuguese developed the various regions and controlled Brazil until 1580. Spain held Portugal as a dependency at that time, but Spain was also at war with the Netherlands, the Dutch. During this period, the Dutch invaded and took charge of many Brazilian territories as part of their military campaigns, instituting their own Protestant regimes and persecuting Catholics. In 1654, the Dutch had to withdraw from Brazil, but they claimed many Catholic lives before being ousted. Ambrosio and his companions were among those persecuted and slain.

His parish on the Uruacu River, in Natal, was a thriving community when the Dutch forces arrived to arrest and execute the faithful. He and his companions were forced by the Dutch to go to a remote area. There, the martyrs were tortured and endured hideous sufferings as prisoners of the Indian allies of the Dutch. Ambrosio and his companions died at the hands of their captors.

Pope John Paul II beatified Ambrosio Francisco Ferro and Companions on March 5, 2000, when he declared:

> The martyrs beatified today came at the end of the seventeenth century,
> from the communities of Cungau and Uruacu in Rio Grande do Norte. .
> . . Fr. Ambrosio Francisco Ferro and twenty-eight lay companions belong

to this generation of martyrs who watered their homeland, making it fertile for a generation of new Christians. They are the first fruits of the missionary work, the protomartyrs of Brazil.

(See also André de Soveral.)

✠

Ana Mogas Fontcuberta — see Maria Anna Mogas Fontcuberta

✠

Anawarite Nengapete — see Maria Clementine Anuarite Nengapete

✠

André Bessette (August 9, 1845 – January 6, 1937)
"Miracle Worker of Montreal"

André Bessette was born in St. Gregoire d'Iberville, near Montreal, Canada, the son of Isaac and Clothilde Foisy Bessette, and was baptized Alfred. After moving to Farnham in 1849, his family suffered a terrible tragedy when Isaac was killed in a logging accident in 1855. Alfred's mother was unable to care for her sons and daughters and put eleven of them up for adoption, but she kept Alfred with her when she moved to St. Césaire d' Iberville. Two years later, she died also, and the local mayor and his family adopted the boy and raised him in a kindly manner.

In 1863, he moved to the United States, where he worked for four years as a laborer, then returned to Canada, where he applied to the Congregation of the Holy Cross and was accepted as a lay brother in 1870. Br. André's poor health put his vocation in doubt, but he was allowed to serve as a porter, or doorkeeper, at Holy Cross College at St. Césaire. His first miraculous cures date to this initial stage of his religious life.

While he performed the duties assigned to him, André visited many individuals or received them at his post, bringing about phenomenal cures. He also had a sincere desire to establish a unique haven of worship on Mount Royal, in Montreal, and started fund-raising. André served as a barber for the college students in order to put aside money for his proposed shrine. Successful in raising sufficient money, he laid the cornerstone of the present basilica on August 31, 1924. The original structure on the site was a wooden chapel called St. Joseph's Oratory. Pope Blessed Pius IX (r. 1846-1878), who declared that St. Joseph was the patron of the Universal Church, was André's inspiration for the shrine.

A famed thaumaturgist, or healer, he spent many hours at the bedside of the ill throughout the region. André took no credit for the miracles, saying: "I am nothing . . . only a tool in the hands of Providence, a lowly instrument at the service of St. Joseph." At the basilica of Mount Royal, André received thousands of visitors until his death on January 6, 1937.

One million people paid him tribute as he lay in state in the Mount Royal crypt chapel for seven days. Now, the basilica there attracts more than two million pilgrims each year.

Pope John Paul II beatified André Bessette on May 23, 1982, declaring:

> Where, then, does his unheard-of radiance, his fame among millions of people, come from? A daily crowd of sick, afflicted, poor of all kinds, and those who were handicapped or wounded by life found in his presence, in the parlor of the college, at the oratory, a welcoming ear, comfort and faith in God, confidence in the intercession of St. Joseph, in short, the way of prayer and sacraments, and with that the hope and often manifest relief of body and soul. Do not the poor today have as much need of such love, of such hope, of such an education in prayer?

☩

André de Soveral (1572 – July 16, 1645)
Martyred at the Altar

One of the protomartyrs of Brazil, beatified with Ambrosio Francisco Ferro and Companions, André was born in Sao Vicente, Brazil on the Isle of Santos. He became a Jesuit in 1593 and made his novitiate in the Society of Jesus in Bahia. He was then sent to the College of Olinda. After his ordination, André was sent to work in the area of Rio Grande do Norte in 1606. He labored among the local Potiquar Indians there. By 1614, André was the parish priest of Cunhau, having left the Jesuits and becoming a diocesan priest. He served Our Lady of the Purification parish there.

Celebrating Mass on the day of his martyrdom, André was accompanied by almost 70 of the devout of the area. Near the end of the Mass, the Dutch, then in control of that part of Brazil and at war with Spain, broke into the church with Indian allies. André told his congregation to prepare themselves for martyrdom, then warned the Dutch and the Indians not to assault the minister of God or the sacred vessels — but they paid no heed, and he was slain by an axe thrown at him by an Indian.

Pope John Paul II beatified André de Soveral with Ambrosio Francisco Ferro and Companions on March 5, 2000, declaring:

> The blood of defenseless Catholics, many of whose names are unknown — children, the elderly, whole families — will be an incentive for strengthening the Faith of new generations of Brazilians, reminding them especially of the value of the family as an authentic and irreplaceable teacher of faith and moral values.

✠

Andrea Giacinto Longhin
(November 23, 1863 – June 26, 1936)
Great Shepherd of Treviso, Italy

Andrew Hyacinth Longhin was born in Fiumicello di Campodarsego (in the diocese of Padua), to Matthew and Judith Marin, tenant farmers. From his early youth, Andrew Hyacinth expressed a desire for the priesthood and religious life. Thus, at the age of sixteen, he entered the novitiate of the Capuchin Order under the name of Andrew of Campodarsego. He studied at Venice was ordained to the priesthood on June 19, 1886.

Assigned to the post of spiritual director and instructor of the young religious, he served with distinction for eighteen years, until his election in 1902 as Provincial Minister of the Capuchins of Venice. During this time, he earned the abiding respect of the patriarch of Venice, Giuseppe Melchior Sarto, the future Pope St. Pius X. It came as no surprise, then that in 1904, soon after Sarto's election as pope, Fr. Andrew was named Bishop of Treviso.

Consecrated by Cardinal Merry del Val in Rome, Bishop Andrew Hyacinth immediately issued two pastoral letters even before he arrived to assume his duties. The letters detailed a program of reform that found expression over the next years as the new bishop visited every church in the diocese and established close pastoral contact with his priests, the religious, and the laity under his care. At the end of the visits, the bishop convoked a diocesan Synod to implement fully throughout the diocese the many reforms that were then being encouraged by Pius X. To assist the clergy, Bishop Andrew ordered improved spiritual and theological studies, spiritual retreats, and ongoing formation.

The bishop also confronted with great determination the immense suffering caused by the First World War (1914-1918). Treviso was devastated by the fighting, including attacks from the air that left much of the diocese in ruins. The bishop remained at his post, even as all civil leaders fled to safety, and encouraged his priests to remain in their parishes to provide care to the people. He organized soup kitchens and medical care for the fallen, both civilians and soldiers.

In the time after the war, Bishop Andrew Hyacinth assisted in the reconstruction, then resumed his pastoral program of reform. He was determined to resist the anti-Catholic efforts of the Fascists, who brought political violence to Treviso and attacked Catholic organizations. As a sign of papal favor and respect, Pope Pius XI named him Apostolic Visitor to Padua and Udine, with the task of bringing reconciliation between priests and their bishop.

The bishop's last years were filled with great sufferings, and hisdeath was greeted with intense mourning. He was beatified by Pope John Paul II on October 20, 2002. The pope declared of him:

"I have called you by name" (Is. 45:4). The words which the prophet Isaiah uses to show the mission entrusted by God to his elect express well the vocation of Andrea Giacinto Longhin, the humble Capuchin who for thirty-two years was Bishop of the Diocese of Treviso at the beginning of the twentieth century. He was a simple, poor, humble, generous Pastor always available for his neighbour, in accord with the genuine tradition of the Capuchins.

They called him the Bishop of essential things. In an age that was noted for tragic and painful events, he was outstanding as a father for his priests and a zealous pastor of the people, always close to the people, especially in moments of difficulty and danger. In this way he anticipated what the Second Vatican Council emphasized when it taught that evangelization was "one of the principal duties of bishops" (*Christus Dominus*, n. 12; cf. *Redemptoris missio*, n. 63).

☩

Andreas Carol Ferrari (August 13, 1850 – February 2, 1921)
Church Builder

One of the most beloved cardinals of Milan, Italy, Andreas Carol Ferrari was an outstanding Churchman of his era. A man of power and esteem, he maintained a close relationship with the faithful of the region, young and old, rich and poor.

He was born in Lalatta di Protopiano, in the diocese of Parma, Italy, the son of Giuseppe and Madellene Langarine Ferrari. They raised him piously and encouraged his vocation. Educated in Parma, Andreas entered the seminary there and was ordained a priest on December 20, 1873.

He was appointed the vice-rector of the seminary in that same year and rector in 1876. In 1878, Andreas was made canon of the cathedral and was consecrated bishop of Guastalla in 1890.  One year later, he was made bishop of Como, Italy. In 1894, his appointment as archbishop of Milan was announced, and Andreas received the rank of cardinal on May 21, 1894.

He attended the conclave in 1903 as an advisor and conducted three diocesan synods in Milan. Andreas also established a Eucharistic Congress and celebrated the centennial of St. Charles Borromeo, the city's patron saint. He erected many churches, the Catholic University of the Sacred Heart, and charitable institutions. He also organized a committee to care for soldiers and prisoners and was decorated with the Grand Cross of Sts. Maurizio and Lazarro in 1919. Andreas celebrated his twenty-fifth anniversary of consecration in Milan that same year.

Stricken with cancer of the throat, Andreas endured three months of agony as the illness reached its terminal stages. He did not remove himself from the faithful of Milan even in that time of intense suffering, however, but allowed thousands of Milanese to come to his bedside. His nights and days were filled with such visits, as men and women of all stations and all walks of life stood in line before his residence to bid him farewell in their own words. These deathbed conversations inspired a whole generation of faithful in Milan and brought about a revival of Catholicism in the archdiocese. At the end, Andreas also wrote a personal letter of farewell to his people in which he promised his prayers for their salvation. He died on Candlemas Day, and he was buried near St. Charles Borromeo, as he had requested.

Pope John Paul II beatified Andreas Cardinal Carol Ferrari on May 10, 1987, extolling his faithfulness to Christ, the Good Shepherd, and praising the fervent charity that he demonstrated for his people.

✛

Andrew of Phú Yên (1625/26 – July 26, 1644)
Protomartyr of Vietnam

Andrew of Phú Yên was born in Phú Yên (Ran Ran), in Vietnam, and educated there by the local Jesuit missionaries. In 1641, he and his mother were baptized in the Catholic Church, and he became a catechist at *Maison Dieu* (the House of God), the local catechetical and missionary center. Within a short time, however, the local mandarin, or chieftain, returned to the area with orders from the ruler of Annam (as Vietnam was called then) to halt the spread of Christianity.

When soldiers were sent to arrest the local Jesuit, Fr. de Rhodes, they discovered Andrew in the catechetical center and promptly beat him. They then took him to the local governor's palace for further investigation. Andrew was interrogated on July 25, 1644, by the mandarin, and as a result of this questioning was imprisoned and sentenced to death. The following day he was taken to a field at Ke Kham, where he was stabbed and beheaded.

Pope John Paul II beatified Andrew of Phú Yên on March 5, 2000, stating:

Today, Blessed Andrew, protomartyr of Vietnam, is given as a model to the Church of his country. May all Christ's disciples find in him strength and support in trial, and be concerned to strengthen their intimacy with the Lord, their knowledge of the Christian mystery, their fidelity to the Church and their sense of mission.

✢

Angela Astorch (September 1, 1592 – December 2, 1665)
Mystic of the Breviary

Angela Astorch was born in Barcelona and orphaned at the age of five. Desperately ill at the time, she was nursed back to health by the saintly Mother Angela Maria Serafina, the foundress of the Capuchin Franciscan convent in Barcelona. Angela remained in the convent and became a religious there at the age of eleven. In 1609, the Capuchin Sisters of Barcelona became members of the Poor Clares, adopting that strict rule and contemplative religious life. Angela welcomed the changes and prospered spiritually as a result.

She displayed a brilliant intellect and was a holy religious. Studying the Breviary, the Divine Office recited by priests and religious, Angela knew the sacred texts and possessed a profound knowledge of spiritual concerns involved in the liturgical prayers of the Church. She became famous for her knowledge and was revered by scholars and the simple people of her region.

At the age of twenty-five, Angela was sent to Zaragoza, where she served as a novice mistress for her order. She then went to Murcia, where she spent the last twenty years of her life as an abbess. Many powerful leaders, as well as the common people, came to her for counsel, and Angela was able to discern their problems and speak to them with wisdom. She died in Murcia, deeply mourned by all who had benefited from her holiness and guidance.

Pope John Paul II beatified Maria Angela Astorch on May 23, 1982, praising her for her scholarly wisdom and holiness. The Holy Father declared:

> From her we can learn to respect the ways of man and at the same time make men open to the ways of God . . . she was able to respect the individuality of each person, helping the one concerned "to keep in step with God," which means something different for each one. In this way, her profound understanding did not become inert tolerance.

✢

Angela Salawa (September 9, 1881 – March 12, 1922)
Franciscan Tertiary

Angela Salawa served the faithful during World War I.

She was born in Siepraw, Poland, and was raised in a devout family. When she was older, Angela moved to Krakow to become a serving woman. There, she began to care for young domestic workers of the city, teaching them the

Faith and protecting them. Her Franciscan spirit inspired her to spiritual maturity as a Tertiary, or lay member, of the order. This same spirit also led her to a heroic apostolate among the needy.

When World War I tore apart her native land, Angela cared for wounded Polish soldiers and gave comfort to all who were afflicted by the military campaigns. Her devotion and commitment to the service of others continued until she died in Krakow, mourned by countless Poles touched by her Franciscan ardor.

Pope John Paul II beatified Angela in Krakow's Market Square on August 13, 1991, announcing:

> This daughter of the Polish people, who was born in nearby Siepraw, was associated for a large part of her life with Krakow. It is in this city that she worked, that she suffered, and that her holiness came to maturity. While connected to the spirituality of St. Francis of Assisi, she showed an extraordinary responsiveness to the action of the Holy Spirit.

✠

Angela Maria Truszkowska
(May 16, 1825 – October 10, 1899)
Cause Opened by Future Pope

The founder of the Felician Sisters, Angela Maria Truszkowska was a remarkable Polish noblewoman who served everyone who came into her sphere of concern. Karol Cardinal Wojtyla, who became Pope John Paul II, opened her Cause.

Angela was born in Kalisz, Poland, the daughter of prosperous noble parents, Joseph and Josepha Truszkowska. She was baptized Sophia Camille and was raised in the Russian-dominated section of Poland.

Sophia was never blessed with robust health. Born prematurely, she was placed in an incubator, a unique, advanced invention devised by her mother. Prayers were also said to Our Lady of Czestochowa to save the infant.

Her childhood was marked by her early charitable activities in Kalisz. In her twelfth year, her family moved to Warsaw, where she contracted tuberculosis and was sent to Switzerland to recover in a sanitarium. Sophia continued her charitable works and became a Franciscan tertiary. In 1857, she received the habit, and the name Angela in religion, when she founded her Franciscan congregation. Because the convent was near the church of St. Felix of Cantalice, the sisters became known as the Felicians.

Within four years, Angela had opened twenty-seven schools; in 1860, she founded a contemplative branch of the congregation to ensure graces for the active apostolate. The Russian occupation in 1864 saw the Felicians lose everything they possessed because they had cared for wounded Polish soldiers. They were disbanded by the conquerors, but Emperor Franz Josef gave Angela and her Sisters refuge in the Austrian sector of Poland; by 1866, the congregation was united in the Austrian area and flowering again. In 1874, Angela sent the first Felician Sisters to the United States. The other houses flourished as well, even in the turmoil of that European era.

By combining the active and contemplative vocations of the congregations, Angela brought all aspects of religious life to bear on the ministry of charity and education. At age forty-four, she withdrew from the active leadership of the Felician Sisters because of her increasing deafness. She accepted this retirement as God's will and served for three decades as a source of grace, inspiration, and prayer. When Angela was diagnosed with stomach cancer in 1899, her physician was astonished at the amount of suffering that she had borne in silence before receiving medical care. She died in Krakow, Poland, and her remains were enshrined in the Krakow motherhouse.

Pope John Paul II beatified Angela Maria Truszkowska on April 18, 1993, praising her as a glory of Poland and the Church. The Holy Father announced:

> Christ led Mother Angela on a truly exceptional path, causing her to share intimately in the mystery of his Cross. He formed her spirit by means of numerous sufferings, which she accepted with faith and a truly heroic submission to his Will: in seclusion and in solitude, in a long and trying illness and in the dark night of the soul. Her greatest desire was to become a "victim of love."

✠

Angelico, Fra (John of Fiesole)
(c. 1387- February 18, 1455)
Patron of Christian Painters

Fra Angelico was born Guido di Piero in Vicchio di Mugello, near Florence, Italy, and baptized John. Granted the grace of a religious vocation, he entered the Dominicans in Fiesole in 1420. For a time he was assigned to the Dominican San Marco Monastery in Florence, and there he started his life-long painting career as a religious after receiving major orders in 1427-29.

Fra Angelico had already been active in painting, a member of the artist Company of San Nichola. During the next year he decorated the church of San Stefano al Ponte. His work there provided a serene religious spirit while reflecting a classical influence that mirrored the revival of the arts in his era. His art reflected an angelic approach from the start, and his figures and scenes were mantled in light, radiant with religious fervor.

Fra Angelico and his brother became embroiled in the political tumult of the era and had to leave Florence because of their loyalty to the Pope. He continued working, however, moving to Cortona, then Fiesole. His art was attracting attention, and Pope Eugenius IV used Fra Angelico's gifts from 1431-1447, asking him to decorate papal chambers. He also served Pope Nicholas V (r. 1447-1455). Pope Eugenius proposed appointing Fra Angelico as the Archbishop of Florence, but he declined out of humility: he understood that his artistic gifts had to be put to use in the service of God.

Throughout his life, Fra Angelico painted masterpieces that display intricate, beautiful interpretations of spiritual events and ideals. His piety and radiance as a Dominican brought about the name by which he is famed in the modern world. He continued painting until his death, at La Minerva Friary, in Rome. He was buried in Santa Maria Church in the Eternal City.

Pope John Paul II beatified Fra Angelico on October 3, 1982, and declared him the patron of Catholic artists in 1984. The Holy Father praised the holiness of his life and honored the profound spirituality evident in the masterpieces that Fra Angelico bequeathed to the Church and the world, masterpieces that mirror his religious life and his interior union with Christ.

✠

Aniceto Adolfo — see Martyrs of Astoria

✠

Anna Katharina Emmerick
(September 8, 1774 – February 9, 1824)

"Mystic of the Land of Münster"

A mystic whose writings have been highly influential, Anna Katharina was born in Flamsche, near Coesfeld, and grew up in a large family. From a very early age, she demonstrated a deep love of prayer, especially the Mass. To assist her family, she worked for three years on a farm, then mastered sewing in Coesfeld. While in that town, she went to Mass with great eagerness and particularly enjoyed walking the Way of the Cross by herself.

Anna hoped fervently to enter the religious life, but she was prevented by her family's inability to provide a suitable dowry. The Poor Clares in Münster, however, accepted her on condition that she play the organ. While she never learned to play the organ, she proved a tireless worker who gave herself entirely for the good of the sisters and the many poverty-stricken families in the area. Finally, she entered the convent of Agnetenberg in Dülmen in 1802, and took her vows the following year.

Sr. Anna again proved an indefatigable laborer in the religious life, despite a lack of respect from some of her fellow nuns who knew her poor background. The convent was suppressed in 1811, and Anna Katharina was forced to work as a housekeeper at the home of Abbé Lambert, a priest who had been forced to flee from France, in Dülmen.

Largely as a result of her mortifications, she fell ill. Her sister took over her duties as housekeeper, but Anna's sufferings were only preparation for the reception of the stigmata. Her condition was confirmed by a doctor, Dr. Franz Wesener, who maintained a detailed record of his care for her and her daily prayers and patience.

Her reputation for holiness soon spread across Europe; she was visited by such prominent figures as Clemens August Droste zu Vischering, Friedrich Leopold von Stolberg, Christian and Clemens Brentano, and Luise Hensel. Clemens Brentano proved instrumental in recording her visions.

Her final months were spent in intense agony, but she died offering up her suffering to Christ. After her funeral, attended by a large throng, she was laid to rest in the cemetery of Dülmen. Her visions were later published and have since found a wide readership. Her visions influenced even the monumentally successful film *The Passion of the Christ* (2004).

She was beatified by Pope John Paul II on Oct. 3, 2004. The pontiff said of her:

> The fact that the daughter of poor peasants who sought tenaciously to be close to God became the well-known "Mystic of the Land of Münster" was a work of divine grace. Her material poverty contrasted with her rich interior life. We are equally impressed by the new Blessed's patience in putting up with physical weakness and her strong character, as well as her unshakable faith. She found this strength in the Most Holy Eucharist. Her example opened the hearts of poor and rich alike, of simple and cultured persons, whom she instructed in loving dedication to Jesus Christ.
>
> Still today, she passes on to all the saving message: Through the wounds of Christ we have been saved (cf. 1 Pt 2: 24).

✠

Anna Rosa Gattorno (October 14, 1831 – May 6, 1900)
Widow and Stigmatic

A religious founder, Anna Rosa Gattorno was born in Genoa, the daughter of a prominent and wealthy local family. At the age of twenty-one, she married her cousin, Gerolamo Custo, and moved with him to Marseilles, where they became poverty-stricken. Her first child, Carlotta, suffered a severe illness and was left blind and dumb as a result. Anna Rosa also lost a young son, and her husband died after only six years of marriage.

Having returned to Genoa, she put her life in order and made perpetual vows of chastity and obedience as a Franciscan Tertiary. Anna Rosa also received daily Communion — an unusual practice at the time. She had the stigmata, but it was hidden throughout her life, bringing suffering to her personally but not visible to others. Despite her losses and her pain, she became involved in many ministries and was respected by Church leaders. Anna Rosa was even received by Pope Pius IX (r. 1846-78), who counseled her to found a religious congregation for women. As a result of this papal invitation, the Daughters of St. Anne, Mother of Mary Immaculate was founded on December 8, 1866, with an original group of twelve members.

This congregation assumed many charitable ministries and spread to Bolivia, Brazil, Chile, Eritrea, France, Peru, and Spain. Anna Rosa led the congregation through the difficult first stages and saw the increase in members and foundations before she died of influenza in Rome.

Pope John Paul II beatified Anna Rosa Gattorno on April 9, 2000, declaring:

> With complete trust in Providence and motivated by a courageous impulse of charity, Blessed Anna Rosa Gattorno had one desire: to serve Jesus in the suffering and wounded limbs of her neighbour, with sensitivity and motherly attention to all human misery.

✠

Anna Monteagudo (c. 1600 – January 10, 1686)
"Anna of the Angels"

She was born in Arequipa, Peru, the daughter of Sebastian and Francisca de León Monteagudo. Her parents were Spaniards, and Anna benefited from both their social status and their piety. Early in her life, she had great devotion to St. Rose of Lima and demonstrated a reverence for the contemplative life at the same time. She was well educated, attending the Dominican Convent of St. Catherine of Siena in Arequipa, where her religious vocation was recognized. The convent, founded in 1577, was reportedly the size of a small city, forming a haven for the devout within its massive walls.

When Anna announced her desire to enter the Dominican convent, however, her parents did not give their consent willingly, having planned a secular life for their daughter, but they relented in the face of her obvious religious vocation, and she entered the Dominican convent, receiving the religious name Anna of the Angels. After her religious training, she resided in a small enclosure of the convent, where she matured spiritually.

Gifted with many remarkable graces, Anna demonstrated the ability to give spiritual counsel and to discern prophecies. She became novice mistress of the convent in 1648. There, she served as a model of prayer and religious fidelity. She died in St. Catherine of Siena Convent, having served faithfully for decades.

Pope John Paul II beatified Anna of the Angels Monteagudo on February 2, 1985, while on a papal visit to Latin America. At the ceremony, Anna was honored before thousands of her own countrymen for her faithfulness to her religious vows. Her graces and gifts did not lead her astray from her commitment to service and to love.

✠

Anna Maria Francesca Rubatto
(February 14, 1844 – August 6, 1904)
Missionary to the New World

A co-founder and inspiration of a religious congregation, Anna Maria Rubatto visited the New World many times to introduce her community. She was born in Carmagnola, Italy the daughter of a devout family. Her father died when she was only four, and her mother raised her in the Faith. She took a private vow of virginity at an early age and demonstrated a profound sense of charity and concern for others even as a child.

After the death of her mother — when Anna Maria was nineteen — she moved to Turin, Italy, where she was welcomed by a noblewoman, Marianna Scoffone. She began to teach catechism to the local children and visited the homes of the sick and needy. She continued in this apostolate until 1882, when her noble patroness died.

Anna Maria went to the Ligurian coastal region after her patroness' funeral, seeking a period of rest and recovery. In the town of Loano, where she attended Mass at the local Capuchin Franciscan church, she witnessed an accident. A young worker was struck on the head by a stone, which fell from a scaffold at a convent being constructed. She cleaned his wound and gave the worker two days' wages so that he could remain at home to rest and recuperate. She then went on her way, but the worker told everyone about her kindness.

The group constructing the convent heard about the event and discussed it as a possible sign. Some of the members contacted Anna Maria and asked her to join the community as their spiritual guide. A Franciscan priest, Fr. Angelico Martini, also urged her to accept the invitation, and she did so a year later. Bishop Filipo Allegro named her the Superior of the new convent, which was called the Institute of the Capuchin Sisters of Mother Rubatto. The name was later changed to the Capuchin Sisters of the Third Order of Loano.

In 1892, Mother Anna Maria Francesca of Jesus began missions in Montevideo, Uruguay, and Argentina. She sailed across the Atlantic Ocean seven times, founding another mission in Alto Alegre, with the aid of Capuchin missionaries and converts. She returned to Montevideo in 1904, intending only a brief stay there. She remained at this mission, however, for over a year and died there. She was buried in Montevideo.

Pope John Paul II beatified her on October 10, 1993, declaring:

Maria Francesca of Jesus . . . who made your life a constant service to the lowest, witnessing to God's special love for the lowly and humble . . . faithfully following the footsteps of Francis, the lover of evangelical poverty, you learned not only to serve the poor, but to make yourself poor.

✠

Anna Maria Sala (April 21, 1829 – November 24, 1891)
United to Christ in Suffering

Anna Maria Sala was born in Brevio, Italy, the fifth of eight children of Giovanni and Giovannina Sala, and was sent to a school operated at Vimercate by the Sisters of St. Marcellina. She asked to enter that convent, but family problems delayed her. Her father had to declare bankruptcy, and her mother became very ill. Finally, however, in February 1848, Anna Maria was accepted by the Sisters and was professed on September 13, 1852.

She was assigned to various educational institutions operated by the Congregation of St. Marcellina in Italy and served faithfully in Cernusco, Chambéry, Genoa, and Milan for almost four decades. In 1883, Anna Maria was diagnosed with throat cancer; she demonstrated no alarm, merely asked to continue her labors for as long as possible. As a member of a large community, she was able to serve without being singled out, and she bore her pain and illness with calm and humility.

In 1891 she collapsed, too infirm to carry on her assigned tasks. She died in the Milan infirmary of her beloved congregation, uncomplaining and joyous. When her Cause was opened in 1920, the body of Blessed Anna was exhumed and found to be intact.

Pope John Paul II beatified Anna Maria Sala on October 26, 1980, and he praised her silent suffering, her resolute commitment to the care of her students, and her fidelity to her religious vows. The Holy Father stated that she demonstrated a spiritual maturity in following Christ Crucified.

✠

Anna Schaffer (February 18, 1882 – October 5, 1925)
Apostle of Reparation

Anna Schaffer was born in Mindelstetten, Bavaria, Germany, to a devout family. Reserved as a child, she was instructed in the Faith by her mother and received First Communion while young. After this ceremony, Anna offered herself to Christ and expressed a desire to enter a missionary congregation.

Lacking a dowry, she worked in the local area after finishing school to raise the necessary funds for her entrance into a convent.

In June 1898, however, going to work in a forester's lodge in nearby Stammham, Anna tried to put a broken stovepipe back in place over the laundry boiler. The stovepipe was difficult to handle, and she slipped while struggling with it and fell into a vat of boiling water, scalding both legs to the area above the knees. Despite immediate medical care, the burns did not heal, bringing her pain and the need for constant cleansing. The doctors, unable to offer more permanent relief, sent Anna home in May 1902, where she was confined to her bed.

Although poverty-stricken and in pain, Anna soon became spiritually transformed. Her parish priest, Fr. Karl Rieger, recognizing the depths of her devotion, brought her Holy Communion every day, supporting her in her apostolate of suffering.

In 1910, Anna began to experience visions and received the stigmata — at first, visible to those around her, but later in a hidden form. Her entire life thus became an act of reparation for sin in the world, and many benefited from her words and prayers.

On April 25, 1923, Anna suffered paralysis in her legs, a stiffening of her spinal cord, and the onset of rectal cancer. She did not falter, however, writing to those who asked her aid and doing embroidery to maintain some financial security. Then, she had a fall from bed that damaged her brain and silenced her vocal cords; Anna died soon after, making the Sign of the Cross and whispering: "Jesus, I live in you."

Pope John Paul II beatified Anna Schaffer on March 7, 1999. The Holy Father praised her apostolate of suffering and reparation and her willingness to embrace the torments of the body in daily acts of surrender to Christ's love.

✠

Annunciata Cocchetti (May 9, 1800 – March 22, 1882)
Protector of Young Women

The founder of a religious congregation for women, Annunciata Cocchetti was born in Rovato, Italy, the daughter of a wealthy local family. When her parents died, Annunciata's grandmother, a devout noblewoman, raised her.

The Ursuline Sisters educated her until they were suppressed by Napoleon. She was then tutored in her home and, there, recognized her calling to the service of others, particularly to the service of the abandoned girls of her region.

When her grandmother died in 1823, her uncle insisted that Annunciata move to Milan, where she resided for six years. In 1831, however, given encouragement by her spiritual director, Annunciata went to Cemmo to join Erminia Panzerini, who was living as a religious and conducting a school for girls. Annunciata undertook the same charitable work and placed herself under the direction of Bishop Girolamo Verzeri. With his aid, at the age of forty, she founded the Sisters of St. Dorothy of Cemmo.

She received her religious training in Venice, then resided in Cemmo in the Val Camonica, near Brescia. There, she remained the inspiration and model for her expanding community for another four decades. Annunciata died at her congregation's motherhouse.

Pope John Paul II beatified Annunciata Cocchetti on April 21, 1991. The Holy Father praised the new Blessed, saying:

> She expressed her love for God . . . with a fidelity that endured every-thing, with a strong asceticism which helped her overcome the difficulties she met throughout her daily life.

⚜

Anselm Polanco Fontecha (April 16, 1881 – 1939)
Martyr of the Spanish Civil War

Anselm Polanco Fontecha was born in Buenavista de Valdavia, Palencia, Spain, and educated by his parents in the Faith. Anselm entered the Augustinians at age fifteen in Valladolid and studied for the priesthood, eventually being ordained. In time, he was elected prior of his monastery, a position he held until he was sent to the Augustinian missions in the Philippines as a provincial councilor. Anselm became Provincial Superior in 1932 and visited China, Colombia, Peru, and the United States.

In 1935, he was consecrated the bishop of Teruel, Spain, and the apostolic administrator of Albarracin. Three years later, the city was taken over by the revolutionary forces of the Republican Army. Anselm had already signed the collective letter of the Spanish bishops denouncing the persecution of the Church, and he refused to deny that signature or document. He was arrested with Felipe Ripoll Morata, his vicar general, and shared a prison cell with him for over a year. In 1939, when the Communist-led troops were retreating, Anselm and Felipe were used as human shields, then taken to a gorge near Gerona, called Can Tretze of Pont de Molins, where they were shot. Their remains were enshrined in the Cathedral of Teruel.

Pope John Paul II beatified Anselm and Felipe on October 1, 1995, announcing:

Martyrdom is a particular gift of the Holy Spirit; a gift for the whole Church. Anselm Polanco, an Augustinian religious, chose as his Bishop's motto, "I will most gladly spend myself and be spent for your souls."

(See also Felipe Ripoll Morata.)

✠

Antoine Marie Chevrier (April 16, 1825 – October 2, 1879)
"To Know, To Love, To Act"

Antoine Marie Chevrier was born in Lyons, France, and baptized Antoine-Marie. Growing up devout, he studied for the priesthood and was ordained in Lyons in 1850. His first assignment was as a curate in a working-class parish. There, he saw the sufferings of the poor and the disabled and began his endless service of caring and working for their spiritual good.

On Christmas 1856, Antoine received a divine revelation concerning his apostolate, and he vowed then and there to follow Jesus Christ "for the salvation of souls." One of his first charitable projects was flood relief in the district. John Vianney, the Curé of Ars, watching Antoine's zeal and prudence, encouraged him to serve as a chaplain for the Town of Infant Jesus, a massive charitable organization. Antoine remained in this work for three years, learning the depths of poverty in his area and seeking innovative ways of teaching the Gospel and the love of Christ.

He decided to reach the poor by opening a charitable institution and purchased an abandoned ballroom in Lyons, called the Prado, for this purpose. There, he opened services to aid the sick and poor, calling the work The Providence of the Prado.

He remained in the renovated ballroom for twenty years, joined by others who came to aid him in his apostolate. As a result, Antoine founded religious congregations to stabilize and extend the various charitable undertakings. He also wrote treatises and devised training programs for priests and seminarians, authoring *The Priest According to the Gospel* and other spiritual works.

The Providence of the Prado set a standard for service to the needy of the region, and Antoine was recognized as a spiritual mentor and servant of the poor. He was called upon often to inspire others who were seeking the same ministries. His Society of the Priests of the Prado and the Society of Sisters of the Prado gave themselves entirely to the elderly, the abandoned, and the suffering. Exhausted by his labors and suffering from painful ulcers, Antoine died in Lyons and was buried in a chapel of the Prado.

Pope John Paul II beatified Antoine Marie Chevrier on October 4, 1986, in Lyons, praising his holiness and the dedication of this patron of the poor. Blessed Antoine was revered for his motto: "To know, to love, to act." His writings testified to the Christian commitment that he made as a priest of the people.

✛

Anton Maria Schwartz (February 28, 1852 – September 1929)
Founder of the Calasantines

Anton Schwartz was a champion of workers and the poor.

He was born in Baden, near Vienna, Austria, the fourth of thirteen children. Introduced to the musical world by his father, he became a singer, also attending the *Schotten-gymnasium* in Vienna. In 1869, he joined the Scalopian or Piarist Congregation, which was threatened with suppression. He left the congregation's seminary to study for the archdiocese of Vienna and was ordained a priest on July 23, 1875, renting vestments and a chalice for his first Mass because he was too poor to purchase them.

After ordination, Anton was assigned to Marchegg, where he became famous for his vigorous concerns. In 1879, he was named chaplain to the Catholic Hospital in Vienna-Sechshaus, and there he started his young workers' apostolate. He founded the Congregation of Christian Workers of St. Joseph Calasanz (also called the *Kalasantiner*, or Calasantines), in Vienna, with the aid of four companions. He also founded an "Oratory for Apprentices" and another training program for workers, where housing, education, and spiritual instructions were freely available. Anton united himself with striking workers and became the patron of tailors and shoemakers.

In 1908, Anton withdrew from most public or controversial activities; the Austrian government did not appreciate his leadership among the poor and disenfranchised, however, and in 1913, he had to be defended by Cardinal Friedrich Piffl. Anton died in Vienna and was buried in Our Lady of Help Church there.

Pope John Paul II beatified Anton on June 21, 1998, declaring:

> In Vienna 100 years ago, Fr. Anton Maria Schwartz was concerned with the lot of workers. He first dedicated himself to the young apprentices in the period of their professional training. Ever mindful of his own humble

origins, he felt especially close to poor workers. To help them, he founded the Congregation of Christian Workers according to the rule of St. Joseph Calasanz, and it is still flourishing. He deeply longed to convert society to Christ and to renew it in him. He was sensitive to the needs of apprentices and workers, who frequently lacked support and guidance.

The Holy Father added:

He leaves us a message: Do all you can to protect Sunday! Show that it cannot be a workday because it is celebrated as the Lord's day! Above all, support young people who are unemployed! Those who give today's young people an opportunity to earn their living help to make it possible for tomorrow's adults to pass the meaning of life on to their children. I know that there are no easy solutions. This is why I repeat the words which guided Blessed Fr. Schwartz in his many efforts: "We must pray more!"

✠

Anton Martin Slomsek
(November 26, 1800 – September 24, 1862)
"Good Samaritan of the Slovenian People"

Anton Martin Slomsek was born at Maribor, the son of a Styrian peasant family. Raised devoutly and receiving the grace of a vocation, he was educated in the seminary and ordained to the priesthood on September 8, 1824. His first Mass was celebrated at Olimje, and he was then assigned as a chaplain in Bizeljsko and Nova Cerkev. He went from that ministry to Klagenfurt, where he remained for nine years as the director of the seminary. From 1838 until 1846, he held other important posts in his diocese and was appointed the Bishop of Lavantal, Austria.

Anton was consecrated on July 5, 1846, went to Sankt Andrá, then to Maribor. where he displayed an ability to use innovative methods of communicating with his people. A writer and poet, he became a printer and published many catechetical and devotional works. He founded confraternities to bring people into the churches and was a noted ecumenist in a time when distrust and disputes between the various faiths of the region were rampant.

Pope Blessed Pius IX learned about the remarkable apostolate of Anton and commissioned him to reform the Benedictine monasteries of Central Europe. Throughout this ministry, Anton remained loyal to the Church and yet handled the various communities and individuals with care and sensitivity. He made continuing apostolic visitations to religious houses, then transferred his see to Lavantal, Austria. There, he demonstrated his oratorical skills and ecumenical visions. When he died, Anton was buried in the Chapel of the Cross, a shrine in Maribor.

Pope John Paul II beatified Anton Martin Slomsek on September 19, 1999, in Maribor, Slovenia — "the first son of this Slovenian nation raised to the glory of the altars." The pope went on to declare:

> He was a vine which yielded abundant fruits of Christian holiness, of remarkable cultural richness and of lofty patriotism. This is why he stands before us today as a splendid example of one who put the Gospel into practice.

✠

Antonia Messina (June 21, 1919 – May 17, 1935)
Symbol of Purity

Antonia Messina was born in Orgosolo, Sardinia, and raised in a pious family in a tightly-knit community. At age sixteen, while walking with a young companion, she was accosted by a young man, Giovanni-Ignacio Catgui. Her companion ran to the nearby village for help as Giovanni assaulted Antonia. When she refused his advances, in a rage, he killed her. Her body bore seventy-four wounds from the stones that he used in his murderous assault.

Antonia's family and neighbors were horrified by the crime and inconsolable over their loss. Giovanni at first denied his guilt and tried to hide the evidence of his crime. The witness identified him, however, and two days later, he confessed. He was eventually tried, condemned, and executed for the murder.

Amid the outpouring of grief by the men and women of the region, the remains of Antonia were laid to rest. All of Sardinia honored this young woman who had defended her purity even in the face of death.

Pope John Paul II beatified Antonia Messina as a martyr on October 4, 1987, praising her innocence, piety, and fidelity to purity.

✠

Antoñio de Sant Anna Galváo (1739 – December 23, 1822)
"Man of Peace and Charity"

A Franciscan missionary, Antoñio de Sant Anna Galváo was born into a prominent family in São Paulo, Brazil. The family lived in the Guaratingueta area of the city, famed for religious devotion. At age thirteen, Antoñio was placed in the Jesuit seminary at Belém. In time, his father directed him to the Alcantarine Franciscans, and he entered St. Bonaventure Friary in Macao, Rio de Janeiro, on April 15, 1760.

After completing his novitiate and seminary training, Antoñio was ordained a priest on June 11, 1762. He was assigned to St. Francis Friary in São Paulo, where he served as a porter (or gate keeper), preacher, and a confessor to the local laymen and women. From 1769-1770, he served as confessor to a unique institution called a *recolhimento*, a convent of Recollects of St. Teresa in São Paulo. He then aided Sr. Helena Maria of the Holy Spirit, a famed mystic, in founding Our Lady of the Conception of Divine Providence in February 1774. Sr. Helena died suddenly in 1775, leaving Antoñio to guide the Recollects.

He wrote the rule for the congregation and built a church and convent, dedicated on August 15, 1802. In 1781, Antoñio was named novice master of the Franciscans in Macao, and in 1798, was appointed guardian of St. Francis Friary in São Paulo. When it became apparent that his duties would take him away from São Paulo, the bishop, religious, and laity notified the Franciscans that "None of the inhabitants of the city will be able to bear the absence of this religious for a single moment." Antoñio remained in São Paulo, holding various posts in the Franciscan Order until his health demanded rest.

In 1811, he founded St. Clare Friary in Sorocaba, São Paulo, then returned to St. Francis Friary. Receiving permission to reside within the Recollect convent, Antoñio died there. He was buried in the convent church, and his tomb became an immediate pilgrimage site.

Pope John Paul II beatified Antoñio de Sant Anna Galváo on October 25, 1998, in Rome, declaring that Blessed Antoñio "fulfilled his religious consecration by dedicating himself with love and devotion to the afflicted, the suffering, and the slaves of his era in Brazil." The Holy Father went on to add:

> His authentically Franciscan faith, evangelically lived and apostolically spent in serving his neighbor, will be an encouragement to imitate this man of peace and charity.

✠

Antonio Lucci (August 1681 – July 25, 1752)
"Angel of Charity"

Antonio Lucci was born in Agnone del Sannio, Italy and baptized Angelo Nicola. He entered the Friars Minor Conventual at Iserni, made his profession as a Franciscan in 1698, and studied at Assisi and other houses. Ordained to the priesthood in 1705, he received his doctorate in theology in 1709. He was then assigned to San Lorenzo Monastery in Naples, where he taught and worked among the people of the city. His contemplative prayer life left its mark upon his ministry, and people recognized his piety and loyalty to the Franciscan ideals and to the faith.

In 1718, Antonio was elected Provincial Superior, a regent of studies, then rector of the College of St. Bonaventure in Rome. He served the pope as a theologian in two synods and as a consultor of the Holy Office. Pope Benedict XIII (r. 1724-1730) consecrated Antonio on February 7, 1729, praising him with the words, "I have chosen a profound theologian and a great saint as Bishop of Bovino."

Charity was a hallmark of Antonio's service as bishop. He reformed the clergy and religious with kindness and began a series of campaigns to protect the poor. He established schools, emptied his own episcopal treasury to provide for the needy, and wrote a *Manual of Theology* — but also served as a simple catechist, preparing children for the sacraments. After twenty-three years of service, Antonio died at Bovino. Pope Blessed Pius IX (r. 1846-1878) declared him Venerable in 1847.

Pope John Paul II beatified Antonio Lucci on June 18, 1989, stating that he was "attentive to the signs of the times," and served as "a great tree" that spread out branches of charitable activities to offer refuge and relief to all in need.

✠

Anwarite Nangapeta — see Maria Clementine Anuarite Nengapete

✠

Arcangelo Tadini (October 12, 1846 – May 20, 1912)
Apostle of the Blessed Sacrament

Arcangelo Tadini was born in Verolanuova, Italy, and entered the seminary in Brescia at age 18. There, he suffered an accident that crippled him for life. Although he was ordained to the priesthood in 1870, Arcangelo had to spend a year at home with his family, trying to restore his health.

In 1871, he was assigned as a curate in Lodrino, staying there for three years, then, transferring to the Shrine of Santa Maria della Noce near Brescia. When a flood devastated the area, Arcangelo organized a soup kitchen and provided 300 meals a day to the displaced residents. In 1885, he was assigned to Botticino Sera parish as a curate, becoming pastor, then dean. Arcangelo would spend twenty-five years there, making the region the focal point of his ministries.

He remodeled the church and used his own inheritance to build a factory and a residence for young workingwomen. To further augment this apostolate, Arcangelo founded the Congregation of Worker Sisters of the Holy House of Nazareth. Confraternities and associations for workers provided care and inspiration for the entire area, but Arcangelo was the true model for his fellow countrymen. He spent hours every day before the Blessed Sacrament, standing rapt in prayer. The Eucharist was his strength and consolation, and he was never far from the altar. When he died, all of Brescia was in profound mourning.

Pope John Paul II beatified Arcangelo Tadini on October 3, 1999, announcing:

> Union with Christ, a spirit of prayer, and strong ascetic effort were the secret of the extraordinary pastoral effectiveness of another generous vineyard worker, the priest Arcangelo Tadini, whom the Church enrolls today among the blessed. In the school of the Eucharist he learned to break the bread of God's Word, to practice charity, and to respond with pastoral resourcefulness to the social and religious challenges that marked the end of the last century. Precisely because he was a person totally given to God, he could also be a priest totally dedicated to others.

✠

Arnold (Jules) Réche (September 2, 1838 – October 23, 1890)
"Ambassador of Jesus Christ"

The future Christian Brother Arnold (Jules) Réche was born in Landroff, France, the eldest of eight children. His parents were Claude and Anne Clausset Réche, and he was baptized Julian Nicholas Réche. As the family was poor, Julian started working early in life, performing menial jobs in his local area. He was honored even then as an exceptionally pious young man with a devout prayer life.

Drawn to the Christian Brothers, who were conducting education programs in the town, Julian asked to enter the congregation and was accepted. He became a novice, taking the name Arnold, in November 1862, and made his solemn profession in 1871. He then began an academic career that included teaching in the Christian Brothers' institute in Reims for fourteen years.

Arnold taught advanced students in many subjects, showing skill and concern. The Franco-Prussian War of 1870 involved him and his confreres, who cared for the wounded on both sides of the conflict. Arnold served with such distinction that he was awarded the Bronze Cross by the military authorities. At the same time, his spiritual maturity and intense prayer life were manifesting themselves in the congregation.

He was appointed the director of novices in 1877 at the Christian Brothers monastery at Thillois, and in 1885 he went to Courlancy (near Reims), the new formation center, where he eventually served as director. He had particular devotion to the Sacred Heart and the Passion of Christ, and he devoutly attended daily Mass and community prayer.

Arnold died of a cerebral hemorrhage and was buried in a cemetery in Reims. His grave was the site of miracles and soon became a famed pilgrimage destination.

Pope John Paul II beatified Arnold Réche on November 1, 1987, and the prayer prepared for this ceremony called this Christian Brother "an admirable guide for the young." Arnold was praised by the Holy Father for his manner of sanctifying the everyday aspects of life and transforming them into heroic acts of love.

✠

Artemide Zatti (October 12, 1880 – March 15, 1951)
Servant of the Sick and Poor of Argentina

Artemide Zatti was was born in Italy but spent his adult life in South America; his family emigrated from Reggio Emilia, Italy, to Bahía Blanca, Argentina, when he was seventeen years old. An uncle of the family was already prospering there and encouraged the family to join him.

Artemide worked in the area and attended a Salesian parish. At the age of nineteen, he entered the Salesians but faced difficulties in the seminary. He developed tuberculosis after caring for a young tubercular priest, and the studies for the priesthood were beyond his prior educational experiences. In 1902, he moved to Viedma, a city located in the upper reaches of the Andes

Mountains, hoping to be cured of his illness. A Salesian, Fr. Evaristo Garrone, operated a hospital and pharmacy in Viedma and took care of Artemide, prompting him to make a vow that he would serve the sick and poor if Our Lady, Help of Christians, obtained his cure.

When his health was restored, Artemide entered the Salesian training programs again and became a religious brother. He was professed in 1908 and worked under the guidance of Fr. Garrone, succeeding him as director of the hospital and pharmacy. He remained in this ministry for four decades. Artemide was prayerful and joyous as he served the sick poor of the area, and in 1913, started building a new hospital.

In 1950, he was diagnosed with cancer of the liver, and he later died in Viedma, where his remains were interred in the Salesian chapel.

Pope John Paul II beatified Artemide Zatti on April 14, 2000, declaring:

> His almost fifty years in Viedma represent the history of an exemplary religious, careful to accomplish his duties in his community and totally devoted to the service of those in need.

✠

Asensio Barroso — see Florentino Asensio Barroso

✠

Augustino Andres — see Martyrs of Asturia

✠

August Czartoryski (August 2, 1858 – April 8, 1893)
Nobleman and Priest

August was born in Paris, France, the firstborn son to Prince Ladislaus of Poland and Princess Maria Amparo, daughter of the Duke and Queen of Spain. The family had been forced to reside in France due to the political situation in Poland, but the members of the noble house still had hopes of reestablishing a unified Poland. The family thus had plans from August's birth for him to become a prime figure in recapturing Polish dominance for the Czartoryskis.

August, however, was graced with a very different destiny. At the age of six, he lost his mother from tuberculosis, a disease that she passed on to him and that caused him poor health for the rest of his life. While raised as nobility, he expressed early on a deep dissatisfaction with the superficial and ultimately empty life of parties and banquets. His tutor, Joseph Kalinsowski, provided spiritual direction and strongly recommended that the young prince be given proper supervision by a priest. Prince Ladislaus found this accept- able and appointed Fr. Stanislaus Kubowicz to August, who was shaped spir- itually by the priest. But the decisive turning point in his life came when he met Don Bosco, founder of the Salesians, at the age of twenty-five.

Embracing what he knew was a vocation to the priesthood and to the Salesians, August rejected his noble lineage. Over Don Bosco's expressed reluctance to accept him into the Salesian community, Pope Leo XIII granted express permission, and August entered the novitiate in 1887. After strenuous objections, at last, Prince Ladislaus acquiesced to his son's decision, and August was ordained a priest on April 2, 1892.

His tenure as a priest, however, was very short: Augusto died a year later, in Alassio, at the age of thirty-five.

Pope John Paul II beatified him on April 25, 2004, saying:

"How lovely is your dwelling place, Lord, God of hosts. My soul is long- ing and yearning, is yearning for the courts of the Lord. . . One day within your courts is better than a thousand elsewhere" (Ps 84[83]: 2, 11).

Blessed Augusto Czartoryski wrote these words of the Psalm, his motto of life, on the holy card of his first Mass. In them is contained the rapture of a man who, following the voice of the call, discovers the beauty of the ministerial priesthood. In them resounds the echo of the different choices that the person who is discerning God's will and wishes to fulfil it must make. Augusto Czartoryski, a young prince, carefully prepared an effective method to discern the divine plan. In prayer, he presented to God all ques- tions and deep perplexities, and then in the spirit of obedience he followed the counsel given by his spiritual guides. In this way he came to understand his vocation and to take up the life of poverty to serve the "least." The same method enabled him throughout the course of his life to make deci- sions, so that today we can say that he accomplished the designs of Divine Providence in a heroic way.

I would like to leave this example of holiness especially to young peo- ple, who today search out the way to decipher God's will relating to their own lives and desire to faithfully forge ahead each day according to the divine word. My dear young friends, learn from Blessed Augusto to ask ardently in prayer for the light of the Holy Spirit and wise guides, so that you may understand the divine plan in your lives and are able to walk con- stantly on the path of holiness.

ℬ

✠

Bartholomew Longo (February 11, 1841 – October 5, 1926)
"Herald of the Blessed Virgin Mary's Rosary"

Bartholomew Longo labored to build the shrine of Our Lady of the Rosary at Pompeii.

He was born in Latiana in southern Italy, the son of a prosperous and devout physician, and educated by the Scalopian or Piarist priests. He then studied law at the University of Naples. On March 25, 1871, Bartholomew became a Dominican tertiary, receiving the name "Brother Rosary." He also received a prediction from a Redemptorist priest that God would ask great things from him. Bartholomew devoted himself to charitable works until 1872, when he went to Pompeii on a legal matter. There, he felt compelled to counteract the growing ignorance of the Faith and the rampant secularism in the region.

Pompeii, the buried city of Italy, has long fascinated people around the world because of its rare glimpse of life in ancient Rome. The city has been restored, rescued from a timeless tomb by modern archaeologists, and tourists flock to the splendid ruins. What many people do not know is that there is a Pompeii that did not die; a modern city that has undergone all of the pressures of political, social, and religious change. Pompeii is also a city that can claim its own apostle, Bartholomew.

He bought a rather unfashionable painting of Our Lady of the Rosary, which he restored, and decorated a shrine for the painting, then initiated the Rosary of the Fifteen Saturdays, a unique Marian devotion. The cornerstone of a new chapel was laid in 1876. Pope St. Pius X (r. 1903-1914) elevated the shrine to the status of a pontifical basilica, as miracles were reported at the site of the holy image almost immediately.

A noblewoman, Countess Marianna De Fusco, had been aiding him in his apostolate. When Bartholomew consulted Pope Leo XIII (r. 1878-1903) about his work, the Holy Father recommended that he marry the countess in order to avoid scandal. They were wed and devoted their lives to the people of Pompeii, while living vows of celibacy. This ancient ruin of a city experienced a spiritual rebirth because of their devotion.

Bartholomew founded the Daughters of the Rosary and the Institute for the Sons of the Imprisoned, which was operated by the Brothers of the Christian Schools and was joined in 1922 by an annex for young women. He also started a periodical, *The Rosary and the New Pompeii.*

In 1906, Bartholomew turned over the entire estate and all properties owned by him and the countess to the Holy See. (Their schools, hospices, and presses are still in operation.) When Bartholomew died, his remains were placed in the basilica, as a year before, he had been made a Knight of the Guard Cross of the Holy Sepulcher. His tomb was prepared beneath the throne in Our Lady's shrine.

Pope John Paul II beatified Bartholomew on October 26, 1980, and in the ceremony he was called the "Herald of the Blessed Virgin Mary's Rosary," honored for his generosity and lifelong commitment to the faith.

✠

Bartholomew Maria dal Monte
(November 3, 1726 – December 24, 1778)
The Missionary of Discretion

Bartholomew Maria dal Monte was born in Bologna, Italy, the son of Orazio dal Monte and Anna Maria Basani. Prospero Cardinal Lambertini, who would become Pope Benedict XIV (r. 1740-1758), confirmed Bartholomew. As a young man, he already displayed great discernment and zeal, and he was revered for his dedication.

Trained by the Jesuits at Santa Lucia College, Bartholomew met with St. Leonard of Port Maurice, who encouraged him in his missionary desires and his vocation to the priesthood. Bartholomew was ordained on December 20, 1749, and completed a degree in theology. He then began his priestly ministry of parish missions, first in Bologna, then in sixty-two dioceses, as he was a popular and powerful orator.

Parish missions, Lenten retreats, spiritual exercises, and conversions were daily activities for Bartholomew for twenty-six years. He opposed the heresy of Jansenism and the philosophical errors of the Enlightenment of his era, but he did so with charm, eloquence, and fervor. Bartholomew was also devoted to Mary, the Mother of Mercy, and to saving souls. He recognized the secular forces loose in the world and worked unceasingly to give the Church a voice amid the materialism and chaos. Bartholomew also had many spiritual graces. Worn out by the unending demands of his mission schedule, he predicted his own death on Christmas Eve. He died in Bologna as he had prophesied and his remains were enshrined in the basilica there.

Pope John Paul II beatified Bartholomew on September 27, 1997, in Bologna, stating: "Blessed Bartholomew dal Monte shines brightly before us as a witness to Christ who was particularly sensitive to the demands of the modern age."

✠

Bartolomeu Fernandes dos Martires
(1514 – July 16, 1590)
Royal Tutor and Court Preacher

This Archbishop of Braga, a friend of Charles Borromeo, was born in Lisbon, Portugal, and raised devoutly. His name was taken from the fact that he was baptized in the church of Our Lady of the Martyrs.

In 1528, he entered the Dominicans, studied with them, and was ordained to the priesthood. A brilliant priest, Bartolomeu was assigned as a teacher after his ordination, serving at St. Dominic of Lisbon College and at the College of Batalha. When word of his holiness and intellect reached the royal court of Portugal, he was asked to serve as the royal tutor and court preacher. In 1558, Queen Catherine of Portugal nominated him as the archbishop of Braga, a nomination approved by Pope Paul IV, and he was consecrated in 1559.

Bartolomeu became known quickly for his austere lifestyle and his concern for the people of his archdiocese. He established schools of moral theology for priests, educating them in the necessities of their ministries. He also produced thirty-two literary works, some of which are still respected in the Vatican. Bartolomeu attended the Council of Trent, 1561-1563, where his counsel was valued. His great work, *Stimulus Pastorum,* was used in Vatican Councils I and II. He was a friend of Pope Pius IV and Charles Borromeo.

Returning to Braga after the Council, Bartolomeu called for a provincial council and established a seminary in Campo Vinha in 1571. He retired in 1582 and resided in the Dominican Convent of the Holy Cross in Viana do Castelo, where he died. Bartolomeu was buried in the Dominican Church there.

Pope John Paul II beatified Bartolomeu Fernandes dos Martires on November 4, 2001, announcing:

Blessed Bartolomeu of the Martyrs, Archbishop of Braga, with great vigilance and apostolic zeal, gave himself to safeguarding and renewing the Church in her living stones . . . He paid special attention to the living stones who had little or nothing to live on. He took from his own pocket to give to them. By his wisdom, his example, and apostolic zeal, he moved and made burn with zeal the souls of the Fathers of the Council of Trent.

✠

Benito de Jesus — see Martyrs of Astoria

✠

Benjamin Julio — see Martyrs of Astoria

✠

Bernard Lichtenburg (December 3, 1875 – November 5, 1943)
Nazi Foe and Martyr

Bernard Lichtenburg was born in Ohlau, Silesia (modern east central Europe), receiving the grace of a priestly vocation and studying at the seminary in Innsbruck, Austria. Bernard was ordained at the age of twenty-four and sent to Berlin, where he studied at St. Hedwig's Cathedral. He was appointed a canon of the cathedral and began his ministry as the Nazis started their vicious campaign for power.

The rise of the Nazis alarmed Bernard, especially as their propaganda was spread through Josef Goebbels's newspaper, *Der Angriff.* So Bernard became politically active; in 1935, he protested the rising tide of Nazism and the persecution of the Jews by going to Herman Göring to make a personal plea for a more humane policy. The Nazis viewed Bernard as naïve and pious at first and dismissed his concerns with nonchalance.

He was not naïve, however, and he did not intend to stand by idly as the Nazis destroyed Germany and the faith. He continued his confrontations with officials and preached again and again for an awareness of the murderous immorality being institutionalized in the land. Bernard was warned by many but did not falter in his opposition to the Nazi dogmas. He distributed copies of Pope Pius XI's (r. 1922-1939) encyclical *Mit brennender Sorge* ("With Burning Anxiety"), which was banned in Germany.

In 1941, Bernard was arrested and held in appalling conditions for two years. He was then given to the Gestapo for "re-education," the Nazi method of controlling adversaries. On his way to Dachau concentration camp, old and ill from abuse, he died near the town of Hof on November 5, 1943. More than 4,000 mourners attended his funeral in Berlin, despite the Nazi announced condemnation of his activities and beliefs.

On June 23, 1996, Pope John Paul II beatified Bernard Lichtenburg in Berlin, along with Carol Leisner, another victim of the Nazis, proclaiming:

> On the basis of his clear principles ... Lichtenburg spoke and acted independently and fearlessly. Nevertheless, he was almost overcome with joy and happiness when his Bishop, Konrad von Preysing, upon his last prison visit at the end of September 1943, relayed to him a message from my predecessor, Pius XII, in which he expressed his deepest sympathy and paternal appreciation. Whoever is not hampered by cheap polemics knows full well what Pius XII thought about the Nazi regime and how much he did to help the countless people who were persecuted by the regime. For Bernard Lichtenburg conscience was "the place, the sacred place, where God speaks to man" (*Veritatis Splendor*, n. 58). And the dignity of conscience always derives from the truth (cf. ibid, n. 63).

☩

Bernard Maria Silvestrelli
(November 7, 1831 – December 9, 1911)
"Second St. Paul of the Cross"

Bernard Maria Silvestrelli was born in Rome, Italy, the third of seven children of Gian Tommasso and Teresa Silvestrelli. Baptized Cesare, he was raised in a devout Catholic home that trained him in the virtues. Cesare was educated at home, then by the Jesuits, and finally at the Roman College. A brilliant man of remarkable administrative abilities, he originally intended to serve as a civil servant but instead entered the Passionist Congregation at the age of twenty-two, receiving the name Bernard Mary of Jesus.

Bernard suffered ill health that forced him to return home for a time, but he continued his studies and was ordained a priest on December 22, 1855. He also returned to the Passionists and was professed on April 28, 1857. One of his novitiate companions was the future St. Gabriel Possenti.

In 1865, Bernard became the master of the novices at Scala Santa Monastery in Rome and was named Superior of the house when international students were enrolled. In 1875, he became a provincial counselor, and on May 4, 1878, Bernard was elected the Superior General of the Passionists. He was an energetic defender of the Passionist ideals, directing restoration and expansion programs and serving as Superior General from 1878 to 1889 and from 1893 until 1903. Bernard died on December 9, 1911, at Morricone Monastery, after suffering a fall. His Cause was opened soon after.

Pope John Paul II beatified Bernard Maria Silvestrelli on October 16, 1988, praising him for holding "steadfast in the profession of faith with exemplary strength and generosity." The Holy Father called Blessed Bernard "an instrument of mercy and grace."

✠

Bernardina Maria Jablonska
(August 5, 1878 – September 23, 1940)
"To Give, Eternally To Give"

Bernardina Maria Jablonska used her spiritual gifts to aid the faithful during the terrible days of World War II.

She was born in Pizuny, Poland. As a child she was reared devoutly, then trained in the spiritual arts by Albert Chmielowski. She entered the Albertine Sisters founded by the future saint and became a hermitess.

Bernardina exhibited many graces and mystical abilities, but she was always mindful of the needs of the common people of Poland. She was elected Superior and served during critical times for her native land. She founded hospices for the sick and the poor, holding firm to the Faith as the Nazi threat overshadowed Europe, before she died in Krakow, Poland.

Pope John Paul II beatified Bernardina Maria Jablonska on June 6, 1997, in Krakow, Poland, announcing:

> The Church places this devout religious before us today as an example. Her motto of life was the words: "To give, eternally to give." With her gaze fixed on Christ, she followed him faithfully, imitating his love.

✠

Bibiana Khampai — see Thailand Martyrs

✠

Blandina Merten (July 10, 1883 – May 18, 1918)
Faithful to the "Little Way"

Blandina was born Maria Magdalena Merten in Duppenweiler, Germany. The ninth child of a pious family, she received the grace of a teaching vocation and entered the Ursuline convent. Blandina would serve for only eleven years as a religious, accomplishing no remarkable feat that could be admired by others. Instead, her life was filled with intense physical pain, and she bore it in calm silence.

After months of ill health and telltale symptoms, Blandina was diagnosed with a terminal illness. She bore the news with no outward signs of resentment or dread, indicating instead that her desire for union with Christ would be fulfilled as a result of her pain. As an Ursuline, she relied upon the rules and ideals of her religious life in order to continue teaching without drawing attention to her sufferings. She would only state, "Whoever loves God does not need to achieve exceptionally elevated actions; it is enough to love." She died in the company of her Ursuline Sisters in Trier.

Pope John Paul II beatified Blandina Merten on November 1, 1987, praising her heroism and her fidelity to the "Little Way" of performing all things for love.

✠

Boleslawa Maria Lament (July 3, 1862 – January 29, 1946)
Foundress of the Missionary Sisters of the Holy Family

Boleslawa Maria was born in Lowicz, Poland, and as she matured in the Faith and in prayer, she took the motto of St. Ignatius as her own: "All for the greater glory of God."

She began her apostolate by establishing Catholic organizations in Lowicz to care for the abandoned or ill. When others came to join her in this ministry, she started the Missionary Sisters of the Holy Family. Her congregation served in St. Petersburg, Mohilev, and Zytomierz. After World War I ended, Boleslawa went to Pinsk, Vilnius, and Bialystak. The times were difficult, and she had to start over on three separate occasions, facing hunger and homelessness because of political unrest. The terrible time of World War II brought more destruction to her houses, forcing her to begin yet again.

While Boleslawa concentrated on the forgotten suffering of the modern world, she also felt a need to work for Church unity. She worked ceaselessly to improve relations between Catholics and the Orthodox faithful in Poland. Long before Vatican Council II, Boleslawa was an instrument of ecumenical accord. When she died in Bialystak, people of all faiths came to mourn her passing from the world.

Pope John Paul II beatified Boleslawa Maria in Bialystak, Poland, on June 5, 1991. He called the beatification a true pilgrimage to honor Boleslawa, who "set herself apart by showing sensitivity to human misfortune." The Holy Father also declared:

> The faithful in Poland and in areas of her apostolate will henceforth be able to acclaim her in liturgical prayer and to follow the example of her life.

✝

Bonifacia Rodríguez Castro (June 6, 1837 – August 8, 1905)

Foundress of the Congregation of the Sisters Servants of St. Joseph

Bonifacia was born in Salamanca, Spain, to Juan (a tailor) and Maria Natalia. Her parents were dedicated to raising their six children in the Faith. Bonifacia learned how to make cord and, at the age of fifteen, began working to assist her family after the early death of her father. Proving successful in her work as a cord-maker, Bonifacia opened her own shop for cord, sewing, and needlework.

During this time, she also developed her spiritual life and soon found support from among her friends from Salamanca, who wished to emulate her dedication to prayer and the Mass. They gathered in her house-shop on Sundays and holy days. After a time, they founded the Association of the Immaculate and St. Joseph, later called the Josephine Association, with the aim of assisting young girls from succumbing to the temptations of the time.

Bonifacia, for her part, desired to join the Dominicans in their convent in Salamanca. Her wishes, however, were transformed when she met the Spanish Jesuit Francisco Javier Butiña y Hospital (1834-1899) in 1870. A gifted spiritual writer who cared especially for the spiritual needs of workers, he soon became Bonifacia's spiritual director as well as a vital director for the other young women. Encouraged by their example and dedication to holiness, Butiña decided to establish a new congregation of religious and asked Bonifacia to assist him.

Together, Bonifacia and Butiña founded the Congregation of the Siervas de San José. With six women from the Josephine Association — including Bonifacia's mother — the new community received permission from the bishop of Salamanca and was begun right in the little sewing shop, on January 10, 1874. From the start, the congregation intended to assist poor and uneducated young women by helping them find work, and thus stay off the streets and away from drifting into financial and moral troubles.

The new congregation was soon attacked by the diocesan clergy of Salamanca, however, who did not recognize the need for the boldly innovative program of service. Butiña was exiled from Spain with his fellow Jesuits, and Bonifacia soon found herself alone in charge of the new community. After interference from some of the local clergy, she was removed as Superior and subjected to severe humiliations and false accusations.

Faced with terrible suffering and slanders, Bonifacia endured in prayerful silence and proposed to the bishop of Zamora to depart the community to establish a new house. Her suggestion was approved. Thus, in 1883, she left Salmanca with her mother. She continued to receive humiliations in various forms until the day of her death. Two full years later, the community at Zamora was finally incorporated into the Congregation.

Bonifacia's profound spiritual gifts and remarkable spiritual vision were slowly, and finally, realized over the next century. Pope John Paul II beatified her on November 9, 2003. At that time, he declared:

> The words of Jesus proclaimed in today's Gospel: "Stop turning my Father's house into a marketplace" (Jn 2:16), question today's society, often tempted to turn everything into commodity and profit, putting aside values and dignity which do not have a price. Since the human person is the likeness and dwelling place of God, a purification is necessary, so as to protect the person beginning with his or her social condition or work.
>
> Bl. Bonifacia Rodríguez Castro was dedicated entirely to this activity; she herself was a worker who understood the risks of the social condition of her age. In the simple and protected life of the Holy Family of Nazareth, she discovered a model of the spirituality of work that gives the human person dignity and makes every activity, however little it may seem, an offering to God and a means of sanctification.
>
> This is the spirit that she wished to instil in working women, starting with the Josephine Association and then with the foundation of the Servants of St. Joseph, who continue their work in the world with simplicity, joy, and renunciation.

✠

Braulio Maria Corres — see Martyrs of the Hospitallers of St. John of God

✠

Brazilian Martyrs — see André de Soveral and Ambrosio Francisco Ferro

✢

Brigida of Jesus Morello
(June 17, 1610 – September 3, 1679)
Prophetess and Miracle Worker

The founder of a religious congregation, Brigida of Jesus Morello endured a lifetime of suffering.

She was born in San Michelle di Pagana, Italy, the daughter of Nicolo and Lavinia Borgese Morello, nobles, who had seven children. Well-educated and trained in the Faith, Brigida married Matteo Zancari from Cremona in October 1633. He lived in Salsomaggiore, an area recovering from the 1630 plague. Brigida and her sister, Agata, aided Matteo in this recovery.

Two years later, in the midst of political upheaval, the family had to seek refuge in the castle of Tabiano. The castle came under siege, and Matteo, leading the defenses, became seriously ill with tuberculosis. Brigida collapsed as well. While she recovered, her husband did not.

After mourning Matteo, she dedicated herself to a life of penance and prayer, aided by the Franciscans of Salsomaggiore and the Jesuits of Piacenza. She displayed particular mystical gifts and served as a prophetess and a miracle worker. When Margherita de' Medici Farnese opened a school for young girls in Piacenza, Brigida was recommended for the position of directress. Out of this apostolate, the Ursuline Sisters of Mary Immaculate was founded. The congregation was started on February 17, 1649. In April 1655, Brigida offered herself as a victim of love. For almost a quarter of a century, she endured a serious illness, borne with joy.

Pope John Paul II beatified Brigida of Jesus Morello on March 15, 1998, declaring:

> In love with God, she was thus ready to open her heart and her arms to brothers and sisters in need. . . . A constant invitation to trust in God shines through her.

C

+

Callisto Caravario (June 8, 1903 – February 25, 1930)
Martyred to Protect Others

Callisto Caravario was born in northern Italy, and moved to Turin with his family as a young boy. Educated in local religious schools, he applied to the Salesians in 1918 and was professed the following year as a member of the congregation. In 1924, he was sent to Shanghai, then to Macao and Timor.

In 1929, Bishop Versiglia ordained him in Shiu Chow. He then accompanied the bishop on a missionary tour, setting out on February 24, 1930. Two young men and three young women, catechetical teachers, were in Bishop Versiglia's party on board a small boat.

On February 25, 1930, Chinese pirates took over the boat and attempted to assault the women. Both Callisto and Bishop Versiglia defended them and were beaten for their efforts, then taken on shore by the pirates. At that point, the two knew they would be slain for defending the women in their company. They were both shot, despite Bishop Versiglia's plea that Callisto be spared.

The martyrs' intervention did save the young women, and other missionaries looking for the group claimed the bodies of the martyrs. Callisto was buried at the door of the church of St. Joseph in Lin Kong How. His death and the martyrdom of Bishop Luigi Versiglia brought new converts to the Faith in that region.

Pope John Paul II beatified Callisto on May 15, 1983, with Bishop Versiglia, saying their martyrdoms served as foundations for the Church in China. The Holy Father honored the martyrs for giving their lives "for the salvation and the moral integrity of their neighbors."

(See also Luigi Versiglia.)

✠

Cándida María Cipitria y Barriola
(May 31, 1845 – August 9, 1912)
Visionary of the Modern World

Cándida María Cipitria y Barriola was born in Berrospe, Andoáin, Guipúzcoa, Spain, and was baptized Juana Josepha Cipitria y Barriola. Under the direction of the Jesuit priest Michael Herranz, Juana started a series of charitable and educational programs. In 1871, she gathered other young women and founded her congregation, The Daughters of Jesus, in Salamanca, taking the religious name Cándida.

Called *Hijas de Jesus* in Spain, the Daughters of Jesus were the result of Cándida's vision of using modern methods for education. She had witnessed the devastation visited upon the people of Spain over the decades, and so designed her congregation to provide educational institutions, retreat houses, medical dispensaries, and social service centers. The congregation spread to Europe, Asia, and South America, inspired by her example. The Daughters of Jesus, approved by Pope Leo XIII in 1902, arrived in the United States in 1950, founding a convent and opening their educational apostolates.

A contemplative, she trusted in Our Lady, whom she called "the Star of our way." Cándida spent long hours in prayer before the tabernacle, and she radiated calm and trust in the Holy Spirit. She also recognized the holiness of the future Blessed Maria Antonia Bandrés y Elosegui, who was raised to the altars with her.

After her death in Salamanca. Cándida's fame grew as the faithful heard of her profound spiritual life. Pope John Paul II beatified Cándida María de Jesus on May 12, 1996, observing:

> Keeping Jesus' commandments is the supreme proof of love (cf. Jn. 14:21). This is how it was understood by Mother Cándida María de Jesús Cipitria y Barriola, who said as a young girl: "I am for God alone" and, at the moment of her death, stated once again: "In all forty years of my religious life, I do not recall a single moment which did not belong to God alone." Her deep experience of God's love for each of his creatures led her to respond with generosity and dedication. She concretely expressed her love of others by founding the Congregation of the Daughters of Jesus, whose mandate was the Christian education of children and adolescents. The attention she showered on her sisters, the benefactors of her works, priests, students, the needy, to the point of becoming universal, are a visible expres-

sion of her love for God, of the radical way she followed Jesus and her total commitment to the cause of his kingdom.

(See also Maria Antonia Bandrés y Elosegui.)

✠

Carol Leisner — see Karl Leisner

✠

Carlos Manuel Cecilio Rodriguez Santiago
(November 22, 1918 – July 13, 1963)
Lay Apostle of the Liturgy

Carlos Manuel Cecilio Rodriguez Santiago was the first Puerto Rican to be raised to the altars of the Church.

He was born in Caguas, Puerto Rico, and suffered a traumatic experience at age six, when a fire destroyed the family home and store. The grandparents of the family provided aid, and Alejandrina Esterás, Carlos' grandmother, trained him in devotion to the Holy Eucharist and in service as an altar boy in the parish church.

Carlos suffered from ulcerative colitis in the first year of high school but graduated and went to the University of Puerto Rico in Rio Piedras. He had to withdraw from the university because of his health, however, and went to work at an agricultural experimental station near his home.

Recognizing the need for his fellow countrymen to have catechetical and liturgical materials readily available to them, Carlos soon began an evangelistic ministry. He published liturgical materials and articles on Christian culture and established Circulos de Cultura Cristiana, groups that met to discuss and learn the beauty of the liturgy and the heritage of the Church. He also organized a *Te Deum Laudamus* choir to provide stunning renditions of the liturgical splendors of the Faith. Christian Life Days — particular efforts to inculcate the Catholic customs and traditions into the everyday life of Puerto Ricans — also flourished.

Carlos was diagnosed with rectal cancer in March 1963 and died less than three months later, accepting his pain and suffering and still offering his fellow islanders the joys and beauty of the liturgy of the Faith.

Pope John Paul II beatified Carlos on April 29, 2001, announcing:

Carlos Manuel Rodriguez emphasized the universal call to holiness for all Christians and the importance for all baptized to respond to it in a conscious and responsible way. May his example help the whole Church of Puerto Rico to be faithful, living with great consistency the values and Christian principles received during the evangelization of the island.

☩

Caroline Kozka (August 2, 1898 – November 18, 1914)
Martyr of Purity

Caroline Kozka was born in Wal-Ruda, Poland, the fourth of eleven children of Jan and Maria Borzecka Kozka. They resided in a devout rural community of Poland where the local parish was the center of the community's life, and Caroline happily attended Mass and devotional services and taught catechism.

When Caroline was sixteen, a Russian soldier made advances to her, which she refused. Angered, he kidnapped her, dragged her to a wooded area near the village, and assaulted and killed her.

Caroline's body was not discovered for a long time, despite the frantic searches conducted by her family and fellow villagers. Finally, on December 4, her remains were found; she was buried two days later in a parish plot at Zabawa. In November 1917, the remains were solemnly interred, and a cross was erected at the site of her cruel slaying. Caroline was revered as a martyr of purity.

Pope John Paul II beatified Caroline Kozka in Tarnów, Poland, on June 10, 1987. Throughout the beatification ceremony, Caroline was honored as a young woman who would never surrender to brutal impurity, even at the cost of her life.

☩

Caspar Stangassinger — see Kaspar Stangassinger

☩

Caterina Cittadini (September 28, 1801 – May 5, 1857)
Servant of the Poor and Needy

Caterina Cittadini was born in Bergamo, Italy and had a sister, Ginditta, who was abandoned with her by their father after their mother's death. The two small girls were sent to the Conventino di Bergamo orphanage, where they received kindly care and the opportunity for an education. In 1823, Caterina earned a diploma in elementary teaching, and she and Ginditta then went to live with two cousins, Fathers Giovanni and Antonio Cittadini, at Calalzio.

Caterina worked in the ministry of her cousins, but she was drawn to her own apostolate and, within two years, moved to found a congregation to aid young girls in her area. Fr. Giuseppe Brena, who had advised them in the orphanage, counseled her to go to Somasco, where she rented a house in 1826. Caterina was inspired by the apostolate of St. Jerome Emiliani and the Oratorians and started to teach young girls, orphans, and the disadvantaged. She opened the Cittadini institute in 1832, adding a boarding school four years later.

Her sister died in 1840, and Fr. Brena passed away in 1841, devastating Caterina, who became very ill in 1844. Despite this, she persevered; in 1855, the Ursuline Sisters of Somasca received approval from Blessed Pope Pius IX. She died in Somasca, just before her congregation was established canonically.

Pope John Paul II beatified Caterina Cittadini on April 29, 2001, saying:

> In her difficult life the new Blessed showed indomitable love for the Lord. Her deep capacity for loving, sustained by great emotional balance, is emphasized by all those who had the opportunity to know her.

╬

Caterina Volpicelli (January 21, 1839 – December 28, 1895)
Society Belle Dedicated to the Sacred Heart

Caterina Volpicelli was born in Naples, where she was well educated and a society belle — until she met the future Blessed Ludovico de Casoria on September 19, 1854, at Las Palmas, Naples. Caterina was instantly inspired to dedicate her life to Christ and joined the Third Order of St. Francis, demonstrating a valiant devotion to the Sacred Heart.

Her family and friends were stunned by her withdrawal from her normal worldly pleasures and watched as she entered the Perpetual Adorers of the Blessed Sacrament. She did not remain in that convent, however, but prayed and sought her own apostolate for reparations, prayer, and charitable works. On July 1, 1874, she founded the Institute of the Servants of the Sacred Heart. Pope Leo XIII (r. 1878-1903) declared his papal approval of the Institute in 1890.

Catarina opened an orphanage and other houses of care in Italy. She also attended the first National Eucharistic Congress in Naples in 1891.

She died in Naples in 1895, and Pope John Paul II beatified her on April 29, 2001, declaring:

Three significant aspects stand out in her life, which was totally consecrated to the heart of the Lamb slain for our salvation: a deep Eucharistic spirituality, an indomitable fidelity to the Church, and a surprising apostolic generosity.

✠

Catherine de Longpré — see Maria Catherine de Longpré

✠

Catherine Jarrige (October 4, 1754 – December 28, 1894)
"Little Nun of the Priests and the Poor"

Catherine Jarrige demonstrated valiant courage during the French Revolution.

She was born in Doumis, France, the youngest of seven children, and as a child was called *Catinon-Menette* — "Cathy, the Little Nun" — because of her humility and gentle ways. At the age of nine, Catherine was sent to work as a maid, and at thirteen, she suffered the tragic loss of her mother. She learned how to make exquisite lace products as a way of earning a living as a result, and moved to Mauriac to support herself.

Catherine became a Third Order Dominican soon after, adapting to the life of a *menette,* or "little nun." She lived in a small room with her sister and kept a vow of chastity, praying daily with other tertiaries. As she cared for the sick and the poor and sheltered orphans, her constant companion was the Rosary. She worked in this apostolate for many decades, even as political conditions in France worsened around her.

In 1791, the French Revolution brought terror and death to the Catholic people of the nation. Priests and religious were driven from their institutions and hunted by authorities for cruel punishments. Catherine, alert to the need for havens for priests, started a network of safe houses. She found devout families willing to aid the priests and kept such havens supplied with food and clothing. She even managed to provide vestments, hosts, and wine, so that the priests could celebrate Mass for the faithful.

After the persecution ended, Catherine resumed her usual ministry among the poor and needy. She also served in prisons and hospitals until her death.

Pope John Paul II beatified Catherine Jarrige on November 24, 1996, declaring:

A Dominican tertiary, the spiritual daughter of St. Catherine of Siena, she preached Christ and his Gospel by her actions. Her message is a message of joy, love, and hope.

✠

Catherine Troiani — see Maria Catherine Troiani

✠

Cecilia Butsi — see Thailand Martyrs

✠

Ceferino Jimenez Malla (August 26, 1861 – August 2, 1936)
"El Pele"

Ceferino Jimenez Malla was the first Gypsy beatified by the Church.

He was born in Fraga, Huesca, Spain, and married a Gypsy woman, Teresa Jimenez Castro. Living in Barbastro and having no children, they adopted a niece, Pepita, and raised her as a devout Catholic. Ceferino was a respected horse dealer, called the patron of the Gypsies. Though illiterate, he was sought as a counsel for the poor and the politically powerful. He continued his religious observances and was revered as a pious Catholic.

In July 1936, Ceferino protested the arrest of a priest by Spanish revolutionary militia and was taken prisoner because of his fervor. Placed in a Franciscan monastery, which had been converted into a prison, Ceferino recited the rosary, which infuriated his guards. One of the leading revolutionists of the area came to Ceferino to warn him to hide his faith; he would be freed, it was promised, if he ceased reciting the rosary.

But "El Pele," a daily communicant, refused. He considered devotion to the Blessed Virgin Mary a matter of honor and refused to deny the Holy Mother of God, even in the face of threats and lies from the revolutionaries. As he calmly continued to recite the Rosary, he was singled out for punishment. He was shot to death in the cemetery of Barbastro, dying with his Rosary in his hands and crying, "Long live Christ the King!"

Pope John Paul II beatified Ceferino Jimenez Malla on May 4, 1997, declaring him a glory of his people and a glory of the Church. As was noted during the ceremony, Blessed Ceferino proved that a "death for the faith" is always rooted deeply in a "life of faith."

✠

Charles of Austria — see Karl of Austria

✠

Charles of Mount Argus Houben
(December 11, 1821 – January 5, 1893)
Saint of Mount Argus

Charles Houben was born in Munstergeleen, in the Netherlands, the fourth of eleven children born to Peter Joseph and Elizabeth Houben. He was baptized John Andrew and was a quiet child, a slow learner who worked on his lessons carefully. He received the grace of a priestly vocation early and realized that he had to master his school assignments.

In 1840, John Andrew enlisted in the military and spent five years on duty, although he saw only three months active service. When this reserve term ended, he worked in his uncle's mill. In 1845, he entered the Passionists and was given the religious name of Charles of St. Andrew. He was ordained on February 21, 1852, and was assigned to England, where he remained for five years.

In July 1857, Charles went to serve in a retreat house in Dublin, in an area called Mount Argus. He returned to England for a time in 1866, but then went back to Mount Argus, where he labored and earned the trust of the local people. Charles was tireless in his efforts to ease the burdens of the poor in his mission. Catholics and non-Catholics alike recognized his holiness, and when he died, exhausted by his labors, the entire city mourned his passing. When Charles was beatified, a 103-year-old woman — a living witness of his work and one who revered his memory — attended the ceremony.

Pope John Paul II beatified Charles of Mount Argus Houben on October 16, 1988, with Bernard Silvestrelli. The Holy Father praised Charles's ecumenical labors and his ministry in the Sacrament of Penance, saying that Charles "was daily concerned with the difficulties of others."

✠

Child Martyrs of Tlaxcala: Christopher, Anthony, and John
(c. 1527-1529)
First Laymen Martyred for the Faith in the New World

Christopher (Cristobal) was born in Atlihuetza about 1514, the son of an influential native resident and one of his sixty wives. He was sent to the Franciscan mission school nearby, where he became a Catholic. Christopher, zealous in the Faith, tried to convert his family and admonished his father for his dissolute lifestyle. His father killed Christopher, who was twelve or thirteen years old, because of these rebukes.

Anthony (Antonio) was born in Tizatlan, circa 1516. He was the son of a local senator and heir to the family fortune. Anthony was baptized at the Franciscan mission at Tlaxcala and was very devout. When the Dominican priest Bernardino de Minaya started his journey to Oaxaca, Anthony volunteered to accompany him into the dangerous territory. He was slain at Cuauhtinchan, near Puebla, in 1529.

John (Juan) was born in Tizatlan and appears to have been a servant in Antonio's family. When Antonio was baptized, John was at his side. This faithful lad accompanied Antonio and the Dominican missionary to Oaxaca, sharing their fate, and probably dying while trying to save his master and friend.

All of the Child Martyrs of Tlaxcala were revered immediately after their deaths. The missionaries gathered up their remains and placed them in the mission church grounds, as the local Christians honored them as true martyrs of the Faith in the New World.

Pope John Paul II beatified Christopher, Anthony, and John at the basilica of Our Lady of Guadalupe in Mexico City, Mexico, on May 6, 1990. The Holy Father praised "these sons of Mexican soil," declaring that they inspired countless generations of Mexicans in the panorama of faith through the centuries.

✠

Chiara Bosatta de Pianello (May 27, 1858 – April 20, 1887)

Spiritual Daughter of Bl. Luigi Guanella

Chiara Bosatta de Pianello was dedicated to the poor and suffering.

She was born Dina Bosatta in Pianello Lario, Italy. She and her sister, Marcellina, were two of the first women to support the work of Luigi Guanella among the poor. In 1886, she joined his congregation and began her spiritual ministry, receiving the religious name of Chiara.

She served in her local parish as a religious, despite an illness that she contracted during her care of the poor in her hometown; the future Blessed Luigi recognized her as a soul especially chosen, saying, "God led her on the way of the strong souls, a life that is difficult and dangerous, he guided her so that her feet would not fail."

Surrendering herself as a victim soul, Chiara worked among the poor, relying upon Divine Providence, until she was physically incapacitated. She died at the age of twenty-nine.

Pope John Paul II beatified Chiara Bosatta de Pianello on April 21, 1991, praising her unending dedication to the religious and charitable ideals of Blessed Luigi and his congregation. The Holy Father also honored Chiara's vocation as a victim soul of love.

✠

Claretian Martyrs — see Martyrs of Barbastro

✠

Claudio Granzotto (August 23, 1900 – August 15, 1947)
"A Glory of the Franciscan Order"

Claudio Granzotto was a gifted sculptor.

He was born at St. Lucia del Piave, Italy, the son of a poor but devout local family. He lost his father when he was only nine and had to go to work in order to aid the family. At fifteen, he was drafted into the army and served throughout World War I, serving an additional three years in peacetime.

Discharged, Claudio enrolled in the Academy of Fine Arts in Venice. In 1929, he received his degree as a "professor of sculpture," with honors and high praise from instructors. He specialized in sacred art and opened his own studio, making a name for himself because of his skills and sensitivity to his subjects.

He felt drawn to the religious life, however, and entered the Franciscans to combine his skills with the devotion of the Order. His parish priest, commenting on Claudio's entrance into the Friars Minor, said, "The Order is receiving not only an artist but a saint."

Throughout his religious life, Claudio displayed humility and great compassion in dealing with others. He spent hours in prayer and sculpted as part of his daily routines. He predicted, however, "I am leaving on the Assumption." Diagnosed in 1947 as suffering from a brain tumor, Claudio died in Padua on that feast day.

Pope John Paul II beatified Claudio Granzotto on November 20, 1994, announcing:

> Love of Christ, "Son of Man," and service to God's kingdom are uniquely resplendent in the life of Blessed Claudio Granzotto. The youngest of nine children, he learned at home how to fear God, how to live a sincere

Christian life, with generous solidarity, willingness to sacrifice, and love of hard work in the fields. Because of his docility to the Spirit and such an effective family upbringing, the earthly life . . . became a constant pilgrimage towards holiness, to the very peaks of Gospel perfection.

A true son of the Poverello of Assisi, he could express contemplation of God's infinite beauty in the sculptor's art, of which he was a master, making it the privileged instrument of the apostolate and evangelization. His holiness was especially radiant in his acceptance of suffering and death in union with Christ's Cross. Thus by consecrating himself totally to the Lord's love, he became a model for religious, for artists in their search for God's beauty, and for the sick in his loving devotion to the Church.

✛

Clemente Marchisio (March 1, 1833 – December 16, 1903)
"The Image of Christ, the Good Shepherd"

Clemente Marchisio was born in Racconigi, Italy, and was raised devoutly by his family. Entering the seminary after receiving a call to the priestly life, he was ordained to the priesthood on September 20, 1856, and the future St. Joseph Cafasso prepared him for his priestly apostolate.

Clemente conducted his ministry with great devotion from the start, caring for those in want. He became the vicar of Cambiano in 1858 and, in 1860, was assigned to Rivalta, where he would remain for forty-three years.

Clemente founded the Congregation of the Daughters of St. Joseph to serve the needs of the poor, stressing to his followers the need for devout prayer lives and union with God. He became known as a loving father of the poor, a holy man of intense piety and hard work: his daily work schedule extended from 5 a.m. until midnight.

Clemente died in Rivalta, Italy, on December 16, 1903, mourned by his spiritual daughters and by the thousands that he had aided in his apostolate.

Pope John Paul II beatified Clemente Marchisio on September 30, 1984, honoring this priest-founder as "the image of Christ, the Good Shepherd." Blessed Clemente was praised as a man who attained perfection "through the Sacrament of the Body and Blood of Christ."

✠

Colomba Joanna Gabriel (May 3, 1858 – September 24, 1926)
A Woman Born for Love

Colomba Joanna Gabriel was born to a Polish family in Stanislaviv (now Ivano-Frankivsk), Ukraine, and baptized Joanna Matylda. A noble by birth, she was highly educated, both in local schools and in Leopoli. During this period, Joanna received the grace of a religious vocation and decided upon the Benedictines at Leopoli, taking the name Colomba. She served in that convent for some time but felt the need to conduct programs for the poor, especially vulnerable young working girls.

In 1900, Colomba moved to Rome and, except for a brief time Subiaco, remained there. Her spiritual director was the Dominican Hyacinth Cormier, who guided her as she started teaching catechism and visiting the sick and poor in the parish of the Prati district of Rome. This apostolate led to the founding of the Benedictine Oblates, a secular group.

In 1908, Colomba was inspired to found the Benedictine Sisters of Charity as a more permanent institute of service. Young women entering the new congregation established homes and other charitable programs for the poor people of Rome. Colomba earned the respect and reverence of the Romans as her congregation spread throughout Italy to Madagascar and Romania. Her patrons included Pope St. Pius X (r. 1903-1914) and Pope Benedict XV (r. 1914-1922). Queen Elena of Italy also aided her apostolate.

Colomba died at Centacelle, a suburb of Rome, mourned by thousands who cherished her vision and her spiritual motherhood.

Pope John Paul II beatified Colomba Joanna Gabriel on May 16, 1993, declaring:

> On the path of suffering the Holy Spirit uprooted her from her homeland, led her to leave everything and begin all over.

The Holy Father also praised Blessed Colomba's special charism: "the gift of the active apostolate of charity."

✠

Columba Marmion (April 1, 1858 – January 30, 1923)
Spiritual Writer

Columba Marmion was born in Dublin, Ireland, the son of an Irishman and a French mother, and baptized Joseph Aloysius. In 1874, Joseph entered the local seminary, then attended the College of the Propagation of the Faith in Rome, where he took the name Columba and was ordained to the priesthood on June 16, 1881.

Following his ordination, Columba visited the Benedictine Abbey of Maredsous in Belgium and was drawn to that monastic way of life. His bishop, however, assigned him to Dundrum and posted him as a professor in Clonliffe Seminary, where he served from 1882-1886. He also served as a prison chaplain. In 1886, Columba received permission from his bishop to enter the Benedictines at Maredsous, where he had to learn a new language and adjust to a new culture while making his novitiate. He made his solemn profession on February 10, 1891, and was sent to aid in the founding of the Abbey of Mont César in Louvain. Columba served as the prior there and preached retreats. He also became the confessor of Bishop Joseph Mercier, the future Cardinal.

On September 28, 1909, Columba was elected the third abbot of Maredsous, charged with the care of over 100 monks, a college, trade school, publishing house, and the grounds. During his term of office, Columba aided the Anglican monks of Coldey to convert to Catholicism. He also sent the young Benedictine monks to Ireland, a neutral country, during World War I. The German Benedictines were sent to Germany to protect them against retaliation because of the German occupation and aggressiveness.

Prayerful, filled with the love of God, Columba also wrote spiritual treatises and conferences that inspired an entire generation. His writings are lucid and inviting, and his works were popular around the world. His *Christ the Life of the Soul* (1917), *Christ in His Mysteries* (1919), and *Christ the Ideal of the Monk* (1922) provided religious and lay people with demonstrations of his spiritual insight and ardor. He was honored by Queen Elizabeth of Belgium and sought after for his personal holiness and wisdom.

Columba died in 1923, during a particularly harsh flu epidemic. Pope John Paul II beatified him on September 3, 2000, announcing:

> Throughout his life Blessed Columba was an outstanding spiritual director, having particular care for the interior life of priests and religious. May a widespread rediscovery of the spiritual writings of Blessed Columba Marmion help priests and religious and laity to grow in union with Christ and bear faithful witness to him through ardent love of God and generous service of their brothers and sisters.

☩

Cyprian Michael (Iwene) Tansi (1903 – January 20, 1964)
"A Man of God and a Man of the People"

A Trappist from Nigeria, Cyprian Michael (Iwene) Tansi was a holy and gentle priest, willing to sacrifice himself for good.

He was born in 1903 in Igboezunu, in southern Nigeria, the son of farmer Tabansi and his wife Ejikweve of the Igbo tribe. Called Iwene at birth, he was sent to a Christian mission at Nduka in 1909, where he received the name Michael.

He earned his first teaching certificate at age sixteen and taught in Onitsha and Aguleri. In 1925, Michael entered St. Paul's Seminary in Igboriam and was ordained in Onitsha Cathedral on December 19, 1937.

He started his ministry then as a pastor in Nnewi. In 1939, he was sent to Dunukofia, in the Umudioka region. There, he confronted the myth of the "cursed forest," putting it to rest. He also started the League of Mary and marriage preparation centers. On foot or on bicycle, from village to village, Fr. Tansi traveled endlessly, raising vocations and giving the Faith a rebirth. In 1945, he was assigned to Akpu; four years later, he went to Aguleri.

In order to assist Bishop Charles Heerey, who wanted to establish a Trappist monastery in the diocese, Michael agreed to undertake the necessary training for such a foundation. Accordingly, he left his homeland and went to the abbey of Mount St. Bernard in Leicestershire, England, after making a pilgrimage to Rome in 1950. There, he received the religious name Cyprian, and took his vows on December 8, 1956.

Much to Cyprian's surprise, however, the plans for the Nigerian Trappist monastic foundation did not materialize. The Trappists chose the neighboring land of Cameroon instead, causing him severe suffering; however, he accepted God's will and continued his cloistered life in a foreign land.

In January 1964, Cyprian developed an aortic aneurysm while in the Trappist cloister. He did not recover and died on January 20. When his death was announced, people came from far and wide to attend his funeral. Among those in attendance was Fr. Francis Arinze, the future cardinal of the Church. Cyprian's remains were taken to Onitsha for burial in 1988. They are now enshrined in Aguleri.

Pope John Paul II beatified Cyprian Michael (Iwene) Tansi in Nigeria on March 22, 1998. During the ceremony, the Holy Father announced:

The life and witness of Fr. Tansi is an inspiration to everyone in the Nigeria that he loved so much. He was first of all a man of God; his long hours before the Blessed Sacrament filled his heart with generous and courageous love.

✠

Cyriac Elias Chavara (February 10, 1805 – January 3, 1871)
Carmelite Visionary and Founder

A devoted son of the Blessed Virgin Mother, Cyriac Elias Chavara was a member of the Syro-Malabar Catholic rite who instituted a ministry fitted to his era and to his region of the world.

He was born in Kainakary, in the Malabar region of India. Cyriac Elias was raised by a pious family and, as a child, was continuously gentle and prayerful. Knowing that he had been called to the priestly life, he entered the local seminary and was ordained in 1829.

In 1831, Fr. Thomas Parukara, the secretary to the vicar apostolic, with Fr. Thomas Palakal, rector of the seminary, erected the Third Order Discalced Carmelites. Before a formal rule could be drawn up, however, both Fr. Palakal and Fr. Parukara died. Cyriac Elias had moved to Mannara, the site of the congregation, so the burden of the new religious community came to rest upon him. The new community already had many priest members and achieved a formal approbation of a rule in 1855, upon which approval Cyriac called the new congregation the Carmelite Brothers of Mary Immaculate. He took vows that same year, on December 8, becoming Cyriac Elias of the Holy Family.

Elected Superior, Fr. Chavara guided the apostolate and the expansion of the Carmelite Brothers of Mary Immaculate, founding six houses. With Fr. Leopold Beccaro, O.C.D., Cyriac Elias also founded a congregation for women at Koonammavu, bringing dedicated young women of the region into the service of the Faith. He was then appointed vicar general of the Syro-Malabar rite in that part of the world. This was yet another burden, as Cyriac Elias had to safeguard ancient rites, stemming schismatic movements of that era.

He organized both contemplative and active apostolates, distinctly Carmelite and devoted to the Blessed Virgin Mary. Prayerful and guided always by fervent charity, Cyriac Elias saw his congregation become the largest in India, with missions in Tanzania, Somalia, Sudan, and in Europe. He died at Koonammavu after a long illness.

Pope John Paul II beatified Cyriac Elias Chavara in Changaachery, India, with Blessed Alphonsa, on February 8, 1986, praising the spiritual heights of Carmel that spurred the new Blessed to heroic service and the dedication of this priest in adapting the ancient truths to the needs of the modern world.

$$\mathcal{D}$$

⊹

Damien de Veuster (January 3, 1840 – April 15, 1889)
Hero of Molokai

Damian Joseph de Veuster served the lepers of Molokai, Hawaii.

He was born in Tremeloo, Belgium, the son of a prosperous couple. Damien followed his brother, Auguste, called Pamphile, into the Congregation of the Sacred Hearts, the Picpus Fathers. He took his final vows on October 7, 1860, then volunteered as Pamphile's replacement to the Hawaiian missions, even though he had not been ordained. Damien arrived in Honolulu on March 19, 1964, and was ordained two days later in the cathedral.

Assigned to the island of Hawaii, called the Big Island, he took up residence at Puna. He then served at Kohala and Hamakua, spending eight years in a mission that covered 2,000 square miles of cliffs, ravines, valleys, and volcanoes. In January 1866, the Hawaiian royal government, recognizing that leprosy (Hansen's Disease) was spreading through the islands, exiled victims of the disease to a settlement on the island of Molokai. Damien had been caring for some of these lepers on Hawaii and had "an undeniable feeling that he should join them."

His prophetic words proved true on May 10, 1873, when he landed at Kalaupapa, Molokai, in the company of Bishop Louis Maigret, SS.CC. At an earlier meeting, Fr. Damien and other Sacred Heart Fathers had volunteered to go to the leper settlement. The first one assigned, Fr. Damien would remain there for the rest of his short life.

He built coffins for the dead and houses for the living, as well as chapels. Going from leper to leper, he washed and bandaged each one. His medical skills were learned by necessity and were matched by his fervent charity and his view of the lepers as individuals worthy of respect, kindness, and courtesy.

In 1876, the first symptoms of leprosy appeared in Damien's left foot. He did not shrink from this cross, and he was thrilled to see the Franciscan Sisters of Syracuse, led by Blessed Marianne Kope, arrive to start an advanced medical clinic. The years of loneliness and isolation from his fellow Sacred Hearts religious had taken their toll, however, and he died of leprosy and was buried on Molokai. At the request of the Belgian government, his remains were returned to his homeland decades later. Fr. Damien, however, is revered in his adopted islands; he also represents Hawaii in Statuary Hall in Washington, D.C.

Pope John Paul II beatified Damien de Veuster on June 4, 1995, honoring him as a "Servant of Humanity" and an inspiration to the world during his years of ministry on Molokai. His dedication and unfailing devotion also changed the way the world viewed lepers. Simple, adamant in his concerns and care, Damien became the Hero of Molokai.

✠

Daniel Brottier (September 7, 1876 – February 28, 1936)
Cathedral Builder in Senegal

Daniel Brottier was born in La Ferté-Saint-Cyr, France, and educated locally. While growing up the Loire Valley town, Daniel received the grace of a priestly vocation and entered the seminary. Ordained in 1899 for the diocese of Blois, Daniel was assigned as a faculty member of the college of Pontlevoy.

He desired missionary work, however, and entered the Congregation of the Holy Ghost at Orly, at age twenty-six. In 1903, Daniel was sent to Saint-Louis in Senegal. He labored in that mission for eight years, returning to France in 1911 because of ill health.

Because of his devotion to Senegal, Daniel agreed to a request from Bishop Jalabert, the vicar apostolic of the region, to launch a fundraising campaign to build a cathedral in Dakar. This cathedral would serve as a memorial to the French men and women who died in Africa — a *Souvenir Africain* — as well as honor Africans who had given their lives for France. Daniel appealed to all of France to contribute to this memorial.

During World War I, serving as a chaplain, he was cited for bravery six times and was awarded both the *Croix de Guerre* and the medal of the Legion of Honor. He attributed his survival on the front lines to the intercession of St. Thérèse of Lisieux and built a chapel for her at Auteuil in the year of her canonization. Daniel also organized war veteran programs and assumed the administration of a work called the Orphan Apprentices of Auteuil. At first, he supervised 175 apprentices; later the number increased to 1,408.

On February 2, 1936, Cardinal Verdier of Paris consecrated the cathedral in Senegal made possible through Daniel's labors. This was also the last day that Daniel was able to rise from his bed. He became very ill and died in Paris, mourned by all of France. More then 15,000 men and women paid their respects, and Cardinal Verdier preached the funeral homily.

Pope John Paul II beatified Daniel Brottier on November 25, 1984, praising his spirit of service, generosity, and true Christian valor that knew no national boundaries or racial designations.

✚

Daudi Okelo (1902 – October 1918)

Ugandan Martyr, with Jildo Irwa

Daudi was born in Ogom-Payira, a village on the road Gulu-Kitgum. The son of pagan parents, Lodi and Amona, he chose to study the Christian faith, and at the age of fourteen or sixteen, was baptized by Fr. Cesare Gambaretto on June 1, 1916. He also received his first Holy Communion on the same day and was confirmed on October 15, 1916. Soon after completing his formation, he started studies as a catechist.

In early 1917, Daudi volunteered to take over as catechist after the death of the catechist in charge of Paimol. Approved in the post by Fr. Cesare, Daudi was instructed to take along Jildo Irwa as his assistant, but the priest was firm in telling them of the many hazards faced by catechists in the task of evangelization. At the time, there was the constant risk of bandits, marauders, and dangers of political and tribal instability. Daudi acknowledged the dangers and set out with Jildo with what was reported to be a fearless determination to emulate Christ even in death.

The two set out in November-December 1917 with Boniface, the head-catechist of Kitgum, to Paimol. Daudi began work immediately as catechist among the children of the area. He taught to them basic prayers, the rosary, and basic teachings in the Faith. Daudi also made regular visits to nearby villages, working in the fields with the local people and assisting with their cattle.

Local troubles soon brought a violent end to his ministry. On October 18-20, 1918, a group of attackers entered the village and demanded that Daudi and Jildo cease preaching the Gospel. The village elder tried unsuccessfully to halt the impending attack, but Daudi courageously asked the elder not to become involved, as it might cost him his life. The attackers gave a final warning to Daudi. When he refused to abandon his work as a catechist, they dragged him out of the hut and stabbed him to death with spears. The body was soon dragged to a nearby empty termite hill. His remains were collected in February 1926 and subsequently placed in the mission church of Kitgum, at the foot of the altar of the Sacred Heart. Pope John Paul II beatified Daudi and Jildo on October 20, 2002.

✠

Dermot O'Hurley and Companions — see Martyrs of Ireland

✠

Diego Oddi (June 6, 1839 – June 3, 1919)
Practice of the Presence of God

A lay brother of the Friars Minor, Franciscans, Diego Oddi was born in Vallinfreda, Italy, and baptizd by his peasant parents as Giuseppe. After a spiritual encounter, he made a pilgrimage to the Franciscan hermitage of Bellegra. He met Mariano of Roccacasale and entered the Franciscans soon after, taking the name Diego, in 1871.

Poorly educated, he nevertheless became known for his holiness and his sermons, which touched the hearts of rich and poor alike. His life in the streets of Subiaco displayed his penance, piety, and awareness of the eternal Presence of God. From the ranking cardinals to the simple beggars in the street, he was a marvel of wit, generosity, and goodness. When he died, the people attended the funeral rites with genuine grief, aware of the fact that Diego had walked as an angel of God among them.

Pope John Paul II beatified Diego Oddi on October 3, 1999, announcing:

> During his long service of alms-begging, he was a genuine angel of peace and goodness towards everyone who met him, particularly because he knew how to care for the needs of the poorest and most severely tried.

✠

Diego Aloysius de San Vitores (1627 – April 2, 1672)
Dedicated to the People of the Marianas

Diego Aloysius de San Vitores was born into a noble family of Bourgos, Spain, and was raised in the Faith and in the royal court of the nation. Diego was educated at the *Colegio-Imperial* of Madrid, which was operated by the Jesuits, and he entered the Society with a desire to be a missionary in China.

Ordained in 1651, Diego was assigned to the Philippines nine years later. He arrived in the Philippines in 1662, but on the voyage came into contact with the Marianas Islands and volunteered to go there to start a mission. He received permission from King Philip III (r.1621-1665) in June 1665. With missionary companions, he had a ship built and sailed to Guam, arriving in June 1668.

Initially successful, Diego and his companions had to face growing opposition from powerful clans that ruled the region. Missionaries were assaulted and slain, but Diego went from island to island to strengthen the efforts of his fellow Jesuits. On one such journey, however, he met up with a convert who had apostasized. That native cursed Diego and attacked him with a spear. The missionary died on the beach of Tumon, near Agana.

Pope John Paul II beatified Diego Aloysius de San Vitores with two other Jesuits, Francis Garate and Joseph Rubio y Peralta, on October 6, 1985. During the beatification, the dedication of Blessed Diego to the apostolate of evangelization was honored. Carrying the Gospel of Christ to the world was the paramount impetus of his life. Diego's willingness to risk all for the Marianas served as the fire that illuminated his priestly vocation.

✠

Dina Belanger (April 30, 1897 – September 4, 1929)
Musician and Mystic

Dina Belanger was born in Quebec, Canada, and was raised devoutly by her family. A skilled musician, she was given special training at academies in Canada and in New York and offered concert opportunities. She did not pursue a musical career, however, receiving the grace of a religious vocation.

In 1920, Dina joined the Sisters of Jesus and Mary in Canada, having entered a mystical state of union. She said, "My hunger for the Eucharist is always growing. A day without bread, is it not a day without sunshine, hours in which evening delays in coming?"

Dina received many extraordinary mystical gifts, but the essence of her religious life remained union with Christ and surrender to divine love. She became ill soon after taking vows, and spent her remaining religious life suffering. She died in Sillery, Canada.

Pope John Paul II beatified Dina Belanger on March 20, 1993, saying:

Her message is handed on to us this evening, brothers and sisters, with a marvelous purity and clarity. Welcoming Jesus in our life, uniting our hearts with his, love of the Blessed Virgin, a fraternal spirit in the community: these are the graces of the Lord through the intercession of Dina Belanger, who leaves us as her last motto: "To love Jesus and Mary and make them loved."

⁜

Dionysius Pamplona and Companions
— see Martyrs of the Scalopian Congregation

⁜

Domenica Brun Barbantini
— see María Domenica Brun Barbantini

⁜

Domenico Lentini (November 20, 1770 – February 25, 1828)
"Angel of the Altar"

Domenico Lentini was revered as a model of the ministerial priesthood.

He was born in Lauria, Potenza, Italy, the youngest of five children raised in the Faith. Domenico desired a priestly vocation and, at age fourteen, entered the seminary at Salerno, beginning his studies for the priesthood. He completed his training and was ordained in 1794. He was then sent to his hometown, Lauria, to perform his ministry.

Domenico had an extraordinary devotion to the Blessed Sacrament, keeping vigil and offering adoration whenever possible. He was a model of piety as well in the celebration of Mass. People from the surrounding area came to participate in his Masses, inspired and spiritually renewed by his devotion and grace. He evangelized Lauria and the entire region and taught everyone to honor Our Lady of Sorrows.

Personally, Domenico was an ascetic, sleeping on the floor, never sparing himself, and practicing severe penances in a spirit of reparation. His purity was evident to all, especially when celebrating the Holy Eucharist or when administering the Sacraments to his parishioners. He also gave everything that he owned to the people of Lauria. Domenico died as a simple parish priest, and the Potenza region of Italy was devastated by the loss.

Pope John Paul II beatified Domenico Lentini on October 12, 1997, declaring:

A priest with an undivided heart, he could combine fidelity to God with fidelity to man. His total dedication to his ministry made him, in the words of Pope Pius XI, "a priest rich only in his priesthood."

⊞

Dominic Iturrate Zubero (May 11, 1901 – April 7, 1927)
"With Generosity and Joy"

Dominic Iturrate Zubero was born in Dima, in the Basque region of Spain, and demonstrated great devotion to the Blessed Virgin Mary. He entered the Trinitarian Order, where he received the religious name of Domenico of the Most Blessed Sacrament. He was sent to the Gregorian University in Rome from 1919-1926. Although ordained to the priesthood, Dominic would never be allowed to actively pursue his ministry.

He was spiritually advancing toward union with Christ as a Trinitarian. In 1922, he wrote, "Our obedience to God's will must be total, without reserve, and constant." Guided by his Order, he vowed "never to refuse God our Lord, but to follow his holy inspiration in everything with generosity and joy." He died in Belmonte, Spain, mourned by his fellow religious and all who knew him.

Pope John Paul II beatified Dominic Iturrate Zubero on October 30, 1983, declaring:

> The faithful fulfillment of God's Will is an aim which in him reached very lofty heights, especially during the last years of his life. As a Trinitarian religious, he strove to live according to two central principles of the spirituality of his Order: the mystery of the Holy Trinity and the work of the Redemption, which lead to a life of intense charity.

$\mathcal{E}$

✠

Edmund Stanislaw Bojanowski
(November 14, 1814 – August 17, 1871)
Founder of the Congregation of the Handmaids
of the Holy and Immaculate Virgin

Edmund Stanislaw Bojanowski was born in the village of Grabonog to a patriotic and devout family, studying at the University of Breslau and noted for his literary skills. Edmund translated Serbian songs into Polish and composed his own poetry.

From an early age, he had a deep concern for the rural populations in Poland, especially abandoned children. To provide them with hope, safety, and education, Edmund founded a home for peasant girls aged 14-30. It was not his intention to start a religious congregation, but the spread of new homes, and the overwhelming need for such care, convinced Edmund to establish a religious community in 1850, the Little Servant Sisters of the Immaculate Conception. In 1858, the Archbishop of Poznan approved the rule for the congregation.

The homes for the new congregation multiplied swiftly across Poland; by the time of Edmund's death, there were twenty-two houses and nearly a hundred sisters. Owing to the difficult political realities of the time (Poland was actually partitioned into three territories belonging to Austria, Prussia, and Russia), the congregation was subdivided. Four congregations survive today, all of which trace themselves back to the initial labors of Edmund, including the Poor Servants of the Mother of God and the Sisters Servants of Mary Immaculate.

Pope John Paul II beatified Edmund Stanislaw Bojanowski on June 13, 1999, in Warsaw during a pastoral visit to Poland, declaring:

> The apostolate of mercy also filled the life of Blessed Edmund Bojanowski. Despite delicate health, this landowner from Wielkopolska, endowed with many talents and a particular depth of religious life by God, undertook and inspired a vast activity on behalf of the rural population, with perseverance, prudence and generosity of heart. Guided by a discernment that was very

sensitive to people's needs, he launched numerous educational, charitable, cultural, and religious works aimed at the material and moral support of the rural family.

He remained in the lay state and founded the Congregation of the Handmaids of the Holy and Immaculate Virgin, which is well-known in Poland. He was inspired in every initiative by the desire that everyone should have a share in the Redemption.

He is remembered as a good man with a big heart, who for love of God and neighbour was able to bring different sectors together, effectively rallying them around a common good. In his many-faceted activity, he anticipated much of what the Second Vatican Council said about the apostolate of the laity. His was an exceptional example of generous and industrious work for man, the homeland, and the Church. The work of Blessed Edmund Bojanowski is continued by the Handmaids, whom I warmly greet and thank for their silent service, filled with the spirit of sacrifice on behalf of their neighbour and the Church.

✠

Edmund Ignatius Rice (June 1, 1762 – August 29, 1844)
Established "Catholic Model School"

The founder of the Congregation of the Brothers of the Christian Schools, Edmund Ignatius Rice was a pioneer in Catholic education and a holy, fearless defender of the Faith as well.

He was born in Westcourt, Ireland, the fourth of seven sons in a farming family. At age seventeen, he began working at his uncle's import-export business in Waterford, which he later inherited. He was married at twenty-five but lost his wife two years later and was left with a sickly infant daughter.

A devout man, Edmund attended Mass and meditated in this time of suffering, also dedicating himself to charitable works. He was living in troubled times: Ireland faced economic and political storms that had a significant impact on the young and the aged. While Edmund saw all of this, he desired a religious vocation in the contemplative life.

The bishop of Waterford put an end to that attraction when he pointed to the ragged youths in the streets and asked Edmund if he planned to abandon them. Encouraged by Pope Pius VII (r. 1800-1823) and Bishop Hussey, Edmund sold his business, arranged for his daughter's care, and opened his first school in 1802. He had three other schools in operation by 1806 and, in 1808, he took the name Ignatius as a religious with companions in a pontifical institute.

He established the "Catholic Model School" and saw the founding of eleven communities in Ireland, eleven in England, and one in Australia, with requests from the United States and Canada. Edmund Ignatius resigned as Superior General in 1838 and died at Mt. Sion, the site of his first school.

Pope John Paul II beatified Edmund Ignatius Rice on October 6, 1996, declaring:

> The Spirit eventually led him to the total consecration of himself and his companions in the religious life. Today his spiritual sons, the Christian Brothers and the Presentation Brothers, continue his mission.

⊹

Edoardo Giuseppe Rosaz (February 15, 1830 – May 3, 1903)
Founder of the Sisters of the Third Order of St. Francis of Susa

Edoardo Joseph Rosaz was born in Susa, near Turin, to devout parents; he entered the seminary and was ordained during a turbulent era in Italy. Edoardo served in various priestly ministries in the region, winning many to the Church. His holiness and zeal were recognized as he was consecrated the bishop of Susa.

Edoardo immediately started a series of renewal programs, instituting charitable programs and focusing on the need for educational facilities to train the young people of the region. The Sisters of the Third Order of St. Francis of Susa were founded by Edoardo to operate schools and orphanages as part of the renaissance. Recognizing the area's needs, the sisters started hospices and geriatric residences as well. In time they expanded their charitable works to Turin, then to Switzerland. When Edoardo died in Susa, he was mourned by the members of the congregation and by the faithful of the diocese.

Pope John Paul II beatified Edoardo Giuseppe Rosaz in Susa on July 14, 1991, and during the ceremony Edward was described as a model of episcopal charity, a man who radiated the redeeming love of Christ for all souls.

☩

Edward Maria Joannes Poppe
(December 18, 1840 – June 10, 1924)
Serving the People of "Poor Flanders"

A spiritual director and guide, Edward Maria Joannes Poppe honored the "Little Way" of St. Thérèse of Lisieux.

He was born in Moerzeke (Temse), Belgium, the son of a family of local bakers, and entered the seminary in May 1909. There, his brilliance was immediately recognized, as well as his aspirations to serve the people of "poor Flanders."

Edward was ordained to the priesthood and assigned to St. Colette's Parish in Ghent, where he instituted programs for the children of the area, especially the poor and the terminally ill. He developed catechetical and Eucharistic associations and raised both the morale and faith of the people. Worn out by unending labor, he was made rector of a religious community in rural Moerzeke; he served in that capacity from 1918-1922, recuperating and beginning to write. Eventually, he produced some 284 articles and many letters about the problems of Flanders at the time. On a pilgrimage to the tomb of the Little Flower, St. Thérèse of Lisieux, he recognized the beauty of that saint's "Little Way."

Edward was revitalized, and returned to his ministry with zeal. He mobilized local educators for a campaign to re-evangelize the region, using the motto "First yourself, then others." He promoted the local priest associations and aided renewal of the liturgy. In October 1922, he was sent to Leopoldsberg as the spiritual director for clerics fulfilling military service. He died there, while contemplating the Sacred Heart of Jesus.

Pope John Paul II beatified Edward Maria Joannes Poppe on June 13, 1999, announcing:

> Today he becomes a model for priests, especially those of his country, Belgium. He invites them to conform their lives to Christ, the Shepherd, in order to be like him, "priests on fire" with love for God and their brethren.

⽕

Elias del Socorro Nieves
(September 21, 1882 – March 10, 1928)
Persevering Through Persecution

An Augustinian Martyr of Mexico, Elias del Socorro was born on the island of San Pedro, Yuriria, Guanajuato, Mexico, on September 21, 1882. Circumstances — among them, a bout of tuberculosis and the death of his father — delayed his vocation, so it was 1904 before Elias could be admitted to the Augustinian college at Yuriria. He took final vows in 1911, putting aside his baptismal name, Mateo Elias, to become Elias del Socorro.

Just as Elias had endured trials and delays in order to realize his eternal vocation, he would demonstrate the same rigorous character as a priest and opponent of the anti-Catholic government of Mexico during the revolution.

He was ordained in 1916 and appointed parochial vicar of La Cañada de Caracheo, where he won the respect and affection of the local Mexicans. When the Mexican authorities restricted religious services and the activities of priests, Elias refused to allow his care of the faithful to be disrupted. He moved to the hills of La Gavia, making them the base of his clandestine ministry.

Elias and two ranchers were arrested because of this defiance. On the way to Cartazar, the local capital, the ranchers were murdered. When the leader of the squad taunted Elias with his coming death, referring to the Mass, the martyr exclaimed "... to die for the Faith is a sacrifice pleasing to God." His last words on March 10, 1928, were "Long live Christ the King."

Pope John Paul II beatified Elias del Socorro Nieves on Sunday, October 12, 1997, declaring:

> His total trust in God and Our Lady of Christians, to whom he was deeply devoted, characterized his whole life and priestly ministry, which he exercised with self-denial and a spirit of service, without letting himself be overcome by obstacles, sacrifices, or dangers. This faithful Augustinian religious knew how to transmit hope in Christ and Divine Providence.

✠

Elizabeth Canori Mora
(November 21, 1774 – February 5, 1825)
Brought Her Spouse Back to the Faith

A Trinitarian Tertiary and mystic, Elizabeth Canori Mora was born in Rome to a wealthy couple, Tommaso and Teresa Primali Canori, and studied with the Augustinian Sisters at Cascia. In 1796, she was wed to Cristofora Mora, a young lawyer of Rome. He proved unfaithful and dissolute, and in no time reduced Elizabeth to poverty. She bore him four children, two of whom died in infancy, but she raised her daughters, Marianna and Luciana, by earning a meager living with her own skills.

In 1801, Elizabeth was stricken with a mysterious illness and miraculously cured. She also had a mystical experience that enabled her to counsel others and to take part in charitable works. Her home became a haven for the needy and the troubled. In 1807, Elizabeth became a member of the Trinitarian Third Order, and her fame spread throughout Rome, Albano, and Marino. She predicted that Cristoforo would eventually repent and become a devout Catholic.

Elizabeth died in Rome, while being cared for by her daughters. She was buried in the Trinitarian church of San Carlino alle Quattro Fontane. Following her death, her husband gave up his dissolute lifestyle, entered the Triniarian Third Order, then became a Conventual Franciscan priest.

Pope John Paul II beatified Elizabeth Canori Mora on April 24, 1994, declaring:

> . . . An ardent faith and an exceptional mystical experience sustained her during the many difficulties she encountered, both in her married life and in bringing up her children. At every moment, her strength was in prayer. She offered her suffering for the conversion of her husband, Christopher, who after her death became a Conventual Franciscan, dying a holy death in the Lord . . . Elizabeth lived her vocation as wife and mother, as a tertiary in the Trinitarian Third Order, aware that it was her duty to show absolute fidelity to God in her own state of life and always to respect the Commandments. Thus her witness is an invaluable example for Christian spouses. As I recall the new Blessed, I am thinking in particular of the Trinitarian Order and of all those whose life is inspired by the luminous example of this faithful Gospel witness.

✠

Elizabeth of the Trinity Catez
(July 18, 1880 – November 9, 1906)
Great Mystical Writer

Elizabeth of the Trinity was born in Camp d'Avor, Bourges, France, and by all accounts was a rather willful child — even called "a little devil" by relatives — until her father died when she was seven. His death made her aware of the spiritual aspects of human existence. She also made her First Communion in April 1891, experiencing a profound spiritual effect as a result of the sacrament. She became a spouse of Christ at the age of fourteen.

Raised with her sister, Margaret, by their mother, Elizabeth was given every advantage as a child. She displayed unique musical talents and studied at the Dijon Conservatory, but she did not develop these talents further, making such gifts a sacrifice to God. In turn, she received the grace of a vocation and mystical consolations. Elizabeth was "dwelt in" by the Holy Trinity; thus, even in the face of her mother's vehement opposition, Elizabeth did not falter in her determination to experience the contemplative life

She entered the Carmel of Dijon on August 2, 1901, at the age of twenty-one, receiving the name Elizabeth of the Trinity. (She also called herself *Laudem Gloriae*, "the praise of glory.") She received the habit on December 8, 1902, little knowing she was destined to have only four more years on earth.

She possessed a rare awareness of the presence of God and the need to unify one's personality in order to offer God praise and service. God dwelt in her in a unique mystical union, and her writings are considered spiritual treasures, attesting to the Divine Indwelling in the soul through sanctifying grace.

On July 1, 1903, Elizabeth displayed the first symptoms of Addison's disease, a rare illness of the adrenal glands. She worsened and collapsed three years later, surrendering herself to her coming death. Spiritual pain was added to her severe physical suffering, but Elizabeth did not deny her commitment, announcing: "In the evening of life, nothing remains but love." She died in her beloved Carmel, declaring: "I go to the light, to love, to life."

Pope John Paul II beatified Elizabeth of the Trinity Catez on November 25, 1984, declaring that this Blessed:

> . . . gives witness to a openness to the Word of God . . . truly nourishing with it her prayer and reflection, to the point of finding therein all her rea-

sons for living and of consecrating herself to the praise of the glory of this Word.

✠

Elizabeth Hesselblad (June 4, 1870 – April 24, 1957)
Returned the Brigittines to Sweden

Elizabeth Hesselblad was born in Fáglavik, Sweden, the fifth of thirteen children in a prosperous family. Raised in the Lutheran faith, she had social and educational advantages until her father went bankrupt. Then, at the age of sixteen, she became a housemaid in local residences. She traveled to the United States in 1888 and worked as a nurse in Roosevelt Hospital in New York. There, she came into contact with Catholics, arranging for priests to come to the bedside of the dying.

In 1900, during a trip to Brussels, Elizabeth attended a massive Corpus Christi procession. When the Blessed Sacrament was carried in front of her, she was forced to kneel in recognition of the Presence and rose from her knees as a Catholic. Elizabeth studied the Faith and, on August 15, 1901, in Washington, D.C., she was baptized conditionally in the Church.

On March 25, 1904, Elizabeth visited the house of St. Bridget of Sweden in Rome, where she recovered from an illness previously diagnosed as terminal. She became a Brigittine nun in 1906 and made plans to return the Brigittine convent to Sweden, where it had been banned centuries before. Elizabeth founded the Order in Sweden in 1923. During World War II, she was able to aid refugees and Jews before she died.

Pope John Paul II beatified Elizabeth Hesselblad on April 9, 2000, announcing:

> The promise of Jesus is wonderfully fulfilled also in the life of Mary Elizabeth Hesselblad. Like her fellow countrywoman, St. Bridget, she too acquired a deep understanding of the wisdom of the Cross through prayer and in the events of her on life. Her early experience of poverty, her contact with the sick who impressed her by their serenity and trust in God's help, and her perseverance despite many obstacles in founding the Order of the Most Holy Saviour of St. Bridget, taught her that the cross is at the center of human life and is the ultimate revelation of our heavenly Father's love.

✠

Elizabeth Rienzi (November 19, 1786 – August 14, 1859)
Foundress of the Sisters of Our Lady of Sorrows

Elizabeth Rienzi served the faithful in the difficult time of Napoleon.

Called Elisabetta at baptism, she was born in Saludecio, near Rimini, Italy. Her parents, John Baptist and Victoria Rienzi, were wealthy and socially prominent, and they raised her in a truly devout home. Elisabetta desired a religious vocation and entered the Augustinian convent at Petrarubbia in 1807, when she turned twenty-one. She was not destined to serve as an Augustinian, however, because the convent was suppressed by Napoleonic proclamations.

Elizabeth returned home and performed charitable works until 1824, and in April of that year she went to Coriano, a town near Rimini, where she became an instructress in a girl's school. She hoped that Magdalen of Canossa would take over the school, and she corresponded with the future saint, offering her the facility. Magdalen, however, advised Elizabeth to assume the responsibility personally, especially in view of the precarious political situations in the region.

So Elizabeth gathered companions to undertake this ministry, studying the religious constitutions of the Canossan and Venerian Congregations. In 1839, she founded the Sisters of Our Lady of Sorrows, a teaching congregation active in Italy, the United States, Bangladesh, Brazil, and Mexico. She died in 1859 and was declared Venerable in 1988.

Pope John Paul II beatified Elizabeth Rienzi on June 19, 1989, calling the faithful to reflect on her ministry of charity that reflects "on the life of the Church, considered in her mysterious and unexpected development in time and among mankind."

✠

Elizabeth Vendramini (April 9, 1790 – April 2, 1860)
Foundress of the Franciscan Tertiary Sisters of St. Elizabeth

Elizabeth Vendramini was born in Bassano del Grappa, Italy, in an era when political and social forces were competing for power across Europe. Sent to the Augustinian convent for her education, she was trained by the nuns until she reached fifteen. She was then considered eligible for marriage but refused such plans, because she had received the grace of religious vocation.

In 1820, Elizabeth joined the staff of an orphanage for girls. The Capuchin Franciscans operated the institution, and she was trained in the spirit of the Order. She became a Third Order Franciscan and practiced a life of religious consecration.

After a move to Padua in 1827, Elizabeth continued to work with children and realized the need for a religious congregation to take up this ministry. So, in 1829, she and two companions started a small house that offered free education for needy children. In the next year, she was aided by the bishop of Padua in forming the Franciscan Tertiary Sisters of St. Elizabeth, a congregation that followed the rule of the Third Order Regular of St. Francis. The constitutions of the congregation were completed in 1830.

Under Elizabeth's guidance, her sisters added the apostolate of caring for the elderly and other charitable labors to their original education ministry. Prayerful, trusting always in the Blessed Trinity, she served as Superior for more than three decades before her death in Padua.

Pope John Paul II beatified Elizabeth Vendramini on November 4, 1990, declaring:

> Today from heaven, Elizabeth exhorts all those who want to give effective spiritual and physical aid to their brothers and sisters to draw their strength from faith in God and the imitation of Christ. Blessed Elizabeth teaches us that wherever faith is strong and sure, our charitable outreach to our neighbor will be more daring. Wherever our sense of Christ is more acute, our sense of the needs of our brothers and sisters will be more correct and on target.

⚜

Emilie Tavernier Gamelin
(February 19, 1800 – September 23, 1851)
Servant of the Poor

Emilie Tavernier Gamelin was born in Montreal, Canada, and grew into an unusually sensitive child who would set a place at mealtimes for the hungry.

In 1823, she married Jean-Baptiste Gamelin, and the couple had three children. Sadly, none of them survived long, and her husband also died young. Suddenly, Emilie had to make her own way in the world.

Having endured terrible sorrow, she decided to care for others who were suffering and took a private vow to serve the poor. Out of this came her House of Providence, in 1830, a haven for orphans, unemployed immigrants, the disabled, and the elderly. In March 1843, aided by Bishop Ignace Bourget, she founded the Daughters of Charity. This congregation eventually became the Congregation of the Religious of Providence of Montreal, or the Sisters of Providence.

The ministry adopted by these gallant women served Montreal and the needs of Canadians, led by Elizabeth, who was a model of courage and generosity of self. She died during a cholera epidemic while working to alleviate the suffering of those stricken by the disease.

Pope John Paul II beatified Emilie Tavernier Gamelin on October 7, 2001, stating:

> She had a heart open to every kind of trouble, and she was especially the servant of the poor and the little ones, whom she wished to treat like kings.

✠

Emilie van der Linden d' Hooghvorst
(October 11, 1818 – February 22, 1878)

Foundress of the Congregation of St. Mary Reparatrix

Emilie was born in Wegimont, Liège, Belgium, to a noble family, and her father served as the Belgian ambassador to the Vatican. She developed a lasting devotion to the Blessed Sacrament at a young age; she knew enough about events in the world to understand the need for atonement and reparation. She also had a special dedication to Sacred Hearts of Jesus and Mary.

In 1837, she married Baron Victor van der Linden d' Hooghvorst, and they had four children before the baron was stricken with a severe illness. Emilie cared for him tenderly until his death in 1847. When the baron died, Emilie knew that she had been chosen by God to fulfill his will in a deeper way, and so she consecrated herself to Christ and set about gathering companions to begin an apostolate of service and reparation.

In 1857, she founded the Congregation of St. Mary Reparatrix and took the religious name of Mary of Jesus. (Her two daughters also entered the congregation, but died young.) This congregation was dedicated to reparation and to conducting retreats.

In 1859, Emilie led her sisters to Madras, India, where she founded a mission. She established houses in other Indian cities, then in Mauritius and La Réunion. The congregation expanded to France, England, Ireland, Italy, and Spain. Her sisters arrived in the United States in 1908.

Emilie's last years were difficult and troubled, and she suffered great spiritual and emotional trials. She died in Florence, Italy, in the company of her son, Adrien.

Pope John Paul II beatified Emilie van der Linden d'Hooghvorst on October 12, 1997, declaring:

> Widowed and motivated by the desire to participate in the paschal mystery, Mother Mary of Jesus founded the Society of Mary Reparatrix. By her life of prayer she reminds us that in Eucharistic adoration, where we draw from the source of life that is Christ, we find the strength for our daily mission.

✠

Emmanuel Domingo y Sol
(April 1, 1836 – January 25, 1909)
Founder of the Pontifical Spanish College

An evangelist dedicated to the care of the young, Emmanuel Domingo y Sol was born at Tortosa, Tarragona, Spain, the oldest of eleven children in his family. Educated in the local school, then by a tutor, Emmanuel received the grace of a priestly vocation and entered the seminary in October 1851. He was ordained a priest in July 1860, and started his priestly ministry by giving missions in regional parishes. He then served as a priest in Aldea.

In 1862, his bishop, recognizing Emmanuel's intellectual and spiritual qualities, sent him to the University of Valencia. There, he earned a degree in theology, using his education as a lecturer at the Tortosa seminary. At the same time, he catechized the young, giving missions to workers and starting *El Congregante*, a publication designed to foster ideals among the youths of the diocese. He also built a theater complex and a sports arena to offer Christian recreational facilities for the young. Here, Emmanuel excelled in winning the trust of the youth of his era.

He was also a devoted friend of another holy man of that era, Henry de Ossó y Cervelló. Emmanuel assisted the future saint at his first Mass in 1867 and maintained a close friendship throughout their lives. He was at Henry's bedside when he died.

In 1881, Emmanuel started the Congregation of Diocesan Workers, a unique group of dedicated individuals to serve in the operation of the local seminary. Recognizing as well the need for a Spanish institution of learning in the Eternal City, he founded the Pontifical Spanish College in Rome in

1882. This institution allowed young Spanish seminarians to complete their studies near the Vatican.

By 1909, Emmanuel was in high regard — and high demand — which took an unending toll on his time and energies. After his death in Tortosa, his Cause was opened in July 1946.

Pope John Paul II beatified Emmanuel Domingo y Sol on March 29, 1987, praising his generosity and priestly ministries, and the fact that this Blessed used all of his talents and intellect in the ministry of safeguarding the future of the Church in the care of the young.

✛

England, Scotland and Wales, 84 Martyrs of — see Martyrs of England, Scotland and Wales

✛

Enrico Rebuschini (April 28, 1860 – May 10, 1938)
"Mystic of the Streets"

Enrico Rebuschini was born in Gravedona, on Lake Como, in Italy, the son of a prominent, wealthy family of the region. He desired a religious vocation at an early age, but his parents opposed such a vocation. In accordance with his parents' wishes, he attended Pavia University in order to prepare himself for the secular career his father expected him to pursue. He did not remain there, however, because he was horrified by the wanton secular environment and disregard for the Faith on the university campus.

Military service soon called him; Enrico fulfilled his obligations, then went to work in a silk plant owned by his brother-in-law. As time went on, the family soon discovered that Enrico was favored by God in unique ways. He was so good, so holy and pure, that his relatives feared that he could not endure the coarse ways of their society and labor sites. In the end, he was sent to the Pontifical Gregorian University, where his family hoped he would thrive.

Unfortunately, he had to return home because of illness and spent a long period in recuperation. But as his body mended, he received mystical gifts. He entered the Camillians (Servants of the Sick) in Verona, and on April 14, 1889, was ordained to the priesthood by the future Pope St. Pius X (r. 1903-1914).

He served in various charitable capacities for the Camillians and eventually was assigned to Cremona, where he labored from 1903 to 1937 as Superior. His gifts of contemplation were evident to others, who remarked on his holiness and recollection. Even when involved in active service, Enrico displayed his mystical gifts, reflecting Christ in action.

His devotion to the service of the sick was a hallmark of his priestly vocation. The last Mass that Enrico celebrated upon the earth was for the intentions of the sick. He fell ill with bronchial pneumonia, and at his death, the people of Cremona mourned the passing of their mystic patron.

Pope John Paul II beatified Enrico Rebuschini on May 4, 1997, declaring:

> Throughout his life Blessed Enrico Rebuschini walked resolutely towards that "perfection of charity" . . . his firm resolution . . . involved him in a demanding ascetic and mystical journey marked by an intense life of prayer, extraordinary love for the Eucharist, and constant devotion to the sick and suffering.

✠

Eugene Bassilikov — see Vincent Eugene Bossilkov

✠

Eugénie Joubert (February 11, 1876 – July 2, 1904)
Devoted to the Hearts of Children

Eugénie Joubert was born in Isingeaux, France, and received training in the Faith and in charity by her mother. Realizing a religious vocation, Eugénie entered the Congregation of the Holy Family of the Sacred Heart in 1895. This religious community, founded by Marie Ignace Melin, served as catechists for the poor and as devotees to the Sacred Heart of Jesus.

Professed, Eugénie was assigned to the congregation's missions at Saint-Denis and at Aubervilles. When her health failed, she was assigned to St. Giles Parish in Liège, Belgium. For two years, Eugénie suffered a severe illness, responding with good-natured calm and a distinct sense of God's presence. Eugénie also practiced the "Little Way" of total reliance upon God, observing obedience and humility in all things. She had a brief trip to Rome before she died in Liège, at the age of twenty-eight. Her silent suffering was at an end.

Pope John Paul II beatified Eugénie Joubert on November 20, 1994, announcing:

Sr. Eugénie Joubert, a religious of the Congregation of the Holy Family of the Sacred Heart, is presented to us as a living example of what God works in a human heart. With her too, a Christian upbringing was decisive for all her subsequent activities. Two years before she died, at the end of a brief life devoted in particular to the catechesis of small children, she expressed this heartfelt cry: "I want to be just like a tiny child carried in her mother's arms." Christ's kingdom can begin in the heart of a child. This is what Sr. Eugénie realized and for this reason she took care in preparing the little ones for their First Confession and First Communion. Each, from the earliest years, is called to witness to the truth. Ceaselessly the Church makes the Lord's words resound: "Let the children come to me!" (Mt 19:14). She was to continue to do so, for she knew that no human child, however poor or humble he might be, is indifferent to God. Each is called to enter the kingdom and the blessed go before us to show us the way.

✠

Eugenia Picco (November 1867 – September 7, 1921)
Serving the Poor During World War I

Eugenia Picco was born in Crescenzago, Italy, to parents dedicated to secular pursuits. Her father was the famous musician, Giuseppe Picco. He disappeared from the lives of Eugenia and her mother, who thereafter devoted herself to social events, opposing any sort of religious aspirations of her daughter.

Eugenia, however, went to Parma to enter the novitiate of the Congregation of the Little Daughters of the Sacred Hearts of Jesus and Mary, founded by Don Chiappi. She took her vows of solemn profession as a religious, becoming novice mistress, then Superior General. All the while, she was the victim of a degenerative bone disease and eventually needed to have her right leg amputated in 1919. Even through great physical pain, however, she directed the work of her congregation, serving the poor and neglected during the terrible era of World War I.

Her death in Parma brought about a great show of mourning from people of all walks of life who had been aided by her vision and her personal courage.

Pope John Paul II beatified Eugenia Picco on October 7, 2001, announcing:

In her life she made every effort to listen to the word of the Lord . . . Even in the face of suffering, with the inevitable moments of difficulty and bewilderment that it entails, Blessed Eugenia Picco knew how to transform the experience of suffering into an occasion of purification and inner growth.

✠

Eugenia Ravasco (January 4, 1845 – December 30, 1900)
Foundress and Educator

Eugenia was born in Milan, Italy, the third of six children to Francesco Matteo and Carolina Mozzoni Frosconi. When she was only three years old, her mother died, and her father was forced to move the family to Genoa to be closer to his other relatives. Eugenia, however, was left behind in Milan in the care of her Aunt Marietta Anselmi; her aunt became like a mother to her and was a key figure in raising Eugenia in the Faith.

For a brief time, the family was reunited in 1852, but three years later, her father also died. She then lived with her uncle Luigi Ravasco and her aunt Elisa and their ten children. Like her Aunt Marietta, her uncle provided Christian upbringing to his nephews and nieces, helping to shape Eugenia in the process. Eugenia developed swiftly in the spiritual life and was imbued especially with a love of the poor and the suffering, as well as an abiding devotion to the Eucharist and the Sacred Hearts of Jesus and Mary.

With the death of her uncle in December 1862, Eugenia assumed the responsibility of caring for her family; she was helped in the task by her aunt. Her aunt hoped she would marry, but Eugenia discerned a vocation to the religious life. She began teaching the catechism to poor young girls in the city and attracted other women to assist her. From this beginning, in December 1868, she founded the religious congregation of the Sisters of the Sacred Hearts of Jesus and Mary, with the purpose of educating poor young girls.

In 1878, Mother Eugenia opened a school for girls, with the particular aim of preparing women to offer Christian instruction in the city. She faced severe opposition from local secularists, Freemasons, and the anti-Catholic press. Despite this, and battling poor health, she journeyed throughout Italy and went to France and Switzerland to establish new communities. The congregation received formal approval in 1882. She and her sisters made their final profession in 1884.

Mother Eugenia remained the guiding force for the congregation until her death. Today, the congregation serves in schools, parishes, and missions in

Europe, Central and South America, Africa, and the Philippines. She was beatified by Pope John Paul II on April 27, 2003.

✛

Eusebia Palomino Yenes
(December 15, 1899 – February 10, 1935)
Victim Soul for Spain

Eusebia was born in Cantalpino, Spain, to Agustin Palomino and Juana Yenes, one of four children. Though her father worked as a seasonal farmhand, the family was reduced to poverty during winter months when there was no work, and her father regularly had to beg for food in the streets.

In the face of such severe financial hardship for the family, Eusebia went to work at the age of twelve. She and her older sister worked as nannies, but she was already displaying unusual maturity for one her age and developing quickly in the spiritual life. Her remarkable maturity was noted by the Daughters of Mary, Help of Christians; they asked if she would be willing to volunteer her time to help them run their local community. She agreed readily and assisted in a variety of errands. She soon became a valued spiritual guide to the students in the school.

Eusebia longed to become a member of the community; at last, she reluctantly confided her hope to a visiting superior, who — despite her lack of education and resources — wasted little time in accepting her into the congregation. She entered the novitiate in August 1922 and made her profession two years later. Sent to Spain, she was at first greeted harshly by the students but set to work in the convent with great zeal; in short order, she both won over the students and gained a reputation for wisdom and holiness among all who came in contact with her.

In August 1932, however, her health deteriorated, and she offered herself as a victim soul on behalf of Spain, then undergoing severe political and social turmoil. Her last days were spent in agony, but she had a prayer always on her lips and greeted her suffering with joy.

She was beatified by Pope John Paul II on April 25, 2004. He said of her:

> The Lord says to Peter in a decisive and penetrating way: "Follow me." Sr. Eusebia Palomino, of the Daughters of Mary, Help of Christians, also heard God's call one day and answered by way of an intense spirituality and a profound humility in daily life. As a good Salesian, she was enlivened by love for the Eucharist and for the Blessed Virgin. Loving and serving

were important for her; the rest did not matter, faithful to the Salesian maxim: *"da mihi animas, caetera tolle."*

With the radicalness and constancy of her choices, Sr Eusebia Palomino Yenes traced out an attractive and demanding path of holiness for us all, especially for the young people of our time.

✠

Euthymia Uffing
(April 8, 1914 – September 9, 1953)
Religious and Nurse

Euthymia Uffing was born in Halverde, Germany, one of eleven children in a poor family. As a child, she had rickets and poor health. At age fourteen, however, she received the grace of a religious vocation. Shortly after her father's death in 1932, she entered the Congregation of the Sisters of Charity on July 23, 1934. Two years later, she made her first vows.

Germany was in a period of chaos and peril at the time, as the Nazis were beginning their rise. Euthymia was still able to receive a nursing degree at St. Vincent's Hospital in Dinslaken and made her final religious vows on September 15, 1940. She cared for victims of World War II, aiding prisoners of war and foreign workers by hiding food in the garbage cans of the prison hospital. At the war's end, Euthymia operated the laundry room in St. Raphael's Clinic, Munster. Although suffering from cancer, she did not complain or seek consolation, even on her deathbed in the clinic.

Pope John Paul II beatified Euthymia Uffing on October 7, 2001, declaring:

> Blessed Euthymia dedicated herself tirelessly to the care of the sick, particularly prisoners of war and of foreign workers. For this reason she was nicknamed "Mamma Euthymia."

$$\mathscr{F}$$

✠

Faustino Míguez (March 24, 1831 – March 8, 1925)
"Seeker of Souls"

Faustino Miguez was born in Xamirás, a village of Rio Calanova, Orense, Spain, the fourth child of a devout family. He studied Latin and the humanities in Orense and received the grace of a religious vocation, being inspired by the spirit of St. Joseph Calasanz and drawn to the Scalopians. He entered St. Ferdinand's novitiate in Madrid in 1850, starting a vocation that would span half a century in the educational ministry.

Ordained a priest, Faustino served the Scalopian institutions in San Fernando, Guanboacoa, Getafe, Monforte de Lemas, Celanova, El Escurial and Sanlúcar de Barrameda. His special concern for the young and remarkable kindness became evident in all of his ministerial assignments. Besides serving as confessor and medical researcher, he was tireless in his efforts to open new scientific and cultural horizons for his students. Faustino opened the Míguez Laboratory in Getafe, one of his great legacies today.

While stationed in Sanlúcar de Barrameda, Faustino became aware of the harsh reality of a lack of educational opportunities for women. To minister to such women, he founded the Calasanctian Institute of the Daughters of the Divine Shepherdess on January 2, 1885. This congregation was devoted to the Blessed Virgin and dedicated to aiding the poor, especially young women. Before he died, Faustino saw the congregation spread to Andalucia, Castile, Galicia, then to Argentina and Chile in South America.

He was not allowed to remain in Sanlúcar de Barrameda to aid in the formation of the Daughters of the Divine Shepherdess. Assigned once more to Getafe, Faustino obeyed his superiors and resumed his medical studies. He died at age ninety-four in Getafe.

Pope John Paul II beatified Faustino on October 25, 1998, declaring:

By renouncing his own ambitions, the new Blessed followed Jesus the Teacher and dedicated his life to teaching children and young people in the style of St. Joseph Calasanz. As an educator, his goal was the formation of the whole person. As a priest, he continually sought the holiness of souls.

As a scientist, he was able to alleviate sickness by freeing humanity from physical suffering.

✠

Felipe de Jesus Munarriz and 50 Companions — see Martyrs of Barbastro

✠

Felipe Ripoll Morata (September 14, 1878 – 1939)
Political Martyr

Felipe Ripoll Morata was born in Teruel, Spain. Raised devoutly, he entered the seminary and was ordained for his diocese. He served as a professor, then as rector of the local seminary. Anselm Polanco Fontecha, bishop of Teruel in 1935, appointed Felipe as the diocesan vicar general.

When the revolutionary military forces took Teruel in 1938, he stood firm with Bishop Anselm against the godless doctrines of the Republican Army. He was arrested and spent more than a year in prison with Anselm. In 1939, Felipe and Anselm were used as human shields for the retreating revolutionaries. They were then taken to a gorge near Gerosa and shot. Their remains are enshrined in the Teruel Cathedral.

Pope John Paul II beatified Felipe on October 1, 1995, declaring that both Felipe and Anselm chose to stay with the faithful in a time of crisis. The Holy Father added:

> The new Blesseds, before the alternative of abandoning the requirements of the Faith, or of dying for it, strengthened by God's grace, put their own destiny in his hands. The martyrs did not defend themselves, not because they thought little of life, but out of their total love of Jesus Christ.

(See also Anselm Polanco Fontecha.)

✠

Ferdinando Maria Bacciliari (May 14, 1821 – July 13, 1893)
"Country Priest"

A founder of a religious congregation and lay associations, Ferdinando Maria Bacciliari was an ardent promoter of devotions.

He was born in Campodosa (Modena), Italy, to a devout family and was educated by the Barnabites and the Jesuits. Ferdinando entered the Jesuit seminary in 1838, but his ill health brought his studies to a temporary halt. After his recovery he re-entered the seminary in Ferrara and, in 1844, was ordained to the priesthood. He started his ministry by preaching missions throughout the archdiocese and also taught Latin and Italian at Finale Emilia Seminary.

In 1848, Ferdinando was sent to the Pontifical University of Bologna, where he studied can and civil law. He was then assigned by the Archbishop of Bologna to administer Galeazza parish, as the people of that region had asked for him personally. Ferdinando would serve as the pastor of the parish for forty-one years. He founded the Confraternity of the Sorrowful Mother, the Servite Third Order, and the Mantellate Servite Congregation of Sisters to aid the parish. The convent opened in 1862. In 1867, Ferdinando lost his voice, but he continued his labors in the region until his death.

Pope John Paul II beatified Ferdinando Maria Bacciliari on October 3, 1999, announcing:

> A poor "country priest," as he liked to describe himself, he cultivated souls with vigorous preaching, in which he expressed his deep inner conviction. He thus became a living icon of the Good Shepherd.

✠

Filippo Rinaldi (1856 – December 5, 1931)
Successor to St. John Bosco

Filippo Rinaldi was born in Lu Monferrato, Italy. When he was only ten years old, met John Bosco at Mirabello, outside of Turin; the boy received the blessings of the saintly founder and a priestly vocation as well. He was ordained a Salesian priest on December 23, 1882, in the cathedral of Ivrea.

John Bosco recognized the extraordinary virtues of Filippo early on and prepared him for his unique role in the Salesian community. Nine months after ordination, he was named director of a community and set about expanding the congregation's ministries in Spain and Portugal. He founded twenty-one houses during this period.

In 1901, Filippo returned to Turin to serve as prefect general of the Salesians; during this time, he earned respect for his ministry as a confessor and spiritual director. In 1922, he became rector major of the Salesians, serving in this capacity until his death in Turin.

Pope John Paul II beatified Filippo Rinaldi on April 29, 1990, declaring that this third successor of St. John Bosco was worthy of the rank of martyr for the faith. The Holy Father said:

Don Rinaldi was an especially tireless promoter of the great Salesian Family in its various groups and worked to help it develop more and more into a worthwhile organized and adaptable force for Christian education of youth and of the popular classes.

╬

Filippo Smaldone (July 27, 1848 – June 4, 1923)
Apostle of Our Lady of Pompeii

Filippo Smaldone served as the father of the deaf, blind, and abandoned of his era, sacrificing himself to educate and protect them.

He was born in Naples, Italy, and studied for the priesthood at Rossano Calabro. Filippo was ordained for the archdiocese of Naples in 1871. He started his ministry by holding evening catechism classes and, during an epidemic, he cared for victims until falling ill himself. Our Lady of Pompeii, for whom Filippo had a special devotion, cured him miraculously.

Interested in the deaf-mutes of Naples at an early age, in March 1885, Filippo went to Lecce, Italy, where he opened an institute for them with Fr. Lorenzo Apicella. Women dedicated to the care of deaf-mutes aided Filippo and formed the Congregation of the Salesian Sisters of the Sacred Heart. He also opened an institute in Bari and took in blind children, orphans, and the abandoned.

Filippo faced many trials throughout his life, but continued his apostolate. He worked as a confessor and as a spiritual director for priests and founded the Eucharistic League of Priest Adorers and Women Adorers. He also served as the Superior of the Missionaries of St. Francis de Sales. He received many honors before dying of a diabetic condition, with fatal cardiac complications, in Lecce.

Pope John Paul II beatified Filippo Smaldone on August 16, 1996, announcing:

"He who loves me will be loved by my Father, and I will love him and manifest myself to him (Jn 14:21)." Filippo Smaldone, the Lecce priest whose life was marked by constant attention to the poor and extraordinary apostolic zeal, also intensely lived and embodied charity to God and neighbor. This great witness to charity realized he had to fulfill his own mission in Southern Italy, and turned specifically to the care and education of the deaf to give them an active role in society. His intense, unwavering priestly spirituality, nourished by prayer, meditation, and even bodily penance, spurred him to provide a social service open to those advanced insights which true pastoral charity can inspire.

✠

Florentino Asensio Barroso
(October 16, 1877 – August 9, 1936)
Bishop and Martyr

Florentino Asensio Barroso was born in Villasexmir, Valladolid, Spain. He studied for the priesthood and was ordained in June 1901, then earned a doctorate at the Pontifical University of Valladolid and began teaching. When his uncle (Cardinal Cos) died, Florentino became a priest in the cathedral, earning a reputation as a preacher and spiritual director for many religious houses in the area. His fame led to his consecration as the bishop of Barbastro on January 26, 1936, where he began programs for the poor.

Florentino had served in this office for a little less than six months when the forces of the Spanish Civil War began their persecutions, and the anti-clerical spirit rose in Barbastro. He was placed under house arrest on July 20, 1936; on August 8, he was placed in solitary confinement, tortured, and mutilated. The bishop was singled out for this harsh treatment because of his holiness and reputation as a leader of the Catholic faith.

On August 9, 1936, he and twelve others were taken by truck to the local cemetery. They were shot, and when the first salvo did not end the saintly bishop's life, he was shot once again in the temple. His remains were dropped into a common grave, and only later identified and placed in the crypt of the cathedral.

Pope John Paul II beatified Florentino on May 4, 1997, declaring:

> At the last moments of his life, after having suffered lacerating humiliations and tortures, in answer to one of his torturers as to whether he knew the destiny that awaited him, he relied serenely and firmly, "I am going to heaven." Thus he proclaimed his staunch faith in Christ, conqueror of death and giver of eternal life.

✠

Florida Cevoli (November 11, 1685 – June 12, 1767)
Dying "Out of Pure Love for God"

A Poor Clare mystic and reformer, Florida Cevoli was an aristocrat of Pisa, Italy, baptized Lucrezia Elena Cevoli. Lucrezia was educated in the convent of the Poor Clares of Pisa, and at eighteen she revealed her desire to enter the cloister. She sought admission to the Poor Clares, the Franciscan Second Order, in Cittá di Castello.

Her family opposed her vocation, however, and the Poor Clares were reluctant to accept someone of her rank, especially in the face of her family's lack of consent. When she did not swerve from her calling, she was finally allowed to enter the novitiate at Cittá di Castello and took the name Florida in religion. Her novice mistress, the future St. Veronica Giuliani, trained Florida to the paths of perfection. Even after taking her vows, she remained in the novitiate to benefit from Veronica's direction. Her assignment in the cloister was to administer the pharmacy.

In 1727, Florida, who was a true contemplative and humble servant of all, was elected abbess. She had served as vicaress when Veronica was Superior and was well prepared for this office. In this capacity, she restored many customs to the cloister and increased the weekly receptions of the Holy Eucharist by the nuns. She also fed the poor who came to the cloister for aid.

Physically, Florida endured pain and fever throughout her religious life. Yet she never indulged herself, and when she died, her confessor said she had expired "out of pure love for God."

Pope John Paul II beatified Florida on May 16, 1993, declaring that her entire life was dedicated to love and service. The Holy Father declared: "Florida was inspired by the Spirit of Truth who leads believers to interiorize the Word of God."

✠

Fra Angelico — see Angelico, Fra

✠

Frances Nisch — see Ulricka Nisch

✠

Francis Coll (May 18, 1812 – April 2, 1875)
Friend of Anthony Claret

Francis Coll was born in Gombeny, in the Catalan Pyrenees of Spain. When Francis was only four, his father died, leaving a widow and ten children in dire straits. Francis' mother raised him devoutly, and he was confirmed in 1818. Four years later, he entered the seminary at Vichy, France, earning his own way by teaching catechism and grammar to local children. One of Francis' classmates was the future St. Anthony Claret.

In 1830, Francis entered the Dominicans at Vichy, but the monastic Orders were suppressed, and he had to study for the priesthood under great stress. He was ordained on March 28, 1836, in his original seminary. Following his ordination, Francis was assigned to the parish of Arles and, in 1839, was sent to Moyá. The area had been devastated by war; the local people were starving. Francis aided them with charitable programs until 1849. Even though he could not reside in a monastery, he also maintained his religious life scrupulously.

In 1846, Francis aided Anthony Claret in forming a new priestly group called the Apostolic Fraternity. He also became the director of the Third Order of Vichy and, in 1850, opened the former Dominican monastery and began preaching throughout the Catalan region. When cholera struck the area four years later, Francis cared for all of the victims. He saw the response to his catechetical and preaching efforts, and in August 1856, started a teaching branch of the Third Order of St. Dominic, calling the congregation La Annunciata. By the time he died, La Annunciata had fifty houses and more than 300 sisters.

In 1872, the Dominicans were able to return to Spain, as part of the Order, under the direction of the master general. It was discovered then that Francis had carefully nurtured all of the Dominican communities and institutions during the suppression, maintaining the Order even under assault.

On December 2, 1869, Francis was struck blind while preaching at Sallent. He endured great pain and suffering until his death, but he bore his last trials with calm and resolve. His remains were enshrined in the motherhouse of the Dominican Sisters of La Annunciata.

Pope John Paul II beatified Francis Coll on April 29, 1979. During the beatification celebrations, Blessed Francis was praised as an apostolic preacher whose popular missions spurred Marian devotions and regenerated the Faith while safeguarding the great Dominican traditions. The spirit of Blessed Francis has endured more than one hundred years.

✠

Francis Fa'a di Bruno
(March 29, 1825 – March 27, 1888)
Leading Mathematician and Astronomer

Called "a prophet of his time," Francis Fa'a di Bruno was born in Alessandria, Italy, the son of the Marquis Louis Fa'a di Bruno and his wife, Caroline. He was the youngest of twelve children.

He was educated in Alessandria and elsewhere in Italy and, at age sixteen, entered the armed forces of Piedmont, reaching the rank of captain. In 1849, Francis was assigned to Paris, where he studied at the Sorbonne — earned his doctorate in mathematics and astronomy — and became a member of the St. Vincent de Paul Society.

As a result of his academic interests, he resigned his commission and studied under the leading mathematicians and astronomy leaders of his age. He returned to Turin, Italy, and became a professor at the university in that city. In honor of his great knowledge and dedication, Francis received degrees of Doctor of Science from the universities of Paris and Turin. He wrote more than forty articles for American and European journals as well as treatises and studies, and his writings are included in the Catalogue of Scientific Papers of the Royal Society in London. He also wrote ascetical studies and sacred melodies, and even invented scientific apparati.

His focus, however, was on charitable works in Turin, and he showed special concern for the safety of women and young girls exposed to the dangers of society. Francis established schools, retirement homes, and other charitable institutions, and in 1868, founded the Society of St. Zita to aid in his ministry. The society began as a place of training for young poor girls, then expanded to include unmarried mothers and others.

Francis accomplished all this as a dedicated layman. He received ordination to the priesthood in Turin only in 1876, having completed his seminary studies while conducting the myriad activities of his apostolates.

He died in Turn in 1888; a century later, Pope John Paul II beatified Francis Fa'a di Bruno on September 25, 1988, calling him "a prophet in the midst of the people of God." The Holy Father praised Francis for knowing how "to find positive responses to the needs of his time" and called him "a giant of faith and charity."

✠

Francis Xavier Seelos
(January 11, 1819 – October 4, 1867)
German-American Missionary

Francis Xavier Seelos served the faithful in America during a troubled time.

He was born in Fussen, Bavaria, Germany, one of twelve children in a devout family, and educated locally. He then attended St. Stephen's Institute in Augsburg, attending the University of Munich in 1839. Four years later, Francis Xavier sailed to New York, where he entered the Redemptorist Congregation of St. James and was ordained to the priesthood on December 22, 1844.

Following his ordination, Francis Xavier was assigned to Pittsburgh, where he served as an assistant to the future St. John Neumann. He assumed religious offices as well, including novice master; he was offered the See of Pittsburgh but declined episcopal honors. Instead, he served in other capacities until 1854, when he was sent to Maryland. While in Maryland, he met with President Abraham Lincoln to ask that Redemptorist seminarians be exempted from service in the Civil War — a request that was granted.

He also traveled to Illinois, Michigan, Missouri, New Jersey, New York, Ohio, Pennsylvania, Rhode Island, and Wisconsin to give missions. He served for a time in a Detroit parish but, in 1866, was assigned to New Orleans. There, while aiding victims of a yellow fever epidemic, he died of the disease.

Pope John Paul II beatified Francis Xavier Seelos on April 9, 2000, announcing:

> Sustained by God's grace and an intense life of prayer, Fr. Seelos left his native Bavaria and committed himself generously and joyfully to the missionary apostolate among immigrant communities of the United States … Today, Blessed Francis Xavier Seelos invites the members of the Church to deepen their union with Christ in the sacraments of Penance and the Eucharist.

✠

Francisca Ana Crier Carbonell
(June 1, 1781 – February 25, 1855)
Foundress At Seventy

Francisca Ana Crier Carbonell was born in Senecelles, Majorca, Balearic Islands Spain, and raised piously. Early in life, she received the grace of a religious vocation, but her family refused permission for her to enter a convent. Francisca accepted the refusal with grace, then suffered the loss of her mother and siblings while she was still young. In 1821, her father passed away as well.

At the suggestion of her spiritual director, Francisca remained in her home, praying, fasting, and caring for the sick and the poor. Her fellow parishioners and others recognized her pious nature, prudence, and wisdom, and soon people began coming to her for advice. Francisca was also reported to be a thaumaturgist, as she cured the sick of her area. Some called her "The Saint of Senecelles."

At age seventy, Francisca used her own home and financial resources to found the Congregation of the Sisters of Charity of St. Vincent de Paul. On December 7, 1851, she and two companions made their vows. These sisters cared for the sick and poor, taught children and adults, and organized school programs. When she died of a stroke during Mass, the entire region was plunged into grief.

Francisca was declared Venerable in 1983, and Pope John Paul II beatified her on October 1, 1989, declaring:

> Throughout her life Francisca-Ana obeyed God's will — a divine will that was sometimes difficult to discern . . . a life full of uncertainty, but a life in which there was no obstacle to serving God in everything . . ."

✠

Francisco and Jacinta Marto — (June 11, 1908 – April 4, 1919; March 11, 1910 – February 20, 1920)

Children of Fatima

Two of the three children who witnessed the apparitions of Our Lady of Fatima, Francisco and Jacinta Marto, were born in Aljustrel, Portugal, the children of Manuel Pedro and Olimpia di Jesus Santos Marto. On May 13, 1917, with a cousin, Lucia de Jesus, the two were reciting the Rosary in the Cova da Iria and saw a light. A second light appeared above a small Holm oak tree (now the site of the Chapel of the Apparition). The children described the figure that appeared to them as a "lady brighter than the sun." The apparition was holding a rosary and told the children to return for five consecutive months, on the thirteenth day of each month.

On the thirteenth of June and July, they witnessed the same apparition. On August 13, the children could not return to the Cova because they were taken away by the mayor of Villa Nova de Ourém and held for a short time. The Lady, however, appeared to the children on August 19, while they were tending their flocks in the area of Dos Valinhos; after that, the apparitions returned on both September and October 13. In October, some 70,000 faithful were with the children during the vision. While no one but the children witnessed the Lady, all witnessed a miracle that occurred on that day: the sun changed colors and spun like a fireball in the sky.

Both Francisco and Jacinta were told by the Lady that they would die very young. They accepted this news with joy. Francisco died first and was buried in the parish cemetery. His remains were transferred to the Basilica on March 13, 1952.

Jacinta died after an operation to remove two ribs. She was under partial anesthesia because she was considered too young for the regular dose, and she did not survive the trauma. Buried at first in the family tomb of Baron Alosiázere in Ourem, her remains were united with those of Francisco on September 12, 1935, then taken to the Basilica on May 1, 1951.

Francisco and Jacinta were declared Venerable on May 13, 1989. Pope John Paul II beatified Francisco and Jacinta on May 13, 2000, announcing:

> According to the divine plan, "a woman clothed with the sun" (Rev. 12:1) came down from heaven to this earth to visit the privileged children of the Father. She speaks to them with a mother's voice and heart: she asks them to offer themselves as victims of reparation, saying that she was ready to lead them safely to God. And behold, they see a light shining from her maternal hands which penetrates them inwardly, so that they feel immersed in God just as — they explain — a person sees himself in a mirror . . .
>
> Father, to you I offer praise, for you have revealed these things to the merest children. Today Jesus' praise takes the solemn form of the beatification of the little shepherds, Francisco and Jacinta. With this rite the Church wishes to put on the candelabrum these two candles which God lit to illumine humanity in its dark and anxious hours. May they shine on the path of this immense multitude of pilgrims and of all who have accompanied us by radio and television.

✝

Francisco Garate (February 3, 1857 – September 9, 1929)
"Brother Courtesy"

Francisco Garate was born in a farming community called Azpeitia, the Basque region of Spain, the second of eleven children, and worked on the family farm. At the age of fourteen, he went to Orduna, where he was employed as a house servant in the Jesuit College of Nuestra Señora de la Antigua. After three years of service there, he asked to be accepted by the Society of Jesus. But the Jesuits had been expelled from Spain by that time, so Francisco entered the novitiate at Poyanne in southern France.

He made his first vows on February 2, 1876. The following year, he was assigned to the College of Santiago Apostolo a La Guardia (Pontevedra). Francisco was named infirmarian there, and he cared for the sick for a decade, serving in the sacristy as well.

In August 1887, Francisco made his final vows and was assigned to Duesto Bilbao soon after, in order to lighten his duties. There, he became a porter, or doorkeeper, at the university. He would remain in this post humbly and devoutly until his death. "Brother Courtesy," as he was called, brought a gentle concern to his day-to-day routines. He was meek and charming, caring for one and all with a quiet joy that was contagious and calming.

Pope John Paul II beatified Francisco Garate on October 6, 1985. During the celebration, this saintly brother was honored as a religious who understood the way of perfection in humble service; one that provided him with gentleness, calm, and recognition of the value of others.

✠

Francisco Palau y Quer
(December 29, 1812 – March 20, 1872)
Founder of School of Virtue

Francisco Palau y Quer was born in Aytona (Lérida), Spain. Trained in the Faith and in the traditions of his people, he also received the grace of a religious vocation. Francisco started his four years of seminary in 1828, at Lérida. He became a Carmelite in Barcelona, being professed on November 15, 1833, and ordained a priest on April 2, 1836.

When the Spanish political situation threatened Catholic religious institutions, Francisco was caught by revolutionary forces and imprisoned for one year. He was then sent to France, serving there in exile from 1840 to 1851. He returned to Spain in 1852 and founded the School of Virtue, an organization for catechetical instruction. Falsely accused of fomenting labor strikes, he was arrested and confined to the island of Ibiza from 1854 until 1860. During this exile, Francisco experienced a mystical union of his soul with Christ.

On his return to Spain, he founded the Missionary Carmelites of St. Teresa and a community of brothers that later became part of the Carmelite Order. Francisco labored to make possible institutions that would carry the Carmelite spirit into a troubled world, responding to God's will and to the needs of men and women facing modern life.

He was a miracle worker and an exorcist of considerable fame in his own age and served as a consultor at Vatican Council I in Rome, inspiring many with his holiness and generosity. When Francisco died in Tarragona, the people of Spain mourned his passing.

Pope John Paul II beatified Francisco Palau y Quer on April 24, 1988, declaring that this Discalced Carmelite "made his priestly life a generous offering to the Church, the flock of Christ." The Holy Father said also:

> However, the most cherished work of Fr. Palau was the foundation of the Carmelite missionaries . . . His spiritual daughters — the Carmelite Missionary Sisters and the Teresian Missionary Carmelites — flesh out and continue in the Church the spirit of that apostle.

✠

Francisco Spinelli (April 14, 1853 – February 6, 1913)
Founder of the Sisters of Perpetual Adoration of the Blessed Sacrament

Francisco Spinelli was born in Milan, Italy, and baptized in the basilica of St. Ambrose. His family moved to Cremona when he was young, and he was raised in Vergo, in the diocese of Bergamo, where the family spent the summer months.

Francisco suffered from a severe spinal problem as a young child but was cured of the condition in 1871, in Vergo. There, he also accompanied his mother on her visits to the poor of the region. An uncle, Fr. Peter Cagliaroli, and a friend, the future Blessed Luigi Palazzolo, also served as mentors for Francisco, who completed his studies and was ordained at age twenty-two.

He was assigned to help his uncle and Luigi until December 1875, when he had a revelation in the St. Mary Major Basilica in Rome: he was being asked to found a religious congregation of women dedicated to adoring Christ in the Eucharist. In 1882, with the future Blessed Gertrude Comensoli, Francisco started the Sisters of Perpetual Adoration of the Blessed Sacrament. He suffered many trials and problems because of this founding but endured, despite pain and illness, until his death in Cremona.

Pope John Paul II beatified Francisco Spinelli on June 21, 1992, in Caravaggio, Italy, declaring:

> The life of the Servant of God, whom today I have been able to number among the choirs of the Church's blessed, assumes a prophetic importance in the holy mystery of the Eucharist . . . Franceso Spinelli, who lived "to love Jesus in the Eucharist and to make him loved." The Church offers him

as a model of an authentic apostle especially to you, the priests whom Providence calls to be stewards of the mysteries of salvation.

✠

Francois de Montmorency Laval
(April 30, 1623 – May 6, 1708)
"A Bishop According to God's Heart"

Francois de Montmorency Laval was a missionary to Quebec and the first bishop of Canada.

He was born in Montigny-sur-Avre, France, the son of Hughes de Laval and Michelle de Péricard. They were members of a distinguished family whose ancestor baptized St. Clovis.

After studying with the Jesuits at La Flèche, Francois received the position of canon at age twelve. He entered the college of Clermont in Paris intending to become a priest, but he received the family estate and titles in 1645 when his two older brothers died. His vocation remained strong, however, and in 1647, Francois was ordained and appointed archdeacon of Evreux, making journeys of visitation throughout the area. He was appointed vicar apostolic of Tongkin (modern Vietnam), in the Paris Foreign Mission Society at age thirty, but never took up residence there because of the political and geographical conditions.

In 1654, Francois resigned his position and spent four years at a hermitage in Caen. Pope Alexander VII (r. 1655-1667) appointed him vicar apostolic of New France in 1658; on December 8 of that year, Francois was consecrated a bishop. Shortly thereafter, he set sail for Canada, reaching Quebec on June 16, 1659.

When he arrived in Canada, he discovered a frontier diocese in need of organization and stability. He was responsible for all of North America except the British-held lands of New England and the Spanish settlements. But this responsibility didn't intimidate him — Francois would only say that his sole mission was to be "a bishop according to God's heart." Contemporaries echoed that spiritual mission, saying about Francois, "His heart is always with us." He was a staunch patron of missionaries who went from Quebec to their far-flung posts.

Francois promoted missions and fought against the rampant liquor trade with the local Indian tribes. He erected a cathedral dedicated to the Immaculate Conception and restored the shrine of St. Anne at Beaupré to foster devotion. Francois also started the Catholic school system in Canada, all the while revered as a man of prayer and mortification. In 1684, he retired to the seminary that he had founded but came out of retirement to assist the effort twice more, in 1701 and 1705, when disastrous fires engulfed the facility. He died in Quebec after three decades of tireless labors for the Canadian Church.

Pope John Paul II beatified Francois de Montmorency Laval on June 22, 1980, praising this episcopal pioneer of the New World as a priest and prelate who gave everything to see the Church thrive and to nurture the inhabitants of towns and wildernesses in the Faith.

✠

Frederico Albert (October 16, 1820 – September 30, 1876)
Founder of the Albertines

Frederico Albert was born in Turin, Italy, to a family facing great needs. Not given the normal opportunities of life as a child, he worked for every penny that he had and saved constantly. He had a vocation to the priesthood but could not attend seminary when he was young; as an adult, though, he took the required exams for candidates and was ordained at last, bringing a wealth of wisdom and basic common sense to his ministry.

Frederico served in various diocesan parishes and gained respect as a concerned pastor who cared for his people and their day-to-day problems. He also proved a remarkable counselor for the priests of the region. His years of trials gave him an insight into souls, and he understood the needs of his own age.

Frederico gathered dedicated young women to conduct charitable programs to ease the suffering of the faithful. He founded the Vincentian Sisters of Mary Immaculate, also called the "Albertines," in order to complete his vision of service. A friend of John Bosco, Frederico was nominated for the bishopric by Blessed Pope Pius IX (r.) but declined out of humility. John Bosco and Michael Rua cared for Frederick after he experienced a fall from a ladder while painting a ceiling. His death in Lanzo Torinese, Italy, was mourned as a great loss for the Faith.

Pope John Paul II beatified Frederico Albert on September 30, 1984, declaring:

> His spirit of faith, his unconditional obedience to the Pope and his bishop, and his priestly charity made him an element of balance among the members of the priesthood and a zealous pastor, particularly attentive to youth and the poor.

✠

Frederick Jansoone (November 19, 1838 – August 4, 1916)
Special Ministry to the Holy Land

Frederick Jansoone was born in the small village of Ghyvelde, near Lille, France. His family was not financially secure; Frederick had already entered the seminary when hie father died young, forcing him to withdraw from studies for the priesthood in order to support his mother. After her death, Frederick applied to the Friars Minor at Amien in 1864 and was professed as a Franciscan on July 18, 1865. He was ordained a priest on August 17, 1870.

He served as a chaplain in the military and spent twelve years in the Holy Land, where he assisted the Church ministries in various capacities, including conducting the Way of the Cross for pilgrims in Jerusalem. In 1888, he was sent to Canada, and there, he labored at the shrine of Our Lady of Cap-de-la-Madeleine. His major ministry was promoting support in Canada for the Christian communities in the Holy Land.

His holiness and profound spirituality drew people to him; they knew that he had wandered through many regions of the world for Christ. Contemplative in nature, he used his spiritual maturity as the foundation for his ministerial zeal, until his death in Montreal.

Pope John Paul II beatified Frederick Jansoone on September 25, 1988, announcing:

A true son of St. Francis, Fr. Frederic gives us the example of contemplative prayer which is able to embrace the works of creation, the events of daily life, and encounters with each person. May we receive as simply as he the Spirit which the Lord bestows on his people (cf. Num 11:29)!

"Good Father Frederic" shows us that the spirit of contemplation, far from inhibiting apostolic zeal, strengthens it. Close to God, he is also close to people. In the Holy Land and in Canada he never ceases to form those who listen to him to commit themselves to the *vita evangelica* along the ways traced by the Secular Franciscan Order, and especially in the very concrete apostolate of family and professional life. Attentive and brotherly towards the little ones "because (they) belong to Christ" (cf. Mt 9:41), Fr. Frederic taught his contemporaries to be consistent and ardent witnesses of the Gospel.

May his glorification by the Church contribute to arouse in the Order of St. Francis and in the Church a renewed burst of holiness and apostolic zeal!

✠

Frederick (Frédéric) Ozanam
(April 23, 1813 – September 8, 1853)
Noted Author of Apologetics

Frederick Ozanam was born in Milan, Italy, where his father served as a military officer. In 1816, the family moved to Lyons. Frederick was educated at the College Royal, and there he had a crisis of faith. While a student in Paris, however, he wrote a treatise on the revolution that attracted noted Catholic thinkers. Another treatise, *Reflections on the Doctrine of St. Simon,* was also well received. His literary efforts on defense of the Faith displayed a brilliant intellect, eloquence, and profound spiritual insight.

He also co-founded a charitable project, the Conference of Charity of St. Vincent de Paul, a society that was destined to serve men and women in countries throughout the world. He founded the society with seven companions, in his words, to "insure my faith by works of charity."

After a period of spiritual aridity and doubt, Frederick promised God "to devote my life to the services of truth which had given me peace," and he kept that vow for his remaining years. In 1836, he left Paris, only to return two years later to defend his thesis on the epic poet Dante for a doctorate in letters. He was given his doctorate and the chair of commercial law at Lyons. In 1841, he married Marie-Josephine Soulacroix and had a daughter; he substituted for a judge at the Sorbonne, becoming a full-tenured judge there in 1844; and was awarded the Grand Prize Gobert two years in a row in Paris.

He had to retire to Italy in 1853 because of ill health, but eventually returned to Marseilles, where he died. He was a member of the Third Order of St. Francis and was buried in the Carmelite Church in Paris.

Pope John Paul II beatified Frederick Ozanam in Paris on August 22, 1997, during the celebrations of World Youth Day. French bishops joined the Holy Father at Notre Dame Cathedral for the ceremony, where he lauded Frederick's zeal and spiritual maturity, calling him: "this student, professor, and family man, burning with faith and inventive in charity."

$\mathcal{G}$

✠

Gabriella Sagheddu — see Maria Gabriella Sagheddu

✠

Gaetana Sterni (June 26, 1827 – November 26, 1889)
Foundress of the Congregation of the Daughters of the Divine Will

Gaetana Sterni understood the Cross of Christ.

She was born in Cassola, Vicenza, Italy, the eldest of six children in the family. In 1835, her parents took the children to Bassano to live; there, a sister died. Gaetana's father also became ill, and the family was in dire need. She helped care for her younger siblings until she married Liberale Conte, a widower with three children. Gaetana was expecting her first child when Liberale died suddenly, and her baby did not survive long after being born. She returned home, knowing that she was needed there.

In 1843, Gaetana entered the Canossan convent, but she had to leave the religious life and come back home when her mother died and no one was caring for her younger brothers. She took charge of the local poor house in 1853, beginning her care of the destitute and the infirm. When other women came to assist Gaetana, she founded the Congregation of the Daughters of the Divine Will in Bassano and saw the rule approved in 1875. After her death in Bassano, her remains were interred in the congregation's motherhouse there.

Pope John Paul II beatified Gaetana Sterni on November 4, 2001, stating:

> She suffered a great deal, above all, in her youth, which, however, refined her sensitivity, rendering her capable of an unselfish love, pardon, and availability for the poor. Living in the continual search for the will of God and of readiness for it, she understood that to do the will of God meant to dedicate herself like Jesus to drawing good from evil with the force of love.

✠

Gaetano Catanoso (February 17, 1879 – April 4, 1963)
"Flying Squad" Leader

An apostle of devotion to the Holy Face of Jesus, Gaetano Catanoso founded a religious congregation for women.

He was born in Chorio di San Lorenzo, Reggio Calabria, Italy, the son of landowners who educated him in the Faith and fostered his vocation. He entered the local seminary and was ordained a priest in 1902, serving in the parishes of Pentedattilo and Reggio Calabria. He was made a cathedral canon in 1930.

While serving as a pastor, Gaetano promoted devotion to the Holy Face as a form of devout reparation for modern sinfulness, establishing the Confraternity of the Holy Face to aid the spread of the devotion. In 1920, he started the *Holy Face Bulletin* and promoted the Poor Clerics Association to sponsor vocations. While serving in Reggio Calabria, he revived the entire region, enlisting "flying squads" of priests who went into individual communities to promote the faith. Gaetano was also a confessor to religious institutions and prisons. He served as a hospital chaplain and spiritual director of the archdiocesan seminary.

He founded the Congregation of the Daughters of St. Veronica, Missionaries of the Holy Face, in 1934, to aid in his apostolate. This congregation was designed as a community devoted to prayer and reparation, worship, and catechesis programs. Gaetano opened the first convent in Reparo, and the first sisters received their habits in 1935. The congregation received diocesan approval in 1958.

Gaetano spent most of his life as "a victim of love" to the Sacred Heart of Jesus, offering his life and work in 1929. This hidden spiritual apostolate prompted his endless charitable works. He died in Reggio Calabria.

Pope John Paul II beatified Gaetano Catanoso on May 4, 1997. At the ceremony, he was honored as a victim of expiation for sins and as a true image of the Good Shepherd. Gaetano's devotion to the Holy Face transformed him during his lifetime. The Holy Father declared: ". . . he worked tirelessly for the good of the flock entrusted to him by the Lord."

✠

Gaetano Errico (October 19, 1781 – October 29, 1860)
Founder and Church Builder

Gaetano Errico was born in Naples, the second of nine children in a devout family. At the age of fourteen, he tried to enter the Capuchin Franciscans and the Redemptorists but was refused because of his youth. At age sixteen, Gaetano was accepted in the archdiocesan seminary of Naples and began his priestly vocation. He did not live at the seminary and had to walk long distances each day in order to attend the required classes. He was ordained to the priesthood on September 23, 1815.

His first assignment was as a teacher in a public school in the city. He served in that capacity diligently until 1818, when he had a vision of St. Alphonsus Ligouri, who told him to build Our Lady of Sorrows Church in Secondigliano and to found a religious congregation.

Gaetano acquired land for the church in 1822, and Our Lady of Sorrows was completed on December 9, 1830. He also began living in a small house near the church, serving the people of the region by hearing confessions and instructing one and all. The small house was to become the first established residence of his congregation, but Gaetano had to endure disappointments in order to establish that second part of his vision's commands. The first companions who came to aid him in starting the congregation left him, and he had to wait for others to accept the hardships of such a foundation.

In March 1836, at last, the Congregation of the Missionaries of the Sacred Hearts of Jesus and Mary came into being. With his new assistants, Gaetano continued his ministerial works until he died in Secondigliano. The townspeople spread word of his death by saying, "A saint is dead."

Pope John Paul II beatified Gaetano Errico on April 14, 2002, announcing:

> True martyr of the confessional, the new Blessed spent entire days giving his best energies to welcoming and listening to penitents.

✠

Gaspar (Kaspar) Stangassinger
(January 12, 1871 – September 26, 1899)
Model Redemptorist Religious

Gaspar Stangassinger was born in Berchtesgarden, Germany, one of sixteen children of a well-to-do farmer who owned a local quarry. The family was devout and well respected. Gaspar was raised in the Faith and received the grace of a religious vocation at a young age (despite his father's opposition to any thought of a religious life). In 1871, having attended local schools, he went to Freising to continue his studies. He entered minor seminary in 1884, major seminary in 1890, and entered the the Redemptorists in 1892, where he was ordained three years later.

Displaying both a mature spirituality and stability, he was named the assistant director of the Redemptorist Juniorate in Durnsberg. There, he taught and counseled the young men enrolled in the Juniorate, gaining many graces and serving as a model religious for the entire congregation.

On the night of September 22, 1899, Gaspar woke up in the middle of the night in severe pain. He was diagnosed as a suffering from acute appendicitis, but peritonitis developed as well, draining his life away. He died at Garsam Inn four days later, at the age of twenty-eight.

Gaspar was declared Venerable in 1986, and Pope John Paul II beatified him on April 24, 1988, declaring:

> Shaped by the deep religious spirit of his family and called very early to the priesthood, his life was wholly centered on God. He did not seek the extraordinary, but wanted "to do what the day demanded."

☩

Gennaro Maria Sarnelli
(September 12, 1702 – d June 30, 1744)
Co-Founder of the Redemptorists

A companion of Alphonsus Ligouri, Gennaro Maria Sarnelli was born in Naples, the son of Baron Angelo Sarnelli of Ciorani, raised in an aristocratic environment and well educated. The baron insisted that Gennaro (Januarius) study law and thus opposed his son's desire to enter the religious life. Obedient to his father's wishes, Gennaro became a lawyer and achieved success in that field before finally refusing his father's pleas and entering the seminary in 1728. Four years later, on July 8, 1732, he was ordained a priest.

Gennaro aided Alphonsus de Ligouri in founding the Redemptorists and worked with the future saint at Salerno until 1735, when his health demanded his return to Naples for recuperation. After he recovered, in 1744, he started a crusade against the immorality of his own era — a crusade that was highly successful. A prolific writer, he also demonstrated a remarkable ability to teach others the efficacy of daily meditation. These teachings were endorsed and indulgenced by Pope Benedict XIV (r. 1740-1758) on December 16, 1746.

Alphonsus was with Gennaro when he died in Naples. He testified that Gennaro's countenance "suddenly became beautiful," and that a sweet aroma remained with his body, which was laid to rest in the Redemptorist church in Naples.

Pope John Paul II beatified Gennaro Maria Sarnelli on May 12, 1996, declaring:

> His human and religious life, like that of St. Alphonsus Maria de Liguori, of whom he was a friend and collaborator, was particularly expressed in a remarkable sensitivity to the poor, whom he approached and accepted in the light of their reality as children of God.

The Holy Father added:

> His evangelizing activity was marked by a great dynamism. He was able to reconcile missionary involvement with his activities as a writer and with the equally demanding ministry of spiritual counselor and guide. Although he followed the cultural patterns of his day, the new Blessed never neglected to seek fresh forms of evangelization to respond to new challenges. For this reason, although he lived in a historical period in many ways very different from our own, Gennaro Maria Sarnelli can be held up to the Christian community today, on the threshold of the new millennium, as an example of an apostle who was open to accepting every useful innovation for a more penetrating proclamation of the eternal message of salvation.

✠

George Haydock and Companions
– see Martyrs of England, Scotland, and Wales

✠

George Matulaitis (Matulewicz)
(April 13, 1871 – January 27, 1927)
Marianist Rebuilder

A Marian prelate, George Matulaitis was called a "truly holy man" by the Pope.

He was born in Lugine, Lithuania, the youngest of eight children in a family of farmers. Both his parents died when he was ten, and at age fifteen, he was diagnosed with tuberculosis of the bone, a disease that would trouble him all of his life.

He was educated by the Marians at Mariampole, Lithuania, and was sent to the seminaries of Kielce and Warsaw, in Poland. He also attended the Ecclesiastical Academy of St. Petersburg, Russia, and the University of Fribourg, in Switzerland. After earning a doctorate, George was ordained a priest in St. Petersburg in 1898.

When he returned to Warsaw, he founded orphanages and organized charitable programs for people of all faiths. He became ill in 1905, and was near death when a community of sisters brought a doctor to his side. These sisters had been driven out of their convents by occupying forces but were operating underground missions. They sheltered George until he recovered. In return, he made a vow to honor the Blessed Virgin Mary in thanksgiving.

In 1907, he became a professor at the Ecclesiastical Academy in St. Petersburg; there, he learned of the oppression inflicted upon the Marians. He became a Marian as a result and adopted the constitution of the congregation in order to revive it. In 1910, he moved to Fribourg and started rebuilding (gaining more than 250 members before he died). George also reclaimed abandoned or confiscated Marian houses. He arrived in the United States in 1913 to open a house in Chicago.

Five years later, he founded the Sisters of the Immaculate Conception and, in 1924, the Sister Servants of Jesus in the Eucharist. George was appointed bishop of Vilnius, Lithuania, in 1918 and, in 1925, became an archbishop and apostolic visitator, appointed by Pope Pius XI (r. 1922-1939) to Lithuania. He urged the Marians to sacrifice themselves for Christ as he revived the revered congregation. Pope Pius XI called him "a truly holy man" and "a man of God." George died in Kaunas, after undergoing surgery for a ruptured appendix.

Pope John Paul II beatified George Matulaitis on June 28, 1987, and at this ceremony, the courage and honor of this Blessed was extolled. He was praised as a prelate and religious who traveled the royal way of the Cross with unstinting fidelity.

✝

Gertrude Catarina Comensoli
(January 18, 1847 – February 18, 1903)
Co-Worker of Francis Spinelli

Revered also as Geltrude, Gertrude Catarina Comnensoli was born in Biennio, Brescia, Italy, the fifth of ten children of a poor local family. She learned quickly to imitate her parents' reverence and received the grace of a religious vocation. She entered the Sisters of Charity, the Maria Bambina Sisters, only to be forced to leave that convent because of ill health.

Turning to a secular institute called the Company of Angela Merici, Gertrude worked and taught catechism. She then served for more than a decade as a companion to a countess. In 1879, she met the future Bl. Francis Spinelli. Together they founded the Sisters of the Blessed Sacrament (Bergamo), a congregation devoted to education and to adoration. Gertrude's sister, Bartolomea, joined the community also, and six houses were opened by 1881.

Differences concerning recognition of the apostolate of the congregation led Gertrude and her sisters to move temporarily to Lodi, Italy, but they were able to return to Bergamo the following year and expand their ministries.

Gertrude imbued her sisters with love for the Blessed Sacrament and for humble service to the Church. She died in Bergamo and was declared Venerable by Pope John XXIII (r. 1958-1963).

Pope John Paul II beatified Gertrude Catarina Comensoli on October 1, 1989, declaring:

> Once again it is the example of the poor and humble Christ, contemplated especially in the eucharistic mystery, which guides the commitment of Gertrude Comensoli on the difficult spiritual journey and the distressing events of the foundation of the Blessed Sacrament Sisters.

✝

Giacomo Alberione
(April 4, 1884 – November 26, 1971)
Founder of the Pauline Family

Giacomo Alberione was born in San Lorenzo di Fossano, Italy, one of six children belonging to Michael and Teresa Alberione. His parents were farmers, but as early as the first grade, Giacomo knew that he would not follow

285

his family's profession. Asked by a teacher what he wanted be when he grew up, he responded forcefully, "A priest!"

When the family moved to Cherasco, in the Alba diocese, Giacomo met the local parish priest, Fr. Montersino. Under his spiritual guidance, the boy discerned his vocation and responded fully to God's call. At the age of sixteen, he entered the seminary of Alba. At the time of his entrance, he met Canon Francesco Chiesa, a priest who served as his friend and mentor for the next four decades.

Ordained a priest on June 29, 1907, he was soon named spiritual director to the seminarians in the diocesan seminary of Alba and was professor on the faculty. He also was a gifted preacher; his abilities in that area helped him in developing what he felt was an important apostolate — using the means of modern communications to spread and proclaim the Gospel. His decision was the fruit of years of pastoral service and the study of contemporary culture. And, in August 1914, Giacomo founded what came to be called the Pauline Family through the establishment in Alba of the Pious Society of St. Paul to bring Christ to the world.

He was joined in the early years by his brothers and sisters and by a young woman, Teresa Merlo. Together with Merlo, Giacomo launched a second Congregation in 1915, the Daughters of St. Paul. In 1924, he started a second congregation for women, the Pious Disciples of the Divine Master. The intent of this second community was to promote the Eucharist and the liturgy; its primary figure in the first years was Sr. M. Scholastica Rivata. In 1938, he founded a third congregation for women, the Sisters of Jesus the Good Shepherd (or Pastorelle Sisters,) to provide assistance to parish priests in their pastoral labors. Between 1957 and 1960, he added a fourth congregation, the Queen of Apostles Institute for vocations (the Apostoline Sisters), along with several secular institutes for the consecrated life: St. Gabriel the Archangel, Our Lady of the Annunciation, Jesus Priest, and the Holy Family.

Giacomo oversaw the steady growth and development of the Pauline family, especially engaging in the fullest possible use of the means of social communications. He promoted the printing of the Bible and started several important periodicals to advance the preaching of the Gospel: *Vita Pastorale* (*The Pastoral Life*, in 1912) for parish priests; *Famiglia Cristiana* (*Christian Family*, in 1931) to promote the Christian life of families; *Madre di Dio* (*Mother of God*, in 1933) to promote Marian devotion; *Pastor Bonus* (*Good Shepherd*, in 1937), a Latin language monthly magazine; *Via, Verità e Vita* (*Way, Truth, Life*, in 1952), a monthly magazine to teach Christian doctrine;

and *Vita in Cristo nella Chiesa* (*Life in Christ and in the Church*, 1952), to encourage the liturgy.

In recognition of the fortieth anniversary of the foundation of the Pauline Family in 1954, Fr. Giacomo agreed to the publication of a book detailing his life. The result was *Mi protendo in avanti* (*I Strain Ahead*). He also accepted the request to write down some of his own reflections on the birth of the Pauline Family. These were published in *Abundantes divitiae gratiae suae*, (English edition, *A Charismatic History of the Pauline Family*).

Fr. Giacomo built the stunning Church of St. Paul in Alba, the two Churches to the Divine Master (in Alba and Rome), and the Sanctuary of the Queen of Apostles (in Rome). He likewise worked to found houses and communities elsewhere in Italy and around the world.

Fr. Giacomo died at the age of eighty-seven. Just before his passing, he was visited by Pope Paul VI, and Pope John Paul II beatified him on April 27, 2003. The pontiff declared of him:

> Bl. James [*sic*]Alberione felt the need to make Jesus Christ, the Way, the Truth and the Life, known "to all people of our time with the means of our time," as he liked to say. He was inspired by the Apostle Paul, whom he described as a "theologian and architect of the Church," remaining ever docile and faithful to the Magisterium of the Successor of Peter, a "beacon" of truth in a world that is so often devoid of sound spiritual references. "May there be a group of saints to use these means," this apostle of the new times was in the habit of repeating.
>
> What a formidable heritage he left his religious family! May his spiritual sons and daughters keep intact the spirit of their origins, to respond adequately to the needs of evangelization in the contemporary world.

✠

Giacomo Cusmano (March 15, 1834 – March 14, 1888)
Patron of the Poor and Imprisoned

Giacomo Cusmano was born in Palermo, Italy, in a turbulent era. Both his faith and his knowledge of the truly appalling conditions around him compelled him to combine a medical and priestly career to benefit the sick and the needy of the area.

Ordained to the priesthood after seminary training and certified as a medical doctor, Giacomo started his ministry by opening a House for the Poor in Palermo. Anyone in need could come to him for medical care and necessary material goods. To support this endeavor, he also started the Morsel for the Poor Association, an organization that awakened the people of Palermo to the needs of those in their midst.

If those around him needed yet another symbol of charity, Giacomo stood before the people seeking aid for those in prison. He did not live in a good district himself, and he did not use salaries or benefits to make himself comfortable. This medical man even begged in the streets of the city for the poor. He collected food, clothing, and other necessities and distributed to the indigent people who gathered around him.

When others came to join in this charitable labor, Giacomo founded the Missionary Servants of the Poor and the Sister Servants of the Poor. The rule of both congregations was Christ-centered and based on the practice of the presence of God in all things.

Giacomo provided the ultimate example of such union with Christ, when an epidemic of cholera struck Palermo in 1888. He did not spare himself but remained on duty throughout the epidemic, bringing whatever medical aid possible to victims and comforting all. This epidemic drained the last of Giacomo's energies, however, and he died at age fifty-four. At his passing, all of Palermo went into mourning.

Pope John Paul II beatified Giacomo Cusmano on October 30, 1983, declaring:

> To heal the wounds of poverty and misery which were afflicting such a large part of the population because of recurring famines and epidemics, but also because of social inequality, he chose the way of charity; love for God which was translated into effective love for his brethren and into the gift of himself to the most needy and suffering, in a service pushed to the point of heroic sacrifice.

The Holy Father hailed Giacomo as the "Servant of the Poor."

☩

Giorgio Preca of Malta
(February 12, 1880 – July 26, 1962)
Malta's Second Father in Faith

Giorgio Preca was born in Valetta, Malta, the son of Vincenzo and Natalina Ceravalo Preca. Receiving the grace of a priestly vocation early, he entered the University of Malta for theological studies and was ordained on December 22, 1906. During this period, he also developed spiritually, becoming a profound contemplative in prayer.

In 1907, he started his Societas Doctrinae Christiane, a group of lay people living as a secular institute, and in 1910, he founded a woman's evangelization group with Giannina Cutajar.

Giorgio suffered attacks from enemies, however, and a Church investigation of his work was opened. On April 12, 1932, after some periods of time being closed, then reopened, the centers of evangelization were at last canonically established and given approval.

Giorgio had suffered during the attacks and the investigation, but he continued his labors and became a Carmelite Tertiary in July 1918. He lived to see his evangelization programs serving the faithful in Albania, England, Kenya, Peru, and the Sudan.

Pope John Paul II beatified Giorgio Preca of Malta on May 9, 2001 in Malta, declaring that Blessed Giorgio was "a pioneer in the field of catechetics and in promoting the role of the laity in the apostolate." The Holy Father added, "He became, as it were, Malta's second father in faith."

⊹

Giovanni Antonio Farina
(January 1803 – March 4, 1888)
"Bishop of Charity"

Giovanni Antonio Farina was born in Gambellara, Italy, the second of five brothers. When his father died, he was adopted by a priest uncle, Fr. Antonio, and educated with care. At age fifteen, Giovanni entered the Seminary of Vicenza. He was ordained at age twenty-one and taught in the seminary, serving also as spiritual director for eighteen years. He then served for a decade as an assistant pastor in parishes and as the headmaster of a local school.

In 1836, after opening a local school, he founded the Institute of the Sister Teachers of St. Dorothy, Daughters of the Sacred Hearts. This congregation was dedicated to the care of the blind, deaf, elderly, and ill. In 1850, Giovanni was appointed the Bishop of Trevino. As part of his episcopal duties in the area, he ordained a priest named Giuseppe Sarto, who would become St. Pius X. Giovanni reformed and educated the priests of his diocese and visited every parish to encourage the lay people to participate in the local evangelization programs and demonstrations of the Faith.

In 1860, Giovanni was made Bishop of Vicenza. There, his charitable works brought him esteem and the title of "Bishop of Charity." However, by 1886, he was exhausted and ill and suffered a stroke that led to his death.

Pope John Paul II beatified Giovanni Antonio Farina on November 4, 2001, announcing: "Bishop Giovanni Antonio Farina presents the glorious image of the Pastor of the People of God after the model of Christ."

⊹

Giovanni Maria Boccardo (1848 – December 30, 1913)
"Good Father" of the Catholic Parish

The founder of the Congregation of the Poor Daughters of St. Cajetan, Giovanni Maria Boccardo was born in Tertona di Moncalieri (Turin), Italy, and raised in a pious family of the Faith. Studying for the priesthood and ordained in Turin in 1871, he was appointed assistant, then spiritual director, of the seminaries in Chieri and Turin. In 1882, he was made a parish priest at Pancalieri, where he would remain for the rest of his life.

He entered the pastoral ministry as a victim for the good of his parishioners, and within two years proved himself valiant and charitable. He cared for the sick throughout an epidemic, and when it was over, he started an apostolate to aid the abandoned aged, orphaned, and homeless. Giovanni opened the Hospice of Charity and founded the Congregation of the Poor Daughters of St. Cajetan, which spread rapidly in Italy. He served as the "good father" of the faithful while practicing penances until his death.

Pope John Paul II beatified Giovanni Maria Boccardo on May 24, 1998, in Turin's Piazza Vittorio, stating that the new Blessed "was a man of deep spirituality and, at the same time, a dynamic apostle, a promoter of religious life and the laity, ever attentive to discerning the signs of the times."

⊹

Giovanni Baptist Mazzucconi
(March 1, 1826 – September 7, 1855)
Martyr of Woodlark Island

Giovanni Baptist Mazzucconi was the first martyr of the Pontifical Institute for Foreign Missions.

He was born in Rancio di Lecco, near Milan, Italy, the ninth of twelve children born to Giacomo and Anna Maria Scuri Mazzucconi. Educated in local schools as a child, Giovanni entered the seminary at Monza. He studied as well in Milan, and was ordained on May 25, 1850.

A charter member of the Pontifical Institute for Foreign Missions, Giovanni became a missionary priest, setting sail for Sydney, Australia, in March 1852. He was assigned to the islands of Woodlark and Rook, where he hoped to begin his priestly labors. The natives on these islands did not welcome Europeans or missionaries, however, and rebuffed all attempts at meetings or understanding. Two years after making their evangelization efforts, the missionaries, including Giovanni, had to leave the islands, returning to Sydney in January 1855. He was very ill, but he recovered in Sydney.

On August 18, 1855, Giovanni boarded the schooner *Gazelle*, planning to rejoin his fellow missionaries, whom he believed had regrouped. That belief was erroneous, as the missionaries of the Woodlark and Rook stations had decided to abandon these posts on a permanent basis; Giovanni had not received word of this official determination. On September 7, 1855, he arrived in Woodlark Bay but ran aground on the coral reef. Natives in canoes came out to greet him, but their greeting was not made with good intentions: one, named Avicoar, used a hatchet to kill Giovanni. The entire ship was then taken over and those aboard were slaughtered.

Eight months later, Fr. Timoleone Raimondi, who would become the bishop of Hong Kong in time, led an expedition to find the schooner. The expedition succeeded in discovering the truth about the martyrdom.

Pope John Paul II beatified Giovanni Baptist Mazzucconi on February 19, 1984, as the first martyr of the Pontifical Institute for Foreign Missions. Giovanni was praised for his angelic purity and generosity, virtues that led him fearlessly across the world with the Good News of Christ.

✠

Giovanni Piamarta
(November 26, 1841 – April 25, 1913)
Laboring Among the Young

Giovanni Piamarta was born in Brescia, Italy, to a poor but devout family, and was educated in local schools. He entered the seminary in 1860 and, five years later, was ordained a priest for the diocese of Brescia.

Having observed the economic and social challenges young people in the region faced, he devoted his time and energies to their needs. He started an institution for the children of local workers, knowing that such young ones often became ill because of the poverty rampant in their neighborhoods. He also provided care for the young men in Brescia, establishing the Institute Artigianelli with Msgr. Peter Capretti. This institute trained youths in professional skills and in Christian ideals.

Giovanni also built houses and workshops for more than 100 Brescian youths, in the process offering them spiritual and educational opportunities. An agricultural colony that he provided even introduced new farming techniques into the region, prompting a rejuvenation of the local farming harvests and management systems.

In 1902, he realized that a religious congregation was needed to carry on his apostolate. So, first, Giovanni founded the Congregation of the Holy Family; then, with his mother, he founded the Humble Servants of the Lord for women. The members of these congregations engaged in rural and urban apostolates designed to strengthen families and offer the Faith to young and old alike.

Giovanni died at Remedello, surrounded by members of his congregation, and thousands of Brescians mourned his passing.

Pope John Paul II beatified Giovanni Piamarta on October 12, 1997, declaring:

> How many, thanks to his pastoral activities, were able to start out joyfully in life, having learned a skill and, above all, having encountered Jesus and his message of salvation! . . . Where did this extraordinary man of God find the energy for all his numerous activities? The answer is clear: assiduous and fervent prayer was the source of his tireless apostolic zeal and beneficial influence that he exercised on everyone he approached. He himself said, as the accounts of his contemporaries recall: "With prayer one is strengthened by the strength of God himself . . . *Omnia possum.*"

☩

Giovanni Baptist Scalabrini
(July 8, 1839 – June 1, 1905)
"Apostle of the Catechism"

The founder of the Missionaries of St. Charles, Giovanni Baptist Scalabrini was born in Fino Mornasco, Italy, one of eight children in the family. He was ordained at Como on May 30, 1863, after which he served as a professor and rector of St. Abundius Seminary, and was consecrated the bishop of Piacenza on January 30, 1876.

Giovanni was a model bishop, visiting every parish in Piacenza and cele-brating three synods designed to bring about renewal programs and the restoration of doctrine. During a cholera epidemic, Giovanni sold all that he possessed to buy the food and medical supplies that saved hundreds of human lives.

He also had great concern for migrants, as he witnessed the great tides of immigrants in his own era. On November 28, 1887, Giovanni founded the Congregation of the Missionaries of St. Charles, called the Scalabrinis; he also convinced Frances Xavier Cabrini to go to America to care for Italian immigrants in the New World. In 1895, Giovanni founded the Missionary Sisters of St. Charles for migrants, and he started a secular institute, the Scalabrinian Lay Missionary Women. All of these institutes were designed to aid the great masses of human beings on the move across the world.

He had a special devotion to the Holy Eucharist and to the Blessed Vir-gin Mary. Dying on the feast of the Ascension, Giovanni's last words were, "Lord, I am ready. Let us go."

Pope John Paul II beatified Giovanni Baptist Scalabrini on November 9, 1997, announcing:

> The universal call to holiness was constantly felt and personally lived by Giovanni Baptist Scalabrini. He loved to say over and over: "Would that I could sanctify myself and all the souls entrusted to me!"
>
> Striving for holiness and proposing it to everyone he met was always his first concern . . . Pope Pius IX called him the "Apostle of the Catechism" because of his efforts to promote the systematic teaching of the Church's doctrine to children and adults in every parish.

✠

Giulia Salzano
(October 13, 1846 – May 17, 1929)
Forerunner of New Evangelization

Foundress of the Catechist Sisters of the Sacred Heart, Giulia Salzano was born in Santa Maria Capua Vetere in the province of Caserta, Italy. She was the daughter of Adelaide Valentino and Diego Salzano, a Captain in the Lancers of King Ferdinand II of Naples. As her father died when she was four, Giulia was given into the care of the Sisters of Charity in the Royal Orphanage of St. Nicola La Strada. She remained under their direction until the age of fifteen. When the family moved to Casoria, in the province of

Naples, in 1865, Giulia earned a teaching diploma that permitted her to teach in the local school.

To assist in the proclamation of the life and the teachings of Jesus through education and catechesis, Gioulia founded the Congregation of the Catechetical Sisters of the Sacred Heart in 1905. For her, the heart of the vocation of the congregation's members was to teach the catechism and so make Jesus Christ known to the world. The members taught parish catechesis in pastoral training centers and in all suitable places where catechesis could be expounded.

The rest of her life was devoted to developing the congregation, and she is revered today as one of the great forerunners of the New Evangelization that was a hallmark of John Paul II's pontificate. The pope beatified her on April 27, 2003. He said of her:

> In advance of her time, she was an apostle of the new evangelization in which she combined apostolic activity with prayer, offered ceaselessly, especially for the conversion of the "indifferent."
>
> This new Blessed encourages us to persevere in faith and never to lose our confidence in God, who does all things. Called to be the apostles of modern times, may believers also be inspired by Bl. Julia Salzano "to instill in many creatures the immense charity of Christ."

✠

Giulia Nemesia Valla
(June 26, 1847 – December 18, 1916)
Member of the Sisters of Charity of St. Jeanne-Antide Thouret

Giulia was born in Aosta, Italy, to a humble family of milliners. She and her brother, however, lost their mother at a young age and were entrusted reluctantly by their father into the care of relatives in Aosta. When Giulia was eleven, she was sent to Besançon, France, and a boarding school run by the Sisters of Charity. There, she received a sound education, but the years in France created what proved to be an insurmountable gulf with her family, especially with her brother.

In 1866, Giulia entered the Sisters of Charity, refusing the hopes of her father that she be married. Her father, however, journeyed with her to the Monastery of Santa Margherita in Vercelli, where she entered congregation's novitiate. At the end of her novitiate, Giulia received a new name: Nemesia, taken from an early martyr.

Sr. Nemesia was sent by her superiors to St. Vincent's Institute in Tortona, where she taught various subjects, including French. She was later nominated the Superior of the community and humbly accepted the position with the understanding that she was being called to serve in another capacity.

In May 1903, she departed Tortona for the small town of Borgaro, near Turin. Her new task was to help give direction to the recently established province of the Sisters of Charity. She spent the rest of her life in the community at Borgaro and had a direct hand in shaping the vocations of over five hundred novices.

Sr. Nemesia was beatified on April 25, 2004. The pontiff said of her:

"Manifest God's love to the little, to the poor, to every person in every corner of the earth." This was the undertaking of Blessed Nemesia Valle throughout her entire life. She left this teaching especially to her Sisters, the Sisters of Charity of St. Joan Antida Thouret, and to the faithful of the Archdiocese of Turin. It is the example of a shining holiness directed towards the high summits of evangelical perfection, which can be translated in the simple gestures of daily living, completely spent in God's service.

✠

Giuseppe Allamano
(January 21, 1851 – February 16, 1926)
Missionary Founder

Giuseppe Allamano was the nephew of St. Joseph Cafasso.

He was born in Castelnuovo d'Asti, Italy, the fourth child of Joseph and Marianna Cafasso Allamano. Educated at Valdocco, the institute operated by St. John Bosco's Congregation. He entered the diocesan seminary at Turin. His education was difficult, as Giuseppe suffered from hemoptysis (coughing up blood) continually. He was ordained on September 20, 1872, in the Turin Cathedral, and became a canon there. Giuseppe also restored the sanctuary and convent of the Consolata, succeeding his uncle, Joseph Cafasso, as head of this ecclesiastical house in 1880.

The hallmark of his priestly life, however, was his concern about the missions. To this end he founded the Consolata Missionary Fathers, which were approved by Rome on January 29, 1901. (It is also called the Consolata Society for Foreign Missions.)

In 1902, two mission priests were sent to Zanzibar, where they baptized the king and opened twelve mission stations. The congregation worked in Africa and in North and South America, conducting hospitals, dispensaries, schools, and seminaries. In 1910, Pope St. Pius X (r. 1903-1914) asked Giuseppe to found the Consolata Mission Sisters. The rule for this congregation was approved on January 29, 1910. Both congregations are devoted to Our Lady of Consolation, and both are concerned with the missionary identity of the Church.

Giuseppe served the needs of his societies until his death in Turin. He tried to continue celebrating Mass until the end, and his death was so peaceful that it was almost unnoticed by those in attendance. He was buried in the Turin cemetery, but his remains were later transferred to the Consolata Motherhouse.

Pope John Paul II beatified Giuseppe Allamano on October 7, 1990, stating:

> Rooted in him was the deep conviction that 'the priest is above all a man of charity, destined to the greatest possible good, to sanctify others by word and example, with holiness and knowledge. He reminds us that in order to stay faithful to our Christian vocation we must know how to share the gifts we received from God.

✠

Giuseppe Baldo (February 19, 1843 – October 24, 1915)
Perseverance in the Face of Mason Opposition

The founder of the Little Daughters of St. Joseph, Giuseppe Baldo was a tireless devotee of Christ in the Eucharist. He was born in Puegnago, near Brescia, Italy, the son of Angelo and Hippolita Casa Baldo. When he was sixteen he entered the seminary at Verona and was ordained on August 15, 1865. This ordination took place with a papal indult, because he was only twenty-two.

Giuseppe served as a curate in parishes after his ordination but was recalled to the seminary as vice-rector. He wrote books on prayers, sermons, and seminary training, and he taught at the seminary for over a decade. He then asked for a pastoral assignment, and in 1877, became parish priest at Ronco all Adige. Anticlerical freemasons threatened him from the first day, but Giuseppe stood up to them and started his ministry in charitable programs.

He founded schools for adults, a Workers' Mutual Assistance Society, a nursery, elementary schools, and a rural savings bank. Giuseppe also started the Servants of Charity of Our Lady of Succor to conduct home visits and care for the sick. In 1888, he opened a hospital, followed by the founding of a nursing congregation, the Little Daughters of St. Joseph, in 1894.

Giuseppe also established an Association of Christian Mothers, a Confraternity of the Blessed Sacrament, and a Society of the Forty Hours. He suffered from an illness for almost two years at the end of his life. Giuseppe died at Ronco all 'Adige, and his remains were enshrined in the chapel of his congregation in 1950.

Pope John Paul II beatified Giuseppe Baldo on October 31, 1989, announcing:

> From the first day as a parish priest, he told his parishioners, "I am your parish priest. Yours — that is, totally yours." [You may] confidently invoke Blessed Giuseppe Baldo, who shines in the glory of the elect, in order to imitate his example of faith, charity, and holiness.

✠

Giuseppe Benedetto Dusmet
(August 15, 1818 – April 4, 1894)
Total Generosity

Giuseppe Benedetto Dusmet was born in Palermo, Sicily, and entered the Benedictine Order at St. Martino della Scale Monastery. After completing his studies, he was professed in 1840 and ordained a priest in 1842.

He served the Benedictine Order in various capacities, displaying his unfailing loyalty and faith as political and social upheaval racked the area. In 1858, Giuseppe was elected the abbot of St. Nicoló de Arenis Monastery in Catania and was named the archbishop of Catania in 1867. He would spend the next twenty-seven years giving his money, time, and energies to the people of the region

Earthquakes, volcanic eruptions, and outbreaks of cholera brought Giuseppe into the streets of the city to care for victims. He also established the Confederation of the Benedictine Order and served Pope Leo XIII (r. 1878-1903) in re-establishing the International College of Sant'Anselmo on the Via Aventina in Rome. Giuseppe was elevated to the rank of Cardinal in 1888.

He died in Catania, at which point it was discovered that he had beggared himself so thoroughly that there were no good linens in his residence for wrapping his remains.

Pope John Paul II beatified Giuseppe Cardinal Dusmet on September 25, 1988, proclaiming:

He gave that example of evangelic charity in times which were particularly difficult for the life of the Church.

The Holy Father praised Giuseppe also for his total generosity, saying:

He literally stripped himself of everything in order to put on poverty, whose humble servant he was.

✠

Giuseppe Nascimbeni
(November 22, 1851 – January 21, 1922)
Founder of the Little Sisters of the Holy Family

Giuseppe Nascimbeni worked to protect the families of his region.

He was born in Torri del Benaco, Italy, and was baptized the same day. The son of Antonio and Amidaea Sartori Nascimbeni, he was raised devoutly, and desiring a religious vocation, he entered the seminary at Verona where he completed his training and was ordained on March 19, 1874. He was then assigned to the village of San Pietro di Lavagno, where he served as pastor and schoolmaster.

In 1877, Giuseppe was sent to Casteletto di Brenzone and served as a curate and assistant in the school. In 1884, he became the pastor, a ministry he would conduct for almost four decades. The village had a population of only ninety, but Giuseppe poured out his charity and priestly care to aid them in their changing world.

On November 4, 1892, he founded the Little Sisters of the Holy Family with Mother Maria Mantovani (beatified on April 27, 2003). He directed the congregation and continued his ministry, displaying an acute awareness of the dangers of the modern era and their devastating effects on the family and young people. Dedicated to charitable works, the congregation spread rapidly, and Giuseppe saw more than 1,000 sisters in his foundation before he died.

Pope St. Pius X recognized Giuseppe's labors in 1911 (r. 1903-1914) and made him a protonotary apostolic. Although he accepted the honor, he would not allow anyone to call him Monsignor.

On December 31, 1916, Giuseppe suffered a stroke and was left partially paralyzed. He did not stop his labors, bearing all things with patience until his death at Casteletto del Garda.

Pope John Paul II beatified Giuseppe Nascimbeni in Verona, Italy, on April 17, 1988. At the ceremony, the Holy Father praised him as a symbol of Christ, the Good Shepherd, and as a pastor of consummate charity and virtue.

✠

Giuseppe Tovini (March 14, 1841 – January 16, 1897)
Lawyer and Public Servant

Giuseppe Tovini was born in Cividate Camuno, near Brescia, the eldest of seven children in a poor family. Sponsored by his uncle, Fr. Giambattista Malaguzzi, he was able to attend a boys' school for the poor in Verona. He subsequently finished his studies there and went on to law school, obtaining his degree at the University of Pavia in 1865.

He found employment in a law office as a notary, continuing to support his younger brothers and sisters, who were left in his care when their parents died young. Aside from his work as a notary and an attorney, Giuseppe was appointed vice rector and professor at the municipal college of Lovere, posts which required great sensitivity and spiritual discernment. In 1867, he moved to Brescia, where he entered a prominent law office. From 1871 to 1874, he served as the mayor of Cividate and brought many improvements to the area, including the founding of the Banca di Vallecamonica in Breno.

In 1875, he married Emilia Corbolani, his former employer's daughter. They had ten children, three of whom entered the religious life, including one who became a Jesuit. Two years after his marriage, Giuseppe joined the Catholic Movement of Brescia and helped found the daily newspaper *Il Cittadino di Brescia*. Giorgio Montini — the father of the future pontiff, Paul VI — edited this paper.

In 1878, Giuseppe aided in the formation of the diocesan committee of the Opera dei Congressi, a Catholic program designed to protect the faithful from the anticlerical attitudes of the era. One year later, he was elected provincial councilor for Pisogne, then became the provincial councilor for Brescia in 1882. Giuseppe understood the Church's essential role in aiding the poor of the region and founded banks in Brescia and Milan to assist the destitute. He also opened Catholic workers' societies and established a school, a college, and education programs, declaring that such institutions were "mission fields."

Although always plagued by poor health, Giuseppe was tireless in his labors. He died in Brescia, much mourned by the local citizens.

Pope John Paul II beatified Giuseppe Tovini in Brescia on September 20, 1998, declaring:

Giuseppe Tovini, this lay Christian whom I had the joy of proclaiming blessed today, stands before us and speaks to us with the example of his life, a life totally dedicated to the defense and promotion of the moral and spiritual values indispensable for renewing society. He was able to combine his vocation as husband and father of a family with his commitment to many Catholic initiatives.

During the hard struggles undertaken out of fidelity to the Gospel in the difficult political and social context of his time, he had recourse to the intercession of Mary, whom he had learned to venerate since childhood. To her motherly heart, he commended the problems of teachers, workers, and young people; it was she who inspired him in fulfilling his duties as a father; he was always confident in her during illness and in the many moments of trial. Today, the new Blessed invites us as well to turn our gaze to the tender Mother of Divine Grace, to draw from her the necessary strength to follow Christ in every circumstance.

Blessed Giuseppe Tovini was certainly a great witness of the Gospel incarnated in Italy's social and economic history in the last century. He is resplendent for his generous efforts to improve society. Between Tovini and Giovanni Battista Montini [Pope Paul VI] there is — as a matter of fact — a close, profound spiritual and mental bond.

In fact, the pontiff himself wrote of Tovini: "The impression he left on those I first knew and esteemed was so vivid and so real that I frequently heard comments and praise of his extraordinary personality and his many varied activities; astonished, I heard admiring expressions of his virtue and sorrowful regrets at his early death" (Preface by Giovanni Battista Montini to the biography of Giuseppe Tovini by Fr. Antonio Cistellini in 1953, p. 1). Fervent, honest, active in social and political life, Giuseppe Tovini proclaimed the Christian message, always in fidelity to the guidance of the Church's Magisterium. His constant concern was to defend the faith, convinced that — as he said at a congress — "without faith our children will never be rich; with faith they will never be poor."

☩

Giuseppina Gabriella Bonino
(September 5, 1843 – February 8, 1906)
Patroness of Modern Family Life

Giuseppina Gabriella Bonino was born in Savigliano, Italy, and raised in a pious family. She moved with her family to Turin when she was twelve and, there, she took a vow of chastity at age eighteen.

In 1869, Giuseppina returned to Savigliano to care for her father, who suffered from a terminal illness. In 1871, she underwent back surgery and journeyed to Lourdes to give thanks to the Blessed Virgin Mary. At Lourdes, Giuseppina was inspired to serve the poor. Upon returning home, she began caring for orphans.

Giuseppina wanted to be a contemplative, and entered the cloister on two occasions, but discovered that this form of religious life was not for her. Upon the advice of her spiritual director, instead, she founded a congregation: the Sisters of the Holy Family, whose members cared for orphans, the elderly sick, and the poor. Giuseppina became Superior in April 1881, and remained in this post until her death. She guided her spiritual daughters and opened four other houses of the congregation before she died in Savona, on the day that she had predicted.

Pope John Paul II beatified Giuseppina Gabriella Bonino on May 7, 1995, announcing:

> The love of Christ, the Good Shepherd, also found a unique expression in the life of Giuseppina Gabriella Bonino, foundress of the Sisters of the Holy Family of Saigliano. Her charism was family love, learned and practiced above all while living with her parents until adulthood, then by following the Lord's call in consecrated life. From the family as the domestic church to the religious community as the spiritual family: this is summary of her humble journey, hidden but of incalculable value, that of the family, the environment of extraordinary love in ordinary things.
>
> Giuseppina Gabriella, an exemplary daughter — she took care of her father and mother until their death — became a mother to numerous infants and children with no family. The message of her life, extended in the institute, remains most timely for today's society: every person who comes into the world hungers for love more than bread, and has a right to a family. The Christian community is called to respond to the situations of need which are inevitable.

✠

Grimoaldo Santamaria (May 4. 1883 – November 18, 1902)
"God's Will Be Done"

A Passionist seminarian called to heaven at a young age, Blessed Grimoaldo was revered for his devotion to the Virgin Mary.

He was born in Pontecorvo (Frosinone), Italy, the eldest of five children. Baptized Ferdinand, he was consecrated to the Blessed Virgin Mary. Ferdinand entered the Congregation of the Passion at Santa Maria di Pugliano and made his first vows on March 6, 1900, receiving the name Grimoaldo. He started his seminary training at Santa Maria di Corniano, near Ceccano, and was revered for his purity and devotion. As a Marian apostle, he inspired everyone he met and demonstrated total reliance upon the Providence of God.

He was not destined for the priesthood, however. Grimoaldo fell ill in the seminary with acute meningitis and did not respond to medical care. He died despite all medical efforts, edifying all who came into contact with him during his final days on earth. As he passed from the world, he repeated the words "God's will be done."

Pope John Paul II beatified Grimoaldo Santamaria on January 29, 1995, declaring:

> His biographers describe him as joyful even amid humiliations, contradictions, and difficulties in his studies. His companions noted that although Grimoaldo did nothing different from them, he did it with an extraordinary and growing intensity of love. Young people today and in the future can see in him a model of simple and generous spirituality, firmly rooted in Christ's paschal mystery.

✠

Guido Maria Conforti
(March 30, 1865 – November 5, 1931)
"Shepherd of Two Flocks"

Guido Maria Conforti was born at Casalora di Ravadese, Italy, the son of Rinaldo and Antonia Conforti. At the age of seven, he entered the Christian Brothers' school in Parma and, each day, visited a crucifix to pray and to receive divine guidance. He read about the life of St. Francis Xavier and soon wanted a missionary life. So, despite parental opposition, he entered the seminary in Parma at age eighteen to begin his apostolate.

A mysterious illness threatened Guido's ordination, but he was healed at a shrine dedicated to the Blessed Mother. He was thus ordained on September 22, 1888, and worked in diocesan positions until December 3, 1895, the feast of St. Francis Xavier. On that day, he founded a seminary for the training of missionaries. Three years later, on that same date, he founded the Congregation of St. Xavier for Foreign Missions.

Guido sent out two missionaries to China the following year and founded a mission aid society to assist the Xaverians overseas. At the time, he was also serving as assistant rector of the diocesan seminary, vicar of priests, and director of the Propagation of the Faith. On June 11, 1902, he made his vows with the Xaverians and began an almost endless series of visits and renewal programs. Four more missionaries were sent to China; in 1912, the first Xaverian bishop of the missions was consecrated.

In September 1907, Guido was appointed archbishop of Parma, being consecrated on November 12. He became the "shepherd of two flocks" — the people of his archdiocese and his missionaries, hundreds of miles across the sea. In August 1918, he became president of the Union of Italian Missionaries and, in 1920, witnessed the Holy See's approval of the congregation's constitution. He visited China in the fall of 1928, returning by train across the wilds of Siberia.

The Xaverians spread to Asia, Africa, Brazil, Japan, the Philippines, Taiwan, Mexico, Spain, and the United States. The missionaries conduct parishes, hospitals, leprosariums, orphanages, schools, and colleges. Guido, having carefully guided the congregation as he had guarded the faithful of Parma, died with his people around him.

Pope John Paul II beatified Guido Maria Conforti on March 17, 1996, announcing:

> Called to be Pastor of a portion of God's people in an area where a disturbing rejection of the Faith was occurring, Guido Maria Conforti discovered, in the way of the mission *ad gentes,* a providential journey by which he could cause a new current of divine life to flow into the souls of believers, increasing in them the fire of great missionary zeal. . . .
>
> But what was the source from which his tireless zeal and total dedication to the mission *ad gentes* drew strength? It was Christ's Cross, a source of inexhaustible love in those who give themselves to their brothers and sisters, near and far. Thus, this new Blessed was a shining example of

priestly spirituality, always motivated by living faith and indomitable missionary spirit. A model of genuine pastoral charity who knew how to invite believers to open their hearts to those who were distant without forgetting the needs of local communities, so that Christ, redeemer of man, might be proclaimed to all.

⊹

Guillaume Joseph Chaminade
(April 8, 1761 – January 22, 1850)
Keeping Christianity Alive in the French Revolution

The founder of the Daughters of Mary Immaculate and the Society of Mary, Guillaume Joseph Chaminade was born in Périgueux, France, the fourteenth child of a deeply Catholic family. Three of his brothers became priests, and in 1771, Guillaume also entered the minor seminary of Mussidan. Ordained a priest in 1785, he served for five years in various clerical positions as France became engulfed in a revolution. In 1790, a year after the outbreak of the Revolution, he transferred to Bordeaux.

He refused to take the oath of the so-called Civil Constitution of the Clergy in 1791 and, despite great risks, continued to serve secretly in his priestly ministry. During this period, he met Marie-Thérèse Charlotte de Lamourous (1754-1836), who became of his closest friends and who later joined him in founding the *Miséricorde* in Bordeaux to aid women in desperate circumstances. In 1795, he was assigned to the dangerous mission of receiving back into the diocese those priests who had repented taking the constitutional oath and desired to return to the Church.

At the height of the oppression in France (1797), Guillaume was forced to flee to Saragossa, Spain, where he remained for three years in exile. During a visit to the Shrine of Our Lady of the Pillar, he first conceived his determination to establish a religious community of both clergy and laity dedicated to Mary.

In November 1800, he was able finally to return to Bordeaux, where he continued to focus on his Marian sodality. He saw the sodality as a possible means to re-Christianize France after so many years of repression. Not long after his return to France, he was named apostolic administrator for the reorganization of the diocese of Bazas and, in 1801, received the title of Missionary Apostolic from the Holy See.

The Sodality of Bordeaux spread to other dioceses of the region, then throughout the rest of France. In 1816, together with (future Venerable) Adèle de Batz de Trenquelléon (1789-1828), he founded the Institute of the Daughters of Mary Immaculate at Agen; the next year, at Bordeaux, he established the Society of Mary, whose members were later called Marianists. The two institutes grew in popularity across France, and in 1839, they received the *decretum laudis* from Pope Gregory XVI. The Society of Mary expanded to Switzerland in 1839, then the United States of America in 1849. (Today, there are over 1,900 members of the Marianists in the world.)

In his last years, Guillaume endured many forms of suffering, including poor health, financial difficulties, and disagreements with some of his own members. He faced these trials with patience and died at peace in Bordeaux.

Pope John Paul II beatified Guillaume Joseph Chaminade on September 3, 2000, declaring:

> The beatification during the Jubilee Year of Guillaume Joseph Chaminade, founder of the Marianists, reminds the faithful that it is their task to find ever new ways of bearing witness to the faith, especially in order to reach those who are far from the Church and who do not have the usual means of knowing Christ. Guillaume Joseph Chaminade invites each Christian to be rooted in his Baptism, which conforms him to the Lord Jesus and communicates the Holy Spirit to him.

Fr. Chaminade's love for Christ, in keeping with the French school of spirituality, spurred him to pursue his tireless work by founding spiritual families in a troubled period of France's religious history. His filial attachment to Mary maintained his inner peace on all occasions, helping him to do Christ's will. His concern for human moral and religious education calls the entire Church to renew her attention to young people, who need both teachers and witnesses in order to turn to the Lord and take their part in the Church's mission.

$\mathcal{H}$

☩

Honorat a Biala Podlaska Kozminski
(October 16, 1829 – December 16, 1916)
A Faith Perfected in Trial

A Polish confessor, Honorat a Biala Podlaska Kozminski founded the Felician congregation.

He was born Florence Wenceslaus John Kozminski in Biala, Poland, the second of four children of an architect and his wife. From a devout, rather wealthy family, Florence attended the Fine Arts School in Warsaw, but when his father died in 1845, the young man turned against his religion.

In 1846, he was accused falsely by the Russian occupiers of Poland and was imprisoned on a charge of treason. This imprisonment became a blessing in disguise: through illness and torment, he endured patiently until his release in 1847 — and regained his faith.

Florence became a Capuchin Franciscan in December 1848, receiving the name Honorat in religion. He was ordained four years later on December 8, 1852, and started his ministry by writing and serving as a spiritual director. Honorat was revered in Warsaw, where he preached against the factions threatening the Church and founded Circles of the Living Rosary, which helped to revive the Faith and bring the people back to prayer and frequent Communion.

With Maria Angela Truszkowska, Honorat founded the Sisters of St. Felix of Cantalice in November 1855, dedicated to charitable missions; he also founded the Sister Servants of Mary Immaculate in 1878. During the Russian period of suppression, he moved to Zakroczym, where he was kept under house arrest in a local monastery but still managed to give great consolation to the people. He promoted the Third Order of St. Francis, using the rules and the spirit of this form of lay dedication to strengthen the Faith in a time of severe trial.

In 1892, Honorat had to move to Nowe Miasto, where he was able to continue his ministry as a confessor and spiritual director under Russian control. In 1895, he was appointed commissary of the Capuchin Franciscans in Poland.

He died in 1916, in Nowe Miasto, after a painful illness.

Pope John Paul II beatified Honorat a Biala Podlaska Kozminski on October 16, 1988, saying:

> He was a man of constant prayer, especially of adoration of the Blessed Sacrament, immersed in God and at the same time open to earthly reality. An eyewitness account said that "he always walked with God." He shows us how to read the signs of the times, how to persevere according to God's will, and work in difficult times.

✠

Hyacinthe Marie Cormier (December 8, 1832 – 1916)
Counselor to Pope Pius X

Hyacinthe Marie Cormier was born in Orléans, France, and baptized Henri-Marie. Raised devoutly, he displayed a brilliant intellect and a disciplined piety that brought him to the attention of many. He was well prepared to pursue a brilliant career, but he entered the Dominican Order in 1856. Completing his seminary training, Henri-Marie was ordained and received the name Hyacinthe, then given the task of restoring the Order in the provinces of Lyons and Toulouse.

At first, he served as a professor of theology, demonstrating considerable knowledge of the Faith and a winning approach in the classroom. He was elected prior, then Provincial Superior for four separate terms, and in these roles he was able to draw on historical perspectives of the religious life to counterbalance the turbulent demands of his own era. In 1891, Hyacinthe was appointed aide to the Master General of the Order, then Procurator General in 1896.

In May 1904, he became the seventy-sixth Master General of the Dominicans. A pious and strict observer of the Dominican religious spirit, he promoted academic studies in the Order. In 1910, he founded the Angelicum in Rome, where he was a close friend and aide to Pope (St.) Pius X. Hyacinthe not only broadened the apostolic scope of the Dominicans but deepened the spiritual and intellectual foundations as well. His Cause was opened in 1935, just decades after his death.

Pope John Paul II beatified Hyacinthe Marie Cormier on November 20, 1994, declaring:

Truth is not an abstract notion. For us it is one person, the person of Christ, King of the universe. In his life, Fr. Cormier never ceased to live the truth and he passed it on to all his Dominican brothers with humility and perseverance. Did he not combine truth with charity in his motto, *Caritas veritatis?* Indeed, the founder of the Angelicum University reminds us that God requires us to use the faculties of our spirit, a reflection of his own, to glorify him.

J

✠

Ignatius Falzon (July 1, 1813 – July 1, 1865)
Evangelist of Malta

Ignatius Falzon was born at Valetta, Malta, and baptized Nazju. His father was a prominent lawyer and judge, and he had two brothers in the priesthood. Nazju was tonsured at the age of fifteen, receiving minor orders and taking the religious name Ignatius. He then went on to earn a doctorate in secular and canon law. He did not, however, feel worthy of the priesthood and began a ministry on Malta as a dedicated layman.

His life was devoted to catechetics — he learned English in order to evangelize the many British soldiers and seamen who were on duty in Malta — and to intense prayer, with a special devotion to the Holy Eucharist. Aided by a group of dedicated Maltese lay people, he prepared 650 British troops for baptism. Ignatius also became a Franciscan Tertiary, translating the Franciscan ideals into his apostolate. His life inspired (the future Blessed) Giorgio Preca and countless others. When he died, Ignatius was buried in the family tomb in the Church of St. Mary of Jesus in Valetta.

Pope John Paul II beatified Ignatius Falzon on May 9, 2001, in Malta, announcing:

> He renounced the worldly success for which his background had prepared him, in order to serve the spiritual good of others, including the many British soldiers and sailors stationed in Malta at the time.

✠

Ignatius Maloyan (April 1869 – June 11, 1915)
Turkish Martyr

Ignatius Maloyan was born in Shouks Allah, Mardin, Turkey, the fourth of eight children in the family. At age fourteen, he was sent to Bzommar, Lebanon, for his education, but after five years, he was forced to return home because of poor health. After a rest and recuperation period of three years, he returned to Bzommar, where he completed his priestly studies and was ordained in 1896.

Ignatius labored in Alexandria and Cairo, Egypt, where he suffered an eye ailment that kept him in Egypt until 1910. He was then sent to the Diocese of Mardin to restore order, becoming the archbishop there in 1911. Three years later, on June 3, 1915, he was arrested by the Turkish officials and taken in chains to the local court, where he and others were told to convert to Islam. When they refused, the archbishop and his companions were beaten and had their fingernails torn out. Some 440 Armenians were taken to a site called Chikhan, where Ignatius had to witness their deaths. The Turkish official in charge of the massacre then shot Ignatius as he prayed.

Pope John Paul II beatified Ignatius Maloyan on October 7, 2001, declaring:

Archbishop Ignatius Maloyan, who died a martyr when he was forty-six, reminds us of every Christian's spiritual combat, whose faith is exposed to the attacks of evil.

✛

Ildephonse (Alfredo) Schuster
(January 18, 1880 – August 30, 1954)
Opponent of Mussolini

The cardinal archbishop of Milan, Ildephonse Schuster rose up to oppose Fascism and its inherent evils.

He was born in Rome, to parents of German descent. Always known for his intense prayer life, he entered the Benedictines and strictly observed the Order's spiritual practices. He served in many capacities, displaying holiness and a firm faith.

In 1929, Ildephonse, recognized for his holiness and qualities of leadership, was consecrated the archbishop of Milan. The Holy See also gave him the rank of cardinal. Italy was in the grip of Fascism when Ildephonse governed Milan. As Mussolini and his confederates tightened their hold on the nation, Ildephonse studied that political system carefully. He made no protests in the early stages, seeing the advances and unity brought to all areas of Italian life. The rampant brutality of Mussolini's government, however, and the rise of the Nazis, alerted Ildephonse to the coming threat. He soon wasted no time in denouncing Fascism as a "heresy," an act that put him in considerable danger.

Small in stature, Ildephonse nevertheless became a powerful presence in Italy; some in the government even suspected him of wanting to overthrow Fascism and began campaigns that smeared his reputation and disgraced him publicly. As the war continued and Italians began to endure the results of Allied military power, the Fascists tried to silence Ildephonse, but he would not surrender his principles. He lived through the last terrible stages of the war, leading the Milanese people and trying to ease their burdens.

He died in Venegono, Italy, having survived World War II and its horrors. Just before his death, Ildephonse told his seminarians, "You want something to remember me by ... All I can give you is an invitation to holiness."

Pope John Paul II beatified Ildephonse Schuster on May 12, 1996, observing:

> Love for Christ, expressed in tireless service to the Church, was the heart of the spirituality and apostolic activity of [...] Schuster, for many years the indefatigable pastor of the Archdiocese of Milan. "A man of prayer, study, and action," as he was described by Archbishop Giovanni Montini in the speech he gave on entering the Archdiocese, "he had no other concern than the spiritual salvation of his people" (*Rivista diocesana Milanese,* January 1955, 9). His pastoral ministry was motivated by the spirit of prayer and contemplation proper to the Benedictine tradition. His monastic spirituality, nourished by daily meditation on Sacred Scripture, thus expanded into active collaboration with the Holy See and into his generous service to the Ambrosian community, "edified and consoled by him until the very end by the regular, devoted celebration of the sacred mysteries and by the example of a clear and consistent life" (Ambrosian Missal, Preface of the Memorial).

☩

Innocencio Immaculada — see Martyrs of Astoria

☩

Isidore Bakanja (c. 1885 – August 15, 1909)
Catechist Martyr

Isidore Bakanja was born in the tribal lands of the Boangi and educated by Christian missionaries in Mbandaka (Coquilhatville). There, he worked as a mason, and there, he was baptized on May 6, 1906.

Isidore was graced with a remarkable faith and heroic devotion to the Blessed Mother. He learned his catechism and began to make converts among his own people while working for a kindly white colonist. When that colonist moved to the settlement of Ikile, Isidore followed him. In Ikile, however, he found himself in the hands of an atheistic, hateful white supervisor who had a particular prejudice against the rosary and scapular. He warned Isidore to put such devotions aside.

When Isidore remained loyal to the Blessed Virgin and wore the scapular, the white man beat him without mercy. Isidore was brutally scourged and dragged in chains to a rubber-processing room, where he was left for dead. An inspector for the colonist's company found him and cared for him at a nearby plantation, but Isidore could not recover from the internal and external wounds inflicted upon him, and he spent days in pain as a result. He died as a child of Mary at Busirá, having publicly forgiven his murderer. The white supervisor subsequently was tried and convicted by a local court.

Pope John Paul II beatified Isidore Bakanja on April 24, 1994, proclaiming:

> You were a man of heroic faith, Isidore Bakanja, young layman of Zaire. As a baptized person, called to spread the Good news, you shared your faith and witness to Christ with such conviction that to your companions you seemed one of those valiant lay faithful, the catechists. Yes, Blessed Isidore, absolutely faithful to your baptismal promises, you were a true catechist, toiling generously for "the Church in Africa and for her evangelizing mission."

⊹

Isidore of St. Joseph de Loor (1881 – October 6, 1916)
Faithful Doorkeeper

A Passionist Lay Brother, Isidore of St. Joseph de Loor protected his monastery during World War I.

He was born in Vrasene, Belgium, the oldest of three children. The family attended daily Mass, and Isidore was raised with prayers and deep religious values. He attended school, but only for six years, as his family needed him in the labor force. At the age of twenty-six, he entered the Passionists as a lay brother, making Christ Crucified the center of his religious life. He was then called Isidore of St. Joseph.

Isidore was drawn to prayer and solitude as a Passionist, strictly observing the customs of his monastic vocation and accepting all things as the will of God. In 1914, he became the porter, or doorkeeper, at the monastery of Kortrijk. When the military destruction of World War I threatened the monastery, the monks evacuated, but Isidore remained behind as a voluntary custodian. He endured the loneliness and military threats with calm, knowing he was fulfilling his obligations, and was able to welcome his fellow Passionists when they returned.

BROTHER ISIDORE
Saintly Laybrother

by Nicholas Schneiders, C.P.
+ + +
A Grail Publication

Isidore then suffered from a painful cancer that developed in his right eye. That eye had to be surgically removed, and he endured the medical treatment with patience and calm, inspiring all who cared for him. In 1916, it was learned that the cancer had spread to his intestines. Isidore collapsed and was confined to his bed. There, he prayed, asking forgiveness from his fellow Passionists for his faults. After his death at Kortrijk Monastery, miracles were reported immediately at his tomb.

Pope John Paul II beatified Isidore of St. Joseph de Loor on September 30, 1984, announcing:

> In Blessed Isidore de Loor it is given to us to contemplate above all the face of the suffering Christ, in whom the infinite love of God is revealed. The new Blessed . . . is surely a fascinating and providential example for our era (taken up with freedom which is sometimes quite equivocal), of a growing conformity to the Will of the heavenly Father in following Christ Jesus.

✠

Ivan Merz (December 16, 1896 – May 10, 1928)
Founder of Youth Movements

Ivan Merz was born in Banja Luka, Bosnia. He studied briefly at the military academy of Wiener Noustadt, then enrolled at the University of Vienna in 1915 with the intention of becoming a teacher.

In March 1916, Ivan was drafted into the Army of the Austrian Empire and sent into combat against the Italians. He spent nearly two years at the front and found the fighting powerfully transforming. He took to daily prayer, developed a deep love of the Mass, and made a vow of personal chastity.

After the war, he returned to school in Vienna (1919-20), then studied in Paris (1920-22). In 1923, he earned a degree in philosophy with the thesis on "The Influence of the Liturgy on French Authors." He was soon appointed a professor of language and French literature and earned the respect and devotion of his students.

To assist the young people of Croatia, he founded two youth movements, the League of Young Croatian Catholics and the Croatian League of Eagles. His intention was to fashion a movement that would encourage holiness in the young and promote the liturgy among them. He also wrote extensively on theology, papal primacy, and the Church.

Sadly, he died young — at the age of thirty-two — and was mourned by the many thousands of young and old who knew him. Pope John Paul II beatified him on June 22, 2003. He declared:

> The name of Ivan Merz has meant in the past a programme of life and of activity for an entire generation of young Catholics. Today too it must do the same! Your country and your Church, dear young people, have experienced difficult times and now there is a need to work together so that life on all levels will fully return to normal. I therefore appeal to each of you; I invite you not to step back, not to yield to the temptation to become discouraged, but to multiply initiatives which will make Bosnia-Hercegovina once more a land of reconciliation, encounter and peace.

> The future of this land depends also on you! Do not seek a more comfortable life elsewhere, do not flee from your responsibilities and expect others to resolve problems, but resolutely counter evil with the power of good.

> Like Blessed Ivan, strive for a personal encounter with Christ which sheds new light on life. May the Gospel be the great ideal guiding your approaches and your decisions! Thus you will become missionaries in word and deed, signs of God's love and credible witnesses of the merciful presence of Christ. Never forget: "one does not light a lamp and put it under a bushel" (cf. Mt 5:15).

J

+

Jacinta Marto of Fatima — see Francisco and Jacinta Marto

+

Jacinto de los Angeles and Juan Bautista (September 16, 1700)
"Guardians of the Faith" of Oaxaca

Jacinto de los Angeles and Juan Bautista were martyred by their pagan neighbors because they opposed the revival of ancient cultic practices.

These two saints lived in San Francisco Cajonos, in Oaxaca, Mexico. Juan was married to Josefa de la Cruz and had a daughter. Jacinto was married to Petrona and had two children. He was also a descendant of tribal chiefs of the region.

Both men had served as "Guardians of the Faith," or religious inspectors, for some time when they heard about idolatrous rituals taking place in the home of a man named José Flores. The men tried to halt the ceremonies and faced an angry mob. They took refuge in the local Dominican convent, but the mob demanded that they be turned over, threatening to burn down the convent and to slay all the Christians if Jacinto and Juan were not given up for torture.

They were taken to Tanga Hill (Monte Fiscal-Sante) in San Pedro, where they were again beaten, then cut by knives. Their hearts were ripped from their chests and given to dogs. Their remains were recovered and buried in Villa Alta Church. In 1889, they were entombed in the Cathedral of Oaxaca.

Pope John Paul II beatified Jacinto de los Angeles and Juan Bautista in Mexico City on August 1, 2002, announcing:

> Faced with the human suffering that accompanies the journey of faith, St. Peter urges, "Rejoice insofar as you share Christ's sufferings, that you may also rejoice and be glad when his glory is revealed" (1 Pt 4:13). With this conviction, Juan Bautista and Jacinto de los Ángeles faced martyrdom, remaining faithful to their devotion to the true, living God and rejecting idols.

As they were being tortured, they were invited to renounce their Catholic faith and save themselves. But they answered bravely: "Once we have professed Baptism, we shall always follow the true religion": a beautiful example of how nothing, not even our life, should be put before our baptismal commitment. This is the same example given by the early Christians, who, born to new life through Baptism, abandoned all forms of idolatry (cf. Tertullian, *De baptismo*, 12, 15).

⁜

Jacques (Jacob) Desiré Laval
(September 18, 1803 – September 9, 1864)
"One Who Is a Saint and Who Always Says That He Does Nothing"

The first beatified member of the Congregation of the Holy Spirit and Immaculate Heart of Mary, Jacques Desiré Laval was born in Croth, France, and spent his childhood watching his mother care for the needy of the region and learning about the priesthood from a pious uncle. Educated in local schools, then at Evreux, he studied at Stanislaus College, earning a medical degree in 1830. Though Jacques started his medical practice in St. André and St. Ivry-la-Bataille, he longed to serve in the missions. Finally, he gave up his practice and entered the seminary of St. Sulpice, where he was ordained a priest in 1838.

Three years later, Jacques entered the Congregation of the Immaculate Heart of Mary, which had joined with the Congregation of the Holy Ghost. He was sent to Mauritius on September 14, 1861, to a parish of 80,000 souls, serving there for twenty-six years. He brought unique medical and scientific procedures and training to his missionary labors, instituted agricultural and sanitation reforms, and converted 67,000 former slaves.

In the Mauretian environment, Jacques was able to establish many sanitation and health standards to protect the people, especially the poor, who were at the mercy of diseases and natural disasters in the region. He was tireless in his efforts to serve their spiritual and physical needs.

Eventually, however, exhausted by his mission work, he died in Port Louis and was mourned by people of all faiths. Jacques' Cause was opened in 1918.

Pope John Paul II beatified Jacques Desiré Laval on April 29, 1979, stating that this missionary brought a true Christian dimension to his labors. As Jacques settled into his mission, the Holy Father declared:

He has no overall plan, he has no theory about the apostolate . . . He has all the kindness of a father, all the pity of a pastor, for these poor people.

One by one they come towards him. He receives them with respect, sweetness, and cordiality.

✛

Jakob Gapp (July 26, 1897 – August 13, 1943)
Enemy of the Nazis

Jakob Gapp was born in Wattens, Austria, the seventh child of Martin Gapp and Antonia Wach. He was educated locally, then by the Franciscans in Hall, an Austrian Tirolean town. Called to military service in May 1915, he was wounded and received a medal after serving a period as a prisoner of war until 1919.

Returning from the war, Jakob entered the Marianist novitiate at Greisinghall, where he made his first vows in 1921; he made his profession at Antony, France, on August 27, 1925, and entered the seminary. On April 5, 1930, he was ordained at Fribourg, then sent to Graz.

He worked for eight years in the Marianist houses in that area of Austria, displaying personal asceticism and charity for the destitute. The Nazis were coming into power in Germany, and he began to warn the faithful about the incompatibility between Nazism and the Church. Not surprisingly, his outspoken opposition forced Jakob to flee Graz, and his own superior sent him home for his safety.

In October 1938, the Gestapo forbade Jakob from teaching religion; in December of that year, however, he denounced the Nazis from the pulpit and was advised to leave the country. He escaped to Bordeaux, France; then, in May 1939, he went to Spain to labor in San Sebastián, Cadiz, and Valencia. However, the Gestapo lured him back to France by sending false word that two people fleeing the Nazis desired catechetical instruction. He was arrested on November 9, 1942 in Hendaye, France, and taken to Berlin.

Jakob was executed at the Platzensee Prison in Berlin at 7:08 p.m., by guillotine, on August 13, 1943. At first he was denied a proper burial, as the Nazis feared his grave would become a center for honoring him as a martyr; they gave his physical remains to the Anatomical Biological Institute at the University. Eventually, however, his burial site became a place of silent protest and opposition to the Third Reich.

Pope John Paul II beatified Jakob Gapp on November 24, 1996, proclaiming:

Fr. Jakob Gapp gave his witness with the power of the courageous word and the deep convictions that between the pagan ideology of National Socialism and Christianity there could be no compromise. In this clash he rightly saw an apocalyptic battle. He knew where he had to stand, and for this reason, he was condemned to death.

✠

Jakob Kern (April 11, 1897 – October 20, 1924)
A Solemn Profession In Heaven

A Norbertine priest and wounded war veteran, Jakob Kern suffred heroically.

He was born in Vienna, Austria, and was baptized Franz Alexander. One of three children in the family, he entered the minor seminary at Hollabrunn at age eleven. Before he could complete his studies, however, he was drafted into military service and sent to Vöklabruck for officer training. In 1916, Franz was assigned to the Italian front. He was wounded on September 11 and evacuated to Salzburg to recuperate.

Franz returned to Vienna after recovering, but he was recalled to military service and served until the end of the war. When he finally returned to his seminary studies, he entered the Premonstratensian Abbey of Geras, taking the place of a Norbertine who had left the monastery previously. Franz entered the novitiate in 1920, receiving his religious name of Jakob, and was ordained on July 23, 1922, in St. Stephen's Cathedral.

He then served in Geras Abbey in lower Austria, near the Czech border, and he was zealous, despite increasing pain. His wounds began to develop severe complications, and he had to have several ribs removed; the operation being performed without anesthetic because of his weakened condition. Jakob did not complain and apologized to the surgeon for being such a problem.

As he recuperated in Geras, he seemed to gain strength and was scheduled for his solemn profession on October 20, 1924. He was also scheduled for surgery that same day. Jakob predicted that his solemn profession would be in heaven. He died during the operation and his remains were interred in Geras Abbey.

Pope John Paul II beatified Jakob Kern in *Heldenplastz*, "Heroes' Square," in Vienna, Austria, on June 21, 1998, announcing:

Blessed Jakob Kern stands before us as a witness of fidelity to the priesthood. At the beginning it was a childhood desire that he expressed in imitating the priest at the altar. Later, this desire matured. The purification of pain revealed the profound meaning of his priestly vocation: to unite his own life with the sacrifice of Christ on the Cross and to offer it vicariously for the salvation of others.

╫

Jan Adelbert Balicki (January 25, 1869 – March 15, 1948)
"Humility in Person"

Jan Adelbert Balicki was born in Staromiescie, Poland, where he was educated in local schools. In September 1888 he entered the Seminary of Przemsyl and was ordained to the priesthood on July 20, 1892. A year later, he was assigned to the Pontifical Gregorian University in Rome to continue his studies. In 1897, Jan became a professor of dogmatic theology in Przemsyl, becoming vice-rector in 1927 and rector in the following year. By 1934, however, his health was so poor that he had to resign his position, although he continued to reside in the seminary and served as confessor and spiritual director there.

In September 1939, Russian troops entered Przemsyl, sharing occupation of the area with the Germans. Jan remained in the Soviet zone to protect the seminary, putting himself at risk. In October 1941, the Soviets were withdrawn, and the bishop and other priests returned. Jan remained active until February 1948, when he was diagnosed with bilateral pneumonia and tuberculosis. He died in Przemysl, recognized immediately as "humility in person" by the faithful of the area, then all of Poland. His Cause was opened and supported by Cardinal Wojtyla, who became Pope John Paul II.

Pope John Paul II beatified Jan Adelbert Balicki on August 17, 2002, announcing:

> Blessed Jan Balicki's life was marked by his service of mercy. As a priest, his heart was always open to the needy. His ministry of mercy, besides offering help to the sick and the poor, found a particularly energetic expression in the confessional, where he was filled with patience and humility, always open to bringing the repentant sinner back to the throne of divine grace.

✠

Jan Beyzym (May 15, 1850 – October 2, 1912)
Apostle to the Lepers of Madagascar

Jan Beyzym was born at Beyzymy Wielkie, Ukraine, and trained in the Faith as a child. On December 10, 1872, he entered the Society of Jesus, being ordained to the priesthood on July 26, 1881, in Krakow, Poland. He was first assigned to teaching faculties of local colleges; then, in 1898, he was sent to the Jesuit mission in Madagascar, the site called Red Island.

His first posting in the mission was to Ambahivoraka, a leprosarium near Antananarivo, where there were 150 lepers needing medical and spiritual attention. Jan had to adjust to the horrors of the leper settlement, but he learned to nurse and inspire each one of the victims entrusted to his care. The needs of the settlement were so great that he called on his fellow Poles for aid and began to collect the necessary funds to bring relief to his charges. In 1903, Jan was able to start a hospital at Mirana, opening the medical facility on August 16, 1911.

He centered his life on the Mass and on Marian devotion, being a man of prayer. The people of Madagascar, seeing his devotion to the lepers and to the needs of many, mourned his passing when he died in Fianarantsoa, Madagascar.

Pope John Paul II beatified Jan Beyzym on August 17, 2002, announcing:

> The charitable work of Blesssed Jan Beyzym was an integral component of his fundamental mission: bringing the Gospel to those who do not know it. This is the greatest gift of mercy: bringing people to Christ and giving them the opportunity to know and savor his love. Therefore I ask you: pray for the birth of missionary vocations in the Church in Poland. Support missionaries unceasingly with your prayers.

✠

Jeanne Jugan — see Marie of the Cross Jugan

✠

Jeremiah of Valachia Kostistik (June 29, 1556 – March 5, 1625)
The First Romanian Beatified

Jeremiah of Valachia Kostistik was a Franciscan healer and Marian devotee.

He was born in Zaro, Romania, the eldest son of a local farmer, and baptized John. Called to the religious life when he matured, John entered the Capuchin Franciscans in Naples and was professed in 1579, receiving his religious name.

He began his apostolate at Sant' Eframo Nuovo, where he would spend decades giving service to the people of the region. They were stunned as they watched him perform his duties with a spirit of the selfless imitation of Christ. He was devoted to Christ Crucified, the Holy Eucharist, and especially to the Blessed Virgin.

The sick and the abandoned were the focus of Jeremiah's apostolate, but his reputation for wise counsel attracted people from all walks of life, and patients clamored for his attention. Bishops, nobles, and many others tolerated no other caregivers when they needed medical care. Jeremiah's union with Christ provided the source of his self-sacrificing, and he radiated calm and comfort.

He took a chill, however, while visiting patients in early March 1625. Jeremiah became very ill as a result and died of pneumonia at age sixty-nine.

Pope John Paul II beatified Jeremiah of Valachia Kostistik on October 30, 1983, declaring:

> The glorification of this faithful Servant of the Lord, after three centuries of mysterious concealment, is reserved to our time, marked by the search for ecumenism and solidarity among peoples on an international level. Jeremiah a Valachia is the first Romanian to ascend officially to the honors of the altar.

✠

Jildo Irwa (c. 1906 – October 1918)
Young Ugandan Martyr

Jildo Irwa was born in the village of Bar-Kitoba, Uganda, to Ato and Okeny, pagan parents (although his father, Okeny, later became a Christian). On June 6, 1916, Jildo was baptized by Cesare Gambaretto; he received his first Communion on the same day and was confirmed on October 15, 1916.

While still a young man, Jildo displayed enormous zeal in proclaiming the faith. When Daudi Okelo was named to serve as catechist in the Ugandan area around Paimol, Jildo volunteered to join him; he proved very popular in this ministry, earning considerable respect for his commitment to the faith.

Jildo and Daudi were threatened with death from a group of raiders who demanded that they cease their evangelization, but neither would stop. Once he knew that Daudi had been murdered — speared to death — Jildo spoke courageously to the attackers, declaring to them that they must kill him as well. He was then set upon, dragged outside of the hut, run through with a spear, and finally, hacked to death with a knife. His age at his martyrdom is uncertain; he was either twelve or fourteen years old.

(See also Daudi Okelo for other details.)

✠

Johann Nepomuk Tsciderer von Gleifheim
(April 15, 1777 – December 3, 1860)
Scholar and Aristocrat

Johann Nepomuk Tsciderer von Gleifheim was a prelate of profound charity.

He was born into a high-ranking noble family at Bolzano, Italy, and was raised devoutly in a family well connected to the outstanding churchmen of the time. He entered the seminary and was ordained on July 27, 1800, by the bishop of Trento, Emmanuel Count Von Thul. Johann began his priestly ministry in the diocese, then was sent to Rome to earn his doctorate in moral and pastoral theology, and returned to the seminary to serve as a professor.

In 1810, Johann was made pastor at Sarnthal and went to Meran nine years later. In 1826, he was made a cathedral canon and pro-vicar of the diocese, so honored by Prince-Bishop Luschin. He demonstrated such holiness that, in 1832, he was nominated a bishop by Prince-Bishop Galura of Brixen; in 1834, was nominated by Emperor Francis I (r. 1804-1835) as bishop of Trento. Johann was consecrated on May 15, 1835. In the role of bishop, he was revered for his virtue, gentleness, and charity.

Johann literally gave away all that he possessed to the sick and the poor, and built churches, libraries, and charitable institutions with his own personal fortune. He left his property to the seminary — now called the Joanneum — and bequeathed a legacy to a school for the deaf and dumb. He also distinguished himself by serving victims of two cholera epidemics in his area.

Pope John Paul II beatified Johann Nepomuk Tschiderer von Gleifheim on April 30, 1995, in Trento, praising his episcopal zeal and apostolic labors of this scholarly holy man. Thousands of the faithful rejoiced at his beatification.

✠

John XXIII (Angelo Giuseppe Roncalli)
(November 25, 1881 – June 3, 1963)
"Good Pope John"

The future Pope John XXIII was born in Sotto il Monte, Italy, the fourth child in a family of fourteen, and baptized Angelo Giuseppe Roncalli. His parents were sharecroppers and poor, but he received an education from his uncle Zaverio and Fr. Francesco Rebuzzini in the local parish. In 1812, Angelo entered the seminary in Bergamo, becoming a Franciscan Tertiary four years later. From 1901 to 1905, he studied at the Pontifical Roman Seminary and was ordained to the priesthood on August 10, 1904.

Following his ordination, he was appointed secretary to the bishop of Bergamo and taught and preached in the region. He was drafted into the Italian military in 1915 and served both as a sergeant in the medical corps and as a chaplain. When World War I ended, he opened a house for students. He was then called to the Vatican by Pope Benedict XV (r. 1914-1922) and given the office of Italian President of the Society for the Propagation of the Faith. In 1925, he was named Apostolic Visitator to Bulgaria, and was consecrated as a bishop on March 19, 1925.

In Bulgaria, the bishop was well respected. He served the people after the earthquake in 1928 and conducted Vatican affairs in Bulgaria with tact and warmth. In 1935, he became the Apostolic Delegate to Turkey and Greece, again displaying sensitivity and diplomacy in dealing with Orthodox and Islamic matters. During World War II, he saved countless Jews by providing them with "transit visas" of the Vatican.

At the close of the war, he became the Apostolic Nuncio to France, appointed to this post by Pope Pius XII (r. 1939-1958). In this capacity, he aided in the rebuilding of France, showing himself both prudent and visionary in dealing with ecclesiastical associations and personnel. In 1953, he was made the Cardinal Patriarch of Venice.

Following the death of Pope Pius XII, Fr. Angelo was elected Pope, choosing the name John XXIII, on October 28, 1958. He was welcomed by people all around the world and issued encyclicals — *Pacem in Terris* and *Mater et Magistra* among them — that had an impact on postwar affairs. His *Journal of a Soul* was one of the best-selling books of his era. On January 25, 1959, he announced Vatican Council II and brought the prelates of the world into session from 1962-65. His motto — "Patience and Peace" — clearly demonstrated his spiritual maturity.

John XXIII died in Rome, and his remains were unearthed in 2001, at which time his body was found to be incorrupt. His remains were put on display in a crystal coffin in St. Peter's Square on June 3, 2001. Pope John Paul II beatified him on September 3 of that year, announcing:

> Today we contemplate in the glory of the Lord another pontiff, John XXIII, the Pope who impressed the world with the friendliness of his manner which radiated the remarkable goodness of his soul. How many people were won over by his simplicity of heart, combined with a broad experience of people and things.

✝

John Andrew Houben — see Charles of Mt. Argus Houben

✝

John Duns Scotus (c. 1265 – November 8, 1308)
"Subtle Doctor"

Called "the Minstrel of the Incarnate Word" and the "Herald of the Blessed Virgin," John Duns Scotus was a defender of the Immaculate Conception and one of the leading Franciscan theologians and philosophers of his time.

He was born in Duns, near Roxburgh, Scotland. His name is "John of Duns, the Scot" as a result.

About 1280, he entered the Franciscan Order and studied theology at Oxford under the brilliant William de Ware. Ordained in 1291, he also studied in Paris. He then taught at Oxford, Paris, and Cologne, but was exiled by King Philip IV the Fair of France, who was in a dispute with Pope Boniface VIII (r. 1294-1303). John went to Cologne and lived there until his death.

His school of philosophical thought was called Scotism, and it had an impact on the Franciscans and others in the historical period called the Middle Ages. John wrote commentaries on the *Sentences* of Peter Lombard, followed by his *Oxford Work* (*Opus Oxontense*), and by his *Parisian Papers* (*Reportatio Parisiensia*). He also produced commentaries on Aristotle and a work called *Selected Questions* (*Questiones Quodlibetales*).

He is called the "Subtle Doctor," affirming the Augustinian tenet while using new techniques of philosophy. He included Aristotelian tenets also, with the use of deduction and mathematics. John held that theology was not a scientific study in the strictest sense, but one also based upon revelation and authority. He viewed theology as a practical science because it pursues a practical end: the possession of God. Above all, although he criticized many of the theologians of his era, John was a truly holy man who gave Europe's faithful new insights into the mysteries of God and the Church.

John Duns Scotus is revered as a genuine Scholastic scholar and a profound intellect. He was the first theologian of note to proclaim the doctrine of the Immaculate Conception, and the Scotist School — chiefly among Franciscans — resulted from John's teachings. All of this is remarkable, given his death at a relatively young age. He is recorded as dying in Cologne.

Pope John Paul II beatified John Duns Scotus on March 20, 1993, giving praise to his philosophical genius and his abiding Franciscan spirituality.

✠

John Faesulanus — see Fra Angelico

✠

John Souzy and Companions — see Martyrs of La Rochelle

✠

José Aparicio Sanz and 232 Companions — see Martyrs of the Spanish Civil War

✠

José de Anchieta (March 19, 1534 — June 9, 1597)
"Great Son of Ignatius"

José de Anchieta was born in San Cristobal de la Laguna, Spain, and was a relative of Ignatius of Loyola.

At age eighteen, José consecrated himself to the Blessed Virgin and entered the Society of Jesus at Coimbra, Portugal, on May 1, 1551. He was sent to Brazil two years later, going to the mission at Quisininga. He would subsequently spend forty-four years in Brazil, founding missions, including Sao Paulo de Piratininga.

After ordination, he learned the native languages and wrote catechisms. In 1567, he was appointed Superior of the Jesuit province of Brazil, and a decade later became the Jesuit Provincial of Brazil. He was a thaumaturgist — a miracle worker — and healed many. Animals and birds came at his call, and witnesses claim that a wall of water rose around him when he prayed in the wilderness.

While serving as a hostage for the Tamuins during negotiations with that native people, José composed a 5,000-verse poem in his mind, remembering it months later in order to commit it to paper. He was able to suppress cannibalism and other pagan customs among the tribes because of the reverence he inspired.

José began a classical school, the first such institute in the New World, to teach Latin in Brazil's missions. Discovering that dramas and plays caught the attention of the local population, he taught actors to perform and stage doctrinal plays to educate his audiences. He continued to heal those who came to him and made his way through the perilous jungles without fear.

He died at Reritiba, Brazil, and the local tribes came in vast numbers to honor his passing. The bishop who preached at his funeral called him a first-rate missionary.

Pope John Paul II designated José de Anchieta as "this great son of Ignatius" at his beatification on June 22, 1980, praising his gifts and his pioneering missionary work as well as the profound spiritual union that sustained his mission labors for so many decades.

✛

Josefa Naval Girbes
(December 11, 1820 — February 24, 1893)
Mystic and Model for Young Women

Josefa Naval Girbes was born in Algemesi, near Valencia, Spain. Taught her catechism by her parist priest, she was confirmed in 1828 and received her First Communion a year later. Josefa took charge of the family residence after the death of her mother in 1833 and vowed perpetual virginity in 1838, allowing her to perform her apostolate at home. She became a Third Order Carmelite, remaining in the world and working to prepare young women of her area for marriage or convent life.

Josefa did excellent embroidery work and gave lessons in the art to young women. When they came to study, they soon discovered that she was a learned mystic as well who could impart the beauty of the Faith. Along with training many young women in needle arts, Josefa taught catechism and led many followers in advanced stages of prayer. She also assisted the dying and displayed heroism in the cholera epidemic of 1885.

A true spiritual daughter of St. Teresa of Ávila and St. John of the Cross, Josefa was revered as a mystic who had achieved mystical union with God at age fifty-five. She was also honored for fostering many religious vocations in her contact with others.

She died in Algemesi at the age of seventy-one, after serving as a quiet, humble personification of penance, prayer, and contemplation. Pope John Paul II beatified her on September 25, 1988, declaring:

> The Church sings a song of joy and praise to God for the beatification of Josefa Naval Girbes, a secular virgin who dedicated her life to the apostolate in her native town. A special characteristic of Josefa is her condition as a member of the laity. She, whose disciples filled the cloistered convents, remained as an unmarried woman in the world.

✛

Joseph-Marie Cassant (March 6, 1878 — June 17, 1903)
Joyful and Humble in Suffering

Joseph-Marie Cassant was born at Casseneuil, Lot-et-Garonne, in the diocese of Agen, France, where his parents worked as orchard keepers. He expressed a desire to become a priest from a young age, but was challenged from the start by a very poor memory. Nevertheless, his local parish priest encouraged his vocation.

Joseph-Marie still needed help with his studies, however, so the priest suggested that perhaps the Trappists might be a suitable place for him. The young man agreed readily, and on December 5, 1894, he entered the Cistercian Abbey of Sainte-Marie du Désert, in the diocese of Toulouse, France. The new novice quickly earned the favor of his fellow monks, who appreciated his joyous, prayerful nature.

Joseph-Marie made his final vows on May 24, 1900, and then began the hard task of studies for the priesthood. By staying focused utterly on the Eucharist — and with help from his superiors, who grasped fully the special qualities of the young monk — he passed his final examinations and was ordained for the priesthood on October 12, 1902.

Immediately, however, he was diagnosed with advanced tuberculosis. He spoke of his severe sufferings only when pressed, even as his health deteriorated steadily. He took the opportunity to use his ordeal to make of himself a sacrifice to Jesus and sought to emulate the Passion of Christ. On the morning of June 17, 1903, he received Holy Communion and died soon afterward.

He was mourned by the monks of the monastery, who recognized the heroic virtue he displayed in the very way that he led his life as a monk. In his humility, obedience, dedication to work, prayer, and — above all — the sacraments, he was a model for his fellow Trappists and for the world.

Pope John Paul II beatified Joseph-Marie on October 2, 2004. He said at that occasion:

> Fr. Joseph-Marie always put his trust in God, in contemplation of the mystery of the Passion and in communion with Christ present in the Eucharist. Thus, he was imbued with love for God and abandoned himself to him, "the only true happiness on earth," detaching himself from worldly goods in the silence of the Trappist monastery. In the midst of trials, his eyes fixed on Christ, he offered up his sufferings for the Lord and for the Church. May our contemporaries, especially contemplatives and the sick, discover following his example the mystery of prayer, which raises the world to God and gives strength in trial!

✠

Jozef Bilczewski (April 26, 1860 – March 23, 1923)
"Living Icon of the Good Shepherd"

The Archbishop of Lviv for the Latin rite, Jozef Bilczewski led the faithful during wars and Communist invasions.

He was born into a devout Catholic peasant family in Wilamowice, in Russian-occupied Ukraine, the eldest of nine children. In August 1880, he fulfilled what he perceived was a vocation to the priesthood by entering the Seminary of Kraków. He was ordained a priest on July 6, 1884.

After ordination, Jozef was sent to Vienna to continue his studies. He earned a doctorate in theology and was sent to Rome, then to Paris, to further his studies in dogmatic theology and Christian archaeology. Upon his return to Lviv in 1891, he was appointed a professor at the University of

Lviv, and later at the Jagiellonian University. There, he was well-respected and known for both his intelligence and his abiding faith.

On December 18, 1900, Pope Leo XIII appointed Jozef the Archbishop of Lviv for Latins by Pope Leo XIII. The see brought with it a host of challenges, especially the terrible destruction of the First World War (1914-18). He intervened frequently with the civil authorities on behalf of Poles, Ukrainians, and Jews in order to alleviate internal strife and prevent misunderstandings or miscarriages of justice. The Polish-Ukrainian War (1918-19) also caused considerable upheaval, including the arrest and murder of many priests.

The Bolshevik invasion (1919-20) brought even more suffering, as it focused its attention especially on merciless persecution of the Church. Between 1918 and 1921, the archdiocese of Lviv alone lost about 120 priests. But Jozef continued to lead his people with fortitude, resisting the oppression wherever possible. He died in Lviv still praying for the freedom of the Ukraine.

Pope John Paul II beatified Jozef Bilczewski on June 26, 2001, with other valiant martyrs of the Church in the Ukraine. The pontiff declared:

> Archbishop Józef Bilczewski invites us to be generous in living the love of God and neighbour. This was his supreme rule of life. From the early years of his priesthood he cultivated a burning passion for revealed Truth, and this led him to make theological research an original way of translating the command to love God into practical behaviour. In his priestly life, as in the various important positions he held at the Jan Casimir University in Lviv and at the Jagiellonian University in Kraków, he always gave example of his great love of neighbour as well as his love of God. He was especially concerned for the poor, and developed warm and respectful relations with his colleagues and students, who invariably reciprocated with esteem and affection.
>
> His appointment as Archbishop gave him the chance to widen and expand the range of his charity. In the especially difficult period of the First World War, Blessed Józef Bilczewski was like a living icon of the Good Shepherd, ready to encourage and support his people with inspired words full of kindness. He came to the aid of the needy, for whom he nurtured such a love that even beyond death he wanted to be with them, choosing to be laid to rest in the Janow cemetery in Lviv, where paupers were buried. A good and faithful servant of the Lord, motivated by deep spirituality and unceasing charity, he was loved and esteemed by all his fellow citizens, regardless of their religious convictions, rite, or nationality.

+

Joseph Gérard (March 12, 1831 – May 29, 1914)
"Friend of the Africans"

A pioneering Oblate missionary of Africa, Joseph Gérard was born at Boux-
ières-aux-Chênes, France, the son of Jean and Ursula Stofflet Gérard. For a
time, Joseph aided his farm parents as a shepherd; then, he was allowed to
study at Pont-á-Mousson. He entered the Nancy seminary on Easter Sunday, 1851, joined the Oblates of Mary Immaculate, and completed his studies at Marseilles.

Joseph was ordained in Natal, South Africa, in February 1854 and began
his missionary labors in the field. His first assignment to the Zulu tribe was
not successful, and he went to the Basotho mission in 1862, determined to
serve the tribes of the area faithfully. He took up residence in a tent in a valley and went from village to village to care for the sick. He baptized his first
converts in 1865. By 1875, he had 500 converts in his Mission of the Mother
of God, winning them with his holiness and devotion.

The following year, Joseph went to St. Monica's mission. He labored there
alone, celebrating his golden anniversary as a priest there in 1894, and continued his work at St. Monica's until 1897. He was beloved by all of the
Africans of the region, as his solitary mission continued decade after decade
in all seasons and all weather. His eyesight was weakening, and by May 1914,
he could no longer use his legs. Joseph offered his last Mass on May 24, and
five days later, at Roma, Lesotho, he simply crossed himself and died.

When word of his death spread, officials of the regional tribes, including
Moshesh, the "Lion of the Mountain" and chief of Basutoland, gathered to
lay him to rest as the "Friend of the Africans." People of all faiths profoundly
mourned his passing.

Pope John Paul II beatified Joseph Gerard in Maseru, in Lesotho, the arena
of his missionary labors, on September 15, 1988, announcing that he was "a
servant of reconciliation and peace." After praying at Blessed Joseph's tomb, the
pontiff further described him as "a missionary eager to understand souls."

+

Joseph Vaz (April 21, 1651 – January 16, 1711)
Apostle of Ceylon (Sri Lanka)

A priest of Goa, India, Joseph Vaz was born in Sancoale, Goa, as a member
of the Konkani Brahmin caste. He was raised as a Christian, however, and

his family was pious and dedicated to the faith, educating Joseph in cate-chetical areas as well as academic fields. He learned Portuguese and Latin, then took pre-seminary courses at the Jesuit College and at the College of St. Thomas. He completed his studies, was ordained in 1676, and was sent to the Kanar mission for three years as vicar forane. From these beginnings came his unique ministry as a confessor and preacher.

In 1686, Joseph went to Ceylon (Sri Lanka), dressed as a coolie with his servant, to undertake the great apostolate that distinguished his life. Ceylon was under Dutch control at that time, and the colonial authorities perse-cuted Catholics, but his arrival marked the beginning of change. He worked in disguise, going from village to village to preach and to console the faith-ful, combining the wisdom and elegance of his own people with the joy of Christ. The Dutch arrested him after a time, and he was imprisoned in Kandy, the capital of a native independent state. But the king, Vimalad-harma Surya II, ordered Joseph's release in 1699 after having met him per-sonally.

The Oratorian Fathers and other missionaries arrived soon thereafter to aid Joseph in his labors. He was already revered by the people because of his holi-ness and genuine concern for one and all. Joseph cared for the abandoned sick of the streets and jungles during a smallpox epidemic and opened a hos-pital for victims, earning respect from all denomination and races. When Cey-lon was erected as a diocese, Joseph was the natural candidate for the episcopacy, but he declined the honor. His health was strained by his constant labors, and, in 1710, he was unable to leave his residence at Kandy. He died there and was buried in the church that he had built. Unfortunately, in 1754, the church was destroyed and his actual grave lost.

Pope John Paul II beatified Joseph Vaz on June 21, 1995, at Colombo, Sri Lanka, declaring that the new Blessed combined the virtues of his own her-itage with the radiance of Christ to serve the needs of his adopted people of Ceylon. As the Apostle of Ceylon, Joseph will forever be honored.

✠

Josaphata Hordashevska (1869 – 1919)
Pioneer in the Basilian Order

The first member of the Sisters Servant of Mary Immaculate, Josaphata Michaelina was born in Lviv and, at the age of eighteen, decided to conse-crate her life to God. Further, she chose to enter a contemplative monastery belonging to the Order of St. Basil the Great; at the time it was the only Eastern-rite woman's congregation.

Soon after she entered the monastery, however, the Basilians decided to establish a woman's congregation that focused on the active life. Josaphata received a great honor when she was elected to be the first leader. She was then sent to the Felician sisters to be trained in the active religious life. She took the name Josaphata in honor of the Ukrainian martyr, St. Josaphat Kuntsevych.

As the first Superior of the young sisters, Josaphata provided them with vital training in the spirit and charisms of the Sisters Servants. One of her favorite maxims was, "Serve your people where the need is greatest."

After immense suffering from bone cancer, she died at the age of forty-nine and was buried in the Generalate of the Sisters Servants in Rome.

Pope John Paul II beatified Josaphata Hordashevska on June 27, 2001, during a pastoral visit to the Ukraine, along with other martyrs and blesseds dear to the Church in that country.

✠

Josephat Chichov — see Martyrs of Bulgaria

✠

Josephine Vannini (July 7, 1859 – February 23, 1911)
Founder of the Daughters of St. Camillus

Josephine Vannini was born in Rome, Italy, and baptized Judith Adelaide, the daughter of Angelo and Annunziata Papi Vannini. The family faced tragedy between 1863 and 1866, when Angelo and Annunziata died. The children — Judith and her sister, Ginlia, and brother, Augusto — were separated, and Judith was given to the care of the Daughters of Charity of St. Vincent de Paul. Inspired by these religious, she wanted to enter the convent, a desire that she maintained steadfastly even when reunited with her brother and sister in 1880.

Judith did enter the Daughters of Charity and took her religious name, but then became ill and spent time in another convent recuperating. Her spiritual director, the future Blessed Luigi Tezza, suggested that she found a new congregation; so, with the aid of her aunt, Anna Maria Papi, she started the Daughters of St. Camillus on February 2, 1892. The congregation was elevated to the status of having a cardinal protector, His Eminence Lucido Maria Parocchi, on January 24, 1894.

The Daughters of St. Camillus served the poor and the infirm, with Josephine as Superior General, and opened houses in Italy, France, Belgium, and Argentina prior to Josephine's death in Rome. Her remains were interred there, then in Grottaferrata.

Pope John Paul II beatified Josephine Vannini on October 16, 1994, declaring:

> To serve the suffering; this was the special charism of Josephine Vannini, foundress of the Congregation of the Daughters of St. Camillus. To belong totally to God, who is loved and honored in the needy, was her constant concern, expressed in a daily, boundless charity towards the infirm, in the footsteps of the great apostle of St. Camillus of Lellis. How contemporary are her witness and message! Mother Vannini makes a strong appeal to today's young men and women who sometimes hesitate to make total and definitive commitments. She invites all who are called to the consecrated life to respond generously, as she does all who fulfill their vocation in family life: God has a plan of holiness for everyone.

✠

Juan Bautista — see Jacinto de Los Angeles

✠

Juan Nepomuceno Zegrí y Moreno
(October 11, 1831 – March 5, 1905)
Queen Isabel II's Royal Chaplain

A priest and founder of the Sisters of Charity of the Blessed Virgin Mary of Mercy, Juan Nepomuceno was born in Granada, Spain, to Antonio Zegrí Martín and Josefa Moreno Escudero. His parents were responsible for instilling in him a great love for the Church and, especially, an abiding concern for the poor. Under their inspiration, he also discerned a vocation to the priesthood at an early age, a desire to serve the Church and those in need.

Juan Nepomuceno entered St. Dionysius Seminary for the diocese of Granada and received ordination to the priesthood on June 2, 1855. He held several assignments in Granada and was subsequently appointed to various diocesan positions, including synodal judge, canon of the cathedral of

Malaga, and preacher to the court of Queen Isabel II. He was next named the queen's royal chaplain.

Even as he fulfilled these other duties, Juan Nepomuceno remained deeply concerned with the needs of the poor and the forgotten. He thus decided to do something about this problem and, in March 1878, established the Congregation of the Sisters of Charity of the Blessed Virgin Mary of Mercy, under the protection of the Blessed Virgin Mary of Mercy. The primary purpose of the new congregation was to undertake a ministry dedicated to the care of the poor; within a few short years, he had opened new houses across Spain.

Despite this early growth, however, the congregation and its founder faced severe trials. Juan Nepomuceno was accused falsely of misconduct and removed as head in 1888 by pontifical decree. Finally, his name was cleared, in July 1894 — but, although he was permitted to return to the congregation, he was not given any kind of a welcome. He then voluntarily chose to stay away from the very community that he had founded.

Juan Nepomuceno died without returning to the congregation. In the succeeding years, his immense contributions were finally realized, thanks in large measure to the sisters who had known and respected him and who preserved dedication to his memory. In 1925, he was declared officially the Founder of the Sisters of Charity of the Blessed Virgin Mary of Mercy.

Pope John Paul II beatified him on November 9, 2003. At that time, the pope said:

> Juan Nepomuceno Zegrí y Moreno, an upright priest of deep Eucharistic piety, understood well how the proclamation of the Gospel needed to become a dynamic reality, able to transform the apostle's life. As a parish priest, he was committed to "visibly providing for all those who, suffering from abandonment, must drink from the bitter chalice and receive nourishment from the bread of tears" (June 19. 1859). He developed his redemptive spirituality with this purpose, born from intimacy with Christ and directed towards charity for the neediest.
>
> He was inspired, through invocation to the Virgin of Mercy, Mother of the Redeemer, to found the Sisters of Charity of the Blessed Virgin Mary of Mercy, with the aim of making God's love ever-present where there was "just one suffering to heal, one misfortune to console, one single hope to instill in hearts." Today this Institute, following in the footsteps of its Founder, continues its dedication to witness and promote redemptive charity.

⊹

Juana María Condesa Lluch
(March 30, 1862 – January 16, 1916)
Help for the Working Poor

Juana was born in Valencia, Spain. Her parents were wealthy and provided her with an excellent education, especially in the Faith. At an early age, she manifested a love of the Eucharist and the Blessed Mother and was concerned for the plight of the poor and those who toiled in factories to feed and care for their families. So, at the age of eighteen, she decided to do what she could to relieve the suffering of the poor workers who had been forced to depart the countryside and find work in the often grim and inhuman conditions of the factories in the cities.

Initially denied permission by Cardinal Antolín Monescillo, Archbishop of Valencia, to start a religious community because of her age, Juana nevertheless did receive authorization to open a shelter for workers in 1884. Soon after, she opened a school for the children of factory workers and attracted a number of other young women who shared her commitment to the cause of the poor laborers.

Juana continued to seek ecclesiastical approval for a new religious congregation and, in 1892, she was at last granted diocesan approval for the Congregation of the Handmaids of the Immaculate Conception, Protectress of Workers. In 1895, Juana and the first members made their initial vows; they made their perpetual profession in 1911. The congregation received final approval pontifical approval from Pope Pius XII on January 27, 1947.

Pope John Paul II beatified her on March 23, 2003. He said at the occasion:

> Blessed Juana Condesa Lluch, guided by her exquisite religious sensitivity
> . . . lived a profoundly Christian youth: assisted at daily Mass in the church
> of the Patriarch, united her faith to an assiduous prayer. In this way she
> was prepared to dedicate herself totally to the love of God, founding the
> Congregation of the Handmaids of Mary Immaculate who, faithful to her
> charism, continue to be involved in the advancement of working women.

✠

Julian Alfredo — see Martyrs of Astoria

✠

Junípero Serra (November 24, 1713 – August 28, 1784)
Father of the California Missions

One of the most famous missionaries in the history of the United States, Junipero Serra was born in Petra-Mallora, Majorca. Raised devoutly, he entered the Franciscans on September 14, 1730, displaying a remarkable brilliance even in his early years. He lectured on philosophy while a seminarian, then taught at the university of Palma. In 1749, Junípero was assigned to the San Fernando College in Mexico. During his stay in Mexico, he seriously injured his leg and was lame for the rest of his life.

He asked to be sent to the Sierra Gorda Indian Mission and served there for nine years, writing a catechism in the Pamé language. He also preached missions and became popular in Mexico. In 1767, Junípero was appointed the Superior of a group of fifteen Franciscans going to the missions in Lower California. Two years later he went north, establishing San Fernando de Velicata and arriving in San Diego on July 1. Junípero founded the first of the California missions on July 15, 1769. Others followed: San Carlos (1770), San Antonio, San Gabriel (1771), San Luis Obispo (1772), San Francisco de Asis (1776), San Juan Capistrano (1776), Santa Clara (1777), San Buenaventura (1782), and Santa Barbara (1782).

He is the "Father of the California Missions" and a remarkable spiritual figure in the opening eras of the New World. He confirmed more than 5,000 native peoples of California, while trying to provide safe havens and civilizing processes considered necessary at the time. Because his missionary foundations overshadow the other elements of his life, Junípero's brilliance and courage have been overlooked. He suffered many trials and severe physical pain throughout his ministry, but he never asked to be spared from his labors. Absolute confidence in the Providence of God was a hallmark of his vocation. He died, exhausted and ill from his years of founding and preaching, at Monterey, California.

Pope John Paul II beatified Junípero Serra on September 25, 1988, stating that this Franciscan:

. . . sowed the seeds of Christian faith amid the mountainous changes wrought by the arrival of European settlers in the New World . . . In fulfilling this ministry, Fr. Serra showed himself to be a true son of St. Francis. Today, his example inspires in a particular was the many Serra Clubs around the world, the members of which do so much praiseworthy work in fostering vocations.

$\mathcal{K}$

Kamen Vitchev — see Martyrs of Bulgaria

✚

Karl (Carol) Leisner (February 28, 1915 – August 12, 1945)
Ordained at Dachau

Karl Leisner was born in Rees, Germany, and was raised in the Faith, showing an early interest in aiding Catholic young people. While a seminarian in
Munster, he tried to teach catechism to the young, but the Nazis took him
out of the seminary and forced him into six months of compulsive labor on
agricultural settlements. The Gestapo also raided his home and confiscated
his personal papers.

Karl was ordained a deacon by Bishop von Galen in 1939, then arrested.
He was confined to Freiburg, Mannheim, then Sachsenhausen, for criticiz-
ing Adolph Hitler. On December 24, 1941, he was sent to Dachau. For three
years, he endured life in the camp. Then, on December 17, 1944, he was
ordained in secret by the French bishop Gabriel Piquet, who had been
admitted to Dachau with the help of local religious authorities. One week
later, Karl was able to celebrate his first Mass.

On May 4, 1945, the Allied military forces captured Dachau, and Karl was
released. But by this time he was so ill that he was placed in a sanitarium in
Planegg, near Munich, where he died of tuberculosis.

Pope John Paul II beatified Karl Leisner on June 23, 1996, with his fellow German martyr, Bernard Lichtenberg, announcing:

> Christ is the Way. Bernard Lichtenberg and Karl Leisner bore witness to
> this at a time when many people had lost their way and, because of oppor-
> tunism or fear, had gone astray. Whoever observes the way of the two mar-
> tyrs knows that their martyrdom was no accidental stroke of misfortune
> along life's journey, but a final and inevitable consequence of a life lived in
> following Christ.
>
> Even in their youth both of them set out on the way in which God had
> called them and on which he wanted to accompany them. "Christ, you

have called me. I say decisively and with conviction: here I am, send me, "
wrote Karl Leisner at the beginning of his theological studies. He, who was
very early to recognize the anti-Christian nature of the ruling party, felt
called, through his desired service as a priest, to show people the way to
God and to make no concessions to the so-called "popular world view."

✠

Karl of Austria (August 17, 1887 – April 1, 1922)
The Last Hapsburg Emperor

Karl was born in the Castle of Persenbeug, in the region of Lower Austria,
and was the son of the Archduke Otto and Princess Maria Josephine of Saxony, daughter of the last King of Saxony; Emperor Franz Joseph I was his
great uncle. Raised in the Faith, early on he developed a great love for the
Eucharist and the Sacred Heart of Jesus.

On October 21, 1911, Karl wed Princess Zita of Bourbon and Parma. The
couple was blessed with eight children, and Karl was a devoted husband and
father. However, the life of the family was changed forever on June 28, 1914,
when Archduke Franz Ferdinand was assassinated. The murder sparked
World War I and made Karl the heir to the throne of the Austro-Hungar-
ian Empire.

Karl succeeded to the Hapsburg throne upon the death of Franz Joseph
on November 21, 1916, and was crowned King of Hungary on December 30,
in the middle of the terrible conflict. Recognizing that the war had to be
brought to some kind of end, Emperor Karl gave his support to the peace
efforts of Pope Benedict XV. As emperor, Karl also promoted extensive social
legislation that took its inspiration from the social teachings of the Church.

Despite his efforts to bring peace, Karl was driven from the throne after the
war and banished from the country to the island of Madeira. Nevertheless, he
succeeded in preventing a civil war in the empire and made possible a relatively smooth transition politically following the final passing of the ancient
Hapsburg Empire. Notably, however, he courteously refused to abdicate, as he
saw his throne as a mandate from God. He thus faced poverty and disgrace
with his family and died with a prayer on his lips for his people. On his
deathbed, he declared, "I strive always in all things to understand as clearly as
possible and follow the will of God, and this in the most perfect way."

Reportedly, among his last words were also a pledge to his wife: "I will love
you forever."

He was beatified by Pope John Paul II on Oct. 3, 2004. At his beatification, the Holy Father greeted pilgrims from various countries, including Archduke Otto, the son of Blessed Karl. The pope said:

> The Christian statesman, Charles of Austria, confronted this challenge every day. To his eyes, war appeared as "something appalling." Amid the tumult of the First World War, he strove to promote the peace initiative of my Predecessor, Benedict XV.

> From the beginning, the Emperor Charles conceived of his office as a holy service to his people. His chief concern was to follow the Christian vocation to holiness also in his political actions. For this reason, his thoughts turned to social assistance. May he be an example for all of us, especially for those who have political responsibilities in Europe today!

✠

Kaspar Stangassinger — see Gaspar Stangassinger

✠

Kateri Tekakwitha (c. 1656 – April 17, 1680)
Lily of the Mohawks

A mystic of the American wilderness, Kateri Tekakwitha was born at Ossernenon, Auriesville, New York, circa 1656, the daughter of a Mohawk war chief and an Algonquin Christian woman named Kahenta. Kateri was orphaned at the age of four, when her parents and an infant brother died in an epidemic of smallpox that left her with a disfigured face and damaged eyesight. An uncle took care of Kateri, and powerful older women of the tribe treated her kindly and raised her as a high-ranking Mohawk maiden. Her refusal of marriage offers, however, distressed her family and strained their relationships, because Indian maidens normally looked forward to the married state.

When a missionary, Fr. Jacques de Lamberville, arrived in Kateri's village, she displayed unusual virtue and astounded him by asking for baptism. Her open Catholic faith and contemplative nature added to the strain with her people, and she was subjected to abuse. To save her life, she fled to the Christian community of Sault Sainte-Marie near Montreal, 400 miles away, walking there under the protection of Christian Mohawk and Iroquois warrior escorts.

In the safety of the Christian missions, Kateri flowered in prayer and in holiness. She endured many trials, including a false accusation by a jealous woman, but she remained steadfast in her devotion. Kateri received her First Communion on Christmas Day, 1677, and this union sped her mystical graces. Actually, Kateri was a mystery not only to her fellow Native Americans but to the missionaries trying to guide her toward perfection. She was so advanced spiritually that she stood as a contradiction to the wild lands and the primitive conditions of the North American continent.

In 1679, Kateri took a private vow of chastity, dedicating herself to Christ. However, when she asked to become a nun, her request was answered with a gentle derision; the concept of Native American vocations was totally alien to the Europeans.

At Kateri's death at Caughnawaga, Sault, Canada, the word of her passing quickly spread as "The saint is dead." Two French trappers lovingly made her coffin; as she lay in state, her face glowed, and all the scars she had in life disappeared. Pope Pius XII (r. 1939-1958) declared Kateri venerable.

Pope John Paul II beatified Kateri Tekakwitha on June 22, 1980. At the ceremony, she was recognized as a unique American who symbolized the flowering of the Faith in the New World. Kateri was honored for her mystical graces, suffering, and loyalty to the Church on earth.

✠

Kuriakose Elias Chavara — see Cyriac Elias Chavara

$$\mathcal{L}$$

☩

Laura Vicuña (April 5, 1895 – January 22, 1908)
Sacrificial Love

Laura Vicuña sacrificed herself for her mother's conversion.

Not long after her birth in Santiago, Chile, her father had to flee to the Andes Mountains because of political upheavals. Laura and her mother, Mercedes, went with him into hazardous exile. He died when Laura was only three, and Mercedes became the mistress of a local hacienda (ranch) owner, one Manuel Mora.

Laura attended the Salesian mission school at the age of eight with her sister, Julia. Even then, Manuel would try to molest her when he was drunk. At the time of her First Communion when she was ten, she was already afraid of Mora because he was focusing his lewd desires on her. After she fought off his assaults, Mora refused to pay for her school tuition. The Salesian Sisters, knowing of her piety and courage, continued educating Laura for no charge.

On Easter Sunday, 1902, Bishop Juan Cagliero comforted Laura, as she offered her life to God for her mother's conversion. The following winter she became very ill, and Mercedes left Mora's hacienda for Junion de los Andes, Argentina, in order to provide her daughter with care and protection.

On January 14, 1904, however, Manuel Mora arrived on their doorstep to demand Laura's surrender to his lusts. When she refused him, he whipped and kicked her, then put her across the saddle to carry her back to his hacienda and force her to submit. By this time, though, the people of the area were watching him, so instead of hauling her off, he threw Laura's unconscious body into the gutter and left.

She lingered just over a week before succumbing to internal injuries. But, before she died, Laura told her mother that she was willingly offering her life for Mercedes' conversion. Her mother reformed and became a devout Catholic again.

Pope John Paul II beatified Laura Vicuña on September 3, 1988, in Turin, Italy, calling her the "Eucharistic flower of Junin de Los Andes, whose life was a poem of purity, sacrifice, and filial love." The Holy Father expressed his hope that "the tender figure of Blessed Laura, pure glory of Argentina and Chile, arouse a renewed spiritual commitment in those two great nations."

✠

Laura Montoya Upegui (May 26, 1874 – October 21, 1949)
Foundress of the Congregation of the Missionary Sisters of Mary Immaculate and St. Catherine of Siena

Laura was born in Jericó, Antioquia, Colombia, to Juan de la Crux Montoya and Dolores Upegui. She endured a very difficult childhood: her father died when she was two years old, and the family was forced into severe poverty. Laura was sent to live with her grandmother — not a good arrangement for the young girl, as her grandmother was unsympathetic — but Laura endured these trials with patience.

When Laura was sixteen, her mother asked her to become a teacher to provide financial assistance to the family. She went on to study at the Normale de Institutoras in Medellín and was noted for her excellent study habits and high grades.

Having earned her teaching certificate, Laura began working as a teacher in different sections of Antioquia. Her life as a teacher was only the first step in her destiny, for she was called to the religious life and soon aspired to become a cloistered Carmelite nun. This proved unsuitable, however — for she was also drawn to the care of the large native population in South America, who were often mistreated and held in contempt by the governments of the continent.

So, on May 14, 1914, she departed Medellín with four other young women and journeyed to Dabeiba, where they took up residence among the native Indian people. They were encouraged in their labors by the Bishop of Santa Fe de Antioquia and became known as the Missionaries of Mary Immaculate and St. Catherine of Siena. To provide a firm foundation for the community, Laura wrote a directory and other useful writings for the sisters, stressing the need to serve God by serving the Indians and teaching the native peoples with love and patience.

Her last years were spent in suffering. She was confined to a wheelchair for the last nine years, but she remained active in teaching and writing to assist the congregation. Her congregation is today found in nineteen countries throughout the Americas, Africa, and Europe.

She was beatified by Pope John Paul II on April 25, 2004. The pontiff said of her:

343

It is possible for a person not to know the Lord, notwithstanding his numerous manifestations in the course of history. Mother Laura Montoya, seeing how many indigenous persons far away from urban centres lived without knowing God, decided to found the Congregation of the Missionaries of Mary Immaculate and St. Catherine of Siena, with the aim of bringing the light of the Gospel to the inhabitants of the forests.

This Blessed Colombian considered herself as mother to the Indians, to whom she wanted to show God's love. Her times were not easy ones, since the social tensions bloodied even then her noble Country. Taking inspiration from her message of peace, let us ask today that the beloved Nation of Colombia may soon enjoy peace, justice, and holistic progress.

✠

Lazlo Batthyáni-Strattmann
(October 28, 1870 – January 22, 1931)
Doctor of the Poor

A layman, doctor, and loving father, Lazlo was born in Dunakiliti, Hungary, into an ancient, large (he was one of ten brothers), and noble family.

As a dedicated Catholic, he was committed not only to assisting the poor but to serving the needs of his family; he focused many of his university studies in Vienna on those talents he would need to run the holdings of the household. He was also a widely talented individual, with courses in chemistry, physics, philosophy, literature, and music. Finally, in 1896, he began working toward a degree in medicine, graduating in 1900.

Meanwhile, on November 10, 1898, Lazlo had married Countess Maria Teresa Coreth. Their happy union was blessed with thirteen children, and the entire family became exemplars of the ideal Christian home: they attended daily Mass, studied the teachings of the Faith, prayed the Rosary together, and strove to perform acts of charity.

In 1902, Lazlo founded a private hospital in Kittsee and served in various capacities, including general practitioner, surgeon, and oculist. The hospital was expanded during World War I (1914-1918), to assist in the care of wounded soldiers returning from the front lines.

Then, upon the death of his uncle, Ödön Batthyány-Strattmann, in 1915, he inherited the family Castle of Körmend in Hungary — and a title of Prince. He moved his family into the castle five years later, then set about utilizing part of the estate as a hospital specializing in ophthalmology. Lazlo was soon renowned as a specialist in that field.

At the same time, he was called the "doctor of the poor" for his deep concern for those in need. He gave them free treatment and prescriptions or accepted their prayers as payment.

Diagnosed with a tumor of the bladder when he was sixty, Lazlo faced his declining health with patience and forbearance. As he declared to his sister, "I am happy. I am suffering atrociously, but I love my sufferings and am consoled in knowing that I support them for Christ." He died in Vienna, after months of pain.

He was beatified by Pope John Paul II on March 23, 2003. The pontiff declared:

> "The weakness of God is stronger than men" (1 Cor 1:25). These words of the holy Apostle Paul also reflect the devotion and life style of Blessed Lazlo Batthyány-Strattmann, father of a family and doctor. He used the rich inheritance of his noble family to give free care to the poor and to build two hospitals. His greatest interest was not material goods; nor even less were success and career the goals of his life. He taught and lived this in his family, and so he was the best teacher of the Faith for his children. Drawing his spiritual energy from the Eucharist, he showed as many as divine Providence led to him the source of his life and mission.
>
> Blessed Lazlo Batthyány-Strattmann never placed earthly riches before our true good which is in heaven. May his example of family life and of generous Christian solidarity be an encouragement for all to follow the Gospel faithfully.

⊹

Liberatus Weiss — see Martyrs of Ethiopia

⊹

Liduina Meneguzie (September 12, 1901 – December 2, 1941)
"Sister Gudda"

An Italian nun and missionary in Ethiopia, Elisa Angela Meneguzzi was born in Giarre, near Abano Terme, Italy, to a poor family of farmers. From her earliest days, she demonstrated a strong commitment to the faith, including daily prayer and Mass and dedicated study of the Catechism. Owing to her family's difficult finances, she willingly went to work in hotels in the nearby town of Abano, but she had already formed a desire to enter the religious life.

On March 5, 1926, Elisa entered the motherhouse of the Sisters Congregation of St. Frances de Sales in Padua. She took the name Sr. Liduina and was filled with immense joy in the life of a religious and worked as a sacristan, a nurse, and, above all, as a beloved spiritual guide to the young girls who were in the care of the sisters. In 1937, however, her fondest dream was fulfilled: she was chosen to be sent to the congregation's missions in Ethiopia.

Arriving at Dire-Dawa, Ethiopia, she was given a post as a nurse in the Parini Civil Hospital. Her duties during World War II (1939-1945) included the care of soldiers who had been wounded in battle. She grieved at their suffering, and her tender care and compassion won the admiration of the soldiers, her fellow sisters, and the people of the town, who called her "Sister Gudda" ("Great Sister"). Her reputation for goodness was especially known among the non-Catholics and non-Europeans — among the local Ethiopians, Coptics, and Muslims.

Sr. Liduina began to suffer herself from deteriorating health. Eventually, it was determined that she needed stomach surgery, but complications ensued and hastened her death. She passed at the age of forty, with a prayer on her lips.

The entire mission and town went into mourning. After her initial burial in the cemetery at Dire-Dawa, she was transferred to the motherhouse in Padua in 1961.

Pope John Paul II beatified her on October 20, 2002, saying:

"Give to the Lord, families of peoples, give to the Lord glory and power" (Ps. 95 [96]:7). The words of the responsorial Psalm express well the missionary yearning, that permeated the heart of Sr. Liduina Meneguzzi, of the Sisters of St. Francis de Sales. In the course of her brief but intense life, Sr. Liduina poured herself out for her poorer and suffering brothers, particularly at the hospital of the mission of Dire Dawa in Ethiopia.

With fervent apostolic zeal, she sought to make known to everyone the only Saviour Jesus. At the school of Him who was "meek and humble of heart" (cf. Mt 11:29), she learned to spread the charity that flows from a pure heart, overcoming mediocrity and inner inertia.

☩

Lodovico Pavoni (September 11, 1784 – April 1, 1849)
Patron of the Poor and Abandoned

The founder of a religious congregation, Lodovico Pavoni was born in Brescia, Italy, and raised devoutly in the Faith. At a young age, he began his apostolate to the young people of his region. The future bishop of Brescia, Fr. Domenico Ferrari, trained Lodovico in this ministry.

Ordained to the priesthood in 1807, Lodovico served as secretary to Bishop Gabrio Nava and operated an oratory for the young. In 1818, he became the rector of St. Barnabas, where he founded an orphanage and school that became the Institute of St. Barnabas. Deaf-mutes were welcomed there in 1823. Lodovico provided support for the ministry by founding the *Pavoniani*, or the Congregation of the Sons of Mary Immaculate. The members of this congregation served in the same spirit of love as their founder.

On March 24, 1849, faced with a regional military conflict, Lodovico took his students to Saiano for safety. The journey exhausted him, and he died there a week later, mourned by all who knew him.

Pope John Paul II beatified Lodovico Pavoni on April 14, 2002, in Rome, announcing:

> Gifted with a particularly sensitive spirit, he was totally given over to the care of poor and abandoned youngsters and even deaf-mutes . . . By his example, he exhorts us to place our confidence in Jesus and to be ever more immersed in the mystery of his love.

⊹

Lorenzo Maria of St. Francis Xavier de Salvi
(October 30, 1782 – June 12, 1856)
Passionist Miracle Worker

Lorenzo Maria of St. Francis Xavier de Salvi was born in Rome on October 30, 1782, the son of Antonio and Marianna Biondi Salvi. His father served as house steward for the Counts of Carpegna and raised Lorenzo Maria devoutly. The young man was encouraged in the Faith in many ways — among them, having the honor of being confirmed by Cardinal Henry of York, the bishop of Frascati.

Lorenzo Maria studied at the Jesuit Roman College (now the Gregorian) and entered the Passionists, taking religious vows on November 20, 1802. He was ordained a priest in Rome on December 29, 1805. As a Passionist, he devoted himself to preaching, prayer, and study. He was also Superior in various Passionist houses and a provincial consultor.

The young priest's consuming devotion was to the Infant Jesus. He carried the image of the Christ Child wherever he went, working marvels through the image. People revered him as a holy man and as a special soul who cured the sick and wounded. Lorenzo Maria's devotion to the Infant Redeemer spread to men and women of all classes, providing inspiration to thousands.

When he died in Viterbo, in Capranica, the faithful of the region mourned his passing. His remains were enshrined at Sant' Angelo di Vetralla. There, they became a source of devotion and a pilgrimage destination.

Pope John Paul II beatified Lorenzo Maria of St. Francis Xavier de Salvi on October 1, 1989, announcing:

> Blessed Lorenzo Salvi, a man of God, not only in intense prayer, but also in untiring dedication to the priestly ministry . . . Blessed Salvi succeeded in being a master of the spiritual life for many people who listened to him in his preaching, in the confessional, in spiritual direction.

☩

Louis Zephyrinus Moreau
(April 1, 1824 – May 24, 1901)
Bishop and Founder

Louis Zephyrinus Moreau was born in Bécancour, Canada. After completing his studies in a local seminary, he was ordained to the priesthood and assigned to various ministries. He was appointed secretary to the bishop of the diocese in 1852; on January 16, 1876, he himself was consecrated as the fourth bishop of St. Hyacinthe.

Louis served St. Hyacinthe with remarkable charity and zeal. He dedicated the new cathedral, sponsored religious communities, and promoted education throughout the diocese. He even founded a unique religious congregation dedicated to St. Joseph — the Sisters of St. Hyacinthe, dedicated to helping priests and religious in their administrative burdens to release them for spiritual ministries. (A group of these sisters arrived in the United States in 1929.) Louis also visited the parishes of the diocese and served as a loving, caring pastor throughout the years, endearing himself to the Canadian Catholic community. After a quarter of a century of service and the promotion of the Faith and a spirit of unity, he died in St. Hyacinthe.

Pope John Paul II beatified Louis Zeferinus Moreau on May 10, 1987, praising him as a pioneer of the Church in the New World and a model of episcopal charity.

✠

Louisa Therese de Montaignac de Chauvance
(May 14, 1820 – June 27, 1885)
Foundress of the Oblates of the Sacred Heart of Jesus

Louisa Therese de Montaignac de Chauvance was born in Le-Havre-de-Grace, France, the daughter of a wealthy financier, Aimée, and his wife Anne de Ruffin Montaignac de Chauvance. She was sent to a boarding school at age seven; there, she developed a profound devotion to the Sacred Heart of Jesus and received the grace of a religious vocation. The Faithful Companions of Jesus at Chateauroux educated Louisa, fostering her desire to enter a convent. She originally wanted to enter the Carmelite cloister but was advised that instead, she should assist her aunt in founding a group dedicated to the Sacred Heart.

So, in 1848, Louisa moved to Montlucon. With her aunt, she formed the Guild of the Tabernacle, a group of women dedicated to restoring faith and ideals in France, in 1852. She also made a private vow of chastity in honor of the Sacred Heart in September 1843. Louisa served the regional community as well, starting a much-needed orphanage for abandoned children.

Seeing the need for a community of women serving the people, Louisa founded the Oblates of the Sacred Heart of Jesus, dedicated to community ministries and reparation, a congregation that received episcopal approbation on December 21, 1874. These sisters were dedicated to the particular ministry of giving of themselves "to renew society by their example and their holy lives." Their duties varied, adapting to local needs. Among other tasks, the congregation's members cleaned and decorated poor parish churches, promoted Eucharistic devotion, and conducted retreats for the laity.

Louisa served as Superior of the congregation, attracting many followers. She was elected Mother General on May 17, 1880, and promoted devotion to the Sacred Heart and to the Holy Eucharist through her entire life. Her congregation received approbation from the Holy See prior to her death in Moulins.

Pope John Paul II beatified Louisa Therese de Montaigne de Chauvance on November 4, 1990, declaring that she was:

> . . . a daughter of the Church, and a woman of the Church [who understood that] serving the Lord and serving the Church are the same thing.

The Holy Father added:

Together, let us ask [her]to help us recognize the Love of the Heart of Jesus and ceaselessly remind people about it, as she was able to do so well during her entire life.

✠

Lucia Khambang — see Martyrs of Thailand

✠

Ludovico of Casoria Palmentieri
(March 11, 1814 – March 30, 1885)
Champion of the Lay Apostolate

Ludovico of Casoria Palmentiere was born in Casoria, near Naples, Italy, and baptized Archangelo Palmentieri. Entering the Franciscans on July 1, 1832, he received the name Ludovico, or Louis. Five years later, on June 4, 1837, he was ordained a priest and was assigned to teach philosophy, chemistry, and mathematics in the Naples Franciscan house. There, he counseled students and came into contact with the secular world, which was overwhelmed with problems.

In 1847, while praying at the Church of St. Joseph in Naples, Ludovico had a profound mystical experience, one that he described as a "cleansing." He focused on the needs of the sick and poor as a result and responded to their deprivations by envisioning programs that would harness the energies of the laity. Starting with small projects, he eventually bought a villa on Naples' Capadimonte, where he founded a fraternity of Franciscans. He also established an infirmary for ailing Franciscans in his province.

Laymen and women who were Franciscan Tertiaries came to aid Ludovico, and he subsequently founded the religious congregations of the Brothers of Charity in 1859 and the Sisters of St. Elizabeth in 1862. These community members were called the Bigi, because of the color of their habits — *bigio,* or gray. With the aid of these religious, Ludovico opened a school for redeemed slaves from Africa, and members of his congregation arrived in the United States in 1919.

He suffered a terrible illness for ten years, even as he served the Franciscans and his congregations, but he was undaunted by suffering and even expanded his charitable works to Assisi, Florence, and Rome. He died in Naples, surrounded by his Bigi religious, and his Cause was opened within a year.

Pope John Paul II beatified Ludovico of Casoria Palmeniteri on April 18, 1993; he was revered for his Franciscan spirit of commitment and generosity of soul. The Holy Father praised him as a true son of St. Francis of Assisi and as a luminary of the Order who understood the power of the laity when directed toward service.

✠

Luigi Maria Monti (July 25, 1825 – 1900)
Caring for "Christ's Poor Ones"

Luigi Monti was born at Bovisio in the archdiocese of Milan, the eighth of eleven children. After his father died when he was only twelve, Luigi was forced to learn a trade as quickly as possible to assist his family. He thus became a woodworker and, despite his youth, started a group of devout artisans and farmers his own age called The Company of the Sacred Heart of Jesus. Locally, however, they were known as The Company of Friars.

The Company distinguished itself by a dedication to prayer, care for the sick and poor, and zeal in preaching among those who had left the Church or who had abandoned their faith. In 1846, Luigi took private vows of chastity and obedience.

The innovative work being undertaken by Luigi and his followers met with envy and opposition from some quarters, however. In 1851, charges of political conspiracy were falsely made against them to the Austrian authorities, then occupying that part of Italy. They spent some seventy-two days in jail, released only after an investigation cleared them of all charges.

Desiring to enter the religious life, Luigi Monti accepted the advice of his spiritual director, Fr. Luigi Dossi, and became a novice in the Sons of Mary Immaculate, the congregation founded by Ludovico Pavoni. As a member of the community, he distinguished himself in caring for cholera victims during the epidemic of 1855 in Brescia, when he willingly went into isolation with victims.

Inspired to care further for the sick, Luigi joined with Fr. Dossi to establish the Congregation of the Sons of the Immaculate Conception, a community that would be dedicated to the sick in Rome. He at first worked as a simple nurse at the Santo Spirito Hospital, then went on to earn a diploma as a phlebotomist from the La Sapienza University in Rome. The following year, in 1877, Pope Pius IX gave him permission to head the new congregation and was a special patron of its work in the Eternal City.

With this sound foundation, Luigi expanded the work of the congregation into other parts of Italy. In 1882, he extended the care of the members to include orphaned children. The Congregation today has houses throughout the world continuing Luigi's vision of care and concern for the sick and the orphaned.

Luigi Monti died at the age of seventy-five, after a lifetime of selfless toil. He was beatified by Pope John Paul II on November 9, 2003. The pope stated at that time,

> "I saw water flowing out from beneath the threshold of the temple... everything will live where the water goes" (Ez. 47: 1, 9). The image of water, which brings everything back to life, illuminates well the life of Bl. Luigi Maria Monti, entirely dedicated to healing the physical and spiritual wounds of the sick and the orphaned. He loved to call them "Christ's poor ones," and he served them, enlivened by a living faith and sustained by intense and continual prayer. In his evangelical commitment, he was constantly inspired by the example of the Holy Virgin and placed the Congregation he founded under the sign of Mary Immaculate.

⳨

Luigi and Maria Corsini Quattrocchi
(1880 – 1951; 1884 – 1965)
Personifying Christian Marriage and Family Life for Modern Times

The first married couple ever beatified, Luigi and Maria spent fifty years as man and wife, working together to raise their family and to take active roles in the lay apostolates of the Church through politically and militarily dangerous eras. During World Wars I and II, they aided refugees and the victims of the political upheaval. Luigi, as the Attorney General of Italy, aided in the rebuilding of the nation at the close of World War II. Maria was a teacher, writer, and member of the Women's Catholic Action programs.

They also tried to live the tenets of the Faith, encouraging others to seek the truth and to serve Christ in all walks of life. Their lay vocations were a matter of daily tasks and the courage to stand for what was right in troubled times. Their own children, immersed in the total Catholic family life, were astounded when they realized how remarkable their parents were, as the virtues and goodness that they witnessed within their home were so real and total that they took such things for granted as part of human existence.

Pope John Paul II beatified Luigi and Maria Corsini Quattrocchi on October 21, 2001, with three of their children (the couple had four children, but one died) present at the ceremonies in Rome. The couple's priest sons, Filippo and Cesare, concelebrated the Mass with Pope John Paul II. A daughter, Enrichetta, was also present.

On that occasion, the pope said:

> The husband and wife lived in Rome in the first half of the twentieth century, a century in which faith in Christ was harshly tried, and gave a positive reply.

The Holy Father added that the new Blesseds

> . . . assumed with full responsibility the duty of collaborating with God in procreation, dedicating themselves generously to their children in educating, guiding, and directing them to the discovery of His design of love. This couple lived married love and service to life in the light of the Gospel and with great human intensity.

✠

Luigi Talamoni (October 3, 1848 – January 31, 1926)
Founder of the Misericordines

Italian priest Luigi Talamoni was born in Monza, Italy, to Maria Sala and Giuseppe Talamoni, a hatmaker. From his youth he expressed a desire to become a priest, and he received encouragement in his vocation from the future Servant of God, Barnabite Fr. Luigi Villoresi, then director of the Oratory of Carrobiolo in Monza.

Luigi lived and studied in the oratory until 1865, when he was permitted to transfer to the Theological Seminary of Milan for additional preparation for the priesthood. On March 4, 1871, he was ordained a priest. He began his ministry as a teacher at St. Charles College in Milan; wiithin a short time, he was sent to the Archdiocesan Seminary to take up a post that he held for the rest of his life.

Aside from his many duties as a seminary instructor, Fr. Luigi was a popular preacher and spiritual advisor. He dedicated many long hours to the confessional, gave retreats for priests, and preached throughout Northern Italy. He also assisted in the local political scene by serving on the city council of Monza (from 1893-1916 and 1923-1926) in order to encourage what he termed "political charity" and promoting the dignity and rights of the poor.

In March 1891, Luigi (with Maria Biffi Levati) founded the Congregation of the Misericordines of St. Gerard, a community of sisters who were to be dedicated to caring for and assisting the sick and elderly. The members dedicated themselves to caring for those who needed help during the night-time hours, so that their family members could find the strength to work during the day.

Fr. Luigi continued in all of these different ministries until the day of his death in Milan. Pope John Paul II beatified him on March 21, 2004, saying at the time:

> The priest Luigi Talamoni was a faithful reflection of God's mercy. Achille Ratti, subsequently Pope Pius XI, the most famous of the Blessed's high school students at the Seminary of Monza, described him as a "gem of the Ambrosian [Milanese] clergy and a spiritual director and father for countless souls because of his holy life, enlightened knowledge, great heartedness, Magisterial expertise, apostolic zeal, and praiseworthy civic services in Monza." The new Blessed was diligent in the ministry of the confessional and in his service to the poor, to prisoners, and especially to the poverty-stricken sick. What a shining example he is to us all!
>
> I urge especially priests and the Congregation of the Misericordine Sisters to keep their gaze on him.

✠

Luigi Tezza
(November 1, 1864 – September 26, 1923)
Apostle of Lima

Luigi Tezza was born in Conegliano Treviso, Italy, the son of a physician who died at a young age. Soon afterward, Luigi and his mother moved to Padua, where he was educated. In 1850, he entered the Order of the Ministers of the Sick of St. Camillus de Lellis in Verona, and his mother became a Visitation nun. Luigi was ordained to the priesthood in 1864.

He served the Camillian Order in various capacities, becoming the master of novices in 1871. That same year, he was sent to France to found Order monasteries there and became the Provincial of the region. Luigi and his companions were expelled from France in 1880 because of religious and social upheavals taking place; he returned secretly to France later, however, and reunited the scattered members of his Order.

In 1891, Luigi became the procurator and vicar general of the Order. One year later, with the future Blessed Josephine Vannini, he founded the Congregation of the Daughters of St. Camillus in 1892.

Then, in 1900, he was sent to Lima, Peru, to found new Camillian houses. The Peruvians were so edified by his holiness and zeal that, when the Order assigned him once again to Europe, Peruvian Church authorities would not give him permission to leave Lima. He died in Los Reyes, Peru, mourned by the entire nation and by his Order. His remains were taken to the Generalate of the Daughters of St. Camillus, Grottaferrata, Rome.

Pope John Paul II beatified Luigi Tezza on November 4, 2001, declaring that he stands as "a glorious example of a life totally dedicated to the exercise of charity and mercy towards those who suffer in body and in spirit."

⊹

Luigi Variara (January 15, 1875 – February 1, 1923)
First Salesian Priest Ordained in Colombia

Luigi Variara was the Apostle to the Lepers.

He was born in Viarigi, Asti, Italy, and entered the Salesian Oratory in Turin at age twelve, where he was trained by Michael Rua. During his training, he also met and heard Fr. Michele Unia, a Colombian priest serving the lepers of that nation, who inspired him to undertake this ministry. In 1894, they sailed to Colombia, where Luigi continued his priestly studies while serving at Agua de Dios leper colony. He was ordained in 1898.

Concerned about the very young lepers in the area, Luigi opened the Michele Unia Youth Hostel to serve their needs. He also founded a congregation of lepers and daughters of lepers — the Daughters of the Sacred Hearts of Jesus and Mary. These courageous young women defied criticism and dedicated themselves to the service of lepers. The future Blessed Michael Rua defended the congregation and Luigi, and the Daughters of the Sacred Hearts of Jesus and Mary proved successful and spiritually mature. Luigi continued his labors, even going for a time to Venezuela to start a ministry there. He returned to Colombia and died in Cucuta.

Pope John Paul II beatified Luigi Variara on April 14, 2002, announcing:

> The first Salesian priest to be ordained in Colombia, he succeeded in bringing together around him a group of consecrated women, some of whom were lepers or the daughters of lepers.

⊹

Luigi Versiglia (June 5, 1873 – February 25, 1930)

Martyred by Chinese Pirates

Luigi Versiglia was born at Oliva Gessi, Italy, and was reportedly a lively lad. Entering St. John Bosco's Oratory, he spent three years there, then became a Salesian in 1886, studying for the priesthood at the Gregorian in Rome. He received his doctorate in 1893 and became master of novices.

In 1905, he was sent to the Salesian mission in China, serving as the Superior of six missionaries there. He also opened a school for more than fifty pupils and fostered Gregorian chant, which fascinated the Chinese. However, the 1910 revolution in China forced the Salesians to go to Hong Kong, then to Heung Shan, and next, to Macao. This was a particularly dangerous mission, as the region was in the control of pirates.

Luigi was consecrated a bishop on January 9, 1921, and headed the Macao missions. Upon arriving there in 1912, he established a Christian community and two leper colonies, and he traveled on foot, on water, and by horseback to reach mission outposts.

On February 24, 1930, he set out with Callisto Caravario on a mission voyage. The next day, pirates boarded the ship, and the sainted bishop and his companion had to defend the young women sailing with them.

The women were not harmed because of their impassioned intervention, but the pirates took Luigi and his companion on shore. When it became obvious that the pirates intended to kill them, Luigi pleaded for Callisto's life, saying, "I am an old man, kill me; but he is still young, spare him." The pirates ignored the pleas and shot them both at a site called Li Thau Tsieu.

When Luigi's remains were recovered, they were enshrined in the cathedral at Lin Kong-How. The Red Guards vandalized his tomb after the Communists gained control.

Pope John Paul II beatified Luigi Versiglia and Callisto Caravario on May 15, 1983, announcing:

> The two martyrs' acts of supreme love find their broader significance in the framework of that evangelical ministry which the Church carries out on behalf of the great and noble Chinese people, beginning from the times of Fr. Matteo Ricci. In fact, in every age and in every place martyrdom is an offering of love for the brethren, and especially for whose benefit the martyr offers himself. The blood of the two new Blesseds is therefore is at the

foundation of the Chinese Church, as the blood of Peter is at the foundation of the Church of Rome.

We must therefore understand the witness of their love and their service as a sign of the profound harmony between the Gospel and the highest values of the culture and spirituality of China. In this witness, the sacrifice offered to God and the gift of self made to the people and to the Church of China cannot be separated.

Monsignor Versiglia and Don Caravario, following Christ's example, have perfectly embodied the ideal of the evangelical shepherd who is at once a "lamb" (cf. Rev 7:17) "who lays down his life for his flock" (Jn (10:11), the expression of the Father's mercy and tenderness, but at the same time the lamb "who sits on the throne" (Rev 7:17), victorious "lion" (cf. Rev 5:5), courageous father for the cause of truth and justice, defender of the weak and the poor, victor over the evil of sin and death.

Therefore today, little more then half a century from their slaughter, the message of the new Blesseds is clear and relevant. When the Church proposes some life model for the faithful, it does so also consideration of the particular pastoral needs of the time in which such proclamations take place.

(See also Callisto Caravario.)

$\mathcal{M}$

✛

Magdalena Catarina Morano
(November 15, 1847 – March 26, 1908)
Spiritual Daughter of St. John Bosco

Magdalena Catarina Moreno was a pioneer in catechetical ministries.

She was born at Chieri, near Turin, Italy. When she was only eight years old, her father and an older sister died, making it necessary for her to find small jobs to aid the family finances. However, she did not neglect her education, and in 1866 earned a diploma as an elementary school instructor. For more than a decade, Magdalena taught in Montaldo, aiding as well the local parish catechetical program. She wanted to become a religious, but she had to wait until she had earned enough money to insure her mother's continued support.

In 1878, Magdalena entered the Daughters of Mary Help of Christians, founded by St. John Bosco and María Mazzarello. In 1881, she took her first vows and was assigned to Trecastagni, Catania, Sicily, to administer an institute for women. Accepting her new life with generosity and zeal, Magdalena remained in Sicily for a quarter of a century, founding new religious houses and educational and catechetical programs. She established catechetical classes in all of the parishes of Catania, laboring faithfully until her death as a spiritual child of St. John Bosco.

Pope John Paul II beatified Magdalena Catarina Morano on November 5, 1994 in Catania, declaring:

> Beloved brothers and sisters, your ancient Church, which has recently celebrated her cathedral's 900th anniversary as a place of worship, is called by circumstances today to serve the city's rebirth, mobilizing the energies which the Lord constantly renews in her, through tireless activity at the service of good. Sr. Magdalena Morano worked with precisely this in mind! She, the "born teacher," had come from Turin, the city of Don Bosco, with her outstanding pedagogical talent and her love for God and neighbor. On this island, Sr. Magdalena carried out an intense and fruitful spiritual and educational activity for the benefit of your people. For

long years she made herself one of you, becoming the model of faithful service to God and to her brothers and sisters. Look to her, beloved faithful, the better to carry out that apostolic and missionary project which all the members of the Church in Catania are striving to promote as they listen to the voice of the Spirit and concentrate their efforts on a diligent discernment of the "signs of the times."

✠

Manuel Barbal Cosan — see Martyrs of Astoria

✠

Manuel Gonzalez Garcia
(February 25, 1877 – January 4, 1940)
Founder of the Eucharistic Missionaries of Nazareth

Manuel Gonzalez Garcia was born in Seville, Spain, educated locally, and ordained to the priesthood on September 21, 1901. In the following year, he was sent to preach at Palomares del Rio, where he displayed a genuine intimacy in prayer with Christ in the Real Presence. Three years later, Manuel was assigned to Huelos; there, he started catechism programs for the young and authored a book on parish life.

On March 4, 1910, he started a union for Eucharistic reparation (adding devotions by children in 1919). With Sr. Maria Antonia, Manuel began the Congregation of the Eucharistic Missionaries of Nazareth and a congregation for Eucharistic priests. He was made the auxiliary bishop of Malaga on January 16, 1919, and succeeded to the see in 1920.

The Spanish Civil War impacted his diocese not long after that; on May 11, 1931, revolutionaries of the Spanish Civil War attacked, and Manuel had to go to Gibraltar with his refugee people. He was then ordered to administer Malaga from Madrid.

On August 5, 1935, he became the Bishop of Palencia, where he served until his death. His remains are in the Cathedral of Palencia.

Pope John Paul II beatified Manuel Gonzalez Garcia on April 29, 2001, declaring:

Blessed Manuel Gonzalez, founder of the Missionaras Eucaristicas de Nazaret, is a model of Eucharistic fraith whose example continues to speak to the Church today.

✠

Manuel Martin Sierra — see Martyrs of Motril

✠

Marcantonio Durando
(May 22, 1801 – December 10, 1880)
A Mission to the Sick and Suffering

Italian priest, promoter of the missions, and founder of the Nazarene Sisters, Marcantonio was born in Mondovì to a prominent family. His mother was a devout Catholic, but his father and two of his brothers became dedicated secularists; his two brothers took part in the *Risorgimento*, the movement to unite Italy that resulted in the end of the Papal States.

Marcantonio, however, followed his mother's path and, at the age of fifteen, entered the Congregation of the Mission to fulfill a desire to be a missionary. He took his perpetual vows at the age of eighteen and received ordination to the priesthood on June 12, 1824. For several years, he served in Casale Monferrato, and he was then transferred to Turin in 1829. He longed to go to China as a missionary, but this was not to be; he was destined instead to remain in the Turin house of the congregation literally for the rest of his life.

In 1837, at the age of thirty-six, he was appointed Visitor (or major Superior) to the Province of North Italy of the Vincentian Fathers, a position he held for the next forty-three years. During that time, he launched the Brignole-Sale School for the foreign missions in 1855, with the aim of training priests for the foreign field. He was also instrumental in introducing the Daughters of Charity into northern Italy.

In 1865, Marcantonio established the Company of the Passion of Jesus the Nazarene — the Nazarene Sisters — with the intention of caring for the sick in emulation of Christ's own suffering. The members were to care for the infirm day and night in their homes, labors that were boldly innovative and that met with some initial opposition.

Marcantonio was beatified on October 20, 2002, by Pope John Paul II. At the ceremony, the pontiff declared:

> "Remembering . . . your work of faith, and labour of love and your steadfastness of hope" (1 Thess. 1:2-3). The words of the Apostle draw the spiritual portrait of Fr. Marcantonio Durando, of the Congregation of the Mission and worthy son of the Piedmont region. He lived the Faith and

a burning spiritual zeal, shunning every kind of compromise or interior tepidity. At the school of St. Vincent de Paul, he learned how to recognize in the humanity of Christ the greatest, most accessible and disarming expression of the love of God for every human being. Still today, he indicates to us the mystery of the Cross as the culminating moment in which the unsearchable mystery of God's love is revealed.

✠

Marcel Callo (December 6, 1921 – March 19, 1945)
Missionary to Nazi Death Camps

Marcel Callo was born in Rennes, France, one of nine children, and was baptized two days later. Educated in local schools, he was apprenticed to a printer when he was almost thirteen. Marcel also belonged to the J.O.C., the Christian Workers' Youth organization, and was conspicuous for his devout nature. He maintained his job, never missed attending the sacraments, and became engaged in August 1942.

His happiness came in the midst of the conquest and occupation of France by the forces of the Third Reich, however. After only a few months of his engagement, the full weight of Nazi oppression reached Rennes, and Marcel was forced to enter the Service of Obligatory Work, a program that transported young French men to Germany as slave labor. He was assigned to a factory in Zella-Mehlis, Germany, and spent his time there organizing the Christian workers and rebuilding their morale under the dangerous and often inhumane conditions of forced labor. He even arranged for a French Mass, an act that brought him to the attention of the Gestapo, the dreaded Nazi secret police.

In April, 1944, Marcel was arrested for being "too much of a Catholic" and sent to Mauthausen, the Gusen 2 concentration camp called "the hell of hells" by the few who survived. There, he prayed and encouraged his fellow prisoners for the five months before his death from malnutrition and related conditions.

Pope John Paul II beatified Marcel Callo on October 4, 1987, declaring:

Yes, Marcel met the Cross. First, in France. Then, torn from the affection of his family and of a fiancée whom he loved tenderly and chastely — in Germany, where he re-launches the J.O.C. with some friends, several of whom also died witnesses of the Lord Jesus. Chased by the Gestapo, Marcel continued until the end. Like the Lord, he loved his own until the end and his entire life became eucharist. Having reached the eternal joy of God, he testifies that the Christian faith does not separate earth from heaven. Heaven is prepared on earth in justice and love. When one loves, one is already "blessed." Colonel Tibodo, who had seen thousands of prisoners die, was present on the morning of March 19, 1945; he testifies insistently and with emotion: Marcel had the appearance of a saint.

✠

Marcellina Darowska — see Maria Marcellina Darowska

✠

Marcellus Spinola y Maestre
(January 14, 1835 – January 19, 1906)
"Either Sanctity or Death"

Marcellus Spinola y Maestre was born at Isla de Spinola, Spain, the son of Marquis Juan and Antonia Spinola y Maestre. Well educated and raised piously, Marcellus was ordained a priest on March 21, 1864. He started his ministry by instituting charitable programs for the sick and abandoned, displaying the spirit of concern that would become the hallmark of his apostolate.

Marcellus served as a pastor, then as a cathedral canon, before becoming the auxiliary bishop of Seville in 1880. In 1885, he was made bishop of Caria, moving a year later to the diocese of Málaga. In 1896, Marcellus was consecrated the archbishop of Seville. He also began programs for young workers and educational institutions. He brought his concern for the poor and the sick to his new office.

Prayerful and kindly, Marcellus recognized the need for a balance in the Christian apostolate, and founded the Conceptionist Sisters of the Divine Heart, a congregation that combines the active and the contemplative life. He also started programs for young workers in Seville and promoted educational reforms in the archdiocese. Revered by his faithful and by the Holy See, Marcellus was designated as a cardinal, but died before he could receive the honor in person.

Pope John Paul II beatified Marcellus Spinola y Maestre on March 29, 1987, giving honor to this great cardinal of Spain and praising his charitable apostolate that led to the founding of his congregation of the active and contemplative ministries.

✠

Marciano Jose — see Martyrs of Astoria

✠

Marco d'Aviano (November 17, 1631 – August 13, 1699)

Standing Firm Against the Ottoman Threat

An Italian Capuchin priest and preacher, Marco d'Aviano was born in Aviano, Italy, to Marco Pasquale Cristofori and Rosa Zanoni. Raised in the Faith by his parents, he was filled with such zeal that, at the age of sixteen, he set out from home for the island of Crete to die as a martyr against the Ottoman Turks, who were then engaged in a struggle against the Christian West. After a few days of travel, however, he arrived at Capodistria and was given food and shelter in the local community of Capuchins.

Overwhelmed by the charity and example of the Capuchins, he chose to remain and entered the order in 1648 at Coneglian Veneto. He professed his vows a year later and was given the name Mark of Aviano. On September 18, 1655, he was ordained a priest in Chioggia and spent the next several years in prayer and service to the community. In 1664, however, he received a license to preach and was sent forth to preach throughout Italy, particularly during the Advent and Lenten seasons. In 1672, he was elected Superior of the community at Belluno; in 1674, Superior of the house in Oderzo.

In 1676, Marco preached in the monastery at Padua and gave his blessing to Sr. Vincenza Francesconi, who had been bedridden for thirteen years. Upon receiving the blessing, she was inexplicably healed. Word of the healing soon spread, and Marco was asked for his blessing by throngs of the sick. He continued to preach throughout Italy and elsewhere, at the behest of his superiors, and found himself approached for spiritual counsel by the Austrian Emperor Leopold I.

Over the course of his final years, Marco served as spiritual guide to the emperor and advised him on a host of issues, including the military and political needs of the Empire. In recognition of his talents and contributions, Pope Innocent XI named Marco apostolic nuncio (or ambassador) and papal legate to the imperial court. Marco's energy and forceful preaching proved instrumental in rallying the people of Vienna to defeat the seemingly invincible assault of the Ottoman Turks in 1683.

He dedicated the next years to promoting unity among the Christian princes as they grappled with the Ottoman threat. Through his labors, the city of Buda was freed in 1686, followed by Belgrade in 1688.

At the time of his death in Vienna, he was still exhorting the leaders of Christendom to maintain the tenuous peace with each other and to stand firm in the Faith against the Turks.

Marco was beatified by Pope John Paul II on April 27, 2003. At that time, the pope said of him:

> In a different time and context, Bl. Mark of Aviano shone with holiness as his soul burned with a longing for prayer, silence, and adoration of God's mystery.
>
> This contemplative who journeyed along the highways of Europe was the centre of a wide-reaching spiritual renewal, thanks to his courageous preaching that was accompanied by numerous miracles. An unarmed prophet of divine mercy, he was impelled by circumstances to be actively committed to defending the freedom and unity of Christian Europe. Bl. Mark of Aviano reminds the European continent, opening up in these years to new prospects of cooperation, that its unity will be sounder if it is based on its common Christian roots.

✠

Margaret Ebner (c.1291 – June 20, 1351)
Mystic of Medingen

Margaret Ebner was born in Donauworth, Germany, to a wealthy family and was given every advantage. But when she received the grace of a religious vocation, she quickly forgot those comforts and privileges to become a nun. She entered the Dominicans at María-Medingen, near Dillingen, completed her novitiate training, and was professed in 1306.

Six years later, Margaret became critically ill. Unable to continue her normal religious obligations, she was sent home by her superior to recover her health. This was an arduous process: ill for three years, she then took seven more years to recover her strength. During that decade of suffering, however, she experienced profound spiritual gifts, including visions and revelations.

Her spiritual director, the remarkable priest Henry of Nordlingen, recognized Margaret's mystical nature and asked her to write of her experiences once she returned to the convent. He was away from Medingen at the time, so, from 1332 to 1351, she carried on an elaborate correspondence with her spiritual director — the first collection of this type in Germany.

Pope John Paul II beatified Margaret Ebner on February 24, 1979, praising the devotions and endurance of the Mystic of Medingen, who was showered with many graces and persevered on a spiritual journey that led to union with Christ. Blessed Margaret Ebner was also the first person beatified in the pontificate of Pope John Paul II.

⊹

Marguerite Bays (September 8, 1815 – June 27, 1879)
Saintly Swiss Laywoman

A mystic and stigmatic, Marguerite Bays lived as a Third Order Franciscan.

She was born at Siviriez (Pierroz), in Fribourg Canton, Switzerland. Baptized the next day, she was raised in the Faith, confirmed in 1823, and made her first Communion at the age of eleven. Four years later, Marguerite was apprenticed as a dressmaker.

When her parents died in 1856, she ran the household, caring for her brother until he married. The introduction of her brother's wife into the house caused Marguerite considerable pain, as the woman appears to have disliked or even resented her. Despite the daily abuse, Marguerite maintained her spiritual life; she continued to serve her parish as a catechist and joined the Society for the Propagation of the Faith.

In 1853, Marguerite suffered cancer of the intestines but was miraculously cured on December 8, 1854. She then received the stigmata — the wounds of Christ — and experienced a deep mystical union with him, in which she was chosen as a victim soul and as a receptor of many graces. Many people came to see Marguerite, inspired by her devotion and sufferings. Her remarkable spiritual advancement was evident, and she displayed courage, fidelity to the faith, and profound graces.

Marguerite had always asked to die on the feast of the Sacred Heart; she expired on the octave of the feast, and her funeral was celebrated with joy by the local Swiss, who believed they had buried a saint.

Pope John Paul II beatified Marguerite Bays on October 29, 1995, observing:

> The mission lived by Marguerite Bays is the mission incumbent upon all Christians . . . Without leaving her country, she nevertheless kept her heart open to the dimensions of the universal Church and world.

✠

Maria Pilar Izquierdo Albero
(July 27, 1906 – August 27, 1945)
"Love For God, For the Cross of Jesus"

Maria Pilar Izquierdo Albero was born in Zaragosa, Spain, to a poor family. Because she had poor health as a child, she was sent to Alfamen to recover, returning to Zaragosa when her illnesses disappeared. As a very young woman she was sent to a shoe factory to work. In 1926, however, she fractured her pelvis, and cysts paralyzed her in the following year. To add to her trials, Maria Pilar also went blind.

But when — still suffering — she began to make plans for the founding of a religious congregation in 1936, Maria miraculously regained both mobility and sight. As a result, she moved to Madrid, gathered young women to join her, and tried to found the Missionaries of Jesus and Mary. Her first efforts failed, but a second congregation — the Pious Union of Missionaries of Jesus, Mary, and Joseph — succeeded. This group then became the Missionary Workers of Jesus and Mary and received approval.

Throughout the ordeals of founding, Maria Pilar displayed a constancy and faith that enabled her to accomplish charitable works for the poor and needy untiringly, until her death in San Sebastiano.

Pope John Paul II beatified Maria Pilar Izquierdo Albero on Novembr 4, 2001, announcing:

> One can sum up her short life: she died when she was thirty-nine years old, noting that she wanted to praise God by offering him her love and her sacrifice. . . . The love for God, for the Cross of Jesus, for her neighbour in need were the great concerns of the life of the new Blessed.

✠

María Antonia Bandrés y Elósegui
(March 6, 1898 – April 27, 1919)
Beatified With Her Foundress

A Spanish religious, María Antonia Bandrés Elósegui served as a model of a beautiful death.

She was born in Tolosa (Guipúzcoa), Spain, the second of fifteen children of Romón Bandrés and Teresa Elósegui. The Daughters of Jesus, founded by the future Blessed Cándida María of Jesus, educated her as a child and were impressed by her pure soul and spiritual maturity. Throughout her childhood, María Antonia demonstrated intense charity and took on tasks others did not normally perform willingly.

She entered the Daughters of Jesus, as Cándida had predicted, on December 8, 1915, in Salamanca, and was professed on May 31, three years later. Soon after, however, María Antonia became very ill. Despite this suffering, she displayed such serenity and joy that people within and outside of her community spoke of her often.

At one point prior to her death, María Antonia declared, "How mistaken we are about life! This, yes, this is what dying means." She died in the convent in Salamanca, singing the praises of Mary, Mother of Mercy.

Pope John Paul II beatified María Antonia Bandrés Elósegui on May 12, 1996, with Blessed Cándida María of Jesus Cipitria y Barriola, declaring:

> One day Mother Cándida said to a student at her school in Tolosa, "You will be a Daughter of Jesus." The young girl was María Antonia Bandrés y Elósegui, who today is raised to the glory of the altars with her foundress.
>
> In love with Jesus, she enabled others to love him as well. As a catechist, an instructor of working people, missionary in her desire since she was already a religious, she spent her short life loving, serving, and sharing with others. United to Christ in her sickness, she left us an eloquent example of participation in the saving work of the Cross.
>
> The witness of life given by these two Blesseds fills the Church with joy and should inspire their congregation, which has spread to many countries in Europe, America, and Asia, to follow their rich teachings, the model of their self-giving and their persevering fidelity to the charism received from the Spirit.

✠

María Domenica Brun Barbantini
(January 17, 1789 – May 22, 1868)
Pioneer in Catholic Action

María Domenica Brun Barbanti was born in Lucca, Italy, and educated in the Faith. She married at age twenty-two but was widowed six months later, while expecting her first child. On the night her husband died, María Domenica vowed to serve only God for the rest of her life. She gave birth to a son and carried on the family business while beginning an apostolate to the poor of the area.

Sadly, Maria also buried her son, who died after a brief illness at the age of eight. She channeled her grief into action, carrying on with the activities she had begun even before her son's illness, among them forming the Pious Union of the Sisters of Charity to expand her apostolate.

For a time, she resided in the local Visitandine convent. Then, in 1829, advised by Fr. Antonio Scalabrini, the Superior General of the order of St. Camillus, she founded a new congregation. The Sisters Servants of the Sick of St. Camillus, her congregation, received archdiocesan approval in 1841.

María Domenica was a pioneer in Catholic action in her era, introducing innovative programs to aid those in need and radiating her love of God. She died in Lucca, surrounded by her spiritual daughters and the many people who had been touched by her devotion.

Pope John Paul II beatified María Domenica Brun Barbanti on May 7, 1995, announcing:

> We rediscover the vigilant and caring image of the Good Shepherd in the newly Blessed Mother María Domenica Brun Barbantini, who, aware of having become "a new creature" in Christ's sacrifice, did not hesitate to respond to divine grace with a love expressed in daily service to her needy brothers and sisters.
>
> She bequeathed to her spiritual daughters a heritage and a mission that is very timely and precious. A practical Gospel love for the lowliest, the marginalized, the afflicted; a love expressed in acts of caring and Christian consolation, of generous dedication and tireless closeness to the sick and the suffering. The power and truth of the words of Jesus, who asked to be loved and served in the persons of his brothers and sisters who are hungry, thirsty, naked, strangers, sick, and in prison, shine out in this apostolic and missionary task.

⊹

María of Jesus Crucified Bouardy
(January 5, 1846 – August 26, 1878)
"The Little Arab"

Sometimes known as María or Maríam of Pau, María of Jesus Crucified Bouardy was a Carmelite founder.

She was born in Abelin, modern Israel, one of thirteen children, and the only surviving offspring of the family. Orphaned at age three, María was adopted by a caring uncle and taken to Alexandria, Egypt, where she was trained as a domestic servant. Interiorly, she was being transformed by divine grace, having her first vision at age thirteen.

María worked for a Muslim family and was treated kindly at first, but later was attacked by one of them when she refused to convert to Islam. After a miraculous cure of the wounds that she received from this brutal assault, she went on to serve as a domestic elsewhere. She worked for families in the cities of Alexandria, Jerusalem, and Beirut. Hired by the Nadjar family, María accompanied them to France. There, she discovered her own religious vocation. She entered the Carmelite monastery at Pau and made her novitiate.

In 1870, María was sent with other Carmelites to Mangalore, India, to start a new foundation. A year later, she was professed as a lay sister, but her mystical experiences were beginning to appear. She bore the stigmata, levitated at prayer, and had visions. She was considered to be a true prophetess by many, although she referred to herself as "the Little Nothing." The Carmelites sent her back to Pau, France, to ease her life, and she remained there until 1875, when she was sent to Bethlehem, Israel, to found a Carmel in that holy city. She also founded a Carmel in Nazareth. But while there, she broke her arm; the injury became gangrenous, and María died of the infection in Bethlehem.

Pope John Paul II beatified María of Jesus Crucified Bouardy on November 13, 1983, praising her fidelity, courage, and sacrifices, and asking her intercession for peace in her home region, where the Catholic Faith has long glorified God and has provided much needed charity and good.

✠

Maria Cristina Brando (May 1, 1856 – January 20, 1906)

Foundress of the Sisters, Expiatory Victims of Jesus in the Blessed Sacrament

Maria Cristina Brando was born in Naples, Italy, to Giovanni Giuseppe and Maria Concetta Marrazzo; her mother died only a few days after Maria's birth. Her childhood was marked by her early determination to become a woman religious, but her first efforts proved failures. She tried to enter the Monastery of the Sacramentine Nuns in Naples, but her father was adamantly opposed to the idea. He did, however, give his permission for her to join the Poor Clare Nuns, but she was twice prevented from entering because of bouts of severe illness. At last, when she was well enough, she was granted permission to enter the Sacramentine Nuns. In 1876, she took the name Sr. Maria Cristina of the Immaculate Conception; but yet again, her health collapsed, and she was compelled to abandon her hopes.

Relinquishing the notion of being a member of an established religious community, Maria instead established a new spiritual venture in 1878, the Congregation of the Sisters, Expiatory Victims of Jesus in the Blessed Sacrament. From its inception, the community proved an effective one and grew rapidly despite the often poor health of its founder. With the assistance of Michelangelo of Marigliano and Ludovico of Casoria, the community flourished and was moved to Casoria, near Naples. At last, in 1897, Maria took her temporary vows. In 1903, the congregation received canonical approval from the Holy See, and in November of that year, Maria and the other sisters took their perpetual vows.

The heart of Maria's spiritual life was the adoration of the Blessed Sacrament, and from this wellspring emerged the other ministries of the congregation, including schools, orphanages, and boarding school. She was beatified by Pope John Paul II on April 27, 2003. The pontiff declared:

> All that God worked through Maria Christina Brando is astonishing. Her Eucharistic and expiatory spirituality is expressed in two lines, like "two branches that stem from the same trunk": love of God and love of neighbour. Her desire to take part in Christ's passion, as it were, "overflowed" into educational works, for the purpose of making people aware of their dignity and open to the Lord's merciful love.

✠

Maria Caritas Brader (August 14, 1860 – February 27, 1943)
Missionary to South America

Mary Josephine Caroline was born in Kaltbrunn, St. Gallen, Switzerland, and received an excellent education in the Faith. Faced with every opportunity and promise in life, she chose the religious life and entered the enclosed Franciscan convent of Maria Hilf on October 1, 1880. The following year, she received the Franciscan habit and took the name Mary Charity (Maria Caritas) of the Love of the Holy Spirit. In August 1882, she professed her religious vows and was chosen immediately to teach in the local convent school.

In 1888, Sr. Maria was given the opportunity for missionary work in South America, at the request of Bishop Pietro Schumacher of Portoviejo, Ecuador. Sr. Maria was delighted to learn that she had been chosen by the future Blessed Maria Bernarda Bütler, Superior of the convent, as one of the six sisters who would comprise the mission. The sisters set out for Ecuador in June 1888. In 1893, they reached Tùquerres, Colombia, with the task of educating the local children.

Sr. Maria demonstrated remarkable evangelizing zeal and genuine courage in trekking through the harsh jungles and forests of the region to reach the poor people and proclaim the Gospel. To assist this work further, she founded the Congregation of the Franciscan Sisters of Mary Immaculate. The new establishment was to be composed initially of young Swiss girls who sought to emulate the labors of their foundress, but the community's numbers soon swelled as local girls from Colombia and elsewhere arrived, eager to join. Mother Maria kept the focus of the congregation firmly upon the education and care of the poor and the forgotten, but she also secured permission for Perpetual Adoration of the Blessed Sacrament in the convent.

Mother Maria remained Superior General of the congregation from 1893 to 1919 and, again, from 1928 to 1940. Formal pontifical approval of the congregation was received in 1933. Her passing was marked by mourning in Colombia, and her grave was soon a site for pilgrims. Pope John Paul II beatified her on March 23, 2003. He declared:

> In the course of history, numberless men and women have proclaimed the Kingdom of God in the whole world. Among them must be counted Mother Caritas Brader, the foundress of the Franciscan Sisters of Mary Immaculate.
>
> From the contemplative life of the enclosed convent of Maria Hilf in her Swiss homeland, one day the new Blessed set out, first in Ecuador, then in Colombia, to consecrate herself entirely to the Mission *ad gentes* (to the nations). With unlimited confidence in divine Providence, she founded schools and homes, above all in poor areas, and in this way spread a deep Eucharistic devotion.
>
> At the moment of death, she said to her sisters, "Do not abandon the good works of the Congregation, the alms and great charity for the poor, great charity among the sisters, allegiance to the bishops and priests." Beautiful lesson of a missionary life dedicated to the service of God and of neighbour.

⳨

María Bernarda Bütler (May 28, 1848 – May 19, 1924)

Foundress of Franciscan Missionaries of Mary, Help of Christians

María Bernarda Bütler was born in Auw, Aargau, Switzerland, the daughter of a peasant family. As she matured in the Faith, she entered the Franciscan convent of María Hilf in Altstätten, Switzerland, and was professed in 1869. She became novice mistress, then Superior, serving until June 1888, when she and six companions went to Portoviejo, Ecuador. In Chone, Ecuador, she founded the Franciscan Missionaries of Mary, Help of Christians.

Forced to leave Ecuador because of difficulties, María Bernarda set out again with fifteen sisters and reached Bahia. Bishop Eugenio Biffi then invited them into Cartagena, Colombia, providing them with a wing of the women's hospital, *Obra Pie*. María Bernarda centralized her congregation there and founded houses in Colombia, Austria, and Brazil.

The congregation was dedicated to the spiritual and physical care of the poor and the sick. Devoted to the Holy Trinity and the Passion of Christ, María Bernarda chose the Blessed Virgin Mary as patroness of her religious community in the New World.

She died at Cartagena, Spain, in 1924; some seventy-one years later, Pope John Paul II beatified María Bernarda Bütler on October 29, 1995, announcing:

> As a perfect daughter of St. Francis of Assisi, she wished to serve God by serving her brothers and sisters. Her generosity was admirable. She radically detached herself from everything and risked her life for Christ, since her greatest wish was to proclaim the Lord to the ends of the earth.

☩

María del Transito Sacramentado Cabanillas
(August 15, 1821 – August 25, 1885)
"Let Divine Love Be the Motive for All Our Actions"

María del Transito Sacramento Cabanillas served others with heroic charity.

She was born in Cordoba, Argentina, the third of eleven children residing with their parents on an estate. She was baptized María del Transito — or María Asunción, in honor of the Assumption of the Blessed Virgin Mary — and was given the name Eugenia de los Dolores. María del Transito was educated at the colleges of Santa Catalina and Santa Teresa. Her father died in 1850, at which point she began taking care of the family on the estate.

In 1858, she became a Franciscan Tertiary and distinguished herself by her charity and generous service during the cholera epidemic of 1867. She also recognized that she had been given the grace of a religious vocation and entered the Carmelite cloister in 1873, but she stayed there only one year. After another year with the Visitation Sisters in Montevideo, María del

Transito came to understand that she was being asked to found a religious congregation.

On December 8, 1878, she and two companions took vows as the first members of the Third Order Franciscan Missionary Sisters of Argentina. Her motto was "Let Divine Love be the motive for all our actions." She died in Cordoba.

Pope John Paul II beatified María del Transito Sacramentado Cabanillas on April 14, 2002, declaring:

> The flame that burned in her heart brought María del Transito to seek intimacy with Christ in the contemplative life . . . she understood a life of poverty, humility, patience, and charity, giving rise to a new religious family.

✠

María Margaret Caiani
(November 2, 1863 – August 8, 1921)
Patroness of Tuscany

María Margaret Caiani was born in Poggio a Caiano, Italy, the third child of Jacob and Luisa Caiani. Called Maríanna Rosa by her family, she was devoted to prayer at a very young age. Her father died in 1884, and she had to work in the family shop until 1890, when her mother passed away. She was then free to respond to a religious vocation.

Maríanna tried to enter the Sisters of St. Maximus convent, but chose not to remain there when she realized that she was called to another life. Anxious to accomplish God's Will, she and two friends opened a school in Poggio a Caiano for neglected and abandoned children, and other young women joined them in their apostolate. This group became the Franciscan Minims of the Sacred Heart on September 15, 1902. In 1915, María Margaret was elected Superior General for life.

Her devotion to the Sacred Heart led her to serve the people of Tuscany with great generosity and care. Her congregation aided the elderly, military wounded, children, rural families, and the poor. She also expanded the labors of her sisters to meet new needs and, in 1920, revised the congregation's constitution, aggregating the Minims to the Order of Friars Minor. María Margaret died in Florence and was declared Venerable in 1986.

Pope John Paul II beatified her on April 23, 1989, declaring:

Blessed María Margaret Caiani made an option for Christ Crucified, whom she loved in the symbol of his divine Heart. She loved him in the needy, the least, and the smallest.

✠

Maria Candida of the Eucharist
(January 16, 1884 – June 12, 1949)
Mystic of the Eucharist

Maria Candida was born Maria Barba in Catanzaro, Italy; her father was a judge in the Appeal Court of Palermo, Pietro Barba. While called to the religious life by the age of fifteen, she was unable to fulfill the call at first, as her family opposed it. It was ten years later, in September 1919, when she was finally able to enter the Teresian Carmel at Ragusa.

Her religious life mirrored her youth in one important way — from a very young age, Maria was profoundly drawn to the Eucharist and looked upon receiving Communion as the greatest joy of her life. Hence, upon joining the Carmelites, she took the name Maria Candida of the Eucharist. The adoration of the Eucharist was one of the principle tasks of her daily life and was at the heart of her consecration of herself to God as a victim on November 1, 1927.

Sr. Maria subsequently was elected prioress in 1924, an office she held until 1947. She dedicated herself to the establishing the Rule of St. Teresa of Jesus for the community and extending the presence of the Carmelites in Sicily. In 1933, she also began writing her famed spiritual work, *The Eucharist*, a deep meditation on the Eucharist that showed that the Sacrament unites all of the aspects of the Christian life, including faith, hope, and charity, and all of the dimensions of the religious life.

Mother Maria was beatified by Pope John Paul II on March 21, 2004, when the pope said of her:

> Maria Barba became a "new creature" who offered her entire life to God in Carmel, where she received the name Maria Candida of the Eucharist. She was an authentic mystic of the Eucharist; she made it the unifying centre of her entire life, following the Carmelite tradition and particularly the examples of St. Teresa of Jesus and of St. John of the Cross.
>
> She fell so deeply in love with the Eucharistic Jesus that she felt a constant, burning desire to be a tireless apostle of the Eucharist. I am sure that Bl. Maria Candida is continuing to help the Church from Heaven, to

assure the growth of her sense of wonder at and love for this supreme Mystery of our faith.

✠

María Sagrario Cantarero
(January 8, 1881 – August 15, 1936)
Martyr of the Spanish Civil War

María Sagrario Cantarero led her cloistered nuns to safety before being arrested by anti-Catholic revolutionaries.

She was born Elvira Moragas Cantarero in Lille, Spain, the third child of Ricardo Moragas and Isabel Cantarero. Her father served as the pharmaceutical purveyor of the royal household and, in 1886, the family moved to Madrid. Elvira was given a good education; in fact, she became the first woman of Spain to earn a degree in pharmacy.

When Elvira's father died, she continued his work, although she was drawn to the religious life. A younger brother was dependent upon her care, and her spiritual director told her to remain in the world for a time. She was in her early thirties when circumstances allowed her to enter the Carmel of St. Anne and St. Joseph in Madrid. On December 21, 1915, she received the name María Sagrario of St. Aloysius Gonzaga. She was solemnly professed on January 6, 1920.

Seven years later, she was elected prioress, then served three years as novice mistress. María Sagrario was elected prioress for the second time in July 1936, just as the Spanish Civil War crashed down upon the nation. Rebel forces, focusing their wrath on priests and religious, attacked the convent, and María Sagrario had to lead the cloistered nuns to safe havens. On August 14, however, she was arrested with a companion by an armed unit of revolutionaries.

The secret police of the rebels questioned her about the "treasures" of the convent and the location of the other nuns, but she remained serenely silent. She was taken to the Pradera of San Isidro on August 15, 1936, and there, was shot to death.

Pope John Paul II beatified María Sagrario Cantarero on May 10, 1998, declaring that this Blessed

> . . . gave up everything to live for God alone in Christ Jesus. She found the strength not to betray priests and friends of the community facing death with an integrity for her state as a Carmelite and to save others.

✠

María of St. Joseph Alvarado Cardozo
(April 25, 1875 – April 2, 1967)
"Mother of the Abandoned"

Maria of St. Joseph Alvarado was born in Choroní, Venezuela, and baptized Laura Evangelista. The faith was important to her family, and Laura made her First Communion at age thirteen. She added to the occasion by making a private vow of consecration to Christ. In time, aided by her pastor, Laura made a vow of perpetual virginity.

This pastor, Fr. Vincente López Aveledo, stationed in Maracay, had founded a hospital, and Laura performed charitable works there. During the smallpox epidemic of 1893, she demonstrated heroic endurance in caring for victims of the disease. She was motivated throughout this ordeal by one desire — to seek Christ in sanctity.

In 1901, aided by Fr. Aveledo, Laura founded the Augustinian Recollects of the Heart of Jesus, a congregation devoted to the care of the aged, orphans, and the sick. On September 13, 1903, she took her religious name and began her ministry, founding thirty-seven homes for the aged and orphans. María of St. Joseph spent hours before the Holy Eucharist and even made hosts to distribute freely to local parishes. Finally, after a long illness, she died in Maracay, Venezuela.

Pope John Paul II beatified María of St. Joseph Alvarado Cardozo on May 7, 1995, announcing:

When she was a small child, Blessed María Alvarado Cardozo discovered love for the Eucharist, in which she found the distinctive charism of her spirituality. She spent long hours of the day and night before the tabernacle. All her life she made with her own hands thousands of hosts in order to distribute them freely to priests. Her example is still followed by her daughters, who have offered the hosts for this Mass today.

Her boundless love for Christ in the Eucharist led her to dedicate herself to the service of the neediest in whom she saw the suffering Jesus. For this reason, she founded in Maracay the Congregation of Augustinian Recollects of the Heart of Jesus, dedicated to the assistance of the elderly, orphans, and abandoned children. Charity, the virtue in which Mother María of St. Joseph most distinguished herself, led her to repeat constantly to her daughters: "Those rejected by everyone are ours; those whom no one wants to take are ours." Her deep piety, anchored in the Eucharist and in prayer, was enriched by a tender devotion to the Virgin Mary, whose name she took and whom she imitated, saying, "I would like to live and die singing the Magnificat."

The witness of this simple woman of our time invites everyone, especially the beloved sons and daughters of Venezuela, to live the Gospel faithfully.

✠

María Vicenta of St. Dorothy Chavez Orozco
(February 6, 1867 – July 30, 1949)
Foundress of Institutions of Mercy in Mexico

María Vicenta of St. Dorothy Chavez was born in Catija, Mexico, in the state of Michoacan, the youngest of four children, and known for her devotion at an early age. In February 1892, she entered Holy Trinity Hospital, a small medical facility started by Fr. Augustin Beas in her neighborhood. While recovering from an illness, she received the grace of a vocation and a special calling to aid the sick.

On July 10 of that year, she started caring for patients in the hospital. In 1895, María Vicenta took private vows with Catalina Velasco and Juana Martin del Campo. On May 12, 1905, she founded her congregation, the Servants of the Poor, which would later be renamed the Servants of the Holy Trinity and the Poor. María Vicenta became Superior General in 1913, leading the congregation for three decades.

During the Mexican Revolution, she and her sisters were in constant danger from anti-Catholic troops. She stayed in St. Vincent's Hospital in Zapotlán during its occupation by such forces in 1926 and endured vile insults and death threats until a commanding officer reprimanded his troops, praising her as a courageous model of charity. She persisted in her works of mercy, even under duress; by 1942, she had established seventeen new clinics, hospitals, and nurseries.

She began to suffer eye problems that year but continued her labors until July 29, 1949, when she was no longer able to attend chapel. Archbishop José Garibi Rivera, who became Mexico's first cardinal, was at María Vicenta's bedside in Holy Trinity Hospital, in Guadalajara, and she died at the moment the archbishop elevated the Host during Mass.

Pope John Paul II beatified María Vicente of St. Dorothy Chavez Orosco on November 9, 1997, declaring her a remarkable symbol of charity and faithful resolve. Her beatification served as an insignia of the thriving devotion of the nation of Mexico, despite the persecutions and trials over the centuries.

✠

María Raffaella Cimatti (June 6, 1861 – June 23, 1945)
"Mamma Cimatti" to Wounded Soldiers

María Raffaella was born in Celle di Faenza, Ravenna, Italy, to a family of modest means. She had five brothers, but only two survived to adulthood, and they both became priests. After her father died in 1882, María Raffaella educated her brothers and served as a parish catechist. Her mother moved into the local rectory, while her brothers entered St. John Bosco's congregation, allowing her to respond to her own call to the religious life. In 1889, she entered the Hospitaller Sisters of Mercy.

Two years later, María Raffaella made her religious profession, adding a vow of hospitality. She was assigned as a pharmacist's assistant in Alatri, then in Frosinone. In 1921, she became the Superior in Forsinone and, in 1928, took the same office in Alatri. She maintained that role until 1940, when she resigned as Superior and asked to live as a simple religious.

In 1944, María Raffaella ministered to so many wounded soldiers that she became the favorite of hardened veterans who had survived the dangers of battle and now found solace in her care. At age eighty-three, she was still working night and day for the steady stream of wounded who were brought from the front. Hearing word that Alatri would be bombed and reduced to rubble to stem the advance of the Allied troops, María Raffaella marched into German headquarters and cofronted the supreme commander himself, Field Marshal Kesselring. Taken aback by the courage and the sincere concern of this venerable religious — and possessed of a certain military chivalry — Kesselring accepted her demand and spared Alatri.

María Raffaella died in Alatri, and her Cause was opened in 1962.

Pope John Paul II beatified María Raffaella Cimatti on May 12, 1996, declaring:

> "Blessed be God, because he has not . . . removed his steadfast love from me!" (Ps 65 [66]: 20).

> Divine Mercy is the key to interpreting the simple, profound spirituality of María Raffaella Cimatti, a religious of the Hospitaller Sisters of Mercy. Her activity was inspired by God's infinite mercy, of which the psalmist speaks, especially in her service to the poor and the suffering. This woman, who is raised to the honors of the altar today, spent herself in total

consecration to God in silent daily service to the sick. She carried out her humble daily duties, as well as the responsible tasks she was constantly required to fulfill, with a spirit of sacrifice and ever-ready willingness, listening and accepting all those who came to her seeking advice or comfort.

✠

Maria Marcellina Darowska
(January 16, 1827 – January 5, 1911)
Polish Educator and Foundress

Maria Marcellina was born in Szulaki, in the Ukraine, to a family of Polish descent named Kotowicz. Prayerful, recollected, and dutiful, Maria Marcellina hoped to enter the religious life. Her parents, however, did not promote this aspiration, and she could not go against their wishes. On his deathbed, Maria Marcellina's father even made her promise that she would wed and raise a family. Accordingly, she married a man named Karol Darowska in 1849.

The couple had two children before Karol died, less than three years after their wedding. One child, a son, followed his father to the grave in 1853. Maria Marcellina buried her son with his father and went to Rome with her daughter, Carolina. There, she met Fr. Hieronim Kajsicwicz, who became her spiritual director. He was aware of her spiritual maturity and holiness, and he understood Maria Marcellina's religious vocation.

With his aid, even while providing for her daughter's upbringing, she was able to co-found the Congregation of the Sisters of the Immaculate Conception of the Blessed Virgin Mary with Josephine Karska. Josephine died in 1860 after being stricken with typhus, and Maria Marcellina carried the burden of the new congregation alone. In 1863, she brought her sisters to Jazlowicz, in the archdiocese of Lviv, Ukraine, where she opened a school for girls. This school proved instrumental in Maria Marcellina's ministry. Through this institution, she was able to influence young and old with the Church's doctrines of family life and a moral society. Countless women experienced a renewal in her schools. Maria Marcellina opened formation institutes, schools, and seven convents, even pioneering tuition-free schools. After a half century of service, she died with her community at her bedside.

Pope John Paul II beatified Maria Marcellina Darowska on October 6, 1996, declaring:

She wanted to do everything so that truth, love, and goodness would triumph in human life and transform the face of her beloved nation.

✠

Maria Teresa Fasce
(December 27, 1881 – January 18, 1947)
Devoted to St. Rita

Maria Teresa Fasce was born at Torriglia, near Genoa, Italy. Raised profoundly in the Faith, she entered the monastery of St. Rita in Cascia in 1906, receiving the Augustinian habit the following year. She performed many roles in the Augustinian convent, serving as novice mistress and vicaress and inspiring her fellow religious. In 1920, she was elected abbess for life.

Her special apostolate was the spread of the devotion to St. Rita. Through her efforts, thousands visited the saint's basilica in Cascia. She also established an orphanage for girls, an Augustinian seminary, and St. Rita's Hospital. Maria Teresa sought ways in which to protect and nurture the abandoned, vulnerable, or needy of the region as well. During the war years, she faced the Nazis with determination and courage, denying them access to her convent and to those in her care on more than one occasion.

The abbess suffered physically but kept silent about her growing infirmities and carried on her work. At her death, she expressed her faith exquisitely, declaring that she was not just leaving the world and her sisters but entering eternity with "faith, hope, and love." When she died, Maria Teresa was laid to rest next to her beloved patroness, St. Rita.

Pope John Paul II beatified Maria Teresa Fasce on October 12, 1997, stating that she was one:

> . . .who lived in the constant contemplation of the mystery of Christ. . . . the Church holds her up today as a radiant example of the living synthesis between contemplative life and a humble witness of solidarity to men and women, especially to the poorest, the humble, the abandoned and suffering.

✠

María Anna Mogas Fontcuberta
(January 13, 1827 – July 3, 1886)
Pioneered Catholic Education

The co-founder of the Congregation of the Capuchins of the Divine Shepherdess, María Anna Mogas Fontcuberta was born in Corró de Vall, Grenollers, Spain. Her father died when she was seven, and her mother died seven years later. An aunt in Barcelona was given the care of María Anna. The aunt was devout and instilled the Faith and the practice of virtues in María Anna's daily life.

When María Anna had matured in the world and in the spiritual life, she met Fr. Joseph Tous Soler, an exclaustrated Capuchin monk — a Franciscan who had been given permission to minister to people in the world. Two former cloistered Capuchin nuns were being directed by Fr. Soler, and they asked María Anna to assist them in founding a new congregation dedicated to the education of children. When she agreed to help them, the Congregation of the Capuchins of the Divine Shepherdess was formed in 1850. Bishop Luciano Casadevail of Vich received the new community and gave them a school in Ripoli. María Anna was clothed in the habit and elected Superior.

The first years were difficult ones, as the congregation lacked financial resources and commitment of the laity. The two former Capuchin nuns returned to the cloister, leaving María Anna to deal with the harsh realities of such an undertaking. She took the necessary academic tests to direct a school and began recruiting new members for the congregation.

María Anna followed the Franciscan spirit in her congregation, but her devotion to the Blessed Virgin Mary was instilled in her sisters as well. The congregation spread rapidly; in time, she went to Madrid, where she directed the congregation, which developed a second group in Barcelona. Her faith and generosity served the Church throughout Spain, until her death in Fuencarral.

Pope John Paul II beatified her on October 6, 1996. He said this of Maria:

> . . . [she] knew how to respond generously to God's intimate love for his children, and thus to yield abundant fruit. Renouncing a well-to-do social position, she forged, in union with the tabernacle and the cross, a spirituality inspired by the Heart of Christ.

✠

Maria Theresa of Jesus Gerhardinger
(June 20, 1797 – May 9, 1879)
"The Strong Woman of God"

Maria Theresa of Jesus Gerhardinger founded the School Sisters of Notre Dame.

She was born in Stadtamhof, Germany, the daughter of Frances and Willibald Gerhardinger. She was baptized Caroline Elizabeth Frances. At age six, Caroline entered a school conducted by the Canonesses of Notre

Dame, but after Napoleon's forces entered the area in 1809, she had to continue her education without the Canonesses, who were forced to leave their religious institutions. In 1812, Caroline became a "royal teacher" at the King's School in Stadtamhof.

The death of her father in 1825 left Caroline with responsibility for the care of her mother, who came to live with her. On October 24, 1833, Caroline, along with Maria Blass and Barbara Weinzierl, founded the School Sisters of Notre Dame with the aid of Bishop Michael Wittman. At that point she took her religious name of Maria Theresa of Jesus.

The congregation received episcopal sanction the following year. On November 16, 1835, she pronounced her vows in a chapel of St. Gall in Regensburg; a year later, six novices entered the congregation.

Steadily building the new foundation, Maria Theresa received a convent from King Louis Philippe (r. 1830-1848) in 1841. The motherhouse of the Notre Dame Sisters was thus erected in Munich.

Two years later, her own mother died, and she suffered a severe illness; but she recovered and sailed to America in 1847 to start the missions among the German immigrants. Baltimore became the first foundation., after which a second group of Notre Dame Sisters arrived in the United States in 1848, and were joined by yet another group the following year.

Having established the American houses, Maria Theresa returned to Europe. There, she was elected Superior General for life, receiving a decree from the Holy See in 1854 (when the congregation was also called the Poor School Sisters of Notre Dame). She sent sisters to many lands and received awards for her aid to the wounded in the wars of that historical era.

Maria Theresa died in Munich, leaving more then 2,500 sisters and countless schools and missions. Pope John Paul II beatified her on November 17, 1985, announcing:

> Maria Teresa of Jesus, a simple but determined and courageous religious, accomplished great things for mankind and the kingdom of God. In the founding of her order she showed herself a "strong woman" who did not shy away from sacrifice or difficulties of any kind in order to fulfill this work, which she always referred to as "God's work." Her order of teachers was a pioneering influence in the development of education in countless European countries and in America. The spiritual heritage of the new Blessed lives on today in some 7,500 School Sisters in Europe, North and Latin America, Asia, Oceania, and Africa . . . May Blessed Mother Teresa of Jesus Gerhardinger continue to be a shining example and intercessor,

not only for the sisters of her own congregation, but for all Christian educators as well.

⊹

Maria Elisabetta Hesselblad — see Elizabeth Hesselblad

⊹

Maria Bernardina Jablonska
(August 5, 1878 – September 23, 1940)
"To Give, Eternally To Give"

A spiritual daughter of St. Albert Chmielowski, Maria Bernardina Jablonska was a servant of the suffering and poor.

She was born in Pizuny, Poland, and raised in a devoutly religious family. Gifted spiritually and a contemplative, she resided in a hermitage for a time and believed she was called to a hidden apostolate of prayer and penance.

As she began to see the suffering around her, however, Maria Bernardina followed the religious trail blazed by St. Albert Chmielowski in Poland. Drawn to his holiness, she entered the Albertine Sisters, recently founded by the saint. Maria Bernardina brought a spiritual insight and a profound awareness of human suffering to the convent. Her holiness and her abilities led to her election as Superior, a role that she fulfilled with energy and prudence.

In the spirit of commitment and dedication, Maria Bernardina founded hospices for the sick and poor and pioneered charitable works to alleviate the needs of others. She died in Krakow, Poland, in 1940.

Pope John Paul II beatified Maria Bernardina Jablonska on June 6, 1997, at Zakopane, Poland, declaring:

> The Church places this devout religious before us today as an example. Her motto of life was the words: "To give, eternally to give." With her gaze fixed on Christ she followed him faithfully, imitating his love.

⊹

Maria Restituta Kafka (May 10, 1894 – March 30, 1943)
Franciscan Martyr of the Nazis

Maria Restituta Kafka was born in Brno, now part of the Czech Republic, and baptized Helena. When her family moved to Vienna, Austria, Helena was raised in that great capital. She worked as a salesgirl, then entered nursing, which brought her into contact with the *Hartmannschwestern*, the Franciscan Sisters of Christian Charity. Helena entered that congregation in 1914 and received her religious name of Maria Restituta.

A surgical nurse, she had served as a medical religious for two decades when the Nazis gained control of Austria. She was unrestrained in her opposition to the Nazis, calling upon the tradition that Viennese speak their minds. Maria Restituta even declared Hitler a "madman," and she retaliated against the Nazis by hanging a crucifix in every room of a new hospital wing.

When the Nazis demanded the removal of the crucifix, they also threatened the hospital with retaliation if Maria Restituta was not dismissed. The hospital administration argued that no one could replace her — and the crucifixes remained on the walls.

Eventually, Maria Restituta was reported to the Gestapo by a hospital physician and, on October 28, 1942, was arrested for plotting high treason against Hitler. Held as a prisoner for a time, she was offered her freedom if she would give up her religious life. She refused and was condemned to death.

A petition for leniency reached the desk of Martin Bormann, one of the most powerful Nazis in the entire Third Reich. He replied merely that Maria Restituta should die to provide "effective intimidation" of those who might think about resisting. While in prison and undergoing personal abuse, Maria distinguished herself by caring for other prisoners, including Communists, who later testified on her behalf. She was led to the execution site and decapitated on March 30, 1943.

Pope John Paul II beatified Maria Restituta on June 21, 1998, in Vienna, announcing:

> Sr. [Maria] Restituta Kafka was not yet an adult when she expressed her intention to enter the convent.... Because of her courage and fearlessness, she did not wish to be silent even in the face of the National Socialist regime. Challenging the political authority's prohibitions, Sr. Restituta had crucifixes hung in all the hospital rooms. On Ash Wednesday, 1942, she was taken away by the Gestapo. In prison her "Lent" began, which was to last more than a year and to end in execution. Her last words passed on to us were, "I have lived for Christ; I want to die for Christ."
>
> Looking at Blessed Sr. Restituta, we can see to what heights of inner maturity a person can be led by the divine hand. She risked her life for her witness to the Cross. And she kept the Cross in her heart, bearing witness

to it once again before being led to execution, when she asked the prison chaplain to "make the Sign of the Cross on my forehead."

✠

Maria Karlowska (September 4, 1865 – March 24, 1935)
Mystic and Foundress

Maria Karlowska was born in Kartowo, Poland, and raised in a pious family and community. As a young woman, she developed a great devotion to the Sacred Heart of Jesus. Maria desired only to live for the Sacred Heart; led by this motivation, she began to care for the poor and sick and concerned herself with young women in her region.

Additionally, our of this devotion grew the Congregation of the Good Shepherd of the Divine Providence. Maria worked mainly in Plock, Pomerania (now considered part of Poland). Her motto was to make Christ "more visible than we ourselves." She lived to see her congregation expand and receive official approbation. Maria died in Pniewita, Poland.

Pope John Paul II beatified Maria Karlowska on June 6, 1997, at Zakopane, Poland, with Maria Bernardina Jablowska, stating that Maria Karlowska:

> . . . worked as a true Samaritan among women suffering great material and moral deprivation. . . . Her devotion to the Savior's Sacred Heart bore fruit in a great love for people. . . . Thanks to this love she restored to many souls the light of Christ and helped them to regain their lost dignity.

✠

Maria Ludovica De Angelis
(October 24, 1880 – February 25, 1962)
Distinguished Hospital Religious

An Italian woman religious, Maria Ludovica was born in Abruzzo, Italy, to a dedicated Catholic family of workers. Baptized Antonina, she loved the outdoors as a child and was tireless in working in the fields. She was also deeply prayerful and, inspired by the example of St. Mary Joseph Rossello, foundress of the Institute of the Daughters of Our Lady of Mercy, Antonina was drawn to the religious life.

Antonina entered the Daughters of Our Lady of Mercy in November 1904 and took the name Sr. Maria Ludovica. Three years later, she was sent Buenos Aires, Argentina, to assist the work of the congregation in South America.

While not well-educated, she proved a tireless woman religious who gave her entire life to others. She distinguished herself in a Children's Hospital by giving love and compassion to the sick and dying children and their families.

To her surprise, she was named the Superior of the hospital, and through her efforts and quiet determination, she assisted the hospital in finding the money needed to expand its services for the care of sick children, including a farm that provided produce for the nutritional needs of the patients. After her death — bringing to a close fifty-four years of selfless work — the Children's Hospital was renamed "Superior Ludovica Hospital." Her favorite (and hallmark) phrase was, "Do good to all, no matter who it may be."

She was beatified by Pope John Paul II on Oct. 3, 2004, at which time the pope said of her:

> "God did not give us a spirit of timidity but a spirit of power and love and self-control" (II Tm 1: 7). St. Paul's words invite us to collaborate in building the Kingdom of God in the perspective of faith. They can be aptly applied to the life of Bl. Ludovica de Angelis whose existence was totally dedicated to the glory of God and the service of her peers.
>
> She was a person with an outstanding mother's heart, leadership qualities, and the daring typical of saints. She also showed concrete and generous love to sick children, making sacrifices to bring them relief; with her co-workers in La Plata Hospital, she was a model of cheerfulness and responsibility, creating a family atmosphere. As a Daughter of Our Lady of Mercy, she set an authentic example to the Sisters in her community. She was sustained in all this by prayer and by making her life a continuous communication with the Lord.

⚜

Maria Domenica Mantovani
(November 12, 1862 – February 2, 1934)
Co-Foundress of the Little Sisters of the Holy Family

Maria Domenica Mantovani was born in Castelletto di Brenzone, Italy. Her parents, Giovanni and Prudenza Zamperini, were farmers and provided their four children with a sound upbringing in the Faith. She received considerable spiritual direction beginning in 1877, when Fr. Giuseppe Nascimbeni (beatified on April 17, 1988) was appointed as a parish priest in Castelletto. He encouraged her development in the spiritual life and the performance of charitable works. In December 1886, Maria made a private vow of perpetual virginity while standing before a statue of Mary Immaculate.

In 1892, Fr. Nascimbeni founded the Congregation of the Little Sisters of the Holy Family, and crucial to the first establishment of the new community was the tireless effort of Maria Domenica. For her immeasurable assistance, she was declared the co-foundress of the congregation and its Superior General. Taking the name Mother Maria of the Immaculate, she led by gentle wisdom and by being a model for prayer and service rooted in her abiding trust in Mary Immaculate.

In 1922, Fr. Nascimbeni died, and the task fell squarely upon Mother Maria to continue the growth and development of the congregation. This she did unitl the day of her death. Today the Little Sisters of the Holy Family serve in Italy, Switzerland, Albania, Africa, and South America.

Pope John Paul II beatified her on April 27, 2003, having already beatified Fr. Nascimbeni in 1988. He said at the ceremony:

> Blessed Maria Domenica Mantovani followed the same path. This praiseworthy daughter of the region of Verona, a disciple of Blessed Giuseppe Nascimbeni, was inspired by the Holy Family of Nazareth to make herself "all things to all people," ever attentive to the needs of the "poor people." She was extraordinarily faithful, in all circumstances and to her last breath, to the will of God, by whom she felt loved and called. What a fine example of holiness for every believer!

✠

Maria Stella Mardosewicz and Companions — see Martyrs of the Holy Family

✠

Maria Romero Meneses (January 13, 1902 – July 7, 1977)
Model Religious Missionary

Called a Mother of the Poor, Maria was was born in Granada, Nicaragua, one of eight children in her family. She was well educated and an artist, versatile on the piano and violin. The Salesian Sisters in the area provided Maria with an education, although her studies were interrupted by an attack of rheumatic fever, which left her heart badly damaged. The Blessed Virgin Mary cured her and inspired her future ministries.

On December 8, 1915, Maria joined the Daughters of Mary, a pious organization of Marian devotion; in 1920, she entered the Congregation of Daughters of Mary, Help of Christians. She was professed on January 6,

1929. As a model religious, Maria went to San Jose, Costa Rica, where she taught, then built schools for local young girls. She also established recreational centers, clinics, and entire villages of homes for local families who had no housing available. Her care and concern were unending, and she served the area's poor and needy until she died in León, Nicaragua. Her remains are now in the Salesian chapel of San Jose, Costa Rica.

Pope John Paul II beatified Maria Romero Meneses on April 14, 2002, announcing:

> With a passionate love for God and an unlimited confidence in the assistance of the Blessed Virgin Mary, Sr. Maria Romero was an exemplary religious, apostle and mother of the poor people, who were her real favourites.

✠

Maria Clementine Anuarite Nengapete
(December 29, 1939 – December 1, 1964)
Martyr of Zaire

Maria Clementine Anuarite Nengapete was slain because she protected her purity.

She was born in Matali, Wamba, in Upper Zaire. Her family was not Christian but, in time, she, her mother, and her sister were attracted to the faith. After instruction at their local mission, all three women were baptized in 1943.

Maria Clementine was devout from her earliest days as a convert, and she realized that she had received the grace of a religious vocation. With her mother's blessing, she entered the Holy Family Sisters at Bafwabaka at age fifteen. Completing her novitiate training and demonstrating spiritual maturity and generosity, she was professed in the religious life on August 5, 1959.

Maria Clementine continued to serve as a Holy Family Sister, even as tragic consequences of political unrest engulfed her native land. On December 1, 1964, she was confronted by military troops led by a Colonel Olombe at Isiro. The colonel was attracted to Maria Clementine and made advances, which she rebuffed in the name of Jesus. Angered, the colonel demanded that she surrender to his desires. When she refused, the colonel killed her. She was instantly recognized as a martyr of purity in Zaire.

Pope John Paul II beatified Maria Clementine Anuarite Nengapete on August 5, 1985, in Zaire, Africa, praising the virginal purity of this Blessed. Blessed Maria Clementine was lauded as a symbol of the strength and courage of the Church in Africa. Her maturity of purpose and her devotedness to her Divine Spouse were honored in the joyful ceremonies.

✢

Maria of Jesus Crucified Petkovic
(December 10, 1892 – July 9, 1956)
Foundress of the Congregation of the Daughters of Mercy

Maria Petkovic was born on the island of Korcula in Blato, Croatia. Her parents, Antun Petkovic-Kovac and Maria Marinovic, were blessed with eleven children and gave considerably to support the poor in the region. She was educated in schools run by the Servants of Charity, who had recently arrived in Croatia from Italy.

Drawn to the religious life, Maria confessed to the local bishop that she desired above all things to be a nun. He assumed her spiritual direction and encouraged her in her vocation. She made a private vow of chastity in 1906 and served as president of the Daughters of Mary from 1909 to 1919. As an outgrowth of this group, with the assistance of twenty young women, she started the Good Shepherd Association, which took up the task of visiting the sick and assisting children to prepare for their First Communion.

At the same time, the death of her father in 1911 made it necessary for Maria to assist her mother in raising the family, a task made all the more difficult by the start of World War I in 1914 and the devastation it brought to the country. She was nevertheless entrusted by the bishops with starting the Society of Catholic Mothers and, in 1917, became the chief figure among the area's Third Order Franciscans.

In March 1919, Maria was at last able to enter the convent of the Servants of Charity in Blato, but the departure of the sisters to Italy made it necessary for Maria and her friend, Maria Telenta, to keep up the needs of the house. She convinced the two Croatian sisters to remain in the house in Blato, and the bishop again provided his support and confidence that she would be able to accomplish the tasks set before her. In short order, Maria opened several needed facilities in Blato, including a place for the care of children and an orphanage.

The following year, in August 1920, Maria established the Congregation of the Daughters of Mercy in Prizba-Korcula. With the official founding of the congregation on October 4, 1920, Maria took the name Maria of the Crucified Jesus and was officially the foundress of the new community. She served five times as Superior General, from 1920 to 1952, and journeyed all over the world to open new houses dedicated providing nursing home care, parish and nursery schools, and assistance in parishes, seminaries, and hospitals.

She was beatified by Pope John Paul II on June 6, 2003, while on a visit to Dubrovnik. He said of her:

> "Good Teacher, what must I do to inherit eternal life?" (Mk 10:17). This is the question that Sr. Maria asked her Lord from the time of her youth in Blato on the island of Korcula, when she took active part in the life of her parish and devoted herself generously to others in the Association of the Good Shepherd, in the Association of Catholic Mothers, and in the people's Kitchen.
>
> The response echoed clearly in her heart: "Come and follow me!" Overwhelmed by the love of God, she chose to consecrate herself to him for ever and to fulfil her aspiration to total devotion to the spiritual and material well-being of those most in need. Later, she founded the Congregation of the Daughters of Mercy of the Third Order Regular of St. Francis, with the specific task of "spreading knowledge of God's love through the spiritual and corporal works of mercy." Difficulties were not lacking, but Sr. Maria persevered with indomitable courage, offering up her sufferings as so many acts of worship and supporting her Sisters by her words and her example.

✠

María Maravaillas de Jesús Pidal y Chico de Guzmán
(November 4, 1891 – December 11, 1974)
Carmelite Leader in the Spanish Civil War

María Maravaillas de Jesus Pidal y Chico de Gúzmán was born in Madrid, Spain, the daughter of Luis Pidal y Mon, the marquis of Pidal, and his wife, Cristina Chico de Guzmán y Munoz. Luis was the Spanish ambassador to the Vatican at the time.

María Maravaillas was extremely devout at an early age, making a vow of chastity at age five. She matured in the Faith and entered the Carmelite Monastery of El Escorial in 1920. Four years later, she and three other

Carmelites founded a daughter convent in Cerro de los Angeles, and there she made her solemn profession. In 1933, María Maravaillas founded another Carmel in Kottayam, India.

When the Spanish Civil War engulfed Spain in chaos and terror, María Maravaillas and her nuns found haven in an apartment in Madrid. The following year, 1937, she founded another Carmel in the Batuescas region of Salamanca. She also erected Carmelite houses in Mancera de Abajo, Duruelo, Cabreira, Arenas de San Pedro, San Calixto, Aravaca, Talavera de la Reina, La Aldehuela, and Montemor-Torremolinas. María Maravaillas was able to restore the damaged Carmel of the Escorial, establishing a community there when the Civil War ended. She combined all of these Carmelite foundations in an association of St. Teresa in 1972.

Throughout her life she demonstrated not only courage and practical wisdom, but also the joy of her religious life. She said, "What happiness to die a Carmelite"— as she did, in the Carmel of Aldehuela.

Pope John Paul II beatified María Maravaillas de Jesús Pidal y Chico de Gúzmán, announcing that she was "another shining example of holiness." The Holy Father went on to say:

> A well-known person in her time, she was able to make the most of this fact to attract many souls to God . . . She lived with heroic faith, formed in response to an austere vocation, by putting God at the center of her life.

✠

María Rafols (November 5, 1781 – August 30, 1853)
Heroine of Charity

Maria Rafols was born in Villafranca del Penedés, to a simple family of modest means. Brilliant and gifted, she was sent to a boarding school in Barcelona. There, she was noted for her life of solitude and prayer. When her education was completed, María joined a group of twelve women being trained by Fr. Juan Bonal for service in Our Lady of Grace Hospital in Saragossa. The ministry of the hospital was quite varied, as the staff cared for the sick, disabled, orphaned, and the mentally ill.

María demonstrated a profound spiritual maturity and was appointed Superior at the age of twenty-three. The hospital employees resented her youth at first, but she earned their respect. During the occupation of Spain (1808-1813) by the forces of Napoleon Bonaparte, emperor of France, María labored in bombed ruins and had to beg for food and medicine. She even went to a French general in the nearby enemy camp, seeking his aid.

In 1825, María and her community took public vows. During the era of the Carlist Wars (the political upheaval that troubled Spain for years after the ending of the Napoleonic Wars), she was unjustly accused and imprisoned. When she was released, she retired to one of the foundling homes that she had opened.

María died in Saragossa in 1853, and Pope John Paul II beatified her on October 16, 1994, declaring:

> In Blessed María Rafols we contemplate God's action, which made a "Heroine of Charity" of the humble young girl who left her home in Villafranca del Penedés (Barcelona) and, in the company of a priest and eleven other young women, began a journey of service to the sick, by following Christ and, like him, giving her "'life a ransom for the many" (Mk. 10:45).
>
> A contemplative in action: this is the style and message María Rafols leaves us. The silent hours of prayer in the chapel loft of Saragossa's Hospital of Grace, known as the *domus infirmorum urbis et orbis* [home for the sick of the city and the world], were continued in her generous service to all the defenseless collected there: the sick, the mentally ill, destitute women and children. Thus she showed that charity, true charity, has its origin in God, who is love (1 Jn 4:8). After spending the better part of her life in selfless, hidden service at the Foundling Home, where she poured out her love, self-denial, and tenderness, she embraced the Cross and made her total surrender to the Lord, leaving to the Church, and especially to her daughters, the great teaching that charity never dies nor passes, the great lesson of a charity without borders, lived in the dedication of each day. All consecrated persons can see in her an expression of the perfection of charity to which they are called and to a deep experience of which the celebration of the present Synod Assembly seeks to contribute.

☦

María Repetto (November 1, 1807 – January 5, 1890)
Patroness of the City of Genoa

María Repetto was born in Voltaggio, in the northern region of Italy, the oldest daughter of Giovanni Battista and his wife, Teresa Gozzola. The family life taught her a strong sense of duty, and she helped to form her eight brothers and sisters, fostering their religious vocations: four of her sisters entered convents, and a brother became a priest.

At age twenty-two, having served her family faithfully, María entered the Conservatory of Our Lady of Refuge in Genoa. There, she was content to serve as an infirmarian, gatekeeper, washerwoman, and general laborer of the community. She did not seek a loftier role, but her lowly status did not hide her holiness or her spiritual graces.

The people of Genoa recognized María's holiness very quickly, and the sick were brought to her for loving treatment. During the cholera epidemics of 1835 and 1854, María went to the aid of countess victims. She served these victims without fear and with extraordinary tenderness. The people of Genoa also recognized her spiritual insight and her mystical awareness. They visited the Conservatory of Our Lady of Refuge every day, seeking her counsel.

When María died, the entire city of Genoa went into profound mourning. Her remains were laid to rest in the chapel of the Conservatory.

Pope John Paul II beatified María Repetto on October 4, 1981, announcing:

> Right from her youth María Repetto learned and lived a great truth, which she has transmitted also to us: "Jesus must be contemplated, loved and served in the poor, at all moments of our life."

The Holy Father added:

> To serve Christ's poor was a program of her Institute, a program which she carried out in fifty years of religious life, serving Jesus above all, growing in the perfection of love.

⊹

María Encarnación Rosal Vásquez
(November 1, 1897 – January 5, 1890)
Reformer of the Bethlehemites

María Encarnación Rosal Vásquez was born in Quetzaltenango, Guatemala, and baptized Vicenta. Raised devoutly, Vincenta received the grace of a religious vocation while young. By age fifteen, she knew that she was called to be a nun and entered the Bethlehemites, a cloistered congregation founded in 1688 and a spiritual institution that was part of St. Pedro de Betancur's ministry.

In the Bethlehemite convent, however, María Encarnación found that laxities and distractions were tearing at the fabric of the cloister. She completed her novitiate training and took her vows, maturing in the spiritual life and attaining virtues. In 1855, she was elected prioress of the community and immediately set about revising the rules of the congregation. Opposed by those who preferred a less demanding way of life, María Encarnación founded a new Bethlehemite house in Quetzaltenango in 1861.

She had unique gifts of contemplation and a special devotion to the Sacred Heart of Jesus that she forged into her new community. She also practiced penance and reparation for the sins of the modern world. María Encarnación died in the odor of sanctity in Quetzaltenango.

Pope John Paul II beatified María Encarnación on May 4, 1997, declaring:

> Mother María Encarnación Rosal, the first woman from Guatemala to be beatified, was chosen to continue the charism of St. Pedro de San Jose Betancurt . . . Giving up many things did not matter to her, as long as the essential was saved; as she said, "May all be lost, except charity."

✠

María Francesca Rubatto (February 14, 1844 – August 6, 1904)
Missionary to the New World

María Francesca Rubatto was born in Carmagnola, Italy, and baptized Anna María. She lost her father when she was only four, and was raised by her mother. Anna made a vow of virginity and refused any thoughts of marriage at an early age, despite her lay status. When she was nineteen, her mother died, and Anna moved to Turin, Italy, where the noblewoman Marianna Scoffone welcomed her.

There, Anna María began to teach catechism to the children of the city and visit the sick and the poor. She continued this apostolate faithfully until 1882, when Marianna Scoffone died. At that point, Anna went to the Ligurian coastal region to rest and recuperate from her labors. In Loano, just after attending Mass at the local Capuchin Franciscan church, Anna María saw a young worker struck on the head by a stone from a convent under construction. She cleaned his wound and gave him two days' wages so that he could rest, then went on her way.

The story of the accident was repeated everywhere, and the group building the convent heard of her kindness. They asked her to enter their convent as spiritual guide, and a Capuchin Franciscan, Fr. Angelico Martini, convinced her to join the group a year later. Bishop Filipo Allegro named her Superior of the group that became the Institute of the Capuchin Sisters of Mother Rubatto, and is now called the Capuchin Sisters of the Third Order of Loano.

In 1892, María Francesca started missions in Montevideo, Uruguay, and in Argentina. She crossed the Atlantic Ocean seven times and founded another mission in Alto Alegre with Capuchin missionaries and converts. She returned to Montevideo in 1904, intending a brief stay; however she remained in Montevideo for a year and died there. She was buried in Montevideo.

Pope John Paul II beatified María Francesca Rubatto on October 10, 1993, declaring:

> [Maria] Francesca of Jesus . . . who made your life a constant service to the lowliest, witnessing to God's special love for the lowly and humble . . . faithfully following the footsteps of Francis, the lover of evangelical poverty, you learned not only to serve the poor, but to make yourself poor.

✛

María Gabriella Sagheddu (March 17, 1914 – April 23, 1939)
Promoter of Church Unity

She was born in Dorgali, Sardinia, the daughter of a devout shepherd family in a region that bred strong-willed, resolute people of the Faith. Willful and difficult as a child, María Gabriella lost her father at age three, a tragedy that had a tremendous impact on the financial and emotional stability of her family.

At age eighteen, María Gabriella experienced a profound and lasting spiritual conversion. She changed totally and began to explore the possibility of a religious vocation. At the age of twenty-one, she entered the Trappistine Monastery at Grottaferrata, now located in Viterbo, but once operating near Rome. There, she made her novitiate; there, she was professed in 1937.

Aware of the ongoing dissension in the Christian faith, María Gabriella offered her life for Church unity. In this heroic act, she displayed faith, courage, and hope. María Gabriella understood the perils of modern society and the need for Christians to unite with the Holy See to achieve a true defense of the Faith.

Soon after her sacrificial offer, María Gabriella was stricken physically and spiritually. She developed tuberculosis and was plagued with a profound spiritual dryness. She did not withdraw her pledge to suffer and to die for unity. All of this was endured in silence. The members of her own community remarked that María Gabriella served quietly and humbly, almost unnoticed in the daily monastic routines. Only her superiors knew of her offer and her sufferings. She died on the Sunday of the Good Shepherd, in which the Gospel proclaimed, "There will be one flock and one shepherd."

Pope John Paul II beatified María Gabriella Sagheddu on June 25, 1983, and representatives of the Anglicans, Lutherans, and Orthodox Church attended the ceremony. Pope John Paul II proclaimed her "voluntary spiritual martyrdom" at her beatification, which was held at St. Paul's Basilica Outside the Walls. The ceremony ended the Week of Prayers for Christian Unity. The Holy Father declared:

> Sr. María Gabriella had never studied the problem of separation or the history of ecumenism, and, in fact, knew very little about it. She was simply dominated by the desire that all men might return to God and that his Kingdom might come in every heart. She had already offered her existence for this by embracing the humble and silent life of a Trappist nun with its daily renouncements and its long hours of hard work and prayer. "'As for my part, I feel that I have already given all that was in my power to give," she had written very frankly to her spiritual father.
>
> Maybe it was exactly for this reason that God wanted to make her a visible sign of the total gift of self that is asked by every Christian. The explicit act of offering her life conformed her even more perfectly to Christ, the Lamb, who immolated himself so that all might be one.

He also declared:

> This strong, little Trappistine nun . . . has taught that to foster the spiritual life and to promote great ideals, one must be prepared to pay the price personally.

✠

María of Mount Carmel Sallés y Baranqueras
(April 9, 1848 – July 25, 1911)
"Solid and Sensible Piety"

María of Mount Carmel Sallés y Baranquers was born in Vich, Spain, the oldest child of José and Francisca Baranqueras Sallés, baptized Carmen Francisca Rosa. Carmen studied at the La Enseñanza school, operated by the Company of Mary, and received the grace of a religious vocation. After graduation, she started educating young women, using the Dominican spirit of combining the active life with contemplation.

In order to achieve the apostolate, she founded the Congregation of the Missionary Teaching Sisters of the Immaculate Conception. The members of this congregation were trained to witness to the presence of Mary Immaculate in the secular world. María of Mount Carmel founded thirteen schools and many convents. Her congregation went to Brazil in 1911, then to Asia and Africa. The Conceptionists, as María of Mount Carmel's Sisters are called, continue to manifest the love of God for humanity through Mary. María died in Madrid on July 25, 1911, speaking lovingly of "our Immaculate Mother."

Pope John Paul II beatified María of Mount Carmel Sallés y Baranqueras on March 15, 1998, declaring that she was "a valiant woman," one who based her life and work on a "Christocentric and Marían spirituality nourished by solid and sensible piety."

✠

María Josefa Sancho de Guerra
(September 7, 1842 – March 20, 1912)
Co-Foundress of the Servants of Jesus of Charity

María Josefa Sancho de Guerra guided her congregation to mission fields around the world.

She was born in Vitoria, Spain, to a poor family. In 1864, María Josefa entered the Servants of Mary, a new religious congregation that sent her into the poorest districts of Madrid. During the plague of 1865, she worked without rest, and she continued her labors until 1871.

In 1871, she and two companions left the Servants of Mary to found a new congregation in Bilbao — the Servants of Jesus of Charity. As the congregation faced terrible financial problems in the beginning, María Josefa cared for the sick while other members worked diligently to raise funds. In time, the Servants of Jesus of Charity spread to other European countries, Latin America, and Asia. María Josefa guided the congregation, despite her own intense sufferings. She died in Bilbao.

Pope John Paul II beatified María Josefa Sancho de Guerra on September 27, 1992, declaring:

> Blessed María Josefa of the Heart of Jesus Sancho de Guerra incarnated the words of Christ . . . she founded the Servants of Jesus of Charity, entrusting to them the mission of finding the face of Christ in so many

brothers and sisters, alone and sick, and soothing them with oil of fraternal love.

✠

Maria Crucifixa Satellico (January 9, 1706 – November 8, 1745)
"Seraphic Splendor"

Maria Crucifixa Satellico was born Elisabeth Maria Satellico in Venice, Italy, the daughter of Pietro and Lucia Mander Satellico. The family lived with a maternal uncle, a priest, who aided in Elisabeth's spiritual formation. The child showed an innate ability for prayer, music, and singing, and grew up desiring a religious vocation as a Poor Clare cloistered nun.

Accepted as a student of the Poor Clare Monastery of Ostra Vitere, Elisabeth played the organ and directed the monastic music. In 1725, she received the Poor Clare habit and her religious name, and she was professed on May 19, 1726. The goal of perfection was the source of her religious life, and Maria Crucifixa was devoted to the Most Holy Trinity and the Holy Eucharist.

Elected abbess, she led by example and also became a patroness of the local poor. She died at age thirty-nine and was buried at the Church of St. Lucy in Ostra Vetere, revered as a woman of seraphic splendor.

Pope John Paul II beatified Maria Crucifixa Satellico on October 10, 1993, declaring:

> The Church . . . salutes you . . . faithful daughter of Francis! You have configured your life to him who for love of humanity let himself be nailed to the Cross . . . and now you contemplate the glory of your Lord.

✠

Maria Theresa Scherer (October 31, 1825 – June 16, 1888)
"Mother of the Poor"

The founder of a religious congregation, Maria Theresa Scherer was born Anna Maria Catherine Scherer in Meggen, Switzerland. When her father died in 1831, two of her uncles raised her as their ward. She was quick, bright, and exuberant, and displayed her concern for the poor at an early age with a profound spiritual maturity. At age sixteen, Maria Theresa, seeing the need for dedicated laborers in the medical institutions of her era, started doing hospital work. She learned quickly, and she attracted companions who were eager to form a religious group dedicated to such a ministry.

With four such companions, Maria Theresa founded the Sisters of Mercy of the Holy Cross on October 27, 1845, assisted by Fr. Theodosius Florentini of Altdorf. She labored to form the congregation in Altdorf for about a year. The congregation was designed to incorporate two separate ministries, nursing and teaching.

Elected Superior, Maria Theresa centered her activities in Ingenbohl, opening a motherhouse there and attracting new religious aspirants. She had a simple but dynamic motto: "No work of Christian love of neighbor may be considered beyond the scope of this institute." With this motto, Maria Theresa was able to adapt her sisters to the compelling needs of the time and to make innovative apostolates to aid all who needed their care.

She quickly became known as the "Mother of the Poor," opening hospitals and schools for the handicapped and embracing the social apostolate for workers in the region. Her labors required a considerable amount of travel, which she endured despite severe physical sufferings. While on a visitation to her Rome house, Maria Theresa became very ill. She was taken to Ingenbohl, where she died. At the time of her death, her congregation had almost 1,700 sisters. A mission was opened in the United States in 1912.

Pope John Paul II beatified Maria Theresa Scherer on October 29, 1995, announcing:

> Maria Theresa Scherer fought the good fight. Through her life and work she reminds us of the essential place of the mystery of the Cross, by which God proclaims his love and grants salvation to the world . . . Maria Theresa remains an example for us. Her inner strength was a result of her spiritual life: she spent many hours before the Blessed Sacrament, where the Lord communicates his love to all who live in close relationships with him.

✛

Maria of the Sacred Heart Schinina
(April 10, 1844 – June 11, 1910)
Protector of the Persecuted

Maria Schinina was born in Ragusa, Sicily, a member of an aristocratic family. Raised to the social status of her lineage, she had the rights and privileges of the nobility from birth. She also developed spiritual graces, being raised devoutly by her family.

At age sixteen, Maria saw Italy and her own region convulsed by the *Risorgimento* and the campaign for unification. Unlike many of her noble class, she was not able to turn away from the suffering caused by the war and by the resulting famine. She set about recruiting companions to aid prisoners of war and the tormented peasantry of her region.

She shocked the nobles of Sicily with her religious labors, as such a ministry spanned the stiff divisions between the social classes. However, the Archbishop of Syracuse came to her defense, then aided her when she and five companions started the Sisters of the Sacred Heart of Jesus. They opened their doors to peasants and nobles, even to prisoners of war, who were despised by others.

Maria of the Sacred Heart (as she was now known) cared for all in need, even providing a safe haven for Carmelites forced to flee their home convent because of political unrest. During a devastating earthquake, Maria opened her motherhouse to the refugees from Messina and Reggio di Calabria. All received food, medicine, and devoted care. There also, secular priests and religious came to learn the newest methods of conducting charitable labors, and she financed seminaries and study programs.

Maria of the Sacred Heart died in Ragusa, mourned by the nobles and the common people of the region as a true heroine of Christian love.

Pope John Paul II beatified Maria of the Sacred Heart Schinina on November 14, 1990, saying:

> The spiritual journey of Blessed Maria Schinina of the Sacred Heart began with a deep penetration by God's love, which is expressed in the symbol of the Heart of Jesus; in order to respond to this love in her spirituality, she emphasized contemplation, adoration, and reparation.

The Holy Father added, "Her charism remains ever alive and timely."

✠

Maria of Jesus Siedliska
(November 12, 1842 – November 21, 1902)
Polish Religious Foundress

Maria of Jesus Siedliska was born in Rozkowa Wola, Poland, and baptized Francisca. The daughter of Adolph and Cecilia Morawska Siedliska, Francisca was quite frail as an infant, needing special care. Her mother also suffered a serious illness, and for this reason, a tutor educated the young Francisca. During her mother's illness, she began an intense devotion to Our Lady of Czestochowa, a devotion that would become a hallmark of her holiness.

After her confirmation in 1855, her growing dedication to the religious life alarmed her parents, who took her on a long journey to France, Germany, and Switzerland to discourage her vocation. But their plans failed, and her father finally agreed to her aspiration while on this sightseeing trip. She returned home and was aided by a Capuchin priest, Fr. Leander Lendzian, in starting her congregation in Rome in 1875.

Francisca eventually became Mother Maria of Jesus, the Good Shepherd. Concerned about neglected and abandoned children, Maria of Jesus began a series of charitable works and founded the Sisters of the Holy Family of Nazareth. Pope Pius IX (r. 1846-1878) approved the congregation on October 1, 1873. The beautiful personality traits that Maria of Jesus possessed won many to her apostolate.

She located her motherhouse in Rome, but returned to Poland in 1881 to begin a foundation there. By 1884, Maria of Jesus was operating four convents in Poland, where her spirit took root; she opened a mission in the United States, and in 1895, began her apostolate in London, which was also well received.

Maria of Jesus of the Good Shepherd died in Rome in 1902. Pope John Paul II beatified Maria of Jesus Siedliska on April 23, 1989, declaring:

> Throughout her whole life she was able in a mature manner to combine prayer with the active apostolate, creating initiative with a concrete obedience to the Will of God in the Church ... The source of inspiration and reference point for her and her spiritual daughters was the model of the hidden life of the Holy Family of Nazareth.

⛧

Maria Dolores Rodríguez Sopeña
(December 30, 1848 – January 10, 1918)
Devoted to the Care of the Forgotten and Needy

Maria Dolores was born in Velez Rubio, Almería, Spain; she was the fourth of seven children born to Tomas Rodríguez Sopeña and Nicolasa Ortega Salomon. Maria grew up in the Andalusia region of Spain, and her father, who became a judge, made sure that his children received every social opportunity. Maria, however, was uninterested in high society. Secretly, she cared for victims of typhoid and leprosy, but she was afraid to tell her parents of her charitable work, lest they forbid her from continuing.

In 1869, Maria moved to Madrid, while her father was sent to Puerto Rico. Once established in Madrid, she dedicated herself to teaching women prisoners the catechism and running Sunday schools. Three years later, the entire family went to Puerto Rico; there, she came under the spiritual direction of the Jesuits. Answering the need to educate the poor children in Puerto Rico, she established the Association of the Sodality of the Virgin Mary.

In 1873, the family moved to Cuba, and Maria expressed a hope of being admitted to the Sisters of Charity; this proved impossible because of her poor eyesight — the result of an eye operation when she was a child — so instead she established Centers of Instruction, schools where poor children could receive instruction in the Faith as well as often badly needed medical care.

With the death of her mother, the family departed Cuba and went back to Madrid in 1877. There, she cared for her family and continued her remarkable spiritual development as well as her charitable efforts. After her father's death in 1883, she was able at last to enter a convent. Her choice, at the encouragement of a Jesuit spiritual advisor, was the Salesians, but she soon realized that the contemplative life was not for her.

Returning to her active apostolate in 1885, she launched social centers for the poor and began a process of visits to the most destitute neighborhoods. In 1892, she founded the Association of the Apostolic Laymen (known today as the Sopeña Lay Movement). Her movement soon spread beyond Madrid to all of Spain. In 1901, she began the Ladies Catechetical Institute and soon after started the Civil Association, today known as OSCUS, or Social & Cultural Work Sopeña. The Association was officially recognized by the Spanish government in 1902 and received papal approval directly from Pope St. Pius X in 1907. Today, her foundations include the Sopeña Catechetical Institute, Sopeña Lay Movement, and Sopeña Social and Cultural Work. Branches are found in Spain, Italy, Argentina, Colombia, Cuba, Chile, Ecuador, Mexico and the Dominican Republic.

Renowned for her holiness even before her death, Maria was beatified by Pope John Paul II on March 23, 2003. The pope said at the time:

> Dolores Rodríguez Sopeña felt this necessity and wished to respond to the challenge of making the redemption of Christ present in the world of work. For this reason, her goal was a "to make all persons one sole family in Christ Jesus" (*Constitutions of 1907*). This spirit is crystallized in the three foundations of the new Blessed: the Sopeña Lay Movement, the Institute of Women Catechists — today called Sopeña Catechists — and the Sopeña Social and Cultural Work. By means of these works, in Spain and in South America, a spirituality continues that fosters the building of a more just world proclaiming the saving message of Jesus Christ.

✠

Maria Helen Stollenwerk
(November 28, 1852 – February 3, 1900)
Spiritual Daughter of St. Arnold Janssen

The founder of the Holy Spirit Missionary Sisters, Maria Helen Stollenwerk was born in Germany and raised devoutly in an era of political unrest. Her childhood experiences made her particularly aware of the need for religious ministries in the world. Active in the Holy Child Association as a young woman, Maria Helen received the grace of a religious vocation in 1882.

She journeyed to Steyl, in the Netherlands, where Arnold Janssen aided her in founding her religious congregation, the Holy Spirit Missionary Sisters, begun on December 8, 1889. She was made Superior and set about recruiting new members and founding new houses. Her motto was "To God, the honor; to my neighbor, the benefit, and to myself, the burden."

In 1896, the congregation was divided into two separate entities: the original missionary institute and a cloister. Maria Helen was directed to enter the cloister, thus having to relinquish her vision for the community and giving control of the congregation to others. Her suffering was intense, but she remained obedient and resigned as Superior. Entering the cloister, she was obliged to undergo another novitiate and take a new religious name, "Maria Virgo." Maria Helen fulfilled all of her new obligations without complaint. One year later she became ill, and she died as a cloistered nun in Steyl. Hidden, possessing no honor or title, Maria Helen died in saintly obedience.

Pope John Paul II beatified Maria Helen Stollenwerk on May 7, 1995, announcing:

If we think of Mother Maria Stollenwerk, we find ourselves before a great feminine personality and missionary pioneer, although she was not able to fulfill her greatest desire: to be send on mission herself. In brief, we can state that her whole life was a sign of her being touched by God.

From her childhood the new Blessed's life of prayer was inspired by the Pontifical Society of the Holy Childhood. She was particularly affected by the loss of those children who were deprived of the right to life. Through her meeting with Blessed Arnold Janssen, she believed she would be able to fulfill her dream of becoming a missionary sister. With him she eventually founded the Congregation of the Missionary Servants of the Holy Spirit. The congregation's name shows how much Mother Maria Stollenwerk had at heart the adoration of the Holy Spirit. The Holy Spirit inspired her to proclaim the Gospel, and, as St. Paul said, to become all things to all men (cf. 1 Cor. 9:16-22). The new Blessed saw the Holy Spirit as the driving force of missionary activity.

Thanks to this basic attitude of trust in the power of God's Spirit and to the Faith flowing from her Eucharistic adoration and her constant closeness to the Lord by whom she felt sent, Mother Maria Stollenwerk could state, "Only God can fill our hearts. He is too great and too vast to be understood by creatures."

✠

Maria Catherine of St. Rose Troiani
(January 19, 1813 – May 6, 1887)
Foundress and Educator

Maria Catherine of St. Rose Troiani was born in Giuliano, near Rome, Italy, and baptized Constanza. The Franciscan Sisters of Terentino taught Costanza; while she was under their tutelage, she received the grace of a religious vocation. She had a missionary spirit as well, and a remarkable love of Egypt and Palestine. These eventually combined in Maria Catherine to lead her far from her native land to serve the young women of the Middle East.

She served as a teaching sister in the Franciscans for thirty years, all the time desiring to aid the peoples of Egypt and Palestine; so, once she was given permission to establish a school in Cairo, Egypt, she gathered companions and began her ministry immediately. Welcomed in Cairo, Maria Catherine saw her apostolate grow and realized that she had to form a new congregation to meet the need of her newly chosen mission. She received approval for such a congregation, calling the new group the Franciscan Missionary Sisters of Egypt.

These Franciscans educated young Egyptian and Palestinian women and opened charitable institutions to aid the poor. María Catherine died in the motherhouse in Cairo, mourned by Christians and Muslims, who respected her vision and her unsparing generosity in service.

Pope John Paul II beatified María Catherine of St. Rose Troiani on April 14, 1985, praising her vision and courage in using the Faith to span time and cultural differences for the benefit of the young and the needy.

✠

María Guadalupe García Zavala
(April 27, 1878 – June 24, 1963)
Being "Poor With the Poor"

María Guadalupe García Zavala was born in Zapopan, Jalisco, Mexico, to Fortino García and Refugio Zavala de García; her father operated a shop specializing in religious goods. She grew up in the Faith and was especially fond of making visits to the Basilica of Our Lady of Zapopan, located next to her father's store.

Maria was initially betrothed to a young man, Gustavo Arreola, but at the age of twenty-three, she suddenly broke off the planned marriage to answer the call to enter the religious life. She found much support in this decision from her spiritual director, Fr. Cipriano Iñiguez. He also confided to her that he hoped one day to establish a religious congregation to assist those who were hospitalized. He went on to ask María to become his co-founder of this new community. María readily and happily agreed, and the new congregation was given its official start in October 1901 under the name of the Handmaids of St. Margaret Mary (Alacoque) and the Poor.

In starting the new community, María filled a variety of tasks and jobs, including work as a nurse. She was soon appointed Superior General, responsible for maintaining the spiritual and material well-being of the swiftly developing congregation. She served especially as a model for the other sisters; she taught them the importance of laboring for the poor with joy and a spirit of interior poverty, and she called upon all of the members to be "poor with the poor." To raise funds for the hospital, she asked permission to beg and ask for financial support, and she proved strikingly successful in the effort. In time, the sisters went on to serve in parishes and as catechists.

During the time of Mexico's political upheaval in the early twentieth century, the Church faced severe persecution, and clergy were regularly arrested and even executed. To help the cause of protecting priests, Mother María willingly risked personal harm and opened the doors of the hospital to the Archbishop of Guadalajara and his clergy, providing them secret sanctuary during the worst days of the oppression.

Mother María's final days were marked by severe suffering, and she died prayerfully at the age of eighty-five. Her congregation is found today in five countries: Mexico, Peru, Iceland, Greece, and Italy. Pope John Paul II beatified her on April 25, 2004. He spoke of her by saying:

With deep faith, unlimited hope and great love for Christ, Mother "Lupita" sought her own sanctification beginning with love for the Heart of Christ and fidelity to the Church. In this way she lived the motto which she left to her daughters: "Charity to the point of sacrifice and perseverance until death."

✠

Mariam Thresia Chiramel Mankidiyan
(April 26, 1876 – June 8, 1926)
Indian Mystic and Foundress

Mariam Thresia Chiramel Mankidiyan was born in Puthenchira, Kerala, India, a daughter of a wealthy family suddenly impoverished by economic troubles. As a result, Mariam's father and brother drank heavily. Her mother, Thanda, was a saintly woman who kept the family together, but she died when Mariam was only twelve. At that point, Mariam's mystical side began to develop freely.

She started to care for the sick of the region, even lepers, and experienced visions of the Holy Family, as well as ecstasies and levitation. Mariam also received the stigmata. She did not shrink from the contemplative vocation that opened before her; in 1903, she asked for permission from the local bishop to build a haven of prayer and solitude.

The bishop did not give his permission for ten years. But finally, on May 14, 1914, the Congregation of the Holy Family was canonically erected. Mariam built three convents, two schools, two hospitals, a study house, and an orphanage as part of her ministry. Currently, members of the congregation serve in India, Italy, Germany, and Ghana.

Mariam continued her labors until she injured her leg and died of complications brought about by diabetes.

Pope John Paul II beatified Mariam Thresia Chiramel Mankidiyan on April 9, 2000, announcing:

"Unless a wheat grain falls on the ground and dies, it remains only a single grain; but if it dies it yields a rich harvest" (Jn 12: 24). From childhood, Mariam Thresia Mankidiyan knew instinctively that God's love for her demanded a deep personal purification. Committing herself to a life of prayer and penance, Sr. Mariam Thresia's willingness to embrace the Cross of Christ enabled her to remain steadfast in the face of frequent misunderstandings and severe spiritual trials. The patient discernment of her vocation eventually led to the foundation of the Congregation of the Holy Family, which continues to draw inspiration from her contemplative spirit and love of the poor. Convinced that "God will give eternal life to those who convert sinners and bring them to the right path" (Letter 4 to her Spiritual Father), Sr. Mariam devoted herself to this task by her visits and advice, as well as by her prayers and penitential practice. Through Blessed Mariam Thresia's intercession, may all consecrated men and women be strengthened in their vocation to pray for sinners and draw others to Christ by their words and example.

✠

Mariano de Jesus Euse Hoyos
(October 14, 1845 – July 13, 1926)
"Padre Marianito"

An evangelist of Colombia, Mariano de Jesus Euse Hoyos was born in Yaru-mal, Colombia, the son of Pedro Euse and Rosalia de Hoyos, the eldest of seven children in this family of farmers. At the age of sixteen, he discerned the grace of a priestly vocation and was sent to his uncle, Fr. Firmino Hoyos, for further training. In 1869, he entered the seminary at Medellin and was ordained to the priesthood on July 14, 1872.

As a curate, Mariano was sent to San Pedro, then to Yarumal in 1876. Two years later he was assigned to Antioquia, where he was called Padre Mari-anito and beloved. He addressed the poor as "Christ's nobles" and served them while he aided the local aged priest. When he became the pastor of the parish, Mariano built a new church, bell towers, chapels, and a cemetery. He taught catechism classes day and night and served the local community for nearly a half century. In July 1926, Mariano became bedridden by enteritis. He died in Antioquia and was buried in Our Lady of Mount Carmel chapel.

Pope John Paul II beatified Mariano de Jesus Euse Hoyos on April 9, 2000, declaring:

> From his intimate experience of meeting the Lord, Fr. Marianito, as he is familiarly known in his homeland, dedicated himself tirelessly to the evangelization of children and adults, especially farm workers. He spared no sacrifice or hardship, giving himself for almost fifty years … for the glory of God and the good of the souls entrusted to his care.

✠

Mariano da Roccacasale
(January 14, 1778 – May 31, 1866)
Blessed Hermit

Mariano da Roccacasale was born in Roccacasale, Italy, and baptized Domenico. One of six children in a family of farmers and herders, he stayed with the flocks in the mountains, accustomed to the solitary existence of such guardians of animals. He entered the Franciscans at St. Nicholas Friary at Arischia, in Abruzzi Province, when he was twenty-four. Professed in the Order, he remained at Arischia for twelve years, serving as a carpenter, cook, gardener, and porter, or gatekeeper.

When Mariano was thirty-seven, he was assigned to the Franciscan hermitage at Bellegram, where he would spend four decades as the porter. Through his service, he became famous for his loving smile, which was always accompanied by the Franciscan greeting of *Pax et bonum*. He influenced the vocation of Diego Oddi (beatified on the same day); he also spent hours in prayer before the Holy Eucharist and lived as a hermit when not on duty. He died in Bellegra, mourned by his fellow Franciscans and by the people of the area.

Pope John Paul II beatified Mariano da Roccacasale on October 3, 1999, announcing:

> As for the life and spirituality of Blessed Mariano of Roccacasale, a Franciscan religious, it could be said that they are symbolically summed up in the Apostle Paul's wish to the Christian community of Philippi: "The God of peace will be with you!" (4: 9). His poor and humble life, led in the footsteps of Francis and Clare of Assisi, were constantly directed to his neighbor, in the desire to hear and share the sufferings of each individual, in order to present them later to the Lord during the long hours he spent in adoration of the Eucharist. Blessed Mariano brought peace, which is God's gift, wherever he went. May his example and intercession help us to rediscover the essential value of God's love and the duty to bear witness to it in solidarity towards the poor. In particular, he serves as an example to us of showing hospitality, which is so important in the present historical and social context and is particularly significant in view of the Great Jubilee of the Year 2000.

✠

Marie-Anne Blondin (April 18, 1809 – January 2, 1890)
Foundress of the Congregation of the Sisters of St. Anne

Marie-Anne Blondin was humiliated by the members of her congregation, yet maintained her faith.

She was born in Terrebonne, Quebec, Canada, to a poor family. At age twenty-two, she became a domestic in the convent of the Sisters of the Congregation of Notre Dame, where she learned to read and write and demonstrated personal holiness. Having achieved literacy, Marie-Anne was allowed to enter that congregation's novitiate but became too ill to continue her studies.

She left the convent and, in 1833, was teaching in a school at Vaudreuil, where she studied the current educational practices and decided that co-educational schools would be advantageous. To further these ends, Marie-Anne founded the Congregation of the Sisters of St. Anne at Vaudreuil on September 8, 1850. The motherhouse was then moved to St. Jacques de l'Achigen. But the chaplain of the congregation, Fr. Louis Marechal, disrupted Marie-Anne's work and promoted her removal as Superior — a decision that eventually came to pass.

Forced to resign, she was kept in seclusion in the motherhouse as a servant in the laundry room; nevertheless, she maintained spiritual tranquility and accepted the abuse of others with calm and charity. She knew her end was near and that she was "happy to go to the good God." Her death, in the motherhouse, ended the terrible trials inflicted upon her at last.

Pope John Paul II beatified Marie-Anne Blondin on April 29, 2001, stating:

> Trials would never lessen her great love for Christ and for the Church, nor her concern to form true teachers of youth. The model of a humble and hidden life, Marie Anne Blondin drew her inner strength from contemplation of the Cross, showing us that a life of closeness to Christ is the surest way to bear fruit mysteriously and to accomplish the mission willed by God . . . Marie Anne Blondin, foundress of the Sisters of St. Anne, is a model of a life given to love and inspired by Christ's death and resurrection . . . Trials would never lessen her great love for Christ and the Church.

✛

Marie of Jesus Deluil-Martiny
(May 28, 1841 – February 27, 1884)
Forgiving to Her Killer

Marie of Jesus Deluil-Martiny was born in Marseilles, France, and educated at the Visitation Convent in Lyons. She became a member of the Guard of Honor of the Sacred Heart of Jesus in the convent. This organization was designed to give praise and acts of reparation to the Sacred Heart, and the devotion inspired Marie of Jesus. She visited John Vianney at Ars to discuss her religious vocation and the tragedies that had befallen her in losing her sisters and a brother.

With the aid of Fr. Colage, S.J., Marie of Jesus planned her new congregation, the Daughters of the Sacred Heart, designed to give praise to the Sacred Heart of Jesus, offering the community to the patronage of the Blessed Virgin Mary. In 1873, Cardinal Deschamps desired a center of reparation established in Belgium and was interested in her work. On June 20 of that year, Marie of Jesus and her companions received their habits in Antwerp. They were given final approbation for the rule on August 2, 1878.

Marie of Jesus erected her first house at Berschem, near Antwerp, Belgium, and erected a shrine to the Sacred Heart there; the congregation observed Perpetual Adoration as part of their ministry.

Unfortunately, Marie's work and life were cut short when a crazed gardener, Louis Chave — an agnostic — killed her in a fit of rage at the La Servianne Convent, Marseilles. Her last words were: "I forgive him . . . for the Work."

Prior to her death, Marie had located the motherhouse in Rome, and this finally received Vatican approbation on February 2, 1902, eighteen years after her death.

The remains of Marie of Jesus were buried in a local cemetery but moved in 1906 to the Basilica of the Sacred Heart in Berschem (Antwerp), and her Cause was opened in 1921.

Pope John Paul II beatified Marie of Jesus Deluil-Martiny on October 22, 1989, declaring:

> Marie of Jesus contemplated the Mother of the Savior at the foot of the Cross and present in the heart of the Church at its birth. The Virgin Mary was her true model. With Mary, the foundress of the Daughters of the Heart of Jesus prays and keeps watch so that God's children do not cease proclaiming to the wonders of his love . . . At a very young age, Marie was

able to share with her neighbors her ardent desire to live in the Sacrifice of the Mass. When she founded the Daughters of the Heart of Jesus, she put Eucharistic adoration at the center of their religious life. Deeply understanding Christ's sacrifice, she wanted to unite themselves continually to the offering of the Blood of Christ to the Blessed Trinity.

✠

Marie Rose Durocher (October 6, 1811 – October 6, 1849)
Canadian Pioneer in Education

Marie Rose Durocher was born in Sainte-Antoine-sur-Richelieu, Canada, the daughter of Oliver Amable Durocher and his wife, baptized Eulalie or Melanie. She was educated by the Notre Dame Sisters in St. Denis and in Montreal, Canada. At age eight, she lost her mother and had to assume maternal responsibilities that matured her rapidly. She was never robust or strong, and this physical weakness kept her from being admitted to the religious congregations in Quebec. To aid in her recovery, she went to Belseil, where her brother, Eusebius, was a parish priest, and served as her brother's housekeeper for thirteen years.

During this time, she took care of sick priests and seminarians, establishing a sodality and operating the charitable programs of the parish. A devout Marianist, she encouraged others to dedicate themselves to the Blessed Virgin. As her work increased, Eulalie was aided by the Oblates of Mary Immaculate. Bishop Ignace Bourget also heard of her and asked her to form a new teaching congregation.

On December 8, 1844, Eulalie took the religious name Marie Rose and she, Mother M. Agnes, and Mother M. Madeleine took their vows as the Sisters of the Holy Names of Jesus and Mary in Longueuil. Marie Rose attracted many new members. Her contemporaries described her as lovable, light-hearted, and kindly. She would live only six more years as a consecrated religious, founding convents and establishing schools, as part of the Catholic renaissance of Canada at that time, but her congregation would eventually carry her spirit and vision to the United States, Brazil, Peru, Haiti, and Lesotho. When Marie Rose died, she was buried at the congregation's motherhouse in Outremont, Quebec, Canada.

Pope John Paul II beatified Marie Rose Durocher in Quebec on May 23, 1982, stating:

Marie Rose Durocher acted with simplicity, prudence, humility, and serenity. She refused to be halted by her personal problems of health or the initial difficulties of her newborn work. Her secret lay in prayer and self-forgetfulness, which, according to her bishop, reached the point of real sanctity.

✠

Marie of the Incarnation Guyart
(October 28, 1599 – April 30, 1672)
Patroness of the Algonquin and Iroquois Nations

The founder of the Ursulines in Canada, Marie of the Incarnation Guyart was born in Tours, France. Married and widowed, she joined the Ursuline convent in Tours, then sailed for Canada with Madame de la Peltrie, a rich widow of Alençon. They arrived in Quebec on August 1, 1639, to found the oldest institution of learning for women in North America. Marie of the Incarnation's son, Dom Claude Martin, became a Benedictine priest and her biographer.

Called the "Theresa of her time and of the New World," Marie of the Incarnation spent three years in the Lower Town, taking over a convent in 1642 that was given to the Ursulines by the company of New France. Their first pupils were Native Americans, and Marie of the Incarnation mastered Algonquin and Iroquois in order to provide her students with a catechism and a sacred history. (Eventually, she would compose dictionaries in both languages.) When the convent was destroyed by fire in 1650, Marie saw a new one built upon the ashes of the old. When her friend, Madame de la Peltrie, died in 1671, Marie continued her labors and her particular devotion to the Sacred Heart of Jesus alone. Bishop Francis de Montmorency-Laval approved the rule of her congregation in 1681.

A devout, brilliant woman who guided the Ursulines through perilous times by combining a contemplative spirituality with acute administrative skills, Marie of the Incarnation was greatly mourned when she died in Quebec. Her correspondence, some 12,000 letters, provides a valuable look at life in Quebec in the seventeenth century.

Pope John Paul II beatified Marie of the Incarnation Guyart on June 22, 1980, declaring that she had come to the New World from France but had completed her life in Quebec, attaining holiness and a record of service that elevated her to the honor roll of Canada's founding settlers. The Holy Father also praised Marie of the Incarnation's contemplative gifts, treasures that she put at the service of her fellow Canadians.

✠

Marie Thérèse Haze
(February 27, 1782 – January 7, 1879)
Foundress of the Daughters of the Cross

Marie Thérese Haze was born in Liège, Belgium, where her father was secretary to the local bishop. As a result of her father's position, the French Revolution and its terrors threatened the family. Her father had to flee Liège — in fact, suffering a heart attack in the process, and dying separated from his family. Marie Thérèse's mother raised her children alone, aided by her daughter's dedication and skills. Marie Thérèse even aided in financing her brother's university education, although he did not live to pursue a career, and their mother died young as well.

Marie Thérèse was a master of the embroidery art. Through this creative skill, she had supported her family and provided her own income. While teaching young women that art of embroidery, she also instructed them in the catechism, and her classes became popular. Soon she was joined by other women, and an apostolate began.

In 1833, Marie Thérèse founded the Daughters of the Cross, becoming Mother Marie Thérèse of the Sacred Heart of Jesus, and dedicating her congregation to the service of the poor. The community spread throughout Europe, Asia, Africa, and America.

Marie Thérèse died, after long and faithful service, at the age of ninety-four. Pope John Paul II beatified her on April 21, 1991, declaring:

In the humility of the Incarnation, in the generosity of the love which makes all of us "children of God" (1 Jn 3:2), the Daughters of the Cross find an example for placing themselves in the service in the poorest of their neighbors. Blessed Marie Thérèse invites them to put into action the Gospel call to serve Christ in the person of the frailest and most suffering members of his Body. This basic inspiration follows that of Peter who proclaims, after the cure of the cripple, that healing comes from the Lord, who was crucified and is risen.

✛

Marie of the Cross (Jeanne) Jugan
(October 25, 1792 – August 29, 1879)
Co-Foundress of the Little Sisters of the Poor

Marie of the Cross Jugan bore a profound cross during the last years of her life.

She was born in Cancale, Brittany, France, and was baptized Jeanne. The sixth child of Joseph and Marie Jugan, she was little more than three when her father died at sea. Economic problems plagued the family, and the political unrest of the era added to their difficulties.

At age sixteen, Jeanne went to the estate of the Viscountess de la Choue to seek employment. This noble person recognized the spiritual graces of the young girl and befriended her; as Jeanne served as a maid on the estate, the viscountess taught her genteel manners and fostered her virtues, especially that of charitable service. In time, the viscountess said goodbye to Jeanne and moved to Saint-Servan. Jeanne, then twenty-five, worked in a hospital and became a member of the Third Order of the Heart of the Admirable Mother, taking her religious name.

In 1837, she and two companions, Françoise Albert and Virginie Tredaniel, founded the Little Sisters of the Poor. They were dedicated to the care of the aged, abandoned, and needy. Her work was so outstanding and well received that she was eventually awarded medals from both the French Academy and the Freemasons, and she opened a second and a third foundation. By 1851, Marie of the Cross had five houses and more than 300 sisters.

Toward the end of her life, a priest named Le Pailleur gained control of the congregation. He abused Marie of the Cross severely, dismissing her as Superior and keeping her hidden from the people of the region. She did not complain about this outrageous behavior, viewing all things as providing grace. She died in obscurity on August 29, 1879, but left behind a thriving congregation of some 2,400 sisters.

Pope John Paul II beatified Marie of the Cross Jugan on October 3, 1982, stating that this woman of the people had dedicated herself entirely and had endured great suffering with dignity and trust in God. Standing as a beatified of the faithful, Marie's vision of service continues in the modern world.

✠

Marie Catherine Simon de Longpré
(May 13, 1632 – May 8, 1668)

Revered in Canada as Marie Catherine of St. Augustine

Marie Catherine Simon de Longpré was called to Canada because of her nursing skills and her spiritual wisdom.

She was born in Saint-Sauveur le Vicomte, France. Dedicated at an early age to the sick and the poor, she entered the Hospitallers of Mercy of St. Augustine, accepting the apostolate of caring for the sick and the needy. As a member of this religious congregation, in fact, she demonstrated heroic devotion, medical skill, and spiritual wisdom when called upon as a counselor in hospital and community matters. Many patients and medical officials came to rely on her practical knowledge and her vast font of spiritual dedication. She had many graces and a beautiful spirit that attracted people of all walks of life.

As word of her medical abilities and holiness spread, Marie Catherine was asked to sail from France to Quebec, where she served as a model for the evolving medical facilities and religious institutions, again impressing many with her wisdom and skill. Her nursing experiences broadened the horizons of care in Quebec, bringing comfort to thousands.

Marie Catherine inspired many forms of praise, including poetic tributes, but she remained obedient to her religious rule and to her vocation. She died in Quebec, mourned by the entire region.

Pope John Paul II beatified Marie Catherine Simon de Longpré on April 23, 1989, announcing:

> In the secret of her soul she received the gift of being ceaselessly present to God, to Christ the Redeemer. She lived in union with the Sacred Heart of Jesus and placed all her confidence in Mary.

The Holy Father also declared:

> A tireless apostle, she was generous in fulfilling her important responsibilities and infinitely capable and patient in lovingly caring for the sick. In the spiritual springtime of the first era of the Church in Canada, one can inscribe among the "founders" Marie Catherine.

☩

Marie de la Passion Hélène Marie de Chappotin de Neuville
(May 21, 1839 – November 15, 1904)

Foundress of the Franciscan Missionaries of Mary

Hélène Marie Philippine de Chappotin de Neuville was born in Nantes, France, to a noble and Catholic family. She was raised solidly in the Faith and, by 1856, she discerned an unmistakable call to the religious life. Her hopes were delayed, however, by her mother's sudden death, which meant Hélène was needed to help with the family.

By the end of 1860, however, she was in a position to ask the local bishop of Nantes for permission to enter the Poor Clares, as she was drawn deeply to the life of austerity and poverty that the order offered. In January 1861, she offered herself as a victim soul on behalf of the Church and the Pope and fell ill soon after. Such was the severity of her illness that she was forced to depart the convent. When Marie had recovered her strength, she was urged by her confessor to enter the religious life again, this time the Society of Marie Reparatrice. She entered the community in 1864 and soon received the habit and the name Marie de la Passion (Mary of the Passion).

In March 1865, while still a novice, Marie was sent by the congregation to India. The sisters were to assist the local Jesuits there in forming the members of the congregation in the Apostolic Vicariate of Madurai. While there, she made her temporary vows in May 1866. Soon after, she was named local Superior; the following year, in July 1867, she was appointed Provincial Superior.

Unfortunately, internal divisions made it necessary for Mother Marie to journey to Rome to settle the matter. In 1877, she secured authorization from Pope Pius IX to establish a new institute called the Missionaries of Mary. She opened a novitiate in Saint-Brieuc in France, at the behest of the Congregation of the Propagation of the Faith, and soon attracted a variety of vocations. Difficulties in the fledgling community forced Marie to go back to Rome again in 1880 and 1882. As a result of the visit, she was permitted to open a house in Rome. In 1882, she was also received into the Third Order of St. Francis.

More troubles emerged in 1883, and Marie was removed form her office as Superior of the Institute. Cleared of all wrongdoing by Pope Leo XIII, she was re-elected Superior in July of the next year. The Institute of the Missionaries of Mary received its constitution initially in 1890 and formally in 1896. The missionaries of the institute were subsequently sent out across the globe; in 1900, seven members were martyred while in the course of their labors in China. They were canonized in 2000 among the members of the Martyrs of China.

Pope John Paul II beatified Marie on October 20, 2002, and declared:

> Mary of the Passion let herself be seized by God, who was able to satisfy the thirst for truth that motivated her. Founding the Franciscan Missionaries of Mary, she burned to communicate the torrents of love that sprang up in her and wished to extend them over the world. At the heart of the missionary commitment she placed prayer and the Eucharist, because for her, adoration and mission blended to become the same work. Drawing on Scripture and the Fathers of the Church, combining a mystical and an active vocation, passionate and intrepid, she gave herself with an intuitive and bold readiness to the universal mission of the Church. Dear Sisters, learn from your Foundress, in profound communion with the Church, and welcome the invitation to live, with renewed fidelity, the intuitions of your founding charism, so that the number of those who discover Jesus, who makes us enter into the mystery of the love that is God, may be more abundant.

☩

Marie-Leonie Paradis (May 12, 1840 – May 3, 1912)
"Little Sister" of Humble Service

Marie-Leonie Paradis brought countless dedicated women into a life of service, humble labor, and spiritual graces.

She was born Alodie Virginia Paradis in Acadie (Sainte Marguerite de Blairfindie), a suburb of Montreal. At age thirteen, Alodie entered the Holy Cross Sisters at Saint-Laurent, where she received her religious name. She made her vows in 1857 and was sent later to St. Vincent's Orphanage in New York City.

In 1864, Marie-Leonie became directress of a group of sisters engaged in household management in Indiana. She had many volunteers for this work and asked permission to establish a new congregation, the Little Sisters of the Holy Family. Canonical erection of the congregation came on January 27, 1896. Marie-Leonie had remained a

Holy Cross Sister but became a "Little Sister" when the congregation was erected. Papal approval from Pope Pius X (r. 1904-1913) was announced May 1, 1905.

Serving the Holy Cross Sisters originally, Marie-Leonie's Little Sisters began keeping households in the apostolic delegation in Canada and in Washington, D.C. They also served in other episcopal residences and operated homes for retired priests.

When Marie-Leonie died at Sherbrooke, Quebec, on May 3, 1912, there were more than 600 sisters caring for clerical and episcopal households in Canada, the United States, and Honduras. The vision that Marie-Leonie shared of humble service to priests continues to inspire generous young women.

Pope John Paul II beatified Marie-Leonie Paradis at Montreal on September 11, 1984, stating that he rejoiced in beatifying her in her homeland. The Holy Father declared further:

> Never doubting her call, she often asked: "Lord, show me your ways," so that she would know the concrete form of her service in the Church. She found and proposed to her spiritual daughters a special kind of commitment: the service of educational institutions, seminaries, and priests' homes. She never shied away from the various forms of manual labor which is the lot of so many people today and which held a special place in the Holy Family and in the life of Jesus of Nazareth himself. It is there that she saw the Will of God in her life. It was in carrying out these tasks that she found God . . . in the sacrifices which were required and which she offered in love, she experienced a profound joy and peace. She knew that she was one with Christ's fundamental attitude: he had "come not to be served, but to serve." She was filled with the greatness of the Eucharist and with the greatness of the priesthood at the service of the Eucharist. That is one of the secrets of her spiritual motivation.

☩

Marie Poussepin (October 14, 1653 – January 24, 1744)
Foundress of the Dominican Sisters of Charity of the Presentation of Tours

Marie Poussepin was born at Dourdan, near Paris, France, in a middle-class family that met financial reverses. At a very young age, Marie took charge of her father's stocking factory and kept the family and local workers secure. In this capacity, Marie also used innovative machines and new methods of training workers. She was a Dominican Tertiary, entering that Third Order in 1693, and served in many other charitable programs.

Her desire to serve the poor prompted Marie to found a Dominican Fraternity in Sainville, France, and to start a school for girls. Twenty such communities were soon established in the area around Paris. From this beginning came the Dominican Sisters of Charity of the Presentation of Tours. The bishop of Chartres, however — who apparently was not in favor of the Dominicans — demanded that Marie renounce all ties to that religious order, and she was compelled to comply. (Eventually, things changed: the congregation was restored to its original spiritual base in the late nineteenth century and was recognized as Dominican in the twentieth century.)

Charity was Marie's sole focus; she was dedicated to the welfare of each parish, the education of young people, and the service of the sick poor. Her congregation mirrored this virtue, as her sisters were trained to accept all labors as their religious commitment.

Her vision and her rule flourished after her death in Sainville, France. The congregation now serves in Burkina Faso, Iraq, Colombia, France, India, and Spain, with 4,000 spiritual daughters of Blessed Marie presently in the world.

Pope John Paul II beatified Marie Poussepin on November 20, 1994, in Rome, declaring:

> The fire of love which Christ came to kindle on the earth would be doomed to being extinguished had not families the courage to keep it burning. During this year dedicated particularly to them, Marie Poussepin brings us a message of joy and hope: born into a family which raised her and which she supported, she is henceforth held up for our veneration as one of our sisters in humanity, a daughter of our humble and generous God, capable of understanding family problems and also of showing us where to seek their solution: in the love which springs from the heart of Christ, King of the universe.

☩

Marie Anne Rivier (December 19, 1768 – February 3, 1838)
"The Woman Apostle"

Marie Anne was born in Montpezat-sous-Bauzon, France. As a child, she had been crippled by a bad fall, and every day her mother carried her to the local parish church, where she prayed at the feet of a statue of the *Pietà* for her child's recovery. This went on for four years, during which time the child learned to pray, believing with a child's faith "the Blessed Virgin will cure me."

On September 18, 1774, Marie Anne began to walk again. At age eighteen, she was devoted to caring for the abandoned children she discovered near her home. Other young women came to her aid, and she realized that a religious congregation was needed to continue this work. With the aid of Abbe Pontanier, Marie Anne founded the Sisters of the Presentation of Mary in Montpezat-sous-Bauzon in 1796. The first novitiate of this congregation was opened in Theuyts, and there, she trained the young volunteers who shared her ideals and devotion.

This was also a time of revolutionary terror in France — priests were tracked down, religious activity was suspect, and executions were frequent. Marie Anne secretly held Sunday assemblies, prayer vigils, and rosaries, despite the bans. While cautious, she continued her efforts for the faith, opening forty-six schools in just eight years in the diocese of Viviers alone. In 1819, she established the motherhouse of the "White Ladies" at Bourg-Saint-Andéol.

Though the motherhouse was terribly poor, Marie Anne taught that welcoming the most destitute is a sacred obligation. Her ideals attracted other faithful, and the Sisters of the Presentation of Mary continued to grow rapidly, operating schools, orphanages, and other charitable institutions. Some of the "White Ladies" went to begin missions in Canada; others went to the United States, where the first foundation opened in Glens Falls, New York, in 1873.

Marie Anne died in the motherhouse of her congregation, revered by her spiritual daughters and many officials and laypersons. Pope John Paul II beatified Marie Anne Rivier on May 23, 1982, announcing:

So what is the secret of Marie Rivier's zeal? One is struck by her boldness, her tenacity, her expansive joy, her courage, "which was enough [for] a thousand lives." There were, however, many difficulties to discourage her: her childhood illness which lasted until she was healed on a feast of Our Lady, a lack of physical growth, a poor state of health throughout the seventy years of her life, the ignorance of religion that surrounded her. But her life demonstrates well the power of faith in a simple upright soul, which surrenders itself entirely to the grace of its baptism. She relied on God, who purified her through the Cross. She prayed intensely to Mary and with her presented herself before God in a state of adoration and offering. Her spirituality is solidly theological and clearly apostolic: "Our vocation is Jesus Christ; we must fill ourselves with his spirit, so that his Kingdom may come, especially in the souls of children."

Marie-Louise of Jesus Trichet (1684 – April 28, 1759)
Dedicated to Wisdom

Marie-Louise of Jesus Trichet was born in Poitiers, France, to a devout Catholic family that remained loyal to the Church in perilous times. She was raised with a concern for others, a virtue that would frame the remarkable apostolate of her life.

In 1703, she founded a group of young women called *La Sagesse*, or "Wisdom." These young women aided the poor, crippled, and blind of their region. Marie-Louise came under the influence of a future saint, Louis de Montfort and grasped his vision of Catholic programs to oppose the secularism and materialism of the age. She guided her companions and adopted a religious life for them, naming the group the Daughters of Wisdom. Louis de Montfort received Marie-Louise's vows and gave the habit to her and the other members of her new congregation.

The Daughters of Wisdom opened a school in 1715 in La Rochelle. Dedicated to the Blessed Virgin Mary in all their ministries, the sisters won the respect of La Rochelle and began new foundations. Some Daughters of Wisdom were martyred during the French Revolution, the ultimate sacrifice for the faith. The motherhouse of the Daughters of Wisdom was established at Saint-Laurent-sur-Sevre by Marie-Louise. When Louis de Montfort died, his remains were enshrined at the motherhouse. Marie-Louise died on April 28, 1759, having founded thirty convents and institutions of charity. Her religious sisters arrived the United States in 1904.

Pope John Paul II beatified Marie-Louise Trichet on May 16, 1993, declaring:

Marie-Louise of Jesus let herself be seized by Christ; she passionately sought the interior union of human wisdom with the eternal wisdom. The natural outcome of this bond of deep intimacy was an activity passionately devoted to the poorest of her contemporaries.

☩

Marthe Le Bouteiller (December 2, 1816 – March 18, 1883)
"Sister Cider"

Marthe Le Bouteiller became the patroness of wounded military personnel in the Franco-Prussian war.

She was born Aimée Le Bouteiller, the third of four children of André and Marie-Française of La Henriére (Percy), France. The family operated a small farm in La Manche province. André Le Bouteiller died in 1827, but the family survived financially. Aimée attended a local school operated by Sr. Marie-Française Farcy in La Henriére, where she received the grace of a religious vocation. The school encouraged vocations among many young women in the area.

At age twenty-four, Aimée entered the Congregation of the Sisters of Saint-Sauveur-le-Vicomte, founded by St. Mary Magdalen Postel, and took the religious name Marthe. She made her novitiate and profession and was assigned to work in the kitchens, storerooms, and gardens. Marthe would perform her convent duties in such menial arenas for four decades, becoming a model religious. Her piety and kindness became the hallmark of her convent life. She had a fall in icy waters, leaving her in severe pain for a year, but she did not complain to anyone.

When the soldiers of the Franco-Prussian War took up residence in her convent, Marthe was able to feed vast numbers for six months, providing food where seemingly there was none available. Finally, exhausted by her years of service, she died, beloved by her community and the laity in Saint-Sauveur-le-Vicomte.

Pope John Paul II beatified Marthe Le Bouteiller on November 4, 1990, announcing:

May this new Blessed help the young people of today and tomorrow find joy in giving themselves to the Lord in religious consecration! May she help them to grasp the primacy of the spiritual life in order to take part in the building up of the Church and perform fruitful activity in the service of mankind! On their life's journey our contemporaries need to see faces that show the true happiness which intimacy with God brings. Sr. Marthe, a true Sister of Mercy, was able to let the love of God shine around her. The extreme simplicity of her life did not prevent the other sisters from recognizing her true spiritual authority. She bore fruit to the glory of the Father: "by this is My Father glorified, that you bear much fruit and become My disciples" (Jn. 15:8).

✠

Martin of St. Nicholas Lumbreras — see Martyrs of Japan

✠

Martyrs of Almeria (d. 1936)
Martyrs of Communism in Spain

Two Spanish bishops and seven Christian Brothers were slain by the military forces of the Communist Popular Front of Almeria in Spain.

The bishops cruelly murdered were Bl. Diego Ventaja Milan of Almeria and Bl. Emmanuel (Manuel) Medina Olmos of Guadix. Five of the Christian Brothers were arrested in their classrooms; the other two religious were hunted down by Communists in the town and captured.

The Christian Brothers were confined to a series of holding areas, sacred places of worship that were profaned, then used to keep the religious in captivity. Both physical and mental abuses were part of the Communist pattern of treatment, and the martyrs endured pain and indignities.

The bishops died first. On August 29, they were taken to an isolated place and shot. The next day, Christian Brothers Edmigio Rodríguez, Amalio Mendoza, and Valerio Bernardo Martinez were also shot by the rebels, and their bodies thrown into a well to avoid any public outcry. On September 8, Evencio Ricardo Uyarra and Teodomiro Joaquin Säiz were slain by the side of a road; on September 12, Aurelio María Acebrón and José Cecilio Gonzalez were martyred in a similar manner.

Pope John Paul II beatified the Martyrs of Almeria on October 10, 1993, announcing:

All of them, faithful servants of the Lord, were like those messengers of the king, who according to what we heard in the Gospel were also "mistreated and killed." (Mt. 22:6) The Church hears these words of the martyrs . . . She looks with veneration at their witness.

⊹

Martyrs of Angers (1792-1794)
William Repin and Ninety-Eight Companions

This group of martyrs is composed of twelve priests, three women religious, and eighty-four lay men and women who were victims of the anti-Catholic forces of the French Revolution.

William (Gulielmus) Repin was born on August 26, 1709, in Thorace, France, and was raised in a devout family. Receiving the grace of a vocation, he entered the seminary of the diocese and was ordained a priest. His first assignment was the parish of Martigne-Brand. He served there for half a century, becoming a part of the daily lives of the people of the region. When the French Revolution swept across the land, William refused to accept the new ideology, which he recognized as pagan, vicious, and bent on destroying the Catholic Church. Accordingly, he refused to sign the oath of allegiance to the new Republic. He was arrested with other Catholics of the region on December 24, 1793.

Taken prisoner also were priest brothers, John and René Lego, and women religious, Rosalie du Verdier de la Sorinire, María Anna Vaillot, and Odilla Baumgarten. They were guillotined on January 2, 1794, at Angers. A remarkable laywoman, Renée-Marie Feillatreau, who was tried for aiding priests, was also among the laity guillotined.

Other martyrs were slain near Avrillé on February 1, 1794. Twenty-four women, including a teacher and a woman surgeon, as well as young Catholic girls, were slain at Angers and Avrillé as part of the revolutionary campaign of terror. The bodies of the victims were not allowed to be viewed by the local citizens but were dumped into a mass grave at Avrillé. Word spread rapidly, and the site became a popular pilgrimage destination for the region. A memorial honoring the deaths was erected at Champs-des-Martyres.

Pope John Paul II beatified the Martyrs of Angers on February 19, 1984. At the ceremony, the Holy Father honored these martyrs who gave their lives for the faith. They are revered as coming from all walks of life, yet bound by their courageous defense of Christ and His Church.

⨯

Martyrs of Armenia (November 22, 1895)

Salvatore Lilli and his Franciscan Companions

These martyrs were slain by the Turkish Muslims because they would not abjure the Faith.

Salvatore was born in Cappadocia-Aquila, Italy, on June 19, 1853, the son of Vincenzo and Annunziata Lilli. In 1870, he entered the Franciscans, making his religious vows on August 6, 1871, at Nazzano. Two years later, he was sent to the Franciscan friary at Bethlehem, Israel, where he studied for the priesthood in the Order's seminary. He also studied in Jerusalem and was ordained on April 6, 1878. He was then assigned to Jerusalem, where he served at St. Saviour and the Holy Sepulchre churches for two years.

In 1880, Salvatore was sent to the Franciscan mission in Marasco, Armenia. He learned the language and the customs and brought his innovative style and spiritual insights to the people of the region, bettering their living conditions. In the process of preaching to the local populations, Salvatore erected schools, clinics, havens, and even entire villages set on prosperous methods of industry, hygiene, and the Faith, and bought land to establish housing units and trade centers. In 1891, he became the hero of the region during a cholera epidemic. For more than six weeks, Salvatore labored unceasingly in treating the victims of the disease.

The Islamic Turks occupied the region in 1894 and took Salvatore and seven companions into custody. Tortured and ordered to abjure Christ and the faith, Salvatore and his fellow religious refused to deny the Church. They were martyred for their loyalty on November 22, 1895.

Pope John Paul II beatified the Martyrs of Armenia on October 3, 1982, declaring that their martyrdom was recognized by the faithful as the fruit of lifelong dedication and service to Christ, and that the Church viewed their sacrifices with reverence.

⨯

Martyrs of Barbastro (1936)

Felipe de Jesus Munarriz and Fifty Companions

These martyrs were slain by local Communist rebels in the Spanish Civil War, supported by more Communists from Catalan. These rebels began a rampage of murder and destruction against Church buildings and personnel in Barbastro, in northern Aragon, Spain. Bishop Florentino Asensio Barroso was one of the first arrested, tortured, and slain as an enemy of the people.

On Monday, July 20, 1936, Communist militia forces entered the house of the Claretians, the Missionary Sons of the Immaculate Heart of Mary, in Barbastro, arresting the entire seminary community. Felipe de Jesus Munarriz, the Superior, was taken prisoner separately with the community's procurator, and members of the local faculty were also arrested. Within two weeks of their arrest — on August 2, 1936 — Felipe and other Claretian faculty members were taken to the local cemetery, where they were shot to death.

The seminarians were imprisoned in a theater with other religious, surrounded by filth and subjected to abuse, their captors even brought prostitutes in to tempt them. Throughout their ordeal, the Claretian seminarians waited with faith and calm, leaving written testimonies of their courage and hope in Christ. They also forgave their tormentors publicly.

Six senior religious were the first of this group to die. They were killed on the morning of August 12, calling out, "*Viva Cristo Rey!*" ("Long live Christ the King!") At midnight, twenty more died with the same religious fervor. On August 15, twenty more Claretians died, many of them celebrating the anniversary of their religious profession as they were martyred. Two other seminarians were taken from their beds in the local hospital and killed three days later. Seven Claretians were spared because of their age; two Claretians from Argentina were exiled.

Pope John Paul II beatified the Claretian Martyrs of Barbastro on October 25, 1992, honoring the profound faith and honor displayed by young and old alike during their frightful torment. The Holy Father declared:

> Since the majority of them were young people and students of theology, their lives can be seen as a direct call to you, novices and seminarians, to recognize the lasting validity of an adequate formation and intense preparation based on a solid piety in fidelity to your vocation and your membership in the Church, serving her through your own congregation; in a life of abnegation in community; in perseverance and the witness of your own religious identity. Without all these prerequisites, our Blessed would not have been able to receive the grace of martyrdom.

(See also Florentino Asensio Barroso.)

✝

Martyrs of Bulgaria (November 11, 1952)
Assumptionist Martyrs

Three Augustinians of the Assumption who were martyred by the Bulgarian Communist officials died with Bishop Vincent Eugene Bossilkov and were honored by Pope John Paul II when he visited Bulgaria. The martyrs were Augustinian Assumptionists Kamen Vitchev, Josephat Chichov, and Pavel Djedjov.

Kamen was born on May 23, 1893, at Strem, Bulgaria, to an Eastern rite family, and baptized Peter. He attended local schools and the Adrianopoli Institute and, in 1907, moved to Phanaraki (near Istanbul). On September 8, 1910, he became an Augustinian of the Assumption in Gemp. He served the Augustinians in various academic and administrative capacities, being an author and lecturer as well. In 1948, he became the rector of the seminary at Plovdiv and provincial vicar of the Bulgarian Assumptionists. But, aware of the coming persecution, he had written to his Provincial Superior: "Obtain for us by prayer the grace of being faithful to Christ and to the Church in our daily life, so that we may be worthy of bearing witness when the time comes." On July 4, 1952, he was arrested.

Josephat Chichov was born on February 9, 1884, in Plovdiv, Bulgaria, and baptized Robert Matthew in the Latin rite. He studied at Kara Agatch in Adrianopoli and entered the Augustinian Assumptionist minor seminary at age nine. After priestly training and studies at the Louvain in Belgium, he was ordained on July 11, 1909, in Malines, Belgium. He then served in administrative positions and as a chaplain to the Oblate Sisters of the Assumption. He was arrested in December 1951 at Varna, on the Black Sea.

Pavel Djedjov was born in Plovdiv, Bulgaria, and baptized Joseph in the Latin rite. He studied locally and at the College of St. Augustine, becoming an Assumptionist on October 2, 1938. Pavel was ordained in Plovdiv on January 26, 1945. He then resided in Varna, where he became the treasurer and procurator of the Bulgarian Assumptionists. He was arrested with Kamen, but only said, "May God's will be done. We await our turn." The three Augustinian Assumptionists and Vincent Eugene Bossilkov were shot to death in Sofia Prison on November 11, 1952.

Pope John Paul II beatified the Martyrs of Bulgaria on May 26, 2002, in Plovdid, Bulgaria, proclaiming:

The courageous fidelity in the face of suffering and imprisonment shown by Fathers Josephat, Kamen and Pavel was acknowledged by their former students — Catholics, Orthodox, Jews, and Muslims — by their parishioners, the members of their religious communities, and their fellow prisoners. By their dynamism, their fidelity to the Gospel, their selfless service to the Nation, the new Beati stand out as models for Christians today, especially for Bulgaria's young people, who are looking to give meaning to their lives and who wish to follow Christ whether as lay persons, in the religious life or in the priesthood.

(See also Vincent Eugene Bossilkov.)

✠

Martyrs of the Christian Brothers (1794)
Solomon Leclerq and Companions

As the Christian Brothers laid down their lives in Spain for the faith, so did they refuse to abjure the Church during the terrors of the French Revolution.

These Christian Brothers refused to agree to the Civil Constitution of the Clergy and were forced out of their schools and residences as a result. Solomon Leclerq was secretary to the Superior General. He was arrested on August 5, 1792, and shot to death on September 2. Léon Mopinot was sixty-eight years old and a teacher in Moulins. Arrested, he was imprisoned in several different rotting hulks of ships anchored in the harbor of Rochefort. Léon died after two months in the hold of one of these ships. Roger Faverge, who had been born in Orléans in 1745, suffered the same imprisonment and fell ill with typhus. Moved to an island in the harbor, he died there. Uldaric Guillaume taught his students secretly until his arrest. He lasted fifteen months and was buried on an island in the harbor of Rochefort.

The horrors of the Christian Brothers' martyrdom were unimaginable, marking a hideous high point in the vicious methods used to try to eradicate Catholic teaching from the land.

Pope John Paul II beatified the Christian Brothers Martyrs of La Rochelle on October 1, 1995. At the ceremony of beatification, the martyrs were praised for their courageous offerings of self, despite their agonies and slow, cruel deaths. The loyalty of these martyrs was recognized as an insignia of their dedication to Christ and the Church.

(See also Martyrs of La Rochelle.)

✠

Martyrs of Daimiel — see Martyrs of the Passionist Congregation

✠

Martyrs of the Diocesan Worker Priests (1936)
Peter Ruiz de los Paños y Angel and Companions

The Diocesan Worker Priests group was formed by Emmanuel Domingo y Sol to sponsor young seminarians and to promote apostolates in Spain that would strengthen the faith. The Communist-led revolutionaries of the Spanish Civil War, aware of the impact of the Diocesan Worker Priests, thus singled out these priests as particular enemies of their atheist agenda.

Peter Ruiz de los Paños y Angel was the director general of the Diocesan Worker Priests at the time, and he and eight of the community's members were arrested by the Spanish revolutionary forces. Peter was born in Mora, Toledo, Spain, on September 18, 1881. Ordained a priest after seminary training, he served in the seminaries of Badajoz, Málaga, and Seville, then became the rector of the Plasencia College and the Spanish College of Rome. Peter also founded the Disciples of Jesus, a women's congregation dedicated to fostering vocations. Peter was martyred on July 23, 1936, in Toledo, Spain, the victim of the revolutionary Communist forces. His eight companions were martyred at different times during the same year.

Pope John Paul II beatified the Martyrs of the Diocesan Worker Priests on October 1, 1995, declaring that Peter and the Diocesan Worker Priests were:

> . . . the mature fruit of the Redeemer's paschal mystery. Pedro Ruiz de los Paños further enriched the Church by founding the Disciples of Jesus, dedicated to the vocations apostolate. Today, these women religious deeply rejoice, together with the Church in Castille, Cataluña, and the community of Valencia, the native land of the new Blesseds.

✠

Martyrs of England, Scotland, and Wales (1584-1679)
George Haydock and Companions

This group — sixty-three ordained Catholic priests, twenty-two laypeople from various social ranks and walks of life — represents Catholics who went to their deaths during one of the most severe anti-Catholic periods in English history. The first was executed in London in 1584, the last hanged in Wales in 1679. They were arrested, tortured cruelly, tried, and executed particularly during the reign of Elizabeth I (r. 1558-1603) and Oliver Cromwell (r. 1653-1658), the Lord Protector, because they refused to accept statutes from these monarchs that denied the Catholic Church's role in their homeland. King Henry VIII (r. 1509-1547) had already enacted legislation to silence Catholic opposition, and Queen Elizabeth I (r. 1558-1603) continued the government's repression with a series of acts that made reconciliation to the Catholic Church a treasonable activity. Missionaries were thus condemned for their efforts at conversions and practicing the liturgies of the Faith. Anyone caught harboring a Catholic priest came under the same treasonable charges.

The martyrs followed in the footsteps of Sts. Thomas More and John Fisher in refusing to deny the declarations of Catholic councils and the traditional beliefs of the Church. Some of these martyrs were the brightest of the young scholars of Britain, a complication that caused considerable dismay among the persecutors, who sometimes tried exile or banishment as a punishment, only to discover the Catholics back in the Isles, again evangelizing among the people.

George Haydock, singularly praised in this beatification, was born in 1556 at Cotton Hall, England, the son of Evan and Helen Haydock. He was sent to Douai, France, then Rome, Italy, to be educated. His uncle, William Allen, was the founder of the English Colleges at Douai, Rome and Valladolid. George was ordained a priest on December 21, 1581, probably at Reims, France. He returned to England to begin a missionary apostolate but was arrested soon after and placed in the Tower of London. Kept in solitary confinement, George suffered from malaria, which he had contracted in Rome. In May 1583, he was given a certain freedom of movement and was able to administer the sacraments to his fellow prisoners.

On February 5, 1583, George was indicted with his companions. On January 11, 1584, he was taken in a cart to his execution, all the while reciting the hymn *Te lucis ante terminum*. Witnesses to the execution reported that he was hanged, drawn, and quartered, the usual method used to slay priests. He was still alive when disemboweled. Some of the noted martyred companions of George Haydock are as follows:

William Carter (1584), a London Catholic bookseller imprisoned for printing "lewd" materials — the designation given to any books or pamphlets concerning the Catholic Faith. When his house was searched and other Catholic articles discovered, William was put to the rack. He spent eighteen months in prison, and his wife died alone. William was condemned to death and was able to confess to a priest. He was hanged, drawn, and quartered at Tyburn on January 11, 1584.

Hugh Grant and Marmaduke Bowes (1585) were a Catholic missionary and a friend who died together at York, England. Hugh was born in Durham, and was sent to Reims, France, for seminary training. He was ordained in 1584. The following year he returned to his native land, where he was arrested immediately.

Marmaduke met Hugh before his arrest and, when he heard that his priest friend had been taken prisoner by the authorities, went to York to intercede for him. Marmaduke was arrested also and tried with the missionary. They were martyred in York on November 26, 1585.

Alexander Crow (1586/7), a priest trained at Douai seminary, worked in northern England. He was born in Yorkshire and was in his twenties when he went to Douai, France, to study for the priesthood. Ordained in 1584, Alexander returned to England, centering his missionary apostolate in the north. He was arrested in Duffield and taken to York. There, he was hanged, drawn, and quartered on November 30, 1586/7.

Nicholas Woodfen (1586), a missionary priest who worked in England under the alias Devereux, may have actually been a Wheeler. He was born in Leominster, Hereforshsire, circa 1530. After studying at Reims, France, Nicholas was ordained a priest in 1581. He returned to England and labored among the lawyers of London until his arrest. Nicholas was hanged, drawn, and quartered on January 21, 1586.

William Pichard (1587), a priest martyr, was exiled from England but returned to serve the faithful. He was born in Battle, Sussex, in 1557, and studied at Oxford. Trained at Reims, France, he was ordained at Laon in 1583. William returned to England and was exiled but re-entered his homeland almost immediately. Arrested, he converted thirty prisoners while in captivity. He was hanged, drawn, and quartered by a cook, who acted clumsily while serving as a substitute executioner, on March 21, 1587, at Dorset.

Edmund Duke and Companions (1590) were priests caught up in the English hysteria following the defeat of the Spanish Armada. They include Edmund Duke, who landed at Tynemouth in 1589, arriving from Rome, Italy, with other priests, Richard Hill, John Hogg, and Richard Holiday. They were imprisoned at Durham, where they were hanged, drawn, and quartered on May 27, 1590.

Roger Thorpe and Thomas Watkinson (1591) were a priest and a friend who died together. Born in Yorkshire, Roger studied for the priesthood and was ordained at Reims, France, in 1585. He returned to England and was arrested in the home of Thomas Watkinson on the eve of Palm Sunday in 1591. They were taken to York, where they were martyred on May 31, 1591.

George Errington and William Gibson (1596) were two English Catholic laymen martyred on the charge of "persuading to popery." Openly devout Catholics, George and William were approached by a Protestant minister who wanted to expose them. The minister claimed to want to convert to the Faith but, instead, betrayed them to the authorities. They were arrested and martyred at York on November 29, 1596.

Peter Snow (1598) was ordained after studying at Douai, France, returned to England in 1597, and labored there. Arrested in 1598, Peter was imprisoned, and **Ralph Grimstow** went to his defense before the authorities. He was also tried for treason as a result. They were martyred in York on June 15, 1598.

Christopher Wharton (1600) was offered a pardon and bribes to abjure Christ and the Church but chose martyrdom. He was born in Middleton, West Riding, England, and was educated at Oxford. He converted to the faith, studied at Douai, France, and was ordained on March 31, 1584. Two years later, he returned to England but was soon arrested. Christopher was tried in York and martyred on March 28, 1600.

The other martyrs honored in this group are: Francis Ingleby (1586), John Fingley (1586), Robert Bickerdike (1586), William Thomson (1586), John Sandys (1586), Richard Sargeant (1586), John Lowe (1586), Robert Dibdale (1586), John Adams (1586), Edmund Sykes (1587), Stephen Rowsham (1587), John Hambley (1587), George Douglas (1587), Richard Simpson (1588), Edward Burden (1588), Henry Webley (1588), William Lampley (1588), Nicholas Garlick (1588), Robert Ludlam (1588), Robert Sutton (1588), Richard (Lloyd) Flower (1588), William Spenser (1589), Robert Hardesty (1589), Thomas Belson (1589), Richard Yaxley (1589), George Nichols (1589), Humphrey Pritchard (1589), Nicholas Horner (1590), Alexander Blake (1590), George Beesley (1591), William Pike (1591), Mountford Scott (1591), Joseph Lambton (1592), Thomas Pormort (1592), William Davies (1593), Anthony Page (1593), Christopher Robinson (1597), John Bretton (1598), Edward Thwing (1600), Thomas Palaser (1600), John Talbot (1600), Robert Nutter (1600), John Norton (1600), Roger Filcock (1600), Thomas Hunt (1600), Thomas Sprott (1600), Robert Middleton (1601), Thurston Hunt (1601), Robert Grissold (1604), John Sugar (1604), Robert Drury (1607), Matthew Flathers (1608), Roger Cadwallador (1610), Thomas Atkinson (1616), Roger Wrenno (1616), John

Thules (1616), William Southerne (1618), Thomas Bullaker (1642), Henry Heath (1643), Arthur Bell (1643), Edward Bamber (1646), John Woodcock (1646), Thomas Whittaker (1646), Nicholas Postage (1679), and Charles Meeham (1679).

Pope John Paul II beatified the Martyrs of England, Scotland, and Wales on November 22, 1987, praising the courage and loyalty of these men of the British Isles, who confounded their oppressors by dying with honor and with joy. They were honored as following in the footsteps of the great English confessor who brought glory to the Faith in that land.

✠

Martyrs of Ethiopia (March 3, 1716)
Martyrs in Ethiopian Civil War

The Martyrs of Ethiopia are Liberatus Weiss, Michele Pio Fasoli, and Samuel Marzorati, Franciscans who embarked on a ministry of evangelization in the remote nation of Ethiopia (ancient Abyssinia).

Dominicans had pioneered missionary efforts in the land, and the Jesuit priest Pedro Páez had won the confidence of Malak Sagad III (Susenyos), who in 1622, commanded his subjects to make allegiance to Rome. A civil war resulted, and Fasilidas took the throne of Ethiopia, expelling missionaries and banning the faith. The major religious body in the nation was the Monophysite Ethiopian Orthodox Church, a group that did not welcome missionaries from Rome.

Liberatus was born in Konnersreuth, Bavaria, Germany, on January 4, 1675, and baptized John Lawrence. Educated by the Bavarian Cistercians , he entered the Franciscans of the Austrian Province of St. Bernardine at Graz in 1693. He was ordained to the priesthood in 1698, then served in Langenlois and became a noted preacher. In 1704, Liberatus was chosen by the Congregation for the Propagation of the Faith to head a mission to Ethiopia after Jasu, the Ethiopian ruler at the time, had contacted the Vatican. Leading seven priests and three lay brothers, Liberatus arrived in Khartoum, in modern Sudan, where the local ruler robbed them and left them to starve. Only Liberatus and Michael Pio Fasali were able to make their way back to Italy.

In 1710, Liberatus was assigned once again to Ethiopia by the Vatican to replace Fr. Joseph of Jerusalem, who had served as apostolic prefect of Ethiopia until he died. This time, Liberatus was joined once more by Michael Pio Fasali, and they took Samuel Marzorati with them.

Michael Pio Fasoli was a Franciscan born near Pavia, Italy, and a missionary priest. Samuel Marzorati was also a Franciscan, born in Varese, Italy, in 1670. He entered the Order at Lugano, where he was ordained. Sent to Rome, Samuel studied medicine and surgery and went to Egypt in 1705. He intended to go to Ethiopia but reached the island of Socotra in March 1706. For five years, he labored in vain, then returned to Egypt in 1711.

Forming a team and avoiding the disasters of the first mission, the Franciscans landed in Massawa on April 18, 1712, going then to Gondor, Ethiopia, on July 20, 1712. They were received by Emperor Justos, the successor of Jasu, who welcomed them cordially and allowed them to set up a hospice and to learn the language, even though he would not give them permission to identify themselves as Roman Catholics or to preach to the people.

Court rivalries threatened the Franciscans, however, and they were sent to Tigre to protect them from critics. Meanwhile, the missionaries spent their time learning the language and converted a priest of the Ethiopian Church. The three Franciscans spent two years in isolation until Fr. Giacomo d'Oleggio joined them. Seeing the situation, Fr. Giacomo left Ethiopia bearing a letter to the Cardinal prefect of the Propagation and seeking reinforcement. The three others planned to leave if aid did not arrive.

The political situation deteriorated rapidly around them, however. Emperor Justos became ill, and the young son of the previous emperor, David III, was proclaimed the true heir to the throne, deposing Justos. As part of this insurrection, the three Franciscans were arrested and condemned to death. On March 3, 1716, Liberatus, Michele, and Samuel were stoned to death at Abbo, Ethiopia.

Pope John Paul II beatified the Martyrs of Ethiopia on November 20, 1988, declaring:

> Deeply convinced that they were not the masters of what they possessed, the blessed martyrs understood that they were representatives and messengers of the gifts they received from Christ. They knew that they were sent by him to the people of Ethiopia.

✠

Martyrs of Guadalajara (1936)

Carmelite Martyrs of Communism

The Martyrs of Guadalajara, Carmelite cloistered nuns caught up in the violence of the Spanish Civil War, include María Pilar of St. Francis Borgia, who was born Jacoba Martinez Garcia on December 30, 1877 in Tarazona (Zaragoza). She entered the Carmelite cloister at Guadalajara on October 12, 1898, taking vows the following year.

With her was María of the Angels of St. Joseph, who was born Marciana Valtierra Tordesillas on March 16, 1905 in Getafe, near Madrid. She entered the Carmel of Guadalajara on July 14, 1929. Teresa of the Child Jesus and St. John of the Cross, the third martyr, was born Eusebia Garcia y Garcia in Mochales on March 5, 1909. She entered the Guadalajara Carmel at age sixteen and made her first profession in 1926.

As the Communist militia groups ravaged sacred buildings and murdered religious, the Carmelites were forced to flee from their convent. They hoped to find places of refuge with devout Catholic families in the area, where they could remain hidden throughout the tragic period, but these Carmelite Sisters did not find the haven they sought. They were confronted by one militia unit while in the town. On July 24, 1936, María of the Angels was killed by gunfire, María Pilar received a mortal wound, and Teresa of the Child Jesus was offered her freedom if she denied Christ, the Church, and Carmel. She refused and was slain.

Pope John Paul II beatified the Carmelite Martyrs on March 29, 1987, announcing:

> The three daughters of Carmel could have addressed these words to the Good Shepherd when the hour came for them to give their lives for their faith in the divine Bridegroom of their souls. Yes, "I fear nothing," not even death. Love is greater than death and "you are with me." You, the Bridegroom on the Cross! You, Christ, my strength! This following of the Master, which should bring us to imitate him even to giving up our lives

for love of him, has been an almost constant call in early times and always, for Christians to give this supreme witness of love — martyrdom — before everyone, especially before their persecutors . . . In this way we see that martyrdom — the ultimate witness in defense of the Faith — is considered by the Church as a very eminent gift and as the supreme test of love, through which a Christian follows the very footsteps of Jesus, who freely accepted suffering and death for the salvation of the world.

✠

Martyrs of the Holy Family (August 1, 1943)
Maria Stella Mardosewicz and Ten Companions

The Holy Family Sisters, founded by Blessed Frances Siedliska, had arrived in Nowogródek, Poland (modern Belarus), in 1929 and had become a vital part of the community. When the Russians, then the Nazis, occupied the area, the Sisters served as a beacon of hope for the local people. The Sisters were also singled out by a special Gestapo unit that conducted mass executions in the region; when a large group of Poles were arrested, the Sisters offered themselves as victims to spare the others. Some of the prisoners were released, others scheduled for deportation to Germany as slave laborers.

On July 31, 1943, the Holy Family Sisters were ordered to appear at Gestapo headquarters. Eleven sisters obeyed the command, knowing they were to be executed without a trial. The Gestapo planned to kill them that same evening, but the word had spread, and too many Polish groups were in evidence. As a result, the martyrdom was delayed until the next morning, August 1, when the sisters were taken to a forest area and shot by the Gestapo.

The martyred Sisters were Maria Stella Mardosewicz, Maria Imelda Zak, Maria Raymond Kolowicz, Maria Daniela Jozwik, Maria Canuta Chrobot, Maria Sergia Rapiej, Maria Gwidona Cierpka, Maria Felicita Borowik, Maria Heliodora Matuszewska, Maria Canisia Mackiewicz, and Maria Boromea Narmontowicz.

Pope John Paul II beatified the Martyrs of the Holy Family on March 5, 2000, declaring:

> God was also a true "protector and helper" for the martyrs of Nowogródek — for Blessed Maria Stella Mardosewicz and her ten sisters, professed religious of the Congregation of the Holy Family of Nazareth. For them he was a helper throughout their lives and at the moment of their terrible test, when for an entire night they awaited death; he was a helper especially

on the way to the place of execution, and finally at the moment they were shot.

Where did these women find the strength to give themselves in exchange for the lives of imprisoned residents of Nowogródek? From where did they draw the courage to accept calmly the death sentence that was so cruel and unjust? God had slowly prepared them for this moment of greater trial. He sowed the seed of his grace in their hearts at the time of holy Baptism, then, tended with great care and responsibility, it developed firm roots and bore the most beautiful fruit, which is the gift of life. Christ says: "There is no greater love than this: to lay down one's life for one's friends" (Jn 15: 13). Yes, there is no greater love than this: to be ready to lay down one's life for one's brothers and sisters.

We thank you, O blessed martyrs of Nowogródek, for your witness of love, for your example of Christian heroism and for your trust in the power of the Holy Spirit. "Christ chose and appointed you that you should go and bear fruit in your lives and that your fruit should abide" (cf. Jn. 15: 16). You are the greatest inheritance of the Congregation of the Holy Family of Nazareth. You are the inheritance of the whole Church of Christ forever!

✠

Martyrs of the Hospitallers of St. John of God (1936-1939)

Braulius María Corres Diaz de Cerio, Federico Rubio Alvarez, and Sixty-Nine Companions

These martyrs were victims of the Communist cruelty in the Spanish Civil War.

Braulius María and his companions died at the hands of the Communist-inspired revolutionary militias at different times in several locations in Spain. Some had come to Spain to train as Hospitallers, dedicated to the care of the sick and abandoned. All died brutally, guilty only of being Catholics and devout religious. They stayed united spiritually throughout, inspired by the holiness of their founder and the community of life which had formed their souls. The martyred Hospitallers were:

Apostolic School of Talavera de la Reina (Toledo)

Federico Carlos Rubio Alvarez, Benavides (Léon), 73 years old; Primo Martínez de S. Vicente Castillo, San Román de Campezo (Alaya), 67 years old; Jerónimo Ochoa Urdangarin, Goñi (Navarre), 32 years old; Juan de la Cruz (Eloy) Delgado Pastor, Puebla de Alcocer (Badajoz) 22 years old.

Sanitarium San Juan de Dios, de Calafell (Tarragona)

Braulius María (Pablo) Corres Díaz de Cerio, Torralba de Río (Navarre), 39 years old; Julían (Miguel) Carrasquer Fos, Sueca (Valencia), 55 years old; Eusebio (Antonio) Forcades Ferraté, Reus (Tarragona), 60 years old; Constancio (Saturnino) Roca Huguet, Sant Sadurní d 'Anoia (Barcelona), 41 years old; Benito José Labré (Arsenio) Mañoso González, Lomoviejo (Valladolid), 57 years old; Vicente de Paúl Canelles Vives, Onda (Castellón), 42 years old; Tomás Urdanoz Aldaz, Echarri (Navarre), 33 years old; Rafael Flamarique Salinas, Mendívil (Navarre), 33 years old; Antonio Llauradó Parisi, Reus (Tarragona), 33 years old; Manuel López Orbara, Puente de la Reina (Navarre), 23 years old; Ignacio Tejero Molina, Monzalbarba (Zaragoza), 20 years old; Enrique Beltrán Llorca, Villareal (Castellón), 37 years old; Domingo Pitarch Gurrea, Villareal (Castellón), 27 years old; Antonio Sanchiz Silvestre, Villamarchante (Valencia), 26 years old; Manuel Jiménez Salado, Jerez de la Frontera (Cadiz), 29 years old.

Colombians

Rubén de Jesús López Aguilar, Concepción (Antioquia, Colombia), 28 years old; Arturo (Luis) Ayala Niño, (Paipa (Boyacá, Colombia), 27 years old; Juan Bta. (José) Velázquez Peláez, Jardin (Antioquia, Colombia), 27 years old; Eugenio (Alfanso, Antonio) Ramírez Salazar, La Ceja (Antioquia, Colombia), 23 years old; Esteban (Gabriel) Maya Gutiérrez, Pácora (Antioquia, Colombia), 29 years old; Melquíades (Ramón) Ramírez Zuloaga, Sonsón (Antioquia, Colombia), 27 years old; Gaspar (Luis, Modesto) Páez Perdomo, La Unión (Huila, Colombia), 23 years old.

Sanitarium San José, de Ciempozuelos (Madrid)

Flavio (Atilano) Argüeso González, Mazuecos, (Palencia), 58 years old; Francisco Arias Martín, Granada, 52 years old; Tobías (Francisco) Borrás Romeu, San Jorge (Castellón), 76 years old; Juan Jesús (Maríano) Ardradas Gonzalo, Conquezuela (Soria), 58 years old; Guillermo (Vicente) Llop Gayá, Villareal (Castellón), 56 years old; Clemente Díez Sahagún, Fuentes de Nava (Palencia), 75 years old; Lázaro (Juan María) Múgica Goiburu, Ideazábal (Guipúzcoa), 69 years old; Martiniano (Antonio) Meléndez Sánchez, (Málaga), 58 years old; Pedro María Alcalde Negredo, Ledesma (Soria), 58 years old; Julián Plazaola Artola, San Sebastián (Guipuzcoa), 21 years old; Hilario (Antonio) Delgado Vílchez, Cañar (Granada), 18 years old; Pedro de Alcántara Bernalte Calzado, Moral de Calatrava (Ciudad Real), 26 years old; Juan Alcalde, Zuzones (Burgos), 25 years old; Isidoro Martínez Izquiero, Madrid, 18 years old; Angel Sastre Corporales, Vallaralbo del Vino (Zamora),

20 years old; Eduardo Bautista Jiménez, La Gineta (Albacete), 51 years old; José Mora Velasco, (Córdoba), 50 years old; José Ruiz Cuesta, Dílar (Granada), 29 years old; Diego de Cádiz (Santiago) García Molina, Moral de Calatrava (Ciudad Real), 44 years old; Román (Rafael) Touceda Fernández, Madrid, 32 years old; Miguel (Miguel Francisco) Ruedas Mejías, Motril (Granada), 34 years old; Arturo Donoso Murillo, Puebla de Alcocer (Badajoz), 19 years old; Jesús Gesta de Piquer, (Madrid), 21 years old; Antonio Martínez Gil-Leonis, Montellano (Seville), 20, years old.

Institute San José de Carabanchel Alto (Madrid)

Proceso (Joaquín) Ruiz Cascales, Beniel (Murcia), 48 years old; Cristino (Miguel) Roca Huguet, Mollins de Rei (Barcelona), 37 years old; Eutimio (Nicolás) Aramendía García, Oteiza de la Solanna (Navarre), 57 years old; Canuto (José) Franco Gómez, Aljucer (Murcia), n.d.; Dositeo (Guillermo) Rubio Alonso, Madrigalejo (Burgos), 67 years old; Cesáreo (Maríano) Niño Pérez, Torregutiérrez, (Segovia), 58 years old; Benjamin (Alejandro) Cobos Celada, (Palencia), 48 years old; Carmelo (Isidro) Gil Arano, Tudela (Navarre), 57 years old; Cosme (Simón) Brun Arará, Santa Coloma de Farners (Girona), 41 years old; Cecilio (Enrique) López López, Fondón (Almeria), 35 years old; Rufino (Crescencio) Lasheras Aizcorbe, Arandigoyen (Navarre), 36 years old; Faustino (Antonio) Villanueva Igual, Sarrión (Teruel), 23 years old.

Hospital San Juan de Dios, de Barcelona, and the Sanitarium of Sant Boi de Llobregat (Barcelona)

Juan Bautista Egozcuezebál Aldaz, Nuin, (Navarre), 54 years old; Pedro de Alcántara (Lorenzo) Villanueva Larráyoz, (Navarre), 54 years old; Francisco Javier Ponsa Casallach, Moiá (Barcelona); Juan Antonio Burró Mas, Barcelona, 22 years old; Asisclo (Joaquín) Piña Piazuelo, Caspe (Zaragoza), 58 years old; Protasio (Antonio) Cubells Minguell, Coll de Nargó (Lleida), 56 years old.

Hospital San Rafael, de Madrid

Gonzalo Gonzalo Gonzalo, Conquezuela (Soria), 27 years old; Jacinto Hoyuelos González, Matarrepudio (Santander), 22 years old; Nicéro Salvador del Río, Villamorco, (Palencia), 23 years old.

Pope John Paul II beatified the martyred Hospitallers of St. John of God on October 25, 1992, declaring:

Unanimous is the witness offered by the Brothers of St. John of God . . . who died giving glory to God and forgiving their assassins. At the moment of their martyrdom, several of them repeated the words of Christ himself: "Father, forgive them, they know not what they do" (Lk 23:24). All of them chose death rather than renounce their faith and their religious life. They went to their execution, rejoicing in the gift of martyrdom, of which they felt unworthy, despite fact that all of them, especially the young ones, had their hearts set on great apostolic ideals of proclaiming the Gospel to others; some of them by caring for the sick, and the others through the ministry of preaching as missionaries. The seven Hospitaller Brothers of Colombia deserve special mention, for they are the first sons of that land to be raised the honors of the altar. They were in Spain to finish their religious and professional formation when the Lord called them to give this witness of their faith. Today, in conjunction with the fifth centenary of the evangelization of America, we publicly acknowledge their martyrdom and present as the first fruits of the Colombian Church.

✝

Martyrs of Ireland (1579-1654)
Dermot O'Hurley and Companions

Cruelty was the hallmark of the English persecution of Catholics in Ireland from 1579 to 1654, in which the archbishop of Cashel and sixteen Irish faithful were slain. These Irish Catholics died because they would not renounce the authority of the pope. The excommunication of Queen Elizabeth I (r. 1558-1603) by Pope Pius V in 1570 unleashed a new persecution in England, and an Irish uprising of nobles spurred the same reprisals in Ireland.

Other martyrs died from 1602-1621, as the Irish refused to surrender the Faith. The insurrection of 1641 brought even more persecutions, and the terrible era of Oliver Cromwell, Lord Protector of England (r. 1653-1658), claimed the last of these courageous followers of Christ. The martyrs of Ireland included:

Dermot O'Hurley (1584), the son of William O'Hurley of Lickadoon, Ireland, he was educated as a Catholic in various European capitals and was revered as a brilliant and eloquent defender of the Faith. Dermot taught at the Louvain, in Belgium; Reims, France; and Rome, Italy. He had a doctorate degree and was deemed courageous in his Catholicism.

In 1581, Pope Gregory XIII (r. 1572-1585) appointed Dermot the archbishop of Cashel, consecrating him on September 11 of that year. Dermot set sail to Ireland to assume his episcopal see but was arrested almost immediately by English authorities. The Irish nobles were in revolt against England at the time, and it was hoped that he was privy to their plans and would be able to betray their military intentions.

In March 1584, the English resorted to hideous tortures to break Dermot's resolute silence. His legs were oiled and roasted over a fire, causing him excruciating pain. As he refused to provide any information, the torment continued day after day without success, and finally, Dermot was returned to his prison cell in a pitiful condition.

When news of his torture reached the outside world, English jurists, horrified as details of his sufferings spread over the land, announced that there was no legal reason for Dermot to endure imprisonment, let alone such hideous punishment. The crown authorities, however, ignored such judicial protests. Sometime in June, between the 19th and the 29th, Dermot, archbishop of Cashel, was hanged on St. Stephen's Green. Other martyrs of this group are:

Patrick O'Healy, O.F.M., the Franciscan bishop of Mayo, Ireland, was arrested and martyred with Conn O'Rourke on August 13, 1579. Patrick's last sermon was a reassertion of papal authority, addressed to all who had gathered to watch his execution.

Conn O'Rourke, O.F.M., the Franciscan priest, he died with Bishop O'Healy at Kilmallock. He gave his life to protest the English attempts to repress the Church in Ireland.

Matthew Lambert was a devout baker martyred at Wexford with several companions in July 1581. He stated that he was not learned enough to comment on the problems between the pope and Queen Elizabeth I, but he believed in the teachings of the Church.

Robert Meyler, a Catholic sailor, professed the Faith and died with Matthew Lambert at Wexford, in July 1581.

Edward Cheevers, another Catholic sailor, was arrested with Robert Meyler and Patrick Cavanagh and died at Wexford, in July 1581.

Patrick Cavanagh was a sailor companion of Matthew Lambert, martyred in Wexford, July 1581.

Margaret Ball, a widowed housewife of Dublin, was arrested for giving priests sanctuary in her home. She was turned over to the English by her apostate son and was thrown into Dublin Castle dungeon. There, she died from abuse and torment in 1584.

Maurice McKenraghty, chaplain of Lord Dermot, was arrested in 1585. He was given the opportunity to deny papal supremacy but refused and was martyred at Clonmel on April 20, 1585.

Dominic Collins, S.J., a Jesuit lay brother living at Youghal, was arrested and tortured by the English, who demanded that he divulge the plans of the Spanish to invade England. Dominic knew of no such plans, and he refused to deny the Holy See. He was hanged at Youghal on October 31, 1602.

Conor O'Devany, O.F.M., Franciscan bishop of Down and Connor, Ireland, was arrested with Patrick O'Loughbrain, O.F.M. The two were tortured, then martyred in Dublin on February 1, 1612.

Patrick O'Loughbrain — see Conor O'Devany, above.

Francis Taylor was the son of a wealthy, landed family of Swords and a merchant of Dublin. In 1595, he became Lord Mayor. He was elected to Parliament but his victory was overturned, and he was thrown into prison. He was martyred for the Faith on January 30, 1621, after seven years of imprisonment and torment.

Peter Higgins, O.P., a Dominican priest of Dublin, was well liked by people of all faiths. He was arrested in the furor of wild rumors following the Insurrection of 1641. Dublin was wracked by rumors that Protestants had been massacred in Ulster at the instigation of priests. Peter died in Dublin on March 23, 1642, innocent of any crime except his loyalty to the Church.

Terence Albert, O.P., Dominican bishop of Emily, Ireland, was captured by Ireton, Cromwell's son-in-law. Terence was visiting Limerick when Ireton's forces took the town. He was arrested and condemned for encouraging the Irish defense and died in Limerick on October 31, 1651.

John Kearney, O.F.M., a Franciscan priest, defied the ban on priests issued by Cromwell. John was arrested and hanged at Clonmel, County Tipperary, on March 11, 1653.

William Tirry, O.S.A., an Augustinian priest, was caught in his vestments and arrested in 1654. Standing on the scaffold, William urged the Irish to endure all things and to remain steadfast to the faith. He was martyred on May 2, 1654.

Pope John Paul II beatified the Martyrs of Ireland on September 27, 1992, declaring:

> And how can we fail to sing the praises of seventeen Irish Martyrs being beatified today? . . . We admire them for their personal courage. We thank them for the example of their fidelity which is more than an example: it is a heritage of the Irish people and a responsibility to be lived up to in every

age. In a decisive hour, a whole people chose to stand firmly by its covenant with God: "All the words which the Lord has spoken we will do" (Ex. 24:3). Along with St. Oliver Plunkett, the new Beati comprise but a small part of the host of Irish Martyrs of Penal Times. The religious and political turmoil through these witnesses lived was marked by grave intolerance on every side. Their victory lay precisely in going to death with no hatred in the hearts. They lived and died for love. Many of them publicly forgave all those who had contributed in any way to their martyrdom. The Martyrs significance for today lies in the fact that their testimony shattered the vain claim to live one's life or to build a model society without an integral vision of our human destiny, without reference to our eternal calling, without transcendence. The Martyrs exhort succeeding generations of Irish men and women: "Fight the good fight of the Faith; take hold of the eternal life to which you were called . . . keep the commandment unstained and free from reproach until the appearing of our Lord Jesus Christ" (1 Tim 6:12-14).

✠

Martyrs of Japan (December 11, 1632)

Martin of St. Nicholas Lumbreras and Melchior Sanchez

These Augustinian missionary priests dared to penetrate the islands of Japan, a nation sealed against the Faith by the Tokugawa Shogunate. For this evangelical ministry, they gave their lives.

Martin was born in Zaragoza, Spain, circa 1592. Ordained an Augustinian priest, he was sent to Japan, where the Order had conducted missions. Melchior Sanchez, also an ordained Augustinian priest, was born in Granada, Spain, in 1599. Both men had served in the Augustinian mission in Manila, the Philippines. With the deaths of missionaries in Japan in 1629, Martin and Melchior were sent out as replacements. They disguised themselves as merchants and carried out their labors among the Christians in the mountains near Nagasaki.

When Melchior became ill, the missionaries went to the city seeking medical assistance. The military forces of Shogun Iemitsu Tokugawa, a formidable foe of Europeans and the Church, arrested them there. Iemitsu was relentless in pursuing Catholic missionaries and the faithful, and cruelty and prolonged horrors were the hallmarks of imprisonment during his reign. Martin and Melchior, imprisoned in Nagasaki, were subjected to almost inhuman tortures before being martyred by being burned alive on December 11, 1632.

Pope John Paul II beatified Martin and Melchior, the Martyrs of Japan, on April 23, 1989, announcing:

> Dear brothers and sisters, the new Blesseds Martin and Melchior are mature fruits of the missionary and evangelizing spirit that has characterized the Church in Spain. Born into the bosom of deeply Christian families and Saragossa and Granada, they left everything to follow Christ. These two martyrs, glory of the Church and the Augustinian family, should be a challenge and a stimulus that arouses in Spanish families that Christian vitality which enables the message of salvation to reach the farthest corners of the earth. May these values not be lost! May such a witness of faith which honors and exalts Spanish history not be forgotten!

⊹

Martyrs of La Rochelle (1794)
John Souzy and Companions

These martyrs refused to support or even recognize the edicts of the French Revolution and its authorities. As a result of their refusal, in 1794, 829 priests and religious were arrested and forced to board two slave ships anchored in the Charente River, near Rochefort. The Martyrs of La Rochelle, also called the Martyrs of Pontini di Rochefort, include John Souzy, Gabriel Pergaud, and sixty-two companions.

These holy and religious exiles (officially they were considered such, but the deportation was not to a place) were crowded into small boats. They sailed in darkness and in inhumane and unsupportable conditions, aggravated by the fact that every morning the crew burned coal (tar), which made the air unbreathable. During the journey, they were forced to remain below decks without food or water. In addition, they were subjected to brutalities and the mockery of the sailors. Prayers or signs of faith were forbidden. Nearly all of the martyrs were stricken by contagious diseases. Deprived of any medical assistance, many prisoners served as nurses for their companions. Among the martyred were:

John Souzy – A priest from La Rochelle, named vicar general of the victims when they were deported. John died after ten months and was buried on Madame Island. His companions included thirteen priests from French dioceses and twelve members of religious congregations.

Gabriel Pergaud – An Augustinian martyr of La Rochelle, Gabriel was born on October 29, 1752, at Saint-Priest-la-Plaine (Creuse), France. He entered the Canons Regular of St. Augustine and took his vows in 1769. Gabriel served in many capacities, including prior of the abbey of Beaulieu (Côtes-d'Arnior). A man of faith and character, he opposed the extreme measures of the government. He reportedly died on July 21, 1794, along with 574 other victims.

Pope John Paul II beatified the Martyrs of La Rochelle on October 1, 1995, declaring:

> This morning, dear brother and sisters, we are thinking of sixty-four French priests who died with hundreds of others on the "decks of Rochefort." . . . They gradually let themselves be identified with the sacrifice of Christ, which they celebrated by virtue of their ordination. Here they are offered to our gaze as a living symbol of the power of Christ, who acts in human weaknesses.

(See also Martyrs of the Christian Brothers.)

✠

Martyrs of Madrid (July 20, 1936)
Rita Dolores Pujatte Sanchez
and Frances of the Sacred Heart of Jesus Aldea Araujo

Rita Dolores Pujatte Sanchez was born in Aspe, Spain, on February 19, 1853, the daughter of Antonio Pujatte and Luisa Sanchez. She had four siblings and was raised in the Faith. As a young woman, Rita Dolores was a catechist and charity worker and a tertiary Franciscan. In 1888, she entered the Sisters of Charity of the Sacred Heart of Jesus, becoming Superior General in 1900 and serving until 1928. She retired to St. Susanna's College in Madrid; by 1936, she was infirm and blind.

Frances of the Sacred Heart of Jesus Aldea Araujo was born in Somolinos, Spain, on December 17, 1881. Orphaned when young, she was a boarding student at St. Susanna's until she entered the congregation at age eighteen. She became a teacher and served as assistant, then General Secretary, of the Sisters of Charity of the Sacred Heart of Jesus.

On July 20, 1936, revolutionary military forces attacked St. Susanna's College, and Rita Dolores and Frances were first allowed to leave because of their age. However, no more than two hours after they took refuge in a nearby apartment, they were taken prisoners by the rebels. They were brought forcibly to a site near Canillejas, a suburb of Madrid, and there, they were shot.

An autopsy performed the next day reported that their remains emitted a fragrant perfume and that rigor mortis had not set in. In 1940, when exhumed as part of the opening of their Cause, their remains still had not decomposed and had lifelike appearances. The remains of Rita Dolores and Frances, still incorrupt, were enshrined in the college of the congregation in 1954.

Pope John Paul II beatified the Martyrs of Madrid on May 10, 1998, declaring:

> The supreme commandment of the Lord had taken deep root during the years of their religious consecration, which they lived in fidelity to the congregation's charism. Their example is a call to all Christians to love as Christ loves, even amid the greatest difficulties.

✠

Martyrs of the Marianist Congregation (September-October, 1936)
Educators and Martyrs

The Martyrs of the Marianist Congregation are three Marianist educators of Ciudad Real, Spain, who were among the countless victims of Communist leadership and hatred for the Church. Carlos Eraña Guruceta, Fidel Fuido, and Jesús Hita were slain by the rebel militias.

Carlos Eraña Guruceta was born in Arechavaleta (Guipuzcoa), Spain, on November 2, 1884. He entered the Marianists, and made his perpetual vows in 1908. Carlos accepted teaching assignments in the congregation's educational institutions and was principal in several schools. He was at the Colegio de Nuestra Señora de Pilar in Madrid when civil war exploded across Spain. In 1936, Carlos went to Alcaros, Ciudad Real, where he had served originally. He discovered many other Marianists in hiding, as the religious Orders of Spain had been suppressed.

Carlos began to aid these fellow religious, enlisting the assistance of former students in amassing the necessary havens and funds. He continued working until September 6, when he was arrested by troops of the Popular Army. The former seminary in the city had been turned into a prison, and Carlos was taken there. He remained a captive for twelve days, standing as a model of faith and true resolve. On September 18, in the company of seven laymen, Carlos was taken into the seminary yard and shot to death.

Jesús Hita was born in Calahorra, Spain, on April 17, 1900. He entered the Marianists and was accepted as a lay brother, making his final vows on August 26, 1928. During the war, Jesús was at the Colegio de Nuestra Señora del Pilar in Madrid, but went to Ciudad Real to teach during the summer. In the summer of 1936, anticlerical militias took over religious facilities and seized members of religious Orders, and Jesús was forced to seek refuge with a Catholic family in the town to avoid arrest. Seeing the desecration and persecutions, he practiced penitential acts in reparation. He was arrested and executed on September 25, with Juan Pedro, Pablo María, and two priests. Their bodies were thrown into a well.

Fidel Fuido was born in Yécora, Spain, on April 24, 1880, and entered the Society of Mary, making his final vows in 1904. He then taught at Colegio Nuestra Señora del Pilar, in Madrid, from 1910-1933. A respected archaeologist with a doctorate in history, Fidel was in the Ciudad Real at the Marianist College when the persecution of the Church began. After being forced out of his seminary, he was arrested in a small boarding house and held prisoner for two months. He was set free, then arrested again and taken to the seminary, where he was executed at dawn on October 17.

Pope John Paul II beatified the Martyrs of the Marianist Congregation on May 7, 1995, proclaiming:

> As Marianists they learned how to love Our Lady intensely and . . . with gentleness they went to their martyrdom, the supreme act of surrender to Jesus and Mary, and like others before them, they died forgiving, thus certain of following the footsteps of Christ himself.

✠

Martyrs of Motril (1936)
Vincente Soler and Companions

The Martyrs of Motril were Augustinian Recollects and others who died as martyrs during the Spanish Civil War.

The martyred Augustinian Recollects were: Vicente Soler, Deogracias Palacios, León Inchausti, José Rada, Vicente Pinilla, Julián Moreno, and José Ricardo Díez. Also martyred was Manuel Martin Sierra, a Spanish priest.

Members of the Augustinian Recollect house, located on the southern coast of Spain, the martyrs were arrested by the violently anti-Catholic Popular Front, which had taken over the region. After being humiliated and abused for their faith, the martyrs were shot to death between July 25 and August 15, 1936, at Motril. Manuel Martín Sierra also was executed.

Pope John Paul II beatified the Martyrs of Motril on March 7, 1999. He praised the courageous fidelity of these individuals to Christ and to the faith.

✠

Martyrs of the Passionist Congregation (July 1936)
Martyrs of Daimiel

The Martyrs of the Passionist Congregation, led by Niceforo of Jesus and Mary Tejerina, were victims of the anti-Catholic rebel forces in the Spanish Civil War. This group of twenty-six martyrs was composed mostly of young men between the ages of eighteen and twenty-one, studying at the Passionist formation house in Daimeil, Spain. The six priests, four lay brothers, and fifteen Passionist students were under the direction of Niceforo.

On the night of July 21, 1936, armed Communist rebel militia troops surrounded the Passionist monastery at Daimiel and the occupants were forced to evacuate to a local cemetery. Destined for immediate execution or to be buried alive, the Passionists were spared by the local mayor. Even so, the students and their Passionist instructors bid one another goodbye, knowing full well the fate that awaited those charged with the crime of "being religious."

Niceforo was an inspiration to the students and the Passionist family. On the night when they were arrested, he declared, "Beloved sons and brothers, this is our Gethsemane. In its weak part, nature faints away and loses courage. However, Jesus Christ is with us. He is going to give us himself who is strength for the weak. An angel comforted Jesus. It is Jesus Christ himself who will comfort and sustain us. In a few moments we shall be with Christ. Inhabitants of Calvary, go on and die for Christ! It is my task to encourage you, but I myself am encouraged by your example!"

Niceforo was killed in Manzanares on July 23, 1936, with five students: José Estalayo Garcia, Epifanio Sierra Conde, Fulgencio Calvo Sanchez, Abilio Ramos Ramos, and Zacarias Fernandez Crespo. On the same day in Carabanchel Bajo, Fr. Germano Perez Gimenez, Fr. Felipe Valcabado Granada, and Brothers Anacario Benito Nozal and Felipe Ruiz Fraile died with students Maurilio Macho Rodriguez, José Oses Sainz, Julio Mediavilla Concejero, José Ruiz Martínez and Laurino Proano Cuesta.

On July 25, 1936, Fr. Pedro Lergo Redondo was executed at Urda with Br. Benito Solana Ruiz and student Feliz Ugalde Iruzun. Fr. Juan Pedro Bengoa

Aranguren and Br. Pablo Leoz Portillo were martyred on September 25 at Carrion de Calatrava.

On October 23, 1936, the remaining martyrs, Fr. Ildefonso Garcia Nozal, Fr. Justiniano Cuesta Redondo, and students Enfracio de Celis Salinas, Tomas Cuartero Garcia, Honorino Carracedo Ramos, and José Cuartero Garcia, were killed in Manzanares.

Pope John Paul II beatified the Martyrs of the Passionist Congregation on October 1, 1989, declaring:

> The majority of them, young men between eighteen and twenty-one years of age, lived dreaming of the priesthood, but the Lord ordained that their first Mass should be their own holocaust. Now we exalt them and give glory to Christ, who has associated them to the Cross. "The Lord loves the just . . . and sustains the orphan and widow, the way of the wicked he thwarts. The Lord reigns for ever" (Ps 145[146]:9-10).

✠

Martyrs of the Piarist Congregation – see Martyrs of the Scalopian Congregation

✠

Martyrs of Plock (1939-1945)
Polish Victims of Nazi Brutality

The Martyrs of Plock, including Archbishop Antoni Julian Nowowiejski of Plock, are 108 victims of Nazi brutality in Poland during World War II. Three of the martyrs were bishops, fifty-two were diocesan priests, three were seminarians, twenty-six were religious priests, eight were religious women, and nine were lay people. Such devout Catholics were deemed dangerous elements by the Nazi occupation forces.

Some of the new Blesseds suffered martyrdom for being in solidarity with the Jews, such as Sr. Ewa Noiszewska and Sr. Martha Wolowska, who were shot in Slomin on December 19, 1942, for protecting Jewish children. Sr. Klemensa Staszewska was killed in Auschwitz for having hidden Jewish girls in a convent.

Of the 108 martyrs, sixty-two were killed immediately and violently, while forty-six died after undergoing torture, forced starvation, and inhuman medical experiments. The majority (seventy-eight) died in the Dachau and Auschwitz concentration camps:

Adam Bargielski, priest (1903-1942); Aleksy Sobaszek, priest (1895-1942); Alfons Mazurek, friar,priest (1891-1944, shot to death in Nawojowa Gora); Alicja Maria Jadwiga Kotowska, sister (1899-1939); Alojzy Liguda, friar, priest (1898-1942); Anastazy Jakub Pankiewicz, friar, priest (1882-1942); Anicet Koplinski, priest, friar (1875-1941); Antoni Beszta-Borowski, priest (1880-1943); Antoni Julian Nowowiejski (1858-1941); Antoni Leszczewicz, friar,priest (1890-1943); Antoni Rewera, priest (1868-1942); Antoni Swiadek, priest (1909-25.1.1945); Antoni Zawistowski, priest (1882-1942); Boleslaw Strzelecki,priest (1896-1941); Bronislaw Komorowski, priest (1889-1940); Bronislaw Kostkowski, alumnus (1915-1942); Brunon Zembol, friar (1905-1922); Czeslaw Jozwiak (1919-1942); Dominik Jedrzejewski, priest (1886-1942); Edward Detkens, priest (1885-1942); Edward Grzymala, priest (1906-1942); Edward Kazmierski (1919-1942); Edward Klinik (1919-1942); Emil Szramek, priest (1887-1942); Ewa Noiszewska, sister (1885-1942); Fidelis Chojnacki, friar (1906-1942); Florian Stepniak, friar, priest (1912-1942); Franciszek Dachtera, priest (1910-1942); Franciszek Drzewiecki, priest (1908-1942); Franciszek Kesy (1920-1942); Franciszek Rogaczewski, priest (1892-1940); Franciszek Roslaniec, priest (1889-1942); Franciszek Stryjas, father of a family, (1882-); Grzegorz Boleslaw Frackowiak, friar (1911-1943); Henryk Hlebowicz, priest (1904-1941); Henryk Kaczorowski, priest (1888-1942); Henryk Krzysztofik, friar, priest (1908-1942); Hilary Pawel Januszewski, friar, priest (1907-1945); Jan Antonin Bajewski, Franciscan friar, priest (1915-1941); Jan Nepomucen Chrzan, priest (1885-1942); Jarogniew Wojciechowski (1922-1942); Jerzy Kaszyra, friar,priest (1910-1943); Jozef Achilles Puchala, friar, priest (1911-1943); Jozef Cebula, friar, priest (1902-1941); Jozef Czempiel, priest (1883-1942); Jozef Innocenty Guz, friar, priest (1890-1940); Jozef Jankowski, friar,priest, (1910-1941, Jozef Kowalski, friar, priest (1911-1942); Jozef Kurzawa, priest (1910-1940); Jozef Kut, priest (1905-1942); Jozef Pawlowski, priest (1890-9.1.1942); Jozef Stanek, friar, priest (1916-1944); Jozef Straszewski, priest (1885-1942); Jozef Zaplata, friar (1904-1945); Julia Rodzinska, sister (1899-1945); Karol Herman Stepien, friar, priest (1910-1943); Katarzyna Celestyna Faron, sister (1913-1944); Kazimierz Gostynski, priest (1884-1942); Kazimierz Grelewski, priest (1907-1942); Kazimierz Sykulski, priest (1882-1942); Krystyn Gondek, friar, priest (1909-1942); Leon Nowakowski, priest (1913-1939); Leon Wetmanski, bishop (1886-1941); Ludwik Gietyngier, priest (1904-1941); Ludwik Mzyk, friar, priest (1905-1940); Ludwik Pius Bartosik, Franciscan friar, priest (1909-1941); Maksymilian Binkiewicz, priest (1913-1942); Marcin Oprzadek, friar (1884-

1942); Maria Antonina Kratochwil, sister (1881-1942); Maria Klemensa Staszewska, sister (1890-1943); Marian Gorecki, priest (1903-22.3.1940); Marian Konopinski, priest (1907-1943 Marian Skrzypczak, priest (1909-1939); Marianna Biernacka laywoman (1888-1943); Marta Wolowska, sister (1879-1942); Michal Czartoryski, friar, priest (1897-1944); Michal Ozieblowski, priest (1900-1942); Michal Piaszczynski, priest (1885-1940); Michal Wozniak, priest (1875-1942); Mieczyslaw Bohatkiewicz, priest (1904-1942); Mieczyslawa Kowalska, siter (1902-1941); Narcyz Putz, priest (1877-1942); Narcyz Turchan, friar, priest (1879-1942); Natalia Tulasiewicz (1906-1945); Piotr Bonifacy Z|ukowski, friar (1913-1942); Piotr Edward Dankowski, priest (1908-1942); Roman Archutowski, priest (1882-1943); Roman Sitko, priest (1880-1942); Stanislaw Kubista, friar, priest (1898-1940); Stanislaw Kubski, friar, priest (1876-1942); Stanislaw Mysakowski, priest (1896-1942); Stanislaw Pyrtek, priest (1913-4.3.1942); Stanislaw Starowieyski, father of a family (1895-1940/1); Stanislaw Tymoteusz Trojanowski, friar (1908-1942); Stefan Grelewski, priest (1899-1941); Symforian Ducki, friar (1888-1942); Tadeusz Dulny, alumnus (1914-1942); Wincenty Matuszewski, priest (1869-1940); Wladyslaw Bladzinski, friar, priest (1908-1944); Wladyslaw Demski, priest (1884-1940); Wladyslaw Goral, (bishop 1898-1945); Wladyslaw Mackowiak, priest (1910-1942); Wladyslaw Maczkowski, priest (1911-1942); Wladyslaw Miegon, priest, commandor leutnant (1892-1942); Wlodzimierz Laskowski, priest (1886-1940); Wojciech Nierychlewski, friar, priest (1903-1942); Zygmunt Pisarski, priest (1902-1943);, Zygmunt Sajna, priest (1897-1940).

Pope John Paul II beatified the Martyrs of Plock on June 13, 1999 in Warsaw, declaring:

If we rejoice today for the beatification of one hundred and eight martyrs, clergy and lay people, we do so above all because they bear witness to the victory of Christ, the gift which restores hope. As we carry out this solemn act, there is in a way rekindled in us the certainty that, independently of the circumstances, we can achieve complete victory in all things through the One who has loved us (cf. *Rom* 8:37). The blessed martyrs cry to our hearts: Believe in God who is love! Believe in him in good times and bad! Awaken hope! May it produce in you the fruit of fidelity to God in every trial!

✠

Martyrs of Podlasie (1874)

Vincent Lewoniuk and Twelve Companions

These martyrs were Byzantine-rite Catholics living in Podlasie, in the eastern region of modern Poland. In 1874, Czar Alexander II of Russia controlled that section of Poland; he intended to suppress the eparchy of Chelm and incorporate all Eastern-rite Catholics loyal to the pope into the Orthodox Church.

Agents of the Czarist government invaded the Catholic parish church of Pratulin, now in the Diocese of Siedlce, Podlasie, Poland, in 1873, and any devotional object deemed "Latin" was torn down and removed. After Christmas of that year, the Catholic priest left the area, and the parish was closed down. The local parish women kept the keys to prevent the Russian-approved priest from taking charge when he arrived on the scene. As a result, Kutanin, a Czarist local governor, was called in by the embattled priest to settle the situation and to install him as the approved pastor. On January 24, 1874, Kutanin arrived with a Cossack unit to perform the installation. He and his troops were faced by the peasants of the area, intent on keeping their parish Catholic.

One after another, these peasants defied Kutanin and the Cossacks, denying the right of Russian government to interfere in their religious observances. Vincent Lewoniuk and his neighbors had heard that the parish was to become Orthodox. The people rejected the Order, despite promises of favors from the czar and threats for disobedience. They had dressed for the occasion, aware of the peril and the possible result of their defense of the Faith. No threats or actions halted their defiance. The officer in charge, quite disturbed by the spontaneous demonstration and the zeal, ordered his soldiers to prepare their weapons.

The people knelt in the street, singing hymns and repeating, "It is sweet to die for the faith." Vincent (Wincenty) Lewoniuk, 26, was the first martyr hit by rifle fire, followed by Daniel Karmasz and Ignacy Franczuk. Lukasz Bojko died next, then Anicet Hyciuk fell. Filip Geryluk, Onufry Wasyluk, Konstanty Bojko, Michael Wawryszuk and Konstanty Lukaszuk died of bullet wounds or the bayonet. Jan Andrzejuk died soon after being carried home. Hawryluk and Bartlomiej Osypiuk also were martyred. Some 180 survivors were chained and imprisoned.

The martyrs were all laymen, most of them married with families; their ages ranged from nineteen to fifty, although most were in their twenties. All thirteen were shot to death before their horrified families and friends.

Their bodies were buried by the Russians, and the families were forbidden to show them any honor. Czar Alexander II suppressed the eparchy of Chelm the following year, but he did not erase the glory of the martyrs or the faith.

Pope John Paul II beatified The Martyrs of Podlasie on October 6, 1996, and greeted a group of Ukrainian pilgrims, declaring:

> I urge you to imitate their courageous perseverance in the Faith and to follow their fervent devotion to the Blessed Virgin.

The Holy Father also honored the martyrs at a special Mass in Siedlce.

⊹

Martyrs of the Scalopian Congregation (1936)
Dionysius Pamplona and Companions

The Scalopians or Piarists — also called the Clerks Regular of the Pious Schools — were founded in 1597 by St. Joseph Calasanctius (Calasanz). In 1621, the Scalopians were made a religious congregation by Pope Gregory XV (r. 1621-1623). Called by some the Poor Clerks of the Mother of God, or the Paulines, the Scalopians were true pioneers in the apostolate of education. As a result, their houses and institutions in Spain drew the wrath of the revolutionaries during the Spanish Civil War.

Dionysius Pamplona and twelve Scalopian companions died as a result of their dedication. Dionysius was a priest, born in 1868 in Calamocha, Teruel, Spain. He was director of the Peralta de la Sol School in Huesca and performed other roles for the congregation. In 1936, he was arrested as a priest, but he escaped from prison in order to go to the parish church to consume all of the consecrated hosts, endangered by the atheist militias. He was recaptured and martyred on July 25, 1936, near Monzon prison. His companions were:

Emmanuel Segura, a priest and educator, was born in 1881 in Almonacid de la Sierra in Saragossa province, Spain. Emmanuel was a novice master in Peralta del Sol. He was martyred on July 23, 1936.

David Carlos, a Scalopian brother from Asorta, Navarre, Spain, was offered his freedom if he would abandon his religious habit but refused. David was slain on July 28, 1936.

Enrico Canadell, a native of Olot, Gerona, Italy, was born in 1890. Ordained as a Scalopian, he was especially devoted to the Holy Eucharist. Enrico was martyred near Castelfullit on August 17, 1936.

Faustino Oteiza, a priest and educator, was born in Aygui, in Navarre, in 1890. He was particularly devoted to the Blessed Virgin. Faustino was slain on August 9, 1936.

Florentino Felipe, a Scalopian lay brother, was born in Alquierzar, in Huesca, Spain, in 1856. He was imprisoned for two weeks while suffering from a severe stomach ailment. He was martyred on August 9, 1936.

Matteas Cardona, a newly ordained Scalopian priest, was born in Vallibona, Castellón, Spain, in 1902. Matteas was devoted and calm throughout his ordeal, and was martyred on August 20, 1936, near his hometown.

Francesco Carceller, a member of a devout family, was born in Forcall, Castellón, Spain, in 1901. He was an ordained priest and a dedicated educator. Francesco was martyred on October 2, 1936.

Ignazio Casanovas, born in Igualada, Barcelona, Spain, in 1893, was noted for his piety and goodness. Ignazio was slain on September 16, 1936.

Carlo Navarro, a newly ordained Scalopian priest, was born in Torrente, Valencia, in 1911. He was martyred on September 22, 1939, calling out: *Viva Cristo Rey!* ("Long live Christ the King!") and invoking the Virgin Mary.

José Ferrer, a Scalopian priest, was born in 1904 in Algemesi, Valencia, Spain. He served as an organist in the cathedral of Albarracín and was noted for his deep piety. José died on December 9, 1936.

Juan Agramunt. A Scalopian priest and educator, was born in 1907 in Almazora, Castellón, Spain. Juan was kept in prison for weeks and was martyred on August 13, 1936.

Alfredo Parte, a Scalopian priest from Cirreluelo de Bricia, Bourgos, Spain, was singled out for a terrible martyrdom. He died on December 27, 1936, after refusing to abjure the Faith and his membership in the Scalopians.

Pope John Paul II beatified the Martyrs of the Scalopian Congregation on October 1, 1995, declaring:

> Dionysius Pamplona and his companion martyrs were not the heroes of a human war, but teachers of youth, who, because of their status as religious and teachers, faced their tragic destiny as authentic witnesses to the faith, giving us with their martyrdom the last lesson of their life.

✠

Martyrs of the Sisters of Christian Doctrine (1936)
Mother Angeles de San José Lloret Martí and Sixteen Companions

These nuns continued their life of prayer even after their Generalate convent was closed. The religious women went into hiding and tried to maintain their spiritual routines. They were discovered and arrested, and spent four months in prison where they calmly and openly lived as a devout community despite the humiliations and abuses. They even knitted jerseys for their captors. Mother Angeles de San José and her nuns were martyred as a community in the fall of 1936.

Pope John Paul II beatified the Martyrs of the Sisters of Christian Doctrine on October 1, 1995, declaring:

> Mother Angeles de San José gathered, in a single apartment, members who had no families or friends to take them in. There, they lived fraternal charity, discovering how persecution, poverty, and suffering are all ways that lead to God ... These sisters, practicing what they had so often passed on in teaching catechism, spent their last few months sewing clothes for those who put an end to their lives. Their death then and their glorification now proclaim the power of the risen Christ and the need to dedicate oneself to the task of evangelization. With them, the communities of Valencia and Cataluña add new names to their martyrology.

✠

Martyrs of the Spanish Civil War (1936-1939)
José Aparacio Sanz and Companions

These martyrs are 233 priests, religious, and lay people from various dioceses and districts of Spain.

The martyrdoms began in 1936 and continued until April 1939, when Spain endured the most extensive religious persecution since the time of the Roman Empire. Before it ended, an estimated 10,000 martyrs were slain. Thirteen bishops, 4,184 diocesan priests and seminarians, 2,365 men religious, 283 religious women, and thousands of devout laymen and women were slain by the Communists. Some thirty-seven dioceses of Spain were overrun and victimized by the Communist rebels.

José Aparacio Sanz, archpriest of Enguera, was slain on December 29, 1936, at Picadero de Paterno, along with about thirty-seven diocesan priests of the Archdiocese of Valencia who suffered martyrdom at the same time.

Laywomen of the Catholic Action in Valencia, along with men and youths of Catholic Action, also died.

In Zaragosa, Dominicans and diocesan priests were slain, and the Order of Friars Minor in Barcelona and other areas suffered barbaric treatment and death. The Order of Friars Minor Capuchin and the Capuchin Sisters of St. Clare also faced martyrdom. A Discalced Augustinian, Josefa de la Purificación María Ferragud, was slain on October 25, 1936.

The Society of Jesus had twelve martyrdoms, and the Salesians of St. John Bosco lost thirty members. Women religious slain include members of the Daughters of Mary, Help of Christians; the Carmelite Sisters of Charity; the Servants of Mary; the Sisters of the Pious Schools; the Claritians; the Little Sisters of the Abandoned Elderly; and the Third Order Capuchins of the Holy Family. The Third Order Capuchins of Our Lady of Sorrows lost priests and brothers, and the Priests of the Sacred Heart of Jesus had martyrs in several areas of Spain.

These priests, religious, and laity are listed as martyrs because they died at the hands of cruel executioners who abused, reviled, and tormented them. Their deaths represent all sectors of the Church in Spain, as the exact number of martyrs is unknown. Other groups are represented under specific titles.

The list of those who have been raised to the glory of the altars for confessing their faith and dying for it is long. There are thirty-eight priests from the Archdiocese of Valencia, with a large group of men and women, members of Catholic Action, also from Valencia; eighteen Dominicans and two priests from the Archdiocese of Zaragoza; four Friars Minor and six Friars Minor Conventual; twelve Friars Minor Capuchin with five Capuchin women religious and a Discalced Augustinian; eleven Jesuits with a young lay man; thirty Salesians and two Daughters of Mary, Help of Christians; nineteen Third Order Capuchins of Our Lady of Sorrows with a laywoman cooperator; one Priest of the Sacred Heart of Jesus (Dehonian); the chaplain of La Salle College of Bonanova, Barcelona, with five Brothers of the Christian Schools; twenty-four Carmelite Sisters of Charity; one Servite Sister; six Sisters of the Pious Schools with two laywomen cooperators from Uruguay, who were the first Blesseds of this Latin American country; two Little Sisters of the Abandoned Elderly; three Third Order Capuchins of the Holy Family; a Claretian Missionary Sister; and lastly, Francisco Castelló y Aleu, a young member of Catholic Action in Lleida.

Pope John Paul II beatified the Martyrs of the Spanish Civil War on March 11, 2001, announcing:

They were men and women of all ages and states; diocesan priests, men and women religious, the fathers and mothers of families, young lay people. They were killed for being Christians, for their faith in Christ, for being active members of the Church. Before dying, all of them, as stated in the canonical processes for their declaration as martyrs, forgave their executioners from their hearts.

How many examples of serenity and Christian hope! All these new Blesseds and many other anonymous martyrs paid with their blood for the hatred of the Faith and of the Church which was unleashed by the religious persecution and the outbreak of the Civil War, the immense tragedy that Spain experienced in the twentieth century. During those terrible years many priests, religious, and lay people were killed simply because they were active members of the Church.

The new Blesseds being raised to the altars today were not involved in political or ideological struggles, nor did they want to be concerned with them. This is well known to many of you who are their relatives and are taking part in this beatification today with great joy. They died solely for religious motives. Now, by this solemn proclamation of their martyrdom, the Church wishes to recognize these men and women as examples of courage and constancy in faith, helped by God's grace. For us they are models of consistency with the truth they professed, while at the same time they honour the noble Spanish people and the Church.

✠

Martyrs of Thailand (1940)
Native Catholic Martyrs

The Martyrs of Thailand were seven native Catholics slain in December 1940, in Songkhon, a community of rice farmers on the Mekong River. During that era, foreign missionaries were being exiled from the region, and no religious or cultural pluralism was tolerated. The local police coerced many into abjuring the Faith, going door-to-door in each village seeking religious sympathizers.

Philip Siphong, called "the man of oak," was the lay religious leader of Songkhon, and he followed behind the police, restoring the Faith throughout the village. Born in Nonseng in 1907, he married Maria Thong and had five children. In Songkhou, Philip taught in the school and was a catechist, replacing the exiled parish priest as leader. He was arrested because of his zeal and success and was shot in a wooded area near the village on December 16.

Agnes Phila, a member of the Congregation of the Lovers of the Cross, led the remaining six martyrs in their ordeals. Born in Ban in 1909, she became a teaching sister of her congregation. Agnes served in various capacities and was appointed Superior of the Songkhon Catholic school in 1932. She served faithfully, and during the persecution encouraged the local Catholics to stand firm. She wrote a defense of the Faith before dying, stating, "You may kill us, but you cannot kill the Church and you cannot kill God."

With her was **Sr. Lucia Khambang,** who was sent to Songkhon in 1940. Born in Viengkuk in 1917, she had entered the Lovers of the Cross Congregation in 1931. Lucia died on December 26. **Agatha Phutta,** an unmarried woman born in 1881, helped in the kitchen of the mission. Refusing to deny the Faith, she was martyred at age fifty-nine. Mission aides **Bibiana Khamphai,** age fifteen, and **Maria Phon,** age fourteen, were slain at the local cemetery.

Cecilia Butsi, the last of the Thai martyrs, was just sixteen when she was martyred. She spoke openly at a public meeting, defying the police and defending the Faith. She died with the others.

Pope John Paul II beatified the Martyrs of Thailand on October 22, 1989, declaring:

> Today, Mission Sunday, we celebrate the beatification of the holy Martyrs of Thailand. In union with the whole Church, we give thanks to the most Blessed Trinity for the witness and example that those martyrs have given to the entire Christian world. It is significant that their generous sacrifice was made within a Christian community that while still young, was prepared to bear witness to Jesus Christ and to the power of his love with full self-giving: "You shall be my witnesses . . . to the end of the earth" (Acts 1:8).

⊹

Martyrs of Ukraine (20th century)

Mykola Charnetsky and Twenty-Four Companions

These martyrs of the Ukraine belonged to the Greek Catholic Church, with the exception of Leonid Fedorov, and were all martyrs for the Faith during the severe persecutions by the Communist authorities dominating Ukraine throughout the Soviet era. The martyrs also endured persecution by the Russian Orthodox Church. The individual members of the group are:

Bishop Mykola Charnetsky (December 14, 1884 – April 2, 1959)

Bishop Mykola Charnetsky was born in the village of Semakivtsi, Horo-denka District, and was ordained to the priesthood on October 2, 1909. After earning a doctorate in dogmatic theology in Rome, he became a spiritual director and professor at the seminary in Stanislaviv (now called Ivano-Frankivsk). In 1919, he entered the Redemptorist Fathers in Zboiska, near Lviv. In 1926, Pope Pius XI appointed Mykola to the post of Apostolic Visitor to Greek Catholics in Volyn and Polissia. Eventually named the Apostolic Exarch of Volyn and Pidlassia, he labored to defend the rights of Greek Catholics. As a result, on April 11, 1945 he was arrested by the NKVD (KGB) and sentenced to six years of forced labor in Siberia. He was later released and died in Lviv.

Sr. Laurentia Herasymiv (September 31, 1911 – August 28, 1952)

Sr. Laurentia was born in the village of Rudnyky, Lviv District and entered the Sisters of St. Joseph in 1931. In 1951, she was arrested by the NKVD (KGB) for being a Catholic and a nun and sent to Borislav. She was then exiled to Tomsk, Siberia, where she faced harsh treatment and forced labor. She was compelled to share a room with, and care for, a paralyzed prisoner, who also suffered from tuberculosis. She died from exhaustion in the Siberian village of Kharsk.

Sr. Tarsykia Matskiv (March 23, 1919 – July 17, 1944)

Sr. Tarsykia was born in the village of Khodoriv, Lviv District, and entered the Sister Servants of Mary Immaculate on May 3, 1938. Sr. Tarsykia made a private oath to her spiritual director that she would sacrifice her life for the conversion of Russia and for the good of the Church. Her oath was fulfilled when the Soviet forces entered Lviv. One of their immediate targets for punishment was the convent of the Sister Servants of Mary Immaculate. On the morning of July 17, a Russian soldier rang the convent door. When Sr. Taryskia answered the door, she was shot dead on the stoop.

Sr. Olympia Bida (1903 – January 28, 1952)

Sr. Olympia was born in the village of Tsebliv, Lviv District, and entered the Sisters of St. Joseph. She distinguished herself as an instructor of catechumens and a director of novices. Appointed Superior of the convent in the town of Kheriv, she worked to promote the Catholic Faith in the midst of Communist oppression. She was arrested with two other sisters in 1951 and, eventually, exiled to the Tomsk region of Siberia. In the camp, she continued to serve as a Superior, maintaining the religious community in the face of the immense sufferings. The harsh conditions and forced labor eventually took away her strength; she died still urging her fellow sisters to pray.

Volodymyr Pryjma (July 17, 1906 – June 26, 1941)

Volodymyr was born in the village of Stradch, Yavoriv District. Known for his musical abilities, he was appointed the cantor and choir director in the village church of Stradch. Volodymyr was arrested by agents of the NKVD (later the KGB) and mercilessly tortured. The NKVD finally murdered him, along with Fr. Nicholas Conrad, in the forest near their village.

Bishop Nicetas Budka (June 7, 1877 – October 1, 1949)

Bishop Nicetas Budka was born in the village of Dobromirka, Zbarazh District. He was ordained in 1905, after graduating from theology in Vienna and Innsbruck. After distinguished service in pastoral ministry, he was consecrated a bishop in Lviv on October 14, 1912. That same year he was appointed by the Holy See as the Apostolic Exarch in Canada. In 1928, he was named vicar general of the Metropolitan Chapter of Lviv. He was arrested by the Communists and sentenced on April 11, 1945 to eight years in a concentration camp in Karaganda, Kazakhstan. There, he endured immense suffering and died without ever returning home.

Bishop Hryhory Lakota – (January 31, 1883 – November 12, 1950)

Bishop Hryhory Lakota was born in the village of Holodivka, in Lemko Region. He was ordained to the priesthood in 1908 and earned a doctorate in theology. After serving as a professor and rector of the Greek Catholic seminary in Przemysl, he was appointed Auxiliary Bishop of Przemysl in1926. On June 9, 1946, he was arrested by the Communists and sentenced to ten years in Vorkuta, Russia. He died there as a result of the harsh conditions in the camp.

Bishop Hryhory Khomyshyn (March 25, 1867 – January 17, 1947)

Bishop Hryhory was born in the village of Hadynkivtsi, Ternopil District. Ordained to the priesthood on November 18, 1893, he studied in Vienna from 1894-1899. In 1902, he was appointed rector of the seminary in Lviv, and in 1904 appointed bishop for Stanislaviv (now Ivano-Frankivsk). In 1939, the NKVD (KGB) arrested him, but he was released. Arrested again in April 1945, he was exiled to Kyiv where he died from the cruel treatment.

Bishop Josaphat Kotsylovsky (March 3, 1876 – November 17, 1947)

Bishop Josaphat Kotsylovsky was born in the village of Pakoshivka, Lemko Region. He was ordained on October 9, 1907 and was appointed vice-rector and professor of theology at the Greek-Catholic seminary in Stanislaviv (now Ivano-Frankivsk). On September 23, 1917 he was named a bishop in Przemysl. In September 1945, the Communist regime in Poland arrested him. He was arrested a second time in 1946, and given over to the Soviet NKVD (KGB) and died a martyr in the Kyiv prison.

Bishop Simeon Lukach (July 7, 1893 – August 22, 1964)

Bishop Simeon Lukach was born in the village of Starunia, Stanislaviv Region. Ordained a priest in 1919 by Bishop Hryhory Khomyshyn, he taught moral theology at the seminary in Stanislaviv (now Ivano-Frankivsk) until April 1945, when it is believed that Bishop Hryhory secretly ordained him a bishop. In October 1949, he was arrested by the NKVD and imprisoned until February 1955. He continued to labor as an underground member of the clergy until July 1962 when he was arrested for a second time. He died in prison from the harsh conditions and from tuberculosis.

Bishop Ivan Sleziuk (January 14, 1896 – December 2, 1973)

Bishop Ivan Sleziuk was born in the village of Zhyvachiv, Stanislaviv (now Ivano-Frankivsk) and was ordained to the priesthood in 1923. In April 1945, Bishop Hryhory Khomyshyn ordained him as his coadjutor, with the right of succession as a precaution in case Bishop Khomyshyn should be arrested. However, in June 1945, Bishop Ivan was arrested and deported for ten years to the labor camp in Vorkuta, Russia. In 1950 he was transferred to the labor camp in Mordovia, Russia. Released in November 1954, he returned to Ivano-Frankivsk but was arrested again in 1962. Released in November 1968, he was regularly tortured by the KGB during required interrogations.

Fr. Leonid Feodorov (November 4, 1879 – March 7, 1935)

Fr. Leonid Feodorov was born to a Russian Orthodox family in St. Petersburg, Russia. In 1902, he departed the Orthodox seminary where he was studying and journeyed to Rome. There, he became Catholic, studied in Rome and Fribourg, and was ordained in March 1911 in the Eastern-rite in Bosnia. In 1913, he became a monk of the Studite monastery, then returned to St. Petersburg, where he was arrested and sent to Siberia. In 1917, he was released and appointed the head of the Russian Catholic Church of the Eastern-rite, with the title of Exarch. But in 1923, he was arrested a second time, sent to Solovky Islands (on the White Sea) and to Vladka, where he died.

Fr. Petro Verhun (November 18, 1890 – February 7, 1957)

Fr. Petro Verhun was born in Horodok, Lviv and was ordained on October 30, 1927. He was appointed pastor of the Greek Catholics in Berlin,

Germany and later made the Apostolic Visitor to Germany. In June 1945, he was arrested by the NKVD (KGB) and sent to Siberia where he died.

Archimandrite Clement Sheptytsky (November 17, 1869 – May 1, 1951)

Archimandrite Clement Sheptytsky, the younger brother of the Servant of God Metropolitan Andriy Sheptytsky, was born in the village of Prylbychi, Lviv. In 1911, he abandoned a promising secular career and, at the age of forty, entered the monastery of St. Theodore the Studite. He then studied in Innsbruck and in August 1915 was ordained to the priesthood. He served for some time as prior of the Studite monastery at Univ. In 1944, he became the Archimandrite (Abbot). During World War II, he gave refuge to Jews seeking to escape the Nazis. In June 1947, he was arrested by the NKVD (KGB) agents and sentenced to eight years of hard labor. He died in the Vladimir prison.

Fr. Severian Baranyk (July 18, 1889 – June 26, 1941)

Fr. Severian Baranyk entered the Krekhiv Monastery of the Order of St. Basil the Great in Krekhiv in September 1904 and made his final vows in September 1910. Ordained to the priesthood in February 1915, in 1932 he became the Prior of the Basilian monastery in Drohobych. Arrested by the NKVD (KGB), he entered a nearby prison and was tortured to death. His mutilated remains were subsequently discovered and given a proper burial.

Fr. Zenobius Kovalyk (August 18, 1903 – 1941)

Fr. Zenobius Kovalyk was born in the village of Ivachev, not far from Ternopil. He entered the Congregation of the Redemptorists and made his vows in August 1926. After studies in Belgium, he was ordained in September 1932. Assigned to the church in Volyn, he was arrested in December 1940 while preaching a sermon in honor of the Immaculate Conception of the Holy Theotokos (Mother of God). In 1941, he was martyred by the Communists in a mock crucifixion against a wall in the Bryhidky prison (formerly a convent of the Sisters of St. Bridgette), Lviv.

Fr. Roman Lysko (August 14, 1914 – October 14, 1949)

Fr. Roman Lysko was born in Horodok, Lviv and was a graduate of the Lviv Theological Academy. He and his wife labored on behalf of young people, and in August 1941 he was ordained to the priesthood. On September 9, 1949, he was arrested by the NKVD (KGB) and put into a prison in Lviv. There, he was tortured with great cruelty for the "crime" of singing Psalms in a loud voice. As a final punishment, he was walled up alive in a part of the prison.

Bishop Vasyl Velychkovsky (June 1, 1903 – June 30, 1973)

Bishop Vasyl Velychkovsky was born in Stanislaviv (now Ivano-Frankivsk) and was ordained to the priesthood in October 1925. After serving as a teacher and missionary in Volyn, in 1942 he became the prior of the monastery in Ternopil, where he was arrested in 1945 and sent to Kyiv under a death sentence. The sentence was commuted to ten years of forced labor. He returned to Lviv in 1955, and in 1963 he was consecrated bishop in Moscow. Arrested a second time in 1969, he was given a three-year sentence. Later released, he traveled to Rome, then to Winnipeg, Canada, where he died.

Fr. Mykola Tsehelskyi (December 17, 1896 – May 25, 1951)

Fr. Mykola Tsehelskyi was born in the village of Strusiv, Ternopil and ordained in April 1925. Assigned to a parish in the village of Soroko, he built a new church there and was noted for his spiritual counsel and personal holiness. In October 1946, he was arrested and sentenced to ten years in prison. Fr. Mykola was sent to the labor camps in Mordovia, where he died.

Fr. Oleksiy Zarytskyi (1913 – October 30, 1963)

Fr. Oleksiy Zarytskyi was born in the village of Biche and was ordained in 1936. In 1948, he was imprisoned by the Communists for ten years and exiled to Karaganda. After his early release in 1957, he was named Apostlic Administrator of Kazakhstan and Siberia. Soon after, however, he was again arrested and died in the Dolynka concentration camp near Karaganda.

Fr. Andriy Ishchak (September 23, 1887 – June 26, 1941)

Fr. Andriy Ishchak was born in Mykolayiv and in 1914 earned his doctorate in theology from the University of Innsbruck just before his ordination. He taught at the Lviv Theological Academy while serving in a parish in the village of Sykhiv, near Lviv. Soviet soldiers murdered him there.

Fr. Ivan Ziatyk (December 26, 1899 – January 5, 1950)

Fr. Ivan Ziatyk was born in the village of Odrekhova, near Sanok (in present day Poland) and was ordained to the priesthood in 1923. In 1935, he entered the Redemptorists. During the Nazi occupation, he was appointed prior of the monastery in Ternopil. The Communists arrested Fr. Ivan in 1950 and sent to Ozerlag, Irkutsk, Russia, where he died.

Fr. Vitaliy Bairak (February 24, 1907 – 1946)

Fr. Vitaliy Bairak was born in the village of Shvaikivtsi and entered the Basilian monastery in September 1924. He was ordained a priest in August 1933, and in 1941 was appointed prior of the Drohobych Monastery. Arrested in September 1945 by the NKVD (KGB), he was sentenced to eight years in a labor camp. He died just after Easter, 1946 from the severe beating given to him by the NKVD guards in the Drohobych prison near Liviv.

Fr. Joachim Senkivskyi (May 2, 1896 – June 29, 1941)

Fr. Joachim Senkivskyi was born in the village of Hayi Velykyi and was ordained a priest in December 1921. He earned a doctorate in theology from Innsbruck and entered the Basilian order in Krekhiv. In 1939, he was appointed prior of the monastery in Drohobych. Arrested in June 1941 by the Communists, he was boiled to death in a cauldron in the Drohobych prison.

Fr. Mykola Conrad (May 16, 1876 – June 26, 1941)

Fr. Mykola Conrad was born in the village of Strusiv and earned a doctorate in theology in Rome, before his ordination in 1899. In 1930, he was appointed to the Lviv Theological Academy and later served as a parish priest in the village of Stradch, near Yakiv. There, he was murdered by Soviet troops.

Pope John Paul II beatified the Martyrs of Ukraine in Lviv on June 27, 2001, during a pastoral visit to the Ukraine. At the beatification ceremony, Pope John Paul II declared:

> The Servants of God who are today inscribed in the Book of the Blessed represent all categories of the ecclesial community: among them are Bishops and priests, monks, nuns, and lay people. They were tested in many ways by the followers of the infamous Nazi and Communist ideologies. Aware of the sufferings which these faithful disciples of Christ were undergoing, my Predecessor Pius XII, sharing in their anguish, expressed his solidarity with those "who are persevering in faith and resisting the enemies of Christianity with the same unswerving fortitude with which their ancestors once resisted." He praised their courage in remaining "faithfully joined to the Roman Pontiff and their Pastors" (Apostolic Letter *Orientales Ecclesias*, 15 December 1952: AAS 45 [1953], 8).
>
> Strengthened by God's grace, they traveled the path of victory to the end. This is the path of forgiveness and reconciliation, the path that leads to the brilliant light of Easter, after the sacrifice of Calvary. These broth-

ers and sisters of ours are the representatives that are known out of a multitude of anonymous heroes – men and women, husbands and wives, priests and consecrated men and women, young people and old – who in the course of the twentieth century, the "century of martyrdom," underwent persecution, violence and death rather than renounce their faith.

✠

Martyrs of the Visitation Order (November 18, 1936)
Martyred Nuns of Madrid

The Martyrs of the Visitation Order were six members of the Madrid convent who remained in the house while other religious of the Order withdrew to Oronoz.

María Gabriela de Hinojosa was in charge and found the nuns a relatively safe place. A neighbor, however, reported them to the revolutionary authorities, and the nuns were arrested. When they were first interrogated, the Visitation nuns rejoiced because they knew "martyrdom is not far off."

The following night, they were taken in a van to a remote, vacant area. They were all shot to death on November 18, 1936, except for María Cecilia Cendoya Araquistain, who fled when her closest companion fell. She surrendered moments later and was executed by a firing squad five days later in Vallecas, a suburb of Madrid. The Martyrs of the Visitation Order are:

María Gabriela de Hinojosa Naveros, (born in Ahlama, Grenada, on July 24, 1872); Josefa María Barrera Izaguire (born in El Ferol, La Coruña, May 23, 1881); Teresa María Cavestany y Anduaga (born in Puerto Real, Cadiz, July 30, 1888); María Angela Olaizola Garagarza (born in Azpietia, Guipúzcoa, November 12, 1893); María Engracia Lecuona Aramburu (born in Oyarzun, Guipúzcoa, on July 2, 1897); María Inés Zudaire Galdeano (born in Echávarri, Navarre, on January 28, 1900); and María Cecilia Cendoya Araquistain (born in Azpietia, Guipúzcoa, on January 10, 1910).

Pope John Paul II beatified the Martyrs of the Visitation Order on May 10, 1998, announcing:

> We are all advancing towards the goal (the heavenly Jerusalem), where the saints and martyrs have preceded us down the centuries. On our earthly pilgrimage these brethren of ours, who passed victoriously through "great tribulations," serve as an example, incentive, and encouragement to us.

⁜

Mary of the Cross MacKillop
(January 15, 1842 – August 8, 1909)

First Australian Raised to the Honors of the Altars of the Church

Mary of the Cross MacKillop was born on January 15, 1842, in Fitzroy, Australia, of Scottish parents, and was baptized Mary Helen. Aided by her father in her education, Mary Helen took courses in teaching and social guidance. Fr. Julian Tenison Woods became her spiritual director and, in 1866, asked her to assume the leadership of a group of women dedicated to educating Catholics in the region. Mary Helen was trained in the religious life and took her final vows in 1869, receiving her convent name.

Four years later, Fr. Woods was removed from control of the congregation in Adelaide. By this time, Mary of the Cross had recruited 127 sisters and had opened thirty-four schools, but the local bishop also excommunicated her for disobedience and dispensed forty-seven sisters from their vows. The following year, near death, the bishop absolved the excommunication and apologized to Mary of the Cross. The Holy See intervened, and the congregation resumed its work.

In 1873, Mary of the Cross made efforts to stabilize her community even more by going to Rome. The constitutions were accepted there in 1875, and she became Superior General. She traveled across Europe seeking financial aid and aspirants for her congregation and worked to enlist support from the Australian hierarchy. As late as 1887, Rome had to intervene again to keep the Sisters of St. Joseph and of the Sacred Heart free of diocesan-level control by certain bishops. In 1888, Pope Leo XIII (r. 1878-1903) approved the congregation, called the Josephite Sisters. Although Mary of the Cross had been replaced as Superior General, she was once again elected to that office.

She continued to serve the local Catholic populations, showing special concern for the Aborigines. As she also fostered conservation, the eucalyptus became her special emblem.

Mary of the Cross saw her sisters spread throughout Australia, New Zealand, and Peru. She died on August 8, 1909, in Sydney.

Pope John Paul II beatified her on January 19, 1995, honoring her as a pioneer in the religious and educational apostolates; a woman who endured suffering to bring graces to her native land and to Australia.

✠

Mary of Jesus of the Good Shepherd
— see Maria of Jesus Siedliska

✠

Matilde del Sagrado Corazón Téllez Robles
(May 30, 1841 – December 17, 1902)

Foundress of the Congregation of the Daughters of Mary,
Mother of the Church

Matilde Téllez Robles was born in Robledillo de la Vera, Spain; her parents, Félix Téllez Gómez and Basilea Robles Ruiz, had four children. Matilde, raised in the Faith, received a good education in a private school in Béjar. At an early age, she knew that she wanted to devote herself entirely to God and to serve the poor and the neglected. Her father, however, wished her to marry and prevented her from attending Mass. Matilde was nevertheless resolved to give her life to God and found support from the Association of the Daughters of Mary. She served as its president and was committed to caring for the poor and the sick.

Matilde experienced a personal turning point one day, while she was deep in prayer before the Blessed Sacrament. She felt an overwhelming call to establish a new religious institute dedicated to Eucharistic Adoration and assisting those in need. With the blessing of her spiritual director, Fr. Manuel de la Oliva, Matilde launched the new community with eight members of the Daughters of Mary. The foundation was started officially on March 19, 1875, in a house in Béjar, and the sisters began immediately to care for orphans, the poor, and the sick; the life of the sisters was full of service, but its heart was always to be the adoration before the Blessed Sacrament.

The new community received local approval from the Bishop of Plasencia in 1884 under the name Daughters of Mary, Mother of the Church; Mother Matilde, with many of her sisters, made their religious profession. The following year, the sisters risked their lives during an outbreak of cholera; the disease claimed the life of one of Matilde's closest collaborators, Sr. María Briz, at the age of thirty-three.

New houses were established in short order, with foundations opened across Spain. Mother Matilde supervised this rapid growth and was the gentle guide for the sisters as they gave themselves utterly for the defenseless, the sick, and the poor. She worked until the very day of her death from a stroke at sixty-one.

Pope John Paul II beatified her on March 21, 2004. He said of her:

"If anyone is in Christ, he is a new creation" (2 Cor 5:17). St. Paul's words can be applied perfectly to Mother Matilde. In love with Christ, she gave herself to him as a true disciple who embodied this newness. This tireless, religious woman devoted herself through an intense prayer life to transforming the society of her time by welcoming young orphan girls, nursing the sick at home, advancing the working woman and collaborating in ecclesial activities. Her deep devotion to the Eucharist and contemplation of Jesus in the Sacrament of the Altar gave rise to her desire to be like the bread that is broken and given to all to share. This is what she also taught her Religious, the Daughters of Mary, Mother of the Church. Her luminous witness is a call to live in adoration to God and in service to our brethren, two fundamental pillars of Christian commitment.

✝

Maurice Tornay (August 31, 1910 – August 11, 1949)
Martyr of Tibet

Maurice Tornay was a Missionary Canon Regular and one of the few Europeans to reach the small Himalayan kingdom in the snowy crests before it became a possession of China in 1950.

He was born in La Rosiére, in the canton of Valais, Switzerland. Educated at St. Maurice Abbey, he entered the Canons Regular of Grand St. Bernard in 1931, was solemnly professed in 1935, and volunteered for the missions. The following year, he was sent to Weixi, Yunnan, China. There, he finished his theological studies and was ordained in Ha Noi in 1938. He served as a catechist in Houa-Lo-Pa until 1945, when he was assigned to Yorkalo, in Tibet.

Established there as the local pastor, he faced opposition from the Buddhist lamas of the region, who forced him into exile, confiscating his church and rectory. Maurice then went to Pamé, where he served Catholic traders and encouraged fidelity among the Catholic Tibetans. He continued his work despite suffering from stomach ulcers, a condition he had developed in his younger years.

As a last resort, Maurice journeyed to Lhasa to seek tolerance from the Dalai Lama to save his Catholic faithful. But he never made it to that meeting; he and his servant were ambushed on the road and slain on August 11, 1949, in To Thong.

Pope John Paul II beatified Maurice Tornay on May 16, 1993, declaring:

Brothers and sisters, let us implore the Holy Spirit. The Church and world need families, which like the Tornay family, will be the forges where parents hand on to their children Christ's call to the Christian life, priestly or religious. Let us offer thanks to the seeds of hope in that Asian land. The mission and suffering of Fr. Tornay, and of his predecessors in the Foreign Mission Society of Paris and the Canons of the Grand Saint-Bernard, are silently bearing fruit in a slow maturation. We cannot fail to rejoice in the respectful dialogue between Tibetan and Catholic monks in order to discover him who is the Way and the Truth and the Life. Vocations are coming, as we can see by the recent ordination of one of our Blessed's students; Christians will continue the work of Fr. Tornay who wanted to teach children and lead them to holiness; a holy life alone is worth being lived.

✠

Mercedes of Jesus Molina (1828 – June 12, 1883)
"Rose of Baba and Guayaquil"

She was born in Baba, Ecuador, and began her apostolate as a laywoman in Guayauil. teaching orphans and aiding the abandoned. Slowly, her efforts took her among the Jibaro Indians, the natives of the region, long misunderstood and ill-treated. Mercedes of Jesus also became protectress of the abandoned children in Cuenca.

She was joined by other dedicated women, and, on Easter Monday, 1873, with the approval of the bishop of Riobamba, Mercedes of Jesus started the Congregation of the Sisters of Maríana of Jesus, also called the Marianites. Her spiritual daughters embraced her apostolate of education, care of orphans and the local Jibaros, and the service of the needy and the abandoned. Pope John Paul II called her "a model for living."

Mercedes of Jesus died, exhausted from her labors, in 1883, mourned by the people of her native land. Pope John Paul II beatified her on the Las Samanes Esplanade in Guayaquil, on February 1, 1985, announcing:

Mother Mercedes was captivated by the poverty of the Child of Bethlehem, by the suffering on the pained face of the Crucified. She wanted to be simply and clearly love for suffering, according to the motto recounted in early biographical notes. "As much love for as many sufferings as there are in the world"; to practice charity toward all those who, in poverty, suffering, and abandonment, reflected the mystery of the poor child of Bethlehem or of Christ suffering on Calvary. She was mother and educator of orphans, a poor missionary and peacemaker among the Indians, foundress of a religious family. To her spiritual daughters she transmitted her same spirit. . . . This was love without limits, able to bring aid and comfort, as Mother summarized in her constitutions, "to as many afflicted hearts as there are in the world."

✠

Mercedes Prat y Prat (March 6, 1880 – July 24, 1936)
Victim of Communist Atrocity

Mercedes Prat y Prat was born in Barcelona, Spain, the daughter of Juan and Teresa Prat y Prat, who both died while she was still a child. Skilled in the domestic arts, Mercedes started her ministry by teaching such activities to poor girls in Barcelona. In 1904, she entered the Society of St. Teresa of Jesus; as a member of the community, taught and labored as an artist.

When the Spanish Civil War began the dreadful persecutions on the nation, Mercedes and her nun companions had to leave their convent to take refuge with families or friends. She was making her way toward the society's safe haven but was halted by four members of the revolutionary militia. They demanded to know if she was a religious, and she joyously admitted her status. Arrested, Blessed Mercedes was executed by firing squad the following day.

Pope John Paul II beatified Mercedes Prat y Prat on April 29, 1990, declaring:

> Her great love for God and neighbor brought her to engage in the apostolic work of catechesis and in Sunday school. Besides her prudence, Mercedes distinguished herself by her virtue of fortitude, which was especially clear in the way she serenely met dangers and suffered persecution. Her love for her neighbor showed itself above all in her act of pardoning those who shot her.

✠

Metodej (Methodius) Trcka (July 6, 1886 – March 23, 1959)
Persecuted for a Christmas Carol

Metodej Trcka was born in Frijdlant nad Ostravici, in the modern Czech Republic. He entered the Redemptorists in 1902 and was ordained in Prague on July 17, 1910. During World War I, Metodej cared for hundreds of refugees and, in 1919, was sent to Lviv to work with Nikols Carneckyj. In 1921, he went to eastern Slovakia and served the Redemptorists in many administrative roles. He became the vice Provincial of the area in 1946.

In 1949, the Communist regime arrested all of the local priests, and Metodej was placed in prison with Peter Gojdic. He was transferred to Leopoldov Prison in April 1958 and put in a punishment cell for singing a Christmas carol. There, Metodej died of pneumonia. In 1969, his remains were taken to the Redemptorist Church of the Holy Spirit in Michalovce.

Pope John Paul II beatified Metodej Trcka on November 4, 2001, declaring that Metodej:

> . . . passed his life in the service of the Gospel and of the salvation of his brothers and sisters, even to the supreme sacrifice of his life . . . His Calvary ended in the prison of Leopoldov, where he died worn out by suffering and sickness, forgiving his persecutors.

✠

Michael Kozal (September 1893 – January 26, 1943)
A Martyr of Dachau

Michael Kozal was born at Ligota (Nowy Folwark), in Poland, and raised staunchly in the Faith. Ordained in 1918, he was assigned to various parishes, teaching in diocesan secondary schools, as well as serving as a seminary instructor for twelve years.

Two weeks before the invasion of Poland and the start of World War II, Michael was consecrated a bishop. He served as an auxiliary, then as bishop of Wloclawek. Because of his status and academic background, he was arrested by the Nazis as soon as their forces occupied his region. He was confined at first to a convent but then, in 1941, was sent to Dachau Concentration Camp. There, he learned of the suffering being endured by Catholics in his native land, and there he offered his own life to save his fellow countrymen. Michael celebrated Mass whenever possible and comforted other prisoners during his camp ordeal. He was given a lethal injection by his Nazi tormentors.

Pope John Paul II beatified Michael Kozal as one of the martyrs of the Faith in Warsaw, Poland, on June 14, 1987, praising this bishop for his courage and generosity in declaring himself a willing victim of love for the Polish people. Blessed Michael was honored for being a prelate of such holiness that he was singled out by the Nazis as an enemy of their godless regime.

✛

Miguel Augustine Pro
(January 13, 1891 – November 23, 1927)
"Viva Cristo Rey!"

A martyred Jesuit priest of Mexico, Miguel Augustine Pro was born in Guadalupe de Zacatecas to a prosperous, devout family. In August 1911, he entered the novitiate of the Jesuits at Michoacán, taking his first vows; soon afterward (1914), he needed to flee the country. He went to Granada, Spain, then to Belgium, to continue his studies and was ordained on August 31, 1925.

After his ordination, he returned to Mexico despite the revolutionary government's ban on all religious practices. Resorting to disguises and the use of safe houses provided by devout families, he administered the Sacraments, taught catechetics, and supported the poor while avoiding government forces.

On November 18, 1927, Miguel was arrested with his brother, Roberto, and was falsely charged of attempting to assassinate the president of Mexico. A stay of execution was arranged, and Roberto was spared, but the stay was too late for Miguel, who was executed by a firing squad.

When he was buried, thousands of the faithful defied the authorities by making a public display of mourning. Vast crowds marched behind the coffin, and more than 500 automobiles formed the procession to Miguel's final resting place. At the funeral, an elderly woman mourner had her sight miraculously restored.

Pope John Paul II beatified Miguel Augustine Pro on September 18, 1988, announcing:

> At the beatification of Fr. Miguel Augustine Pro, a Jesuit priest, whose virtues we today exalt and propose to the People of God, is a reason for joy for the universal Church, especially for the Church in Mexico. He is a new glory for the beloved Mexican nation, as well as for the Society of Jesus. His life of sacrificing and intrepid apostolate was always inspired by a tireless evangelizing effort . . . Neither suffering nor serious trouble, neither the exhausting ministerial activity, frequently carried out in difficult and dangerous circumstances, could stifle the radiating and contagious joy which he brought to his life for Christ and which nothing could take away (cf. Jn 16:22). Indeed, the deepest root of self-sacrificing surrender for the lowly was his passionate love for Jesus Christ and his ardent desire to be conformed to him, even unto death.

✠

Modestino of Jesus and Mary Mazzarella
(September 5, 1802 – July 24, 1854)
"Servant of the Poor"

Modestino of Jesus and Mary Mazzarella was born at Frattamaggiore, Naples, Italy, and baptized Dominic. Raised in a humble, working-class family, he served as an altar boy and attended parish services. At age eighteen, he was sponsored by Bishop Agostino Tommasi in the seminary but, in 1821, the death of this patron forced him to study at home.

One year later, Dominic entered the Franciscans at Grumo Nevano and was sent to the novitiate of Santa Lucia, in Naples. He took the religious name Modestino, was professed in 1824, and was ordained a priest on December 22, 1827, in Aversa. His assignments in the Order were varied; he served as Superior in two Franciscan houses and, in 1839, was transferred to Naples to serve in Santa Maria della Sanitá, a parish in a slum area of the city.

A devotee of Our Lady of Good Counsel, Fr. Modestino worked night and day to care for the sick and the poor. He was a marvelous champion of the Faith, inspiring spiritual and moral resolve in his apostolate. Even in the dreaded cholera epidemic of 1854, he went out to the people, caring for the victims of the disease,. Eventually, he succumbed to it himself, after tireless efforts caring for the faithful of Naples.

Pope John Paul II beatified Modestino of Jesus and Mary Mazzarella on June 29, 1995, announcing:

"For you are my hope, O Lord; my trust, O God, from my youth" (Responsorial Psalm, 70 [71]: 5). Thus sings the Church, which is constantly enlivened by the breath of the Holy Spirit. Today this is echoed by Blessed Modestino of Jesus and Mary, a priest of the Franciscan Order of Friars Minor, an outstanding witness to God's mercy, who instilled hope in Southern Italy during the first half of the last century. From boyhood, God was pleased to reveal to him the mysteries of the kingdom of heaven (cf. Mt 11:25; Gospel acclamation), leading him to discover the authentic value of the person who is fulfilled through generous devotion to the poor and crucified Christ in the gift of self to others.

Fr. Modestino lived in a society of marginalization and moral suffering, and was able to share fully the expectations and anxieties of the weakest, responding to the deep need for God found in his brothers and sisters who thirsted for justice and love. He thus became a leaven of renewal and a living sign of hope. The hand of the Lord was truly upon him, making him a minister of mercy and comfort to every social class, especially through his diligent, patient celebration of the sacrament of Reconciliation.

Fr. Modestino was a true "universal brother": everyone could rely on him, finding someone who would listen, welcome, and share. This love led him to give of his very self, and he did not hesitate to expose himself to the threat of death in order to help his brothers and sisters struck by a cholera epidemic. Indeed, he shared their fate to the very last, dying as a victim of love.

$\mathcal{N}$

✠

Narcisa de Jesus Martillo Morán (1837- December 8, 1869)
Ecuadorian Mystic

Narcisa de Jesus Martillo Morán was born in Daule (Nobol), a small village in the diocese of Guayaquil, Ecuador, the fifth of nine children of Pedro and Josef Morán. After her parents' deaths, while she was still very young, she moved to Guayaquil to work as a seamstress to help support her brothers and sisters. This time in her life was one of spiritual maturation for Narcisa, who spent hours in prayer and penance and was strongly drawn to Christ.

Sometime about 1865, when she moved to Cuenca, the bishop invited her to enter the Carmelite cloister. However, Narcisa believed that she was called upon to remain a laywoman. She returned to Guayaquil for three years, then went to Lima, where she took up residence in a Dominican convent. Although Narcisa was not a religious, she was allowed to remain within the convent and attend the religious ceremonies conducted there.

Serving as a catechist for children and adults, she visited the poor sections of Guayaquil to teach the families there about the faith. But her life was largely quiet, a hidden life of devotion, service, and recollection — until she died in Lima, Peru, at the age of thirty-six. At that point, her obscurity ended; pilgrims began devotions at her tomb, and her Cause was opened in 1889.

Pope John Paul II beatified Narcisa de Jesus Martillo Morán on October 25, 1992, declaring her a glory of Ecuador and praising her devotion to Nazareth and the mysteries of Calvary.

✠

Nazaría Ignacia of St. Teresa of Jesus March Mesa (January 10, 1889 – July 6, 1943)
Patroness of the Barrios

Nazaría Ignacia of St. Teresa of Jesus March Mesa was born in Madrid, Spain, one of eighteen children of Juan and Nazaría Mesa Ramos March y Reve. When she received her First Communion at age nine, Nazaría knew that she was destined to be a religious. Her family's move to Mexico in 1906 did not alter her resolve or her zeal.

In Mexico, Nazaría was encouraged by local religious in her efforts to evangelize the people of her area. Day after day, she went to the poor sections to teach the Faith and conduct catechism classes. In time she attracted other young women, and with them, Nazaría went to Oruro, Bolivia.

On December 23, 1912, she founded the Missionary Crusaders of the Church at Oruro. Her congregation grew rapidly, and Nazaría was able to establish houses in Argentina, Uruguay, and Spain. Her vision of carrying Christ's banner into a troubled world formed the members of her congregation and attracted dedicated young women of many walks of life. They opened soup kitchens and aided the poor in cities and mining camps. On two occasions her life was threatened, once in a violent persecution in Bolivia in 1932, and again in the Spanish Civil War in 1936, but she was not deterred. Her motto was "For Christ . . . for the Church . . . for souls," and she died in Buenos Aires, Argentina, with those words on her lips. Her remains were enshrined in her community house at Oruro.

Pope John Paul II beatified Nazaría Ignacia of St. Teresa of Jesus March Mesa on September 27, 1992, declaring:

> Blessed Nazaría Ignacia of St. Teresa March Mesa . . . was drawn interiorly by the message of the prophet Isaiah, which she heard: 'The Lord . . . has sent me . . . to heal the brokenhearted' (61:1). Moved by this apostolic concern, she founded in Bolivia the Missionary Crusaders of the Church, with whom she meant to 'go out into the streets' to meet people, to be in solidarity with them, to help them, especially if these people were covered with sores of material need, as was Lazarus, the poor man in the Gospel (cf. Lk 16:21), but primarily to bring them to God.

✠

Niceforo of Jesus and Mary Tejerina
— see Martyrs of the Passionist Congregation

✠

Nicholas Roland (December 8, 1642 – April 26, 1678)
Founder of the Sisters of the Child Jesus (Holy Child)

Nicholas was born in Reims, France, and received the grace of a religious vocation at an early age. He attended the Jesuit College in Reims, then went to Paris to complete his studies in philosophy and theology. Upon his return to Reims, he was made a canon of the cathedral. There, he served with John Baptist de la Salle, encouraging him in his ministry.

Nicholas also understood the need for a religious congregation to foster educational institutions particularly designed to shelter and to aid in the development of young women. In 1670, he began to recruit dedicated women to establish such a congregation. He founded the Sisters of the Child Jesus (or Holy Child) with two educators and worked diligently to counsel and guide the new community. Nicholas also labored to provide constitutions for the congregation and to obtain the necessary papal approbation that was given on May 9, 1678, to John Baptist de la Salle and Archbishop Le Tellier.

Nicholas died a victim of an epidemic in Reims. He named John Baptist de la Salle the executor of his will. The future saint revered Nicholas for his holiness and his concern for the young of his era.

Pope John Paul II beatified Nicholas Roland on October 16, 1994, announcing:

> This morning, dear brothers and sisters, we are forcefully reminded of the mystery of Redemption. Yes, we have "a great high priest who has passed through the heavens" (Heb. 4:14). He is Christ Jesus, the crucified Lord, risen and living in glory. He was the soul of Nicolas Roland's activity. During his short but spiritually intense life, he continually allowed the Redeemer to use him to accomplish his mission as high priest. Conformed to the person of Christ, he shared his love for those he guided to the priesthood, in order to "receive mercy" (Heb. 4:16) for them: "Jesus' immense love for you," he used to say, "is even greater than your infidelity." This unfailing faith and hope in the merciful love of the Incarnate Word led him to found the Congregation of the Sisters of the Infant Jesus. They would consecrate themselves to the apostolate of educating and evangelizing poor children. Indeed, he admirably said, "Orphans represent us to Jesus Christ in his childhood."

✠

Nicholas Barré (October 21, 1621 – May 31, 1686)
Spiritual Director of John Baptist de la Salle

Nicholas Barré was born in Amiens, France, to a devout family, at a time of enormous upheaval in France. He studied under the Jesuits and displayed stunning brilliance. It was thus a surprise that he entered, not the Jesuits, but the humble religious community of the Third Order of Minims of St. Vincent de Paul, in 1640. Five years later, he was ordained a priest, then worked as a professor of theology in Paris.

Nicholas then settled in Rouen, where he became the leader of the Minims. He promoted education and distinguished himself as a holy mystic, a profound spiritual advisor, and one of the great patrons of the young, especially the forgotten and neglected children of the cities. In 1666, he established the Sisters of the Infant Jesus to care for the young. He observed that those who cared for the poor and neglected child cared doubly for Christ. He also assisted the spiritual development of the young John Baptist de la Salle. He died in Paris.

Pope John Paul II beatified Nicholas Barré on March 7, 1999, noting that he enshrined in his mission the unceasing contemplation of the mystery of the Incarnation.

✠

Nicolas Bunkerd Kitabamrung (January 31, 1895 – 1944)
Victim of World War II

Nicolas Bunkerd Kitabamrung was born in Nakhom Pathom, Thailand, one of five children in a devoutly Catholic family. Attending Bang Xang and Penang Seminaries, he was ordained to the priesthood on January 24, 1926 in Assumption Cathedral, Bangkok.

He was then assigned to Bang Nokkhuek in Samut Songkhram Province, where he aided the Salesian Missionaries, who arrived in 1927. He also ministered to the faithful in Chiang Mai and other Catholic communities.

The persecution of the Catholic Church started in Thailand in 1940, as Catholics were viewed as tainted remnants of the French interventions. Nicolas, aware of the perils around him, went to Ban Han on January 11, 1941. The next day he was arrested for ringing Church bells and for being a French spy.

Sentenced to fifteen years' imprisonment, Nicolas continued his priestly labors in prison, baptizing some sixty-eight individuals. He died of tuberculosis, exacerbated by the abuse he had already suffered.

Pope John Paul II beatified Nicolas Bunkerd Kitbamrung on March 5, 2000, announcing:

> "I shall praise your name unceasingly and gratefully sing its praises" (Sir. 51:10). Fr. Nicolas Bunkerd Kitbamrung's priestly life was an authentic hymn of praise to the Lord. A man of prayer, Fr. Nicolas was outstanding

in teaching the faith, in seeking out the lapsed, and in his charity towards the poor. Constantly seeking to make Christ known to those who had never heard his name, Fr. Nicolas undertook the difficulties of a mission through the mountains and into Burma. The strength of his faith was made clear to all when he forgave those who falsely accused him, deprived him of his freedom, and made him suffer much. In prison, Fr. Nicolas encouraged his fellow prisoners, taught the catechism, and administered the sacraments. His witness to Christ exemplified the words of St. Paul: "We are afflicted in every way, but not crushed; perplexed, but not driven to despair; persecuted, but not forsaken; struck down but not destroyed; always carrying in the body the death of Jesus, so that the life of Jesus may also be manifested in our bodies" (2 Cor. 4:8-10). Through the intercession of Blessed Nicolas, may the Church in Thailand be blessed and strengthened in the work of evangelization and service.

╫

Nicolas da Gesturi (August 5, 1882 – June 8, 1958)
"Brother Silence"

Nicolas da Gesturi was born in Gesturi, Sardinia, Italy, and was baptized Giovanni. Orphaned at a young age and raised by his sister, he becoming devout, noble and refined. At age twenty-nine, Giovanni developed severe rheumatism but was cured suddenly. He entered the Franciscan Capuchins at Cagliari as an oblate, and received the habit and the name Nicolas. He was professed in 1914 and made his solemn profession on February 16, 1916.

Nicolas served as a cook in Capuchin friaries and, in 1924, was assigned to Cagliari, where he spent thirty-four years begging in the streets for the community. He walked the streets of the area in total silence from 1924-1958, earning the respect and affection of the local people. When some stopped him to give him donations or to ask his aid, miraculous cures took place, and soon Nicolas was being called to sickbeds and hospitals. More cures took place in his presence, but he seldom carried on lengthy conversations or chatted freely. "Brother Silence" died in Cagliari, mourned by the people of the region.

Pope John Paul II beatified Nicolas da Gesturi on October 3, 1999, declaring:

Affectionately called "Brother Silence" by the people, Nicolas of Gesturi displayed an attitude that was more eloquent than words: freed from the superfluous and in search of the essential, he was never distracted by what was useless or harmful, preferring to bear witness to the presence of the Incarnate Word beside every person.

In a world often sated with words but poor in values, there is a need for men and women who, like Blessed Nicolas of Gesturi, emphasize the urgent need to recover the capacity for silence and for listening, so that their whole life can become a "song" of praise to God and of service to their brothers and sisters.

☩

Nicolaus (Niels) Stensen
(January 11, 1638 – December 5, 1686)
"Pilgrim of the World"

A convert and bishop, Nicolaus Stensen was an eminent anatomist and geologist, sometimes called Niels Stensen or Nikolaus Stens.

Nicolaus was born in Copenhagen, the son of Lutherans, Sten Peterson and his wife, Anna Nielstochter. Educated locally, he entered the university of Copenhagen, where he became famous as a scientist for his discovery of important aspects of the thyroid gland. At the university of Leiden, Nicolaus made further discoveries concerning glands, muscles, the heart, and the circulatory system. He was also esteemed as a physiologist, crystollogist and paleontologist, able to identify a range of fossils.

In 1664, Nicolaus was denied a chair — a position of academic importance — at the University of Copenhagen. He received his doctorate in medicine from Leiden, then went to Paris for two years, gaining fame for his research in embryology and the anatomy of the brain. While in Florence, Italy, to continue his academic career, he converted to Catholicism and entered the Church on November 4, 1667. Ferdinand II, Archduke of Tuscany, gave Nicolaus a warm welcome into the Faith and enthusiastic support. His conversion came as a result of his attendance at a Livorno Corpus Christi procession, which moved him deeply.

By 1669, Nicolaus was back in Denmark, where King Christian IV gave him the rank of Royal Anatomist. But in 1674, he was again in Florence. There, Cosimo III appointed him tutor to Prince Ferdinand. Nicolaus was also studying for the priesthood and was ordained in 1675. Two years later, he was consecrated a bishop, and he labored almost a decade in the northern missions of Germany, in Hanover. A vibrant preacher, he brought countless souls back into the Faith as the suffragan bishop of Munster. He then became the vicar apostolic of the Hanover area and held that position until his death at the age of forty-eight.

His remains were enshrined in a vault in the basilica of St. Lawrence. The diocese of Hildesheim has always venerated Nicolaus, and many have been blessed by his intercession on their behalf.

Pope John Paul II beatified Nicolaus Stenson on October 23, 1988, announcing:

> At a distance of centuries, there reaches us, as it were, a cry from all those whose death is recorded in the Book of Life. Through their lives full of the Spirit of Christ, united to his paschal mystery . . . blessed son of the Danish land! You enliven the choir of those great people who have preceded you on the way to holiness. With them you cry, "He who is mighty has done great things for me." This cry of yours is heard in heaven and on earth. May it be received in the hearts of your brothers and sisters today and cause in them an abundant harvest of good, in faith, charity, and communion.

⊹

Nikolaus Gross (September 30, 1898 – January 23, 1945)
Early Opponent of Hitler

A martyr of the Nazis, Nikolaus Gross was a journalist and Catholic activist.

He was born in Niederwenigern, Germany, and attended local schools from 1905-1912. He then worked in rolling mills and as a coal miner. In 1918, he joined the Christian Miners' Trade Union and the Centre Party, as well as the St. Anthony's Miners Association. Nickolaus settled in Bottrop in the Ruhr Valley and married Elizabeth Koch. They had seven children.

He became the assistant editor of the West German Worker's Newspaper in 1927, then the editor-in-chief. Moving to Cologne to conduct this media apostolate, Nikolaus began attacking the Nazis with editorials and commentaries. The paper was banned in November 1938, and Nikolaus was subject to searches and questions by the Gestapo.

He was harassed, but allowed to remain free, until the attempted assassination of Hitler. On August 12, 1944, Nikolaus was arrested and taken to Ravensbruck Concentration Camp, then to Berlin, where he was hanged. The remains of his cremated corpse were scattered into sewage.

Pope John Paul II beatified Nikolaus Gross on October 7, 2001, announcing:

Let us focus on Blessed Nikolaus Gross, journalist and father of a family. With the clear insight that the Nazi ideology was incompatible with Christian faith, he courageously took up his pen to plead for the dignity of human beings.

☩

Nimatullah Youssef Kassab Al-Hardini
(1808 – December 14, 1859)
Mentor of Sharbel Maklouf

A Maronite scholar, Nimatullah Youssef Kassab Al'Hardini was born in Hardin, Lebanon. Four of his brothers entered the monastic orders of the Maronite Church, as the family was devout and generous. Nimatullah entered the Lebanese Maronite Order in 1828 and was sent to St. Anthony Monastery in Qozhaya, near the Qadisha, the "Holy Valley," for two years. There, he became known for his love of the Blessed Sacrament.

After his profession, Nimatullah was assigned to the monastery of Sts. Cyprian and Justina in Kfifan, where he studied philosophy and theology. As an ordained priest, he became director of the scholasticate, where the future St. Sharbel was one of his students. Nimatullah was a model religious, believing community life led to perfection.

He had great devotion to the Virgin Mary and honored her as the Immaculate Conception. In 1845, the Holy See appointed Nimatullah a general assistant of the Order. He served in this capacity for two years, declining an appointment as Abbot General.

Nimatullah came down with pneumonia at the monastery of Kfifan and died there. He held an icon in his hands as he died, commending his soul to the Blessed Virgin Mary.

Pope John Paul II beatified Nimatullah Youssef Kassab Al'Hardini on May 10, 1998, declaring:

> Blessed Al-Hardini is a model of Christian and monastic life for the Maronite community and for all Christ's followers in our time. As a man of prayer he calls his brothers and sisters to trust in God and to commit all their efforts to following Christ, in order to build a better future.

O

✠

Omeljan Kovè (August 20, 1884 – March 25, 1944)
"Righteous Ukranian"

Omeljan Kovè was born near Kosiv, in the Ukraine. At an early age, he discerned a vocation to the priesthood and was subsequently sent to Rome to study. In 1911, after graduating from the College of Sts. Sergius and Bacchus in Rome, he was ordained to the priesthood. He spent the next years in various forms of pastoral ministry.

In 1941, the German Army invaded the Soviet Union and launched a wholesale persecution of the Church and the Jews. Omeljan resisted the Nazis on both fronts, and was especially dedicated to providing assistance to the Jews who stood in danger of being arrested or executed. In the spring of 1943, he was arrested himself by the Gestapo on the charge of aiding Jews.

After enduring severe torture, Omeljan was sentenced to the concentration camp at Majdanek, where he died, burned to death in the ovens of the camp. For his labors on behalf of the Jews of the Ukraine, Omeljan was honored on September 9, 1999 with the title, "Righteous Ukrainian" by the Jewish Council of Ukraine.

Pope John Paul II beatified Omeljan Kovè on June 26, 2001 with other Ukrainian martyrs. Of these martyrs, the pontiff declared:

> The Servants of God who are today inscribed in the Book of the Blessed represent all categories of the ecclesial community: among them are Bishops and priests, monks, nuns, and lay people. They were tested in many ways by the followers of the infamous Nazi and Communist ideologies. Aware of the sufferings which these faithful disciples of Christ were undergoing, my Predecessor Pius XII, sharing in their anguish, expressed his solidarity with those "who are persevering in faith and resisting the enemies of Christianity with the same unswerving fortitude with which their ancestors once resisted." He praised their courage in remaining "faithfully joined to the Roman Pontiff and their Pastors" (Apostolic Letter *Orientales Ecclesias*, 15 December 1952: AAS 45 [1953], 8).

☦

Otto Neururer (March 25, 1882 – May 30, 1940)

First Catholic Priest to Die in a Nazi Concentration Camp

Otto Neururer was arrested was born in Piller, Austria, the twelfth child of an industrious peasant family. His father died when Otto was still young, and his mother had to operate the family farm and mill while raising her children.

Otto attended the minor seminary at Brixen, demonstrating a brilliant intellect and many virtues. In the diocesan seminary, he completed his studies for the priesthood and was ordained on June 29, 1907, celebrating his first Mass in Piller, his hometown. He was then assigned as a curate or teacher in several parishes, finally going to Götzens, near Innsbruck.

By the time Otto arrived in Götzens, the Nazis had invaded and set up vast political governments in this Tirol region. A reign of terror began, but Otto did not withdraw or show timidity in his priestly duties. At Götzens, in December 1938, he advised a young woman not to marry a divorced man with an evil reputation. The man, a member of the Nazi SA, was enraged when he discovered Otto's involvement and went to his close friend, the Gauleiter, the leading Nazi official of the Tirol region. At this point, Otto was arrested for slander to the detriment of German marriage. He was imprisoned, first in Innsbruck, then in the Dachau concentration camp. He was moved to Buchenwald soon after, where he endured hideous tortures.

Otto comforted and aided his fellow prisoners throughout his ordeal and remained steadfast in the Faith and in prayer. Then, a prisoner asked to be baptized. Otto suspected a Nazi trap, as such ceremonies were forbidden in the camp. He was correct; two days later, he was transferred to "a bunker of extreme punishment" called "the Black House." He was hung upside down until he died. His ashes are enshrined in Götzens.

Pope John Paul II beatified Otto Neururer as a martyr on November 24, 1996, stating:

> The simple parish priest, Otto Neururer, gave his witness to Christ's truth, by defending the sanctity of Christian marriage in the most difficult and dangerous circumstances, and for this reason he was imprisoned by the Gestapo. In the concentration camp, it was his sense of priestly duty that spurred him to give lessons in the faith, despite the severe prohibition of the camp authorities. As punishment, he was hung upside down until he died. The two martyrs, Otto Neururer and Jakob Gapp, offer us all, in an era which would like to make Christianity something optional and rela-

tivize all obligations, a witness of uncompromising loyalty to Jesus' truth, where it always shines as such. Thus, they can be our heavenly intercessors as patrons of courageous preaching and of the holiness of marriage and priestly service.

(See also Jakob Gapp.)

P

✠

Paolo Manna (1872 – September 15, 1952)
Promoter of the Missions Through Modern Technology

An evangelist of non-Christians, Paolo Manna was born in Avellina, Italy, the fifth of six children in his family. He was educated locally, then studied Latin and philosophy at the Gregorian University in Rome. In 1891, he entered the Seminary for the Foreign Missions in Milan, preparing for the priesthood, and was ordained in August 1895. He was assigned immediately to Burma — now modern Myanmar — where he labored until 1907, although, having been diagnosed with tuberculosis during his missionary term, he returned to Italy on three occasions for medical care.

Working then to spur concerns about the worldwide missions, Paolo became editor of *La Missioni Cattoliche* and re-launched the Mission Society for the Propagation of the Faith and the Holy Childhood. In 1916, he started the Missionary Union of the Clergy, now the Pontifical Missionary Union. Three years later he opened the *Italia Missioneria* magazine. In 1924, Paolo became the Superior General of the Lombard Seminary for Foreign Missions and Superior General of PIME. He founded a congregation of PIME Sisters in 1936, the Missionaries of Mary Immaculate.

Paolo taught that bishops and clergy are responsible for spreading the Gospel among non-Christians, even if they are not assigned to actual mission territories. This theme was used by Pope Pius XII (r. 1939-58) in the 1957 encyclical, *Fidei Donum*. Paolo died in a Naples hospital, and his Cause was opened in 1974.

Pope John Paul II beatified Paolo Manna on November 4, 2001, announcing: "In Fr. Paolo Manna we perceive a special reflection of the glory of God. He spent his entire life promoting the missions."

✠

Pauline von Mallinckrodt (June 3, 1817 – April 30, 1881)
Aristocrat and Religious

The founder of the Sisters of Christian Charity, Pauline von Mallinckrodt was a member of the German nobility.

She was born in Minden, Westphalia, Germany. Her father was a Lutheran, and her mother a solidly practicing Catholic. Pauline was the oldest of four children, and her brother, Herman, became a famous Catholic political leader.

Raised in the comforts and opportunities of the aristocratic world, she was taught the Faith by her mother. When her mother died during Pauline's seventeenth year, she took care of the family. She was not blind to events and sufferings outside of her home, and she responded generously to these sufferings by opening a school in 1842 for infants and the blind at Paderborn. Innovative and alert to the needs of her charges, Pauline molded the letters of the alphabet so that her students could learn to read, despite their handicaps.

Realizing that simple laywomen could not expand and renew the apostolate that she had started, Pauline offered her facilities to St. Sophie Barat. St. Sophie Barat was unable to assume the responsibility for the school because of political turmoil and prior commitments. Pauline thus came to a critical juncture in her life of service, and she responded again with generosity.

On August 21, 1849, she founded the Sisters of Christian Charity, also called the Daughters of the Blessed Virgin Mary of the Immaculate Conception, and was soon joined by other faithful women who realized the need for such sacrifices. Blessed Pope Pius IX (r. 1846-1878) approved the congregation on February 21, 1863.

A short time later, Bismarck and other German leaders forced the congregation out of Germany. The anti-Catholic *Kulturkampf* (the program in German lands that sought to subordinate the Church to the will of the State) was in operation at the time and was set on limiting the Catholic influence. Pauline went to Belgium when her Paderborn school was closed, and she established a house near Brussels. She labored endlessly to expand her community, visiting the United States in 1873 and 1879. Her sisters began their teaching ministry in America as a result of her visit.

Pauline remained faithful to Christ and to the impaired, the needy, and the young until her death from pneumonia at Paderborn. Her noble and devout manners and her indomitable dedication won many to her apostolate in the Old and New Worlds.

Pope John Paul II beatified Pauline von Mallinckrodt on April 14, 1985, praising her untiring efforts and the spiritual legacy that she left for dedicated souls in the apostolates of truly caring for those in need.

☩

Pavel Djedjov — see Martyrs of Bulgaria

☩

Pavel Peter Gojdic (July 17, 1888 – July 17, 1960)
"The Man With a Heart of Gold"

Pavel Peter Gojdic was born in Ruske Pekl'any, the third child in a devout family, and raised in Cikel'ke, where he received the grace of a priestly vocation. In 1907, he entered the seminary at Presov (Prjasev), then at Budapest. Pavel was ordained to the priesthood and served in local parishes, becoming an assistant chancellor in 1914.

On July 20, 1922, he entered the Order of St. Basil the Great, making his profession on November 28, 1926. In 1927, Pavel became the Titular Bishop of Harpassa, consecrated on March 25 in Rome. He received his gold pectoral cross from Pope Pius XI (r. 1922-39). During World War II, Pavel served as the Bishop of Presov, working tirelessly to protect his people and to ease their sufferings.

At the close of the war, the Soviets entered the region and threatened the Church and its personnel. Pavel was arrested in 1950 and tortured in an attempt to make him break with Rome. He was moved to several prisons and died of cancer in Leopoldov Prison, buried in the anonymous grave H681. Later, his remains were recovered and moved to Presov.

Pope John Paul II beatified Pavel Peter Gojdic on November 4, 2001, announcing:

> Known to the people as "the man with a heart of gold," he became known to the representative of the (Communist) government as a real "thorn in the side" . . . He was arrested and imprisoned. This for him began a long Calvary of suffering, mistreatment and humiliation, which brought about his death on account of his fidelity to Christ and his love for the Church and the Pope.

☩

Pedro Calungsod of Visayas (c. 1655 – April 2, 1672)
Attacked for Baptizing a Child

A young Filipino catechist martyred on Guam, Pedro Calungsod was born in the Visayas region of the Philippines and worked with the Jesuits in his home area, traveling extensively on catechetical missions with Fr. Diego Luis San Vitores. Going to the Ladrones Islands (modern Marianas) in 1668, he proved himself reliable and courageous. The missionaries them sailed to Guam, where they visited the village of Tomkom. Pedro was asked to baptize a local child, and as a result faced the spears of an enraged populace. He received a spear wound in his chest and was struck on the head. Both he and Diego were murdered and hurled into the sea. Their bodies were never recovered.

Pope John Paul II beatified Pedro on March 5, 2000, declaring:

"If anyone declares himself for me in the presence of men, I will declare myself for him in the presence of my Father in heaven" (Mt 10: 32). From his childhood, Pedro Calungsod declared himself unwaveringly for Christ and responded generously to his call.

Young people today can draw encouragement and strength from the example of Pedro, whose love of Jesus inspired him to devote his teenage years to teaching the Faith as a lay catechist. Leaving family and friends behind, Pedro willingly accepted the challenge put to him by Fr. Diego de San Vitores to join him on the Mission to the Chamorros. In a spirit of faith, marked by strong Eucharistic and Marian devotion, Pedro undertook the demanding work asked of him and bravely faced the many obstacles and difficulties he met. In the face of imminent danger, Pedro would not forsake Fr. Diego, but as a "good soldier of Christ" preferred to die at the missionary's side.

Today Blessed Pedro Calungsod intercedes for the young, in particular those of his native Philippines, and he challenges them. Young friends, do not hesitate to follow the example of Pedro, who "pleased God and was loved by him" (Wis. 4: 10) and who, having come to perfection in so short a time, lived a full life (cf. ibid., v. 13).

✝

Pere (Peter) Torrés i Claret (May 30, 1905 – August 31, 1950)
Concerned for the "Poorest of the Sick"

A Spanish priest, Pere was born in Manresa, a province of Barcelona, Spain; his parents were Francesc Tarrés Puigdellívol and Carme Claret Masats. He grew up in a devout Catholic family and, in his youth, was a leader in the Federation of Young Christians of Catalonia and active member of Catholic Action. His two sisters, Francesca and Maria, both entered the convent.

After earning a degree in medicine, Pere began his residency in Barcelona. He soon founded (with Dr. Gerardo Manresa) a medical clinic for poor patients. This was only one example of Pere's deep charity and commitment to those in need. During the Spanish Civil War (1936-1939), however, he spent part of his time in hiding, following the murder of Catholics by Revolutionary forces. This time apart was an occasion for him to deepen his prayer life.

In 1938, Pere was compelled to join the Republican army and to serve as a battlefield physician. He devoted his time to caring for the many wounded in the fighting, and he wrote extensively in his War Diary of the horrors of battle that he saw on a daily basis.

Partly due to the horrors of the war, and determined to be a "Doctor of Souls," he entered the Seminary of Barcelona and was ordained a priest on May 30, 1942. He devoted his energies to the care of sick, the poor, and Catholic Action. He died from cancer and made his sufferings an offering. He was beatified by Pope John Paul II on Sept. 5, 2004. The pope said of him:

> Pere Torrés i Claret, first a doctor, then a priest, dedicated himself to the lay apostolate among the young people of Catholic Action in Barcelona, whose adviser he subsequently became. As a medical practioner, he devoted himself with special concern to the poorest of the sick, convinced that "the sick person is a symbol of the suffering Christ."
>
> Ordained a priest, he devoted himself with generous daring to the tasks of his ministry, ever faithful to the commitment he had made on the eve of his Ordination: "A single resolution, Lord, cost what it may." He accepted with faith and heroic patience a *serious illness* from which he died at the age of only forty-five. Despite his suffering, he would frequently repeat: "How good the Lord is to me! And I am truly happy."

✠

Peter Donders (October 27, 1805 – January 14, 1887)
Apostle to the Lepers

A Redemptorist missionary, Peter Donders was born in Tilburg, in the Netherlands, a child of Arnold and Petronella Donders. While still quite young, he and his brother, Martin, had to leave school to aid the family by working for extra income. Peter had received the grace of a priestly vocation, and eventually he would concentrate all of his energies on earning a seminary degree.

He worked in a factory to earn money, then took a position as a servant in the local seminary. At age twenty-six, he applied to the Franciscans, Jesuits, and Redemptorists, but was refused. Peter had centered on a foreign missionary vocation, inspired by the chance reading of the Annals of the Propagation of the Faith.

While studying at Herlaar, he received financial aid from a patron, a sum that enabled him to complete his priestly studies. He was ordained in 1840 for the missions in Surinam (Dutch Guiana). One year later he was sent to Paramibo, where he served until 1865. By 1850, he had baptized 1,200 plantation workers. During the epidemic of 1851, Peter displayed superhuman energies and concern for victims until falling ill himself.

When he recovered, he went to Batavia to care for the lepers, and his outstanding labors earned him an invitation to join the Redemptorists. He was received into the congregation and was given the opportunity to be reunited with his beloved lepers in Batavia again. Peter was always dedicated and loving in caring for the victims of leprosy. He even learned to play musical instruments to bring his patients moments of comfort and consolation.

He was not handsome, but he radiated Christ's compassion. A contemporary stated that Peter's "beauty was mainly within." He labored in Batavia until his death and was interred there.

Pope John Paul II beatified Peter Donders on May 23, 1982, praising the Blessed for his authentic evangelical life in imitation of Christ. The Holy Father stated:

> We can say that he was an apostle of the poor. In fact, he was born into a poor family and had to lead the life of a worker before he could pursue his priestly vocation. He dedicated his whole priestly life to the poor . . . In addition, he is an invitation and an incentive for the renewal and reflourishing of the missionary thrust which in the last century and in this one has made an exceptional contribution to the carrying out of the Church's missionary duty. Joining the Congregation of the Most Holy Redeemer late in life, he practiced in an excellent way what St. Alphonsus proposed as an ideal for his religious: imitate the virtues and examples of the Redeemer in preaching the divine word to the poor.

✠

Peter Friedhofen (February 25, 1819 – December 21, 1860)
Founder of the Brothers of Charity of Mary, Help of Christians

Peter Friedhofen was born in Weitersburg, Germany, near Koblenz, the sixth of seven children born to a poor family. His father died one year later, adding to the burden of the family. As a result, the children had to find work and extra income as soon as they were able to enter the marketplace.

Peter and his older brother, Jacob, traveled to various villages in the region working as chimney sweeps. He often sang Marian hymns while he worked high above the ground, and even invited the children who watched from the street to join in. When his brother died, he tried to care for his widowed mother and eleven children but was unable to manage the burden physically or financially. His desire had always been to aid the sick and the suffering, particularly children, and he was led to dedicate himself to their care. He started charitable projects for them in Adenau, Cochem, and Wittlich. He also built a shrine for the Blessed Virgin Mary to foster Marian devotions.

The Brothers of Charity of Mary, Help of Christians (also called the Brothers of Mercy) evolved from Peter's first charities; Bishop Arnoldi of Trier approved the constitution of the congregation on July 2, 1848. The congregation adapted itself to Alexian Brothers' rule, and the Alexians at Aachen trained him and his first companion, Karl Marchand.

Peter opened his first house on June 21, 1850, and wore the habit of the congregation after March 25, 1851. He opened other houses, aided by the bishop of Trier and the president of the Rhineland. The congregation served the sick and needy, quickly expanding throughout Europe and into Brazil, China, and Malaysia.

Peter directed the increasing demands and the swelling membership of his congregation until his death, at age forty-one, from tuberculosis in Koblenz. He was buried with honors in Trier.

Pope John Paul II beatified Peter Friedhofen on June 23, 1985, declaring:

"The love of Christ constrains us" — this is what St. Paul avows of himself. It was this same love that constrained the newly beatified Peter Friedhofen at the age of thirty to consecrate his life totally to God and to the service of the sick. Although himself poor and in bad health, he gave up his lay calling as a chimney-sweep, in order to make a new start out of his religious conviction and his burning love of neighbor. He saw the wretched situation of uprooted, sick, and needy people, and recognized his own apostolic mission. Thus, he founded in 1850 the community of the Brothers of Charity of Mary Help of Christians with the task of serving God in poor, sick, and old people.

✠

Peter Ruiz de los Paños y Angel and Companions – see Martyrs of the Diocesan Priest Workers

✠

Peter To Rot (1912 – 1945)
New Guinea Martyr

A native of the Pacific islands, Peter To Rot was a martyr who suffered at the hands of the Japanese invaders. He was born in Rakunai, New Britain, an island off the northeast coast of Papua New Guinea, in 1912. His father was To Puia, the chief of his village, and his mother was Maria Ia Tumul. Peter's father had invited missionaries to his village, and he and his family were baptized.

Peter was trained as a catechist of the Catholic Faith at a young age, and was trained to administer at the local school. He also conducted prayer services and instructional sessions to aid missionaries and, in 1933, took up the role of chief catechist in his own village. He married Paula Ia Varpit, a former student, and the couple had three children.

When the Japanese military forces arrived in New Britain to occupy the region, they interned the missionary priests. Peter, harassed as a possible objector, was arrested several times. The Japanese tried to win the favor of the local populations by legalizing polygamy and making resistance to this legislation a punishable offense. When their efforts failed, the military authorities instituted rules and regulations designed to limit the Catholic presence. Peter openly opposed the regulations, knowing that he had to witness for the faith. As a result, he was arrested again, and singled out for harsh treatment. Realizing the danger he was in, Peter asked his wife to bring him his good clothes — he wanted to go to God properly attired.

About a month before the Japanese surrendered to the Allied forces in the Pacific region, thirty-three-year-old Peter was taken to a hut in the secluded Vunaiara region. There, he was given a lethal injection and was held down while he died in agony. The next day his body was returned to his village for burial.

Pope John Paul II beatified Peter To Rot in Port Moresby, Papua New Guinea, on January 17, 1995, declaring the heroic virtue of this devout catechist who dared the wrath of the occupying military forces in order to fulfill his commitment as a Christian by fostering the Faith in a time of peril.

✠

Petra of St. Joseph Perez Florida
(December 7, 1845 – August 16, 1906)
Apostle of St. Joseph of the Mountain

Petra of St. Joseph Perez Florida was born in Málaga, Spain, and was raised in a devout family. Her childhood was a time of preparation for the apostolate, as she recalled, "I thought about nothing else but becoming a nun." Petra also suffered for the poor, understanding their heartache when their pleas for aid were met with indifference.

Petra started begging for the poor, an activity that her father opposed vehemently. In time she was able to enlist his support, and she began living with three companions who desired to aid her in ministry to the poor. In 1880, the Congregation of the Mothers of the Helpless and of St. Joseph of the Mountain was the result of this first effort. The bishop of Málaga, watching Petra and her companions, proposed the congregation's title.

In 1895, Petra began working on Montaña Pelada, a royal sanctuary of St. Joseph of the Mountain in Barcelona. The church was dedicated in 1901. Guiding her growing communities and promoting more efforts for the poor, Petra continued her labors until her death in Barcelona.

Pope John Paul II beatified Petra of St. Joseph Perez Florida on October 16, 1994, declaring her heroic virtues and praising her for being consumed by divine love.

✠

Piedad de la Cruz Ortiz Real
(November 12, 1842 – February 26, 1916)

Founder of the Congregation of Salesian Sisters
of the Sacred Heart of Jesus

Tomasa Ortiz Real was born in Bocairente, Valencia, Spain; she was the fifth of the eight children of José and Tomasa Ortiz. Remarkably, Tomasa knew at the age of ten that she was called by God to be a nun, and her desire never wavered over the next years. Thus, even as she finished her studies at Loreto College, run by the Religious of the Holy Family of Burdeos, she made the request to enter their community. Her father, however, judged her too young to be a nun — and the political situation in Spain at the time to be too dangerous.

In the succeeding years, Tomasa attempted twice to enter the cloistered community of Carmelite nuns in Valencia. Both times, her health declined so severely that she was compelled to withdraw. At last, while deep in prayer, she came to the understanding that God wished her to establish a new congregation.

Acting on the call, Tomasa requested and, in 1884, received permission from her bishop to found the Community of the Third Order of Our Lady of Mt. Carmel near Alcantarilla with the purpose of caring for the sick and orphans. Tomasa adopted the new religious name of Piedad de la Cruz Ortiz Real (Piety of the Cross). As the facilities soon proved too small, Sr. Piedad found it necessary to open a new house in Caudete.

The new establishment created difficulties with the older community; a division erupted during which Sr. Piedad was essentially abandoned by her sisters save for one member, Sr. Alfonsa, who remained alone with her in the original house. She faced these troubles with patience and prayerful acceptance. At the suggestion of Bishop Bryan y Livermore, Sr. Piedad and Sr. Alfonsa took part in retreat at the Salesian Convent of the Visitation in Orihuela, with the idea that she should ponder founding a new community.

Sr. Piedad did exactly that. In September 1890, she founded the Congregation of the Salesian Sisters of the Sacred Heart of Jesus. The purpose of the community was to care for orphans, the elderly, neglected, and sick. The new congregation grew swiftly and was guided by Mother Piedad until the day of her death. She was beatified by Pope John Paul II on March 21, 2004. During the ceremony, the pope said that Mother Piety:

. . . is a marvellous example of the reconciliation that St. Paul suggests to us in the Second Reading: "God was in Christ reconciling the world to himself" (2 Cor 5:19). But God asks us to collaborate with him to achieve his work of reconciliation (cf. vv. 19-20). Mother Piety gathered various young women who were eager to show the lowly and the poor the love of the provident Father as it is expressed in the Heart of Jesus, thereby giving life to a new religious family. A model of Christian and religious virtues and in love with Christ, the Blessed Virgin, and the poor, she leaves us the example of austerity, prayer, and charity to all the needy.

✠

Pietro Bonilli (March 15, 1841 – January 5, 1935)
"To Be a Family, To Establish the Family, To Build Up the Family"

A founder of a religious congregation, Pietro Bonilli was born in San Lorenzo Trebiani (di Trevi) in Umbria, Italy, the son of Sebastian and Maria Allegretti Bonilli. He was brought up in a devout family and received the grace of a priestly vocation.

Upon completing his studies, Pietro was ordained in 1863, then sent to Cannaiola. He would serve as a pastor there for more than three decades, sharing the trials and tribulations of the Catholic people of that region. Pietro had great devotion to the Holy Family and tried to dedicate himself to the daily needs of his parish. Alert to the changing moral attitudes of his age, he did not turn aside from the most vulnerable of society.

In 1884, Pietro started "the Little Orphanage of Nazareth" in Cannaiola. There, he took care of orphaned young girls and abandoned boys. He attracted many generous souls who aided him in this apostolate. With some of these devout women, he started a congregation, the Sisters of the Holy Family, and was soon able to expand his ministries.

In 1893, he opened a hospice for the deaf and blind. The Sisters of the Holy Family took over the operation of this institution and moved it to Spoleto. Pietro followed, going to Spoleto to supervise operations. Already famous as an apostle of charity, he served as a spiritual director and, in Spoleto, was made a canon of the cathedral and the rector of the regional seminary. Pope Pius X honored him in 1908.

Pietro, exhausted by his many labors, died at last in Spoleto. Pope John Paul II beatified him on April 21, 1988, declaring:

He understood that it was necessary to be present in the flock, also to give his life which would look after and nourish them in whatever situation, even that of sharing times of danger, going into unhealthy places and the humblest and most despised areas. He remained for thirty-five years in a parish in the most depressed area of the Diocese of Spoleto, where religious and moral conditions were exceptionally poor and disheartening, marked by degrading profanity, licentiousness, gambling, and drunkenness. A generous imitator of Christ the Good Shepherd, Fr. Bonilli lavished his charity on all who needed assistance. Experienced since childhood in the sufferings, hardships, humiliations, and needs of the country people, he devoted himself to 'nourishing' his people and leading them to more fertile pastures (cf. Ps 22[23]:2). He who 'knew his flock' wished to find suitable food for it . . . He also guided them in his own experience of prayer, so that they might find pasture in contact with God and in the Eucharist. In particular, he saw in the family the basis of the renewal of society and ecclesial life. "To be a family, to establish the family, to build up the family," was his motto and program. The family, every family, ought to have its vocation and mission renewed according to the example of the Holy Family.

✠

Piero Giorgio Frassati (April 6, 1901- July 4, 1925)
Model of a Holy Death

Piero Giorgio Frassati was born in Turin, Italy, the son of Alfredo and Adelaide Amelia Frassati. His father was a senator of Italy, ambassador to Germany, and the founder of the *La Stampa* magazine. Piero and his younger sister, Luciana, were educated in the Faith, although their parents were not devout.

He demonstrated many virtues and a certain spiritual maturity, even as a child. As an adult, he chose a mining career, a lifestyle that brought him close to the poor, and he aided them with charitable gifts and service through the St. Vincent de Paul Society. Piero was a daily communicant and had great devotion to the Blessed Virgin Mary. He was also athletic, outgoing, and a charming companion to people of all classes. Piero was an avid skier and mountain climber, who met life with cheerfulness and joy.

When asked why he performed so many acts of charity, Piero replied: "Jesus comes to visit me each morning in Holy Communion. I return his visit to him in the poor."

In June 1925, Piero contracted polio while visiting an abandoned sick person, and he faced the terminal illness with calm, patience, and holy resolve. He wrote just before his death, "We should always be cheerful. Sadness should be banished from all Christian souls. . . . Even in the midst of intense physical suffering it[life] is one of joy." The last thing he wrote displayed his charity; he asked for medication for an ill friend who was unable to afford the needed dosage.

He died in Turin, mourned and revered for his special union with Christ and his remarkable joy. Literally thousands came to pay their respects, remembering his personal kindness.

Pope John Paul II beatified Piero Giorgio Frassati on May 20, 1990, announcing:

> "Sanctify Christ as Lord in your hearts. Always be ready to give an explanation to anyone who asks you for a reason for your hope" (1 Pet. 3:15). . . .
> In our century, Piero Giorgio Frassati, whom I have the joy of declaring blessed today in the name of the Church, incarnated these words of St. Peter in his own life. The power of the Spirit of Truth, united to Christ, made him a modern witness to the hope which springs from the Gospel and to the grace of salvation which works in human hearts . . . Thus he became a living witness and courageous defender of this hope in the name of the Christian youth of the twentieth century.
> Faith and charity, the true driving forces of his existence, made him active and diligent in the milieu in which he lived, in his family and school, in the university and society; they transformed him into a joyful, enthusiastic apostle of Christ, a passionate follower of his message and charity. The secret of his apostolic zeal and holiness is to be sought in the ascetical and spiritual journey which he traveled; in prayer, in persevering adoration, even at night, of the Blessed Sacrament, in his thirst for the Word of God, which he sought in Biblical texts; in chastity lived as a cheerful, uncompromising discipline; in his daily love of silence and life's "ordinariness." It is precisely in these factors that we are given to understand the deep wellspring of his spiritual vitality.

✠

Pierina (Petrina) Morosini
(January 7, 1931 – April 6, 1957)
Martyr of Purity

Pierina was born in Fiobbo di Albino, the eldest and only daughter of a farm family. Raised in the Faith, she was trained to take responsibility and to serve others. Pierina helped her mother with household duties and, when she was old enough, she started working in a local cotton mill.

Very devout, she attended Mass daily and aided the local parish as a member of the Catholic Action organization. Pierina also took private vows of poverty, chastity, and obedience, probably hoping to embrace the religious life in time.

But before she attained her desire of the religious life, Pierina was raped and beaten to death by an assailant. The people of the village were horrified by the violent crime, especially since Pierina's personal holiness and singular devotion to Christ were well-known in the region. Pierina's funeral was one of the largest ever held in that part of Italy, and she was laid to rest in her hometown. Today, a small monument with her picture at the place her body was found has replaced the wooden cross put up by her father and brothers.

Pope John Paul II beatified Pierina Morosini on October 4, 1987, as a young woman who symbolizes purity in this modern world of rampant violence and suffering. Her personal vows and her daily service were honored as acts that graced her family and neighbors, and her death as a true martyrdom.

✠

Pierre Bonhomme (July 4, 1803 – September 9, 1861)
Founder and Preacher

Pierre Bonhomme was born in Gramat, France, and was drawn from a very young age to the priesthood. He made his life's first aim preparing to enter the seminary; thus, upon finishing studies at the Royal College, he entered the major seminary of Cahors in November 1818. On December 23, 1827, he was ordained a priest.

From the start, Fr. Pierre proved an exemplary priest. As a parish priest in Gramat, he was aware immediately of the severe plight of the forgotten, poor, and sick in his area. Despite the limited financial resources available to him, he launched a dedicated program of care that relied upon young people to provide crucial assistance. His assistants came chiefly from a school for boys that he had opened while still a deacon. Within a short time, he was able to open a home for those most in need of help.

In 1831, Fr. Pierre opened a preparatory school for young men planning on entering the seminary. He also started a group called the Daughters of Mary to foster the spiritual life of young girls in Gramat. These young women became the Congregation of the Sisters of Our Lady of Calvary, started in Gramat.

Meanwhile, Fr. Pierre became renowned for his brilliant preaching. He traveled extensively to proclaim the Gospel and attract new members for the congregation. His advancing years, however, brought increasing difficulties from a throat disease that slowly took away his voice. This infirmity compelled him to start a school for deaf-mute children in 1854; in 1856, he dispatched members of the congregation to Paris to begin a home for deaf-mutes. The congregation today is found in France, Brazil, Argentina, Guinea, the Ivory Coast, and the Philippines.

Pope John Paul II beatified him on March 23, 2003. The pope proclaimed:

> "The commandment of the Lord is pure, enlightening the eyes" (Ps 18 [19]:10). This naturally applies to Fr. Pierre Bonhomme, who in listening to the Word of God, notably the Beatitudes and the accounts of the Passion of the Lord, with Mary's guidance, found the way to live in intimacy with Christ and imitate him. The meditation of the Scripture was the incomparable source of all his pastoral activity, especially of his dedication to the poor, the sick, deaf-mutes, and the disabled, for whom he founded the Institute of the "Sisters of Our Lady of Calvary." Following the example of the new Blessed, we can repeat, "My model will be Jesus Christ; I am delighted to be like him whom I love." May Fr. Bonhomme encourage us to become familiar with Scripture, to love our Saviour in order to be his untiring witnesses by our words and our life.

✢

Pierre François Jamet
(September 13, 1762 – January 12, 1845)
Patron of the Deaf

Pierre Francois Jamet was born in Fresnes, France, where he was raised with a deep reverence for the faith. While growing up, Pierre received the grace of a priestly vocation and became aware of the suffering of the handicapped in his region. He entered the local seminary, where he completed his studies for the priesthood.

Ordained in 1787, Pierre was assigned to the position of chaplain and confessor to the convent of the Sisters of the Good Savior. The French Revolution began taking a toll on Catholic institutions at the same time. When Pierre and other priests were ordered to take an oath of allegiance to the anti-Catholic state authorities. herefused to take such an oath in good conscience. As a result, he had to seek shelter and conduct his ministry in secret.

Pierre had started his apostolate of caring for the handicapped and mentally ill sometime before having to hide from the authorities, and the terrors unleashed in his region of France did not stop him. In seclusion or disguise throughout this period, he began a sign language dictionary for his deaf and mute charges. (He wrote 10,000 entries but did not complete the masterwork before his death.)

When the French Revolution came to an end, Pierre went to Caen University, where he was revered. He served as rector of the university there from 1822-1830. At first, he combined this role with his care of the handicapped, then spent the remaining years of his life dedicated solely to these patients.

Pope John Paul II beatified Pierre Francois Jamet on May 10, 1987. At his beatification ceremony, 200 deaf-mutes signed the entire proceedings. Pierre was praised as a father of the needy and an individual who could not be terrorized into abandoning the people entrusted to him by Christ.

✢

Pierre Vigne (August 20, 1670 – July 8, 1740)
French Foundress of the Sisters of the Blessed Sacrament

Pierre was born in Privas, France; his father, also Pierre, was a textile merchant and his mother was Frances Gautier. Provided with a solid Catholic upbringing, he was active in his parish and was asked by the pastor to serve as witness to baptisms, marriages, and deaths, despite the fact that he was only eleven years old.

In 1690, Pierre entered the Sulpician Seminary in Viviers and was ordained a priest in 1694 in Bourg St. Andeol. For the next six years, he served as a parish priest. In 1700, however, he joined the Vincentians in Lyon and made preparation for work among the poor. Six years later, he departed the Vincentians, but he was as dedicated as ever to work among the poor and those in spiritual need.

For the next three decades, he conducted missions in Vivarais and Dauphiné. He preached, said Mass, heard confessions, and, especially, promoted the adoration of the Eucharist. In 1712, he arrived at Boucieu-le-Roi and established a Way of the Cross. The construction of the stations attracted several young women who expressed a desire for the religious life. Thus was established the Congregation of the Sisters of the Blessed Sacrament in 1715, with the purpose of promoting the Eucharist and providing Christian instruction to children.

Fr. Pierre continued his other labors, including writing books on spirituality and performing a vast array of charitable works. In 1724, he became an associate member of the Priests of the Blessed Sacrament, a society that was dedicated to the enrichment of the lives of priests.

In 1740, he was at a mission in Rencurel, in the Vercors Mountains, when he fell ill during and died soon after. He was beatified by Pope John Paul II on Oct. 3, 2004. The pope said:

> Contemplating Christ present in the Eucharist and the saving Passion, Fr. Peter Vigne was led to be a true disciple and a faithful missionary of the Church. May his example give the faithful the desire to draw daring for the mission from the love of the Eucharist and from the adoration of the Blessed Sacrament! Let us ask him to move the hearts of the young so that, if God calls them, they are ready to dedicate themselves to him without reserve in the priesthood or in the Religious life. May the Church in France find in Fr. Vigne an example to raise up new sowers of the Gospel!

✠

Pietro Casani (September 8, 1570 – October 13, 1647)
Co-Founder of the Scalopians

Petro Casani was a companion of Joseph Calasanz.

He was born in Lucca, Italy, the only son of Gaspar and Elizabeth Drogo Casani. His father was not religious and was openly opposed to Catholic devotions, but Pietro was dedicated to the Blessed Virgin Mary at an early age. In 1591, when his mother died, he realized that he had a religious vocation and turned his back on the world to study for the priesthood.

In 1594, Pietro entered the Congregation of the Blessed Virgin, impressing his superiors with holiness and dedication. He completed his religious and seminary training and was ordained in the Lateran Basilica in Rome on September 23, 1600. He worked in the congregation's various institutions until he met Joseph Calasanz, who was involved in a religious and social revolution — forming special schools for the poor. The religious of the Blessed Virgin of Lucca undertook the ministry of the Pious Schools, and the Congregation of the Mother of God was founded. When the two congregations were recognized by the Holy See in March, 1617, Pietro became a Clerk Regular of the Mother of God of the Pious Schools. He was invested by Cardinal Benedetto Giusitiniani on March 25.

Pietro served as the first novice master, demonstrating extraordinary concerns about religious formation and the educational apostolate. He taught that "patience and prayer are enough." He served as a leading figure in the expansion of the congregation, in time becoming the Provincial Superior of Genoa and Naples and commissary general of Moravia. Pietro also served the Scalopians or Piarists as an assistant Superior General for twenty years, bringing a quiet resolve and commitment to that post in the congregation. Pietro died in Rome, mourned by his fellow religious and all who benefited from the heroic performance of his religious duties.

Pope John Paul II beatified Pietro Casani on October 1, 1995, stating:

> Pietro Casani, a native of Lucca, joined Joseph Calasanz in 1614 "to educate" Roman children "in piety and letters." Open to love of neighbor and dedicated to the education of poor children, he said before his death, "Much can be accomplished by patience and prayer."

✠

Philip Ripoll Morata — see Felipe Ripall Morata

✠

Philip Munarriz — see Martyrs of Barbastro

✠

Philip Rinaldi — see Filippo Rinaldi

✠

Philip Siphong — see Martyrs of Thailand

✠

Philip Smaldoni — see Filippo Smaldone

✠

Pina Suriano (February 18, 1915 – May 19, 1950)

Foundress of the Association of the Daughters of Mary

Giuseppina Suriano was born in Partinico, near Palermo, Sicily, to Giuseppe and Graziella Costantino. Always called "Pina" by those who knew her, she grew up in a busy parish and was an ardent supporter of Catholic Action and the Association of the Daughters of Mary. She served as secretary of Catholic Action from 1939 to 1948 and as president of Youth Catholic Action from 1945 to 1948.

While eager to enter the religious life and convinced by prayer that she should do so, she was prevented in fulfilling her vocation by her family's determination for her to marry. They resisted any inclination on her part to enter the convent and went so far as to declare that it would be better to have a daughter who was dead than one who was a nun. She faced this torment with acceptance and made of her suffering a sacrifice for Christ. Having made a vow of chastity, she courteously declined the various offers of marriage and remained steadfast in her desire to become a nun.

Finally, in 1940, she was permitted to enter the Institute of the Daughters of St. Anne in Palermo. After only eight days, however, she was forced to leave when a medical exam discovered she had a heart problem. Undaunted, she kept to her intention; in 1948, along with three other women, Pina consecrated herself to Christ in founding the Association of the Daughters of Mary, for which she served as president until she died suddenly of a heart attack two years later, at the age of thirty-five.

She was beatified by Pope John Paul II on Sept. 5, 2004, when he said:

Bl. Pina Suriano, a native of Partinico in the Diocese of Monreale [Sicily], loved Jesus with an ardent and faithful love to the point that she wrote in all sincerity: "I do nothing other than live for Jesus." She spoke to Jesus from her bride's heart: "Jesus, make me more and more your own. Jesus, I want to live and die with you and for you."

Since childhood, she had been a member of the female branch of Catholic Action, of which she later became parish director, finding important incentives in the Association for human and cultural growth in an intense atmosphere of fraternal friendship. She gradually developed a simple, steadfast desire to give her young life to God as an offering of love and especially for the sanctification and perseverance of priests.

✠

Pio Campidelli (April 29, 1868 – November 2, 1889)
Model of Youthful Piety

A Passionist priest, Pio Campidelli was granted only a brief life on earth.

He was born in Trebbio, near Rimini, Italy, and was baptized Luigi on the same day. The fourth of six children, he was the son of Joseph and Filomena Belpani Campidelli, farmers of the region. Luigi's father died of typhoid fever in 1874, at which time an uncle came to the farm to help with the heavier work. Luigi labored on the farm, a tract of land that demanded the time and energies of the entire family, but still managed to attend school and served as an altar boy, becoming devoted to the prayer life after his First Communion at age ten.

Two and a half years later, Luigi and his family attended a Passionist mission. He applied for admission to the congregation and was accepted in 1882, taking the religious name Pio of St. Aloysius Gonzaga. Pio took his first vows on April 30, 1884, and began studying for the priesthood. In 1871, he received the tonsure and minor orders at San Entizio, near Viterbo.

It was then discovered that Pio was in the last stages of tuberculosis, doomed to an early death by the ravages of the disease. He accepted the medical prognosis serenely, declaring that he was a willing victim of love for the Church. Surrounded by the Passionists, whom he thanked for their concern and care, Pio died in Casale.

Pope John Paul II beatified Pio Campidelli on November 17, 1985, declaring that the boy of only fourteen years of age was spiritually advanced. The Holy Father praised Pio for offering his life and honored the new Blessed for his spirit of penance, Christlike ideals, and serenity. The Holy Father honored Pio in the International Youth Year, declaring:

It is fitting that this year should see him honored and put before all young people as a model and an inspiration.

☩

Pius IX, Pope (May 13, 1792 – February 7, 1878)
Longest Reigning Pontiff in Church History

The Vicar of Christ from 1846-1878, Pius IX witnessed the demise of the Papal States and the end of the temporal power of the papacy; Vatican Council I; the definition of the Immaculate Conception; and the expansion of the Church's vast global missionary enterprise.

He was born Giovanni Maria Mastai-Ferretti in Senigallia, in the March of Ancona, the fourth son of a count. After overcoming epilepsy as a child, he studied at Viterbo and Rome and was ordained in 1819. From 1823-1825, he took part in a papal mission to Chile. Despite his comparative youth, in 1827, he was appointed archbishop of Spoleto and, in 1832, bishop of Imola. Known for his open mind and considered by many to be liberal with strong Italian nationalist tendencies, he was made a cardinal in 1840 by Pope Gregory XVI and was a leading candidate to succeed him at the conclave of 1846. After two days, he was elected pope on June 16, 1846.

Pope Pius IX inaugurated his reign with conciliatory measures toward supporters of Italian unity and democracy that made him immensely popular. He made it clear, however, that he had no intention of surrendering his authority to a constitutional regime, then angered reactionaries by adopting a neutral stand in the war that erupted to oust the Austrians from Italy. Pius, denounced as a traitor, soon was faced with a crisis that grew violent with the murder of his prime minister, Count Rossi, on November 15, 1848. Besieged on the Quirinal by rebels, he assumed a disguise and fled to Gaeta on November 24. A Roman republic was established in February 1849, and Pius appealed for aid from the Catholic powers. He returned to the Eternal City on April 12, 1850, with the help of French troops.

Pius subsequently set a politically conservative course for the Papal States, with the capable help of Secretary of State Cardinal Giacomo Antonelli. This included resisting the process of the *Risorgimento,* the movement to unite all of Italy. Nevertheless, he could not stop the loss of the Papal States in 1860 after the defeat of the papal forces at the Battle of Castelfidardo; nor could he prevent the eventual seizure of Rome and the last temporal possessions of the papacy by Italian soldiers on September 20, 1870. The pope was given assurances of the inviolable nature of the Vatican and his person by the Law of Guarantees (May 13, 1871), but Pius protested vehemently and declared himself a prisoner of the Vatican from which he would never leave. He issued the decree *Non Expedit* (1868), forbidding Catholics from participating in Italian political affairs, and thus began a conflict that would not be resolved until 1929 and the Lateran Treaty.

While overshadowed by political events, Pius's long reign was also filled with remarkable vitality and energy and was noted for its many successes in ecclesiastical areas. He restored the hierarchy in England (1850) and the Netherlands (1853), negotiated a number of concordats with various states in Europe and beyond, and worked with bishops to respond to the loss in political power by devoting even greater emphasis to spiritual concerns.

In 1864, Pius denounced several errors that had sprung up in Church teaching with the encyclical *Quanta Cura,* to which he attached the *Syllabus Errorum.* He also gave a definition of the Immaculate Conception (1854), convened the First Vatican Council (1869-1870), and promoted the international missions.

On September 5, 1999, Pope John Paul II beatified Pope Pius IX, "Pio Nono," along with Pope John XXIII. The Holy Father said of Pius IX:

Listening to the words of the Gospel acclamation, "Lord, lead me on a straight road," our thoughts naturally turn to the human and religious life of Pope Pius IX, Giovanni Maria Mastai Ferretti. Amid the turbulent events of his time, he was an example of unconditional fidelity to the immutable deposit of revealed truths. Faithful to the duties of his ministry in every circumstance, he always knew how to give absolute primacy to God and to spiritual values. His lengthy pontificate was not at all easy and he had much to suffer in fulfilling his mission of service to the Gospel. He was much loved, but also hated and slandered. However, it was precisely in these conflicts that the light of his virtues shone most brightly: these prolonged sufferings tempered his trust in divine Providence, whose sovereign lordship over human events he never doubted. This was the source of Pius IX's deep serenity, even amid the misunderstandings and attacks of so many hostile people. He liked to say to those close to him, "In human affairs we must be content to do the best we can and then abandon ourselves to Providence, which will heal our human faults and shortcomings."

$\mathcal{R}$

✠

Rafael Arnáiz Barón (April 9, 1911 – April 26, 1938)
Trappist Oblate and Mystic

Rafael Arnáiz Barón was born in Burgos, Spain, the eldest of four children in a prominent family. Raised devoutly and developing spiritual maturity at an early age, he was educated by the Jesuits, then studied architecture in Madrid. He was described by contemporaries as being lively, extroverted, and artistic.

At age eighteen, Rafael realized that the religious life was his goal. He started an intense prayer life, even while involved in the secular world. In 1933, after completing military service, he joined the Trappists at San Isidro de Dueños Monastery. Shortly after joining, however, he was found to be suffering from diabetes mellitus, and he was forced to return home to recuperate properly. When he could return, Rafael rejoinedthe Trappists as an oblate, as he was unable to assume regular monastic roles because of his illness. After suffering another attack of the disease, he died at age twenty-seven.

Rafael was also a writer of profound spiritual and ascetical works. These writings spread quickly throughout Spain, and his grave at San Isidro Monastery became a pilgrimage site.

Pope John Paul II beatified him on September 27, 1992, declaring:

"Fight the good fight of faith," the reading urges us, and adds, "Take firm hold on the everlasting life to which you were called when, in the presence of many witnesses, you made your noble profession of faith" (1 Tim. 6:12). With great joy we can proclaim today that the new Blessed born in Spain incarnated in [his] life these words of St. Paul. Blessed Rafael Arnáiz Barón incarnated them in his brief but intense monastic life as a Trappist, being an example, especially for young people, of a loving and unconditional response to the divine call. "God alone!" he often repeated in his spiritual exercises.

✠

Rafael Melchior Chylinski
(January 8, 1690 – December 2, 1741)
Noble Patron of the Poor

Rafael Melchior Chylinski was a noble, born in Wysoczka, Poland, and raised in an era of self-indulgence and extravagance. But he turned his back on his hereditary rights and privileges to become a Conventual Franciscan.

As a Franciscan priest, he attained a remarkable degree of holiness and became known as a patron of the poor. During the terrible epidemic of Krakow in 1736, Rafael, living in Lageiewniki (part of Lodz), cared for the sick without sparing himself; he received victims of the plague and offered them shelter and medical aid. He lived out his religious vows faithfully with a resolve and piety that inspired others.

He died at Lageiewniki in 1741, and Pope John Paul II beatified Rafael Melchior Chylinski on June 9, 1991, in the square of Farmer's Park in War-saw. He spoke of Rafael this way:

> Fr. Rafael was never a deputy, a Member of Parliament. He chose the voca-tion of a poor son of St. Francis, but his witness is very similar. His life was hidden, hidden in Christ; it was a protest against the conscience, the atti-tude, and the self-destructive behavior of the nobility in those Saxon times, and we know how the story ended. But why does Providence remind us of this today? Why only now has this process matured through all the signs of earth and heaven, and we can proclaim Fr. Rafael blessed? Look for the answer to this question. We are searching for an answer to this question. The Church does not have the answers at hand; the Pope does not want to suggest any interpretation to you. All of us, 35 million Poles, should reflect together on the meaning of this beatification in the year of our Lord 1991.

✠

Rafael Guizar y Valencia (April 26, 1878 – June 6, 1938)
Bishop of the Poor

Rafael Guizar y Valencia was born in Cotija, Michoacan, Mexico. Receiv-ing the grace of a religious vocation, he entered the seminary at Zamora and completed his priestly studies. He was ordained on June 1, 1901, and started his ministry with exceptional zeal — just four years later, he was appointed apostolic missionary and spiritual director of the seminary.

The revolutionary government in control of Mexico at the time was anti-Catholic and widespread in its denunciation of the Faith. To combat this evil, Rafael published *La Nación*, a periodical that kept the faithful informed and inspired. He was singled out for harassment as a result and had to move to Mexico City, where he disguised himself as a junk dealer so that he could move about freely to minister to those in need. Rafael was sentenced to death by the Mexican courts *in absentia*, and left the country to work in Cuba and in the United States.

He was consecrated the bishop of Veracruz, Mexico, in 1919, and started revitalizing the diocese, writing a catechism of Christian doctrine, and rebuilding the seminary, which was later confiscated by the government. Rafael then moved his program for priest formation to Mexico City, where it operated successfully for fifteen years. He sold all that he had during this period to nurture the poor.

At the same time, he was suffering from cardiac problems, diabetes, obesity, and phlebitis. Forced into exile again, Rafael worked in the United States, Cuba, and Colombia. He finally made the dramatic decision to return to Veracruz and continue his apostolate. Taken ill from overwork, he died in Mexico City.

Pope John Paul II beatified Rafael on June 29, 1995, proclaiming:

> He carried out his apostolate as a priest and Bishop amid almost constant persecution and situations of danger. For many years he had no fixed residence, yet no difficulty prevented him from fulfilling his missionary tasks. He said repeatedly: "I will give my life for the salvation of souls," like the Good Shepherd. Those who knew him said there was no power or obstacle which could weaken his evangelizing zeal. Teaching catechism and giving popular missions were the focus of his activity. His native Mexico, the United States, Guatemala, and Cuba were to benefit from his pastoral zeal. His spirituality was based on Eucharistic devotion and love of the Virgin Mary. Fostering priestly vocations, administering the sacraments, particularly Penance and Matrimony, regularizing many common-law unions, preaching the word of God, as well as constant devotion to prayer, also made him a man of faith and action who was concerned for the salvation of souls.

✠

Rafaela Ybarra de Villalongo
(January 16, 1843 – February 23, 1900)

An Apostolate to Forgotten Souls

Rafaela Ybarra de Villalongo was born in Bilbao, Spain, to a noble and pious family. As was the custom then, she was married quite young, but her husband passed away within a short time. She had always been drawn to the service of the Church; after much prayerful reflection, she decided that she was called by God to devote her life to an apostolate of service to others.

This commitment to service manifested itself in a very specific way. She established a new religious congregation, the Institute of the Holy Guardian Angels. Under her care, the young women who joined the institute labored to found hospitals, maternity homes, and programs designed to give comfort, protection, and hope to the many children who were left without parents through disaster, neglect, abandonment, or social upheaval. Rafaela also administered programs to aid the poor of all ages and relieve the suffering found throughout Spain among the needy, chronically ill, and forgotten souls. Her work continued right up until her death in Bilbao in 1900.

Pope John Paul II beatified Rafaela Ybarra de Villalongo on September 30, 1984, saying:

> Her unconditional dedication to God and others in the different circumstances of her life is admirable . . . From the Cross and prayer she was able to draw strength to offer herself on the altars of Christian love.

✠

Regina Protmann (1552 – January 18, 1613)

Founder of the Congregation of the Sisters of St. Catherine

Regina Protmann dedicated her life to plague victims and the needy.

She was born in Warmia, Poland, the daughter of a wealthy sixteenth-century family. Raised solidly in the Catholic faith, noted for her beauty and intelligence, she chose to join a Marian sodality founded by the Jesuits.

In 1571, Regina committed herself to a life of prayer, eventually working to establish a contemplative institute with perpetual vows. The proposed sisters would not follow the strict enclosure, however, so that they might be able be able to visit the sick in their homes. Thus, the congregation would be able to minister to many plague victims in northeastern Poland, a situation all too common at that time. Her foundation was called the Congregation of the Sisters of St. Catherine, and the rule was approved in 1583 by the bishop of Warmia.

Over the next few years, three houses were established through Regina's tireless efforts. She also revised the rule for the congregation with the help of the local Jesuits. From these origins, the congregation spread to different parts of the globe. Today, the Sisters are found in nine countries on three continents.

Pope John Paul II beatified Regina on June 13, 1999, announcing:

> Blessed Regina Protmann, Foundress of the Congregation of the Sisters of St. Catherine, a native of Braniewo, dedicated herself with all her heart to the work of renewal of the Church at the end of the sixteenth and beginning of the seventeenth centuries. She engaged in this activity, which arose from her love for Christ above all things, after the Council of Trent. She took an active part in the post-conciliar reform of the Church, carrying out a humble work of mercy with great generosity. She founded a Congregation, which united contemplation of the mysteries of God with the care of the sick in their homes and the instruction of young children and older girls. She gave particular attention to the pastoral care of women. With no thought of herself, Blessed Regina looked to the needs of the people and the Church, meeting them with foresight. The words "As God wills" became the motto of her life. Ardent love urged her to fulfill the Heavenly Father's will, following the example of the Son of God. She did not shrink from the cross of daily service in giving witness to the Risen Christ.

☩

Rosalie Rendu (September 9, 1786 – February 7, 1856)
A Lifetime of Service to the Poor

A member of the Daughters of Charity who cared for the poor in Paris for fifty years, Jeanne Marie Rendu was born at Confort, France, in the Jura Mountains; her parents were simple middle-class mountain people, and she was the eldest of four daughters. Jeanne Marie was only three years old when the French Revolution began, and the family decided to take the immense risk of aiding priests during the dark days of the persecution of the Church by the French revolutionary government. Among those to whom they gave sanctuary was the Bishop of Annecy, who lived among them as a "laborer" named Pierre.

Having been raised in an atmosphere of heroic faith, Jeanne Marie understood well what was being asked of her when, in May 1796, her father died, followed by her youngest sister in July of the same year. She assisted her mother in the difficult time that followed and helped care for her sisters.

Once the political situation eased in France, Jeanne Marie's mother sent her for a proper education to the Ursuline Sisters in Gex. She lived in the boarding school for two years, during which time she discovered the important work being done in the local hospital by the the Company of the Daughters of Charity of St. Vincent de Paul in caring for the sick and dying. At once, she knew that she was destined to join the Daughters. So, in 1802, she set out with her mother's permission to enter the Daughters of Charity in Paris. She took the religious name of Sr. Rosalie, making her first vows in 1807, and embarked with great zeal upon the religious life.

She was soon sent to the house of the Daughters in the Mouffetard District. The neighborhood was one of the most destitute in the sprawling city; there, Sr. Rosalie entered a time of service directly to the poor that lasted for fifty-four years.

In 1815, Sr. Rosalie was named Superior of the community, and she supervised the opening of a free clinic, a pharmacy, a school, an orphanage, a childcare center, a youth club for young workers, and a home for the elderly.

Mother Rosalie earned a far-ranging reputation for holiness and commitment to the poor. She was able to secure financial assistance from the wealthiest citizens of Paris; when she was visited by the most powerful figures in the country, they soon understood that she had only once concern — to care for those unable to help themselves, and to do so in Christ's name. Among her guests were Emperor Napoleon III and his wife, Empress Eugenie. She was also consulted for her wisdom and advice by other spiritual giants of the age, such as Frederick Ozanam, co-founder of the Conferences of St. Vincent de Paul, and Jean Léon Le Prevost, later the founder of the Religious of St. Vincent de Paul.

In 1852, Napoleon III bestowed upon her the Cross of the Legion of Honor for her work on behalf of the poor. She intended to refuse the honor, but the Superior General of the Priests of the Mission and the Daughters of Charity begged her to accept.

She continued working even as her health faded, and in the face of growing blindness. Her death was the cause of mourning throughout the French capital. Pope John Paul II beatified her on November 9, 2003. At that time, he declared:

In an era troubled by social conflicts, Rosalie Rendu joyfully became a servant to the poorest, restoring dignity to each one by means of material help, education and the teaching of the Christian mystery, inducing Frédéric Ozanam to place himself at the service of the poor.

Her charity was inventive. Where did she draw the strength to carry out so many things? From her intense prayer life and the continuous praying of the Rosary, which she never abandoned. Her secret was simple: to see the face of Christ in every man and woman, as a true daughter of St. Vincent de Paul and like another Sister of her epoch, St. Catherine Labouré. Let us give thanks for the witness of charity that the Vincentian family gives unceasingly to the world!

⊹

Rupert Mayer (January 23, 1876 – November 1, 1945)
Martyr of Sachsenhausen

He was born in Stuttgart, Germany, the son of Kolumban and Maria Schaürer Mayer. Raised devoutly in the Catholic Faith and well educated, Rupert entered the seminary and, after some years of study, was ordained on May 2, 1899. A year later, he entered the Society of Jesus.

The Jesuits sent Rupert to Lichtenstein to study, then assigned him to the Society's various apostolates. He became chaplain during World War I and was severely wounded. When he recovered, Rupert went on to serve as a chaplain of a Sodality and conducted a mission for travelers.

He saw the troubled condition of Germany in the beginning of the 1930s and tried to alert the faithful of the coming disasters. As a result, the Nazis warned Rupert to cease his sermons and attacks in 1933. Although they threatened him with severe retaliations, however, he was not cowed by their words. He continued to attack the Nazis from the pulpit and, in 1936, was arrested for his activities for a brief period. He did not allow the Nazis to silence him completely, however, and he earned their enmity.

On November 3, 1939, Rupert was sent to Sachsenhausen concentration camp, where he experienced severe abuse and torture. He was there only a short time when he was sent to Ettal Abbey, then was detained in the abbey until Germany surrendered to the Allied forces. He returned to Munich at the war's end, on May 11, 1945. Exhausted by his sufferings, Rupert died later that year, in Munich. He was buried in the Sodality Church in Munich, revered for his heroism in opposing the brutal Nazi regime.

Pope John Paul II beatified Rupert Mayer on May 3, 1987, praising him as a steadfast priest who understood that the Church could not survive the new barbarism of the world without champions who risked life and limb to reverberate Catholic truths in the world.

$\mathcal{S}$

✠

Salvator Lilli of Cappadocia and Companions
— see Martyrs of Armenia

✠

Sancja Szymkowiak (July 11, 1910 – August 29, 1942)
"Angel of Goodness"

Sancja Szymkowiak was born in Mozdzanów (Ostrów Wielkopolski), Poland, to Augustine and Mary Duchalska, the youngest of five children and the only girl. In 1929, she entered the University of Poznan, focusing on Languages and Foreign Literature.

During the summer of 1934, Sancja went on a pilgrimage to the Shrine of Lourdes, France, and here offered herself to the Blessed Virgin, placing her life into the hands of the Mother of God. After devoting a year with the Congregation of the Oblate Sisters of the Sacred Heart at Montluçon, Sancja returned to Poland in June 1936 and entered the Congregation of the Daughters of Our Lady of Sorrows, the "Seraphic Sisters." She took the religious name Mary Santia. On 30 July 1938 she made her first vows, then worked for a year in the nursery school of Poznan-Naramowice; she also began studies in pharmacology. Her eventual graduation, however, was prevented by the outbreak of the Second World War in September 1939.

The German army occupied Poznan, and the Polish sisters were put under house arrest and forced to care for a company of 100 German soldiers. Also housed there were English and French prisoners of war who had been captured and moved to the convent. Sancja's skill with languages proved very helpful, as she was able to translate for the foreign prisoners.

In February 1940, the religious persecution of Poland by the Nazis worsened, and Sancja received permission to return to her family for safety. Instead, she remained in the convent and submitted to the demands of hard labor that were imposed by the German occupiers. Such was the care she gave to the English and French prisoners that they took to calling her the "angel of goodness" and "Saint Santia."

The forced labor and endless hours of nursing care eventually took their toll, and Sancja contracted tuberculosis. The tuberculosis spread to her pharynx, but she carried on with her work despite the pain and exhaustion. She professed her solemn vows on July 6, 1942 and died, a little more than a month later, at the age of thirty-two.

Pope John Paul II beatified Sanja Szymkowiak on Aug. 18, 2002, declaring:

> The work of mercy traced out a path in the religious vocation of Blessed Sancja Szymkowiak, Sr. "Seraphica." She had already received from her family an ardent love for the Sacred Heart of Jesus, and in this spirit she was filled with goodness towards others, especially the poor and the needy. She began to lend help to the poor, first as a member of the Marian Guild and of the St. Vincent Mercy Association; then, having embraced the religious life, she devoted herself to the service of others with greater fervour. She accepted the difficult times of the Nazi occupation as an occasion to give herself completely to the needy. She considered her religious vocation a gift of Divine Mercy. As I greet the Congregation of the Daughters of Our Lady of Sorrows, the "Seraphic" Sisters, I turn to all religious and consecrated persons. Let Blessed Sancja be your patron. Make your own her spiritual witness, summarized in a simple phrase: "To give yourself to God, you have to give yourself to the point of totally losing yourself."

✠

Savina Petrilli (August 29, 1851 – April 18, 1923)
In the Footsteps of St. Catherine of Siena

The founder of the Sisters of the Poor, Savina Petrilli was encouraged in her ministry by Pope Pius IX.

She was born in Siena, Italy, where she was raised in a pious home and introduced at age ten to the life of St. Catherine of Siena. Savina began to practice devotion to Christ in the Eucharist and to Christ Crucified. She also became aware of the needs of the poor. The Children of Mary Sodality in her parish aided in her formation, and her parish priest was an active confessor and spiritual guide.

In 1869, Savina made a pilgrimage to Rome. In an audience with the future Blessed Pope Pius IX, Savina was told by the Holy Father to walk in St. Catherine's footsteps. She returned home to pray; in 1872, she confided to her dying sister, Emilia, that she planned to found a religious congregation. She approached the archbishop of Siena with the same aspiration and, in 1873, this prelate instructed Savina to draw up rules for a community to be called the Sisters of the Poor.

One year later, Savina and her companions moved into a small apartment and cared for an abandoned baby, the first of many. Savina faced severe trials, but her Sisters of the Poor received diocesan approval and approbation from the Holy See in 1875. New foundations were made in Italy and Brazil, then in Argentina and Italy. In 1922, Savina was diagnosed with malignant cancer. She continued work until her death.

Pope John Paul II beatified Savina Petrilli on April 24, 1988, declaring:

> You are my God . . . I extol you with my life, with all my strength, Mother Savina seems to say, but I extol you by gathering before you, my God, the most neglected brothers and sisters seeking along the ways of the world all those whom people despise, in order to lead every person to the joy of the banquet of the Kingdom. Therefore, I extol you by extending the work of the Sisters of the Poor to the most neglected areas of the earth and the most difficult working conditions, so that everyone may find joy and peace and "give thanks to the Lord, for he is good; for his kindness endures forever" (Ps. 117[118]:29).

✠

Scubilion (John Bernard Rosseau) (March 22, 1797- April 13, 1867)
Religious Catechist of the Slaves

Scubilion was a Christian Brother who was born Jean-Bernard Rousseau in Anny-Côte (Tharaigeau), France. His Burgundian family was very devout, and Jean-Bernard performed labors for his local parish, including the activities of a catechist. Dedicated and eager to serve others, he received the grace of a religious vocation and applied to the Christian Brothers. He entered the Paris Christian Brothers novitiate in 1822, receiving the religious name of Scubilion. In the decade following his profession, he served in the Christian Brothers' schools in France, where he was much loved by his students because he was kind and treated everyone who came to him with dignity and respect.

That Christlike presence would change the lives of men and women in a distant land when Scubilion was assigned to the island of Réunion in the Indian Ocean. In 1833, he accepted this missionary assignment and sailed to

Réunion, where he would remain for thirty-four years. The people to whom Scubilion would dedicate his time and energies on Réunion were the enslaved natives. As he began to work with them, he was stunned to realize that no one had given them any level of education or catechism. So, bringing his kindly manner and his profound sense of worth of individual human beings into his mission, he began classes for the slaves.

The slaves came to him in the evenings, after long hours of labor and ill-treatment. He provided Catholic doctrine on many levels, designed to interest the slaves and to prepare them for reception of the sacraments. When the slaves were emancipated in 1848, they turned to Scubilion to guide them through their transition to freedom.

During his last years, Scubilion was exhausted and ill, but he labored in the local parish, winning all to Christ. He died at Sainte-Marie, Isle de Réunion, revered by the islanders.

Pope John Paul II beatified Scubilion on May 2, 1989 — on Réunion — proclaiming:

> The love of God and the love of neighbor were inseparable in him. In the eyes of everyone, he shone with a power of love that revealed the God of Love. He was light, as Christ wished it: "You are the light of the world." He allowed himself to be enlightened by Jesus Christ, and he enlightened others in the light of Jesus Christ by this example and, in particular, by his catechesis among the slaves.

⊹

Secondo Pollo (January 2, 1908 – December 26, 1941)
Italy's Symbol of the Chaplaincy

Secondo Pollo was born in Caresanablot, Italy, near Vercelli, and was raised in a devout family and trained in reverence for the Blessed Sacrament and the Blessed Virgin. Secondo received as well the grace of a religious vocation and entered Montecrivello seminary. He was then sent to the Pontifical Lombard Seminary in Rome and was ordained upon completing his studies.

After ordination, Secondo was assigned to Montecrivello but also served in surrounding parishes. There, he taught catechetical classes to children, using a stable as a classroom in one parish. He rejoiced in being a parish priest, but he was assigned as spiritual director for the major seminary of the archdiocese, where he earned a reputation as a preacher and confessor. In September 1936, Secondo was named archdiocesan chaplain to the Italian Youth of Catholic Action and went to serve as a chaplain in the local prison.

In 1940, Secondo was named administrator of a parish in Larizzate; one year later, he was drafted as a military chaplain. Assigned to the Val Chisone battalion of the Alpine Regiment, he was sent to Montenegro, where he served with honor.

Secondo was fatally wounded while caring for the fallen on the battlefield. With the final words, "I am going to God, who is so good," he bowed his head and died.

Pope John Paul II beatified Secondo Pollo on May 23, 1998, in Vercelli, Italy, with 20,000 faithful in attendance. The Holy Father declared:

> The secrets of Fr. Secondo's ascent to the peaks of holiness were two: continual rootedness in God through prayer, and the most tender devotion to our heavenly Mother, Mary. . . . Let us give thanks to the Lord for the gift of this Blessed and for all the saints and blesseds who, in Christ, the one Mediator of Salvation, build a "bridge" between God and the world by reflecting and radiating heaven's brightness upon humanity making its pilgrim way on earth.

✛

Samuel Marzorati — see Martyrs of Ethiopia

✛

Stanislas Kazimierczyk (1433 – May 3, 1489)
Canon Regular of the Lateran of Corpus Christi

Stanislas Kazimierczyk was born in Casimiria, at the time a part of modern Krakow, Poland. He was the son of a devout couple, Soltyn Matthias and his wife, Hedwige. Stanislas was educated in the local schools, displaying brilliance, and attended Jagiellion University, where he earned a doctorate with honors.

In 1456, he entered the Canons Regular of the Lateran of Corpus Christi, taking his vows as a religious. Stanislas completed his novitiate, was educated for the priesthood, and was then ordained. His austerity and mortification were attracting people even then, and he assumed many roles in the community. Stanislas served as a preacher, master of novices, and sub-prior in his monastery.

His devotion to the Blessed Virgin Mary and the Passion of Christ distinguished Stanislas, but he centered his priestly life on the Holy Eucharist, drawing his strength from the Blessed Sacrament. Stanislas became famous as a peacher, confessor, and spiritual director. He was also a powerful foe of the Wycliffe and Hus heresies.

Although a collection of his homilies was destroyed in World War II, his written spiritual sermons and lectures have survived in part. These display his generous concern for the poor and sick, as well as his towering intellect and spirituality.

Stanislas died in Casmiria and was buried in the church of Corpus Christi. Pope John Paul II beatified himon April 18, 1993, praising him as a glory of Poland and the Church, a giant of the intellect and Faith who helped to preserve his nation's Catholic heritage.

✝

Stefan Wincenty Frelichowski
(January 22, 1913 – February 23, 1945)
Nazi Opponent

A diocesan priest, Stefan Vincenz died caring for prisoners in the Nazi death camps.

He was born in Chelmza, Poland, to Ludwik Frelichowski and Marta Olszewska, both devout Catholics. While in school, Stefan demonstrated a desire to be of service and became a scout, an activity that helped to shape his development, teaching him to have a love of God and country. The time in the scouts also helped Stefan to recognize a priestly vocation. He thus entered the seminary at Pelplin and earned considerable respect from fellow seminarians and teachers for his tranquil nature and his modesty. He also dedicated his life and priesthood to the Heart of Jesus.

Ordained a priest on March 14, 1937, by Bishop Stanislaw Wojciech Okoniewski, Stefan was assigned as an assistant pastor in July 1938 in Torun. While there, he also became chaplain to the local scouts, called the Band of Pomerania. This time of happiness ended abruptly on September 7, 1939, when the German Army entered Torun, as part of the invasion of Poland by the Nazis from the west and the Soviet Red Army from the east. On September 11, all of the priests of the parish were arrested by German security forces, and Stefan began his own emulation of the passion of Christ. He spent the rest of his life in various German prisons and concentration camps: Stutthof, Grenzdorf, Oranienburg-Sachsenhausen and finally Dachau. While in each camp, Stefan demonstrated boundless pastoral zeal and became the spiritual leader of the prisoners. Finally, at Dachau, Stefan became a caregiver for prisoners suffering from typhus. He contracted the disease himself and endured immense suffering before his own death.

Pope John Paul II beatified Stefan Wincenty Frelichowsky during one of his pastoral visits to Poland on June 7, 1999, declaring:

"Blessed are the peacemakers." The dignity of such a designation rightly belongs to Fr. Stefan Wincenty Frelichowsky, raised today to the glory of the altars. His whole life, in fact, is a kind of mirror reflecting the light of that teaching of Christ according to which true happiness is attained only by those who, in union with God, become men and women of peace, peacemakers who bring peace to others. This priest of Torun, whose pastoral service lasted less than eight years, offered a very clear witness of his giving himself to God and to others. Drawing his sustenance from God, from the very first years of his priesthood, with the wealth of his priestly charism he went wherever the grace of salvation needed to be brought. He learned the secrets of the human heart and adapted pastoral methods to the needs of every person he met.

✠

Sygmunt Gorozdowski — see Zygmunt Gorozdowski

ᴛ

✛

Teodor Romza (April 14, 1911 – November 1, 1947)
Eparch of Mukachevo

Teodor Romza was born in the village of Veliky Bychkiv, Transcarpathia. Recognizing from an early age that he was called to the priesthood, he studied philosophy in Rome from 1930-1933; his theological studies were also undertaken in Rome from 1933-1937, culminating in his reception of a licentiate in Sacred Theology. Soon after, he was appointed an administrator of the parish in Berezovo.

In 1939, Teodor was named a professor of philosophy at the seminary in Uzhorod. He held this position with great distinction and, on September 24, 1944, he was ordained to the episcopacy for the Mukachevo eparchy. His appointment came at a dark time: the Second World War was ending, and the Ukraine had once more fallen under the harsh atheistic domination of the Soviet Union.

As eparch, Teodor labored ceaselessly to resist the cruel activities and defend the rights of the Catholic Church against the Red Army in the Carpathian region of Ukraine. He became such a force against Communism that the Soviets singled him out for murder. On October 27, 1947, Soviet troops failed in their initial attempt to kill the eparch. Gravely wounded but still alive, he was taken to the hospital in Mukachiv; however, there his care was sabotaged, and the Soviets had him poisoned.

Pope John Paul II beatified Teodor Romza on June 27, 2001, during a pastoral visit to the Ukraine, along with a group of other revered martyrs for the Faith in the Ukraine. The pontiff said of the martyrs:

> The Servants of God who are today inscribed in the Book of the Blessed represent all categories of the ecclesial community: among them are Bishops and priests, monks, nuns, and lay people. They were tested in many ways by the followers of the infamous Nazi and Communist ideologies. Aware of the sufferings which these faithful disciples of Christ were undergoing, my Predecessor Pius XII, sharing in their anguish, expressed his solidarity with those "who are persevering in faith and resisting the

enemies of Christianity with the same unswerving fortitude with which their ancestors once resisted." He praised their courage in remaining "faithfully joined to the Roman Pontiff and their Pastors" (Apostolic Letter *Orientales Ecclesias*, 15 December 1952: AAS 45 [1953], 8).

☩

Teresa Bracco (February 24, 1924 – August 28, 1944)
Victim of the Nazis

Teresa Bracco was born in Santa Giulia, the daughter of Giacomo and Anna Pera Bracco, Catholic farmers. The family was pious, reciting the rosary each evening, and Teresa learned her devotions in her home. She was also taught the Faith by the local parish priest, Fr. Natale Olivieri, who gave her religious books. Teresa was well-behaved in school and attended Mass each day. Her inspiration was St. Dominic Savio.

In the fall of 1943, guerrilla warfare began in the Acqui region of Italy, Teresa's home. The local people watched these clashes between the partisans and German troops and tried to avoid becoming involved. On July 24, 1944, however, the partisans fought the Germans on the road between Cairo Montenotte and Cortemilia. The next day, the Germans began punitive assaults on the region, entering Santa Giulia on August 28. The Germans believed Santa Giulia was a partisan stronghold and put repressive measures into place.

Three young women, including Teresa, were taken prisoner in the town. Teresa was dragged to a deserted area by one of the Germans. Resisting and trying to escape, she enraged her attacker, who choked the young woman, then shot her, shattering her skull. Teresa was killed for the simple reason that she would not surrender her purity.

Pope John Paul II beatified Teresa Bracco on May 24, 1998, in Turin's Piazza Vittorio, and the people of the Piedmont attended in large numbers. At the ceremony, the Holy Father declared:

> To young people in particular, I hold up this young woman whom the Church is proclaiming blessed today so that they may learn from her clear faith, witnessed to in daily commitment, moral consistency without compromises and the courage of sacrificing even life if necessary, in order not to betray the values that give it meaning.

✠

Teresa of Calcutta (August 26, 1910 – September 5, 1997)
Devotion to the "Poorest of the Poor"

Mother Teresa of Calcutta has become one of the most respected and beloved figures of charity and compassion of the twentieth century.

She was born Agnes Gonxha Bojaxhiu at Skopje, Macedonia, the daughter of an Albanian grocer. At the age of seventeen, she entered a congregation of Irish Loretto sisters and arrived in Ireland in 1928 to begin training. A mere six weeks later, she set sail for Calcutta, India, where she taught at St. Mary's School, an institution for the daughters of prosperous families.

After a number of years of teaching, however, she asked permission to give up her teaching and devote herself to caring for the poor of the city. Granted approval by authorities, she adopted the sari as her dress and, barefooted, began tending to the sick, teaching the children of the slums, and caring for the dying so as to allow them to pass into the next life with dignity. She was granted her request of a small hostel, which then became the cradle of her new religious order, begun in 1948. She had already been receiving help from various sources, but the desire of young women to join her made the foundation of an order of nuns inevitable. Formal approval was granted by Pope Pius XII in 1950 for the Order of the Missionaries of Charity.

Mother Teresa, who had adopted Indian citizenship in the same year, provided the sari as the habit of the sisters. In 1965, Pope Paul VI granted the order special status as a pontifical congregation, meaning that the nuns were answerable only to the pope.

From the one hostel located near the temple of Kali, in Calcutta, the order established a wide variety of hospitals, schools, and shelters, as well as places for lepers, especially the leper colony Shanti Nagar, near Asansol, India. For her efforts on behalf of the most unfortunate, the Indian government awarded Mother Teresa with the order of Padmashri, or Lord of the Lotus, its honor for those who have aided the people of India. Pope Paul VI, an enthusiastic supporter of her endeavors, asked Mother Teresa to open a hostelry in the Vatican in 1968 and, in 1971, gave her the first ever Pope John XXIII Peace Prize. In 1979, she won the Nobel Peace Prize. Despite frequent bouts of poor health, she continued to travel the world, speaking on the rights of the poor and on the dangers of abortion and contraception right up until her death.

Her passing was greeted with international sorrow, following as it did the tragic death of Princess Diana — to whom Mother Teresa had been a friend and advisor — in Paris, barely a week before. She was succeeded by one of her most trusted assistants, Sr. Nirmala Joshi. The order is now in nearly thirty countries, including Tanzania, Great Britain, Australia, the United States, and even Jordan.

Soon after Mother Teresa's death, a worldwide movement arose to promote her cause for canonization. After one of the swiftest investigations for a cause, including the verification of a miracle through her intercession, she was approved by the Congregation for the Causes of Saints for beatification.

Pope John Paul II beatified Mother Teresa on October 19, 2003. During the ceremony at St. Peter's Basilica, the pope declared:

> The cry of Jesus on the Cross, "I thirst" (Jn. 19: 28), expressing the depth of God's longing for man, penetrated Mother Teresa's soul and found fertile soil in her heart. Satiating Jesus' thirst for love and for souls in union with Mary, the Mother of Jesus, had become the sole aim of Mother Teresa's existence and the inner force that drew her out of herself and made her "run in haste" across the globe to labour for the salvation and the sanctification of the poorest of the poor.
>
> "As you did to one of the least of these my brethren, you did it to me" (Mt. 25:40). This Gospel passage, so crucial in understanding Mother Teresa's service to the poor, was the basis of her faith-filled conviction that in touching the broken bodies of the poor, she was touching the body of Christ. It was to Jesus himself, hidden under the distressing disguise of the poorest of the poor, that her service was directed. Mother Teresa highlights the deepest meaning of service — an act of love done to the hungry, thirsty, strangers, naked, sick, prisoners (cf. Mt. 25: 34-36), is done to Jesus himself.
>
> Recognizing him, she ministered to him with wholehearted devotion, expressing the delicacy of her spousal love. Thus, in total gift of herself to God and neighbour, Mother Teresa found her greatest fulfilment and lived the noblest qualities of her femininity. She wanted to be a sign of "God's love, God's presence, and God's compassion," and so remind all of the value and dignity of each of God's children, "created to love and be loved." Thus was Mother Teresa "bringing souls to God and God to souls" and satiating Christ's thirst, especially for those most in need, those whose vision of God had been dimmed by suffering and pain.

✠

Teresa Garcia y Garcia — see Martyrs of Guadalajara

✠

Teresa Grillo Michel (Chavez)
(September 25, 1855 – January 25, 1944)

Foundress of the Congregation of the Little Sisters of Divine Providence

Teresa Grillo Michel was born in Alessandria (Spinetta Marengo), Italy, the fifth child of Giuseppi and Maria Antonetta Parvopassau Grillo. Her father was the chief physician at the Civil Hospital of Alessandria, and her mother was a member of an illustrious local family. She was baptized Maddalena.

Her father died while she was still young, and Maddalena and her family moved to Turin, where she attended the school operated by the Ladies of Loretto in Lodi. Upon graduation, she was introduced to society in Alessandria. On August 2, 1877, Maddalena married Giovanni Michel, and they moved to several towns before finally settling in Naples. Giovanni died of sunstroke in 1891, and Maddalena went through the ordeal of profound and lasting grief.

Restored through spiritual reading and the help of family members, Maddalena embarked on a new apostolate. She opened her home to children and the needy and sold her house to purchase a building on the Via Fa'a di Bruno (honoring that Blessed) in 1893. This was called the Little Shelter of Divine Providence.

On January 8, 1899, Maddalena took the religious name Teresa and, along with eight companions, received the habit of the Congregation of the Little Sisters of Divine Providence. She spent the remaining years of her life guiding her rapidly spreading congregation, which at her death had twenty-five houses in Italy, nineteen in Brazil, and seven in Argentina. Luigi Orioni (the future Blessed) asked her to accept the apostolate in Argentina in 1927.

Teresa made eight voyages to Latin America to establish hospitals, nurseries, homes for the aged, orphanages, and schools. She lived to see her congregation approved by the Holy See in 1942 before her death in Alessandria.

Pope John Paul II beatified Teresa Grillo Michel on May 24, 1998, in Turin's Piazza Vittorio, announcing:

She was called by the Lord to spread love, especially among the poor. . . .
This generous daughter of Piedmont follows in the steps of the saints and
blesseds who, down the centuries, have brought the world the message of

divine love through active service to their needy brethren. Let us thank God for the living witness given by the holiness of this woman.

✛

Teresa Maria of the Cross Manetti
(March 2, 1846 – April 23, 1910)
Foundress of the Third Order Carmelite Sisters

Teresa Maria of the Cross Manetti had many mystical graces.

She was born Teresa Adelaida Cesina Manetti at San Martino a Campo Bisenzio, near Florence, Italy, the daughter of Salvatore and Rosa Bigali Manetti, who called her "Bettina." The family was quite poor, and Teresa was not well educated, but she displayed a beautiful radiance of joy and innocence.

In 1865, Teresa and other young women started a house of devotion and retreat, and she became a Third Order Discalced Carmelite, taking the name Teresa Maria of the Cross. On December 7, 1888, Teresa Maria and twenty-six other virgins received the habit of the Discalced Carmelites, founding the Third Order Carmelite Sisters, in Florence. The Holy See approved the congregation in 1904.

A hallmark of Teresa Maria's spirituality was her devotion to the Blessed Sacrament and the Passion of Christ. She experienced many spiritual and mystical graces and displayed heroic virtue in the many trials facing her new religious foundation. Teresa Maria died in Campo Bisenzio, mourned by all who had come into contact with her. Her Cause was approved in 1937.

Pope John Paul II beatified Teresa Maria of the Cross Manetti on October 19, 1986, honoring her founding, her Carmelite spirituality, and her mirroring of Christ in a troubled time.

✛

Théodore-Anne Thérèse Guerin
(October 2, 1798 – May 14, 1856)
Pioneer in Education in America

The founder of the Sisters of Providence of St. Mary-of-the-Woods, Théodore-Anne Thérèse Guerin was born in Etables, France, the daughter of Laurent and Isabelle Guerin. Théodore-Anne-Thérèse received her First Holy Communion at the age of ten and, on that day, announced her desire to become a nun. On September 6, 1825, she received the habit of the Sisters of Providence at Ruillé-sur-Loire, making her final vows on September 5, 1831. She became Sr. Théodore in the convent.

During her novitiate, Sr. Théodore suffered from a serious illness, probably smallpox, and the medicines administered to her at that time severely damaged her digestive system, leaving her physically frail for life. Yet she continued her vocation, serving the various schools of the congregation and receiving the Medal of Honor in Angers for her teaching methods. Sr. Théodore also studied medicine and cared for the sick poor.

In 1839, at the request of the bishop of the diocese of Vincennes, Indiana, she led five Sisters of Providence into the American frontier. They arrived at Saint-Mary-of-the-Woods, Indiana, on October 22, 1840. There, Sr. Théodore established the motherhouse and novitiate of the congregation, starting with a chapel made of logs. While learning English and adapting to the American lifestyle, she began her first academy for young girls. The first student arrived on July 4, 1841.

Sr. Théodore opened schools as well in Jasper, Indiana, St. Mary-of-the-Woods Village, and at St. Francisville, Illinois. She also founded two orphanages and pharmacies to serve the poor. She faced poverty, fires, persecution by local Protestants, and the separation of her house from the congregation in France. She remained steadfast and resolute, declaring, "Have confidence in the Providence that so far has never failed us. The way is not yet clear. Grope always slowly. Do not press matters; be patient, be trustful."

Mother Guerin's final illness began during Holy Week, in March 1856. Writing her final words, she rejoiced: "I am obliged to keep to my bed. What a beautiful week to be upon the Cross. O good Cross, I will love thee with all my heart." She was buried in the Church of the Immaculate Conception at Saint-Mary-of-the-Woods.

Pope John Paul II beatified Mother Théodore-Anne Thérèse Guerin on October 25, 1998, in Rome, declaring:

"The Lord stood by me and gave me strength to proclaim the word fully" (2 Tim. 4:17). In these words to Timothy, St. Paul looks back across the years of his apostolic ministry and affirms his hope in the Lord in the face of adversity. The words of the apostle were engraved on Mother Théodore Guerin's heart when she left her native France in 1840 with five companions to face the uncertainties and dangers of the frontier territory of Indiana. Her life and work were always guided by the sure hand of Providence, in which she had complete confidence. She understood that she must spend herself in God's service, seeking always his will. Despite initial difficulties and misunderstandings, and subsequent crosses and afflictions, she felt deeply that God had blessed her Congregation of the Sisters of Providence, giving it growth and forging a union of hearts among its members. In the congregation's schools and orphanages, Mother Théodore's witness led many young boys and girls to the loving care of God in their lives. Today she continues to teach Christians to abandon themselves to the providence of their heavenly Father and to be totally committed to doing what pleases him. The life of Blessed Théodore Guerin is a testimony that everything is possible with God and for God. May her spiritual daughters and all who experienced her charism live the same spirit today.

NOTE: Mother Théodore Guerin was canonized by Pope Benedict XVI on October 15, 2006.

✠

Timothy Giaccardo (June 13, 1896 – January 24, 1948)
Offered His Life for a New Congregation

Timothy Giaccardo was born at Narzole, Cueneo, Italy, and was baptized Giuseppe Domenico Giaccardo the same day. At an early age, he had met Don Alberione, the Founder of the Society of St. Paul, who encouraged the boy's devout nature. Giuseppe entered the seminary of the diocese of Alba and took his religious name. But then, even knowing full well that joining an as-yet-unapproved society could result in his not being ordained, he transferred to the Society of St. Paul in 1917. Two years later, on October 19, 1919, he was ordained the first priest of the Society.

In 1926, Timothy was sent to found the first house of the congregation in Rome. He faced the difficulties with a spirit of faith and prayer, accepting his roles as teacher, confessor, spiritual director, and administrator ,as well as editing a weekly periodical, *The Voice of Rome*. After a decade serving in Rome, he was named the Superior of the motherhouse in Alba, where his calm reserve and prayers were needed in directing the growing congregation. In 1946, Timothy was called back to Rome, where he was appointed Provincial Superior for the Society of St. Paul in Italy and the Vicar General of the Pauline Family.

Timothy was revered for his intense spiritual life and endless activities. He offered his own life so that the Disciples of the Divine Master might be approved as a separate religious congregation. Clearly, his prayer was heard, as he was stricken with acute leukemia and died just twelve days after celebrating a Mass of thanksgiving with the members of the new congregation. He was buried in the lower crypt of the Basilica of Mary, Queen of Apostles, beside the house that he had founded.

Pope John Paul II beatified Timothy Giaccardo on October 22, 1989, declaring:

> In the face of a world in which the Faith encounters difficulties and insidious ideas of every kind which threaten the very survival of many souls, Timothy Giaccardo, the first disciple of Don Alberione, interpreted fidelity to his own priestly vocation as proclaiming the Gospel through the press, thereby having an ever broader and deeper effect on his brothers and sisters. Thus he proposed to spread the Gospel and the Church's teaching through the modern means of social communications, which he saw as the principal and typical apostolate of the modern world. All this was to be in absolute fidelity to the Church's Magisterium, in a spiritual life nourished daily through Eucharistic adoration and devotion to Our Lady, in the persuasive example of his humility and meekness which made him so beloved by the entire Pauline family, which today, seventy-five years after its foundation, finds in him a model in continuing the mission entrusted to it by Don Alberione.

✠

Titus Brandsma (February 23, 1881 – July 16, 1942)
Victim of Dachau

A Carmelite theologian, Titus Brandsma was born at Bolsward, the Netherlands, and baptized Anno Sjoerd. The young Anno displayed an intellectual brilliance even at a young age, earning his doctorate at 28.

After entering the Carmelites and receiving the religious name of Titus, he announced that he had reached his spiritual home. His brilliance and dedication were recognized, and Titus was assigned as a professor at the

Catholic University of Nijmegen. He served in this capacity for nineteen years, becoming an authority on mystical theology.

Titus earned fame as well as a journalist and author. He lectured in the United States and was well received because of his scholarship and his evident holiness. Alarmed by the Nazi propaganda and military power, Titus began to speak out against the anti-Semitic laws passed in Germany. In 1935, he warned that Catholic newspapers could not print Nazi propaganda in good conscience. This stand brought him to the attention of the Nazis, who called him "that dangerous little friar."

When the Nazis invaded the Netherlands, they jailed Titus and kept him confined. The SS and the Gestapo interrogated him and offered him solitude in a monastery if he would make a statement that Catholic papers could publish Dutch Nazi Party proclamations. He refused. Not without grudging admiration — one SS official declared, "Brandsma is genuinely a man of character and firm convictions" — the SS decided that the sixty-one-year-old Titus needed to be silenced.

He was sent to Amersfoort Prison in Holland, then to Dachau concentration camp. There, he worked as a laborer, managing to console his fellow prisoners even as his health was nearing a state of collapse. He lived by the simple motto: "They who want to win the world for Christ must have the courage to come in to conflict with it."

Hospitalized in the dreaded medical facility that conducted horrifying experiments on prisoners, Titus was condemned to death because he was too ill for further tests. A prisoner serving as a nursing aide prepared a lethal injection, and Titus gave her his rosary. Three days after the injection of poison, Titus' body was placed in the Dachau crematorium, and his ashes were deposited into a mass grave. The nursing aide who administered the injection testified at Titus' Cause.

Pope John Paul II beatified Titus Brandsma on December 3, 1985, speaking of the terrible trial of this "dangerous little friar" who answered hate with love:

"The souls of the righteous are in the hands of God" (Wis. 3:1). The Church listens to the word of God today, 3 November, the Sunday after the solemnity of All Saints and after the day commemorating all the faithful departed. The Church listens to this word on the day that she raises to the glories of the altar Titus Brandsma, son of the Netherlands and a religious of the Carmelite Order. Once again, a man who passed through the torments of a concentration camp — in this case, Dachau — is raised to the glories of the altar. A man who "was punished," in the words of today's liturgy (Wis. 3:4). And precisely in the midst of this "punishment," in the midst of a concentration camp, which remains the shameful blot upon this century, God found Titus Brandsma worthy of himself (cf. Wis. 3:5). Today, the Church rereads the signs of this divine approval and proclaims the glory of the Holy Trinity, professing with the author of the Book of Wisdom, "The souls of the righteous are in the hand of God, and no torment will ever touch them." And yet, Titus Brandsma suffered torments; in the sight of men he was punished. Yes, God tested him. The ex-deportees of the concentration camps know very well what a human Calvary were those places of affliction. Places of great trial for men and women. The trial of moral force . . . in this regard, perhaps, we are best spoken to by today's Gospel, which recalls the commitment to love our enemies. The concentration camps were organized according to the program of disdain for man, according to the program of hate. Through what trials of conscience, of character, of heart must have passed a disciple of Christ who recalled his words concerning the love of one's enemies! Not to answer with hate, but with love. This is perhaps the greatest trial of man's moral strength.

⳨

Tommaso Maria Fusco
(December 1, 1831 – February 24, 1891)
Founder of the Congregation of the Daughters of Charity of the Most Precious Blood

Tommaso Maria Fusco was born in Pagani, Salerno, the seventh of eight children, to Dr. Antonio, a pharmacist, and Stella Giordano, of noble descent. His parents were devout Catholics and raised their children solidly in the Faith. In 1837, when Tommaso was only six years old, his mother died of cholera and a few years later, in 1841, he also lost his father. Fr. Giuseppe, an uncle on his father's side and a schoolteacher, agreed to becaome the guardian of the children and the chief source of their education.

Deeply moved in his youth by the example of St. Alphonsus Liguori, Tommaso early on discerned a vocation to the priesthood. In 1847, he entered diocesan seminary of Nocera, the same seminary from which his brother Raffaele was ordained a priest in 1849. On December 22, 1855, Tommaso was ordained a priest by Bishop Agnello Giuseppe D'Auria. The young priest continued to endure family losses, including his uncle in 1847 and his brother Raffaele in 1852.

In order to provide a decent religious education for the children of the area around Pagani, Italy, Tommaso opened a morning school; for young people and adults desiring to increase their Christian faith, he organized evening prayers at the parish church of S. Felice e Corpo di Cristo. This was a true place of conversion and prayer, just as it had been for St. Alphonsus.

In 1857, Tommaso was admitted to the Congregation of the Missionaries of Nocera under the special patronage of St. Vincent de Paul, and subsequently served as an itinerant missionary, especially in the regions of Southern Italy. Three years later, he was named chaplain at the Shrine of our Lady of Carmel (known as "Our Lady of the Hens") in Pagani. There, he built up the men's and women's Catholic associations and established the altar of the Crucified Christ and the Pious Union for the Adoration of the Most Precious Blood of Jesus.

In 1862, he opened a school of moral theology to provide training for priests in the ministry of confession. Soon after, he founded the (Priestly) Society of the Catholic Apostolate to provide missions among the common people. The Society received the formal approval of Pope Pius IX in 1874. After seeing the suffering of an orphan girl who was alone and forgotten on a city street, Tommaso founded the Congregation of the Daughters of Charity of the Most Precious Blood on January 6, 1873. Inaugurated at the Church of Our Lady of Mount Carmel, the daughters also received papal approbation.

Tommaso devoted the last years of his life to preaching spiritual retreats and popular missions, and traveling to the growing number of religious houses and orphanages that he had founded. Sadly, he was envied for his many achievements and faced severe persecutions, including cruel slander on the part of a brother priest. In the midst of his sufferings, he repeated to himself, "May work and suffering for God always be your glory and in your work and suffering, may God be your consolation on this earth, and your recompense in heaven. Patience is the safeguard and pillar of all the virtues." Eventually, he was entirely vindicated on all accusations and calumny.

Tommaso died, after more suffering, from a liver disease. Pope John Paul II beatified him on October 7, 2001, declaring:

> The outstanding vitality of faith, extolled in the Gospel for today, emerges in the life and activity of Tommaso Maria Fusco, founder of the Institute of the Daughters of Charity of the Precious Blood. By virtue of the Faith,

he knew how to live in the world the reality of the Kingdom of God in a very special way. Among his aspirations, there was one which was his favourite: "I believe in you, my God, increase my faith." It is this prayer that the Apostles direct to the Lord in the Gospel reading today (cf. Lk. 17:6). Blessed Tommaso understood that faith is, first of all, a gift and a grace. No one can conquer it or obtain it by himself. One can only ask for it, implore it from on high. For that reason, enlightened by the teaching of the new Blessed, we never tire of asking the gift of faith, because "the just man will live by faith" (Heb. 1:4).

✠

Tommaso Reggio (January 9, 1818 – November 22, 1901)
Catholic Newspaper Founder

Tommaso Reggio was born in Genoa, Italy, to the Marquis of Reggio and Angela Pareto. He was provided with a solid Catholic upbringing and had every opportunity to embark upon a brilliant secular career. At the age of twenty, however, Tommaso informed his family that he was determined to become a priest. He was subsequently ordained on September 18, 1841.

By the age of twenty-five, he was serving as the vice-rector of the Genoa seminary and, later, the rector of the Chiavari seminary. At the same time, he became one of the founders of the Catholic newspaper, *The Catholic Standard.* In 1877, he was appointed by Pope Pius IX to serve as Bishop of Ventimiglia.

The diocese was a very poor one, so much so that Tommaso was forced to travel from parish to parish on a mule. He saw as an essential first step bringing about a genuine spiritual revival. He visited every parish — especially the long neglected ones — and organized three diocesan synods in just fifteen years. New parishes were opened, the liturgy was reinvigorated, and pastoral programs for the laity encouraged in every corner of the diocese. In 1878, Tommaso also founded the Sisters of St. Martha, a religious congregation charged with caring for the poor wherever they were found. The poor were such a source of intense concern to Tommaso that he could declare in all honesty that he had become poor himself in their service. His old, patched cassock and the string he used to hang his watch attested to the truth of his claim.

In 1887, the diocese suffered massive damage from an earthquake. The bishop was one of the most active rescue workers, despite his age. He commanded his priests to follow his example and to determine the pastoral and financial needs of those in their parish. Of special anxiety to Tommaso were the many orphans created in the earthquake. He thus founded orphanages in Ventimiglia and San Remo.

Exhausted by his labors, Tommaso requested Pope Leo XIII to relieve him of his duties as bishop in 1892. The Holy Father accepted the resignation, but instead of permitting Tommaso's retirement, the pontiff appointed him Archbishop of Genoa. The ministry of serving as archbishop was a grueling one, especially for a seventy-four-year old prelate. He soon proved equal to the task, however, earning the respect of often hostile government leaders and the love of his Catholic flock. He died just before he was scheduled to go on a pilgrimage to Monte Saccarello.

Pope John Paul II beatified Tommaso Reggio on September 3, 2000, declaring:

> "Be doers of the word, and not hearers only" (Jas. 1: 22). These words of the Apostle James make us think of the life and apostolate of Tommaso Reggio, a priest and journalist who later became Bishop of Ventimiglia and, finally, Archbishop of Genoa. He was a man of faith and culture, and as a Pastor he knew how to be an attentive guide to the faithful in every circumstance. Sensitive to the many sufferings and the poverty of his people, he took responsibility for providing prompt help in all situations of need. Precisely with this in mind, he founded the religious family of the Sisters of St. Martha, entrusting to them the task of assisting the Pastors of the Church especially in the areas of charity and education. His message can be summed up in two words: truth and charity. Truth, first of all, which means attentive listening to God's word and courageous zeal in defending and spreading the teachings of the Gospel. Then charity, which spurs people to love God and, for love of him, to embrace everyone since they are brothers and sisters in Christ. If there was a preference in Tommaso Reggio's choices, it was for those who found themselves in hardship and suffering. This is why he is presented today as a model for Bishops, priests, and lay people, as well as for those who belong to his spiritual family.

U

✠

Ukrainian Martyrs — see Martyrs of Ukraine

✠

Ulricha Nisch (September 18, 1882 – May 8, 1913)
Holiness and Humility

A Sister of Mercy of the Holy Cross, Ulricha Nisch (also revered as Francisca Nisch) bore the cross with patience.

She was born at Obersdorf-Mittelbiberach on the Ress River of Germany. Ulricha's parents were not married at the time, and she was raised for the first six years of her life by her grandmother and godmother. Her parents married after her birth, so finally, at age seven, she went to live with them. But as the oldest child of a poor family, Ulricha had to assume household duties. She was a prayerful young woman, even as she performed her chores or attended the local school.

When she was old enough, Ulricha was sent to various regions in Germany, then to Switzerland, to work as a domestic servant. In Rorschach, Switzerland, she became ill and was placed in a hospital operated by the Sisters of Mercy of the Holy Cross of Ingenhohl. Ulricha received the grace of a religious vocation through this contact and entered the congregation on October 17, 1904, at Hegne, Germany. She was professed on April 24, 1907.

Her domestic experiences led to assignments in the kitchens of the convent in Bühl and in St. Vincent's in Baden-Baden. Spiritually, Ulricha had great devotion to the Cross and the Holy Eucharist. She was a profoundly holy religious, suffering physically with no complaint and reporting no discomfort. She predicted the way she would die — hidden — by saying, "God wills that I die as I have lived." Ulricha collapsed and was diagnosed with advanced tuberculosis. She died in Hegne with no one at her bedside as she breathed her last; even her nurse had been called away.

Pope John Paul II beatified Ulricha Nisch on November 1, 1987, and at the ceremony she was revered as a holy woman of the "Little Way" of the spirit. Ulricha was honored as a soul that lived the true spiritual union in a profound and hidden manner, unnoticed by the world.

✠

Ursula Ledochowska (April 17, 1865 – May 29, 1939)
Sisterhood and Service

Ursula Ledochowska was the sister of Blessed Theresa Ledochowska. These sisters' dedication, zeal, and endurance brought graces and good to thousands of their contemporaries, and their vision provided the modern world with continuing service.

Ursula was born in Loosdorr, Austria, the daughter of Count Anthony Ledochowska and his wife, and was baptized Julia. She was raised devoutly, undertaking many charitable projects while still young, even as her family suffered a financial reverse in 1873 and moved to St. Poelten. Then, in February of 1885, Ursula's father died of smallpox, and the family was aided by an uncle, Cardinal Lebo, who was in Rome.

Receiving the grace of a religious vocation, Ursula founded the Ursulines of the Sacred Heart, also called the Gray Ursulines. Ursula submitted the rule and constitutions of the congregation to Pope Benedict XV (r. 1914-1922) for approval. The actual motherhouse is in Pniewy, Poland, but the Holy See asked Ursula to make her permanent residence in Rome. There, her example inspired many Catholic institutions. She died on May 29, 1939, in her convent on the Via del Casalet in Rome, and was mourned by Romans and the people of Poland.

Pope John Paul II beatified Ursula in Poznan, Poland, on June 20, 1983, announcing that her vision and devotion enabled countless souls to witness for Christ and to provide Christ's charity to all in need.

$\mathcal{V}$

✠

Valentin Paquay (November 17, 1828 – January 1, 1905)
Humble Franciscan Servant

Valentin Paquay was born in Tongres, Belgium, the fifth of eleven children of Henry and Anna Neven. Early on, he discerned a vocation to the priesthood and, in 1845, he entered the seminary of St-Trond. Two years later, with his widowed mother's approval, he transferred to the Order of Friars Minor. He started his novitiate at Thielt in October 1849, was ordained a priest on June 10, 1854, in Liege.

After ordination, he was sent to serve in Hasselt, where he spent the rest of his life in humble service. He remained throughout a humble Franciscan, even as he served with distinction in various posts, including Provincial in 1890 and 1899. He also served as the director of the Fraternity of the Franciscan Secular Order of Hasselt for twenty-six years.

Valentin was best known for his remarkable preaching, spirituality, and labors as a confessor. Moreover, he demonstrated a special veneration of the Immaculate Conception; notably, he was ordained for the priesthood in the same year that the Dogma of the Immaculate Conception was proclaimed by Pope Pius IX (1854).

Valentin died in Hasselt at the age of seventy-seven, bringing to a close a life that was seemingly limited in its earthly achievement. In truth, however, he had demonstrated immense holiness and had guided the spiritual lives of countless people through his own commitment to the priesthood and Franciscan zeal.

Pope John Paul II beatified him on November 9, 2003. He said of him at the time:

> Fr. Valentin is truly a disciple of Christ and a priest according to the heart of God. As an apostle of mercy, he spent long hours in the confessional, with a special gift to place sinners anew on the right path, reminding men and women of the greatness of divine forgiveness. Placing the celebration of the Eucharistic mystery at the centre of his priestly life, he invited the faithful to come frequently to communion with the Bread of Life.

Like many saints, at a young age Fr. Valentin was entrusted to the protection of Our Lady, who was invoked under the title of "Cause of our Joy" in the Church where he grew up, in Tongres. Following his example, may you be able to serve your brothers and sisters to give them the joy of meeting Christ in truth!

☩

Vasil' Hopko (April 21, 1904- July 23, 1976)
Guided Restoration of Greek Catholic Church

Vasil' Hopko was born in Hrabské, a small village in eastern Slovakia. As his father died when Vasil' was only a year old, his mother assumed the sole responsibility for raising her son. In 1908, however, it became necessary for her to travel to the United States in the hope of finding work, and Vasil' was placed into the care of his grandfather. In 1911, the boy was sent to live with his uncle, Fr. Demeter Petrenko, a Greek-Catholic priest; not surprisingly, Vasil' discerned a vocation to the priesthood as well. In 1923, he entered the Greek-Catholic Seminary of Presov.

He was ordained a priest on February 3, 1929, and was sent to assist in the pastoral care of the Greek-Catholics in the capital city of Prague. Aside from his regular pastoral duties, Vasil' founded the Movement of Greek-Catholic Students and the Greek-Catholic Youth Union. He likewise helped to construct a church for the city's Greek-Catholic parish; while serving there, he met his mother, who came home from America after over two decades.

In 1936, Fr. Vasil' returned to Slovakia and took up a post in the Greek-Catholic Seminary of Presov. Five years later, he was named secretary of the episcopal curia. In 1943, he was appointed professor of moral and pastoral theology at the Theological Faculty in Presov. At the same time, he worked as a gifted writer and was the first editor of the magazine *Blahovistnik* (*The Gospel Messenger*).

In the period after the Second World War (1939-1945), the Czechoslovakian Republic was taken over by the Communists under the dark influence of the Soviet Red Army and the machine of Communist oppression. A vicious totalitarian, atheistic, and harshly anti-Christian Marxist system was soon installed in the country. To assist in the increasingly difficult task of maintaining the Church's independence in the face of this development, Bishop Gojdic of Presov requested an auxiliary bishop. Fr. Vasil' was named the auxiliary and was consecrated on May 11, 1947.

Bishop Vasil' proved a major assistant to the bishop, but the country was soon overwhelmed by Soviet terror. On April 28, 1950, Communists launched a wave of persecution; the Greek Catholic Church was declared liquidated and all of its property transferred to the Orthodox Church. At the same time, Bishops Gojdic and Hopko were arrested.

Bishop Vasil' received harsh treatment from authorities, including torture, in the hope that he would deny the Faith and "confess" to various false charges. On October 24, 1951, the bishop was condemned by the State Court to fifteen years in prison and a loss of all civil rights for ten years. His time in prison was marked, among other things, by slow, cruel poisoning with small doses of arsenic.

Released at last in May 1964, in poor health from the torture and inhuman prison conditions, Bishop Vasil' returned to his episcopal ministry and helped to guide the restoration of the Greek Catholic Church in 1968. He then returned to Presov, and in December 1968, Pope Paul VI confirmed his appointment as Auxiliary Bishop for all Greek-Catholics in Czechoslovakia.

Bishop Vasil' died in Presov, after devoting his last years to encouraging the clergy of the diocese and providing spiritual guidance to Greek Catholics. Pope John Paul II beatified Bishop Vasil' on September 14, 2003, during a visit to Bratislava, Slovakia. At that time, he praised Bishop Vasil's commitment to the Faith and his steadfast refusal to repudiate his love of Jesus Christ.

Victoria Diez y Bustos de Molina (November 11, 1903 – August 12, 1936)

Victim of the Spanish Civil War

Victoria Diez y Bustos de Molina was born in Seville, Spain, the only child of a devout family. Victoria was raised modestly and became a teacher. She also studied art and demonstrated many abilities. Her life, however, was formed by her profound faith and by a desire to help others.

When Victoria met Peter Posedo Castroverde, she recognized the opportunity to fulfill her heart's desire. She joined Peter's newly formed Teresian Association and began training in the Carmelite spiritual way. Her first assignment was as a teacher in Cheles, a small town near the Portuguese border. A year later, she returned to Seville, where she was able to aid her family. She taught at Hornachuelos until 1936, when the Church there was brutally attacked.

On August 11, 1936, Victoria was arrested and taken to the town hall, then to a makeshift prison. She was calm and kind to her companions, displaying her joy and her profound beliefs. At daybreak, Victoria and seventeen others were escorted to an abandoned mine shaft at Rincón and cruelly martyred. Victoria encouraged the others with her promise of their "reward." Her last words were "Long live Christ the King."

Pope John Paul II beatified Victoria Diez y Bustos de Molina on October 10, 1993, saying:

> Victoria Diez y Bustos de Molina . . . was able to incarnate the spirituality of the Teresian Association, where she made her total gift to God, pronouncing these words: "If it is necessary to give one's life to be identified with Christ, our divine model, from now on I no longer exist for the world, because my life is Christ and to die is gain." This Blessed is an example of openness to the Spirit and apostolic fruitfulness. She was able to sanctify herself in her work as a teacher in a rural community, at the same time helping out in parish activities, particularly in catechesis. The happiness she transmitted to all was a faithful reflection of that unconditional surrender to Jesus, which led her to the supreme witness of offering her life for the salvation of many.

✠

Victoria Rasoamanarivo (1848- August 21, 1894)
Lay Defender of the Church

A model laywoman of Madagascar, Victoria Rasoamanarivo was born to a leading Malagasy family in Tamanarive; her maternal grandfather was the prime minister for many years, and other relatives held high offices. After Jesuit missionaries and the Sisters of St. Joseph of Cluny educated Victoria, she asked to become a Catholic and was baptized on March 1, 1863.

Thereafter, a series of trials tested her faith: King Radama II was overthrown and the missionaries were persecuted, but Victoria clung to the Faith despite that. On May 13, 1864, she married the son of the prime minister, a marriage that turned out disastrous. Her husband so openly abused her that even the young man's father counseled divorce, but Victoria refused and stayed true to her marriage vows until 1887, when her husband died.

Four years before, the French Catholic missionaries had been expelled, yet Victoria used her influence to keep the churches open and schools in operation. She was present in 1886 when the missionaries returned and turned over a prosperous Catholic community to their care.

Victoria spent six hours a day in prayer and still found time to care for the poor and the sick. In her later years, she had many illnesses but remained a powerful protector of the Church, revered by all. She was declared Venerable in 1983.

Pope John Paul II beatified Victoria Rasoamanarivo on April 30, 1989, at Antananarivo, declaring:

> Today, we honor a woman who loved Christ authentically, a woman who remained faithful to the Word of the Lord: Victoria Rasoamanarivo. The Church recognizes her sanctity, with her brothers and sisters of this land who admire her example, and count on her intercession. The Church in Madagascar and the Church throughout the world greet her as one in whom God dwells, as a sister to whom one remains close in the mysterious reality of the communion of saints.
>
> Victoria has lived the gift of faith intensely, from the time of her Christian initiation as a catechumen. She received the Spirit of Christ. Throughout her life she knew how to keep the living memory of the Word of Jesus (cf. Jn. 14:26). With the power of the "Counsellor," she found the courage for a fidelity without weakness. In the depth of her being, Victoria remained constantly in God's presence. All were struck by the intensity of her prayer. Familiar with the presence of God, she knew how to draw others into intimacy with the Lord. Like the Blessed Virgin Mary, she advanced daily in the pilgrimage of faith. Had she not given to the Catholic Union the maxim: "Let us sanctify ourselves first; then we shall see to sanctifying others"?
>
> The witness of her action shows well that it is not a question of a piety that was closed in on itself. On the contrary, Victoria did not think that she could bring the Good News to her brothers and sisters without opening her whole being to the power of grace. That is why, in the midst of her activities and cares, she always found much time for prayer. . . .
>
> We pray to Victoria that she may help the sons and daughters of Madagascar to receive the gift of faith in the generous way she received it; we ask her to draw her Malagasy brothers and sisters to put their whole life in the light of Christ which enlightens the baptized, guides their decisions, supports them in difficulty, and accompanies them in joy.

☩

Victoriano Pio — see Martyrs of Astoria

╬

Vilmos Apor (February 29, 1892 – April 2, 1945)

"The Cross Strengthens the Weak and Makes Gentle the Strong"

Vilmos was the sixth child of a noble Hungarian family; his father died when he was very young, but his mother, fortunately, raised her children quite devoutly. Educated by the Jesuits, he then entered the seminary and was sent to Innsbruck, Austria, where he earned a doctorate in theology.

Vilmos was ordained a priest for the diocese of Nagyváradon on August 2, 1915. He performed ministerial apostolates in the diocese and served for a brief time as a military chaplain. Throughout his ministries, Vilmos displayed a love of the poor and a fine sense of the religious life, sponsoring religious communities and parochial life.

On February 24, 1941, Vilmos, appointed a bishop by Pope Pius XII (r. 1939-1958), was consecrated for the diocese of Győr. His episcopal motto summed up his apostolate: "The Cross strengthens the weak and makes gentle the strong."

He would need both graces and resolve as Hungary was ravaged by war. When Vilmos read the racial laws enforced by the Nazis, he put himself in danger by protesting against them and working with the Popular Democratic Catholic Party in resisting the Nazis until the war's end. Russian troops then occupied Hungary, and new horrors began for the faithful.

On Good Friday 1945, Russian troops demanded that Vilmos turn over the one hundred women and young girls who had taken refuge in the cellar of his episcopal palace. When he refused, a Russian officer shot him, and the troops fled. Vilmos was operated on for wounds to his hand, forehead, and stomach, but to no avail, and he died of complications on Easter Monday. He was buried in the Carmelite church and his Cause was opened immediately. Vilmos' remains are now enshrined in the cathedral of Győr.

Pope John Paul II beatified Vilmos Apor on November 9, 1997, proclaiming:

> The intimate sharing in the mystery of Christ, the new and perfect Temple in whom full communion between God and man is realized (cf. Jn . 2:21), shines forth in the pastoral service of Blessed Vilmos Apor, whose life was crowned with martyrdom. He was the "parish priest of the poor," a ministry which he continued as a Bishop during the dark years of the Second World War, working as a generous benefactor of the needy and the defender of the persecuted. He was not afraid to raise his voice to censure, on the basis of Gospel principles, the injustices and abuses of power

towards minorities, especially towards the Jewish community . . . The heroic witness of Bishop Vilmos Apor honors the history of the noble Hungarian nation and is held up today for the admiration of the whole Church. May it encourage believers to follow Christ in their lives without hesitation. This is the holiness to which all the baptized are called!

✠

Vincent Eugene Bossilkov
(November 16, 1900 – November 11, 1952)
Bulgarian Bishop and Martyr

Vincent Eugene Bossilkov was born in Belene, Bulgaria, to a Latin-rite Catholic family. He was educated at local schools until age eleven, when he entered the Passionist seminary, then studied in Nikopol, in Belgium, and later, in the Netherlands.

In 1919, he received the Passionist habit and the religious name of Eugene of the Sacred Heart. His took final vows in 1923 and was ordained on July 25, 1926. This was followed by theological studies in Rome leading to his doctorate.

In 1933, Vincent returned to his diocese, where he became secretary to the bishop and a priest of the cathedral. He asked to be made a parish priest and was sent to Bardaski-Gheran. Vincent served as the official orator for the 250th anniversary of the Catholic uprising against the Turks in 1938.

Following World War II and the invasion of Russian Communist troops into Bulgaria, Vincent was appointed bishop of Nikopol. He was consecrated in 1947 and made an *ad limina* visit to Rome, the following year. Pope Pius XII (r. 1939-1958) encouraged Vincent in his apostolate, giving him blessings. Soon after, the apostolic delegate (representative of the Holy See) was expelled from Bulgaria by the Communists. They also exiled all foreign missionaries and tried to crush Catholics who maintained allegiance to Rome. Throughout 1950-1951, Vincent and other Church leaders suffered severe persecutions.

Vincent and Bishop Romanov, the elderly Catholic exarch, were arrested on July 16, 1952, while on vacation near Sofia. Vincent was imprisoned, tortured, and tried, from September 29 to October 3, in a typical Communist-sham court procedure. He was executed in a Sofia prison, his body dumped into a common grave. He had seen his own peril and had assured friends and a relative, "Don't worry about me; I am already clothed with God's grace and have remained faithful to Christ and the Church."

Pope John Paul II beatified Vincent Bossilkov on March 15, 1998, declaring that the martyred bishop has become "the Church's radiant glory in his country," and that Vincent was "a fearless witness to the Cross of Christ."

✠

Vincent Vilar David (June 28, 1889 – February 14, 1933)
Lay Martyr of the Spanish Civil War

Vincent Vilar David was born in Manises, Valencia, Spain, the youngest of eight children in the David family, He was educated in the Scalopian or Piarist Schools and studied engineering in Valencia.

Vincent labored as an industrial engineer in the family ceramics firm, was active in civic affairs, married Isabel Rodes Reig, and was involved in parish activities and in Catholic youth groups. Thus, he was well prepared to render service to the Church when the Spanish Civil War engulfed that nation. He maintained his devout routines and openly declared his faith as he gave shelter to priests and religious. These activities brought him to the attention of the rebel authorities, who arrested him. Vincent said goodbye to his wife, who told him, "See you tomorrow!" His wife and others heard shots ring out and knew that Vincent had been murdered.

Pope John Paul II beatified Vincent Vilar David on October 1, 1995, stating:

> ". . . Blessed Vincent Vilar David, who with his martyrdom crowned his life of total dedication to God, to his neighbor, and to the promotion of justice in the world of work . . . enriched the martyrology of Valencia. His prayer and deep devotion to the Eucharist nourished his whole life, so that his work bore the stamp of God's presence."

✠

Vincent Lewoniuk and Twelve Companions
— see Martyrs of Podlasie

✠

Vincente Soler and Companions — see Martyrs of Motril

W (X - Y)

✠

William Joseph Chaminade — see Guillaume Joseph Chaminade

✠

William Repin and Companions — see Martyrs of Angers

✠

Wisenty Lewonjuk and Companions — see Martyrs of Podlasie

✠

Zdenka Schelingová (December 24, 1916 – July 31, 1955)
Nurse and Martyr

Cecilia Schelingová was born in Krivá in Orava, in northeastern Slovakia; her parents, Pavol Schelingová and Zuzana Pániková, were blessed with ten children and instilled in them a deep love of the Catholic faith. Cecelia was educated by the Congregation of the Sisters of Charity of the Holy Cross, and the example of the sisters so impressed her that she was herself drawn to the religious life. In 1931, she entered congregation and was sent to the motherhouse in Podunajské Biskupice. Prior to her entry into the novitiate, however, the young girl was sent to study nursing and radiology. Finally, on January 30, 1937, she made first vows and received the new name of Zdenka.

Sr. Zdenka applied her nursing skills in a hospital near Ukraine, then in a hospital in Bratislava in 1942, where she served in the radiology department. She was still in Bratislava in the period after World War II (1939-1945) when Czechoslovakia fell under the totalitarian and atheist regime of the Communists installed by the Soviet Red Army and the Soviet machinery of terror.

In her capacity as a nurse in the hospital, Sr. Zdenka treated many political prisoners brought in for treatment and discovered among them many priests who had been arrested and cruelly tortured. In early 1952, when she learned that one of the priests had been falsely charged with being a "Vatican spy" and was going to be sent to certain death in the gulags of Siberia, Sr. Zdenka helped the priest to escape literally from under the guard's nose.

Another effort to free several priests and seminarians, however, proved a disaster, and Sr. Zdenka was arrested. The enraged Communist authorities tortured her and arranged for a court to sentence her to twelve years in prison and the loss of her civil rights for ten years. The next years were filled with the horrors of torture and humiliation at the hands of the guards and Communist officials. She accepted each day of agony, offering it all to Christ.

Finally, in 1955, she was diagnosed with a malignant tumor and was released, solely to ensure that she did not die in custody. Sent back to

Bratislava, she found welcome only in the home of a friend; others feared that the police might take them away for offering her assistance. She was at last taken to the hospital in Trnava. There, she died, soon after receiving the sacraments, at the age of thirty-eight.

On April 6, 1970, the regional court of Bratislava declared that Sr. Zdenka was completely innocent of the false charges made against her. Pope John Paul II beatified her on September 14, 2003, during a visit to Bratislava; she was beatified on the same day as another Slovak martyr, Bishop Vasil' Hopko.

✠

Zeferino Agostini (September 24, 1813 – April 6, 1896)
Founder of the Ursuline Daughters of Mary Immaculate

Zeferino Agostino was born in Verona, Italy, the older of two sons of Antonio and Angela Frattini Agostini. Four days later, he was baptized in the church of Sts. Nazarius and Celsus, where his family was actively involved in the local parish (and where he eventually would begin his priestly ministry). His mother, widowed while still young, raised Zeferino and his brother. She was revered in the area for her gentleness and spiritual awareness.

Receiving the grace of a religious vocation, Zeferino studied at the local schools, then the diocesan seminary. On March 11, 1837, he was ordained to the priesthood by the bishop of Verona and celebrated his first Mass in the local parish of Sts. Nazarius and Celsus. He was assigned there as an assistant priest, teaching Christian doctrine and directing parish activities for local young men, and became the pastor in 1865.

Sts. Nazarius and Celsus was a large parish that served the poverty-stricken section of the city, and Zeferino carried out his ministry alone. The overwhelming tasks facing him did not deter him — he had recourse to hours of prayer and devotion in order to foster his apostolic zeal. He focused on the education of the young women of the parish, speaking always of St. Angela Merici and celebrating her feast day.

When three young women came to Zeferino to offer themselves as religious for the service of the poor, he founded a Pious Union of Sisters devoted to St. Angela Merici. That rule was approved by Bishop Ricabona in 1856. In that same year, Zeferino opened a school for destitute girls. The women involved in this apostolate entered Zeferino's newly founded Congregation of Ursulines, Daughters of Mary Immaculate, and they made their first vows on September 24, 1869. Zeferino cautioned them in 1874, saying: "Do not be dismayed by toil or suffering, nor by the meager fruit of your labors. Remember that God rewards not according to results but efforts." He lived according to that great spiritual truth until his death.

Pope John Paul II beatified Zeferino Agostino on October 25, 1998, in Rome, declaring:

> He stands before us today as a humble, steadfast witness to the Gospel in the latter half of the nineteenth century, a fruitful period for the Church in Verona. His faith was steadfast, his charitable work effective, and ardent was the priestly spirit that distinguished him.

✠

Zygmunt Gorazdowsky (1845 – 1920)
Religious Founder

Zygmunt Gorazdowsky was born to a Ukrainian family and raised in the Faith. An intelligent youth, he initially embarked upon studies to become a lawyer, but by the end of his second year of law school, he had decided to enter the Latin Catholic seminary in Lviv. He subsequently completed his theological studies and was ordained to the priesthood in 1871.

Zygmunt had suffered from childhood from a severe lung ailment, but he did not permit the weakness to deter him from the priesthood or from his active life of ministry. He founded two houses for the poor and homeless in Lviv, a dormitory for poor students of the local teachers' college, and the House of the Child Jesus, which provided refuge for single mothers with children and the many abandoned children wandering the streets.

In 1884, Zygmunt founded a convent for the Sisters of Mercy of St. Joseph, to create a community of religious sisters with the aim of works of charity. He also wrote a catechism and a host of other books providing instruction in the Faith for parents, teachers, and students.

Pope John Paul II beatified Zygmunt Gorazdowsky (along with a group of other Ukrainian martyrs and Blesseds) on June 26, 2001, during a pastoral visit to the Ukraine. At that time, he declared:

> He had a burning passion for the Gospel, which led him into schools, into the field of publishing and various catechetical undertakings, especially on behalf of young people. His apostolic activity was bolstered by a commitment to charity which knew no pause. In the memory of the faithful of Lviv, he remains "the father of the poor" and "the priest of the homeless." His creativity and dedication in this area were almost boundless. As sec-

retary of the "Institute of Poor Christians," he was present wherever he heard the anguished cry of the people, to which he strove to respond with many charitable institutions right here in Lviv.

Because of his total fidelity to the poor, chaste, and obedient Christ, he was acknowledged when he died as "a true religious, even if he had no special vows," and he remains for everyone a privileged witness to God's mercy. For you in particular he is a witness, dear Sisters of St. Joseph, as you seek to follow him faithfully in spreading love for Christ and for our brothers and sisters through your educational and charitable work. From Blessed Zygmunt Gorazdowsky, you have learnt to nourish your apostolic activity with an intense life of prayer. It is my hope that you will be able, like him, to combine action and contemplation, strengthening your piety with an ardent devotion to the Passion of Christ, a tender love of Mary Immaculate, and a very special veneration for St. Joseph, whose faith, humility, prudence, and courage Fr. Zygmunt strove to imitate.

✠

Zygmunt Szezesny Felinski
(November 1, 1822 – September 17, 1895)
The "Holy Polish Bishop"

Zygmunt Szezesny Felinski was born to Gerard Felinski and Eva Wendorff, in Wojutyn, Volinia (present-day Ukraine), in what was then Russian-occupied territory. When Zygmunt was eleven years old, his father died, and five years later, in 1838, his mother was arrested by the Russians and sent into exile in Siberia for her involvement in illegal patriotic activity. (Actually, her crime was providing pastoral care to suffering farmers.)

A talented and intellectually gifted youth, Zygmunt studied mathematics at the University of Moscow from 1840-1844 and French literature at the Sorbonne and the Collège de France in Paris in 1847. In France, he became acquainted with Polish independence leaders and, in 1848, took part in the failed revolt in Poznan against Russia. Discerning a priestly vocation, he returned to Poland in 1851, entered the diocesan seminary of Zytomierz, and studied at the Catholic Academy of St. Petersburg.

On September 8, 1855, Zygmunt was ordained a priest, then assigned to the Dominican Fathers' Parish of St. Catherine of Siena in St. Petersburg. In 1857, he was appointed spiritual director of the Ecclesiastical Academy and professor of philosophy. That same year, he founded the Congregation of the Franciscan Sisters of the Family of Mary.

On January 6, 1862, Pope Pius IX appointed Zygmunt the Archbishop of Warsaw. Zygmunt served as archbishop for only sixteen months; during that time, he sought to steer a course between the oppressive Russian government and suspicious Polish Catholics, who feared that he might collaborate with the Russian overlords.

When he arrived in Warsaw in early February, he found the city in a state of siege owing to harsh Russian efforts to crush all efforts at Polish independence. So, one of his first acts was to consecrate the cathedral of Warsaw that had been desecrated by Russian troops in October 1861, and he took as his chief concerns the gradual reduction of Russian interference in Church affairs, and the reform of the diocese's charitable institutions, seminaries, and program of studies at the Ecclesiastical Academy of Warsaw.

Following the bloody suppression by the Russians of the "January Revolt" of 1863, Zygmunt resigned from the Council of State and, on March 15, wrote a letter to Tsar Alexander II, urging him to end the oppression. The Russian reply was to exile Zygmunt to Siberia. He spent the next twenty years in Jaroslavl, Siberia, entirely ignorant of events in Warsaw, but devoting his time there to the pastoral care of prisoners. Even in this lonely place of imprisonment, he was able to collect funds to build a Catholic church; it later served as the center of a Catholic parish, and the people in the area — even the Orthodox — referred to him as the "holy Polish bishop."

In 1883, negotiations between the Holy See and Russia led to the release of the archbishop. Pope Leo XIII transferred Zygmunt from the See of Warsaw to the titular See of Tarsus, and for the last twelve years of his life he lived in semi-exile in southeastern Galicia at Dzwiniaczka, as chaplain of the public chapel of the manor house of local Counts. There, Zygmunt paid for a small school and a kindergarten, built a church, and founded a convent for the Franciscan Sisters of the Family of Mary.

Zygmunt died and was buried in Kraków. In 1895, his remains were transferred to Dzwiniacza; in 1920, to Warsaw — where, on April 14, 1921, they were solemnly interred in the crypt of the Cathedral of St. John.

Pope John Paul II beatified Zygmunt Szezesny Felinski on August 18, 2002, declaring:

Blessed Zygmunt Szezesny Felinski, Archbishop of Warsaw during a difficult period marked by the lack of national freedom, urged everyone to persevere in generous service to the poor and to establish educational institutions and charitable works. He himself founded an orphanage and a school; he also brought the Sisters of Blessed Virgin Mary of Mercy to

Warsaw and supported the work they began. After the failure of the insurrection of 1863, in a spirit of mercy towards his brothers and sisters, he openly defended the persecuted. This fidelity cost him deportment to the interior of Russia, which lasted twenty years. Even there he continued to be mindful of the poor and distressed, showing them great love, patience, and understanding. It has been written of him that "during his exile, oppressed on every side, in the poverty of prayer, he remained always alone at the foot of the Cross, commending himself to Divine Mercy."

AFTERWORD

Pope John Paul II's extraordinary pontificate drew to a close on April 2, 2005, at 9:37 p.m., in the Apostolic Palace in the Vatican. His unprecedented reign included some truly staggering milestones. He was the longest-reigning pope elected in the twentieth century, the third longest-reigning pontiff in the history of the Church, the most-traveled pope of all time, and the most prolific successor to Peter, having issued fourteen encyclicals, fourteen apostolic exhortations, eleven apostolic constitutions, forty-five apostolic letters, and thirty *motu proprio*.

No less significant was the final list of the saints and blesseds proclaimed during his time as pope. John Paul II declared 1,338 Blesseds in 147 ceremonies and 482 Saints in 51 liturgical celebrations. His seventeen predecessors, from Pope Clement VIII to Pope Paul VI, canonized a total of 302 people. The stress he placed upon universal holiness and the recognition of sanctity as deeply relevant to the modern world are all well-known and will be the source of fruitful reflection for many years — even centuries — to come.

It is the source, then, of great joy that the pope who may in the years to come be honored as a Doctor of the Church and who is hailed even now as "the Great" should have his own cause for canonization officially started. On May 9, 2005, Pope Benedict XVI, John Paul II's successor, officially waived the five year waiting period for a cause for beatification to be opened. On May 13, at a meeting with priests of the Diocese of Rome in the Basilica of St. John Lateran, the Pope made the news public by reading the announcement in Latin:

Instante Em.mo ac Rev.mo Domino D. Camillo S.R.E. Cardinali Ruini, Vicario Generali Suae Sanctitatis pro Dioecesi Romana, Summus Pontifex BENEDICTUS XVI, attentis peculiaribus expositis adiunctis, in audentia eidem Cardinali Vicario Generali die 28 mensis Aprilis huius anni 2005 concessa, dispensavit a tempore quinque annorum exspectationis post mortem Servi Dei Ioannis Pauli II (Caroli Wojtyla), Summi Pontificis, ita ut causa Beatificationis et Canonizationis eiusdem Servi Dei statim incipi posset. Contrariis non obstantibus quibuslibet.Datum Romae, ex aedibus huius Congregationis de Causis Sanctorum, die 9 mensis Maii A.D. 2005.

Datum Romae, ex aedibus huius Congregationis de Causis Sanctorum,
die 9 mensis Maii A.D. 2005

[At the request of His Most Eminent and Reverend Cardinal Camillo Ruini, Vicar General of His Holiness for the Diocese of Rome, the Supreme Pontiff BENEDICT XVI, taking into consideration the exceptional circumstances put forward during the Audience granted to the same Cardinal Vicar General on 28 April 2005, has dispensed the five-year waiting period following the death of the Servant of God John Paul II (Karol Wojtyla), Supreme Pontiff, so that the cause of Beatification and Canonization of the same Servant of God can begin immediately. Notwithstanding anything to the contrary.

Given in Rome, from the See of this Congregation for the Causes of Saints, 9 May 2005.]

Cardinal José Saraiva Martins, C.M.F.
Prefect

Archbishop Edward Nowak
Titular Archbishop of Luni
Secretary

The date for this public announcement had its own significance; it was not only the feast of the Virgin of Fatima but the anniversary of the attempted assassination of John Paul II on May 13, 1981.

BEATIFICATIONS BY POPE JOHN PAUL II, 1979-2004

1979: Margaret Ebner (Feb. 24); Francis Coll, O.P., Jacques Laval, S.S.Sp. (Apr. 29); Enrique de Ossó y Cervelló (Oct. 14; canonized June 16, 1993).

1980: José de Anchieta, Peter of St. Joseph Betancurt (canonized July 30, 2002), Francois de Montmorency Laval, Kateri Tekakwitha, Marie Guyart of the Incarnation (June 22); Don Luigi Orione (canonized May 16, 2004), Bartolomea Longo, Maria Anna Sala (Oct. 26).

1981: Sixteen Martyrs of Japan (Lorenzo Ruiz and Companions) (Feb 18; canonized Oct. 18, 1987); Maria Repetto, Alan de Solminihac, Richard Pampuri (canonized Nov. 1, 1989), Claudine Thevenet (canonized March 21, 1993), Aloysius (Luigi) Scrosoppi (canonized June 10, 2001) (Oct. 4).

1982: Peter Donders, C.SS.R., Marie Rose Durocher, Andre Bessette, C.S.C., Maria Angela Astorch, Marie Rivier (May 23); Fra Angelico (equivalent beatification) (July); Jeanne Jugan, Salvatore Lilli and Seven Armenian Companions (Oct. 3); Sr. Angela of the Cross (Nov. 5; canonized May 3, 2003).

1983: Maria Gabriella Sagheddu (Jan. 25); Luigi Versiglia, Callisto Caravario (May 15); Ursula Ledochowska (canonized May 18, 2003) (June 20); Raphael (Jozef) Kalinowski (canonized Nov. 17, 1991), Bro. Albert (Adam Chmielowski), T.O.R. (June 22; canonized Nov. 12, 1989); Giacomo Cusmano, Jeremiah of Valachia, Domingo Iturrate Zubero (Oct. 30); Marie of Jesus Crucified (Marie Bouardy) (Nov. 13).

1984: Fr. William Repin and 98 Companions (Martyrs of Angers during French Revolution), Giovanni Mazzucconi (Feb. 19); Marie Leonie Paradis (Sept. 11); Frederico Albert, Clemente Marchisio, Isidore of St. Joseph (Isidore de Loor), Rafaela Ybarra de Villalongo (Sept. 30); José Manyanet y Vives (canonized May 16, 2004), Daniel Brottier, C.S.Sp., Sr. Elizabeth of the Trinity (Elizabeth Catez) (Nov. 25).

1985: Mercedes of Jesus Molina (Feb. 1); Anna de los Angeles Monteagudo (Feb. 2); Pauline von Mallinckrodt, Catherine Troiani (Apr. 14); Benedict Menni (canonized Nov. 21, 1999), Peter Friedhofen (June 23); Anwarite Nangapeta (Aug. 15); Virginia Centurione Bracelli (canonized May 18, 2003) (Sept. 22); Diego Luis de San Vitores, S.J., Jose M. Rubio y Peralta, S.J. (canonized May 4, 2003), Francisco Garate, S.J. (Oct. 6); Titus Brandsma, O.Carm. (Nov. 3); Pio Campidelli, C.P., Marie Teresa of Jesus Gerhardinger, Rafqa Ar-Rayes (canonized June 10, 2001) (Nov. 17).

1986: Alphonsa Muttathupandatu of the Immaculate Conception, Kuriakose Elias Chavara (Feb. 8); Antoine Chevrier (Oct. 4); Teresa Maria of the Cross Manetti (Oct. 19).

1987: Maria Pilar, Maria Angeles of St. Joseph, Cardinal Marcellus Spinola y Maestre, Emmanuel Domingo y Sol (Mar. 29); Teresa of Jesus "de los Andes" (canonized March 21, 1993) (Apr. 3); Edith Stein (Teresa Benedicta of the Cross) (May 1; canonized, Oct. 11, 1998); Rupert Meyer, S.J. (May 3); Pierre Francois Jamet, Cardinal Andreas Carol Ferrari, Benedicta Cambiagio Frassinello, Louis Moreau (May 10); Carolina Kozka, Michael Kozal (June 10); George Matulaitis (Matulewicz) (June 28); Marcel Callo, Pierina Morosini, Antonia Mesina (Oct. 4); Blandina Merten, Ulricka Nisch, Jules Réche (Bro. Arnold) (Nov. 1); 85 Martyrs (d. between 1584-1689) of England, Scotland and Wales (Nov. 22).

1988: Giovanni Calabria (canonized April 18, 1999), Joseph Nascimbeni (Apr. 17); Pietro Bonilli, Kaspar Stangassinger, Francisco Palau y Quer, Savina Petrilli (Apr. 24), Laura Vicuña (Sept. 3); Joseph Gerard (Sept. 11); Miguel Pro, Giuseppe Benedetto Dusmet, Francisco Faa di Bruno, Junipero Serra, Frederick Jansoone, Josefa Naval Girbes (Sept. 25); Bernard Maria Silvestrelli, Charles Houben, Honoratus Kozminski (Oct. 16); Niels Stensen (Nicolaus Steno) (Oct. 23); Katharine Drexel (canonized Oct. 1, 2000), 3 Missionary Martyrs of Ethiopia (Liberato Weiss, Samuel Marzorati, Michele Pio Fasoli) (Nov. 20).

1989: Martin of St. Nicholas, Melchior of St. Augustine, Mary of Jesus of the Good Shepherd, Maria Margaret Caiani, Maria of Jesus Siedliska, Maria Catherine of St. Rose Troiani(Apr. 23); Victoria Rasoamanarivo (Apr. 30); Bro. Scubilionis (John Bernard Rousseau) (May 2); Elizabeth Rienzi, Antonio Lucci (June 17); Niceforo de Jesus y Maria (Vicente Diez Tejerina and 25 Companions (martyred in Spain), Lorenzo Salvi, Gertrude Caterina Comensoli, Francisca Ana Cirer Carbonell (Oct. 1); 7 Martyrs from Thailand (Philip Siphong, Sr. Agnes Phila, Sr. Lucia Khambang, Agatha Phutta, Cecilia Butsi, Bibiana Khampai, Maria Phon), Timothy Giaccardo, Mother Maria of Jesus Deluil-Martiny (Oct. 22); Giuseppe Baldo (Oct. 31).

1990: Nine Martyrs of Astoria during Spanish Civil War (De la Salle Brothers Cirilo Bertrán, Marciano Jose, Julian Alfredo, Victoriano Pio, Benjamin Julian, Augusto Andres, Benito de Jesus, Aniceto Adolfo; and Passionist priest Innocencio Inmaculada; canonized Nov. 21, 1999), Mercedes Prat, Manuel Barbal Cosan (Brother Jaime), Philip Rinaldi, Tommaso da Cori (canonized Nov. 21, 1999) (Apr. 29); Juan Diego (confirmation of Apr. 9 decree; canonized July 31, 2002), 3 Child Martyrs (Cristobal, Antonio and Juan), Fr. Jose Maria de Yermo y Parres (May 6; canonized May 21, 2001); Pierre Giorgio Frassati (May 20); Hanibal Maria Di Francia (canonized May 16, 2004), Joseph Allamano (Oct. 7); Marthe Aimee LeBouteiller, Louisa Therese de Montaignac de Chauvance, Maria Schinina, Elisabeth Vendramini (Nov. 4).

1991: Annunciata Cocchetti, Marie Thérèse Haze, Ciara Bosatta (Apr. 21); Jozef Sebastian Pelczar (June 2; canonized May 18, 2003); Boleslawa Lament (June 5); Rafael Chylinski (June 9); Angela Salawa (Aug. 13); Edoardo Giuseppe Rosaz (July 14, Susa, Italy); Pauline of the Heart of Jesus in Agony Visentainer (canonized May 19, 2002) (Oct. 18, Brazil); Adolph Kolping (Oct. 27).

1992: Josephine Bakhita (canonized Oct. 1, 2000), Josemaria Escriva de Balaguer (May 17; canonized Oct. 6, 2000); Francesco Spinelli (June 21, Caravaggio, Italy); 17 Irish Martyrs, Rafael Arnáiz Barón, Nazaria Ignacia March Mesa, Léonie Françoise de Sales Aviat (canonized Nov. 25, 2001), and Maria Josefa Sancho de Guerra (canonized Oct. 1, 2000) (Sept. 27); 122 Martyrs of Spanish Civil War, Narcisa Martillo Morán (Oct. 25); Cristóbal Magellanes and 24 companions, Mexican martyrs, and Maria de Jesús Sacramentado Venegas (Nov. 22; canonized May 21, 2000).

1993: Dina Belanger (Mar. 20); John Duns Scotus (Mar. 20, cult solemnly recognized); Maria Angela Truszkowska, Ludovico of Casoria, Faustina Kowalska (canonized April 30, 2000), Paula Montal Fornés (canonized Nov. 25, 2001) (Apr. 18); Stanislaus Kazimierczyk (Apr. 18, cult solemnly recognized); Maurice Tornay, Marie-Louise Trichet,

Colomba Gabriel and Florida Cevoli (May 16); Giuseppe Marello (Sept. 26; canonized Nov. 25, 2001); Eleven martyrs of Almeria, Spain, during Spanish Civil War (2 bishops, 7 brothers, 1 priest, 1 lay person); Victoria Diez y Bustos de Molina, Maria Francesca (Anna Maria) Rubatto; Pedro Castroverde (canonized May 4, 2003), Maria Crucified (Elisabetta Maria) Satellico (Oct. 10).

1994: Isidore Bakanja, Elizabeth Canori Mora; Dr. Gianna Beretta Molla (Apr. 24; canonized May 16, 2004); Nicolas Roland, Alberto Hurtado Cruchaga, Maria Rafols, Petra of St. Joseph Perez Florida, Josephine Vannini (Oct. 16); Magdalena Caterina Morano (Nov. 5); Hyacinthe Marie Cormier, Marie Poussepin, Agnes de Jesus Galand, Eugenia Joubert, Claudio Granzotto (Nov. 20).

1995: Peter ToRot (Jan. 17); Mary of the Cross MacKillop (Jan. 19); Joseph Vaz (Jan. 21); Rafael Guizar Valencia, Modestino of Jesus and Mary, Genoveva Torres Morales (canonized May 4, 2003), Grimoaldo of the Purification (Jan. 29); Johann Nepomuk von Tschiderer (Apr. 30); Maria Helena Stollenwerk, Maria Alvarado Cordozo, Giuseppina Bonino, Maria Domenica Brun Barbantini, Agostino Roscelli (May 7; canonized June 10, 2001); Damien de Veuster (June 4); 109 Martyrs (64 from French Revolution — Martyrs of La Rochelle — and 45 from Spanish Civil War), Anselm Polanco Fontecha, Felipe Ripoll Morata, and Pietro Casani (Oct. 1); Maria Theresa Scherer, Maria Bernarda Butler and Marguerite Bays (Oct. 29).

1996: Daniel Comboni (canonized Oct. 5, 2003) and Guido Maria Conforti (Mar. 17); Cardinal Alfredo Ildefonso Schuster, O.S., Filippo Smaldone and Gennaro Sarnelli (priests) and Candida Maria de Jesus Cipitria y Barriola, Maria Raffaella Cimatti, Maria Antonia Bandres (religious) (May 12), Bernhard Lichtenberg and Karl Leisner (June 23), Vincent Lewoniuk and 12 companions, Edmund Rice, Maria Ana Mogas Fontcuberta and Marcelina Darowska (Oct 6); Otto Neururer, Jakob Gapp and Catherine Jarrige (Nov. 24).

1997: Bishop Florentino Asensio Barroso, Sr. Maria Encarnacion Rosal of the Sacred Heart, Fr. Gaetano Catanoso, Fr. Enrico Rebuschini and Ceferino Jimenez Malla, first Gypsy beatified (May 4); Bernardina Maria Jablonska, Maria Karlowska (June 6); Frédéric Ozanam (Aug. 22); Bartholomew Mary Dal Monte (Sept. 27); Elías del Socorro Nieves, Domenico Lentini, Giovanni Piamarta, Emilie d'Hooghvorst, Maria Teresa Fasce (Oct. 12); John Baptist Scalabrini,

Vilmos Apor, María Vicenta of St. Dorothy Chávez Orozco (Nov. 9).

1998: Bishop Vincent Bossilkov, María Sallés, Brigida of Jesus (Mar. 15); Fr. Cyprian Tansi (Mar. 22); Nimatullah al-Hardini (canonized May 16, 2004), 11 Spanish nuns (May 10); Secondo Pollo (May 23); Giovanni Maria Boccardo, Teresa Grillo Chavez, Teresa Bracco (May 24); Jakob Kern, Maria Restituta Kafka, and Anton Schwartz (June 21); Giuseppe Tovini (Sept. 20); Cardinal Alojzije Stepinac (Oct. 3); Antônio de Sant'Anna Galvão, Faustino Miguez, Zeferino Agostini, Mother Theodore Guérin (Oct. 25).

1999: Vicente Soler and six Augustinian Recollect Companions, Manuel Martin Sierra, Nicolas Barre, Anna Schaffer (Mar. 7); Padre Pio (May 2; canonized June 16, 2002); Fr. Stefan Wincenty Frelichowski (June 7); 108 Polish Martyrs, Regina Protmann, Edmund Bojanowski (June 13); Bishop Anton Slomsek (Sept. 19); Ferdinando Maria Baccilieri, Edward Maria Joannes Poppe, Arcangelo Tadini, Mariano da Roccacasale, Diego Oddi, Nicolas da Gesturi (Oct. 3).

2000: André de Soveral, Ambrósio Francisco Ferro and 28 Companions, Nicolas Bunkerd Kitbamrung, Maria Stella Mardosewicz and 10 Companions, Pedro Calungsod and Andrew of Phú Yên (March 5); Mariano de Jesus Euse Hoyos, Francis Xavier Seelos, Anna Rosa Gattorno, Maria Elisabetta Hesselblad, Mariam Thresia Chiramel Mankidiyan (April 9); Jacinta and Francisco Marto of Fatima (May 13); Pope Pius IX, Pope John XXIII, Tommaso Reggio, Guillaume-Joseph Chaminade, Columba Marmion (September 3).

2001: José Aparicio Sanz and 232 Companions of the Spanish Civil War (March 11); Manuel Gonzalez Garcia, Marie-Anne Blondin, Caterina Volpicelli, Caterina Cittadini, Carlos Manuel Cecilio Rodriguez Santiago (April 29); George Preca, Ignatius Falzon, Maria Adeodata Pisani (May 9); Abp. Jósef Bilczewski and Fr. Sygmunt Gorazdowski, Ukrainian martyrs (June 27); Ignatius Maloyan (Oct. 7).

2002: Gaetano Errico, Lodovico Pavoni, Luigi Variara, Maria del Transito Sacramentado Cabanillas, Artemide Zatti, Maria Romero Meneses (Apr. 14); Kamen Vitchev, Pavel Djedjov, Josaphat Chichov (May 26); Juan Bautista and Jacinto de Los Angeles (Aug. 1); Zygmunt Szezesny Felinski, Jan Balicki, Jan Beyzym, Sancja Szymkowiak (Aug. 18); Daudi Okelo, Jildo Irwa, Andrea Giacinto Longhin, O.F.M. Cap., Marcantonio Durando, Marie de la Passion Hélène Marie de Chappotin de Neuville, Liduina Meneguzzi (Oct. 20).

2003: Pierre Bonhomme, María Dolores Rodríguez Sopeña, María Caridad Brader, Juana María Condesa Lluch, László Batthyány-Strattmann (Mar. 23); Eugenia Ravasco, Giacomo Alberione, Giulia Salzano, Marco d'Aviano, Maria Cristina Brando, Maria Domenica Mantovani (Apr. 27); Maria of Jesus Crucified Petkovic (June 6); Ivan Merz (June 22); Vasil' Hopko, Zdenka Schelingová (Sept. 14); Mother Teresa of Calcutta (Oct. 19); Juan Nepomuceno Zegrí y Moreno, Valentin Paquay, Luigi Maria Monti, Bonifacia Rodríguez Castro, Rosalie Rendu (Nov. 9).

2004: Luigi Talamoni, Matilde del Sagrado Corazón Téllez Robles, Piedad de la Cruz Ortiz Real, Maria Candida of the Eucharist (Mar. 21); Augusto Czartoryski, Laura Montoya, María Guadalupe García Zavala, Giulia Nemesia Valle, Eusebia Palomino Yenes, Alexandrina Maria da Costa (Apr. 25); Pere Torrés i Claret, Alberto Marvelli, Pina Suriano (Sept. 5); Peter Vigne, Joseph-Marie Cassant, Anna Katharina Emmerick, Maria Ludovica De Angelis, Charles of Austria (Oct. 3).

CANONIZATIONS BY POPE JOHN PAUL II, 1982-2004

JUNE 20, 1982, Vatican Basilica
Crispin of Viterbo (1668-1750)

OCTOBER 10, 1982, St. Peter's Square
Maximilian Maria Kolbe, O.F.M. (1894-1941)

OCTOBER 31, 1982, Vatican Basilica
Marguerite Bourgeoys (1620-1700)
Jeanne Delanoue (1666-1736)

OCTOBER 16, 1983, St. Peter's Square
Leopold Mandic (1866-1942)

MARCH 11, 1984, Vatican Basilica
Paola Frassinetti (1809-1882)

MAY 6, 1984, Seoul (Korea)
103 Korean Martyrs

OCTOBER 21, 1984, Vatican Basilica
Miguel Febres Cordero (1854-1910)

APRIL 13, 1986, St. Peter's Square
Francis Anthony Fasani (1681-1742)

OCTOBER 12, 1986, Vatican Basilica
Giuseppe Maria Tomasi (1649-1713)

OCTOBER 18, 1987, St. Peter's Square
Lawrence Ruiz

Dominic Ibáñez de Erquicia, O.P.
James Kyushei Tomonaga, O.P. and Thirteen Philippine Companions

OCTOBER 25, 1987, St. Peter's Square
Giuseppe Moscati (1880-1927)

MAY 16, 1988, Asuncion (Paraguay)
Roque González de Santa Cruz (1576-1628) and two Spanish
Companions, Alonso Rodríguez and Juan de Castillo, S.I. (+1628)

JUNE 11, 1988, Messina
Eustochia Smeraldo Calafato (1434-1485)

JUNE 19, 1988, St. Peter's Square
Martyrs of Vietnam (+1745-1862)
— Andrew Dung-Lac
— Tommaso Thien and Emanuele Phung
— Girolamo (Jerome) Hermosilla
— Valentino Berriochoa, O.P., and Six Bishops
— Teofano Venard and 105 companions (1745-1862)

JULY 3, 1988, Vatican Basilica
Simón de Rojas, O.SS. (1552-1624)
Rose-Philippine Duchesne (1769-1852)

OCTOBER 2, 1988, St. Peter's Square
Magdalen of Canossa (1774-1835)

DECEMBER 11, 1988, Vatican Basilica
Maria Rosa Molas y Vallvé (1815-1876)

APRIL 9, 1989, Vatican Basilica
Clelia Barbieri (1847-1870)

NOVEMBER 1, 1989, Vatican Basilica
Gaspar Bertoni (1777-1853)
Richard Pampuri, O.H. (1897-1930)

NOVEMBER 12, 1989, Vatican Basilica
Agnes of Bohemia (1211-1282)
Albert Adam Chmielowski of Krakow (1845-1916)

DECEMBER 10, 1989, Vatican Basilica
Mutien-Marie Wiaux, F.S.C. (1841-1917)

DECEMBER 9, 1990, Vatican Basilica
Marguerite d'Youville (1701-1771)

NOVEMBER 17, 1991, Vatican Basilica
Raphael Kalinowski, O.C.D. (1835-1907)

MAY 31, 1992, Vatican Basilica
Claude La Colombière, S.I. (1641-1682)

OCTOBER 11, 1992, Santo Domingo
Ezequiel Moreno y Díaz (1848-1906)

MARCH 21, 1993, Vatican Basilica
Claudine Thévenet (1774-1837)
Teresa de Jesús "de los Andes" (1900-1920)

JUNE 16, 1993, Madrid (Spain)
Enrique de Ossó y Cercelló (1840-1896)

SEPTEMBER 8, 1993, Riga (Latvia)
Meinard (1134/36-1196)

MAY 21, 1995, Olomouc (Czech Republic)
Jan Sarkander (1576-1620)
Zdislava of Lemberk (1220-1252)

JULY 2, 1995, Kosice (Slovak Republic)
Martyrs of Kosice (+1619)
— Marek Krizevcanin
— Stefan Pongracz
— Melichar Grodziecki, S.I.

DECEMBER 3, 1995, Vatican Basilica
Eugene de Mazenod (1782-1861)

JUNE 2, 1996, St. Peter's Square
Jean-Gabriel Perboyre (1802-1840)
Egidio Maria of St. Joseph (Francis Anthony Postillo) (1729-1812)
Juan Grande Román, O.H. (1546-1600)

JUNE 8, 1997, Kraków (Poland)
Hedwig, Queen of Poland (1374-1399)

JUNE 10, 1997, Krosno (Poland)
John Dukla (1414-1484)

OCTOBER 11, 1998, St. Peter's Square
Teresa Benedicta of the Cross (Edith Stein) (1891-1942)

APRIL 18, 1999, St. Peter's Square
Marcellin Joseph Benoît Champagnat (1789-1840)
Giovanni Calabria (1873-1954)
Agostina Livia Pietrantoni (1864-1894)

JUNE 16, 1999, Sajcz, Poland
Sr. Cunegunda (Kinga) (1234-1292)

NOVEMBER 21, 1999, Vatican Basilica
Cirilo Bertrán and Eight Companions
and Inocencio de la Inmaculada (+1934, +1937)
Benedict Menni, O.H. (1841-1914)
Thomas of Cori, O.F.M. (1655-1729)

APRIL 30, 2000, St. Peter's Square
Mary Faustina Kowalska (1905-1938)

MAY 21, 2000, St. Peter's Square
Cristóbal Magallanes Jara and 24 Companions (1869-1927)
José Maria de Yermo y Parres (1851-1904)
María de Jesús Sacramentado Venegas de la Torre (1868-1959)

OCTOBER 1, 2000, St. Peter's Square
Augustine Chao (+1815) and 119 companions, Martyrs of China
María Josefa of the Heart of Jesus Sancho de Guerra (1842-1912)
Katharine Drexel (1858-1955)
Josephine Bakhita (1869-1947)

JUNE 10, 2001, St. Peter's Square
Luigi Scrosoppi (1804-1884)
Agostino Roscelli (1818-1902)
Bernard of Corleone (1605-1667)
Teresa Eustochio Verzeri (1801-1852)
Rafqa Pietra Choboq Ar-Rayès (1832-1914)

NOVEMBER 25, 2001, St. Peter's Square
Giuseppe Marello (1844-1895)
Paula Montal Fornés de San José de Calasanz (1799-1889)
Léonie Françoise de Sales Aviat (1844-1914)
Maria Crescentia Höss (1682-1744)

MAY 19, 2002, St. Peter's Square
Alphonsus de Orozco, O.S.A. (1500-1591)
Ignatius of Santhià, O.F.M. (1686-1770)
Humilis de Bisignano, O.F.M. (1582-1637)
Pauline of the Agonizing Heart of Jesus (1865-1942)
Benedetta Cambiagio Frassinello (1791-1858)

JUNE 16, 2002, St. Peter's Square
Pio da Pietrelcina, O.F.M. (1887-1968)

JULY 30, 2002, Guatemala de la Asunción
Hermano Pedro de San José de Betancurt (1887-1968)

JULY 31, 2002, Ciudad del Messico
Juan Diego Cuauhtlatoatzin (1474-1548)

OCTOBER 6, 2002, St. Peter's Square
Josemaría Escrivá de Balaguer (1902-1975)

MAY 4, 2003, Spain
Pedro Poveda Castroverde (1874-1936)

José María Rubio y Peralta (1864-1929)
Genoveva Torres Morales (1870-1956)
Ángela de la Cruz, (María de los Ángeles Guerrero González) (1846-1932)
María Maravillas de Jesús, (Pidal y Chico de Guzmán) (1891-1974)

MAY 18, 2003, St. Peter's Square
Józef Sebastian Pelczar (1842-1924)
Urszula Ledóchowska (1865-1939)
Maria De Mattias (1805-1866)
Virginia Centurione Bracelli (1587-1651)

OCTOBER 5, 2003, St. Peter's Square
Daniel Comboni (1831-1881)
Arnold Janssen (1837-1909)
Joseph Freinademetz (1852-1908)

MAY 16, 2004, St. Peter's Square
Luigi Orione (1872-1940)
Hannibal Mary di Francia (1851-1927)
Josep Manyanet y Vives (1833-1901)
Nimattullah Kassab Al-Hardini (1808-1858)
Paola Elisabetta Cerioli (1816-1865)
Gianna Beretta Molla (1922-1962)

Other Proclamations by Pope John Paul II

JUNE 10, 1997
Thérèse of Lisieux (1873-1897) — proclaimed Doctor of the Universal Church

INDEX OF SAINTS AND BLESSEDS